T0336244

Design Solutions for Improving Website Quality and Effectiveness

G. Sreedhar
Rashtriya Sanskrit Vidyapeetha (Deemed University), India

A volume in the Advances in Web Technologies and Engineering (AWTE) Book Series

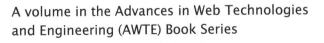

An Imprint of IGI Global

Published in the United States of America by
Information Science Reference (an imprint of IGI Global)
701 E. Chocolate Avenue
Hershey PA, USA 17033
Tel: 717-533-8845
Fax: 717-533-8661
E-mail: cust@igi-global.com
Web site: http://www.igi-global.com

Library of Congress Cataloging-in-Publication Data

Names: Sreedhar, G. 1974- editor.
Title: Design solutions for improving website quality and effectiveness / G.
   Sreedhar, editor.
Description: Hershey, PA : Information Science Reference, 2016. | Includes
   bibliographical references and index.
Identifiers: LCCN 2015041971| ISBN 9781466697645 (hardcover) | ISBN
   9781466697652 (ebook)
Subjects: LCSH: Web sites--Design. | Web site development--Quality control.
Classification: LCC TK5105.888 .D464 2016 | DDC 006.7--dc23 LC record available at http://lccn.loc.gov/2015041971

This book is published in the IGI Global book series Advances in Web Technologies and Engineering (AWTE) (ISSN: Pending; eISSN: pending)

British Cataloguing in Publication Data
A Cataloguing in Publication record for this book is available from the British Library.

All work contributed to this book is new, previously-unpublished material. The views expressed in this book are those of the authors, but not necessarily of the publisher.

For electronic access to this publication, please contact: eresources@igi-global.com.

Advances in Web Technologies and Engineering (AWTE) Book Series

Ghazi I. Alkhatib
Princess Sumaya University for Technology, Jordan
David C. Rine
George Mason University, USA

ISSN: Pending
EISSN: pending

MISSION

The **Advances in Web Technologies and Engineering (AWTE) Book Series** aims to provide a platform for research in the area of Information Technology (IT) concepts, tools, methodologies, and ethnography, in the contexts of global communication systems and Web engineered applications. Organizations are continuously overwhelmed by a variety of new information technologies, many are Web based. These new technologies are capitalizing on the widespread use of network and communication technologies for seamless integration of various issues in information and knowledge sharing within and among organizations. This emphasis on integrated approaches is unique to this book series and dictates cross platform and multidisciplinary strategy to research and practice.

The **Advances in Web Technologies and Engineering (AWTE) Book Series** seeks to create a stage where comprehensive publications are distributed for the objective of bettering and expanding the field of web systems, knowledge capture, and communication technologies. The series will provide researchers and practitioners with solutions for improving how technology is utilized for the purpose of a growing awareness of the importance of web applications and engineering.

COVERAGE

- Case studies validating Web-based IT solutions
- Quality of service and service level Agreement issues among integrated systems
- Web systems engineering design
- IT education and training
- Web systems performance engineering studies
- Information filtering and display Adaptation techniques for wireless devices
- Data and knowledge capture and quality issues
- Human factors and cultural impact of IT-based systems
- Web user interfaces design, development, and usability engineering studies
- Virtual teams and virtual enterprises: communication, policies, operation, creativity, and innovation

IGI Global is currently accepting manuscripts for publication within this series. To submit a proposal for a volume in this series, please contact our Acquisition Editors at Acquisitions@igi-global.com or visit: http://www.igi-global.com/publish/.

Titles in this Series

For a list of additional titles in this series, please visit: www.igi-global.com

Handbook of Research on Redesigning the Future of Internet Architectures
Mohamed Boucadair (France Télécom, France) and Christian Jacquenet (France Télécom, France)
Information Science Reference • copyright 2015 • 621pp • H/C (ISBN: 9781466683716) • US $345.00 (our price)

Artificial Intelligence Technologies and the Evolution of Web 3.0
Tomayess Issa (Curtin University, Australia) and Pedro Isaías (Universidade Aberta (Portuguese Open University), Portugal)
Information Science Reference • copyright 2015 • 422pp • H/C (ISBN: 9781466681477) • US $225.00 (our price)

Frameworks, Methodologies, and Tools for Developing Rich Internet Applications
Giner Alor-Hernández (Instituto Tecnológico de Orizaba, Mexico) Viviana Yarel Rosales-Morales (Instituto Tecnológico de Orizaba, Mexico) and Luis Omar Colombo-Mendoza (Instituto Tecnológico de Orizaba, Mexico)
Information Science Reference • copyright 2015 • 349pp • H/C (ISBN: 9781466664371) • US $195.00 (our price)

Handbook of Research on Demand-Driven Web Services Theory, Technologies, and Applications
Zhaohao Sun (University of Ballarat, Australia & Hebei Normal University, China) and John Yearwood (Federation University, Australia)
Information Science Reference • copyright 2014 • 474pp • H/C (ISBN: 9781466658844) • US $325.00 (our price)

Evaluating Websites and Web Services Interdisciplinary Perspectives on User Satisfaction
Denis Yannacopoulos (Technological Educational Institute of Piraeus, Greece) Panagiotis Manolitzas (Technical University of Crete, Greece) Nikolaos Matsatsinis (Technical University of Crete, Greece) and Evangelos Grigoroudis (Technical University of Crete, Greece)
Information Science Reference • copyright 2014 • 354pp • H/C (ISBN: 9781466651296) • US $215.00 (our price)

Solutions for Sustaining Scalability in Internet Growth
Mohamed Boucadair (France Telecom-Orange Labs, France) and David Binet (France Telecom, France)
Information Science Reference • copyright 2014 • 288pp • H/C (ISBN: 9781466643055) • US $190.00 (our price)

Adaptive Web Services for Modular and Reusable Software Development Tactics and Solutions
Guadalupe Ortiz (University of Cádiz, Spain) and Javier Cubo (University of Málaga, Spain)
Information Science Reference • copyright 2013 • 415pp • H/C (ISBN: 9781466620896) • US $195.00 (our price)

www.igi-global.com

701 E. Chocolate Ave., Hershey, PA 17033
Order online at www.igi-global.com or call 717-533-8845 x100
To place a standing order for titles released in this series, contact: cust@igi-global.com
Mon-Fri 8:00 am - 5:00 pm (est) or fax 24 hours a day 717-533-8661

Table of Contents

Section 1
Design Solutions for Website Quality

Section 2
Design Solutions for Web Usability

Section 3
Design Solutions using Web Analytics

Section 4
Design Solutions for Website Effectiveness

Detailed Table of Contents

Section 1
Design Solutions for Website Quality

Chapter 1
G. Sreedhar, Rashtriya Sanskrit Vidyapeetha (Deemed University), India

In the present day scenario the World Wide Web (WWW) is an important and popular information search tool. It provides convenient access to almost all kinds of information – from education to entertainment. It also makes global information available at our fingertips. This problem of 'long download time' is relevant not only to Web users but also to the authors and designers of websites, as websites that take a long time to download are rarely or less frequently visited. In fact it is felt necessary that the website shall adhere strictly the W3C guidelines to achieve optimum web design and promote quality of websites so as to make the website safer and user friendly and to address the possible reduction of down load waiting time of web pages. A case study with reference to the various Universities in India is discussed in this chapter and assesses the quality of web design about their status of Quality and user friendliness.

Chapter 2
Wing Shui Ng, The Hong Kong Institute of Education, Hong Kong

To improve the quality of a website, many principles or guidelines have been suggested in the literature. However, the application of related principles is not a straightforward issue. It requires the web developer with high level of self-awareness to continuously review his own works and to justify the design based on related web design principles. The web developer should behave as a reflective practitioner for creating a high-quality website which fulfilled web design principles in various aspects. However, reflection cannot be implicitly assumed as an inborn ability. Certain experiences or training must be provided so as to enable the web designer to develop high level of self-reflection. In this connection, this chapter introduces a series of assessment for learning strategies with self- and peer-assessment components for transforming a web developer into a reflective practitioner. Detailed implementation, its effectiveness and participants' opinions of the self- and peer-assessment strategy of a case study will be reported.

Chapter 3

Dorie Pandora Kesuma, STMIK Global Informatika MDP, Indonesia
Achmad Nizar Hidayanto, Universitas Indonesia, Indonesia
Meyliana, Bina Nusantara University, Indonesia
Kongkiti Phusavat, Kasetsart University, Thailand
Dina Chahyati, Universitas Indonesia, Indonesia

Today's internet technology has been utilized in various fields, one of which is to provide services in the field of education. Internet technology in the form of website enables organizations to provide anywhere anytime services to their customers, thus it is expected increasing customers' satisfaction. This research aims to develop a service design framework that can be used to evaluate the quality of website service at the university and formulate solutions for its improvement, by combining E-SERVQUAL, Kano Model, and Quality Function Deployment (QFD). To demonstrate the use of the proposed framework, we conducted a case study in one of the private universities in Palembang, Indonesia. Step by step of the framework usage is discussed, to provide a better understanding of the framework we are proposing.

Chapter 4

Sandeep Kumar Panda, KIIT University, India
Santosh Kumar Swain, KIIT University, India

The chapter introduces the definition of usability, usability assessment techniques to be adopted during the whole application life cycle for promoting usability. Then, the chapter includes design features for evaluating e-commerce websites such as navigation, content, design, ease of use and structure features and designing usable e-commerce websites. Then the chapter discussed the user testing method followed by a case study which comprises data collection by users' preferences, data analysis and the results. The latter in the chapter, we briefly describe the effectiveness of usability evaluation methods. Lastly, we describe the usability problem areas, strength and weaknesses on different features and sub-features of e-commerce websites followed by a conclusion.

Chapter 5

Adiraju Prasanth Rao, Anurag Group of Institution, India

The Semantic Web is a standard of Common Data Formats on WWW with aim to convert the current web data of unstructured and semi-structured documents into a common framework that allows data to be shared and reused across applications, enterprises. The main purpose of the Semantic Web is driving the evolution of the current Web by enabling users to find, share, and combine information more easily. Humans are capable of using the Web to carry out tasks such as searching for the lowest price for a LAPTOP. However, machines cannot accomplish all of these tasks without human direction, because web pages are designed to be read by people, not machines. The semantic web is a vision of information that can be readily interpreted by machines, so machines can perform more of the tedious work involved in finding, combining, and acting upon information on the web. The chapter presents the architecture of semantic web, its challenging issues and also data quality principles. These principles provide a better decision making within organization and will maximize long term data integration and interoperability.

Section 2
Design Solutions for Web Usability

Chapter 6

The primary objective of this chapter is to propose Biclustering Optimization Techniques (BOT) to identify the optimal web pages from web usage data. Bio-inspired optimization techniques like Firefly algorithm and its variant are used as optimization tool to generate optimal usage profile from the given web usage dataset. Finally, empirical study is conducted on the benchmark clickstream datasets like MSNBC, MSWEB and CTI and their results are analyzed to know the performance of the proposed biclustering optimization techniques with respect to optimization techniques available in the literature.

Chapter 7

A Concern is any important property or area of interest of a system that can treat in a modular way. One of the most important Concerns is Usability which is considered one of the key principles in Software Engineering. The importance of Usability Evaluation has dramatically increased due to extremely fast growth in Internet technology. The website design is directly related to the purpose of the website. Website with poor usability can easily destroy the purpose of website. So, the authors have chosen one of the concern "usability" which is the core component of web applications. The purpose of this chapter is to analysis and proposes an appropriate web usability metric for evaluation of universities website. The proposed method will be based partly on a literature study and partly on the survey analysis response by visitors.

Chapter 8

Gregory Wabuke Wanyembi, Mount Kenya University, Kenya

This chapter aims at examining the concept of content management (CM) and the need to identify it as a global best practice in light of its emergence in modern organizations, and specifically so in the context of institutions of higher learning in developing economies. The chapter also examines a number of models and approaches used in the adaptation of web content management systems (CMS), which provide a guide to the separation of digital content that is relevant to an institution of higher learning and also point out relevant management issues. The merits and demerits of these approaches are discussed. The stages in Content Life Cycle (CLC), information architecture and infostructure, quality of good online content, types of content suitable for a website, and are discussed. Content management tools and system have also been covered in some detail, which offers an institution part of the solution that they require to effectively manage and maintain their content. The chapter concludes with a set of recommendations and points at possible areas for further research.

Chapter 9

Harpreet Singh, DAV University, India
Parminder Kaur, Guru Nanak Dev University, India

The structure of a website can be represented in the form of a graph where nodes represent pages and edges represent hyperlinks among those pages. The behaviour of website users changes continuously and hence the link structure of a website should be modified frequently. The problem of optimally rearranging the link structure of a website is known as Website Structure Optimization problem. It falls in the category of combinatorial optimization problems. Many methods have been proposed and developed by the researchers to optimize the web graph structure of a website. In this chapter taxonomy of the website link structure optimization models is presented. The formulation and explanation of the working of the models have also been provided so that the readers could easily understand the methodology used by the models.

Section 3
Design Solutions using Web Analytics

Chapter 10

Balamurugan Balusamy, VIT University, India
Venkata Krishna P, VIT University, India
Jayashree Sridhar, VIT University, India

Over the decades, people are using internet for interconnecting distances across the universe which acts as an information hub. Internet changed the face of business, communication, etc. Consumers are overloaded with the abundance of websites and information offered. This creates a need to foster the quality of websites. Nowadays website designing trends has been evolved with numerous characteristics. This involves design simplicity, performance, improved bandwidth rate, content is designed first and device agnostic where interoperability and portability comes into action. Web analytics is a measure that can be utilized to optimize web usage and to improve the quality of websites. It is used to improve the effectiveness of the website and for optimizing web usage to an extent. This chapter deals with how website quality can be improved using web analytics. The quality of website is evaluated using web analytics with respect to the website metrics that matters.

Chapter 11

Web plays an important role in running business organizations, governments, societies, education sector, scientific organizations, social networks etc. As soon as web application has been deployed into the production environment, some or all of its features are available to the users. Web analytics is used to understand the usage pattern and its behaviour of users. The Web analytics is a procedure of measuring, collecting, analyzing and reporting of Internet data to optimize the business processes and maximize their revenue. Web Analytics is processes of inspecting, analyzing, tracking, measuring and reporting of web data for the purpose of discovering useful information, understanding web site quality, assess and improve the effectiveness of a website.

Chapter 12

There is a remarkable association between an organization's analytics intricacy and its competitive enactment. The biggest problem to adopting analytics is the lack of knowledge of using it to improve business performance. A website is believed and considered as 'face' of the company. In present era, there are more than 200 million people who buy goods online across the globe. Business Analytics helps companies to find the most profitable customer and allows them to justify their marketing effort, especially when the competition is very high. Predictive analytics helps organizations to predict churn, default in loan payment, brand switch, insurance loss and even the outcome in a football match. There is ample evidence from the corporate world that the ability to make better decisions (by management executives) improves with analytical skills. This chapter will provide an in-depth knowledge of business analytic techniques and their applications in improving business processes and decision-making.

Section 4
Design Solutions for Website Effectiveness

Chapter 13

Web security threats have undergone much sophistication compared to their initial introduction and they are becoming more & more evolved every day. The evolution might be in terms of new ways of attack or bringing in resistance to using simulated OS or VM environments. Web service architecture is a set of standard protocols to communicate secure web services. Which include policy, security, trust, secure conversation, reliable messaging and automatic transactions. Security is one of the major issues which reduces the growth of computing and complications with data privacy and data protection continue to plague the market. A new model targeting at improving features of an existing model must not risk or threaten other important features of the current model. The architecture of web poses such a threat to the security of the existing technologies when deployed in a web-based environment. In this chapter, the different security risks presented and specific to the different security issues that has emanated due to the nature of the service delivery models.

Tithi Hunka, KIIT University, India
Sital Dash, KIIT University, India
Prasant Kumar Pattnaik, KIIT University, India

Due to advancement of internet technologies, web based applications are gaining popularity day by day. Many organizations maintain large volumes of web site based data about individuals that may carry information that cannot be revealed to the public or researchers. While web-based applications are becoming increasingly pervasive by nature, they also present new security and privacy challenges. However, privacy threats effects negatively on sensitive data and possibly leads to the leakage of confidential information. More ever, privacy preserving data mining techniques allow us to protect the sensitive data before it gets published to the public by changing the original micro-data format and contents. This chapter is intended to undertake an extensive study on some ramified disclosure threats to the privacy and PPDM (privacy preserving data mining) techniques as a unified solution to protect against threats.

Madana Kumar Reddy C, Annamacharya PG College of Computer Studies, India

The use of Information Technology through Web services has been a major technology trend in the IT industry. IT promoted as a means of reducing costs, increasing reuse, simplifying integration and creating more active infrastructures. Web services replace other methods and technologies used in design, development, deployment and integration, and management services. It also allows different applications to exchange data with one another. SOA separates functions into distinct units or services, thus users can combine and reuse them in the production of various applications via modularity of functions. Here we are taken Signature verification application for dealing all these activities like online verification, offline verification, pressure, thickness, strength, etc. Software is componentized and the components are distributed among the devices available in the distributed environment with respect to their computational strength.

Web 2.0 is a new generation of web applications where the users are able to participate, collaborate and share the created artefacts. Web 2.0 is all about the collective intelligence. Web 2.0 applications are widely used for all the educational, professional, business and entertainment purposes. But a methodology for quantitative evaluation of web2.0 application quality is still not available. With the advancement of web technology various dimensions to evaluate web2.0 application quality is changing. So studies will be made to select a quality model that is required for web 2.0 application. Then the quantitative analysis will be done on the basis of questionnaire method and statistical formula. Quantitative analysis is necessary to know the weakness and strength of a website and then to improve the web quality. Quantitative evaluation can also be used for comparing two or more websites. In this study, quantitative analysis is done for each quality attribute of two social networking sites. Then the two sites are compared on the basis of the quantitative value of quality.

Foreword

The book Design Solutions for Improving Website Quality and Effectiveness is really a good attempt in present scenario by the author, since it presents innovatively new ideas and literature in the field of web engineering especially concerning the Quality aspect of web designing. The book consists of novel ideas and design solution in this direction. The book provides some of the most interesting metrics and web analytics towards the effort of improving Quality of web design and assist in the process of improving the Quality of web design in general. The book Extends helping hand for web designers and also provides concepts and tools for researchers in the field of Web mining and Engineering to contribute and enhance the theoretical foundations in the area of web engineering and web Quality assurance. By and large the effort of the author is quite appreciable to channelize the recent ideas in the field of Web mining and Web Engineering together in a single window in this book. I sincerely congratulate the effort of the author for bring this book to suit the present day need of the IT for its growth.

A. A. Chari
Rayalseema University, India

A. A. Chari *is Emeritus Professor (UGC), Department of Operations Research & SQC, Rayalaseema University, Kurnool, India.*

Preface

This book presents recent investigations and enhancements in the field of web engineering, with specific emphasis on quality assurance and development of web applications. Today, web is a major information resource and is becoming an obvious automated tool in various applications. Due to increased growth and popularity of WWW, one needs to be very cautious in designing the website as per standard and norms. Poor and careless web design will lead to hardship to public utility and does not serve the purpose. If the website does not adhere to the design guide lines and norms, the user may face difficulties in using the website. Despite of many recommendations, ideas and guidelines, designing a quality website is still a burning problem. The majority of web sites have usability and accessibility problems, which result in confusion to users. Some web pages are so clustered that users can easily miss the link or the feature that they are looking for. An estimated 90% of websites from projected growth of 196 million websites severely suffered with usability and accessibility issues. Web Engineering must be explored in a systematic, disciplined way for development, operation and maintenance of web based applications using certain guidelines. In the last few years a set of web site metrics were defined and specified based on the web based data. There are hundred and fifty automated web metrics catalogued till date. Among these metrics for Link and Page Faults, metrics for Navigation, metrics for Information, metrics for Media, metrics for Size and Performance and metrics for Accessibility are important categories for evaluation of quality of web site.

The book comprises of the ideas of various researchers and website quality design experts to evaluate the optimum website design and to offer design solutions for overall website quality process. These design solutions include design solutions for website quality, web usability, website effectiveness and role of web analytics in quality assurance of web engineering. The quality assurance techniques for web applications generally focus on the prevention of web failure or the reduction of chances for such failures.

The book is organized in four sections that cover the main concepts and studies for improving website quality and effectiveness. The Section 1 provides the design solutions for improving the quality of website on various areas that include web metrics, Quality Functional Development model for website, enhancing the quality of website through learning strategies and quality assurance aspects of web design.

The Section 2 deals with web usage using bio clustering techniques, web usability metrics, web content management and web link structure optimization. The Section 3 covers details about web analytics that are used as design solutions for website quality improvement, Assessment of website quality and for the future developments of web usage. The section 4 provides research insights of various authors about security aspects of web environment, web based privacy threats and control, reliability and scalability of service oriented architecture on web services and about web 2.0 application in quality evaluation process.

The present book is an attempt to investigate various solutions for improving website quality for developer. In this book, all areas of website quality are thoroughly discussed for finding desired solutions for enhancing quality of website development process. The book is a step forward towards presenting recent studies for designing website with Quality and serves the purpose for the present trend in web engineering. Hence the book focuses important aspects of web designing process to improve website quality and effectiveness.

Acknowledgment

I am very much happy and thankful to IGI Global for giving me the opportunity to produce the book *Design Solutions for Improving Website Quality and Effectiveness*, which is very much desired in the present scenario. I also would like to express a deep sense of gratitude to Caitlyn Martin, Lindsay Johnston, Courtney Tychinski, Kayla Wolfe, Jan Travers and other members of IGI Global who directly or indirectly supported this book project.

I am thankful to all the authors who contributed their valuable efforts and ideas in the form of the chapters in this book. I would like to express my sincere thanks to Prof. A. Anandaraja Chari for his continuous support and encouragement of my career.

I am thankful to the vice chancellor, the registrar and other faculty members of Rashtriya Sanskrit Vidyapeetha, Tirupati, for their support and kindness in completing this book.

Finally, I am very thankful for the support of my parents Smt. G. Sujatha and Sri. G. Veeranna and the support of my family members and for their encouragement in achieving this target goal in my academic career.

Section 1
Design Solutions for Website Quality

Chapter 1
Identifying and Evaluating Web Metrics for Assuring the Quality of Web Designing

G. Sreedhar
Rashtriya Sanskrit Vidyapeetha (Deemed University), India

ABSTRACT

In the present day scenario the World Wide Web (WWW) is an important and popular information search tool. It provides convenient access to almost all kinds of information – from education to entertainment. It also makes global information available at our fingertips. This problem of 'long download time' is relevant not only to Web users but also to the authors and designers of websites, as websites that take a long time to download are rarely or less frequently visited. In fact it is felt necessary that the website shall adhere strictly the W3C guidelines to achieve optimum web design and promote quality of websites so as to make the website safer and user friendly and to address the possible reduction of down load waiting time of web pages. A case study with reference to the various Universities in India is discussed in this chapter and assesses the quality of web design about their status of Quality and user friendliness.

INTRODUCTION

A Web site is the collection of web pages organized on a Web server. Web pages are of two types, static and dynamic. Static Web pages are static in nature and requires no change in the content. Dynamic Web pages are dynamic in nature and their content is changing frequently. Dynamic Web pages use database for storing end-user information, product information, transaction data and content. Static Web pages are designed using Hypertext Markup Language (HTML) files. Dynamic Web pages are designed using Dynamic HTML, Scripting Languages and other Web Programming techniques. The organization of web application can be divided into three major tiers according to the placement of components. They are

Web Browser Tier: A Web browser is a software application that is used to search, view and navigate Web pages hosted by Web Server over the Internet. The end user requests a Web page by entering a URL in the address bar of the Web browser. The Web browser in turn sends the request to the Web server,

DOI: 10.4018/978-1-4666-9764-5.ch001

which sends an HTML page back to Web browser. The end user then views the returned page. The Web browser acts as the client in the client/server architecture of Web server technology. Some of the popular Web browsers are Internet Explorer, Netscape Navigator and Mozilla.

Web Server Tier: A Web server acts as a gateway between client and DBMS residing on the server. It is an application that serves Web pages over the Internet using the HTTP protocol. The HTTP is a Hypertext Transfer Protocol used by the WWW to establish client and server interactions. Web servers publish Web sites, maintain network traffic and manage user data. Web servers also help in incorporating the network hierarchy in a Web site. Some of the Web servers are Apache Web Server, Microsoft Internet Information Server (IIS) and Web star.

Database Server Tier: Database access interfaces such as ODBC and JDBC are used to connect web applications with database servers. The communication between web application components may also flow through plain TCP sockets, Java RMI or CORBA. Architecture of Web application is shown in the following Figure 1.

Growth of Internet Users: The Internet users have been growing rapidly. The growth rate of internet was increased year by year since 1990s. The Scholar Prof. Robert H. Jackon (2003) conducted the survey on internet users and he concluded how the number of internet hosts is increasing day by day. It is shown in Figure 2.

Figure 1.

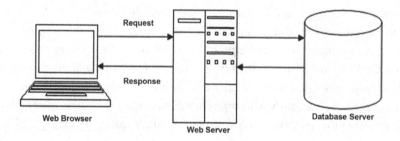

Figure 2. Growth of Internet Users

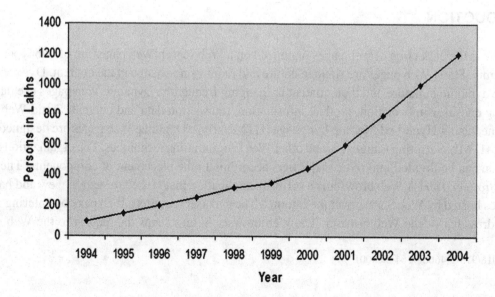

The growth of internet together with the increasing number of personal computers in the world makes for an increase in accessibility. That is, internet is now available to almost every person in the world. It is the fact that web now reached almost all possible target groups; it makes it inevitable that new businesses enter the web. New businesses demand new features. All this adds to the growing complexity of the sites on the web. Previously most sites of the websites did not offer much of interactivity. Today the possibilities for interactivity are endless. Today, web is not only an information resource but also it is becoming an automated tool in various applications. Due to the increasing popularity of WWW, one can be very cautious in designing the website. Poor and careless web design leads to hardship to public utility and does not serve the purpose. If the website is not designed properly, the user may face many difficulties in using the website. Despite of many recommendations, ideas and guidelines, designing a quality website is still a burning problem. The quality assurance techniques for web applications generally focus on the prevention of web failure or the reduction of chances for such failures. Due to the unceasing growth of web sites and applications, developers and evaluators have interesting challenges not only from the development but also from the quality assurance point of view. The majority of web sites have usability and accessibility problems, which can result in confusion to users. Some web pages are so clustered that users can easily miss the link or the feature that they are looking for. An estimated 90% of websites from projected growth of 196 million websites severely suffered with usability and accessibility issues. Tools and methodologies are needed to accelerate and improve the website design process. To achieve software quality in a system, the software's attributes must be clearly defined. Otherwise, assessment of quality is left to the intuition or the responsibility to the persons who are in charge of the process. In this sense, a quality model must be built and evaluation methods should be used during design and implementation stages based on these quality models. Web Engineering must be applied in a systematic, disciplined and quantifiable approach for development, operation and maintenance of web based applications using certain guidelines. These guidelines are useful to the developers in writing well-formed of code with respect to established standards, but also the validity of the code as an integral part of the quality. In the last few years a set of web site metrics were defined and specified based on the data collection point of view. Among hundred and fifty automated web metrics catalogued up to now, metrics for Link and Page Faults, metrics for Navigation, metrics for Information, metrics for Media, metrics for Size and Performance and metrics for Accessibility are important categories for evaluation of quality of web site. A Web site is a collection of Web pages containing text, images, audio and videos. The complete structure of the Internet is made up of Web sites, a mode of sharing information on the Internet. Web sites are designed and developed for a wide variety of organizations in areas such as education, business, research and e-commerce. In order to use any methodology for quality assessment, it has to present a complete and structured list of possible areas of complete web site. Based on interviews and different authors' opinions, a quality assessment must cover all components of web site. The complete list for quality assessment is as follows.

- **Links:** Links are the main feature on web sites. They constitute the mean of transport between pages and guide the user to certain addresses without the user knowing the actual address itself.
- **Forms:** Forms are used to submit information from the user to the host, which in turn gets processed and acted upon in some way. Forms can used both on client side and server side and they can be designed using scripting languages such as JavaScript, VBScript, Perl, etc.,
- **Cookies:** Cookies are used often used to store information about the user and his actions on particular site. When a user accesses a site that uses cookies, the web server sends information about

the user and stores it on the client computer in form of a cookie. These can be used to create more dynamic and custom made pages.

- **Web Indexing:** There are number of different techniques and algorithms used by different search engines to search the internet. Depending on how the site is designed using Meta tags, frames, HTML syntax, dynamically created pages, passwords or different languages, the site will be searchable in different ways.
- **Dynamic Interface Components:** Web pages are not just presented in static HTML any more. Demands for more dynamic features, custom made sites and high interactivity have made the internet a more vivid place than before. Dynamic interface components reside and operate both on server and client side of the web, depending on the application. The most important include java applets, java servlets, Active X Controls, JavaScript, VBScript, CGI, ASP, CSS and third party plug-ins.
- **Programming Language:** Differences in web programming language versions or specifications can cause serious problems on both client and server side. For example, when HTML is generated dynamically it is important to know how it is generated. When development is done in a distributed environment where developers, for instance, are geographically separated, this area becomes increasingly important. Make sure that specifications are well spread throughout the development organization to avoid future problems.
- **Databases:** Databases play an important role in web application technology, housing the content that the web application manages, running queries and fulfilling user requests for data storage. The most commonly used type of databases in web applications is the relational database and its managed by SQL to write, retrieve and editing of information.
- **Navigation:** Navigation describes the way users navigate within a page, between different user interface controls (buttons, boxes, lists, windows, etc.,) or between pages via links.
- **Graphics:** The graphics of web site include images, animations, borders, colors, movie clips, fonts, backgrounds, buttons etc.
- **Content:** Content should be correct, accurate and relevant to the information presented in the website.
- **Platform (OS):** There are several different operating systems that are being used on the market today, and depending on the configuration of the user system, compatibility issues may occur. Different applications may work fine under certain operating systems.
- **Browsers:** The browser is the most central component on the client side of the web. Browsers come in different brands and versions and have different support for Java, JavaScript, ActiveX, plug-ins or different HTML specifications.
- **Settings and Preferences:** Depending on settings and preferences of the client machine, web applications may behave differently. These settings include screen resolution, color depth, etc.,
- **Connection Speed:** Users may differ greatly in connection speed. Users expect minimum download time of the website.

LITERATURE SURVEY

The web is playing a central role in diverse application domains such as business, education, industry and entertainment. As a consequence, there are increasing concerns about the ways in which web applications are developed and the degree of quality delivered. Thus, there are compelling reasons for a systematic and disciplined use of engineering methods and tools for developing and evaluating web sites and applications according to Enruqui Herrera-Viedma, Antonio G. Lopez-Herrera and Carlos Porcel (2006). There is a need of sound evaluation methods for obtaining reliable information about the product's quality. There are many potential attributes, both general and domain specific that contribute to the quality of web applications. Software quality consists of a number of factors, which have been comprehensively listed by Fitzpatrick R and Higgins C, (1998). Bevan N and Macleod M (1994) interpreted the software quality factors in the context of use. Each factor is fully interpreted in the context of the World Wide Web. These factors include Suitability, Installability, Functionality, Adaptability, Ease of use, Learnability, Interoperability, Reliability, Safety, Security, Correctness, Efficiency, Maintainability, Testability, Flexibility, Reusability and Portability. Web site quality research is not yet well established. Researchers addressing this issue include Stern J (1995), Bevan N (1998), Dreyfus P (1998), Keeker K (1998), Nielsen J (1998). Their work focuses mainly on usability issues. Their publications are focused on heuristics and lists of good practice relating to desirable usability features. However, web site quality embraces much more than usability checklists. Additional quality issues, specific to the World Wide Web, include the ease with which users can find a site, user trust and confidence in the web site owner and the extent to which knowledge is enhanced following a visit. Quality web sites also need strategies for return-on-investment which include appeal, brand promotion and which encourage visitor loyalty. These issues are not addressed by traditional quality factors and are the subject of on-going research. Many of existing criteria for evaluating web sites quality require methods such as heuristic evaluations and empirical usability tests. The ISO standard defines three views of quality: users' view, developers' view and managers' view. Users are interested in the quality in use, which is mainly an external characteristic, while developers and managers are concerned with issues like maintainability, portability cost effectiveness and so on, mainly related to internal quality. Web sites are generally evaluated from the users' standpoint, so mainly considering external quality. The quality of web sites is often unsatisfactory and designers ignore or scarcely consider basic web principles, like interoperability and accessibility. There are several reasons for this scarce quality, in spite of the attention paid to the quality in other sectors like Software Engineering. Among the others we can certainly mention the mix of continuously evolving technologies, ease of writing HTML and tolerance of browsers, which display even not correctly coded pages. The last two points, and the presence in the development teams of several professionals, not necessarily with a specific background, have certainly been among the reasons of the diffusion of the web. However, as a result scarce attention has been paid to the internal quality. According to Scharl A (2000), the evolution of the web towards a more complex XML based architecture requires greater attention to the correct usage of technologies and a higher skill. In addition, national regulations are more and more requiring that web sites are accessible and usable as specified by Signore, Oreste and marucci, Luisa and Leporini, Barbara (2004). As the web technologies developed, users began to register their own domain names and create their own websites. At this time, the focus was not on how well designed the site was, but on simply getting a site on the web and having it accessible for others. The increasing popularity of websites has led to a significant focus on web design. The cluttered, jumbled design of website's web pages is no longer accepted. Web users are demanding clear, neat and easily navigated pages. The area of website's quality assessment is relatively new one in the IT industry. Therefore books written on the subject are comparatively limited. Instead, much of the information needed for this research work was gathered using the internet medium, articles, magazines and other resources given by experts in the field. A thorough literature survey is conducted with the available resources in pursuing the research project work. When searching for information regarding websites' quality assessment, large amount of information is found written by diverse knowledgeable authors describing their approach on how to evaluate quality of website design. As we know, the quality assurance was and is one of the challenging processes in software engineering as well as for the web engineering, as a new discipline.

BACKGROUND

There are many design guidelines, and metrics for the evaluation of web sites and applications, most of them lack a well-defined specification framework and even worse a strategy for consultation and reuse. Some initial efforts have been recently made to classify metrics for some entity type as for example metrics for software products. Particularly, in last few years a set of web site metrics were defined and specified based on the data collection point of view. The quality model must be able to assess the quality of each and every aspect of the website and it should cover the process of all web engineering activities. A set of guidelines are evolved to build a qualitative model of a website. A guideline consists of a design and evaluation principle to be observed to get and to guarantee a usable user interface. Guidelines can be found in many different formats with contents varying both in quality and level of detail, ranging from ill-structured common sense statements to formalized rules ready for automatic guidelines checking. Certain rules are validated by experimental results provided by user tests, experiments in laboratory or other techniques. Guidelines can be classified (Figure 3) by type ranging from the most general to the most specific. *Principles* are general objectives guiding conceptual User Interface (UI) decisions. They reflect the knowledge around human perception, learning and behavior and are generally expressed in generic terms like "Use images and metaphors consistent with real world" so that they can be applied for a wide range of cases. *Guidelines* are based on principles specific to a particular design domain. For example, a web design rule can stipulate to "use a consistent look and a visual language inside the site". Some guidelines have to be interpreted more and altered to reflect the needs of a particular organization or a design case. *Recommendations* determine conceptual decisions specific to a particular domain of application and should reflect the needs and the terminology of a given organization. They are un-

Figure 3. Types of Guidelines and Sources

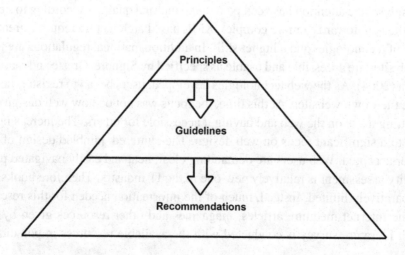

ambiguous statements so that no place for interpretation is left. Recommendations include ergonomic algorithms, user interface patterns and design rules. Design rules are functional and operational requirements specifying the design of a particular interface, e.g. "Every web page needs an informative title".

Beirekdar A, Vanderdonckt J, Noirhomme-Fraiture M (2002) mentioned a tool KWARESMI to define a Guideline Definition Language (GDL) to investigate quality evaluation procedure. The GDL expresses guideline information in a sufficiently rich manner so that evaluation engine can perform GDL-compliant guideline.

$$
\begin{aligned}
U(p) &= f_{kwaresmi}(Web\_page, UES_{i,j}) \\
&= EXEC(EC_{i,j}\{INST\_UES_{i,j}\}) \\
&= \{"\mathrm{Re}\,spected" \mid "Violated" \mid "Partially\,\mathrm{Re}\,spected"\}
\end{aligned}
\tag{1}
$$

Where $UES_{i,j}$ be the set of evaluation sets associated to the guideline i in the source j and that will be used for the evaluation of the evaluated web page. $EC_{i,j}$ be the set of evaluation conditions associated to $UES_{i,j}$. $INST\_UES_{i,j}$ is the set of captured instances of $UES_{i,j}$ in the evaluated page. In practice, the $f(Web\_page, UES_{i,j})$ executes each $EC_{i,j}$ condition and then it combines the results to have the overall result for the guideline i. We say that a web page satisfies a guideline $G_{i,j}$, if the execution of all $EC_{i,j}$ on all the $INST\_UES_{i,j}$ is true. Using the above evaluation parameters allows us to define a kind of quality model to balance the evaluation result. In the accessibility field, Bobby, Valet, and EvalIris define a set of accessible evaluation tools. All these tools are based on accessibility guidelines. It does this through automatic checks as well as manual checks. It also analyzes web pages for compatibility with various browsers (equation 2). Accessibility tools use a binary model to evaluate the accessibility of web pages (eq. 2).

$$
Accessibility\ errors = \sum_{i=1}^{guidelines} a_i x_i
\tag{2}
$$

where a_i is 0 when guideline is violated and 1 when guideline is not violated and x_i is a guideline. A set of guidelines are considered to establish the procedure for Correctness of the Website. The World Wide Web Consortium (W3C Recommendations, 2008) is an open source organizations and it defines various web standards for designing a website. The W3C is led by web inventor Tim Berners-Lee and CEO. The standards defined by W3C are considered as guidelines and these guidelines help in assessing the quality of website content in presenting the web content. The guidelines are as summarized as follows.

Guideline 1: *Provide a text equivalent for every non-text element.* This includes images, graphical representations of text, image map regions, animations, applets and programmatic objects, frames, scripts, spaces, audio and video files.

Guideline 2: *Do not rely on color scheme only.* The content of web page must match with foreground and background color. Also provide sufficient contrast to the content for visibility.

Guideline 3: *Use markup and style sheets instead of images to convey information.* Style sheets controls the layout and presentation of the web page and decreases the download time of the web page.

Guideline 4: *Clearly mention the text information of web page with natural language.* Specify the expansion of each abbreviation or acronym in the document.

Guideline 5: *Use tables properly in the web document.* For data tables, clearly specify row and column headers and number of rows and columns exactly.

Guideline 6: *Ensure that web pages featuring new technologies transform gracefully.* When dynamic contents are updated, ensure that content is changed. Ensure that pages are available and meaningful when scripts, applets or other programmatic objects are not supported by the browsers. If this is not possible, provide equivalent information as alternative in the web page.

Guideline 7: *Ensure user control of time sensitive content changes.* Until user agents provide the ability to stop the refresh, do not create periodically auto-refreshing pages.

Guideline 8: *Ensure direct accessibility of embedded user interfaces.* Make programmatic elements such as scripts and applets directly accessible or compatible with assistive technologies.

Guideline 9: *Design for device-independence.* Ensure that any element that has its own interface can be operated in a device-independent manner.

Guideline 10: Provide context orientation information. Title each frame to facilitate frame identification and navigation. Divide large blocks of information into more manageable groups wherever appropriate.

Guideline 11: *Provide clear navigation mechanisms.* Clearly identify the target of each link. Provide information about the general layout of a site such as site map or table of contents.

Guideline 12: *Ensure that documents are clear and simple.* Create a style of presentation that is consistent across pages.

Characteristics of Website Quality

Authors like Signore O et al (1997), L Marucci et al. (2000) summarized the characteristics of the website quality into six categories. They are:

- **Usability:** The website must easy to use, understand, operate, find information or navigate the site. The factors consider in usability characteristic are Understandability, Learn ability, Graphic Interface, Operability and Agreement respect to standards.
- **Functionality:** Functionality is the system's capacity to do the work for which it was designed and the functionality is orthogonal to the structure. The factors considered in functionality characteristic are Adjustment to purposes, Precision, Interoperability, Security and Correctness
- **Reliability:** The website must have appropriate address, short download time, multi browser support and compatible in different screen settings. The website must be available 7 days/week, 24 hours/day once it is hosted. The factors considered in reliability characteristic are Tolerance to failures, Recuperation, Maturity, Security and Correctness.
- **Efficiency:** Efficiency can be measured on the basis of amount of information and communication between system components. There must be efficient usage of resources in terms of CPU usage, memory usage and processing speed. The factors considers in efficiency characteristic are Behavior, Usage of resources, Non-redundant and Effective
- **Maintainability:** Maintainability is the important characteristic in architectural design. The factors considered in maintainability are Capacity of Analysis, Modifiability, Stability and Testability.

- **Portability:** Portability is an architectural-nature characteristic and it defines the compatible issues among different browsers and systems. The factors considered in portability are Adaptability, Capacity of implementation, Capacity of replace and Consistent.

All these characteristics are determined as part of quality evaluation process and these are shown in Figure 4.

METHODOLOGY

The contents of website must be presented in such a way that the user has to get 100% satisfaction in viewing all web pages of the website so that complete content of website visible and all pages are accessible. A set of quality assurance aspects are identified in website quality analysis module and these are used to satisfy the quality factors for optimizing website content. These quality assurance aspects of website include Accessibility, Usability, Standards, Errors, Compatibility, Privacy and Search. The process of methodology mainly focuses on the quality of website Design. The methodology evaluates various quality assurance parameters of the website. The quality assurance parameters include errors, accessibility, compatibility, privacy, search, standards according W3C guidelines and usability aspects of website. The website quality analysis module accepts URL address of a Website and processes the first 100 web pages in the website. The output report of the website quality analysis module demonstrates the number of pages that suffer with quality issues due to lack of accessibility, lack of compatibility, lack of privacy, lack of search facilities, lack of standards and lack of usability factors. The screen shot of Website Quality Analysis is shown in Figure 5.

Figure 4. Quality parameters of Website

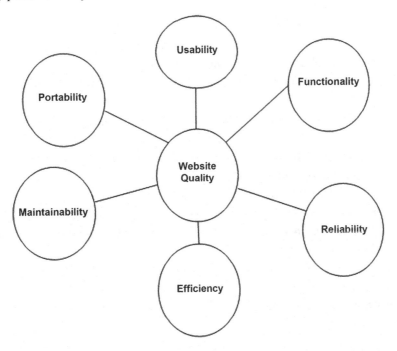

Figure 5. Website Quality Analysis

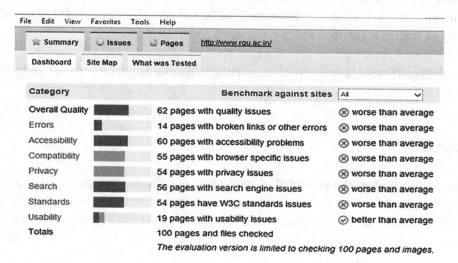

1. **Errors:** Website Quality Analysis module identifies the errors related to
   a. **HTML:** Check for missing images and broken links
   b. **CSS:** Check for missing background graphics and broken @import statements
   c. **Flash:** Check for missing movie files and find broken links inside movie files
   d. **RSS:** Check for broken RSS feeds
   e. **Script Errors:** Find errors and warnings produced by ASP, ASPX and PHP
   f. **Plus:** Find server configuration errors, expired domains and faulty SSL certificates
   g. **Spell and content checking features** include:
      i. Check English Spelling
      ii. Find placeholder
      iii. Find blank pages with no content
      iv. Custom dictionary for unusual words like product names
      v. Uses page LANG attributes to choose spelling dictionary
      vi. Choice of default spelling language for pages without LANG attributes

A Screen shot of various errors issues of a website is shown in Figure 6.

2. **Accessibility Issues:** Accessibility issues are identified in website quality analysis module. The issues identified and analyzed in accessibility check are
   a. **Text Alternatives Issues:** In a website for every non-text content, equivalent text alternatives must be defined in various tags like <Applet>, <Img>, <embed> etc.,
   b. **Time Based Media Issues:** Include equivalent alternatives for audio description, video content and signed language content.
   c. **Adaptable Issues:** Include relationship between heading and content, meaningful sequence and sensory characteristics.
   d. **Distinguishable Issues:** Include use of color, audio control, contrast, resize text, images of text and visual presentation.

Figure 6. Various errors issues of website

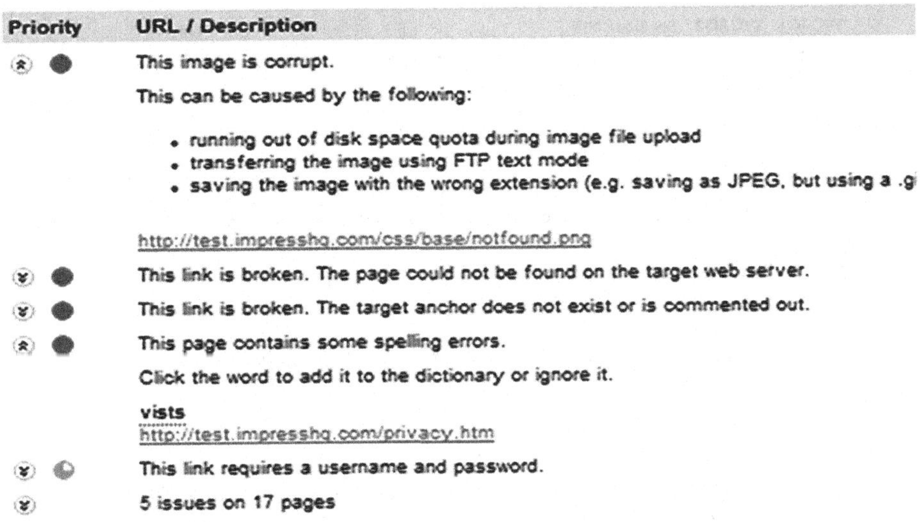

Priority	URL / Description
⊛ ●	This image is corrupt.
	This can be caused by the following:
	• running out of disk space quota during image file upload • transferring the image using FTP text mode • saving the image with the wrong extension (e.g. saving as JPEG, but using a .g
	http://test.impresshq.com/css/base/notfound.png
⊛ ●	This link is broken. The page could not be found on the target web server.
⊛ ●	This link is broken. The target anchor does not exist or is commented out.
⊛ ●	This page contains some spelling errors.
	Click the word to add it to the dictionary or ignore it.
	vists http://test.impresshq.com/privacy.htm
⊛ ◐	This link requires a username and password.
⊛	5 issues on 17 pages

e. **Keyboard Accessible Issues:** Determines that event handlers or subroutines must be defined as input device independent such as an event can execute base on mouse click or key down, key up etc.,

f. **Enough Time Issues:** Are related to time interval, scrolling marquees, pause, stop, hide, interruptions etc.,

g. **Seizures Issues:** Are related to the web pages that contain large images.

h. **Navigable Issues:** Are related to frames, broken links, document title, tab order, link purpose etc.,

i. **Readable Issues:** Related to language of page, unusual words, abbreviations, reading level, pronunciation, etc.

j. **Predictable Issues:** Are related to pop up appearance in page loading, consistent navigation, consistent identification, etc.,

k. **Input Assistance Issues:** Help, instructions, error identification, error suggestion, error prevention, etc.,

l. **Robust Issues:** Include parsing, name, role and value.

A screen shot of accessibility issues is shown in Figure 7.

3. **Compatibility issues:** are related to those websites that don't work correctly, or behave differently, on different browsers. These issues include

    a. HTML tags that don't function correctly on all browsers

    b. CSS features that don't function correctly on all browsers

    c. Vendor specific HTML and JavaScript

    d. Image formats not supported by all browsers

    e. Technologies not supported by some browsers

Figure 7. Accessibility issues for web site

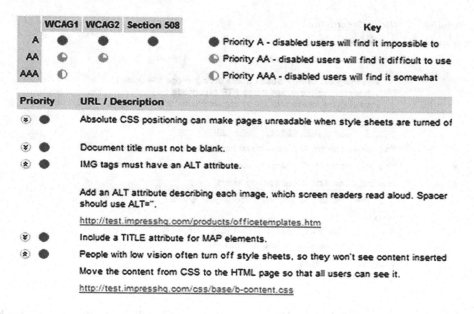

A screen shot of compatibility issues is shown in Figure 8.

4. **Privacy issues:** Privacy has been described as an adjustment process in which humans continuously adjust the views of themselves that they present to others. Privacy issue are related to the hacking issues of website, server log information, etc., The screen shot of privacy issues is shown in Figure 9.

Figure 8. Compatibility issues of website

Browser	Internet Explorer					Firefox		Safari		Opera	Chrome		iOS			Android		BlackBerry	
Version	6.0	7.0	8.0	9.0	10.0	≤20	21	≤5.0	6.0	≤12.0	≤26	27	4.0	5.0	6.0	≤3.0	4.0	≤7.1	10.0
Critical Issues	●	●	●	⊘	⊘	●	⊘	⊘	⊘	⊘	⊘	⊘	●	●	●	⊘	●	⊘	⊘
Major Issues	◐	◐	⊘	⊘	⊘	⊘	⊘	⊘	⊘	⊘	⊘	⊘	⊘	⊘	⊘	⊘	⊘	⊘	⊘
Minor Issues	◐	◐	◐	◐	⊘	⊘	⊘	◐	⊘	⊘	⊘	⊘	⊘	⊘	⊘	⊘	⊘	⊘

Priority	URL / Description
●	Flash is not supported on iPhone, iPad, BlackBerry and older Android phones.
●	The innerText property is a non-standard extension not supported by Firefox.
●	The OnReadyStateChange event is not implemented in Firefox 3.6.
●	The ReadyState property is not implemented in Firefox 3.
●	The W3 DOM textContent property is not supported by IE 8 and earlier.
◐	IE 5 and 6 do not support PNG images with alpha-channel transparency - the transparent an IE7.
◐	Nested tables cause rendering problems on small screen mobile devices.
◐	The :visited CSS selector only supports limited style changes.
◐	The clear: CSS property is not supported by BlackBerry 5.0 and earlier.

Figure 9. Privacy issues of website

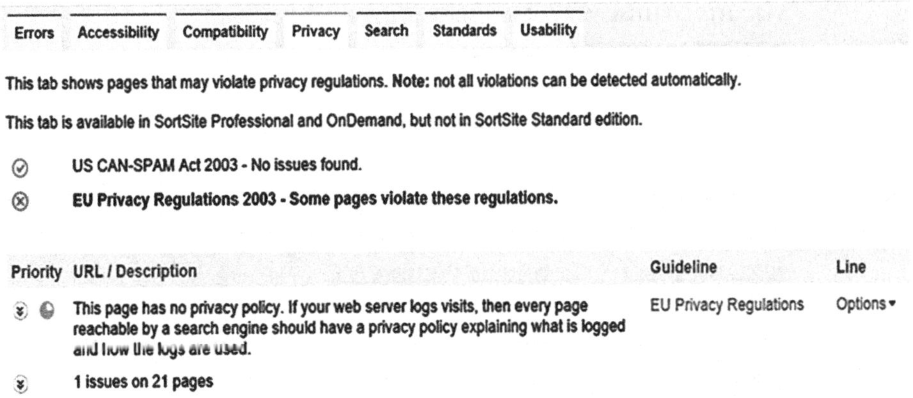

Errors	Accessibility	Compatibility	Privacy	Search	Standards	Usability

This tab shows pages that may violate privacy regulations. Note: not all violations can be detected automatically.

This tab is available in SortSite Professional and OnDemand, but not in SortSite Standard edition.

⊘ US CAN-SPAM Act 2003 - No issues found.

⊗ EU Privacy Regulations 2003 - Some pages violate these regulations.

Priority	URL / Description	Guideline	Line
⚡ ◖	This page has no privacy policy. If your web server logs visits, then every page reachable by a search engine should have a privacy policy explaining what is logged and how the logs are used.	EU Privacy Regulations	Options ▾
⚡	1 issues on 21 pages		

5. **Search issues:** related to check for hidden text, popups, check for keyword stuffed links and ALT Tags, etc., A screen shot of search issues is shown in Figure 10.

6. **Standards:** To display data in a manner that is consistent for users standards must be followed in web designing. The W3C enforces web standards for website against W3C HTML/XHTML norms. A screen shot of issues related to standards of web site is shown in Figure 11.

7. **Usability issues:** Usability relates not only to understanding what taking a particular action means in the context of a particular interaction, but also to whether the user understands the implications of his or her choices in a broader context. The usability issues related to slow loading pages, hard to read pages, text too small to read, duplicate page titles are analyzed in quality analysis module. A screen shot of usability issues is shown in Figure 12.

Figure 10. Search issues of website

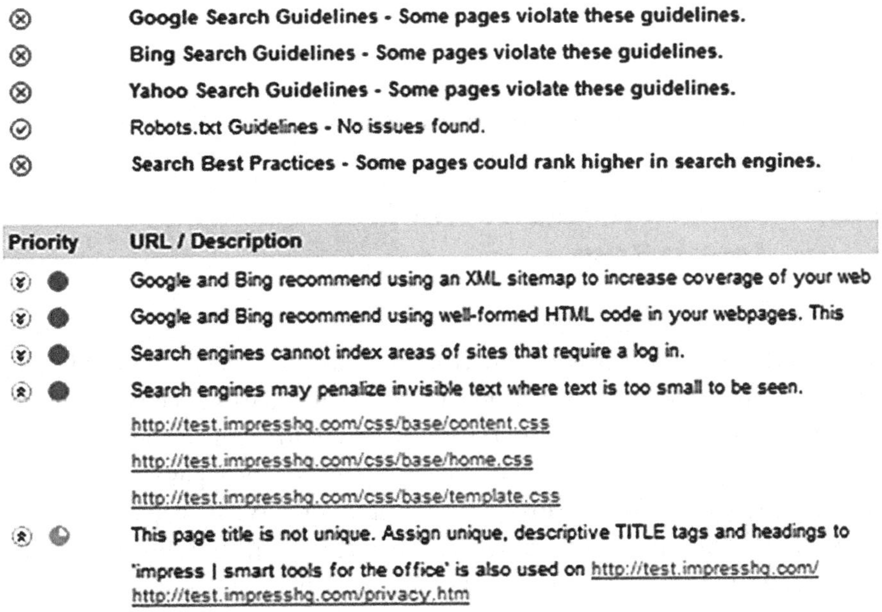

⊗ **Google Search Guidelines** - Some pages violate these guidelines.

⊗ **Bing Search Guidelines** - Some pages violate these guidelines.

⊗ **Yahoo Search Guidelines** - Some pages violate these guidelines.

⊘ **Robots.txt Guidelines** - No issues found.

⊗ **Search Best Practices** - Some pages could rank higher in search engines.

Priority	URL / Description
⚡ ●	Google and Bing recommend using an XML sitemap to increase coverage of your web
⚡ ●	Google and Bing recommend using well-formed HTML code in your webpages. This
⚡ ●	Search engines cannot index areas of sites that require a log in.
⚡ ●	Search engines may penalize invisible text where text is too small to be seen.
	http://test.impresshq.com/css/base/content.css
	http://test.impresshq.com/css/base/home.css
	http://test.impresshq.com/css/base/template.css
⚡ ◖	This page title is not unique. Assign unique, descriptive TITLE tags and headings to
	'impress	smart tools for the office' is also used on http://test.impresshq.com/ http://test.impresshq.com/privacy.htm

Figure 11. Issues related standards of website

⊗   **W3C HTML/XHTML Validation - Some pages fail validation.**

⊘   W3C CSS Validation - All pages valid.

⊘   W3C Style Guide - No issues found.

⊗   **W3C Deprecated Features - Issues found.**

Priority	URL / Description
⊛ ●	An attribute specification must start with a name or name token.
	http://test.impresshq.com/products/chartstore.htm
	http://test.impresshq.com/products/perfectpitch.htm
⊛ ●	An attribute value specification must be an attribute value literal unless SHORTTAG
⊛ ●	Character "&" is the first character of a delimiter but occurred as data.
	This often occurs in text or JavaScript code when a bare angle bracket is used instead
	http://test.impresshq.com/products/chartstore.htm
	http://test.impresshq.com/products/officetemplates.htm
	http://test.impresshq.com/products/outlooktemplates.htm
⊛ ●	Document type does not allow element "div" here.

Figure 12. Usability issues of website

Priority	URL / Description
⊛ ●	This image is corrupt.
	This can be caused by the following:
	• running out of disk space quota during image file upload
	• transferring the image using FTP text mode
	• saving the image with the wrong extension (e.g. saving as JPEG, but using a .gi
	http://test.impresshq.com/css/base/notfound.png
⊛ ●	This link is broken. The page could not be found on the target web server.
⊛ ●	This link is broken. The target anchor does not exist or is commented out.
⊛ ●	This page contains some spelling errors.
	Click the word to add it to the dictionary or ignore it.
	vists
	http://test.impresshq.com/privacy.htm
⊛ ○	This link requires a username and password.
⊛	5 issues on 17 pages

In optimizing the correctness of website content different qualitative measures need to be investigated. These measures derived from the Web page errors that are generated using the W3C Validation Service. This process uses the standard web tool W3C HTML Validator to validate and identify the number of different errors according syntax errors of HTML tags, properties of web page and standards mentioned by various organizations such as W3C. Most pages on the World Wide Web are written in computer languages (such as HTML) that allow Web authors to structure text, add multimedia content, and specify what appearance or style, the result should have. As for every language, these have their own *grammar*, *vocabulary* and *syntax*, and every document written with these computer languages are supposed to follow these rules. Markup languages are defined in *technical specifications*, which generally include a *formal grammar*. The tool compares HTML document to the defined syntax of HTML and reports any discrepancies. The outputs of the Markup Validator are a list of error messages and their interpretation W3C HTML Validator helps to ensure that documents are free of potential problems that can result in unexpected output when users view the bad documents with different browsers. The errors related to website content cause incorrect display of some components of Web pages. These errors include:

A. **Table Tag Errors (TTE):** All the sub tags in table tag should be properly used in the web page design. Errors in table tag cause for display problems of web page.
B. **Body Tag Errors (BTE):** Body Tag Errors cause the errors in displaying the contents of the web page.
C. **Image Tag Errors (ITE):** Image Tag Errors cause for errors in downloading the image in a website.
D. **Head Tag Errors (HTE):** Head Tag Errors cause for errors in displaying heading and title of the web page.
E. **Font Tag Errors (FoTE):** Font Tag Errors cause the errors in textual display of the web page.
F. **Script Tag Errors (STE):** Script Tag Errors cause the errors in programming at client side scripting.
G. **Style Tag Errors (StTE):** Style Tag Errors cause errors in dynamic display features of the web page.
H. **Form Tag E rrors (FmTE):** Form Tag Errors cause errors in input and output display of the script programming in a web page.
I. **Link Tag Errors (LTE):** Link Tag Errors cause errors in linking various web components.

The web content errors are occurred due to non-standards of web site design. The developer must be attentive in using HTML tags so that appropriate tags should be used in web design process. All the tags and their attributes properly set and closed accordingly. This will reduce the problem of web page display and avoids the problem in downloading of the web page. Website optimization is required in the following areas in order to improve the correctness of the website.

Text Presentation: Text Presentation is an important issue in display of the web content. These issues should be properly handled in presenting 100% correct text presentation. Several literature sources provide guidance about appearance of text on the web page. To format the text on web page the developer should consider following properties in text presentation.

1. Fonts must be chosen among the most readable ones.
2. Font size must be defined as relative size.
3. Use fonts designed for computer screens rather than fonts designed for print.
4. In a single page, the number of different fonts must be limited.
5. When using different fonts and font sizes, they should have some specific meaning (e.g. notes, links, and navigation location).
6. Avoid italicizing and underlining text.

These properties can be detected and measured by parsing both the text and CSS. The above properties are defined as attributes in various HTML tags. These tags include <HEAD>, <BODY> and <FONT> tags. The errors in attributes of tag errors cause incorrect or semi correct display of text on web page. The algorithm QAPM identifies the errors related to text presentation. Thus the Head Tag Errors (HTE), Font Tag Errors (FoTE) and Body Tag Errors (BTE) identify the problems in the text presentation of web page.

Link Presentation: The link presentation is important aspect in organization of web pages. The links in a website may be internal or external links. There are differences among the internal and external links. While internal links must all be valid and links pointing to external domains are out of control of the webmaster, but can be checked. Link topology is an often neglected aspect. Some sites are just trees of nodes, with links from a node pointing to children and to ancestors. Some others have a much more complex link topology, with many horizontal or traverse links. To format the links on the web page perform following functions.

1. Use moderate levels of breadth with minimal in the information architecture.
2. Minimize depth.
3. Avoid broken links.
4. Use corresponding text links.
5. Redundant links may cause confusion and avoid them.
6. Effective navigation requires small pages, few clicks between pages and strong scent.

Thus Link Tag Errors (LTE) and broken links identify the problems in link presentation.

Page Layout: The page layout is probably the principal characteristic perceived by the user. Layout must be clean, and the whole content should be well structured. A page layout is designed using tables, <div> tag or <frame> tag. Layout must adaptable to different devices. This implies that page must avoid making reference to specific device settings, like screen resolution or fixed size page components. An automated analysis of CSS usage and coding can supply information about the layout and the adoption of an organization wide standard. The algorithm QAPM generates table tag errors (TTE), frame tag errors (FTE), style tag errors (StTE), font tag errors (FoTE), frame tag usage errors and document type declaration errors if any attribute of tag element deviate the properties of page formatting. The Page Formatting Measures assess the following features of website.

1. Use browser-safe colors.
2. Use no more than 6 discriminable colors.
3. Use 256 (8-bit) color palettes.
4. Avoid using black backgrounds.
5. Use high contrast between background and text.
6. Keep line lengths to 40-60 characters.
7. Keep text between 9 to 15 words per line.
8. Avoid using framesets.
9. Text should cover no more than 25-30% of the screen.
10. Greater text density facilitates page scanning.

Graphics Presentation: The graphic presentation is the important issue in presenting pictorial and multimedia components. To format Graphics on the web page perform following properties should be followed.

1. Avoid using graphical text links.
2. Use corresponding text links instead of graphical links.
3. Avoid using animation unless it is appropriate.
4. Proper contrast between foreground image and background (color or image).

The image tag error (ITE), body tag errors (BTE) and image load errors related to image identifies the errors in display of images and hence Graphic Element Measures to be evaluated. Graphics Element Measures developed for assessing the following features of web interfaces.

Page Performance: correctness is a merely technical aspect, which can be easily checked. In many cases inconsistent behaviour with different browsers can be originated by lack of conformance to the published grammars (HTML, XHTML) and the default actions taken by the browsers themselves. Correctness is easily checked as an internal quality factor. The important aspects to consider in some environments are the professionalism and effectiveness of the web site that could be measured through how many different platforms are supported and it supports adaptivity and adaptability for a personalization. The form tag errors (FmTE), script tag errors (STE) and title tag with no keyword errors identify the need of page performance measure. The page performance measures developed to answer the following questions related to the website. To increase the performance of the web page following guidelines are considered.

1. Avoid gratuitous use of technology.
2. Minimize the use of video.
3. Avoid using sound files.
4. Effective navigation requires small pages.
5. Avoid using 'Click Here' for link text.

WEB METRICS FOR EVALUATING QUALITY ASSURANCE ASPECTS

As part of Quality Assurance process, each website is analyzed and first 100 pages of the website and it shows the number of pages with issues related to correctness, accessibility, compatibility, privacy, search, standards and usability. The contents of website must be presented in such a way that the user has to get 100% satisfaction in viewing all web pages of the website so that complete content of website visible and all pages are accessible. At this part of the research paper, it is tried to evolve 10-point scale. Thus 10-point scale is a metric towards defining quality of web content. In this connection it is interpreted the 10-point scale indicates such that '0' always represent poorer side and '10' always represent the best side of quality aspect. The 10-point scale metrics for various qualitative measures are formulated using empirical evaluation. Here 10-point scale of web content depends on the value computed using measures and its level competence based on performance. Thus the 10-point scale measurements of various quality assurance aspects are defined below.

$$Accessibility = \left(10 - \left(\frac{No.\ of\ Accessibility\ issues}{10} \right) \right) \qquad (3)$$

$$Usability = \left(10 - \left(\frac{No.\ of\ Usability\ issues}{10}\right)\right) \qquad (4)$$

$$Privacy = \left(10 - \left(\frac{No.\ of\ Privacy\ issues}{10}\right)\right) \qquad (5)$$

$$Compatibility = \left(10 - \left(\frac{No.\ of\ Compatibility\ issues}{10}\right)\right) \qquad (6)$$

$$Search = \left(10 - \left(\frac{No.\ of\ search\ issues}{10}\right)\right) \qquad (7)$$

$$Correctness = \left(10 - \left(\frac{No.\ of\ errors}{10}\right)\right) \qquad (8)$$

$$Standards = \left(10 - \left(\frac{No.\ of\ standards\ issues}{10}\right)\right) \qquad (9)$$

The 10-point metric for website content derives the values for quality assurance parameters such as correctness, accessibility, compatibility, privacy, search, standards and usability using Equations (3) to (9).

$$Overall\ Quality = Average \left(\begin{array}{l} Accessibility,\ Usability, \\ Privacy,\ Compatibility, \\ Search,\ Correctness, Standards \end{array}\right) \qquad (10)$$

As an example, the quality assurance aspects of Sri Venkateswara University, Tirupati is evaluated based on the above methodology. Website Quality Analysis of Sri Venkateswara University, Tirupati is shown in Figure 13. The issues related to Quality Assurance Parameters of Sri Venkateswara University are given in Table 1. The 10-point scale values for quality assurance factors of Sri Venkateswara University Website is given in Table 2.

In this chapter quality assurance aspects of various Central University websites in and these are shown in Table 3. During the quality evaluation process, the quality issues such as errors, accessibility issues, compatibility issues, privacy issues, search issues, standards issues and usability issues of Cen-

Figure 13. Quality Assurance Aspects of Sri Venkateswara University, Tirupati

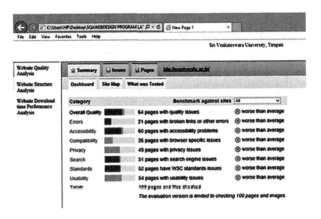

Table 1. Issues related quality assurance parameters of SVU Website

S. No	Issues Category	Issues in Number of Pages
1	Errors	21
2	Accessibility Issues	60
3	Compatibility Issues	26
4	Privacy Issues	49
5	Search Issues	51
6	Standards (W3C) Issues	52
7	Usability Issues	54

Table 2. 10-Point Scale values for Quality Assurance Factors for SVU Website

S. No	Quality Assurance Factor	10-Point Scale Value for Quality Factor	Overall Quality	Performance
1	Correctness	7.9	5.8	Below Average
2	Accessibility	4		
3	Compatibility	7.4		
4	Privacy	5.1		
5	Search	4.9		
6	Standards (W3C)	4.8		
7	Usability	4.6		

tral University websites are shown in Table 4. The 10-point metric quality assurance values related to website design viz., correctness, accessibility, compatibility, privacy, search, standards, usability, website structural complexity, website download time performance, overall quality and performance of various Central University websites are summarized in Table 5.

Table 3. Central Universities with Codes

S. No	Central University Name	Code
1	English and Foreign Language University, Hyderabad	EFLUH
2	Moulana Azad National Urdu University, Hyderabad	MANUUH
3	University of Hyderabad, Hyderabad	UOH
4	Rajiv Gandhi Nagar University, Itanagar	RGUI
5	Assam University	AUS
6	Tezpur University	TU
7	Central University of Bihar	CUB
8	Nalanda University	NU
9	Central University of Haryana	CUH
10	Central University of Himachal Pradesh	CUHD

Table 4. Quality Issues of Central University Websites

S. No	University	Errors	Accessibility Issues	Compatibility Issues	Privacy Issues	Search Issues	Standards Issues	Usability Issues
1	EFLUH	29	88	13	88	23	88	62
2	MANUUH	93	95	19	0	95	95	95
3	UOH	96	96	0	96	96	96	96
4	RGUI	14	60	55	54	56	54	19
5	AUS	38	66	43	18	46	47	48
6	TU	45	62	27	47	48	48	49
7	CUB	87	88	8	88	90	88	90
8	NU	13	35	17	30	31	33	31
9	CUH	45	74	10	47	47	47	47
10	CUHD	8	15	11	8	8	8	8

Table 5. Quality Status of the Central University Websites

S. No	University	Correctness	Accessibility	Compatibility	Privacy	Search	Standards	Usability	Overall Quality	Overall Performance
1	EFLUH	7.1	1.2	8.7	1.2	7.7	1.2	3.8	3.9	Very Poor
2	MANUUH	0.7	0.5	8.1	10	0.5	0.5	0.5	3.8	Very Poor
3	UOH	0.4	0.4	10	0.4	0.4	0.4	0.4	2	Very Poor
4	RGUI	8.6	4	4.5	4.6	4.4	4.6	8.1	5	Below Average
5	AUS	6.2	3.4	5.7	8.2	5.4	5.3	5.2	4.9	Poor
6	TU	5.5	3.8	7.3	5.3	5.2	5.2	5.1	4.7	Poor
7	CUB	1.3	1.2	9.2	1.2	1	1.2	1	2	Very Poor
8	NU	8.7	6.5	8.3	7	6.9	6.7	6.9	6.3	Average
9	CUH	5.5	2.6	9	5.3	5.3	5.3	5.3	5.6	Below Average
10	CUHD	9.2	8.5	8.9	9.2	9.2	9.2	9.2	8.8	Good

Figure 14. Quality Status of Central University Websites

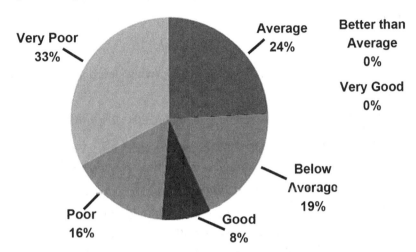

The quality status of 10 Central University websites is shown in Table 5 after thoroughly evaluating quality assurance aspects of the various Central University website in this minor research project. Also the status of the all Central University websites in terms of quality of web design is depicted in Figure 14.

CONCLUSION

The chapter identifies the various factors that influence the quality of website design. The methodology is very much comprehensive and will applicable to web application product because web application is the integration of number of different components. In this chapter, a significant effort is made to evaluate the quality assurance aspects related to website design. The chapter has shown the path and cautiousness to be adopted in web design process for the web designers not only on design but also quality of design. The importance of the quality assurance of Web Design is essential in the light of enormous growth of web applications. In this connection the theme of the chapter shows a direction to improve the web applications more viable to the need of common man and to achieve user friendly websites. Thus the presented methodology is quite helpful to address this and to achieve the end user accessibility of website which is imperative in today's context. Also, the quality web design process removes the unnecessary contents of the website and provides information that was quite useful for the user.

REFERENCES

Beirekdar, A., Vanderdonckt, J., & Noirhomme-Fraiture, M. (2002). Kwaresmi – Knowledge based Web Automated Evaluation with reconfigurable guidelines optimization. In P. Forbig, Q. Limbourg, B. Urban, & J. Vanderdonckt (Eds.), *DSV-IS 2002, LNCS, 2545* (pp. 362–376). Heidelberg: Springer.

Bevan, N. (1998). Usability Issues in Website Design. *Proceedings of UPA'98, Washington DC*, USA.

Bevan, N., & Macleod, M. (1994) Usability measurement in context, Behaviour and Information Technology, Taylor & Francis Ltd. Basingstoke, UK, 1&2.

Bobby. (n. d.). Retrieved from http://webxact.watchfire.com/

Dreyfus, P. (1998). Principles of usability. Retrieved from http://www.devedge.netscape.com/viewsource/arcive/editior98.3.23.htm

EvalIris. (n. d.). Retrieved from http://www.sc.ehu.es/acwbbpke/evaliris.html

Fitzpatrick, R., & Higgins, C. (1998). Usable software and its attributes: A synthesis of software quality, European Community law and human-computer interaction. *Proceedings of HCI'98 Conference*, Springer, London, UK. doi:10.1007/978-1-4471-3605-7_1

Herrera-Viedma, E., Lopez-Herrera, A. G., & Porcel, C. (2006). Evaluating the information quality of Web sites: A methodology based on fuzzy computing with words. *Journal of the American Society for Information Science and Technology*, 57(4), 538–549. doi:10.1002/asi.20308

Keeker, K. (1998). Improving Website Usability and Appeal. *MSN Usability Research*. Retrieved from http://www.microsoft.com/workshop/management/planning/

Marucci, L., & Patrno, F. (2000, March 27-31). Adaptive Interfaces for Web Museums Applications: the Virtual Marble Museum. Proceedings of EVA2000 – electronic Imaging & the Visual Arts, Conference, Training & Workshops, Firenze (pp. 151-155).

Nielsen, J. (1998). *Content usability, NPL: Usability Forum-Making Webs Work (Tutorial)*. Middlesex, UK: NPL.

Nielsen. (1998). Using link titles to help users predict where they are going. Retrieved from www.useit.com/alertbox/990530.html

Zakon, R.H. (2003). *Hobbes' Internet Timeline*. Retrieved from www.zakon.org/robert/internet/timeline/

Leavitt, M.O., & Shneiderman, B. (n. d.). Research-Based Web Design & Usability Guidelines.

Scharl, A. (2000). *Evolutionary Web Development (Applied Computing)*. Springer.

Signore, O., & Bartoli, R. Fresta Ga, Loffredo M (1997, September 3-5). Implementing the Cognitive Layer of a Hypermedia – Museum Interactive Multimedia 1997: Cultural Heritage Systems Design and Interfaces. In D. Bearman and J. Trant (Ed.), *Selected papers from ICHIM 97 the Fourth International Conference on Hypermedia and InterActivity in Museums*, Paris, France (pp. 15-22).

Signore, O., Marucci, L., & Leporini, B. (2004). Web accessibility: principles, international context and Italian regulations. *Proceedings of Euro CMG 2004*, Vienna.

Stern, J. (1995). *World Wide Web marketing*. New York, USA: John Wiley & Sons Inc.

Valet. (n. d.). Retrieved from http://valet.webthing.com/access/url.html

Web Content Accessibility Guidelines. W3C Recommendation (2008). retrieved from http://www.w3.org/TR/WCAG20/

Website Standards and Guidelines. (n. d.). Release 2012, version 6.0. Retrieved from http://www.state. nj.us/it/ps/web/index.html

KEY TERMS AND DEFINITIONS

Database Server Tier: Database access interfaces such as ODBC and JDBC are used to connect web applications with database servers.

Efficiency: Efficiency can be measured on the basis of amount of information and communication between system components. There must be efficient usage of resources in terms of CPU usage, memory usage and processing speed. The factors considers in efficiency characteristic are behavior, usage of resources, non-redundant and effective.

Functionality: Functionality is the system's capacity to do the work for which it was designed and the functionality is orthogonal to the structure. The factors considered in functionality characteristic are Adjustment to purposes, Precision, Interoperability, Security and Correctness.

Maintainability: Maintainability is the important characteristic in architectural design. The factors considered in maintainability are capacity of analysis, modifiability, stability and testability.

Portability: Portability is an architectural-nature characteristic and it defines the compatible issues among different browsers and systems. The factors considered in portability are adaptability, capacity of implementation, capacity of replace and consistent.

Reliability: The website must have appropriate address, short download time, multi browser support and compatible in different screen settings. The website must be available 7 days/week, 24 hours/day once it is hosted. The factors considered in reliability characteristic are Tolerance to failures, Recuperation, Maturity, Security and Correctness.

Usability: The website must easy to use, understand, operate, find information or navigate the site. The factors consider in usability characteristic are Understandability, Learn ability, Graphic Interface, Operability and Agreement respect to standards.

Web Browser Tier: A Web browser is a software application that is used to search, view and navigate Web pages hosted by Web Server over the Internet. The end user requests a Web page by entering a URL in the address bar of the Web browser. The Web browser in turn sends the request to the Web server, which sends an HTML page back to Web browser. The end user then views the returned page.

Web Server Tier: A Web server acts as a gateway between client and DBMS residing on the server. It is an application that serves Web pages over the Internet using the HTTP protocol. Web servers publish Web sites, maintain network traffic and manage user data.

Website Content: Web site content is the collection of web pages organized on a Web server. Web pages are of two types, static and dynamic.

Chapter 2
Enhancing the Quality of Educational Website Design through Assessment for Learning Strategies

Wing Shui Ng
The Hong Kong Institute of Education, Hong Kong

ABSTRACT

To improve the quality of a website, many principles or guidelines have been suggested in the literature. However, the application of related principles is not a straightforward issue. It requires the web developer with high level of self-awareness to continuously review his own works and to justify the design based on related web design principles. The web developer should behave as a reflective practitioner for creating a high-quality website which fulfilled web design principles in various aspects. However, reflection cannot be implicitly assumed as an inborn ability. Certain experiences or training must be provided so as to enable the web designer to develop high level of self-reflection. In this connection, this chapter introduces a series of assessment for learning strategies with self- and peer-assessment components for transforming a web developer into a reflective practitioner. Detailed implementation, its effectiveness and participants' opinions of the self- and peer-assessment strategy of a case study will be reported.

INTRODUCTION

Large number of websites with various themes and applications have been developed in past decade. The creation of a general purpose website has become relatively easy with the development of different web design software which help to remove lots of technical hurdles. The emphasis of web design has shift from the foundation of how to create a website to the requirement on the quality of a website. A website can be regarded as an electronic medium to convey information. Whether the presentation of information and the design of a website can enhance users' comprehension is a challenging and important issue in web design. In the literature, criteria, guidelines and principles were suggested to improve the quality of

DOI: 10.4018/978-1-4666-9764-5.ch002

web design (W3C, 2008; Zaphiris et al., 2005; Ivory & Hearst, 2002; Farkas & Farkas, 2000). However, although many web design guidelines or principles are available for reference, the application of related guidelines for creating a high-quality website is not a straightforward process. It depends very much on the ability of the web developer to continuously review his own works. The web developer should be able to sustain the awareness on related guidelines during the process of web design. It involves a high level of self-reflection to monitor the design procedure. In the literature, few studies can be found to suggest strategies to enhance the web designer's competence of reflection in the process of creating a high quality website.

To transform a web designer into a reflective practitioner, strategies are required to allow him or her to engage in a mindful process of web design. In this connection, the self- and peer-assessment strategies have been recognized with the impact of encouraging individuals to become more reflective in their own working process (Dochy et al., 1999). The underlying rationale is based on the assessment for learning initiative which has been advocated in recent years especially after the contribution of Black and Wiliam (1998) who conducted extensive review on related research and confirmed beneficial evidences in improving performance. For the sake of improving the quality of a website, this chapter aims to introduce a self- and peer-assessment strategy to enhance a web developer's awareness on the application of web design principles in the web creation process. The chapter will also reports the experience of implementing the strategy. Actual improvements on the web design and participants' opinions toward the strategy will also be elaborated.

BACKGROUND

This section provides a discussion on what competence a web developer should acquire so as to create a high-quality website. The author attempts to elaborate the challenge of creating a high-quality website. It follows with an introduction on some suggested web design principles or guidelines on various aspects for improving the quality of web design. The issue on the requirement of a web developer to mindfully reflect on the application of web design principles in the process is identified at the end of this section.

The Challenge of Creating a High-Quality Website

The design of a website can be regarded as a complicated process since it demands knowledge and skills in various domains. The fundamental purpose of creating a website is to convey information to the target audiences. The strategy to appropriately arrange texts, graphics and other elements in the website is critical for creating an effective communication with target users. Research can be found to address the communication issues in web design. For example, in Burch's (2001) article, it explored the communications issues in web-based distance education and discussed related web design considerations. Geissler, Zinkhan, and Watson (2001) also conducted a study on web page complexity and further suggested that communication effectiveness is related to web page complexity. As reflected in the nature of a website, a web developer should equip with certain level of understanding on communication theory for creating a high-quality website.

The aesthetic design of a website can also be regarded as an important attribute of a high-quality website. A website is required to be appealing so as to attract target users to explore the website. It is interesting that most users' first impression on a website was the impression of beauty (Schenkman &

Jonsson, 2000). Research suggested that users will make the decision on whether or not to continue navigating the website during the first few seconds (Tractinsky et al., 2006; Tractinsky et al., 2004). Some researchers further argued that the first impression on the website is constructed in about 50 ms and it will remain stable over time (Lindgaard et al., 2006). In addition, the positive emotional effects brought from the beautiful design make users perceive difficult tasks easier to perform (Chawda et al., 2005; Norman, 2002). The web designer should therefore equip with art knowledge so as to appropriately manipulate web page elements such as color, texture, graphics and page layout for creating a beautiful website.

As the purpose of a website is to convey information to the target users or to facilitate users' on-line activities, a careful consideration on the attributes of the target users is critical for the success of a website. As mentioned by Ng (2014), the "User Oriented Aspect" is one of the critical web design considerations. A website has to be designed in a user-friendly format which involved the consideration of web navigation, web usability and web accessibility (Harper & Yesilada, 2008; Farkas & Farkas, 2000). Therefore, the web developer should have knowledge in the area of human computer interaction for creating a highly usable website.

A web developer should also equip with sufficient knowledge on internet technologies and multimedia manipulation skills so as to create an effective website from technological concerns. Furthermore, as the contents in the website are published materials which can be accessed by people around the world, the web developer must have strong sense on legal aspect and high level of ethics so as to avoid any possible infringement of intellectual property. As reflected in this discussion, the creation of a high-quality website can be regarded as a complicated process. A web developer must equip with lots of skills and knowledge in many areas together with good attitude on respecting intellectual property so as to create a high-quality website. Although different web design software are available to alleviate the technological hurdles, it is still a great challenge to create a high-quality website.

Web Design Principles

In view of the difficulties of creating a high quality website, web design guidelines in various aspects have been suggested to assist web developers in the design process. In this section, related principles or guidelines in the Multimedia Oriented Aspect, User Oriented Aspect and Educational Oriented Aspect (Ng, 2014) will be systematically introduced so as to better understand the development of web design principles for improving the quality of a website.

Multimedia Oriented Aspect

A website can be considered as a container to incorporate different multimedia elements. Multimedia elements are the building blocks to create a website. Thus, to appropriate manipulate multimedia elements is the foundation of creating a high-quality website. In this Multimedia Oriented Aspect, principles on handling multimedia elements, such as text, color, graphics, audio and video, will be elaborated.

Text and Typography

In information technology, text is a human-readable sequence of characters and the words they form that can be encoded into computer-readable formats such as ASCII. Typography is the art and technique of arranging type in order to make language visible. It involves the selection of typefaces, point size, line length, leading which concerns the line spacing, tracking which considers the adjustment of the spaces between groups of letters and kerning that adjusts the space between pairs of letters. It is suggested that a screen should use only one font unless certain materials are required to be emphasized (Bailey & Milheim, 1991). Similar advices were provided by Garner (1990) that varying the size and font of text can be used to attract attention and Hannafin and Hooper (1989) that the control of selective perception and the attention of identified information can be achieved by highlighting of text. Moreover, it has been identified that san-serif fonts work better on computer screen (Poncelet & Proctor, 1993) and flashing of text should never be used due to the difficulty to read and distracting (Jonassen & Hannum, 1987). In addition, titles and headings should be centered while text should be left justified with upper and lowercase letters to enhance readability (Garner, 1990).

Color

The first impression of visiting a website from users' perspective is the impression of beauty (Shenkman & Jonsson, 2000) and color plays an important role. Based on the literature review by Stemler (1997), a maximum of three to six colors per screen should be used since the more color that is used, the less effective it becomes. The use of colors should be consistent. Important information should be presented using bright colors. A neutral gray is a good choice of background color. High level of contrast between text and background color should be maintained for better text readability. Using dark letters with light background for text is recommended. Moreover, complementary colors, such as red and green, should be avoided. The common meaning of colors, such as red for stop or warning, should also be observed.

Graphics

Graphics and images are more effective than text when conducting presentations. Complex idea can be conveyed using a single still image. Examples of graphics include photographs, drawings, line art, graphs, diagrams, etc. According to Skaalid (1999), it is recommended to use the amount of graphics only if it is absolutely necessary so as to maintain the simplicity of a webpage. Superfluous graphics should be avoided since it can interfere with understanding. The style of graphics should be keep consistency. To maintain the harmony of a webpage, pictures should match the topic and graphics should be similar in tone.

Audio

Audio is sound within the acoustic range available to humans. To use audio in web design is a controversial topic since users may find it irritating to listen to sound effects on a webpage and may feel uncomfortable when users are not able to turn it off (Kyrnin, 2015). Although audio is generally not favorable, it is especially suitable for music websites to showcase audio tracks. Online game websites also make extensive use of audio effects for making the games more fun. In addition, audio embedded in a webpage is a good strategy to stimulate and to engage children (Kyrnin, 2015). On the other hand, audio can be used to provide instructions, feedback and to promote interaction (Kaushansky, 2012). To include audio in a web page, Kyrnin (2015) suggested that control of the sound should be provided to users, audio should not be played automatically when a webpage is loaded, link to sound files should be provided to allow users decide whether to play the audio and copyrighted audio should not be used without permission.

Video

Video is a major element in presenting multimedia contents since it can provide vivid descriptions to articulate tacit information and knowledge difficult to describe through text (Steeples, 1998). The Research-Based Web Design & Usability Guidelines (Department of Health and Human Services, 2006) stressed that although video can add value to a website's content and help direct users to the most important information, cautions must be observed in its applications. Video should be used only when they help to convey a website's message. If it is used carelessly, videos can distract users and dramatically decline download speeds. For examples, a video of talking head lectures, a how-to video, a video of real events are some effective applications of video on a website (VideoAktiv, 2006).

User Oriented Aspect

Since the main purpose of creating a website is to convey information to target users, the User Oriented Aspect focuses on the consideration of users and their interaction to the webpage. The design of a web page should be usable and cater for a wide spectrum of users. It includes web design guidelines of web usability, web accessibility and web navigation.

Web Usability

Web usability is generally referred to an approach to make websites easy to use for an end user who does not require to undertake any specialized training. The concept of usability was rooted in human-computer interaction (HCI) which defined as "the extent to which a product can be used by specified users to achieve specified goals with effectiveness, efficiency and satisfaction in a specified context of use" (ISO, 1997). In this area, Nielsen (1995) suggested 10 good heuristics for user interface design. First of all, the system should from time to time keep users informed its current status and what will happen next. The second heuristic concerns the presentation of information. Natural, real word language with users' familiar words, phrases and concepts should be used. Regarding the third heuristic, Nielsen suggested that the system should allow users to freely exit any unwanted state. The fourth heuristic focuses on the requirement of consistency on words, situations and actions provided by the system. The fifth heuristic requires the system to eliminate any possible error as far as possible. The sixth heuristic is to minimize users' memory load by making objects, actions and options visible so that recall of information is not required. The seventh heuristic addresses the flexibility and efficiency of use. It requires the system to cater for both experience and inexperience users and allows users to customize their actions. The next heuristic suggests that any dialogues of the system should only contain related information. Irrelevant information should be removed. The ninth heuristic requires the system to express error messages and suggested solutions precisely in plain English. The last heuristic suggests the system to provide help and documentation to assist users. All these suggested heuristics provide the direction for a web designer to create a more usable website.

Web Accessibility

Web accessibility refers to the practice of making pages on the web accessible to all users, especially to those with disabilities (Thatcher, 2006). The international organization W3C (2008) suggested a set of web content accessibility guidelines (WCAG) 2.0 which grouped into 4 categories, namely perceivable, operable, understandable and robust. Regarding the requirement of perceivable, the design of webpage should provide text alternatives for any non-text content so that it can be changed into other forms people need, such as large print, braille, speech, symbols or simpler language. In addition, a webpage should provide alternatives for time-based media. For example, captions should be provided for all prerecorded audio content in synchronized media. Another guideline of perceivable is to create contents that can be presented in different ways without losing information and structure. In addition, the design of a web-page should make it easier for users to see and hear content including separating from foreground and background so as to make it more perceivable. In the category of operable, related guidelines include to make all functionality available from a keyboard, to provide users enough time to read and use content, to avoid the design that causes seizures and to provide ways to help users navigate, find contents and determine where they are. In the understandable category, it is suggested that contents should be readable and understandable, web pages should appear and operate in predictable ways and efforts should be paid to help users avoid and correct mistakes. Concerning the robust category, the design of a web page should maximize compatibility with current and future user agents, including assistive technologies.

Web Navigation

The design of a website should allow users effectively navigate a network of information within the website. In this connection, Farkas and Farkas (2000) suggested 12 guidelines on web navigation. The first category of guideline emphasizes the importance of designing an effective link. Web designer should ensure that all links indicate that they are links, users will be able to view and notice links, and all links clearly indicate their destinations. When there are large numbers of links, the web designer should manage them effectively. The guidelines are to plan effective ratios of breadth and depth in web site hierarchies, supplement the primary links of a web site with secondary links when appropriate, allow branches of a hierarchy to converge when appropriate and design the interface to readily reveal the underlying information structure. On the other hand, the design of a website should provide orientation information. It can be achieved by providing clear, brief and highly conspicuous orientation information on the home page and to provide orientation information on lower-level pages to support continued exploration of the website. Furthermore, web navigation can also be improved by augmenting link-to-link navigation. The strategies are to employ site maps to show the global structure of a site and to provide direct access to nodes, and to provide a search facility or an index for direct access to content.

Educational Oriented Aspect

The Educational Oriented aspect focuses on web design guidelines for improving the quality of educational websites. An educational website is referred to an online electronic platform to store resources for facilitating educational purposes (Ng, 2014). Web design guidelines concern the strategies to improve the comprehension of information and to enhance learning effectiveness.

Multimedia Learning Principles

Since multimedia elements are the building blocks of a webpage, appropriate manipulation of related elements is significant to assist users' learning when browsing the website. In this connection, Mayer (2009) suggested 12 principles of multimedia learning. The first principle is the Coherence Principle. It states that people learn better when extraneous material is excluded rather than included. The Signaling

Principle suggests that people learn better when cues that highlight the organization of the essential material are added. The next is the Redundancy Principle. It points out that people learn better from graphics and narration than from graphics, narration and printed text. Besides, the Spatial Contiguity Principle advises that students learn better when corresponding words and pictures are presented near rather than far from each other on the screen. While the Spatial Contiguity Principle concerns the positions of elements, the Temporal Contiguity Principle focuses on time issue. It suggests that students learn better when corresponding words and pictures are presented simultaneously rather than successively. On the other hand, people learn better when a multimedia message is presented in user-paced segments rather than as a continuous unit which refers to the Segmenting Principle. For the Pre-training Principle, people learn more deeply from a multimedia message when they know the names and the characteristics of the main concepts. It suggests that materials for pre-training should be included in the website. Moreover, the Modality Principle states that people learn more deeply from pictures and spoken words than from pictures and printed words. The idea of Multimedia Principle is straightforward that people learn better from words and pictures than from words alone. Another principle is the Personalization Principle which states that people learn better from multimedia presentations when words are in conversational style rather than formal style. The last two principles are the Voice Principle and the Image Principle. Voice Principle points out that people learn better when the narration in multimedia presentations is spoken in a friendly human voice rather than a machine voice. The Image Principle states that people do not necessary learn better from a multimedia presentation when the speaker's image is added to the screen. All these principles assist the web designer to create a high-quality educational website.

Further to abovementioned web design principles or guidelines, a relatively comprehensive set of guidelines can be found is the Research-Based Web Design & Usability Guidelines published by the U.S. Department of Health and Human Services (2006) which incorporated more than two hundred guidelines in different categories. More guidelines on designing educational websites can also be found in the literature (Ng, 2014; Hsu et al., 2009). In addition, Ivory and Hearst (2002) developed a quality-checker that was similar to grammar-checkers in word processors to help web designers in creating high quality websites and Zaphiris et al. (2005) introduced a set of age-centered research-based web design guidelines. It is undeniable that related guidelines are good references to improve the quality of a website. However, an integrated application of these guidelines or principles in web design is not a straightforward process. It depends very much on the ability of the web developer to continuously review his own works. The web developer should be able to sustain the awareness on related guidelines during the process of web design. It involves a high level of self-reflection to monitor the design procedure. To tackle the difficulty, the self- and peer- assessment strategies may be a possible solution.

Reflection by Self- and Peer-Assessment

Reflection was broadly defined by Habermas (1973) as a process of critical self-determination and by Calderhead (1989) as an acquisition of attitudes and skills in thinking. Schon (1991) suggested the "reflection in action" which describes the spontaneous process of framing and reframing in professional practice. To transform a web designer into a reflective practitioner, strategies are required to allow him or her to engage in a mindful process of web design. In this connection, the self- and peer-assessment strategies have been recognized with the impact of encouraging individuals to become more reflective in their own working process (Dochy et al., 1999). The underlying rationale is based on the assessment for learning initiative which has been advocated in recent years especially after the contribution of

Black and Wiliam (1998) who conducted extensive review on related research and confirmed beneficial evidences in improving performance. Self-assessment refers to the involvement of individuals in making judgments about their own works (Boud & Falchikov, 1989) while peer- assessment is defined by Topping (1998, p. 250) as *an arrangement in which individuals consider the amount, level, value, worth, quality, or success of the products or outcomes of the works of peers of similar status.* Actually, the benefit of self- and peer- assessment strategies in improving performance has been well documented (Topping, 1998; Dochy et al., 1999). During the process of web design, the web developer is required to continuously review whether the design of website fulfilled different sets of web design principles. The reflective ability is therefore critical in the process. However, an individual's self-reflection process cannot be assumed as an inborn ability. It requires an individual to experience some related strategies for developing necessary self-reflection abilities.

SOLUTIONS AND RECOMMENDATIONS

In this section, a case study on applying assessment for learning strategies with self- and peer-assessment components to improve the quality of educational websites design will be elaborated. Detailed implementation and its effectiveness on improving web design will be presented. A number of examples on actual improvements of web design will be discussed so as to explore to what extent does the self- and peer- assessment strategy improves the quality of web design. In addition, participants' perspectives on the process and effectiveness of applying the self- and peer- assessment strategy in improving web design will also be reported.

Context of the Case Study

The case study was conducted in a course entitled Principles and Practice of Web Design taught by the author. The course with 13 sessions was offered to a class of first-year undergraduates of a science and web technology bachelor programme. Principles and concepts for visual design of modern website were covered in the course. It also explored the criteria of web design for meeting specific needs of different target users. Participants were required to critically evaluate and to develop high quality websites with related web design principles and concepts. There were 31 participants with 21 males and 10 females. Four participants reported to have experience on learning information technology courses in post-secondary education. The case was conducted from January to April in 2012.

In order to obtain participants' consent to the collection of data during the web design process, a consent form was given to the participants at the early stages of the course which clearly stated that the data were being collected solely for academic use. Participants were requested to participate in lesson activities as usual and were told that information about individuals would never be disclosed. They were also advised that their assessment results would not be affected by any data analysis procedure. The participants were invited to sign the consent form to indicate their agreement and all eventually did so.

Procedure of the Self and Peer Assessment Strategy

Principles or guidelines on web design were covered in the first nine sessions of the course to enrich participants' foundation knowledge. Related guidelines in "Multimedia Oriented Aspect", "User Oriented Aspect" and "Education Oriented Aspect" suggested by Ng (2014) were elaborated. Guidelines in "Multimedia Oriented Aspect" focus on manipulating multimedia elements effectively to improve the quality of a website. Skills and knowledge such as appropriate usage of text and typography, texture, color, graphics, audio, video and animation were covered. Regarding the "User Oriented Aspect", principles on web usability, web accessibility and web navigation were elaborated. Since the course was focused on education, principles concerning the "Education Oriented Aspect" such as the application of multimedia learning theory suggested by Mayer (2009) in web design were also discussed. Participants were also provided opportunities to evaluate some educational websites based on related web design principles. At the early stage of the course, participants were requested to form groups by themselves of size about 3-4 members to create educational websites on any topics. A total of 8 groups were formed. Each group was required to prepare a first draft of the educational website before the 10th session of the course. By giving lectures on related web design principles, participants were expected to obtain sufficient understanding on web design principles in different aspects.

The self- and peer-assessment activities were arranged in session 10 of the course. All assessment activities were carried out in a wiki platform prepared by the author. Actually, wiki has been used in a number of studies as an environment for implementing assessment strategies (Ng, 2011; Lai & Ng, 2011; Xiao & Lucking, 2008). The primary purposes of the wiki technology are to facilitate generation, collaboration and distribution of contents in a quick and easy way and it has been regarded as an effective tool for online collaboration and discussion (O'Leary, 2008). The rationale of using wiki for the implementation of self- and peer- assessment was also supported by Topping (1998) that computer-assisted assessment is an emerging growth area due to the rapid development of Internet technologies and Stodberg (2012) that more research is recommended to expand the knowledge of e-assessment, including the application of Web 2.0 technologies in assessment.

Participants were instructed to carry out self- and peer-assessment on the draft educational website created by each group based on three chosen aspects which were text and typography, color and multimedia learning principles. Reichenstein (2006) stressed the important for web designers to get acquainted with the discipline of shaping written information since the proportion of written language is as high as 95% of web information. On the other hand, color was considered as a critical design element since most users' first impression of a website was that of beauty and it also influences users' subsequent navigation (Lindgaard et al., 2006, Shenkman & Jonsson, 2000). Since the participants were requested to create an educational website, how to appropriately arrange multimedia elements in a website to support learning is an important issue. The multimedia learning principles suggested by Mayer (2009) were therefore chosen as one of the aspects in the self- and peer-assessment activities. Since the purpose of the self- and peer-assessment activities were to provide an experience for participants to reflect their own works, three aspects of web design principles were considered as sufficient to achieve the purpose for transforming participants into reflective practitioners.

Self-Assessment

Session 10 of the course started with participants' self-assessment on the educational website created by their own group. They were required to evaluate whether the design of the website fulfilled related web design principles or guidelines and to provide evidence to support their judgments. For those designs which did not fulfill related principles, they had to provide suggestions on how to improve the web design.

The self-assessment learning activity aimed at giving an opportunity for them to reflect on their own work by critically evaluate their own website according to related principles. They were also expected to develop a better understanding of web design principles so as to prepare for the peer-assessment activity.

Peer-Assessment

After the self-assessment, participants were instructed to carry out a reciprocal peer-assessment on the educational website created by another group. The procedure of assessment was similar to that in self-assessment which used the same set of web design principles for evaluation except that they were requested to assess the website created by peers. Through being engaged in peer-assessment, participants were expected to learn from the strengths and weaknesses of peers and thereby reflect on their own work on the applications of web design principles. Similarly, for those designs of the website which did not fulfill related principles, they had to provide constructive feedback to peers on how to improve the website.

After the self- and peer-assessment activities in session 10, participants were invited to fill out a questionnaire adapted from that developed by Falchikov (1986) so as to collect their opinions on the strategy. For example, they were asked whether they thought more, learned more and were more critical on web design in the self- and peer-assessment process. Participants were invited to express their comments on different impacts initiated from the strategy by rating in the scale from 1 to 10. Results are shown in Table 1 and Table 4. After the self- and peer-assessment activities, they were encouraged to revise the website based on the feedback obtained from themselves or peers for preparing the finalized website. In addition to submit the finalized website, participants were required to submit a Website Revisions Record Form prepared by the author to report under which web design principles the revisions were made and the source of feedback whether it was from self, peers or both.

After participants' grades were announced at the end of the course, representatives of four groups were invited to attend an interview. Participants were requested to illustrate how revisions on the created website were made due to reflection on comments given in the self- and peer-assessment process. They were also invited to express their overall opinions on the self- and peer-assessment strategy.

Results

In this study, data from different sources was collected to explore the effectiveness of the strategy. It includes the questionnaires filled out by students in session 10, the Website Revisions Record Forms which reported revisions made on web design, the draft and final educational websites created by participants and their opinions provided in the interview. A total of 24 questionnaires were returned which constituted about 83% response rate given that 29 students attended the class. In the following section, participants' opinions toward the strategy expressed in the questionnaires will be reported first. Results obtained from the Website Revisions Record Form and examples on actual improvement will be elaborated subsequently. Lastly, participants' overall comments on the self- and peer-assessment strategy on improving web design will be discussed.

Participants' Opinions on the Strategy

Since participants were invited to express their opinions in the range from 1 to 10 with 1 indicates less impact and 10 indicates more impact on a particular aspect, value 5.5 as the mid-point of the range could

Table 1. One-sample t-test descriptive statistics of the effects of self-assessment strategy on web design process

	N	Mean	Std. Deviation	Std. Error Mean
Self Active	24	6.00	1.414	.289
Self Serious	24	6.17	1.373	.280
Self Independent	24	6.21	1.250	.255
Self Think	24	6.42	1.613	.329
Self Learn More	24	6.38	1.813	.370
Self Confident	24	6.50	1.351	.276
Self Critical	24	6.38	1.377	.281
Self Time Saving	24	5.54	1.865	.381
Self Enjoyable	24	5.08	1.840	.376
Self Easy	24	5.67	1.579	.322
Self Challenging	24	6.25	2.005	.409
Self Helpful	24	5.92	1.501	.306
Self Beneficial	24	6.13	1.424	.291

be regarded as representing the neutral stance. In Table 1 and Table 2, the code "Self Active" means "The self-assessment strategy made me more active in the learning process." As shown in Table 1, the mean values of participants' opinions toward different effects of the self-assessment strategy fell in the range 5.08 to 6.50. In order to verify whether there were significant differences between participants'

Table 2. One-sample t-test results of the effects of self-assessment strategy on web design process

	Test Value = 5.5					
	t	df	Sig. (2-tailed)	Mean Difference	95% Confidence Interval of the Difference	
					Lower	Upper
Self Active	1.732	23	.097	.500	-.10	1.10
Self Serious	2.379	23	.026	.667	.09	1.25
Self Independent	2.775	23	.011	.708	.18	1.24
Self Think	2.784	23	.011	.917	.24	1.60
Self Learn More	2.364	23	.027	.875	.11	1.64
Self Confident	3.625	23	.001	1.000	.43	1.57
Self Critical	3.113	23	.005	.875	.29	1.46
Self Time Saving	.109	23	.914	.042	-.75	.83
Self Enjoyable	-1.110	23	.279	-.417	-1.19	.36
Self Easy	.517	23	.610	.167	-.50	.83
Self Challenging	1.832	23	.080	.750	-.10	1.60
Self Helpful	1.360	23	.187	.417	-.22	1.05
Self Beneficial	2.151	23	.042	.625	.02	1.23

opinions and the neutral stance, the one sample t-test on mid value 5.5 was executed. Also executed was a K-S test on the 24 questionnaires returned, which confirmed that the normal distribution hypothesis of all items related to the effects of the strategy could be retained. As shown in Table 2, participants' opinions on the effects of self-assessment including serious, independent, think, learn more, confident, critical and beneficial showed significant values with 95% confidence interval. The mean values of all these aspects fell in the range 6.13 to 6.50 which were higher than the mid value 5.5. It suggests that the self-assessment strategy made them more serious, more independent with more critical thinking. They also learned more, more confident and found the self-assessment strategy beneficial. In other words, the self-assessment strategy engaged them with critical independent reflection with serious attitude and they found it beneficial in the web design process.

Similar analysis was conducted for the impacts of peer-assessment strategy in the web design learning process. The code "Peer Active" means "The peer assessment strategy made me more active in the learning process". As shown in Table 3, the mean values of participants' opinions toward different effects of the peer-assessment strategy fell in the range 5.04 to 6.57. The one sample t-test on mid value 5.5 was also executed to verify whether there were significant differences between participants' opinions and the neutral stance. As shown in Table 4, participants' opinions on the effects of peer-assessment including active, serious, independent, think and learn more showed significant values with 95% confidence interval. The mean values of all these aspects fell in the range 6.29 to 6.57 which were higher than the mid value 5.5. It reflects that the peer-assessment strategy made them more active, more serious independent thinking and learned more. The results were similarly to that obtained from the impacts of self-assessment strategy. The peer-assessment strategy made participants more reflect in the web design process and they had better learning on web design.

To explore whether any difference existed on participants' opinions of the effectiveness between self- and peer-assessment strategies, the pair sample t-test analysis was conducted on mean values of different aspects (see Table 5 and Table 6). Results show that no significant difference was found in all aspects.

Table 3. One-sample t-test descriptive statistics of the effects of peer-assessment strategy on web design process

	N	Mean	Std. Deviation	Std. Error Mean
Peer Active	24	6.46	1.668	.340
Peer Serious	24	6.33	1.465	.299
Peer Independent	24	6.29	1.488	.304
Peer Think	23	6.57	1.409	.294
Peer Learn More	24	6.50	1.588	.324
Peer Confident	24	5.92	1.558	.318
Peer Critical	24	6.17	1.685	.344
Peer Time Saving	23	5.70	2.512	.524
Peer Enjoyable	23	5.04	2.078	.433
Peer Easy	23	5.70	1.663	.347
Peer Challenging	23	5.91	1.474	.307
Peer Helpful	23	6.04	1.665	.347
Peer Beneficial	23	6.09	1.593	.332

Table 4. One-sample t-test results of the effects of peer-assessment strategy on web design process

	Test Value = 5.5					
	t	df	Sig. (2-tailed)	Mean Difference	95% Confidence Interval of the Difference	
					Lower	Upper
Peer Active	2.815	23	.010	.958	.25	1.66
Peer Serious	2.788	23	.010	.833	.21	1.45
Peer Independent	2.606	23	.016	.792	.16	1.42
Peer Think	3.627	22	.001	1.065	.46	1.67
Peer Learn More	3.085	23	.005	1.000	.33	1.67
Peer Confident	1.310	23	.203	.417	-.24	1.07
Peer Critical	1.938	23	.065	.667	-.05	1.38
Peer Time Saving	.373	22	.712	.196	-.89	1.28
Peer Enjoyable	-1.054	22	.303	-.457	-1.35	.44
Peer Easy	.564	22	.578	.196	-.52	.91
Peer Challenging	1.344	22	.193	.413	-.22	1.05
Peer Helpful	1.566	22	.132	.543	-.18	1.26
Peer Beneficial	1.767	22	.091	.587	-.10	1.28

It suggests that participants perceived the impact of both self- and peer-assessment strategies on web design process were similar. In addition to the results shown in Table 1 to Table 4, participants' views on the applied strategy were generally positive. However, although no significant result was found in their views of whether the strategy was enjoyable, it is valuable to note that the mean values were below the midpoint (5.5) of the response scale. It may indicate that students did not find the strategy enjoyable even though they engaged in reflection on web design and the quality of the website was improved eventually.

Effectiveness on Improving Web Design

As mentioned in previous section, participants were required to submit a Website Revisions Record Form together with the final website. The form allows students to report under which web design principles the revisions on web design were made. They also had to indicate whether the revisions were made according to feedback obtained during the self-assessment, peer-assessment or both. Based on the Website Revisions Form received from 8 groups, total number of reported revisions in various web design principles was 100 in which 56% of revisions were made based on feedback from self-assessment, 19% of revisions were made based on feedback from peers and 25% of revisions were made based on feedback from both self- and peer-assessment. These results suggest that most of the improvements made on the website were based on self-reflection and comments from peers had less impacts on participants. Regarding the distribution of revisions in different categories of web design principles, the revisions involved 60.7% of the provided web design principles in the aspect of text and typography, 62.5% of the provided web design principles in the aspect of color and 63.5% of the provided web design principles in the aspect of multimedia learning principles respectively.

Table 5. Pair-sample t-test descriptive statistics of the effects of self- and peer-assessment strategy on web design process

		Mean	N	Std. Deviation	Std. Error Mean
Pair 1	Self Active	6.00	24	1.414	.289
	Peer Active	6.46	24	1.668	.340
Pair 2	Self Serious	6.17	24	1.373	.280
	Peer Serious	6.33	24	1.465	.299
Pair 3	Self Independent	6.21	24	1.250	.255
	Peer Independent	6.29	24	1.488	.304
Pair 4	Self Think	6.52	23	1.563	.326
	Peer Think	6.57	23	1.409	.294
Pair 5	Self Learn More	6.38	24	1.813	.370
	Peer Learn More	6.50	24	1.588	.324
Pair 6	Self Confident	6.50	24	1.351	.276
	Peer Confident	5.92	24	1.558	.318
Pair 7	Self Critical	6.38	24	1.377	.281
	Peer Critical	6.17	24	1.685	.344
Pair 8	Self Time Saving	5.52	23	1.904	.397
	Peer Time Saving	5.70	23	2.512	.524
Pair 9	Self Enjoyable	5.00	23	1.834	.382
	Peer Enjoyable	5.04	23	2.078	.433
Pair 10	Self Easy	5.61	23	1.588	.331
	Peer Easy	5.70	23	1.663	.347
Pair 11	Self Challenging	6.26	23	2.050	.427
	Peer Challenging	5.91	23	1.474	.307
Pair 12	Self Helpful	5.87	23	1.517	.316
	Peer Helpful	6.04	23	1.665	.347
Pair 13	Self Beneficial	6.13	23	1.456	.303
	Peer Beneficial	6.09	23	1.593	.332

Improvement Examples

During the interviews, students elaborated a number of examples on website revisions as a result of the self- and peer-assessment strategy. Some typical examples are presented in this section to elaborate the effectiveness of the self- and peer-assessment strategy in improving web design.

Example 1

A website related to sex education was created by one of the groups. The first draft of a subpage with sex education of boys is shown in Figure 1. In the first draft, the style of the word "Boys" including the font and size was similar to that of its contents. During the self-assessment activity, participants reflected on the quality of the website based on principle suggested by Stemler (1997) that *varying the size and*

Table 6. Pair-sample t-test results of the effects of self- and peer-assessment strategy on web design process

		Paired Differences					t	df	Sig. (2-tailed)
		Mean	Std. Deviation	Std. Error Mean	95% Confidence Interval of the Difference				
					Lower	Upper			
Pair 1	Self Active - Peer Active	-.458	1.693	.346	-1.173	.257	-1.326	23	.198
Pair 2	Self Serious - Peer Serious	-.167	1.204	.246	-.675	.342	-.678	23	.504
Pair 3	Self Independent - Peer Independent	-.083	1.283	.262	-.625	.458	-.318	23	.753
Pair 4	Self Think - Peer Think	-.043	1.692	.353	-.775	.688	-.123	22	.903
Pair 5	Self Learn More - Peer Learn More	-.125	1.676	.342	-.833	.583	-.365	23	.718
Pair 6	Self Confident - Peer Confident	.583	1.792	.366	-.173	1.340	1.595	23	.124
Pair 7	Self Critical - Peer Critical	.208	1.285	.262	-.334	.751	.794	23	.435
Pair 8	Self Time Saving - Peer Time Saving	-.174	2.103	.439	-1.083	.736	-.397	22	.695
Pair 9	Self Enjoyable - Peer Enjoyable	-.043	1.692	.353	-.775	.688	-.123	22	.903
Pair 10	Self Easy - Peer Easy	-.087	1.621	.338	-.788	.614	-.257	22	.799
Pair 11	Self Challenging - Peer Challenging	.348	1.873	.391	-.462	1.158	.890	22	.383
Pair 12	Self Helpful - Peer Helpful	-.174	1.696	.354	-.907	.560	-.492	22	.628
Pair 13	Self Beneficial - Peer Beneficial	.043	1.430	.298	-.575	.662	.146	22	.885

Figure 1. First draft webpage of example 1

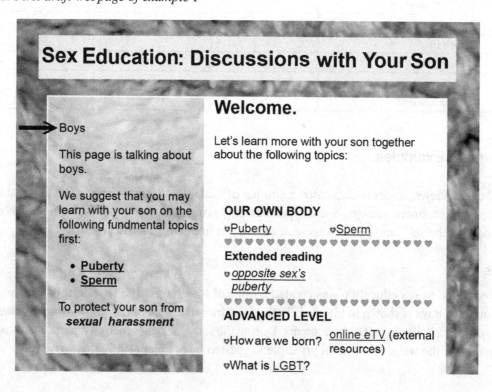

font of text can be used to attract attention. Participants realized that the word "Boys" was a subtitle of the page and should be made outstanding. It was changed to larger size and bold face subsequently to attract users' attention (Figure 2).

Example 2

Another subpage of the sex education website was related to Lesbian, Gay, Bisexual and Transgender (LGBT). The first draft website is shown in Figure 3. Participants assessed their own website and suggested that the letters "L", "G", "B" and "T" should be more outstanding so that users could know what these letters stand for. In this connection, participants reviewed the principle *highlighting of text helps to control selective perception and focus attention on identified information* (Stemler, 1997) and came up with the revised version webpage (Figure 4) with related letters in bold face. With this change, users could easily identify what these letters stand for.

Example 3

A website of handicraft was created by another group. As reported by the participants, white color was used in the background of the first draft (Figure 5). After reviewed the website, the authors reflected that color and texture used should be in harmony with the theme of the website. With this consideration, wood texture of brown color was applied in the background as participants regarded that wood is a raw material of making handicrafts (Figure 6).

Figure 2. Final version webpage of example 1

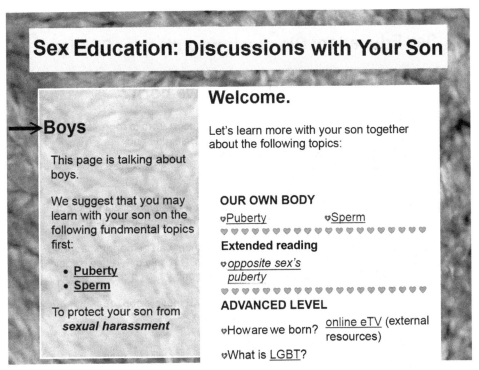

Figure 3. First draft webpage of example 2

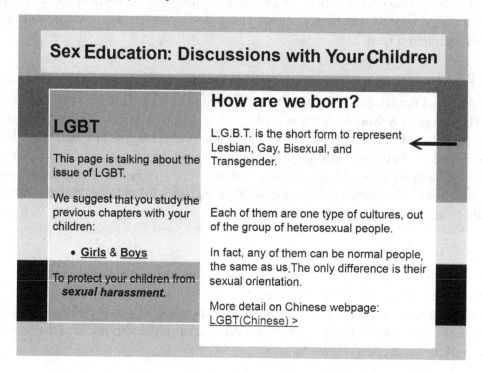

Figure 4. Final version webpage of example 2

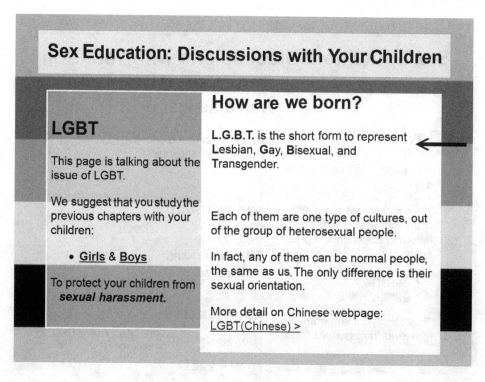

Figure 5. First draft webpage of example 3

Figure 6. Final version webpage of example 3

Example 4

As shown in Figure 7, teaching examples of bamboo carving were included in the subpage. In the first draft, text contents were displayed and followed by related images. During the peer assessment activity, it was suggested that images should be put closed to related text to fulfill the Spatial Contiguity Principle (Mayer, 2009) that *students learn better when corresponding words and pictures are presented near rather than far from each other on the page or screen.* After reviewed the design and reflected on the principle with peer comments, texts and images were displayed in a tabular format closed to each other so as to fulfill the principle (Figure 8).

Figure 7. First draft webpage of example 4

Teaching Examples

1. intaglio:

Carved into the surface depression, capacity just as the pen moves, rely on skilled and accurate techniques, so that the lines have the effect of the origins and destinations and frustrated, the knife can not Gou, mistaken pen or paint to cover up the carved bamboo is not the knife down, no change.

2.Yang carved:

The pattern carved up as that raised the candle, and some have several layers of, in particular, is the landscaping works as a theme more to bring out its characteristics. The Qing Dynasty antique contact pattern painting is the sun carved masterpiece.

3. Relief

Divided into deep relief and bas-relief. Department of deep relief carving three-dimensional or quasi three-dimensional figure or landscape theme in the thick bamboo or bamboo, but also the so-called "sticks to the outer leaves".
Most bas-relief carving of one or two levels, generally there are two kinds, a protruding layer of bamboo things, not to the base scraped; only things carved the edges scraped off that foundation and pattern is as high as this technique is that "thin sun carving.

4. Sculpture in the round (three-dimensional carving):

Zhugen part of such works as the main properly feed material, such as flowers, birds, insects, animal all-encompassing view from the use of water Sheng, printed on buttons, pen holder, cleverly designed as figures or auspicious beast.

5. Leaving Qingyang text carved:

This is the only carved bamboo have the technology, the pattern carved raised the candle, this candle is all set aside a thin layer of bamboo skin formed.

Figure 8. Final version webpage of example 4

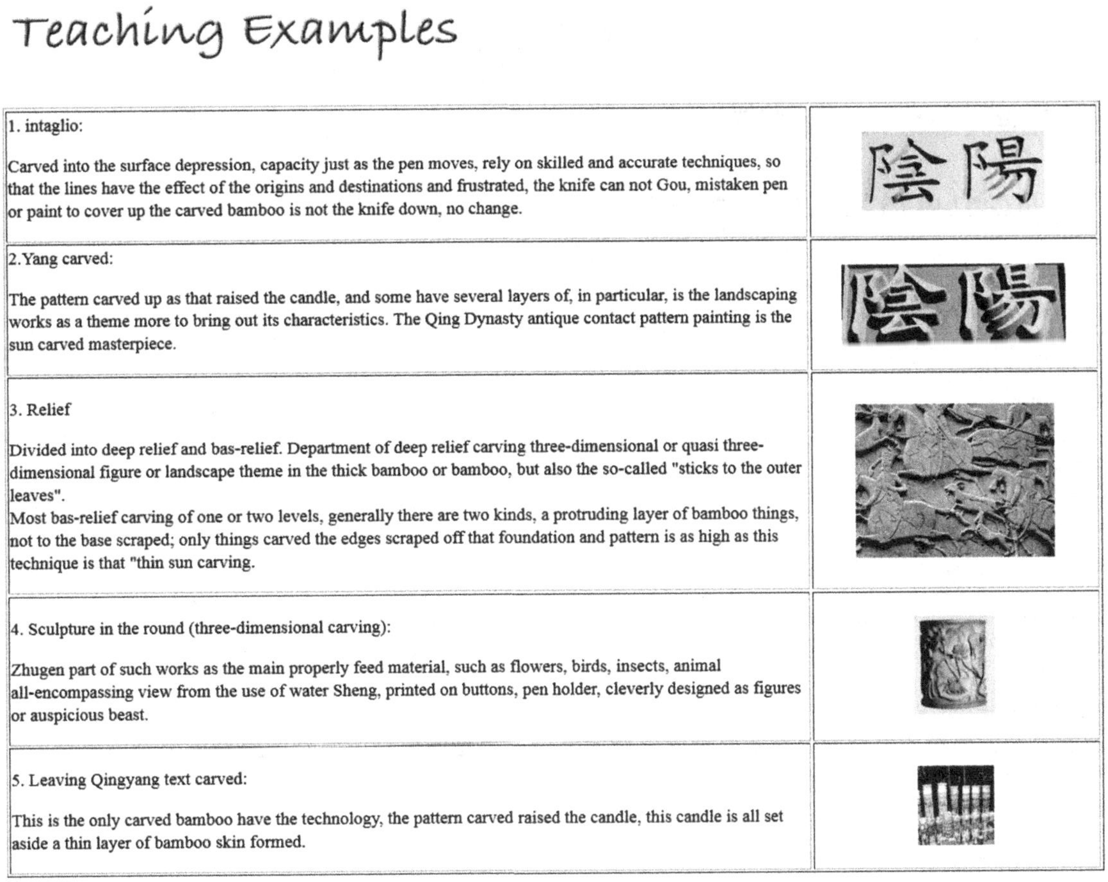

Teaching Examples

1. intaglio: Carved into the surface depression, capacity just as the pen moves, rely on skilled and accurate techniques, so that the lines have the effect of the origins and destinations and frustrated, the knife can not Gou, mistaken pen or paint to cover up the carved bamboo is not the knife down, no change.	陰陽
2.Yang carved: The pattern carved up as that raised the candle, and some have several layers of, in particular, is the landscaping works as a theme more to bring out its characteristics. The Qing Dynasty antique contact pattern painting is the sun carved masterpiece.	陰陽
3. Relief Divided into deep relief and bas-relief. Department of deep relief carving three-dimensional or quasi three-dimensional figure or landscape theme in the thick bamboo or bamboo, but also the so-called "sticks to the outer leaves". Most bas-relief carving of one or two levels, generally there are two kinds, a protruding layer of bamboo things, not to the base scraped; only things carved the edges scraped off that foundation and pattern is as high as this technique is that "thin sun carving.	
4. Sculpture in the round (three-dimensional carving): Zhugen part of such works as the main properly feed material, such as flowers, birds, insects, animal all-encompassing view from the use of water Sheng, printed on buttons, pen holder, cleverly designed as figures or auspicious beast.	
5. Leaving Qingyang text carved: This is the only carved bamboo have the technology, the pattern carved raised the candle, this candle is all set aside a thin layer of bamboo skin formed.	

Example 5

In the bamboo carving subpage, "Teaching Example" and "Useful Links" were the only categories of contents in the first draft (Figure 9). After participants reviewed their own website, they reflected on the Pre-training Principle (Mayer, 2009) that *people learn more deeply from a multimedia message when they know the names and the characteristics of the main concepts.* Thus, in the final version, contents of introduction of bamboo carving and required materials were included to serve the pre-training purpose (Figure 10).

Example 6

In the first draft design, contents in the bamboo carving subpage were displayed continuously from top to bottom without any tool to aid browsing (Figure 11). Participants reviewed their own website and realized that the Segmenting Principle was not fulfilled. According to Mayer (2009), *people learn better when a multimedia message is presented in user-paced segments rather than as a continuous unit.* In order to fulfill the principle, navigation with buttons and anchors settings were intentionally inserted so that users were allowed to browse the webpage at their own pace. (Figure 12).

Figure 9. First draft webpage of example 5

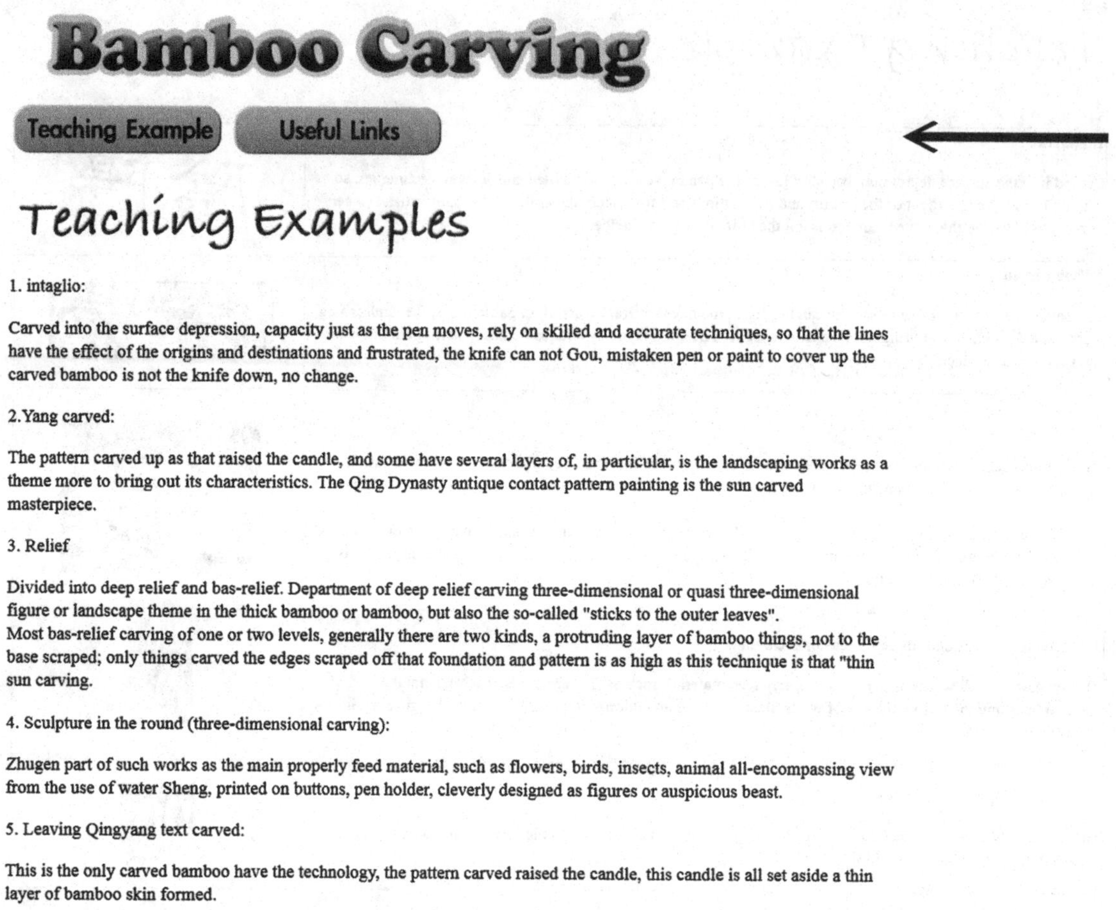

Bamboo Carving

[Teaching Example] [Useful Links] ⬅

Teaching Examples

1. intaglio:

Carved into the surface depression, capacity just as the pen moves, rely on skilled and accurate techniques, so that the lines have the effect of the origins and destinations and frustrated, the knife can not Gou, mistaken pen or paint to cover up the carved bamboo is not the knife down, no change.

2. Yang carved:

The pattern carved up as that raised the candle, and some have several layers of, in particular, is the landscaping works as a theme more to bring out its characteristics. The Qing Dynasty antique contact pattern painting is the sun carved masterpiece.

3. Relief

Divided into deep relief and bas-relief. Department of deep relief carving three-dimensional or quasi three-dimensional figure or landscape theme in the thick bamboo or bamboo, but also the so-called "sticks to the outer leaves".
Most bas-relief carving of one or two levels, generally there are two kinds, a protruding layer of bamboo things, not to the base scraped; only things carved the edges scraped off that foundation and pattern is as high as this technique is that "thin sun carving.

4. Sculpture in the round (three-dimensional carving):

Zhugen part of such works as the main properly feed material, such as flowers, birds, insects, animal all-encompassing view from the use of water Sheng, printed on buttons, pen holder, cleverly designed as figures or auspicious beast.

5. Leaving Qingyang text carved:

This is the only carved bamboo have the technology, the pattern carved raised the candle, this candle is all set aside a thin layer of bamboo skin formed.

Figure 10. Final version webpage of example 5

Bamboo Carving

[Introduction] [Materials] [Teaching Example] [Useful Links] ⬅

Introduction

The bamboo is the engraving text book "book", the book the word is two bamboo middle wearing a strap connected into a pictograph. Previously recorded as historical facts, written on the bamboo or carved text and symbols, the ancients called "Jane", the modern so-called book, a lot of bamboo, called the book.

Figure 11. First draft webpage of example 6

Bamboo Carving

Introduction

The bamboo is the engraving text book "book", the book the word is two bamboo middle wearing a strap connected into a pictograph. Previously recorded as historical facts, written on the bamboo or carved text and symbols, the ancients called "Jane", the modern so-called book, a lot of bamboo, called the book.

Figure 12. Final version webpage of example 6

Bamboo Carving

| Introduction | Materials | Teaching Example | Useful Links |

Introduction

The bamboo is the engraving text book "book", the book the word is two bamboo middle wearing a strap connected into a pictograph. Previously recorded as historical facts, written on the bamboo or carved text and symbols, the ancients called "Jane", the modern so-called book, a lot of bamboo, called the book.

Example 7

Figure 13. shows the first draft of the subpage related to materials used in tear painting. No image was included in the original design. As suggested by peers according to the Multimedia Principle (Mayer 2009) that *people learn better from words and pictures than from words alone*, related images were included in the final version to enable users have better understanding on related contents (Figure 14).

As shown in these examples, if students did not engage in a reflection process, they inclined to design the website based on their past experiences or intuitive judgments. The quality of the website would inevitably become unsatisfactory since they neglected those research-based web design principles or guidelines and behaved as laymen during the process. By providing opportunities for students to reflect on their own works, actual improvements could be obtained.

Overall Comments

In addition to the above examples, participants also expressed their overall comments on the self- and peer-assessment strategy on learning web design during the interviews. For example, students mentioned that

Even though comments were received from peers, student has to accept the comments. If we do not reflect on peers' comments and make respective revisions, it is hard to make improvement…

Figure 13. First draft webpage of example 7

Materials

Colored tissue paper	Glue	Small Pens
This is the basic material of the tissue tear painting. After staining, a more diversified use. There are two kinds of thick and thicker, fibers longer, most likely performance of various tear painting techniques, so the most commonly used.	Paste can be for daily use. Diluted with water, or to change shades according to the paste method.	Tip above water is used to take the pattern, or for posted by precision painting.
Cutter or sessors	Plate	Forceps
Want to show the flower, thin, or straight line tool.	Prepare two plates loaded paste with water, used to adjust the concentration of the paste, water portrayed take pattern.	Commonly used to paste the dense part of, or use of the fiber of the mulberry leather.
News paper	Paper or Color paper	Water Color
Absorbent	For Background	for dying

Figure 14. Final version webpage of example 7

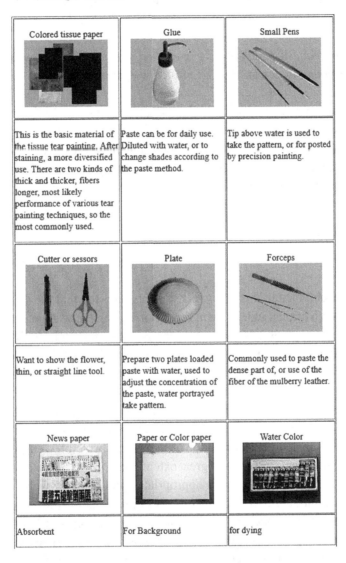

Under this instructional design, participants had more opportunities to reflect on web design and more serious to review whether the website fulfills related web design principles… The revisions were mainly due to self-reflection since peers may not fully understand the objectives of my website…

The Website Revision Record Form provided by lecturer served as a checklist for reflection. Participants could specifically check whether related principles were fulfilled or not. If it is not fulfilled, improvement can be made accordingly.

Participants usually thought that the original website created was good at the early stage. After self-reviewing the website according to principles, participants could identify possible improvements... Participants could learn from peers in the peer assessment process. Participants could also benefit from comments given by peers. Self-weaknesses were more easily identified by peers.

The instructional design requested students to engage in a number of reflection processes. Participants could develop more profound understanding on related web design principles.

As shown in the comments given by students, reflection could be regarded an important element to improve their learning of web design. When participants reviewed their own website, they directly engaged in self-reflection. During the process of peer-assessment, they also reflected on the design on their own website when they reviewed peers works. After engaged in a series of reflections, students developed a better understanding on related principles and were more aware of its applications. The quality of website was also found improved.

CONCLUSION

According to the results obtained in this study, participants reported that the self- and peer-assessment strategy engaged them with critical independent reflection during the web design process. This echoed previous findings (Dochy et al., 1999) that self- and peer-assessment strategy with the effect of transforming students into reflective learners. Participants were also satisfied with the self- and peer-assessment strategy as they expressed that they found it beneficial, learned more and were more confident in applying web design principles in creating high quality website. The high percentage of revisions reported in the Website Revisions Records for improving the quality of website also served as a triangulation on the effectiveness of the self- and peer-assessment strategy in improving web design. Together with examples on the improvement of web design due to reflection of web design principles, empirical evidence suggests that the self- and peer-assessment strategy to a great extent transformed a web developer into a reflective practitioner and it enhanced the awareness on appropriate application of web design principles in the web design process. Without the reflection process, participants inclined to behave as laymen and did not concern related research-based web design principles or guidelines. Further to the favorable results, it should be noted that participants generally did not consider the experience as enjoyable which might affect their attitudes in the reflection process. This chapter contributes to the field by introducing an assessment for learning strategy with self- and peer-assessment components to transform web developers into reflective practitioners for improving the quality of web design for future reference.

REFERENCES

Bailey, H. J., & Milheim, W. D. (1991). A comprehensive model for deigning interactive video based materials. *Proceeding for the Night Conference on Interactive Instruction Delivery at the 2991 Society for Applied Learning Technology Conference.* Orlando, FL.

Black, P., & Wiliam, D. (1998). Assessment and classroom learning. *Assessment in Education: Principles, Policy & Practice, 5*(1), 7–74. doi:10.1080/0969595980050102

Boud, D., & Falchikov, N. (1989). Quantitative studies of self-assessment in higher education: A critical analysis of findings. *Higher Education, 18*(5), 529–549. doi:10.1007/BF00138746

Burch, R. O. (2001). Effective web design and core communication issues: The missing components in web-based distance education. *Journal of Educational Multimedia and Hypermedia, 10*(4), 357–367.

Calderhead, J. (1989). Reflective teaching and teacher education. *Teaching and Teacher Education, 5*(1), 43–51. doi:10.1016/0742-051X(89)90018-8

Chawda, B., Craft, B., Cairns, P., Rugor, S., & Heesch, D. (2005). Do "Attractive Things Work Better"? An Exploration of Search Tool Visualisations. *Proceedings of British HCI Group Annual Conference* Edinburgh, UK, (pp. 46-51). The Bigger Picture.

Department of Health and Human Services. (2006). *Research-based web design & usability guidelines*. Washington: U.S. Government Printing Office.

Dochy, F., Segers, M., & Sluijsmans, D. (1999). The use of self-, peer and co-assessment in higher education: A review. *Studies in Higher Education, 24*(3), 331–350. doi:10.1080/03075079912331379935

Falchikov, N. (1986). Product comparisons and process benefits of collaborative peer group and self assessments. *Assessment & Evaluation in Higher Education, 11*(2), 146–166. doi:10.1080/0260293860110206

Farkas, D. K., & Farkas, J. B. (2000). Guidelines for designing web navigation. *Technical Communication (Washington), 4*(3), 341–358.

Garner, K. H. (1990). 20 rules for arranging text on screen. *CBT Directions, 3*(5), 13–17.

Geissler, G., Zinkhan, G., & Watson, R. T. (2001). Web home page complexity and communication effectiveness. *Journal of the Association for Information Systems, 2*, 1–46.

Habermas, J. (1973). *Knowledge and Human Interests*. London: Heineman.

Hannafin, M. J., & Hooper, S. (1989). An integrated framework for CBI screen design and layout. *Computers in Human Behavior, 5*(3), 155–165. doi:10.1016/0747-5632(89)90009-5

Harper, S., & Yesilada, Y. (2008). Web accessibility and guidelines. In S. Harper & Y. Yesilada (Eds.), *Web Accessibility* (pp. 61–78). London: Springer-Verlag. doi:10.1007/978-1-84800-050-6_6

Hsu, C. M., Yeh, Y. C., & Yen, J. (2009). Development of design criteria and evaluation scale for web-based learning platforms. *International Journal of Industrial Ergonomics, 39*(1), 90–95. doi:10.1016/j.ergon.2008.08.006

ISO. (1997). *ISO 9241: Ergonomics Requirements for Office Work with Visual Display Terminal (VDT)* Parts 1–17.

Ivory, M. Y., & Hearst, M. A. (2002). Towards quality checkers for web site designs. *IEEE Internet Computing, 6*(2).

Jonassen, D. H., & Hannum, W. H. (1987). Research based principles for designing computer software. *Educational Technology, 27*(11), 7–14.

Kaushansky, K. (2012). *Designing With Audio: What Is Sound Good For?* Retrieved from http://www.smashingmagazine.com/2012/04/18/designing-with-audio-what-is-sound-good-for/

Kyrnin, J. (2015). *Pros and Cons of Adding Sound to Web Pages.* Retrieved from http://webdesign.about.com/od/sound/a/aa080607.htm

Lai, Y. C., & Ng, W. S. (2011). Nurturing information literacy of early childhood teachers through web-based collaborative learning activities. *Hong Kong Journal of Early Childhood, 10*(1), 77–83.

Lindgaard, G., Fernandes, G. J., Dudek, C., & Brownet, J. (2006). Attention web designers: You have 50 ms to make a good first impression! *Behaviour & Information Technology, 25*(2), 115–126. doi:10.1080/01449290500330448

Mayer, R. E. (2009). *Multimedia learning.* Cambridge: Cambridge University Press. doi:10.1017/CBO9780511811678

Ng, W. S. (2011). Innovative pedagogy for enhancing web-based collaborative learning in tertiary teacher education using wikis. *Proceedings of the Work-in-Progress Poster of the International Conference on Computers in Education: ICCE 2011.* Chiang Mai: National Electronics and Computer

Ng, W. S. (2014). Critical design factors of developing a high-quality educational website: Perspectives of preservice teachers. *Issues in Informing Science and Information Technology, 11*, 101–113.

Nielsen, J. (1995). *10 Usability Heuristics for User Interface Design.* Retrieved from http://www.nngroup.com/articles/ten-usability-heuristics/

Norman, D. A. (2002). Emotion and design: attractive things work better. *Interactions Magazine*, 36-42.

O'Leary, D. E. (2008). Wikis: From each according to his knowledge. *IEEE Computer, 41*(2), 34–41. doi:10.1109/MC.2008.68

Poncelet, G. M., & Proctor, L. F. (1993). Design and development factors in the production of hypermedia based courseware. *Canadian Journal of Educational Communication, 22*(2), 91–111.

Reichenstein, O. (2006). *Web design is 95% typography.* Retrieved from http://informationarchitects.net/blog/the-web-is-all-about-typography-period/

Schenkman, B. N., & Jonsson, F. U. (2000). Aesthetics and preferences of web pages. *Behaviour & Information Technology, 19*(5), 367–377. doi:10.1080/014492900750000063

Schon, D. A. (1991). *The reflective practitioner: how professionals think in action.* Aldershot, England: Ashgate.

Skaalid, B. (1999). *Multimedia & Web Page Design Principles.* Retrieved from http://www.usask.ca/education/coursework/skaalid/page/design/webdsgn.htm

Steeples, G. P. (1998). Creating shareable representations of practice. *Advance Learning Technology Journal, 6*(3), 16–23.

Stemler, L. K. (1997). Educational characteristics of multimedia: A literature review. *Journal of Educational Multimedia and Hypermedia, 6*(3/4), 339–359.

Stodberg, U. (2012). A research review of e-assessment. *Assessment & Evaluation in Higher Education, 37*(5), 591–604. doi:10.1080/02602938.2011.557496

Thatcher, J. e. (2006). *Web Accessibility: Web Standards and Regulatory Compliance.* New York: Friends of ED.

Topping, K. (1998). Peer assessment between students in colleges and universities. *Review of Educational Research, 68*(3), 249–276. doi:10.3102/00346543068003249

Tractinsky, N., Cokhavi, A., & Kirschenbaum, M. (2004). Using Ratings and Response Latencies to Evaluate the Consistency of Immediate Aesthetic Perceptions of Web Pages. Workshop Program & Proceedings AIS SIGHCI, Washington. *HCI Research in MIS, 04*, 40–44.

Tractinsky, N., Cokhavi, A., Kirschenbaum, M., & Sharfi, T. (2006). Evaluating the consistency of immediate aesthetic perceptions of web pages. *International Journal of Human-Computer Studies, 64*(11), 1071–1083. doi:10.1016/j.ijhcs.2006.06.009

VideoAktiv. (2006). *Handbook on Digital Video and Audio in Education.* UK: The VideoAktiv Project.

W3C. (2008). *Web content accessibility guidelines (WCAG) 2.0.*

Xiao, Y., & Lucking, R. (2008). The impact of two types of peer assessment on students' performance and satisfaction within a Wiki environment. *The Internet and Higher Education, 11*(3-4), 186–193. doi:10.1016/j.iheduc.2008.06.005

Zaphiris, P., Ghiawadwala, M., & Mughal, S. (2005). Age-centered research-based web design guidelines. *Proceedings of the conference on Human Factors in Computing Systems Chi 2005: Technology, Safety, Community,* Portland, Oregon, USA (pp. 1897-1900).

KEY TERMS AND DEFINITIONS

Assessment for Learning: The design and practice of assessment for collecting evidence to adapt teaching and improve learning.

Educational Website: A website with fundamental purpose to serve educational purposes.

Peer-Assessment: The practice of an individual to evaluate the works or performance of peers of similar status or ability.

Reflection: The practice of an individual to engage into serious thought on his/her own works or performance.

Self-Assessment: The practice of an individual to evaluate his/her own works or performance.

Web Design Principle: Rule or guideline for developing a better quality website.

Wiki: A web application to facilitate collaborative modification, extension or deletion of its content and structure.

Chapter 3

Integrating E–SERVQUAL and Kano Model into Quality Function Deployment to Improve Website Service Quality: An Application to University's Website

Dorie Pandora Kesuma
STMIK Global Informatika MDP, Indonesia

Meyliana
Bina Nusantara University, Indonesia

Achmad Nizar Hidayanto
Universitas Indonesia, Indonesia

Kongkiti Phusavat
Kasetsart University, Thailand

Dina Chahyati
Universitas Indonesia, Indonesia

ABSTRACT

Today's internet technology has been utilized in various fields, one of which is to provide services in the field of education. Internet technology in the form of website enables organizations to provide anywhere anytime services to their customers, thus it is expected increasing customers' satisfaction. This research aims to develop a service design framework that can be used to evaluate the quality of website service at the university and formulate solutions for its improvement, by combining E-SERVQUAL, Kano Model, and Quality Function Deployment (QFD). To demonstrate the use of the proposed framework, we conducted a case study in one of the private universities in Palembang, Indonesia. Step by step of the framework usage is discussed, to provide a better understanding of the framework we are proposing.

DOI: 10.4018/978-1-4666-9764-5.ch003

INTRODUCTION

The internet growth in 1990's has triggered the appearance of world-wide-web (www) or website, a global information media where everyone can access or interact with certain information via internet-connected computer. Internet has changed the way organizations provide services to their customers and allows co-creation value, especially with the Web 2.0 technology. Internet allows organizations to provide interactive services, with the expectation that customers can get closer to the organization (Mathwick, Wiertz, & de Ruyter, 2008; Shin, 2014; Verhagen et al., 2015; Van Doorn et al., 2010; Wagner &Majchrzak, 2007).

One of the sectors that use a lot of Internet technology is the education sector. The Internet has changed how the university runs both its primary and supporting business processes. Internet technologies allow prospective customers to perform various administrative tasks that previously had to be done manually, for example an online admission process. Students as the main customers of universities are also able to perform various activities such as online course registration, online consultation with their advisor, etc. Moreover, Internet technology has also altered how the learning process is done, from the conventional one through face-to-face method to blended learning (combination of face-to-face and online learning) and fully online learning or commonly known as e-learning. E-Learning allows the learning process becomes more collaborative in nature, especially since the emergence of Web 2.0 technologies (Hew & Cheung, 2013, Cheng et al., 2014). There are also many efforts to use and integrate social media (like Facebook) as part of Web 2.0 technologies in the learning process (Balakrishnan, Liew, & Pourgholaminejad, 2015; Chen, Fan, & Sun, 2015; Mao, 2014; Won et al., 2015). The use of the internet is expected to be one of the tools to improve higher educations' service quality and compete in global level (Aldridge & Rowley,1998; Athiyaman, 1997; de Jager & Gbadamosi, 2013; Moogan, Baron, & Bainbridge, 2001; Oldfield & Baron, 2000).

Now, Internet is considered as the backbone for universities to deliver their services to both prospective and main customers, and one of them is in form of web-based services such as online course registration. The internet usage has changed customer's way of thinking due to the existence of a more intense interaction and the expectation of a better and faster service quality from the university. This challenges the university management side to define and provide web-based service that can fulfill customer's requirement and get the desired service performance (Goldstein et al., 2002). Regarding this, the management needs to be able to formulate a website service attribute and quality that can be a guide for the developers to plan, implement, operate, and evaluate the website service made for university customer.

In the service design context, the university management surely wants to implement a service with high quality by considering and responding customer's requirements in all service's processes (Edvardsson, 1997; Lin, Yeh, & Wang, 2015). Unfortunately, the meaning of "quality" might be different for each person due to its various criteria. Juran & Godfrey (1999) said that quality can be meant as product's features that can fulfill the user's' needs and in the end create satisfaction to the users. Quality can also mean free from flaws, or in other words free from mistakes or errors that can lead to users' dissatisfaction. The concept of quality itself often times taken as a relative measurement of a product's or service's goodness, which consists of design quality and suitability quality. Design quality means product's specification, while suitability quality means a measurement of how far a product fulfill the requirement or quality specification that has been decided (Tjiptono et al., 2003).

With the service design concept, the management is expected to be capable in creating a high quality website, thus be able to give the best online experience to the customer. This experience will surely trigger satisfaction from the user, and in the future it is expected to improve loyalty and engagement level from the customer, including the desire to do a positive word-of-mouth about the university's service. Good website service quality is also an important factor because it shows that the web owner is not a newcomer (not a 'fly-by-night' operator) in the online business environment (Wingfield cited from Holsapple & Wu, 2008), but a reliable service provider (Bramall, Schoefer, & McKechnie, 2004). Fogg et al. (2003) said that in some past researches, one main reasons why people are not interested in using online service is because the website does not have a professional interface design, which indicates that the lack of credibility from the web owner, and creates a feeling that the web is not reliable. This factor has grown into an important thing because in online business environment, physical factors and direct, personal contact (between users and service provider) has become almost non-existent (Gefen, 2002) and websites has become the main media for service providers to interact with their customers (Yang & Lester, 2004).

Even though service quality is an important thing to improve customer's satisfaction and loyalty, not all organization put enough effort to improve their website service quality. There are still a lot of university websites that are poorly managed and do not fulfill their customers' demands (Kuo, 2006; Kuo & Chen, 2011). Prospective students also find difficulties in looking for information regarding registration, current curriculum, etc. It is a shame because website is the first gate for prospective students to assess the quality of a university. Prospective students have to make sure that the university's service quality fits their expectation, especially considering the type of education service where it is long term and customers cannot easily change their university. Poor website service quality can create a perception that the university's education service quality is also poor (Hidayanto, Rofalina, & Handayani, 2015).

In Indonesia, education is one of the sectors that ranks high in the government's priority list. With 20% of the nation's yearly budget is allocated to education. Regarding university as one of Indonesia's national education systems, up until 2014, there are 3.151 universities Indonesia, where 3.068 or 97% of them are private universities, and 83 or 3% of them are state universities (http://kuliahmurahjakarta. blogspot.com/2014/01/jumlah-perguruan-tinggi-swasta-dan.html). Unfortunately, according to the international ranking system, Indonesian university's rank is still low. QS World Ranking Asia's survey in 2015 for example, placed Universitas Indonesia as the best university Indonesia with rank 79th in Asia. Webometrics ranking also shows those Indonesian universities only have 518th as their highest rank per January 2015 compared to global rank. Although Webometrics ranking itself measures more on the quality of content information instead of evaluates the quality of the website, this can be an indicator of how weak the quality of education in Indonesia, which one of them is related to IT facility management, including website service management from the universities themselves.

To improve Indonesia university's website service quality, an integrated framework that can be a guide to the university is necessary. The simplest approach possible is by identifying the website service quality attribute and measure the customer satisfaction level based on the service quality attribute. SERVQUAL (Parasuraman, Zeithmal, & Berry, 1988) is one of the most commonly used framework to calculate satisfaction level on a service and often times also adapted to calculate website and IT service satisfaction level (Hidayanto et al., 2013; van Iwaarden et al., 2003), which commonly termed as E-SERVQUAL.

Some approaches were also suggested in the past to help improving the website quality in order to improve users' satisfaction. One of the approaches is by using Quality Function Deployment (QFD) (Kuo & Chen, 2011; Islam, Ahmed, & Alias, 2007) which formerly used in industry sector to translate users' demands into technical conditions in every production process, from creating concept into sales or sales service (Akao, 1990). Unfortunately, QFD does not have its own tools to calculate quality aspects that are important for the users. Aside of that, QFD does not have good ability to classify the services attributes according to how a product or service can fulfill the users' demands as Kano Model has (Kano et al., 1984).

Thus, this research aims to propose a framework for improving website service quality by integrating E-SERVQUAL, Kano Model and QFD. The three model integration is expected to help universities improving their website service quality, from the scoring process into the technical response necessary to overcome the flaw. We demonstrate the use of the proposed framework for evaluating a university website.

BACKGROUND

Service Design Concept

One of the emerging disciplines right now is service design. Service design is an activity of planning and organizing people, infrastructure, communication, and material components of a service in order to improve its quality and the interaction between service provider and customer (Tan et al., 2010). The purpose of service design methodologies is to design according to the needs of customers, so that the service is user-friendly, competitive, relevant and providing added value to the customers. Service design is one of the activities in service design process (Shostack 1982; Shostack 1984) aimed to create a "service blueprint" and gives service specification offered to the customer.

In order to make the customer enjoys the service from an organization, the service has to be created systematically and consistently, and also complemented with functions that can improve customer's experience in using the service effectively (Shostack, 1984). The good experience in using a service will improve customer's satisfaction and loyalty to the service provide (Human & Naude, 2014; Rodger, Taplin, & Moore, 2015; Shi, Prentice, & He, 2014). According to Lee & Chen (2009), a service design has to be an integral experience felt by the customer, where the service provider has to fulfill customer's expectations, providing a service that suits the customer's needs, and in the end, the customer can feel the satisfaction on the service provided.

In a service design process, the service designer team has to show service attributes that decides the service's quality to the customer. The service attributes can be tangible such as building cleanliness, or intangible such as speed and responsiveness in handling the customer. In the electronic service context, interface quality is an example for a tangible service attributes. SERVQUAL (Parasuraman, Zeithaml, & Berry, 1985) is one of the frameworks that provide a guideline of service attributes that need attention in designing and evaluating a service.

In practice, service attributes the customer expects will be a lot and widely varied. Service designer won't be able to consider all the service attributes in designing a service, since it will cost a lot of money. Thus, service designer has to be able to decide the critical service attributes. Therefore, a mechanism to decide priority on each attribute is required. By identifying the critical service attributes concerned by the customer, service designer can calculate the trade-off of every single service design option prepared, therefore the service delivered to the customer will be the best product that can bring satisfaction to the customer without servicing service provider's interest. In order to give a comprehensive experience to the customer, service provider should not only focus on the experience gained while using the service, but also all attributes felt by the customer, both before and after using the service (Marentakis & Emiris, 2010). Considering this issue, we integrate Kano Model in the QFD process to design a high-quality website service.

Service Quality Based on SERVQUAL

Service quality concept is something really important for company because it is a vital factor in creating superior value for customers. Service quality in a lot of literature has strong relation to users' satisfaction, loyalty, and even profitability as explained in some researches such as Rodger, Taplin & Moore (2015), Shi, Pretince & He (2014), Orel & Kara (2014), Lee et al. (2015), Kuppelwieser & Sarstedt (2014), and de Reuver, Nikou & Bouwman (2015). The goal of providing service quality is to satisfy the users. Measuring the service quality is a better way to find out whether a service is good or bad, or whether the users are satisfied or not. Gronroos (1984) said that users compare their expectation with their experience they get from the service quality in form of rating. Gronroos (1992) the developed three dimensions in identifying service quality, which are functionality quality, technical quality, and service provider image.

One of the service quality models that is well-known and applied in various industries is SERVQUAL introduced by Parasuraman, Zeithaml, & Berry (1985). SERVQUAL is a method used to measure service quality by looking into the gap between users' perception and expectation on a service. With the method, we can know how much the gap is between customer's perception and expectation on a service. The gaps that will be possibly occurred and affect the service quality are:

1. The gap between customer's expectation and management perception. The difference between user's expectation and management's perception about the customer's expectation.
2. The gap between management perception and service quality specification. The gap of management's perception on customer's expectation and service quality specification.
3. The gap between service quality specification and service presentation.
4. The gap between service presentation and marketing communication. The gap of service presentation with external communication team.
5. The gap in the service that is felt.

SERVQUAL scales include five service quality dimensions, which are: Tangibles, Reliability, Responsiveness, Assurance, and Empathy, which are explained as the following (Parasuraman, Zeithaml, & Berry, 1988):

1. Tangibles portray physical facilities, equipment, and appearance of staffs and users attendance.
2. Reliability refers to the ability to provide the promised service accurately reliably.
3. Responsiveness is the willingness to help and give the right attention to users.
4. Assurance is the polite and knowledgeable employees that create trust and conviction.
5. Empathy includes individual's awareness and care to the users.

SERVQUAL is the most commonly used method to measure service quality (Brysland & Curry, 2001). Aside from that, SERVQUAL is perceived to statistically fulfill validity requirements (Arasli, Mehtap-Smadi, & Katircioglu, 2005). This SERVQUAL was first built for assumption that customer compares the ideal performance attributes for each attribute. If the performance attribute exceeds the desired standard, the perception on service's quality will be improved as a whole. In short, this model analyzes gaps between two core variables: the expected service and the actual experience of the service felt by customer. From various gaps found in SERVQUAL, the 5th gap, which is the gap between the service received with the service expected usually comes as the main focus.

Parasuraman, Zeithaml, & Berry (1988) stated operational perceived quality approach (Q) as the difference degree and direction of customer perception and expectation by defining and measuring the service performance (P) the customer gets and customer expectation (E). The key to maximize service quality is maximizing the difference between the two measurement (Q = P – E), or in other word to maximize the value of service received by customer compared to the customer's expectation to the service. Service quality measurement with SERVQUAL includes calculating the differences between the value given to customer for every pair of questions related with expectation and perception.

Company's service quality in the five SERVQUAL dimensions can be calculated for all respondents by calculating their SERVQUAL average score on the statements that shows all service quality's dimension. The data from SERVQUAL instruments can then be used to calculate the service's gap score on various levels in detail. With the analysis on the gap scores, service manager no only be able to measure all of their service quality perceived by the customer, but also be able to identify the key dimensions and aspects in all of the dimensions that requires quality improvement.

The SERVQUAL score that turns into a gap score between perception score and expectation score can be used to diagnose where the performance improvement needs to be done. A highly negative gap score will be prioritized to be improved. On the other hand, if the gap score is positive, the over-supplying can be analyzed. This will be an evaluation to share the resource to improve the low-performance attribute.

SERVQUAL Modification to Measure IT Service Quality

In the past decades, there was a development that focuses on creating concept, measuring, and managing the service quality and its effects on electronic environment (Carlson & O'Cass, 2011) as well as an effort to evaluate traditional service quality to then adapt it into the information technology context (Bressolles, Durrieu, & Senecal, 2014). The experiences from the customers when using an IT-based services (especially web-based) is certainly different than the traditional services, where in the web-based service (or also known as e-services), customers have to be actively involved in the service delivery, and even have to make their own time and effort to gain the service. Parasuraman, Zeithaml, & Malhotra (2005) identified e-service quality as *how far a website can facilitate product shopping, purchase, and delivery process efficiently and effectively*.

This web-based service quality dimension is different compared to traditional service quality, even though the early basis is taken from the established theory such as SERVQUAL. There are some measurement dimensions that are widely used by some researchers in their research to measure an e-service quality (or known as E-SERVQUAL), such as tangibles dimension (Zeithaml, Parasuraman, & Berry, 1990; Aladwani & Palvia, 2002; Madu & Madu, 2002; Ranganathan & Ganapathy, 2002; Wan, 2000; Cox & Dale, 2001), website usability dimension (Parasuraman, Zeithaml, & Malhotra, 2005), information quality dimension (Li, Tan, & Xie, 2002), services reliability dimension (Zeithaml, Parasuraman, & Berry, 1990; Madu & Madu, 2002; Wan, 2000), assurance dimension (Zeithaml, Parasuraman, & Berry, 1990; Madu & Madu, 2002; Ranganathan & Ganapathy, 2002), and empathy dimension (Zeithaml, Parasuraman, & Berry, 1990; Madu & Madu, 2002; Wan, 2000).

Table 1 shows some sample researches related to SERVQUAL usage in IT field.

Table 1. Samples of SERVQUAL Implementation in Information Technology

SERVQUAL Application	Measure	Empirical Findings	Source
SERVQUAL is combined with usability measures to model usability of *web* based information systems	Perception of service performance	The service quality dimensions of SERVQUAL are an important aspect of usability for *web* based information systems	Oztekin, Nikov, & Zaim (2009)
SERVQUAL is tested as a measure of service quality of online systems to complement teaching quality	Perception of service performance less expectation of service (difference score)	All SERVQUAL dimensions determine satisfaction of online learning systems along with teacher quality	Sohn, Park, & Chang (2009)
Developed and applied a modified SERVQUAL model for online shopping (as an independent variable)	Perception of service performance	Eight dimensions were found in a perception only measure and they were significantly related to satisfaction	Lee & Lin (2005)
Measured the service quality of *web* sites	Perception of service performance less expectation of service (difference score)	Concluded that a gap score SERVQUAL was applicable to web sites	van Iwaarden et al. (2003)
Measured the service quality of virtual community websites with a modified SERVQUAL	Perception of service performance less expectation of service (difference score)	Gap measure found that perceptions fall below expectations	Kuo (2003)
Measured the service quality of web-based customer support systems (as an independent variable)	Perception of service performance less expectation of service (difference score)	Information and system quality determined user satisfaction while the gap score SERVQUAL had no impact	Negash, Ryan, & Igbaria (2003)
Measured web-based service quality	Perception of service performance	A perception-only SERVQUAL measure indicated a need to modify SERVQUAL for the context of the web-based service	Li, Tan, & Xie (2002)

Kano Model

In 1980's, Noriaki Kano developed a highly useful diagram to classify the attributes of a product or service based on how the product or service can satisfy the users' demands. The classification process can be useful for the new design guide as a solution to innovation element that can be attained by SERVQUAL. This diagram was then known as Kano Diagram or Kano Model.

Kano Model is usually used in activities such as users' demands identification, functional requirements determination, concept development, and competitive product analysis. In Kano Model, users' demands can be divided into three attributes (Tan & Pawitra, 2001), which are:

1. The must be (basic needs) (M)
2. The one dimensional (performance needs) (O)
3. The attractive (excitement needs (A)

The must be attribute is an attribute based on product or service the users automatically expect from it. Users will be satisfied if the attributes from this category are fulfilled, but will also be dissatisfied if the attributes are not fulfilled. However, the attributes from this category cannot improve users' satisfaction and can only trigger dissatisfaction if not fulfilled. The one-dimensional attribute is an attributes that can create satisfaction and dissatisfaction from the users. The satisfaction comes from the fulfillment of this attribute. In other words, the higher this attribute performs, the higher the users' satisfaction level will be. Attractive attribute is an attribute that creates satisfaction if fulfilled, but will not trigger dissatisfaction if not fulfilled. The attributes from this category is the attributes that are not really expected by the users. Thus, if the attribute is not there, users will not be disappointed. However, if the attribute is included in the product or service, users will be happy (Ratanasawadwat, 2015). The relation between these three needs can be seen in the Figure 1.

In addition to the categories above, Kano Model also has three other categories to classify users demand, which are Indifferent (I), Reverse (R) (Rashid et al., 2011), and Questionable (Q) (Sauerwein et al., 1996). If one of the users demands are included in the (I) category, it shows that users do not care about the attribute, thus the (I) category can be ignored. The (Q) category indicates contradiction on users demands (Ji et al., 2014), while the (R) category shows displeasure on certain quality attributes where if this category is fulfilled, it will trigger dissatisfaction from the users because they feel uncomfortable and seen as an obstacle for other service attributes (Byun, Lee & Rye, 2014).

Regarding Kano Model implementation in measuring website service quality, there are several sample researches including research by Lee, Shih & Tu (2002) for performance improvement on web-based learning application, Chu, Wang & Lai (2010) which studied digital storage system based on Web 2.0, Khalid, Mustafa & Haqua (2008) which evaluated information quality on university web, Oh, Yoon & Park (2011) which used structured approach to test quality attributes on e-shopping mall.

Quality Function Deployment (QFD)

The QFD concept was first announced by Yoji Akao from Japan in 1966 in an article published in 1972 with the title "Hinshitu Teinkai System" or also known as Quality Deployment and for the first time

Figure 1. Kano Model
(Source: Berger et al., 1993)

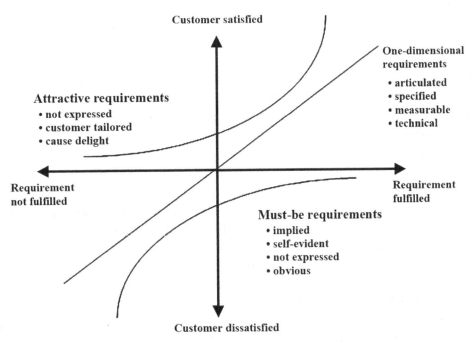

implemented to Mitsubishi Company in 1978. The main goal of QFD is to translate subjective quality criteria into the objective one that can be accumulated and measured, and then used to design and create a product (Reilly, 1999).

QFD uses comprehensive matrix to document information, perception, and decision or also known as House of Quality (HoQ) and often times treated as the whole process of QFD. HoQ is used to translate a set of customer requirements, customer importance level, as well as customer satisfaction level on product/service from market and data research from benchmarking process into technical target priority required to satisfy the customer requirements. There are various version of HoQ that are not significantly different one to another. HoQ's ability to be adjusted based on requirements from certain problem type is one of the strength it has.

According to Herzwurm, Shockert & Mellis (1999), Quality Function Deployment on software development has started in the year of 70's and end of 80's in America. Some sample QFD implementation on web development includes by Ioannou, Pramataris & Prastacos (2004) for electronic retailing, Chang & Kim (2010) for health information website, Islam, Ahmed, & Alias (2007) for redesigning web TV3, Barutcu (2006) for web e-store design, Kuo & Chen (2011) for web internet shopping interface design quality improvement.

E-SERVQUAL, KANO MODEL, AND QFD INTEGRATION PROPOSAL TO IMPROVE WEBSITE SERVICE QUALITY

To improve website service quality, this research adapts the model developed by Tan & Pawitra (2001) that combine SERVQUAL, Kano Model, and QFD to help service provider to evaluate users' satisfaction, provide guidance on empowering the weak service attributes, and quicken innovative services development by identifying attractive attributes and including it to the future service. The combination between Kano Model and SERVQUAL can cover each other's weaknesses, compared to if used separately. According to Bhardwaj & Menon (1997), Kano Model cannot evaluate attribute's performance. Using Kano Model with SERVQUAL will provide better overview on the relationship between product attributes and customer requirements.

The information created is useful to fix and improve the quality of those attributes. However, both will not be done systematically and operationally since the combination of SERVQUAL and Kano Model doesn't provide a device for that. Therefore, the integration of SERVQUAL and Kano Model into QFD will cover that weakness. With HoQ from QFD, there will be connection between customer requirements attributes and company's or service provider's technical responses. The integration of SERVQUAL and Kano Model combination into QFD will provide systematic and operational steps to fix and improve those attributes' quality.

In this research, the SERVQUAL context is used to measure website service's quality, thus in this research we will use the term E-SERVQUAL. The E-SERVQUAL, Kano Model, and QFD combination frame used in this research can be seen in the Figure 2 below.

In this theoretical framework, there are three part of processes required. The first is measurement on the E-SERVQUAL which includes identifying the gap score between expectation and perception score, as well as importance level measurement process taken from expectation score. The second process is measurement on Kano Model where the Kano categories are identified and the categories' scores are determined. Then, with the result of E-SERVQUAL and Kano Model's measurements, we will measure

Figure 2. The proposed E-SERVQUAL, Kano Model, and QFD combination frame

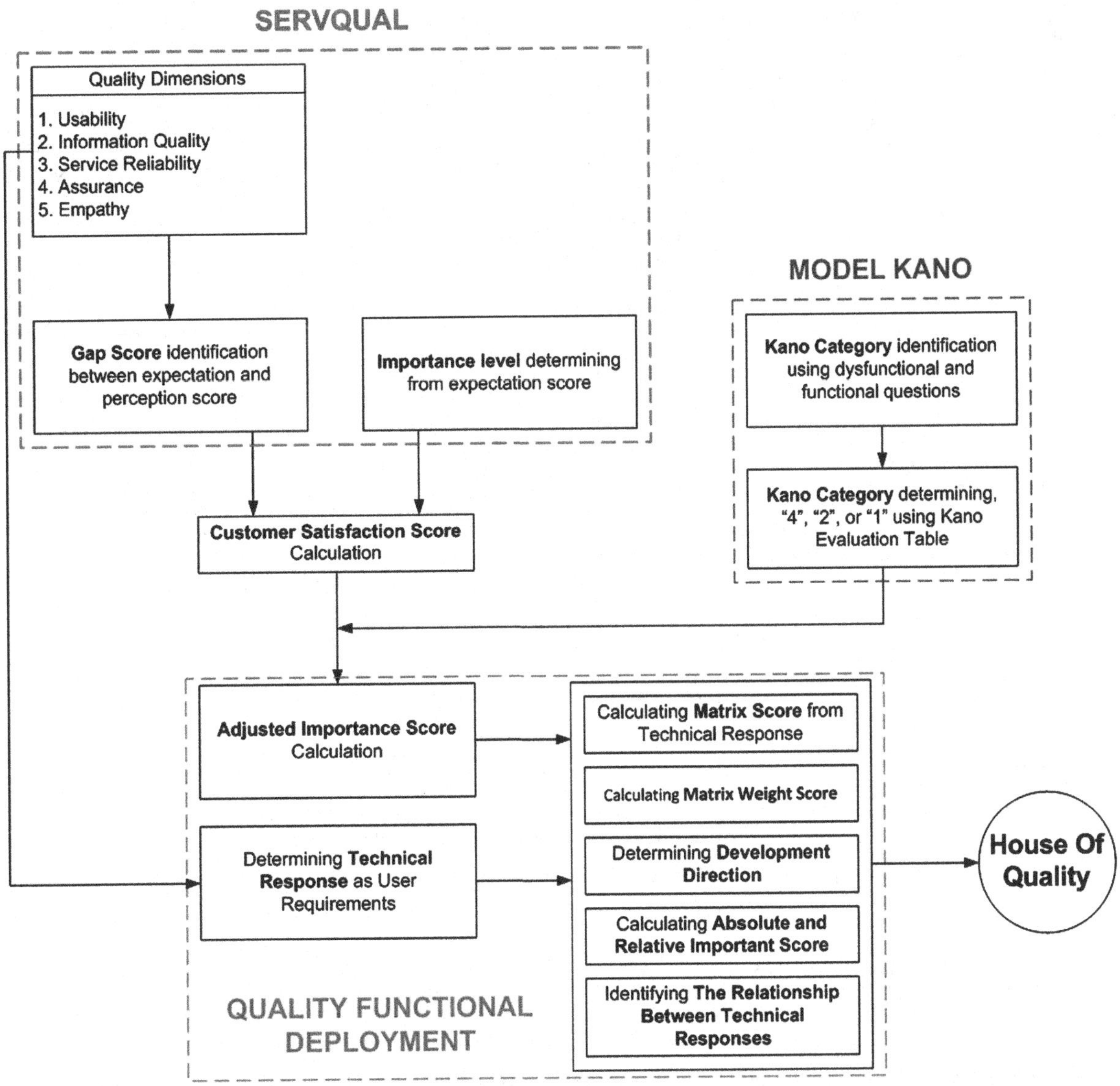

SERVQUAL

```
Quality Dimensions

1. Usability
2. Information Quality
3. Service Reliability
4. Assurance
5. Empathy
```

Gap Score identification between expectation and perception score

Importance level determining from expectation score

MODEL KANO

Kano Category identification using dysfunctional and functional questions

Kano Category determining, "4", "2", or "1" using Kano Evaluation Table

Customer Satisfaction Score Calculation

Adjusted Importance Score Calculation

Determining **Technical Response** as User Requirements

Calculating **Matrix Score** from Technical Response

Calculating **Matrix Weight Score**

Determining **Development Direction**

Calculating **Absolute and Relative Important Score**

Identifying **The Relationship Between Technical Responses**

QUALITY FUNCTIONAL DEPLOYMENT

House Of Quality

the Customer Satisfaction Score. The third process is the combination process with the QFD, where there are several measurement process required, which are finding Adjusted Importance score, deciding the technical response, finding matrix score, calculating matrix weight, deciding development direction, calculating absolute and relative importance, as well as identifying the relationship between technical responses to create House of Quality as the overall process of QFD.

In the E-SERVQUAL model measurement process, the thing that has to be paid attention to is selecting the quality dimension that will be used to create questionnaire. The quality dimension selection will decide quality attributes measured to find the gap score. Table 2 shows the dimensions that we summarized from various researches to show website service quality attributes. The quality dimensions used are the combination of quality dimensions proposed by Swaid & Wigand (2009) with reference provided by van Iwaarden et al. (2003).

Table 2. E-SERVQUAL Dimensions and Attributes

Quality Dimension	Definition	Quality Attributes	References
Usability	Shows users' perception level on website's ease of navigation and level of user-friendliness (Swaid & Wigand, 2009)	1. The web appearance is interesting 2. The web appearance is not confusing	Zhang (2006), Djajadikerta & Trireksani (2006), Mebrate (2010)
		3. The menus are shown and placed clearly (menu appearance) 4. The web's content is related to education 5. The grammar in the web is good and correct 6. The navigation process in the web is not confusing 7. The web has good search engine facility 8. The web can show up perfectly in different browsers	Stockdale & Borovicka (2006)
Information Quality	Users' perception on website content's benefit and quality	9. The information in the web is useful 10. The information in the web is complete 11. The information in the web is clear 12. The information in the web is up to date 13. The information in the web is accurate 14. The information in the web is concise	Djajadikerta & Trireksani (2006)
Services Reliability	Users' perception on website's reliability level (Swaid & Wigand, 2009)	15. The website address is active and directs into the correct web 16. The web name is easy to remember 17. All links in the web are valid 18. The web is accessible anytime 19. The web can be opened quickly every time it is accessed 20. The web reactivates quickly when damaged 21. All forms in the web function well 22. Email and contacts are active 23. There is a notification on newest information	Mebrate (2010), Stockdale & Borovicka (2006)
Assurance	Users' perception on website's assurance	24. The web's security is good 25. The website service provider has good reputation 26. The web management staffs are reliable in their task	Swaid & Wigand (2009)
Empathy	Users' perception on website's personalization/customization that can give personal care (Ratanasawadwat, 2015)	27. Users are comfortable when looking for information in the web	Zhang (2006)

The last process is combining all the measurement results based on theoretical framework above into House of Quality structure from QFD. The used HoQ structure can be seen in the Figure 3.

1. Part 1 is Total row and the content is taken from Absolute Importance score.
2. Part 2 is Percentage row and the content is taken from Relative Importance score.
3. Part 3 is Priority Order row and the content is the sorting of absolute importance to see which score has the highest priority and all the way to the lowest.
4. Part 4 is Customer Importance column and the content is the Expectation Score.
5. Part 5 is Kano Category column and the content is the Kano category classification of each attribute.
6. Part 6 is Importance Level column and the content is taken from adjusted importance score.
7. Part 7 is Development Direction column and the content is the development direction for every existing technical response.

Figure 3. Website Service's House of Quality Structure

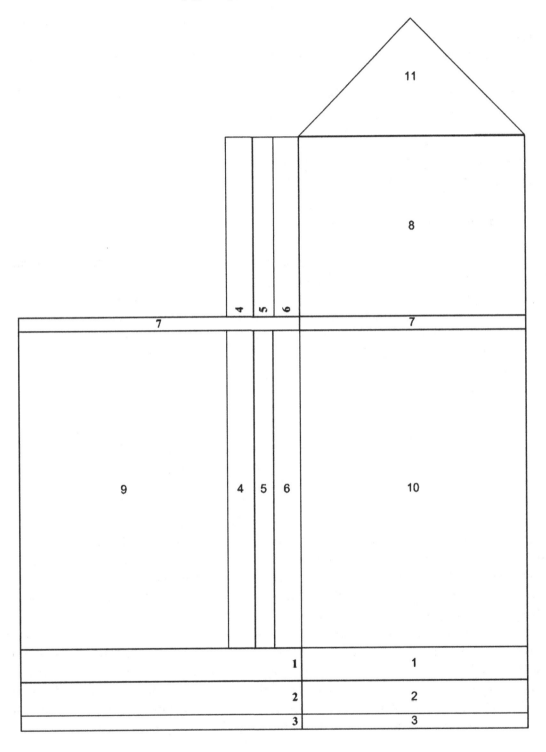

8. Part 8 consists of Technical Response on website service.
9. Part 9 is website service quality attributes included in A, M, and O classification in Kano Model category.
10. Part 10 is Relationship Matrix that portrays the relationship between service attributes and technical response.
11. Part 11 is Correlation Matrix or often called as roof of HoQ which contains Relationship Matrix between technical responses.

APPLICATION OF THE FRAMEWORK FOR UNIVERSITY WEBSITE EVALUATION

Case Study Profile

University that is selected to be the place for case study of this research is STMIK MDP located in Palembang, South Sumatera. STMIK MDP is one of private universities in Palembang that is oriented to computer education for the bachelor and diploma level with around 2000 students. As one of computer universities in Palembang, STMIK MDP has its own website-based online service since 2001 using www.stmik-mdp.net as the address. On the further development, STMIK MDP website got a lot of changes from technical to functional side and has changed its address into www.mdp.ac.id since 2009.

Data Collection

One of the required steps in this research is survey on the STMIK MDP website service users. The survey is conducted to measure the quality of the website service measured by the E-SERVQUAL dimensions defined prior to the survey. The survey is made in form of 27 question items questionnaire arranged using Likert scale and divided into two question groups, group for expectation variable and group for perception variable. The expectation variable will use the scale of Unimportant, Less important, Quite important, Important, Really important. The perception variable will use the scale of Really bad, Bad, Enough, Good, Really good. On the other hand, the measurement for Kano Model will use functional questionnaire list and dysfunctional question developed based on research attribute used on E-SERVQUAL method. The Kano Model will also use Likert scale as answer choice for the respondents. There are five scales, which are Satisfied, It should be like that, Neutral, Not satisfied but can tolerate, Totally not satisfied, marked with the number 1 (Satisfied) to 5 (Totally not satisfied).

The population in this research is the user of STMIK MDP web, which is the students and lecturers. The overall total population, both student and lecturers is around 2000 people. The number of sample that will be used is 200 respondents. The respondents selected are students at least in the second year with the expectation that they are familiar and frequently access the STMIK MDP website. The lecturers selected are the permanent lecturers because they access the website most frequently compared to the part-time lecturers. The questionnaire will be distributed offline to the targeted respondents.

E-SERVQUAL Measurement Results

Result summary from the questionnaire distributed to 200 respondents, for both expectation variable and respondents' perception on STMIK MDP website service attributes can be seen in the Table 3.

Table 3 shows the gap between expectation and perception dimension from E-SERVQUAL measurement conducted before. The table shows that the gap score results are all in negatives, thus creates the conclusion that respondents' expectations are not matched by their perception therefore affect the gap score into negative. This proves that STMIK MDP's website service has not fulfilled its users' expectations.

Table 3. Respondents Expectation Score on Service Quality Attributes

Quality Attributes	Expectation Score	Perception Score	Gap Score	Average Gap Score
The web appearance is interesting	4.02	3.54	-0.48	-0.42
The web appearance is not confusing	4.17	3.84	-0.33	
The menus are shown and placed clearly (menu appearance)	4.23	3.86	-0.37	
The web's content is related to education	4.23	3.92	-0.31	
The grammar in the web is good and correct	4.37	4.16	-0.21	
The navigation process in the web is not confusing	4.18	3.75	-0.43	
The web has good search engine facility	4.00	3.34	-0.66	
The web can show up perfectly in different browsers	4.26	3.68	-0.58	
The information in the web is useful	4.46	4.02	-0.44	-0.62
The information in the web is complete	4.39	3.67	-0.72	
The information in the web is clear	4.32	3.78	-0.54	
The information in the web is up to date	4.48	3.58	-0.91	
The information in the web is accurate	4.43	3.68	-0.75	
The information in the web is concise	4.05	3.68	-0.37	
The website address is active and directs into the correct web	4.52	4.25	-0.27	-0.70
The web name is easy to remember	4.50	4.32	-0.18	
All links in the web are valid	4.31	3.85	-0.46	
The web is accessible anytime	4.49	3.53	-0.96	
The web can be opened quickly every time it is accessed	4.41	3.27	-1.14	
The web reactivates quickly when damaged	4.40	3.25	-1.15	
All forms in the web function well	4.27	3.25	-0.54	
Email and contacts are active	4.17	3.72	-0.90	
There is a notification on newest information	4.44	3.76	-0.68	
The web's security is good	4.51	3.62	-0.89	-0.65
The website service provider has good reputation	4.31	3.79	-0.52	
The web management staffs are reliable in their task	4.33	3.78	-0.56	
Users are comfortable when looking for information in the web	4.42	3.82	-0.60	-0.60

Kano Model Measurement

On the Kano Model measurement process, the most important thing is to decide each attribute's classification. Sauerwein et al. (1996) explained that attribute classification based on Kano Model is conducted by asking functional (positive) and dysfunctional (negative) questions in the questionnaire. Each question has five types of answers, which are "I like it that way", "It must be that way", "I am neutral", "I can live with it that way", and "I dislike it that way" or can be rephrased into "Satisfied", "That's how it should be", "Neutral", "Not satisfied, but can tolerate", and "Totally not satisfied".

For the illustration of each attribute's classification to identify its category, whether it's included in Attractive, Must-be, One-Dimensional, Indifferent, and Questionable, can be seen in the Figure 4.

For each functional and dysfunctional question, we will find the intersection on each question's answers. According to the picture above, it can be explained as the following. For instance, question number 1 in functional question is answered "Satisfied", while the dysfunctional question is answered "Totally not satisfied". Therefore according to the Kano Model Evaluation Table intersection, the attribute of the number 1 question is included into one-dimensional classification. Keep in mind that for 1 question attribute, the total number of Kano Model categories has to be equal with the number of respondents.

Next, using Kano Evaluation Table (Sauerwin et al., 1996), we figured out the classification of each attributes.

After each attribute's classification is identified, the next step is to determine the Kano Category Score on each of those attributes into Table 4 using this set of rules: The Kano Category Score of 4 belongs to attractive category, 2 belongs to one-dimensional category, and 1 belongs to must-be. Table

Figure 4. Attribute Classification Process into Kano Model Categories

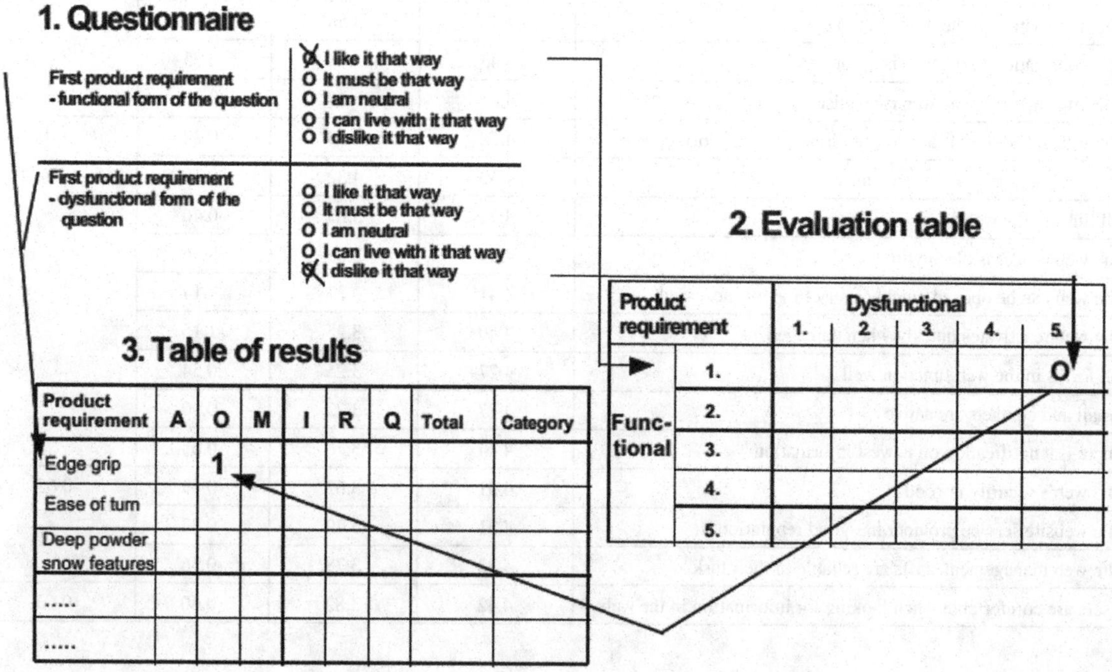

Figure 5. Kano Model Evaluation Table

Customer requirements →		Dysfunctional (negative) question				
	↓	1. like	2. must be	3. neutral	4. live with	5. dislike
Functional (positive) question	1. like	Q	A	A	A	O
	2. must-be	R	I	I	I	M
	3. neutral	R	I	I	I	M
	4. live with	R	I	I	I	M
	5. dislike	R	R	R	R	Q

Customer requirement is ...

A: Attractive   O: One-dimensional
M: Must-be   Q: Questionable
R: Reverse   I: Indifferent

4 shows the classification total recapitulation result from respondents' scoring regarding Kano Model of functional question and dysfunctional question about STMIK MDP website service and Kano category for each attributes.

According to the Table 4 above, from 27 STMIK MDP website service attributes, 11 of them are included into Kano Category "I" or indifferent. The rest, or 16 of the attributes are included into Kano Category "A" or attractive, "M" or must-be, and "O" or one-dimensional. The attributes included into indifferent category will be ignored and deleted, thus not included in the next calculation process, which is finding adjusted importance score.

QFD House of Quality Creation

In the House of Quality creation process, we use the data related to customer requirements that are also the website service attributes, as well as the data from technical responses from STMIK MPD website service management.

Adjusted Importance Score

Adjusted Importance score is found with this formula:

‖Customer Satisfaction Score (CSS)‖ * Kano Category Score
The Customer Satisfaction Score is found with this formula:
Customer Satisfaction Score = Gap score * Importance Level

Table 4. Attribute Classification Choices of STMIK MDP Website Service

No	Quality Attributes	Classification Total						Category Kano	Kano Category Score
		A	M	O	I	R	Q		
1	The web appearance is interesting	30	68	32	66	0	4	M	1
2	The web appearance is not confusing	19	68	38	64	3	8	M	1
3	The menus are shown and placed clearly (menu appearance)	19	59	51	66	1	4	M	1
4	The web's content is related to education	31	51	32	84	2	0	I	-
5	The grammar in the web is good and correct	24	58	51	65	2	0	I	-
6	The navigation process in the web is not confusing	25	58	25	89	3	0	I	-
7	The web has good search engine facility	42	44	29	82	2	1	I	-
8	The web can show up perfectly in different browsers	40	55	61	43	1	0	I	-
9	The information in the web is useful	38	53	54	51	4	0	O	2
10	The information in the web is complete	57	46	49	47	1	0	A	4
11	The information in the web is clear	25	71	38	62	3	1	M	1
12	The information in the web is up to date	42	49	48	56	2	3	M	1
13	The information in the web is accurate	23	63	62	50	2	0	M	1
14	The information in the web is concise	34	36	38	90	2	0	I	-
15	The website address is active and directs into the correct web	22	76	45	55	1	1	M	1
16	The web name is easy to remember	51	29	28	92	0	0	I	-
17	All links in the web are valid	21	73	48	56	2	0	M	1
18	The web is accessible anytime	28	60	58	51	1	2	M	1
19	The web can be opened quickly every time it is accessed	47	53	52	46	1	1	M	1
20	The web reactivates quickly when damaged	26	62	55	54	1	2	M	1
21	All forms in the web function well	22	56	39	81	0	2	I	-
22	Email and contacts are active	27	54	25	92	2	0	I	-
23	There is a notification on newest information	32	62	43	58	2	3	M	1
24	The web's security is good	19	58	68	54	1	0	O	2
25	The website service provider has good reputation	34	53	54	56	2	1	I	-
26	The web management staffs are reliable in their task	22	59	51	66	2	0	I	-
27	Users are comfortable when looking for information in the web	26	45	65	61	1	2	O	2

The gap score in the formula is from the E-SERVQUAL calculation. The Importance Level score is from calculating users' expectation total score from E-SERVQUAL. Users' expectation scale (not important, less important, quite important, important, and very important) is given the score of 1 to 5 respectively. Considering the research has 200 respondents, the users' expectation total score from E-SERVQUAL will be in the range of 200x1 (= 200) until 200x5 (= 1000). The range will be broken down into 5 parts to reflect Importance Level of an attribute according to the Table 5.

Using the Table 5, the Importance Level for each E-SERVQUAL attributes can be determined, which result can be seen in the Table 6. The table also shows customer satisfaction score, adjusted importance score, and also priorities for attribute development gained by sorting the attributes based on the adjusted

Table 5. Service's Importance Level's Category Score

E-SERVQUAL Total Expectation Score	Importance Level	Score
900-1000	Very Important	5
700-899	Important	4
500-699	Quite Important	3
300-499	Less Important	2
200-299	Not Important	1

importance score. From the Table 6, it is seen that the top priority is attribute number 10, while the lowest one is attribute number 2. Keep in mind that this table only shows quality attributes that have the Kano category of attractive, must-be, and one-dimensional.

Deciding Technical Response

Technical response is the translation of customer requirements on a service they're getting into organizational language. Organizational language means process, procedure, or solution organization has or uses to fulfill customer requirements. To decide the technical response in this research, writer conducted a discussion with STMIK MPD web manager, who are Information Technology unit staffs. From the discussion with the Information Technology unit staffs, we gained some technical response information regarding university's website service requirements.

1. Server capacity improvement.
2. Backup server addition.
3. Database and application synchronization.
4. Bandwidth addition.
5. Optimization and efficiency improvement on the current web coding.
6. Software technology upgrade for the web.
7. Web database optimization and efficiency improvement.
8. Redesigning layout.
9. Staff addition.
10. Staff training for web security matters.
11. Adding communication media for users.
12. Mobile web implementation.
13. Cooperation with other organization unit.
14. Notification feature implementation.

Matrix Score and Matrix Weight from Technical Response

To gain the relationship matrix score between technical responses, we will use this set of rules:

1. Strong relationship (●), which is a strong relationship between technical response and service's attribute, with relationship weight of 9.

Table 6. Quality Attribute Priority Level on University's Website Service

No	Quality Attributes	Total score of expectations	Gap Score	Importance Level	CSS	Kano Category Score	Adjusted Importance Score	Priority No
1	The web appearance is interesting	803	-0.48	4	-1.92	1	1.92	12
2	The web appearance is not confusing	834	-0.33	4	-1.32	1	1.32	16
3	The menus are shown and placed clearly (menu appearance)	845	-0.37	4	-1.48	1	1.48	14
9	The information in the web is useful	892	-0.44	4	-1.76	2	3.52	8
10	The information in the web is complete	878	-0.72	4	-2.88	4	11.52	1
11	The information in the web is clear	863	-0.54	4	-2.16	1	2.16	11
12	The information in the web is up to date	896	-0.91	4	-8.19	1	8.19	3
13	The information in the web is accurate	885	-0.75	4	-3.00	1	3.00	9
15	The website address is active and directs into the correct web	904	-0.27	5	-1.35	1	1.35	15
17	All links in the web are valid	861	-0.46	4	-1.84	1	1.84	13
18	The web is accessible anytime	898	-0.96	4	-3.84	1	3.84	7
19	The web can be opened quickly every time it is accessed	881	-1.14	4	-4.56	1	4.56	6
20	The web reactivates quickly when damaged	879	-1.15	4	-4.60	1	4.60	5
23	There is a notification on newest information	887	-0.68	4	-2.72	1	2.72	10
24	The web's security is good	902	-0.89	5	-4.45	2	8.9	2
27	Users are comfortable when looking for information in the web	884	-0.60	4	-2.4	2	4.8	4

2. Moderate relationship (O), which is a moderate relationship between technical response and service's attribute, with relationship weight of 3.

3. Weak relationship (Δ), which is a weak relationship between technical response and service's attribute, with relationship weight of 1,

The Relationship Matrix's weight score is shown in Table 8, where to gain it, we used this formula:
Relationship Matrix's Weight Score:
Adjusted importance score* relationship matrix score between technical response and service attribute.

The adjusted importance score can be found in Table 6.

With the rules above, each relationship decided by the Table 8 can have its relationship matrix score figured out. These scores, 9, 3, or 1, will be multiplied by the adjusted importance score.

As an example, for the "server capacity improvement" technical response, there are 4 types of relationship, which are 3 strong relationships, and 1 moderate relationship. As already known, the strong relationship weight is scored 9, and moderate is 3. Those 4 attributes, which are "The web is accessible any time", "The web can be opened quickly every time it is accessed", "The web reactivates quickly after damaged", and "User is comfortable searching for information in the web have adjusted importance score of 3.84, 4.56, 4.60, and 4.8 respectively. Each of these score will be multiplied with its relationship weight 3.84 * 9, 4.56 * 9, 4.60 * 9, and 4.8 * 3.

Table 7 shows the relationship between each technical response with each university's website service attribute. Each service attribute can have relationship with more than one technical response. On the other hand, Table 8 shows the results of the weighting for each relationship between technical response and service attribute.

Technical Response Development Direction

Table 9 shows the feedbacks on the development directions of STMIK MPD website service's technical response based on the discussion with the web management staff.

From the 14 technical responses created, there are 10 technical responses which development direction needs to be improved, and 4 which development direction is stagnant. For the technical responses that require improved development direction, an improvement action is required since it is not planned yet. On the other hand, the technical responses with stagnant development, an improvement is not required since the improvement plan is there or currently ongoing, but needs attention to prevent any drop.

Absolute and Relative Importance Score

Technical Response Weight is a measurement for each technical response calculated based on relationship level (relationship matrix) between technical responses on customer requirements that has relationship with the said technical response. The technical response weight is a measurement that shows technical response that requires attention or priority from the web manager since it has relationship with customer requirements fulfillment. The technical responses calculation is also called as absolute importance (AI) calculation and relative importance (RI).

The calculation of both uses these formulas:

1. Absolute Importance score $= \sum$ (importance level score * relationship matrix score between technical response and service attribute)

In the other words, the absolute importance score for each technical responses from total of each relationship matrix weight score in Table 9.

2. Relative Importance score $= Absolute\ importance$

    $\sum$ technical response

Table 7. The Relationship between Service Attribute and Technical Response

	Server capacity improvement	Backup server addition	Database and application synchronization	Bandwidth addition	Optimization and efficiency improvement on the current web coding	Software technology upgrade for the web	Web database optimization and efficiency improvement	Redesigning layout	Staff addition	Staff training for web security matters	Mobile web implementation	Adding communication media for users	Cooperation with other organization unit	Notification feature implementation
The web appearance is interesting						○		●	△					△
The web appearance is not confusing						○		●	△					
The menus are shown and placed clearly (menu appearance)						○		●	△					
The information in the web is useful									●					
The information in the web is complete									●			△	○	
The information in the web is clear									●			△	○	
The information in the web is up to date			●						●			△	○	
The information in the web is accurate			●						●			△	○	
The website address is active and directs into the correct web						△			●					
All links in the web are valid	●	△		●		●		●	△					
The web is accessible anytime	●				○	○	●				○			
The web can be opened quickly every time it is accessed				●	○	○	●				○			
The web reactivates quickly when damaged	●	●			○	○			○	○				
There is a notification on newest information								○	●			○		●
The web's security is good		○			○	●			○	●		△		
Users are comfortable when looking for information in the web	○			○	○	○		●	●	○		○	○	

Table 8. The Relationship Weight between Service Attribute and Technical Response

	Server capacity improvement	Backup server addition	Database and application synchronization	Bandwidth addition	Optimization and efficiency improvement on the current web coding	Software technology upgrade for the web	Web database optimization and efficiency improvement	Redesigning layout	Staff addition	Staff training for web security matters	Mobile web implementation	Adding communication media for users	Cooperation with other organization unit	Notification feature implementation
The web appearance is interesting						5.8		17.3	1.9					1.9
The web appearance is not confusing						4		11.9	1.3					
The menus are shown and placed clearly (menu appearance)						4.4		13.3	1.49					
The information in the web is useful									31.7					
The information in the web is complete									103.7			11.5	34.6	
The information in the web is clear									19.4			2.2	6.5	
The information in the web is up to date			73.7						73.7			8.2	24.6	
The information in the web is accurate			27						27			3	9	
The website address is active and directs into the correct web						1.4			12.2					
All links in the web are valid						16.6		16.6	1.8					
The web is accessible anytime	34.6	3.8		34.6	11.5	11.5	34.6				11.5			
The web can be opened quickly every time it is accessed	41	4.6		41	13.7	13.7	41				13.7			
The web reactivates quickly when damaged	41.4	41.4			13.8	13.8			13.8	13.8		13.8		
There is a notification on newest information					8.2	8.2		8.2	24.5			2.7	8.2	24.5
The web's security is good		26.7			26.7	80.1			26.7	80.1		2.67		
Users are comfortable when looking for information in the web	14.4			14.4		14.4		43.2	43.2	14.4		14.4		4.8

Table 9. Technical Response Development Direction

No	Technical Response	Development Direction
1	Server capacity improvement	↑
2	Backup server addition	↑
3	Database and application synchronization	↑
4	Bandwidth addition	↑
5	Optimization and efficiency improvement on the current web coding	o
6	Software technology upgrade for the web	↑
7	Web database optimization and efficiency improvement	↑
8	Redesigning layout	o
9	Staff addition	↑
10	Staff training for web security matters	o
11	Adding communication media for users	↑
12	Mobile web implementation	o
13	Cooperation with other organization unit	↑
14	Notification feature implementation	↑

Where $\sum$ technical response score is 14

The calculation result of absolute importance and relative importance score can be seen in the Table 10 below.

Table 10 above shows priority order of the existing technical responses. The priority order is based on relative importance scores sorted from the highest to the lowest. The priority order portrays what technical

Table 10. Absolute Importance and Relative Importance Score

No	Technical Response	AI	RI	Priority Order
1	Server capacity improvement	131.4	9.4%	3
2	Backup server addition	76.5	5.5%	9
3	Database and application synchronization	108.9	7.8%	5
4	Bandwidth addition	90	6.4%	7
5	Optimization and efficiency improvement on the current web coding	73.9	5.3%	11
6	Software technology upgrade for the web	173.9	12.4%	2
7	Web database optimization and efficiency improvement	75.6	5.4%	10
8	Redesigning layout	110.5	7.9%	4
9	Staff addition	382.4	27.3%	1
10	Staff training for web security matters	108.3	7.7%	6
11	Adding communication media for users	58.5	4.2%	12
12	Mobile web implementation	25.2	1.8%	14
13	Cooperation with other organization unit	82.9	6%	8
14	Notification feature implementation	31.2	2.2%	13

responses that need priority attention from web management and staff to fulfill customer requirements. According to the table above, the technical response with the highest priority is "staff addition" and the lowest one is "mobile web implementation".

Relationship between Technical Responses

The relationship between technical responses is a relationship between each other existing technical responses. The relationship between technical responses is decided by identifying the trade off required in deciding the technical responses that need to get attention from service provider. The relationship is based on interview with university's UPT Information System staffs. The relationship between technical responses is portrayed using the following symbols:

1. **Strong Positive Relationship (●):** The linear relationship between technical responses, where if one of the technical responses has an improvement or drop, it will strongly affect on the improvement or drop of other related items.
2. **Positive Relationship (○):** The relationship where if one technical response has an improvement or drop, it will affect on the improvement or drop of the related technical responses.

Figure 6 shows the end result of relationship matrix between technical responses used to fulfill customer requirements according to the service attribute gained. From the picture above, we can find that from 14 technical responses, there are 10 relationships between technical responses, where 7 of them are positive strong relationships and 3 are positive relationships.

Figure 6. Relationship Matrix between Technical Responses

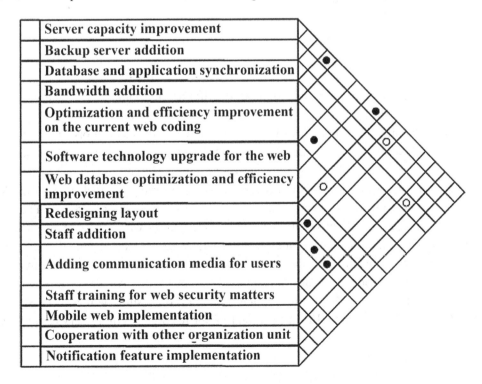

Server capacity improvement has strong positive relationship with bandwidth addition and web database optimization and efficiency improvement. Web coding optimization and efficiency improvement has strong positive relationship with software technology upgrade for the web, while software technology upgrade for the web has strong relationship with redesign layout. Redesign layout has strong positive relationship with staff addition, while staff addition has strong positive relationship with adding communication media with users and staff training for web security matters. Backup server addition has strong relationship with staff addition. Database and application synchronization has strong positive relationship with cooperation with other organization unit, and finally, bandwidth addition has strong relationship with mobile web implementation.

After each of the House of Quality creation process is done, each part of the process is combined into one thus creating website service House of Quality as seen in Figure 7.

FUTURE RESEARCH DIRECTIONS

This study only considers website services in organization, whereas currently social media is also a popular channel to provide services, for example through the use of Facebook and Twitter. Moreover, social media is one of the most effective forms of channel for electronic word of mouth (e-WOM). It would be interesting if this study can be extended to evaluate university services that utilize social media. In addition, this study can also be applied to evaluate website-based service in other fields such as online-gaming that involves intense interaction with the user or news portals that focus on the provision of information services.

THEORETICAL SIGNIFICANCE

SERVQUAL is a theory that is widely used to evaluate the quality of services. The SERVQUAL concept is then spread to evaluate electronic service quality (or also known as E-SERVQUAL) like what was done by Carrasco et al. (2012), Udo, Bagchi, & Kirs (2011), Büyüközkan & Çifçi (2012), and so on. The SERVQUAL usage allowed organizations to identify the electronic service quality dimensions' condition. In the design service context, the SERVQUAL concept is often times integrated with Kano Model, especially to identify the dimensions that have to be prioritized by the organizations, like what was done by Zhao & Dholakia (2009). Unfortunately, so far we only find few literatures discussing integrated framework for end-to-end electronic services design, from evaluating their quality to formulating responses to improve the quality. This study successfully confirms integration of E-SERVQUAL, Kano Model and QFD can be applied also in the context of website services of universities. The integration between the three frameworks on university website service quality was implemented successfully to evaluate website service quality which includes at least three things: (1) identifying the strong and weak university website service quality dimensions, (2) identifying website service quality dimensions that need to be focused on, (3) decide the technical response required to improve the website service quality. This research is also successfully the result of Tan & Pawitra (2001) study which successfully applied the SERVQUAL, Kano Model, and QFD integration to improve organization's service quality.

Figure 7. University's Website Service House of Quality

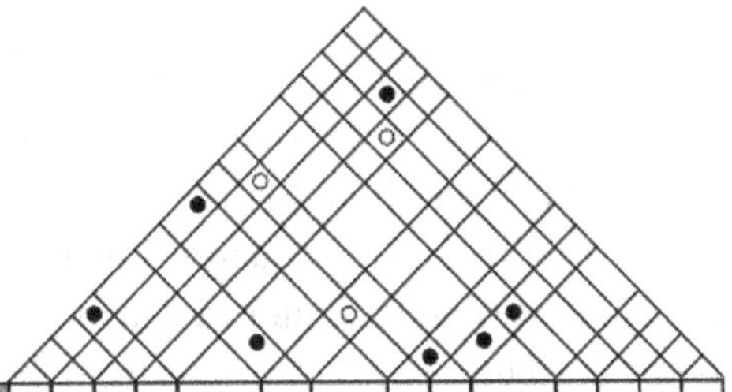

Development Direction	Customer Importance	Kano Category	Importance Level	Server capacity improvement	Backup server addition	Database and application synchronization	Bandwidth addition	Optimization and efficiency improvement on the current web coding	Software technology upgrade for the web	Web database optimization and efficiency improvement	Redesigning layout	Staff addition	Adding communication media for user	Staff training for web security matters	Mobile web implementation	Cooperation with other organization unit	Notification feature implementation
				↑	↑	↑	↑	O	↑	↑	O	↑	↑	O	O	↑	↑
The STMIK MDP's web appearance is interesting	4.02	M	1.92						o		●	Δ					Δ
The STMIK MDP's web appearance is not confusing	4.17	M	1.32						o		●	Δ					
The menus are shown and placed clearly (menu appearance)	4.23	M	1.48						o		●	Δ					
The information in the STMIK MDP's web is useful	4.46	O	1.76								●						
The information in the STMIK MDP's web is complete	4.39	A	2.88								●				Δ	o	
The information in the STMIK MDP's web is clear	4.32	M	2.16								●				Δ	o	
The information in the STMIK MDP's web is up to date	4.48	M	8.19								●				Δ	o	
The information in the STMIK MDP's web is accurate	4.43	M	3.00			●					●				Δ	o	
The website address is active and directs into the correct web	4.52	M	1.35						Δ		●						
All links in the STMIK MDP's web are valid	4.31	M	1.84						●		●	Δ					
The STMIK MDP's web is accessible anytime	4.49	M	3.84	●	Δ		●			●							
The STMIK MDP's web can be opened quickly every time it is accessed	4.41	M	4.56	●	Δ		●			●							
The STMIK MDP's web reactivates quickly when damaged	4.40	M	4.60	●	●												
There is a notification on newest information	4.44	M	2.72			o		o	o		o	●			Δ	o	●
The STMIK MDP web's security is good	4.51	O	4.45		o			o	●			o	●			o	
Users are comfortable when looking for information in the STMIK MDP's web	4.42	O	2.4	o			o		o		●	●	o			o	Δ
Total				131.4	76.5	108.9	90	73.9	173.9	75.6	110.5	382.4	58.5	108.3	25.2	82.9	31.2
Percentage (%)				9.40	5.50	7.80	6.40	5.30	12.40	5.40	7.90	27.30	4.20	7.70	1.80	6.0	2.20
Priority Order				3	9	5	7	11	2	10	4	1	6	12	14	8	13

CONCLUSION

This study successfully integrates E-SERVQUAL, Kano Model and Quality Function Deployment (QFD) to evaluate the quality of website services in the universities. E-SERVQUAL attributes used in this study were grouped into five (5) dimensions of quality attributes, namely usability dimension as much as eight attributes, information quality dimension as much as six attributes, service reliability dimension as much as nine attributes, assurance dimension as much as three attributes and empathy dimension as much as one attribute. The dimensions from the electronic service are then evaluated with Kano Model to identify the dimensions that are prioritized by the electronic service customer in the university. And finally, QFD is applied successfully to decide the technical response required to improve the university's electronic service quality. Framework that we developed is also successfully applied to one of the private universities in Palembang, Indonesia. Based on our processing results by using Kano Model, we found 1 attribute classified as A (attractive) category, 3 attributes classified as O (one-dimensional) category, 12 attributes classified as M (Must-Be) category and the remaining 11 attributes classified as I (indifferent) category. Of the 14 technical responses were found at the stage of QFD, acquired five major action priorities to be carried out by the university, namely: adding staff, upgrading software technology for the web, increasing server capacity, redesigning the layout and database synchronization between applications.

REFERENCES

Akao, Y. (1990). *Quality Function Deployment*. Cambridge, MA: Productivity Press.

Aladwani, A. M., & Palvia, P. C. (2002). Developing and validating an instrument for measuring user-perceived web quality. *Information & Management, 39*(6), 467–476. doi:10.1016/S0378-7206(01)00113-6

Aldridge, S., & Rowley, J. (1998). Measuring customer satisfaction in higher education. *Quality Assurance in Education, 6*(4), 197–204. doi:10.1108/09684889810242182

Arasli, H., Mehtap-Smadi, S., & Katircioglu, S. T. (2005). Customer Service Quality In The Greek Cypriot Banking Industry. *Managing Service Quality: An International Journal, 15*(1), 41–56. doi:10.1108/09604520510575254

Athiyaman, A. (1997). Linking student satisfaction and service quality perceptions: The case of university education. *European Journal of Marketing, 31*(7), 528–540. doi:10.1108/03090569710176655

Balakrishnan, V., Liew, T. K., & Pourgholaminejad, S. (2015). Fun learning with Edooware – A social media enabled tool. *Computers & Education, 80*(1), 39–47. doi:10.1016/j.compedu.2014.08.008

Barutcu, S. (2006). Quality Function Deployment in Effective Website Design, An Application in E-Store Design. *İşletme Fakültesi Dergisi, 7*(1), 41-63.

Berger, C., Blauth, R., Boger, D., Bolster, C., Burchill, G., DuMouchel, W., & Walden, D. et al. (1993). Kano's Methods for Understanding Customer - defined Quality. *Center for Quality Management Journal, 2*(4), 3–36.

Bharadwaj, S., & Menon, A. (1997). Discussion in applying the Kano methodology to meet customer requirements. *Quality Management Journal, 4*(3), 107–109.

Bramall, C., Schoefer, K., & McKechnie, S. (2004). The determinants and consequences of consumer trust in e-retailing: A conceptual framework. *Irish Marketing Review, 17*(1/2), 13–22.

Bressolles, G., Durrieu, F., & Senecal, S. (2014). A consumer typology based on e-service quality and e-satisfaction. *Journal of Retailing and Consumer Services, 21*(6), 889–896. doi:10.1016/j.jretconser.2014.07.004

Brysland, A., & Curry, A. (2001). Service Improvements in Public Services Using SERVQUAL. *Managing Service Quality: An International Journal, 11*(6), 389–401. doi:10.1108/09604520110410601

Büyüközkan, G., & Çifçi, G. (2012). A combined fuzzy AHP and fuzzy TOPSIS based strategic analysis of electronic service quality in healthcare industry. *Expert Systems with Applications, 39*(3), 2341–2354. doi:10.1016/j.eswa.2011.08.061

Byun, H., Lee, B., & Rye, J. (2014). A Comparative Study on Evaluating the Service Quality Attributes based on Kano Model: A Case of Low-cost Carrier and Full-service Carrier. *SHS Web of Conferences 12*.

Carlson, J., & O'Cass, A. (2011). Developing A Framework For Understanding E-Service Quality, Its Antecedents, Consequences, And Mediators. *Managing Service Quality: An International Journal, 21*(3), 264–286. doi:10.1108/09604521111127965

Carrasco, R. A., Muñoz-Leiva, F., Sánchez-Fernández, J., & Liébana-Cabanillas, F. J. (2012). A model for the integration of e-financial services questionnaires with SERVQUAL scales under fuzzy linguistic modeling. *Expert Systems with Applications, 39*(14), 11535–11547. doi:10.1016/j.eswa.2012.03.055

Chang, H., & Kim, D. (2010). A Quality Function Deployment Framework for the Service Quality of Health Information Website. *Healthcare Informatics Research, 16*(1), 6–14. doi:10.4258/hir.2010.16.1.6 PMID:21818418

Chen, Z.-Y., Fan, Z.-P., & Sun, M. (2015). Behavior-aware user response modeling in social media: Learning from diverse heterogeneous data. *European Journal of Operational Research, 241*(2), 422–434. doi:10.1016/j.ejor.2014.09.008

Cheng, B., Wang, M., Mørch, A. I., Chen, N.-S., Kinshuk, , & Spector, J. M. (2014). Research on e-learning in the workplace 2000–2012: A bibliometric analysis of the literature. *Educational Research Review, 11*(1), 56–72. doi:10.1016/j.edurev.2014.01.001

Chu, C.-J., Wang, S.-L., & Lai, Y.-C. (2010). A Study of Web 2.0 Based Digital Archives System Using Kano Model. *Paper presented at the 2010 International meeting of the Computer Symposium*, Tainan.

Cox, J., & Dale, B. G. (2001). Service Quality And Ecommerce: An Exploratory Analysis. *Managing Service Quality: An International Journal, 11*(2), 121–131. doi:10.1108/09604520110387257

de Jager, J., & Gbadamosi, G. (2013). Predicting students' satisfaction through service quality in higher education. *The International Journal of Management Education, 11*(3), 107–118. doi:10.1016/j.ijme.2013.09.001

de Reuver, M., Nikou, S., & Bouwman, H. (2015). The interplay of costs, trust and loyalty in a service industry in transition: The moderating effect of smartphone adoption. *Telematics and Informatics*.

Djajadikerta, H., & Trireksani, T. (2006). Measuring University Web Site Quality: A Development of a User-Perceived Instrument and its Initial Implementation to Web sites of Accounting Departments in New Zealand's Universities. *School of Accounting, Finance and Economics & FIMARC Working Paper Series*, 1-23.

Edvardsson, B. (1997). Quality in new service development: Key concepts and a frame of reference. *International Journal of Production Economics*, 52(1-2), 31–46. doi:10.1016/S0925-5273(97)80765-7

Fogg, B. J., Soohoo, C., Danielson, D. R., Marable, L., Stanford, J., & Tauber, E. R. (2003). How do users evaluate the credibility of Web sites?: a study with over 2,500 participants. *Proceedings of the 2003 conference on Designing for user experiences* (pp. 1-15). doi:10.1145/997078.997097

Gefen, D. (2002). Reflections on the dimensions of trust and trustworthiness among online consumers. *The Data Base for Advances in Information Systems*, 33(3), 38–53. doi:10.1145/569905.569910

Goldstein, S. M., Johnston, R., Duffy, J., & Rao, J. (2002). The service concept: The missing link in service design research. *Journal of Operations Management*, 20(2), 121–134. doi:10.1016/S0272-6963(01)00090-0

Gronroos, C. (1984). A service quality model and its marketing implications. *European Journal of Marketing*, 18(4), 36–44. doi:10.1108/EUM0000000004784

Gronroos, C. (1992). *Service Management and Marketing*. Massachusetts: P Lexington Books.

Herzwurm, G., Schockert, S., & Mellis, W. (1999). Higher Customer Satisfaction With Prioritizing And Focused Software Quality Function Deployment. *Proceedings of the Sixth European Conference on Software Quality*, Vienna.

Hew, K. F., & Cheung, W. S. (2013). Use of Web 2.0 technologies in K-12 and higher education: The search for evidence-based practice. *Educational Research Review*, 9(1), 47–64. doi:10.1016/j.edurev.2012.08.001

Hidayanto, A.N., Mukhodim, W.M., Kom, F.M., & Junus, K.M. (2013). Analysis of Service Quality and Important Features of Property Websites in Indonesia. *Pacific Asia Journal of AIS*, 5(3).

Hidayanto, A. N., Rofalina, F., & Handayani, P. W. (2015). Influence of Perceived Quality of Official University Websites to Perceived Quality of University Education and Enrollment Intention. In P. Isaias, P. Kommers, &T. Issa (Eds.), The Evolution of the Internet in the Business Sector: Web 1.0 to Web 3.0. Hershey, PA, USA: IGI Global Publishing. doi:10.4018/978-1-4666-7262-8.ch013

Holsapple, C. W., & Wu, J. (2008). Building effective online game websites with knowledge-based trust. *Information Systems Frontiers*, 10(1), 47–60. doi:10.1007/s10796-007-9060-5

Human, G., & Naudé, O. (2014). Heterogeneity in the quality–satisfaction–loyalty framework. *Industrial Marketing Management*, 43(6), 920–928. doi:10.1016/j.indmarman.2014.05.006

Ioannou, G., Pramataris, K. C., & Prastacos, G. (2004). Quality Function Deployment Approach to Web Site Development: Applications for Electronic Retailing. *Les Cahiers du Management Technologique*, 13(3), 1–18.

Islam, R., Ahmed, M., & Alias, M. H. (2007). Application of Quality Function Deployment in redesigning website: A case study on TV3. *International Journal of Business Information Systems, 2*(2), 195–216. doi:10.1504/IJBIS.2007.011619

Ji, P., Jin, J., Wang, T., & Chen, Y. (2014). Quantification and integration of Kano's model into QFD for optimising product design. *International Journal of Production Research, 52*(21), 6335–6348. doi:10.1080/00207543.2014.939777

Juran, J. M., & Godfrey, A. B. (1999). *Juran's Quality Handbook.* New York: McGraw-Hill Professional.

Kano, N., Seraku, N., Takahashi, F., & Tsuji, S. (1984). Attractive quality and must-be quality. Hinshitsu. *The Journal of the Japanese Society for Quality Control, 14*(2), 39–48.

Khalid, M. S., Mustafa, A., & Haque, I. (2008). Application of Kano's Model for Evaluating Information Quality of University Websites. *Proceedings SWWS* (pp. 277-280).

Kuo, H.-M. (2006). Discussion of the interfering factors for internet shopping. *Conference on Theories and Practices in International Business*, Chang Jung Christian University (p. 52).

Kuo, H.-M., & Chen, C.-W. (2011). Application of quality function deployment to improve the quality of Internet shopping website interface design. *International Journal of Innovative Computing, Information, & Control, 7*(1), 253–268.

Kuo, Y. F. (2003). A study on service quality of virtual community websites. *Total Quality Management & Business Excellence, 13*(4), 461–473. doi:10.1080/1478336032000047237a

Kuppelwieser, V. G., & Sarstedt, M. (2014). Exploring the influence of customers' time horizon perspectives on the satisfaction–loyalty link. *Journal of Business Research, 67*(12), 2620–2627. doi:10.1016/j.jbusres.2014.03.021

Lee, D., Moon, J., Kim, Y. J., & Yi, M. Y. (2015). Antecedents and consequences of mobile phone usability: Linking simplicity and interactivity to satisfaction, trust, and brand loyalty. *Information & Management, 52*(3), 295–304. doi:10.1016/j.im.2014.12.001

Lee, G.-G., & Lin, H.-F. (2005). Customer perceptions of e-service quality in online shopping. *International Journal of Retail & Distribution Management, 33*(2), 161–176. doi:10.1108/09590550510581485

Lee, W.-I., Shih, B.-Y., & Tu, L.-J. (2002). The Application of Kano's Model for Improving Web-based Learning Performance. *Paper presented at the meeting of the 32nd ASEE/IEEE Frontiers in Education Conference*, Boston. doi:10.1109/FIE.2002.1157975

Lee, Y. C., & Chen, J. K. (2009). A new service development integrated model. *Service Industries Journal, 29*(12), 1669–1686. doi:10.1080/02642060902793573

Li, Y., Tan, K., & Xie, M. (2002). Measuring Web-based Service Quality. *Total Quality Management, 13*(5), 685–700. doi:10.1080/0954412022000002072

Lin, L.-Z., Yeh, H.-R., & Wang, M.-C. (2015, February). Integration of Kano's model into FQFD for Taiwanese Ban-Doh banquet culture. *Tourism Management, 46*, 245–262. doi:10.1016/j.tourman.2014.05.007

Madu, C. N., & Madu, A. A. (2002). Dimensions of e-Quality. *International Journal of Quality & Reliability Management, 19*(3), 246–258. doi:10.1108/02656710210415668

Mao, J. (2014). Social media for learning: A mixed methods study on high school students' technology affordances and perspectives. *Computers in Human Behavior, 33*(1), 213–223. doi:10.1016/j.chb.2014.01.002

Marentakis, C., & Emiris, D. (2010). Location aware auctions for tourism services. *Journal of Hospitality and Tourism Technology, 1*(2), 121–143. doi:10.1108/17579881011065038

Mathwick, C., Wiertz, C., & de Ruyter, K. (2008). Social capital production in a virtual P3 community. *The Journal of Consumer Research, 34*(6), 832–849. doi:10.1086/523291

Mebrate, T. W. (2010). *A Framework for Evaluating Academic Website's Quality From Students' Perspective*. Netherlands: Delft University of Technology.

Moogan, Y. J., Baron, S., & Bainbridge, S. (2001). Timings and trade-offs in the marketing of higher education courses: A conjoint approach. *Marketing Intelligence & Planning, 19*(3), 179–187. doi:10.1108/02634500110391726

Negash, S., Ryan, T., & Igbaria, M. (2003). Quality and effectiveness in web-based customer support systems. *Information & Management, 40*(8), 757–768. doi:10.1016/S0378-7206(02)00101-5

Oh, J.-C., Yoon, S.-J., & Park, B.-I. (2012). A structural approach to examine the quality attributes of e-shopping malls using the Kano model. *Asia Pacific Journal of Marketing and Logistics, 24*(2), 305–327. doi:10.1108/13555851211218075

Oldfield, B. M., & Baron, S. (2000). Student perceptions of service quality in a UK university business and management faculty. *Quality Assurance in Education, 8*(2), 85–95. doi:10.1108/09684880010325600

Orel, F. D., & Kara, A. (2014). Supermarket self-checkout service quality, customer satisfaction, and loyalty: Empirical evidence from an emerging market. *Journal of Retailing and Consumer Services, 21*(2), 118–129. doi:10.1016/j.jretconser.2013.07.002

Oztekin, A., Nikov, A., & Zaim, S. (2009). UWIS: An assessment methodology for usability of web-based information systems. *Journal of Systems and Software, 82*(12), 2038–2050. doi:10.1016/j.jss.2009.06.047

Parasuraman, A., Zeithaml, V. A., & Berry, L. L. (1985). A Conceptual Model of Service Quality and It's Implication for Future Research. *Journal of Marketing, 49*(4), 41–50. doi:10.2307/1251430

Parasuraman, A., Zeithaml, V. A., & Berry, L. L. (1988). SERVQUAL: A Multiple-item Scale for Measuring Consumer Perception of Service Quality. *Journal of Retailing, 64*(1), 12–40.

Parasuraman, A., Zeithaml, V. A., & Malhotra, A. (2005). E-S-QUAL: A Multiple-Item Scale for Assessing Electronic Service Quality. *Journal of Service Research, 7*(3), 213–233. doi:10.1177/1094670504271156

Ranganathan, C., & Ganapathy, S. (2002). Key dimensions of business-to-consumer web sites. *Information & Management, 39*(6), 457–465. doi:10.1016/S0378-7206(01)00112-4

Rashid, M. M., Tamaki, J., Ullah, A. M. M. S., & Kubo, A. (2011). A Kano Model Based Linguistic Application for Customer Needs Analysis. *International Journal of Engineering Business Management*, *3*(2), 29–36.

Ratanasawadwat, N. (2015). E-Service Attribute Analysis: An Application of Kano's Model. *Journal of Economics. Business and Management*, *3*(11), 1076–1079.

Reilly, N. B. (1999). *The Team Based Product Development Guidebook*. Milwaukee, Wisconsin: ASQ Quality Press.

Rodger, K., Taplin, R. H., & Moore, S. A. (2015, October). Using a randomised experiment to test the causal effect of service quality on visitor satisfaction and loyalty in a remote national park. *Tourism Management*, *50*, 172–183.

Sauerwein, E., Bailom, F., Matzler, K., & Hinterhuber, H. H. (1996). The Kano Model: How to delight your customers. *Proceedings of the International Working Seminar on Production Economics*, Innsbruck, Austria (pp. 313-327).

Shi, Y., Prentice, C., & He, W. (2014, July). Linking service quality, customer satisfaction and loyalty in casinos, does membership matter? *International Journal of Hospitality Management*, *40*, 81–91. doi:10.1016/j.ijhm.2014.03.013

Shin, D-H. (2014). Effect of the customer experience on satisfaction with smartphones: Assessing smart satisfaction index with partial least squares. *Telecommunications Policy*.

Shostack, G. L. (1982). How to Design a Service. *European Journal of Marketing*, *16*(1), 49–63. doi:10.1108/EUM0000000004799

Shostack, G. L. (1984). Designing services that deliver. *Harvard Business Review*, *62*(1), 134–135.

Sohn, S. Y., Park, H. Y., & Chang, S. I. (2009). Assessment of a Complementary Cyber Learning System to Offline Teaching. *Expert Systems with Applications*, *36*(3), 6485–6491. doi:10.1016/j.eswa.2008.07.075

Stockdale, R., & Borovicka, M. (2006, Autumn). Ghost towns or vibrant villages? Constructing business-sponsored online communities. *International Journal of Communications Law & Policy*, *11*, 1–22.

Swaid, S., & Wigand, R. T. (2009). Measuring the Quality Of E-Service: Scale Development and Initial Validation. *Journal of Electronic Commerce Research*, *10*(1), 13–28.

Tan, A. R., Matzen, D., McAloone, T. C., & Evans, S. (2010). Strategies for designing and developing services for manufacturing firms. *CIRP Journal of Manufacturing Science and Technology*, *3*(2), 90–97. doi:10.1016/j.cirpj.2010.01.001

Tan, K. C., & Pawitra, T. A. (2001). Integrating SERVQUAL and Kano's model into QFD for service excellence development. *Managing Service Quality: An International Journal*, *11*(6), 418–430. doi:10.1108/EUM0000000006520

Tjiptono, F. (2003). *Strategi Pemasaran, Edisi Kedua*. Yogyakarta: Penerbit Andi.

Udo, G. J., Bagchi, K. K., & Kirs, P. J. (2011). Using SERVQUAL to assess the quality of e-learning experience. *Computers in Human Behavior*, *27*(3), 1272–1283. doi:10.1016/j.chb.2011.01.009

Van Doorn, J., Lemon, K. E., Mittal, V., Naß, S., Pick, D., Pirner, P., & Verhoef, P. C. (2010). Customer Engagement Behavior: Theoretical Foundations and Research Directions. *Journal of Service Research, 13*(3), 253–266. doi:10.1177/1094670510375599

van Iwaarden, J., van der Wiele, T., Ball, L., & Millen, R. (2003). Applying SERVQUAL to Web sites: An exploratory study. *International Journal of Quality & Reliability Management, 20*(8), 919–935. doi:10.1108/02656710310493634

Verhagen, T., Swen, E., Feldberg, F., & Merikivi, J. (2015, July). Benefitting from virtual customer environments: An empirical study of customer engagement. *Computers in Human Behavior, 48*, 340–357. doi:10.1016/j.chb.2015.01.061

Wagner, C., & Majchrzak, A. (2007). Enabling Customer Centricity Using Wikis and the Wiki Way. *Journal of Management Information Systems, 23*(3), 17–43. doi:10.2753/MIS0742-1222230302

Wan, A. H. (2000). Opportunities to enhance a commercial Website. *Information & Management, 38*(1), 15–21. doi:10.1016/S0378-7206(00)00048-3

Won, S. G. L., Evans, M. A., Carey, C., & Schnittka, C. G. (2015). Youth appropriation of social media for collaborative and facilitated design-based learning. *Computers in Human Behavior, 50*(1), 385–391. doi:10.1016/j.chb.2015.04.017

Yang, B., & Lester, D. (2004). Attitudes toward buying online. *Cyberpsychology & Behavior, 7*(1), 85–91. doi:10.1089/109493104322820156 PMID:15006173

Zeithaml, V. A., Parasuraman, A., & Berry, L. L. (1990). *Delivering Quality Service: Balancing Customer Perceptions and Expectations*. New York: The Free Press.

Zhang, T. (2006). *A Study of Government e-Service Quality and Its Effect on Public Satisfaction*. China: Macau University of Science and Technology.

Zhao, M., & Dholakia, R. R. (2009). A multi-attribute model of web site interactivity and customer satisfaction: An application of the Kano model. *Managing Service Quality: An International Journal, 19*(3), 286–307. doi:10.1108/09604520910955311

ADDITIONAL READING

Al-Qeisi, K., Dennis, C., Alamanos, E., & Jayawardhena, C. (2014). Website design quality and usage behavior: Unified Theory of Acceptance and Use of Technology. *Journal of Business Research, 67*(11), 2282–2290. doi:10.1016/j.jbusres.2014.06.016

Carmona, C. J., Ramírez-Gallego, S., Torres, F., Bernal, E., del Jesus, M. J., & García, S. (2012). Web usage mining to improve the design of an e-commerce website: OrOliveSur. *Expert Systems with Applications, 39*(12), 11243–11249. doi:10.1016/j.eswa.2012.03.046

Cebi, S. (2013). A quality evaluation model for the design quality of online shopping websites. *Electronic Commerce Research and Applications, 12*(2), 124–135. doi:10.1016/j.elerap.2012.12.001

Chou, W.-C., & Cheng, Y.-P. (2012). A hybrid fuzzy MCDM approach for evaluating website quality of professional accounting firms. *Expert Systems with Applications*, *39*(3), 2783–2793. doi:10.1016/j. eswa.2011.08.138

Das, R., & Turkoglu, I. (2009). Creating meaningful data from web logs for improving the impressiveness of a website by using path analysis method. *Expert Systems with Applications*, *36*(3), 6635–6644. doi:10.1016/j.eswa.2008.08.067

Ellahi, A., & Bokhari, R. H. (2013). Key quality factors affecting users' perception of social networking websites. *Journal of Retailing and Consumer Services*, *20*(1), 120–129. doi:10.1016/j.jretconser.2012.10.013

Elling, S., Lentz, L., de Jong, M., & van den Bergh, H. (2012). Measuring the quality of governmental websites in a controlled versus an online setting with the 'Website Evaluation Questionnaire'. *Government Information Quarterly*, *29*(3), 383–393. doi:10.1016/j.giq.2011.11.004

Garibay, C., Gutiérrez, H., & Figueroa, A. (2010). Evaluation of a Digital Library by Means of Quality Function Deployment (QFD) and the Kano Model. *Journal of Academic Librarianship*, *36*(2), 125–132. doi:10.1016/j.acalib.2010.01.002

Grigoroudis, E., Litos, C., Moustakis, V. A., Politis, Y., & Tsironis, L. (2008). The assessment of user-perceived web quality: Application of a satisfaction benchmarking approach. *European Journal of Operational Research*, *187*(3), 1346–1357. doi:10.1016/j.ejor.2006.09.017

Hu, Y.-C. (2009). Fuzzy multiple-criteria decision making in the determination of critical criteria for assessing service quality of travel websites. *Expert Systems with Applications*, *36*(3), 6439–6445. doi:10.1016/j.eswa.2008.07.046

Kim, S., & Stoel, L. (2004). Dimensional hierarchy of retail website quality. *Information & Management*, *41*(5), 619–633. doi:10.1016/j.im.2003.07.002

Kim, S., & Stoel, L. (2004). Apparel retailers: Website quality dimensions and satisfaction. *Journal of Retailing and Consumer Services*, *11*(2), 109–117. doi:10.1016/S0969-6989(03)00010-9

Lin, H.-F. (2010). An application of fuzzy AHP for evaluating course website quality. *Computers & Education*, *54*(4), 877–888. doi:10.1016/j.compedu.2009.09.017

Thorleuchter, D., den Poel, D. V., & Prinzie, A. (2012). Analyzing existing customers' websites to improve the customer acquisition process as well as the profitability prediction in B-to-B marketing. *Expert Systems with Applications*, *39*(3), 2597–2605. doi:10.1016/j.eswa.2011.08.115

Vasto-Terrientes, L. D., Fernández-Cavia, J., Huertas, A., Moreno, A., & Valls, A. (2015). Official tourist destination websites: Hierarchical analysis and assessment with ELECTRE-III-H. *Tourism Management Perspectives*, *15*(July), 16–28. doi:10.1016/j.tmp.2015.03.004

KEY TERMS AND DEFINITIONS

House of Quality (HoQ): A comprehensive matrix that is used to translate a set of customer requirements, customer importance level, as well as customer satisfaction level on product/service from market and data research from benchmarking process into technical target priority required to satisfy the customer requirements.

Kano Model or Kano Diagram: A highly useful diagram to classify the attributes of a product or service based on how the product or service can satisfy the users' demands.

Quality Function Deployment (QFD): Is a method that is used to translate subjective quality criteria into the objective one that can be accumulated and measured, and then used to design and create a product.

Quality: The standard of something as measured against other things of a similar kind; the degree of excellence of something.

Service Design: An activity of planning and organizing people, infrastructure, communication, and material components of a service in order to improve its quality and the interaction between service provider and customer.

Service Quality: A comparison of expectations with performance. A business with high service quality will meet customer needs whilst remaining economically competitive. Improved service quality may increase economic competitiveness.

Service: Assistance or advise given to customers during and after the sale of goods.

SERVQUAL: A method used to measure service quality by looking into the gap between users' perception and expectation on a service. With the method, we can know how much the gap is between customer's perception and expectation on a service.

Technical Response: The translation of customer requirements on a service they're getting into organizational language.

Chapter 4
Quality Assurance Aspects of Web Design

Sandeep Kumar Panda
KIIT University, India

Santosh Kumar Swain
KIIT University, India

ABSTRACT

The chapter introduces the definition of usability, usability assessment techniques to be adopted during the whole application life cycle for promoting usability. Then, the chapter includes design features for evaluating e-commerce websites such as navigation, content, design, ease of use and structure features and designing usable e-commerce websites. Then the chapter discussed the user testing method followed by a case study which comprises data collection by users' preferences, data analysis and the results. The latter in the chapter, we briefly describe the effectiveness of usability evaluation methods. Lastly, we describe the usability problem areas, strength and weaknesses on different features and sub-features of e-commerce websites followed by a conclusion.

INTRODUCTION

Due to highly suited capabilities, the World Wide Web continues to generate substantial frustration among users. The difficulty was downloading content that is text based formats, audio, video and 3D graphics. Poorly designed websites can lead to lost productivity and revenue.

Web site quality is dependent on the quality of the software. In the early years, the quality of software provided effective support to develop the websites' performance. Nevertheless the quality assurance process became the challenges for the new discipline of website application. There were a number of experts or organizations who researched on different proposals to improve website quality, including quality frameworks, criteria, evaluation methodologies, approaches and metrics. In fact, since the website quality process became a particularly valuable topic which is ongoing and commercially researched, especially in website quality metrics. A set of metrics has been proposed for quantifying website quality

DOI: 10.4018/978-1-4666-9764-5.ch004

attributes since the 2000s (Consortium 2000, Offut 2002). Although the quality of website has valuable background and been well developed in recent years, a big question is "why is the quality of websites still poor and lack of quality characteristics cause user dissatisfaction in most websites." (Brajnik 2001, Calero 2005) There are some reasons shown below.

Web site software technologies evolve extremely fast, possibly many new software tools are developed each year. Websites blindly applied these software tools. Some of them support websites that have become very successful (e.g. YouTube, Blog and Ask.com), but some are not (Sqrum & Medaglia 2009). So these new website technologies need to be verified and may or may not be used and some may even be eliminated (e.g. Auto-refresh, image ALT). In this case, a complicated website can contain multiple elements: "massive website" is no longer exists. The application domains of websites are developing widely. Websites are becoming the preferred media instrument for information search, company presentation, shopping, entertainment, education, and social contacts. Traditional quality of websites issues does not fit the new multiple-technology website application. Based on the above factors, the new website quality features determine to establish a new website quality metric which will have more practical measurement criteria and appropriate approaches for website quality evaluation needs.

Although most prominent web sites are created by professional design firms, many smaller sites are built by consequence, web sites those belonging to non profits and small businesses often have substandard usability. What makes a high quality web site design? A crucial element in website success is usability among the different Quality factors they are functionality, reliability, usability, efficiency, maintainability, portability.

Usability is a quality attribute that assesses how easy user interfaces are to use. The word "usability" also refers to methods for improving ease-of-use during the design process. On the Web, usability is a necessary condition for survival. If the quality is poor, the user will simply leave the website and go elsewhere. Generally, there is no second chance to get a user back to the website. Therefore, in order to improve the quality of a website. The quality of a website makes a website profitable, user friendly and accessible, and it also offers useful and reliable information, providing better design and visual appearance to meet the users' needs and expectations (Hartmann 2008). This can be done by defining the measurable website criteria (Gledec 2005). When home pages consist of address usability and incorporate other essential design criteria, it gives higher traffic, more repeat visitors and greater customer satisfaction. To attract and maintain online users, web site designers must offer interfaces that address specific needs and functions.

To consider these key points, We now review the chapters covered in sequence, section by section.

Section 1 begins with an overview of quality. Section 2 gives a brief definition of usability according to the different authors. Basic aspects of usability evaluation methods are introduced to facilitate the discussion of different types of usability evaluation methods, which include user-based, heuristic-based and tool-based evaluation methods. Section 3 provides designing issues for e-commerce websites followed by different characteristics of e-commerce websites from the users' perspective. The role of the designing features such as navigation, content, ease of use, design and structure for evaluating e-commerce websites are explored. Section 4 illustrates a case study of the concepts introduced in section 2 and section 3 on e-commerce websites. The data collection, data analysis, and the results are described sequentially in this section. Section 5 presents the effectiveness of usability evaluation methods. Typical usability problems with different features and sub-features are described. Section 6 concludes the chapter with remarks. The references and authors' biographies are present.

WEB SITE QUALITY

"What is quality?" Dr. Tom DeMarco (1999) says "Quality is the function of a product that changes the world for the better." Definition of website quality is how well a website is designed and how well the design meets with the user's satisfaction. Website Quality (or Quality of Websites) could be measured from two perspectives: Developers, and End-users (Liburne & Devkota 2004). The aspects of website quality from developers focus on the degree of Maintainability, Security, Functionality, etc. While the end-users are paying more attentions to Usability, Efficiency, Effectiveness, Creditability, etc. Expanding these concepts, the usages of website quality may depend on, Task-related factors that affect end users such as presentation quality and contrast, Performance-related factors that affect the efficiency for end users and the technologies of websites, for example, response time, transaction output and reliability, Development-related factors that affect developers and maintainers of a website. For instance code complexity, code readability, portability and modifiability. "How to clearly define these factors?" A concept (quality model) will be the leading factor in achieving website success and will apply to the majority of current live websites. From previous research, the quality website is developed from quality of software. Gerald Weinberg (Weinberg 1997) defined that the quality of software is inherently subjective and different people who will experience a different quality even in the same software. It can also apply in a website as meaning that user satisfaction is more important than anything (This issue is reinforced in this study).

With a well thought-out strategy and realistic expectations, a business or organization can have a highly successful Web site created for them. The Web is a new medium with new rules, and in order to achieve an effective presence, one must be aware of the various types of Web site quality and the roles that they can play.

Figure 1 is represents the hierarchy of the Web Site Quality model. Looking from the top, the quality of characteristics depends on the quality of its sub-characteristics, which in turn depend on the quality of their indicators. However, looking from the perspective of the indicator, the quality of each indicator influences the quality of the appropriate sub-characteristic, which in turn influences the quality of the appropriate characterization in the quality model.

DEFINITION OF USABILITY

Usability is generally taken as a software quality factor that aims to provide the answer to many frustrating problems caused by the interaction between people and technology. It describes the quality of products and systems from the point of view of its users.

DEFINITION OF USABILITY OF WEBSITE

Web usability is the ease of use of a website. Some broad goals of usability are the presentation of information and choices in a clear and concise way, a lack of ambiguity and the placement of important items in appropriate areas. One important element of web usability is ensuring that the content works on various devices and browsers. Another concern for usability is ensuring that the website is appropriate for all ages and genders.

Figure 1.

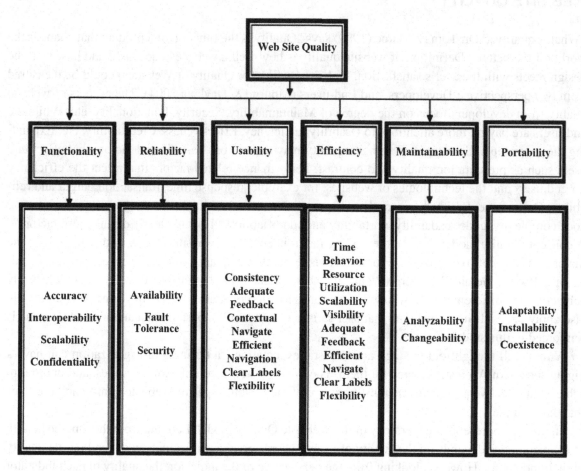

Usability Assessment Techniques

There are a variety of usability assessment techniques. Certain techniques use data from customers, while others depend on usability professionals. There are usability assessment techniques for all levels of design and growth, from product definition to final design modifications. When selecting a technique, consider the cost, time limits, and suitability. The important assessment techniques are mentioned in the following subsections:

- **The User Testing Method:** Includes the set of parameters that involves different types of users (novice and expert) for finding the different types of usability problems, aims to capture the users' performance through different types of observation and satisfaction (interviews and question-naire) of the user while they are tested the interfaces.
- **Heuristic Testing:** Is a usability engineering method for finding and assessing usability problems in a user interface design as part of an iterative design process. It involves having a small set of evaluators examining the interface and using recognized usability principles (the "heuristics") (Nielsen 1994).

- **Tool Based Testing:** Includes using various types of software tools for finding different types of usability problems. Under this method, the tools automatically assess whether the website follows a set of commonly accepted principles. Many of these tools focus on finding whether HTML scripts follow specific guidelines.

EVALUATION METHODOLOGY ADOPTED

We have adopted the method derived from Agarwal and Venkatesh's (2002) that includes the assessment of usability by rating and weights. As such, we have conducted two surveys:

1. The first survey includes the weights given to the different features, sub features in aspects of usability by the users on the 100 points-parameters on the all five features.
2. The second survey includes the ratings given by users to each e-commerce websites.

Here, it is worth mentioning the facts that the help of Alexa.com (one of the major popular international ranking e-commerce websites, mostly used by the customers) has been taken whose survey method significantly varies from our methods of survey since its rank calculation uses a 'combination' of the estimated average daily unique visitors to the site and the estimated number of page views on the site over the past 3 months and the data is collected from a subset of internet users using one of 25,000 browser extensions for Google Chrome, Firefox and/or Internet Explorer.

However, taking the support of Alexa rank calculation serves two purposes i.e:

1. Hopefully it helps minimize some of the biases and take a quick peek at for a very rough idea of how popular a website is.
2. In spite of its lack of credibility, it can provide preliminary level information as well as scopes to go for evolving some alternative reliable methods to measure the user friendliness of a website.

As such, in order to select ten e-commerce websites selected by Alexa.com for the year of 2013, have been used to study the samples for this research. The website of 10 Indian electronics commerce online shopping website was considered in our experiments. To keep anonymity, we have represented these as W1 to W10 respectively. These selected ten highest-ranking websites as shown in Table 1 shown below:

Features and the Sub Features of the Methods

In this section, we first discuss user-testing method followed by usability method and its sub features.

User Testing Method

To conduct the user testing method, several supplementary techniques were used. This involved using different types of observation, including the observer taking notes and using Camtasia software to capture performance data while questionnaires were used to assess users' satisfaction with the tested sites. A think aloud protocol is one of the techniques that can be used during user testing. This has several advantages

Table 1. The Alexa.com for the year of 2013 rank information of Indian e-commerce websites

SI.No	E-Commerce Websites	Symbol
1	www.flipkart.com	W1
2	www.snapdeal.com	W2
3	www.ebay.com	W3
4	www.homshop18.com	W4
5	www.quikr.com	W5
6	www.jabong.com	W6
7	www.myntra.com	W7
8	www.futurebazzar.com	W8
9	www.naaptol.com	W9
10	www.yepme.com	W10

such as obtaining immediate feedback regarding what the participants think about the interface and any problems or surprises they face (Stone et al. 2005).

However, this technique was not used in this research because it was believed that, according to its stated disadvantages, it might influence the performance of the users who were expected to perform tasks on ten websites. These disadvantages included: this technique is considered by some participants unnatural and distracting (Stone et al. 2005); it can slow the participant's thought processes which therefore influence their performance of the task; also, users' problem-solving behavior can be influenced as users verbalize their thoughts (Stone et al. 2005; Nielsen 1993). Furthermore, sometimes it is very exhausting for the participants to verbalize their thought processes during the evaluation session (Stone et al. 2005).

User testing does not have to be conducted in an extensive lab setting for most web development projects do not have the budget to rent a usability lab (Lazar 2005). In this research, the user testing sessions were conducted in an office in one of the colleges in Odisha where the researcher has access. The office was equipped with one desktop computer. This was connected to the Internet and the Camtasia software was installed on it. Since it was estimated that the user testing session would take a long time (3 hours), incentives were paid to the participants. Incentives were a small amount of money rupees one thousand for travel expenses (basic expenses). This section discusses the user testing materials that were developed for the user testing, the pilot study, and the recruitment and evaluation procedures. Afterwards a two week evaluation procedure (during May 2013) was adopted to welcome the users and introduce the research for which necessary formal written consent along with the user agreement to participate in the testing and observation process through the testing session was developed. A task scenario was then developed for each of the ten studied websites, which includes the tasks for the ten e-commerce websites to represent the actual use of the corresponding websites. Further, in order to collect the preference information from the users regarding the tested websites, post-test questionnaires were also developed. Accordingly, each user responded to the appropriate post-test questionnaire after having subjective interactions with each website that could lead to filling up of a post evaluation questionnaire in the context in the form of the feedbacks (satisfaction). Twenty participants were recruited for the usability testing (public newsletter, Email broadcasting to different Internet groups and telephone calls were made to provide details of the place of the study and to schedule the time of the test).

(Note: There may be the chance of the content change in the websites over a period)

Pre-Test Questionnaire

A pre-test questionnaire was developed and had to be filled out by the users after they had signed the consent form (see Table 3 in the Appendix). The pre-test questionnaire was designed to gather users' background information. It involved three sections: background and experience, online shopping experience and perceptions of online shopping. Questions in the first section were based on two earlier studies (Barnard and Wesson 2003; Brinck et al. 2001). The questions in the second and third sections were based on earlier studies regarding consumer attitudes or perceptions towards online shopping or e-commerce (Alsmadi 2002; Obeidat 2001; Aladwani 2003; May So et al. 2005; Shergill and Chen 2005).

Pilot

A pilot test was conducted before the main test to test the user testing methods. This is an essential step which helps to practice the test and to discover and refine any bugs in the testing process, such as un-applicable tasks or ambiguous questionnaire (Rubin 1994).

Before conducting the pilot study, the user testing materials were translated into English. They were then sent to two checkers. The technical checker checked the accuracy of translating the different terms and the grammar checker checked the grammatical accuracy of the translated materials. The testing materials were pilot tested using two Indian Internet users, one of the postgraduate and one an undergraduate student at KIIT University, using both the English and the Odia language versions. The number of pilot users and the method for selecting them (by convenience sampling) coincided with Nielsen's (1993) recommendation. The pilot study identified ambiguity in the questionnaires and the user tasks, and helped to confirm the time limit which was assigned for each task. Results from the pilot test were taken into consideration and changes were made to the user testing materials.

Number of Users and Users' Profile

In order to determine the number of users to perform the user testing, an investigation into the literature was undertaken. For example, Brinck et al. (2002) suggested, if the budget allowed, recruiting eight to ten users to perform user testing. Rubin (1994) also suggested testing with more than five users, suggesting at least eight participants. It is worth noting that, in order to obtain statistically valid results, enough participants should be tested to perform the appropriate analysis and to generalize to a target population (Rubin 1994). In this context, Nielsen (2006) recommended testing 20 users in quantitative studies that included collecting quantitative usability metrics such as learning time, efficiency of use, memorability, user errors, and subjective satisfaction. However, while performing the user testing, it is suggested that there is a need to balance acquiring participants with the practical constraints of time and resources so issues such as the availability of the type of participants required and the duration of the test session need to be considered. Based on the illustration above, it was decided that twenty users would be recruited in this research.

Regarding users' profiles, it was decided that information about the target users of the websites would be helpful to identify typical users for user testing (Preece et al. 2002). Therefore, an email was sent to each of the studied companies asking them to provide information about their current and prospective users (such as demographic information, experience using the computer, and experience using the Internet). This method was used by Barnard and Wesson (2003) in their study. Based on the answers from the ten companies, a matrix of users' characteristics was designed (see Table 4 in the Appendix). The matrix was similar to a table suggested by Rubin (1994) to identify the user profile for a tested product. The designed matrix included five characteristics of the studied websites' users: gender, education level, age, experience in using a computer, and experience in using the Internet. Based on the ten companies' answers, an approximate percentage was calculated regarding each characteristic; then the average of those approximate percentages was calculated. From the calculated percentage, an approximate number of users who should match each characteristic were also calculated.

Evaluation Procedure

All user testing sessions followed the same procedure. Data were gathered using screen capture software (Camtasia) with five questionnaires and observations of the users working through the tasks. The user session began with the researcher welcoming the user and reading the test script that explained the objectives of the study, the number of websites that would be evaluated, number of questionnaires that needed to be filled out, and the user's right to withdraw from the session at any time. It was also explained to the user that he/she would be observed and his/her screen would be recorded using screen capture software (Camtasia) during the session. The user was then asked to read and sign the consent form. After signing the consent form, a pre-test questionnaire was given to the user to fill out in order to obtain information regarding his/her background and experience. Before beginning the tasks related to each website, the user was asked to explore the website for a maximum of 10 minutes, as suggested by Preece et al. (2002). They suggested using a familiarization task at the beginning of the usability tests so that the user would get used to the tested site before the session started. After the exploration, the user was given the tasks for a particular website from the ten tested sites. The time for each task was determined beforehand and checked throughout the pilot study. As the user worked on each task, the observer noted the sequence of pages, the time taken to complete each task, and any comments made by the user.

After completing the tasks for the tested website, the user was given the post-test questionnaire to fill out in order to get his/her feedback. Then the user took a break before beginning to test the second website. A similar procedure was followed by the user while testing the second to tenth sites. After completing the post-test questionnaire for the tenth website, the user was asked to explore each website for a maximum of five minutes and to remember his/her experience of evaluating each website. Then, he/she was given the post evaluation questionnaire to fill out in order to get his/her feedback about the usability of ten tested websites. (Note: There may be the chance of the content change in the websites over a period).

Usability Methods and Its Sub Features

The chapter presented the usability features of the websites based on the related works (Nielsen, J. (1994), Kantner, L. and Rosenbaum, S.(1997), Agarwal, R. and Venkatesh, V. (2002), Nielsen, J. (2000), Mustafa, S. and Al-Zoua'bi, L. (2008), Toit, M. and Bothma, C. (2010), Tarafdar, M. and Zhang, J. (2005)). This section describes these briefly in the following

- **Navigation Feature**: This feature includes search results and navigation menu as key attributes, which not only gives links to a user to assess the site, but also helps the user to find the required piece of information. In website usability, navigation is the key factor in the design that is discussed in the extensive literature (Tarafdar, M. & Zhang, J. (2005), Zhang, P., Von Dran G., Blake P., and Pipithsuksunt V. (2000), Pearson, J., Pearson, A., and Green, D. (2007)). This section covers five sub features, namely:
  - Link supports i.e. The links are very clear on pages for which a user can navigate the site easily.
  - Search result, i.e. This feature enables a user to find a product very fast, its results for easy interpretation.
  - No misleading links, i.e. The obvious links work perfectly without misleading the user and the user can pre-suppose the content from the final page.
  - No broken links: The entire site remains free from any broken links.
  - No orphaned pages, i.e. The entire site does not have the disadvantage of the null end pages.
- **Structure-Feature**: This feature deals with the architecture of the websites that includes various information like logical, clear groups etc. This involves:
  - The architecture of a site, i.e. The architecture of the site appears very simple and clear.
  - No depth structure, i.e. The structure is not so deep to reach the destination page with not more than three clicks only.
  - Link path, i.e. The link paths is very simple as providing clear visibility.
- **Ease of use Feature**: This feature is required to relate the cognitive effort to use a website (Nielsen, J. (1994)) and provide information through which the user communicates with the online shopping in different ways. In website usability, ease of use is the key factor in the design, which is discussed in the extensive literature (Nielsen, J. (1994), Tilson, R., Dong, J., Martin, S. & Kieke E., (1998), Freeman, M.B. & Hyland, P., (2003), Brinck, T., Gergle, D. & Wood S.D., (2001)). It covers the following four sub features:
  - *Downloading time,* i.e. the information is arranged in such a way that it needs less amount of time to download.
  - *Simple communication with sites,* i.e. this sub-feature is used for finding the information, backtrack to the home page, navigate through the site is easy when various types of user interaction with the website.
  - *Contact us information,* i.e. This sub features provide company name, their address, fax number, telephone number, email address through which a user can easily interact with the provider.
  - *Multilingual support,* i.e. the information is provided by website in various types of languages.
- **Design Feature**: This feature deals with the aesthetic aspects of the site design which include efficient page designing, efficient image display, appropriate fonts and color combination. It has the following six sub advantageous features.
  - *Attractiveness of sites,* i.e. the website home page should look beautiful, attention catching and attractive for the customers.
  - *Image display,* i.e. the apparent image quality, properly sized and projected with good resolution without breaking images; the task of understanding and downloading the images is easy and less time consuming.
  - *Fonts clarity, i.e.* The appropriate readable and user-friendly fonts.

- ○ *Color combination,* i.e. appropriate color combination of both fonts along with background colors.
- ○ *Page structure,* i.e. Better display of the page margins with appropriate alignment and the page title
- ○ *Consistency,* i.e. Consistency in the text, types of font, font sizes, color combination, page layout, and link bar position on each page.
- **Content based Feature:** In website usability, content, the key factor in the design, discussed in the extensive literature (Nielsen, J. (1994)) .This feature studies whether the a consists of adequate information which is needed by the user It has the following seven sub features:
  - ○ *Updated information* (updated and current information)
  - ○ *Relevant information* (user friendly and unambiguous texts, non-repetitive terminologies, and very relevant as well as concise content.)
  - ○ *No under construction pages* (no under construction page, which might lead to broken links.)
  - ○ *True information* (correctness of information with all accuracy.)
  - ○ *The shopping information* (providing information on shopping.)
  - ○ *Product information* (Displaying adequate product information about size, cost etc.)
  - ○ *Company information* (providing a company's product-lists and their cost information.)

User Testing Analysis

The data collected during the user testing were analyzed in several ways. It is worth mentioning that the participants of the user testing were categorized into two groups: novice and expert, as suggested by Nielsen (1993). He stated that: "one of the main distinctions between categories of users is that between novice and expert users". The participants' experience in using the Internet was used as a criterion to categorize the participants. Participants in the novice group had less than three years' experience using the Internet and those in the expert group had more than three years'. In the analysis of each user testing method, allocation to the novice or expert groups was taken into consideration.

Pre-Test Questionnaires

Data collected from the pre-test questionnaires were analyzed in various ways. Descriptive analysis was used in Sections 1 and 2 to describe the characteristics of the novice and expert participants and their experience in online shopping. Likert scores were calculated for each statement in Sections 2 and 3 to describe participants' overall perceptions and experiences regarding online shopping. It is worth mentioning that, for the purpose of the analysis in this research that used the Likert scale, a Likert score of 1-3 was regarded as a negative response, 5-7 a positive response and 4 a neutral one. The response values for the negative statements were reversed before calculating the Likert score. This was taken into consideration in the analysis of the pre-test questionnaires and the post-test (satisfaction) questionnaires.

To determine if there was a statistically significant difference between novices' and expert users' ratings regarding the perception of the online shopping statements, the Mann-Whitney test was used. This test is a nonparametric test and was the most appropriate statistical technique to use since the statements were measured on an ordinal scale (Conover 1971). The Likert score of seven points was considered as an ordinal scale because it cannot specify if the differences between the scores will be identical.

Performance Data and the Observation Method

The performance data were summarized in different ways. The task timing (in seconds) was computed, and descriptive statistics were used to obtain the mean time (in seconds) and the standard deviation. The tasks' accuracy was also determined. This represents the percentage of users who completed each task successfully within the time benchmark. It is important to note that the average of the performance data includes values from users who performed the tasks within the time limit and users who exceeded the time limit. Users who exceeded the time limit of a task were asked to stop performing the task and the benchmark time was used for this task. In order to identify the usability problems from the performance data, two steps were used, as suggested by Rubin (1994):

Identifying the Problematic Tasks

In order to compile a comprehensive list of usability problems for each site, all the problematic tasks were considered. Instead of identifying the most problematic tasks (e.g. The tasks that have success rates below 70 percentage as suggested by Rubin (1994)), all the tasks that one or more users could not complete successfully within the time benchmark were considered.

Identifying Users' Problems and Conducting a Source of Error Analysis

To explain the overall usability of the sites, the summary of the total number of tasks successfully performed by all users was used, as well as the sources that identified the different usability problems. The analysis of variance (ANOVA) test was used to obtain statistically significant results. The one-way within-subjects ANOVA test used.

The one-way within-subjects ANOVA test was employed for each of the ten tasks. This was used to determine if the time spent performing each task was significantly different. The within-subject factor, the sites, had ten levels: site 1, site 2 to site 10. The dependent variable was the total time in seconds taken by users to perform a task. However, this test does not provide detailed analysis.

If the time for performing all the tasks on the ten sites was significantly different for novice and expert users.

If the time spent on each site to perform all the tasks was significantly different from the ten sites.

The mixed design employed was a 2*10*10 mixed ANOVA. The first factor was the between-subjects factor of the group with two levels: novices and experts. The second factor was the within-subjects factor of sites with ten levels: site 1, site 2 to site 10. The third factor was the within-subjects factor of tasks with ten levels: the ten tasks: task 1 to task 10. The dependent factor was the time in seconds the user took to perform a task.

Post-Test Questionnaires: Quantitative Data

Data collected from the post-test questionnaires were used to find evidence of usability problems with the sites. Likert scores were calculated for each statement in Section 1 of the post-test questionnaire for each site in order to obtain the overall results concerning the participants' satisfaction with the sites. The post-test statements were grouped under four categories from the developed guidelines: (architecture and navigation, content, design, and purchasing process), and their corresponding sub-categories with the exception of three statements (17, 26, 28). These statements related to the overall evaluation of the tested sites and were grouped under a new sub-category: the overall evaluation of the sites. The statements were grouped to facilitate the pinpointing of usability problems. The post-test questionnaire did not include statements related to the accessibility and customer service category of the guidelines and its subcategories and therefore this category was not considered for grouping the post-test questionnaire statements.

A Likert score rating of 1 to 3 (negative) on a post-test questionnaire statement was interpreted as indicating there was a usability problem from the users' point of view. Negative statements identified a number of usability problems with the sites. These statements were mapped to the problem themes and subthemes identified by the previous method. Four statements identified three new problem sub-themes. To explain the overall usability of the sites, two inferential statistical tests were used for each statement of the post-test questionnaire:

The Mann-Whitney test was used to determine if there was a statistically significant difference between the ratings of novice and expert users.

The Friedman test was used to determine if there was a statistically significant difference between users' ratings of the three sites. The Friedman test and the Mann-Whitney test is nonparametric tests and were the most appropriate statistical techniques due to the ordinal scale of measurement that was used with the collected data.

Post-Test Questionnaires: Qualitative Data

Qualitative data obtained from users' responses to the open-ended questions on the post-test questionnaires were taken into account in determining the usability problems. Users' answers were then combined for each site and grouped under five categories from the heuristic guideline categories that had been developed: (i.e. Architecture and navigation, content, accessibility and customer service, design, and purchasing process), and their corresponding sub-categories. Several usability problems were identified from the answers of users. These answers were mapped to the problem themes and sub-themes identified by the previous methods; nine new sub-themes were generated. Seven of these sub-themes were mapped to appropriate problem themes and the other two sub-themes generated new problem themes.

Post-Evaluation Questionnaires: Qualitative Data

Data obtained from the post-evaluation questionnaires were represented answers to questions that asked users to indicate the site with the best six features. The answers were grouped under the six features of the sites that related to: navigation, internal search, architecture, design, purchasing process, and security and privacy.

Reliability and Validity

The validity of an evaluation technique concerns whether a technique measures what it is supposed to measure; this involves the technique itself and how it is performed (Preece et al. 2002). For example, the validity of the user testing method, according to Nielsen (1993), relates to if the results actually reflect the usability issues the researcher wishes to test. Nielsen (1993) provided examples regarding typical validity problems which included involving the wrong users, or designing the wrong tasks, or not including time constraints and social influences. Furthermore, Gray and Salzman (1998) defined threats to validity of experimental studies within the context of HCI research. They examined the design of five experiments that compared usability evaluation methods and provided recommendations for addressing different types of validity that are most relevant to HCI research. For example: To ensure internal validity, they recommended considering two issues which are instrumentation and selection:

Instrumentation for usability evaluation methods concerns biases in how human observers identify or rate the severity of usability problems. In the case of comparing methods or groups, the instrumentation is only valid if there is a way of rating the results that do not inappropriately favor one condition over the others. This means that the same evaluators or experimenters should not be assigned to different UEMs and asked to identify, classify or rate usability problems. Also, usability problem categories that are defined by one UEM should not be used by the experimenter to categorize problems found by another UEM.

Selection concerns the characteristics of the participants: whether they are related to the manipulation of interest and whether the participants assigned to different groups are equal in terms of certain characteristics (e.g. Knowledge or experience) related to the conditions of the experiment.

To ensure causal construct validity, a researcher should provide explicit information regarding the exact operation and method used so that a UEM should be applied according to the understanding of the reader of that method. For example, in the case of heuristic evaluation, evaluators should use guidelines and should explain whether evaluators work together or independently in the process of identifying the usability problems. Furthermore, in order to avoid the problem of interactions of different treatments, it is highly recommended not to use the same participants to conduct two or more UEMs; each group of participants should conduct only one UEM. These recommendations were considered in this research in order to ensure its validity. The internal validity of this research concerned instrumentation and selection. The researcher/experimenter was not assigned to different UEMs and identified usability problems. Despite the fact that the researcher was involved in the collection of data and played the role of observer in the user testing sessions identified the usability problems themselves.

The selection issue was also considered while recruiting participants in the user testing method. The characteristics of the participants in the user testing were based on the companies' profiles of their users.

Causal constructs validity was also taken into consideration in this research. It is worth mentioning that the multiple case study design which was used in this research would enhance the external validity or the generalization of the findings, as stated by Merriam (1998). The reliability or consistency of an evaluation technique, as indicated by Preece et al. (2002), is related to "how well a technique produces the same results on separate occasions under the same circumstances". For example, in the case of user testing, reliability is related to whether the same result would be obtained if the test were to be repeated (Nielsen 1993). Preece et al. (2002) stated that, in the case of experiments, if an experiment is controlled carefully, then it will have high reliability so that if another evaluator follows exactly the same process then they should achieve the same results. In this research, it was difficult to employ the same methods for a second time in order to investigate whether the same results would be achieved because of the time limitation. However, the reliability of some techniques used in this research can be measured, such as the reliability of the post-test questionnaire. In the case of questionnaires, reliability means that "a measure should consistency reflect the construct that it is measuring" (Field 2009). The most common measure of reliability is Cronbach's alpha, where a value of 0.7 to 0.8 is acceptable, and indicates a reliable measure while values that are substantially lower indicate an unreliable measure (Field 2009).

The post-test questionnaire was based on a reliable measure (CSUQ), in addition to other questions proposed in earlier research, that are specifically designed to measure users' satisfaction with an interface.

The Cronbach's alpha for this measure exceeded 0.89 (Lewis 1993). However, this measure was adapted to evaluate e-commerce websites. The reliability of the developed post-test questionnaire was calculated using the overall Cronbach's alpha for each site. It showed that this measure had high reliability since all Cronbach's alpha for each site were higher than 0.8. The value of Cronbach's Alpha for sites 1 to 10 were varied in between0.911 to 0.947, respectively.

User Testing Results

This section presents the findings obtained from the analysis of the different user testing methods. It presents an overview of the users in terms of their characteristics, and their perceptions and experience of online shopping. This is followed by a presentation of the findings of the performance data and observations; the quantitative and qualitative analysis of the post-test (satisfaction) questionnaires; and the post-evaluation questionnaires. Here we discussed the user testing result of three websites as a sample.

Pre-Test Questionnaires

Sections 1 and 3 of the pre-test questionnaire were answered by all the users, while Section 2 was only answered by users experienced in online shopping (see Table 3 in the Appendix).

Participants' Characteristics

There were ten novice participants: five females and five males. The majority (seven) had more than three years' experience using computers, while only three participants had less experience. All had less than three years' experience using the Internet and none reported having used the Internet for purchasing.

There were ten expert participants: five females and five males. All had more than three years' experience using computers and the Internet. Less than half (four) reported having used the Internet for purchasing. For full details of the users' characteristics and the frequency distribution, (Table 5 in the Appendix).

Participants' Perceptions of Online Shopping

The Mann-Whitney test showed that there were no statistically significant differences between novice and expert users in their ratings regarding their perceptions towards the online shopping statements, except for one. That statement related to users' interest in information about companies presented on the sites. Novices were not interested whilst experts were. The Likert scores for the other statements (Table 6 in the Appendix) showed that novice and expert users:

- Considered the cost of using the Internet as generally unreasonable.
- Liked websites to be easy to navigate and to be well organized.
- Considered compulsory registration frustrating when shopping online.
- Worried about the security of their financial information, the privacy of their personal information, and the absence of legal regulations that govern online transactions when shopping online.

Participants' Experience in Online Shopping

The four expert users who had purchased from the Internet provided information about their experience of online shopping (Table 7 in the Appendix):

- Two thirds (three) used the Internet annually for purchases, whilst one participant indicated his/ her usage was monthly.
- The first purchase from the Internet was made less than a year ago for two participants and between one and two years for the others.
- Two thirds (three) used their credit card as the method of payment, whilst one used the cash on delivery method.
- The products bought in their last purchase were a mobile phone, a digital camera, books and dresses.
- The Likert scores for the online shopping experience (Table 8 in the Appendix) showed that these four users:
- Shopped online because it saved time and they were able to buy products at any time of day from any location.
- Preferred to shop online from: well known sites with a good reputation; sites that provided alternative methods of ordering/payment/delivery; and sites that did not have limited delivery areas.
- Found the website's search function useful when shopping online. A detailed description of the products was also important. They preferred to research products in detail before purchasing and were encouraged to shop online from sites with a clear return and refund policy.
- Received the products within the time period specified by the company and were satisfied with the goods received. The products were accurately represented by the websites.
- Obtained good customer service from online companies. They felt more comfortable with sites which kept them informed about the status of their order.
- Did not find delivery costs reasonable. It was not important for a shopping site to have the ability to deliver the order to an address different from their own.

Performance Data and Observation Method

The summary of the performance data is presented in two tables in the Appendix (Tables 9 and 10). Table 9 presents the mean time in seconds and the standard deviation for each task for novice and expert users. Table 10 presents the accuracy of the tasks for each task across the sites. The problematic tasks, as shaded in the tasks, accuracy table, were:

- Tasks 3, 5, 6 and 8 across the three sites. These related to changing the content of the shopping cart, changing the shipping address, using the internal search of the site, and finding shipping information.
- Using the advanced internal search on site 1 (Task 10).
- Purchasing a product from sites 2 and 3 (Task 2 for sites 2 and 3 and Task 4 for site 3).
- Finding a product and finding information on site 3 (Tasks 1, 4, 9 and 10).

- The observation notes, the notes generated from reviewing the sixty Camtasia files, and users' comments from the user testing were summarized in terms of tasks.
- Noncritical problems/obstacles. The user made a mistake/error, but was able to recover and complete the task within the time limit.

Similar problems in each site were grouped together to generate a list of problems for each. The three lists, then generated were examined to identify similar problems across the three sites. Consequently, sixteen common areas of usability problems were identified which suggested identifying sixteen problem sub-themes. These sixteen problem sub-themes suggested identifying seven problem themes based on the types of the identified problems. The seven problem themes related to: navigation, content, design, architecture, internal search, purchasing process and accessibility and customer service. Table 11 in the Appendix shows the common areas of usability problems, the tasks that identified each problem, and the location of each problem on each site. The location of the problems was named either "entire-site" or by the title of the page with the problem. Entire site problems were identified as problems users faced in any page on the site. Table 11 in the Appendix also shows that during some tasks more than one problem was identified.

Description of the Overall Usability of the Sites

Analysis of the performance data and observations provided the following general findings regarding the overall usability of the sites:

The observation summary showed that expert and novice users experienced many similar problems, obstacles or difficulties performing the different tasks across the sites. The difference between experts and novices is the fact that experts recover faster. This explains why novice users had a larger number of problematic tasks, as shown in Table 14 in the Appendix. The total number of tasks successfully performed by all the users (experts and novices) was lowest on site 3 (Table 9). This indicates that sites 1 and 2 were noticeably better than site 3.

As expected, the percentage of experts who successfully completed each task was higher than the percentage of novices. This was due to their higher level of knowledge.

A one-way within-subjects ANOVA test showed the time spent performing the majority (eight) of the ten tasks was significantly different from the three sites. Table 12 in the Appendix shows the results of the ANOVA test for each task.

Post-Test Questionnaires: Quantitative Data

A list of usability problems was identified from the negative statements (statements with a Likert score rating of 1 to 3) in the satisfaction questionnaires. Each problem in the list and the problem sub-themes which were identified by the performance data and observation method, were compared for agreement. Consequently, these statements were mapped to the identified problem themes and sub-themes. Four statements identified three new problem sub-themes that were mapped to the navigation, design and purchasing process problem themes. The negative statements, their Likert scores and the problem themes and sub-themes identified by these statements, are shown in Table 13 in the Appendix.

Description of the Overall Usability of the Sites

The following points represent the general findings for the overall usability of the sites:

The Mann-Whitney test showed there were no significant differences between novice and expert users for a large number of the post-test statements (Table 14 in the Appendix). Consequently, the ratings of novice and expert users were combined for each statement concerning the post-test questionnaire.

The Friedman test was used after combining the ratings of novice and expert users. This showed that there were statistically significant differences between users' ratings of the three sites for all the statements, as shown in Table 15 in the Appendix. In these statements, site 3 had the lowest ratings for all the following aspects except one: navigation and architecture, content, design and purchasing process. Site 1 had the lowest rating for one statement (21) that related to navigation. The Likert scores for the overall evaluation statements also showed that site 3 rated negatively with the lowest rating for all statements. Site 1 rated positively with the highest rating and site 2 rated neutral.

However, the Friedman test was not used for seven statements. For these statements, site 3 had no ratings for six statements and sites 1 and 2 had no ratings for one statement. Site 3 had no rating for four statements (3, 11, 12, 13) concerning the internal search as it did not have such a facility and for two statements (4, 15) as it did not enable registration. Sites 1 and 2 had no ratings for one statement (16) as they did not have optional registration.

Post-Test Questionnaires: Qualitative Data

Analysis of the qualitative data from the post-test questionnaires showed novice and expert users experienced similar usability problems on the sites. For this reason (and since the results of the Mann-Whitney test showed no significant difference between novice and expert users for many of the post-test statements (Table 14 in the Appendix), answers from novice and expert users for each question of the post-test questionnaire were combined. However, usability problems identified only by expert users were highlighted by noting 'expert' next to these answers. These problems were compared and then mapped to the appropriate problem themes and sub-themes identified by the previous two methods (performance data and observation, and the quantitative data from the satisfaction questionnaires). No match was found between nine problems and the identified problem sub-themes. Therefore, two new problem sub-themes identified two new problem themes relating to an inconsistency problem and missing capabilities. Seven new subthemes were also identified. These sub-themes were mapped to six appropriate problem themes (navigation, internal search, content, design, purchasing process and accessibility and customer service). Table 16 in the Appendix summarizes all the usability problem themes and sub-themes identified by the qualitative data of the post-test questionnaires and their location of the sites.

Description of the Overall Usability of the Sites

Question 35 on the post-test questionnaire was designed to gather users' opinions regarding the overall usability of the sites and showed that the majority (sixteen) of the twenty users were not satisfied with the performance of site 3. They indicated that the general performance of site 3 would discourage them from purchasing from it in the future. However, all the users indicated that there were personal issues, which did not relate to the usability of sites, but which would discourage them from purchasing a product from all three sites. These issues related to feeling that the security of their financial information would not be protected. The preference for physically touching a product before purchasing it was another reason.

Post-Evaluation Questionnaires: Qualitative Data

The qualitative data obtained from experts and novices were combined. Analysis of the seven open-ended questions on the post evaluation questionnaire (relating to the site with the best features from the users' point of view) did not explicitly identify specific usability problems. It only provided information on the overall usability of the sites from the users' point of view in terms of six features of the sites:

Navigation: The answers to two questions (2, 6) indicated that the navigation support of sites 1 and 2 enabled users to find products and information easily. The number of users who recommended site 1 was higher than the number who recommended site 2. Site 1 had the most obvious and simplest methods for finding products and was the easiest site to find information related to the tasks. A few users (two) who used the Arabic interface of site 3 recommended it as the easiest site to navigate and find products or information. The English and Arabic interfaces were similar in terms of their design and architecture. Users preferred the Arabic interface because it used their first language.

Internal Search: Answers to two questions (2, 6) indicated that the internal searches of sites 1 and 2 enabled products and information to be easily located.

Architecture: Answers to two questions (2, 6) on the post-evaluation questionnaire indicated that the simple, straightforward architecture of sites 1 and 2 enabled users to find products and information easily. More users recommended site 1 than site 2. A few users (two) preferred the architecture of the Arabic interface of site 3 to the architecture of the other two sites because it used their first language.

Design: The answer to one question (1) on the post-evaluation questionnaire indicated that site 1 had the most professional appearance. Few users recommended site 2 and none recommended site 3.

Purchasing Process: The answers to three questions (3, 4, 7) showed that most users recommended site 1 as the site with the most obvious method for ordering items. Most users recommended site 1 as having the best support for customers (to continue shopping) and to change the contents of their shopping cart. Most users recommended site 2 as the easiest for changing customer information. No user recommended site 3.

Security and Privacy: The answers to question 5 (related to the site users trusted the most) recommended site 1. Few users recommended site 2 and none recommended site 3. Only two users indicated that their reason for trusting sites 1 and 2 related to the sites' use of the secure socket layer. All the users who recommended site 1 indicated other reasons for their recommendations which did not relate to the site's design issues. They mentioned that this site is a famous and well-known company with a good reputation.

Analysis of Results of Ten E-Commerce Websites and their Overall Usability Value

This section presents an overview of the users in term of their characteristics, their perceptions, and experience of online shopping. For the purpose, ten novices and ten expert participants (five female and five male) were taken as subjects and the average weight was calculated and analyzed from the collected data in several ways. These are:

1. Collection of the weights of the usability features (five main features and corresponding sub features) from the users was done.
2. Carrying out the descriptive analysis (the mean and standard deviation) of the weights of the developed usability features based on the users (novice and expert).
3. Determining the possibility of statistically significant difference in the website usability features on the basis of one-way analysis of variance (ANOVA) used for each feature and the corresponding sub features of the developed usability featurism for rating the ten e-commerce websites by using the Likert scale ranging (Range analysis: 1-3 represents the negative response, 4 for neutral, and 5-7 for positive response).
4. Calculating the overall usability of the individual e-commerce websites related to each sub features and five main features by multiplying the rating with the weights i.e. average weights of the sub features.
5. Adding the usability values of the related sub features for each website to produce the usability values for each site with regard to the five main features of the developed usability features.
6. Producing an overall usability value for each website by adding the usability values of the five features related to each website.

This section, deals with the influence of usability features on ten e-commerce websites from the quantitative and qualitative data collected from the above case study using our usability evaluation methodology. The impacts of the features in e-commerce websites are shown in Table 2.

Strength and Weaknesses of Design, Usability Features

In this section from the user' perspective, we discuss the strength and weaknesses of design, usability features that are used to investigate the ten e-commerce websites.

Strengths

The analysis and interpretation of the results found that the e-commerce websites have strong in respect of the below mentioned usability features:

- **Navigation:** Nine out of ten e-commerce websites have good navigation feature except Jabong. com, which relates to link support, search result, no-misleading link, no broken links, and no orphan pages. Users are satisfied to visit these sites.
- **Content:** Eight out of ten e-commerce websites have good content feature except Quikr.com and ebay.com. Whose users are very delighted when they found the up to date, relevant and true company information, and its product information (price, and size).
- **Design:** The users have indicated that seven out of ten websites have good design feature other than Quikr.com, futurebazzar.com, and naaptol.com. They express their dissatisfaction with fonts, and colors unattractiveness.

Table 2. Ten e-commerce websites and their overall usability value

S.No: Assigned Rank As per user's Preference	E-Commerce Websites	Overall Calculated Usability Value	User's Satisfaction in Respect of	User's Dissatisfaction in Respect of
1	www.naaptol.com (W9)	962.64	Noticeable images in content, easy navigation, and discount offer by web sites	Camouflaged information on the home page.
2	www.yepme.com (W10)	937.58	Easy registration, easy navigation, easy understanding of the information, and fast downloading of the images	Content, and ease of use and use of Multilanguage
3	www.snapdeal.com (W2)	910.69	Easy registration, no misleading link, no orphan pages, no broken links, aesthetic appeal	Use of Multilanguage, inadequate company information and irrelevant product information
4	www.jabong.com (W6)	897.05	The content information was good, adequate images and text size, company and product information are not complex	Use of Multilanguage, inadequate company information, irrelevant product information
5	www.myntra.com (W7)	886.84	The structure of the website, navigation, and design of the website	Missing shopping information, and lack of easy search facility
6	www.flipkart.com (W1)	880.28	Easy navigation, the structure of the website and design of the website	Content provided, more download time, and non supporting Multilanguage
7	www.quikr.com (W5)	877.32	Downloading time of images is less, simple communication with the site, and true information was provided by the site	Content aspect, more download time and non-supporting Multilanguage
8	www.futurebazzar.com(W8)	873.99	Up to date information, relevant and true information, no misleading link, no broken link, and no orphan pages	Design aspects i.e lack of page structure, poor visibility of font, non-proper color combination, non-supporting Multilanguage
9	www.ebay.com (W3)	749.51	Easy navigation, and structure of the website was good	The content, and ease of use of the website, and non-supporting Multilanguage
10	www.homeshp18.com (W4)	742.45	The content of the site, easy navigation, and good design	The structure, and ease of use of the website, and non-supporting Multilanguage

Weaknesses in Respect of Ease of Use and Structure

In spite of the above strong points, the results also reveal that the most of the investigated e-commerce websites do not support the multilingual feature, non-clarity of Contact us information, more time consuming downloading process of the images, non-clarity of Link paths, more depth structure and a few other attributes. In nutshell Consistency level in respect of the mentioned features, which is the biggest factor for those websites, is not properly maintained.

CONCLUSION

In this chapter, we have presented an overview of the definition of usability, usability assessment techniques to be adopted during the whole application life cycle for promoting usability. The idea was to provide some basic concepts and definitions that will be helpful to understand the work in the subsequent sections. We have tried to keep the amount of information to a minimum by presenting only that information which is directly relevant to our work.

We have started by presenting the design features for evaluating e-commerce websites such as navigation, content, design, ease of use and structure features and designing usable e-commerce websites an overview of Usability features that are relevant to our work. Then, the chapter discussed the user testing method followed by a case study which comprises data collection by users' preferences, data analysis and the results. The latter in the chapter, we briefly describe the effectiveness of usability evaluation methods. Lastly, the chapter describes the usability problem areas, strength and weaknesses on different features and sub-features of e-commerce websites.

The outcomes indicate the users' (novice and expert user related to usability features) priority or the order of preference based evaluation of usability of websites, i.e. first - NAVIGATION, second - CONTENT, third - DESIGN, fourth - EASE OF USE and the least important features - STRUCTURE. Based on the qualitative data related to what features they liked and disliked provided by the users. The presented the usability of ten e-commerce websites using the design features and calculated the usability value for each website. Accordingly, it was observed that naaptol.com e-commerce website gets maximum overall usability value, whereas homeshop18.com is of the minimum value. This outcome of the usability features based researches reflecting the strength and weaknesses of ten e-commerce websites may help the founders of the websites to consider it as an evidence to go for further developments on the functioning style of their websites. However, the current research has two limitations: The first limitation is that we have used the user testing method only though questionnaire for evaluating the ten e-commerce websites without using the Heuristic testing and tool based testing and the second limitation deals with the number of clicks, which may influence the outcomes while evaluating the usability of e-commerce websites.

REFERENCES

Agarwal, R., & Venkatesh, V. (2002). Assessing a Firm's Web Presence: A Heuristic Evaluation Procedure for the Measurement of Usability. *Information Systems Research*, *13*(2), 168–186. doi:10.1287/isre.13.2.168.84

Aladwani, A. M. (2003). Key Internet characteristics and e-commerce issues in Arab countries. *Information Technology & People, 16*(1), 9–20. doi:10.1108/09593840310462998

Alsmadi, S. (2002) Consumer attitudes towards online shopping in Jordan: opportunities and challenges. *Proceedings of the Marketing Workshop*, UAE.

Liburne, B., Devkota, P., & Khan, K. M. (2004). Measuring Quality Metrics for Web Applications. *Proceedings of the 2004 IRMA International Conference*, New Orleans, USA.

Barnard, L., & Wesson, J. (2003) Usability issues for e-commerce in South Africa: an empirical investigation. *Proceedings of SAICSIT 2003* (pp. 258-267).

Barnes, S., & Vidgen, R. (2002). An integrative approach to the assessment of ecommerce quality. *Journal of Electronic Commerce Research, 3*(3), 114–127.

Brinck, T., Gergle, D., & Wood, S. D. (2001). *Usability for the web: designing websites that work.* Morgan Kaufmann Publishers.

Calero, C., Ruiz, J., & Piattini, M. (2005). Classifying Web Metrics Using the Web Quality Model. Online Information Review, 29(3), 227-248. doi:10.1108/14684520510607560

Clutter Consortium. (2000). Poor Project Management – Problem of E-Projects. Cutter Consortium: The Cutter Edge.

Conover, W. J. (1971). *Practical nonparametric statistics.* New York, Chichester: Wiley.

Field, A. (2009). *Discovering statistics using SPSS* (2nd ed.). London: Sage.

Freeman, M. B., & Hyland, P. (2003). *Australian online supermarket usability (Technical report). Decision Systems Lab*, University of Wollongong.

Brajnik, G. (2001). Towards Valid Quality Models for Websites. *Proceedings of the 7th Conference onHuman Factors and the Web*, Madison, Wisconsin.

Gledec, G. (2005). Quality Model for the World Wide Web. *Proceedings of the 8th International Conference on Telecommunications - ConTEL2005*, Zagreb, Croatia (pp 281-287). doi:10.1109/CONTEL.2005.185873

Weinberg, G. M. (1997). *Quality Software Management: Anticipating Change*. USA: Dorset House Publishing Co Inc.

Gray, W., & Salzman, C. (1998). Damaged merchandise? a review of experiments that compare usability evaluation methods. *Human-Computer Interaction, 13*(3), 203–261. doi:10.1207/s15327051hci1303_2

Sqrum, H., Medaglia, R., & Normann Andersen, K. (2009). Assessment of Website Quality: Scandinavian Web Awards Right on Track? *Proceedings of the 8th International Conference on Electronic Government*, Linz, Austria (pp. 198 – 209). Springer-Verlag.

Hartmann, J., Angeli, A. D., & Sutcliffe, A. (2008). Framing the User Experience: Information Biases on Website Quality Judgement. *Proceeding of the Twenty-sixth Annual SIGCHI Conference on Human Factors in Computing Systems*, Florence, Italy (pp 855-864). doi:10.1145/1357054.1357190

Offutt, J. (2002). Quality Attributes of Web Software Applications. *Software, IEEE, 19*(2), 25–32. doi:10.1109/52.991329

Kantner, L., & Rosenbaum, S. (1997). Usability Studies of WWW sites: Heuristic Evaluation vs. Laboratory Testing. *Proceedings of ACM 15th International Conference on Systems Documentation*, Salt Lake City, UT, USA (pp. 153-160). doi:10.1145/263367.263388

Kuniavsky, M. (2003). *Observing the user experience: a practitioner's guide to user research.* San Francisco, Calif; London: Morgan Kaufmann.

Lazar, J. (2006). *Web usability: a user-centered design approach. Pearson.* Addison: Wesley.

Lewis, J. R. (1995). IBM computer usability satisfaction questionnaires: Psychometric evaluation and instructions for use. *International Journal of Human-Computer Interaction, 7*(1), 57–78. doi:10.1080/10447319509526110

May So, W. C., Danny Wong, T. N., & Sculli, D. (2005). Factors affecting intentions to purchase via the Internet. *Industrial Management & Data Systems, 105*(9), 1225–1244. doi:10.1108/02635570510633275

Merriam, S. (1998). *Qualitative research and case study applications in education.* Jossey-Bass Publishers.

Mustafa, S., & Al-Zoua'bi, L. (2008). Usability of the Academic Websites of Jordan's Universities. *Proceedings of the International Arab Conference on Information Technology*, Tunisia (pp. 2-9).

Nielsen, J. (1993). *Usability engineering.* London: Aademic Press.

Nielsen, J. (1994). Heuristic Evaluation. In J. Nielsen & R. L. Mack (Eds.), *Usability Inspection Methods* (pp. 25–64). New York: John Wiley & Sons.

Nielsen, J. (2000). *Designing Web Usability: The Practice of Simplicity.* New Riders Publishing.

Nielsen, J. (2006). *Quantitative studies: how many users to test?.* Useit.com.

Obeidat, M. (2001). Consumer protection and electronic commerce in Jordan (an exploratory study). *Proceedings of the Public Voice in Emerging Market Economies Conference*, Dubai, UAE.

Panda, S. K., Swain, S. K. Mall, R. (2015). An Investigation into Usability Aspects of E-Commerce Websites Using Users' Preferences. Advances in Computer Science: an International Journal, 4(13), 65-73.

Panda, S. K. (2014). A Usability Evaluation Framework for B2C E-Commerce Websites. *Journal of Computer Engineering and Intelligent System, 5*(3), 66–85.

Pearrow, M. (2000). *Website usability handbook.* Charles River Media.

Pearson, J., Pearson, A., & Green, D. (2007). Determining the Importance of Key Criteria in Web Usability. *Management Research News, 30*(11), 816–828. doi:10.1108/01409170710832250

Preece, J., Sharp, H., & Rogers, Y. (2002). *Interaction design: beyond human computer interaction.* John Wiley & Sons, Inc.

Rubin, J. (1994). *Handbook of usability testing: how to plan, design, and conduct effective tests.* Wiley.

Shergill, G., & Chen, Z. (2005). Web-based shopping: Consumers' attitudes towards online shopping in New Zealand. *Journal of Electronic Commerce Research*, 6(2).

Shneiderman, B. (1998). *Designing the user interface, strategies for effective human computer interaction* (3rd ed.). Addison Wesley.

Stone, D., Jarrett, C., Woodroffe, M., & Minocha, S. (2005). *User interface design and evaluation*. The Open University, Morgan Kaufmann.

Tilson, R., Dong, J., Martin, S., & Kieke, E. (1998). Factors and principles affecting the usability of four e-commerce sites. *Proceedings of the 4th Conference on Human Factors and the Web (CHFW)*. AT&TLabs, USA.

DeMarco, T. (1999). *Management Can Make Quality (Im) possible*. Boston: Cutter IT Summit.

Toit, M., & Bothma, C. (2010). Evaluating the Usability of an Academic Marketing Department's Website from a Marketing Student's Perspective. *International Retail and Marketing Review*, 5(1), 15–24.

Tarafdar, M., & Zhang, J. (2005). Analyzing the Influence of Website Design Parameters on Website Usability. *Information Resources Management Journal*, 18(4), 62–80. doi:10.4018/irmj.2005100104

Zhang, P., Von Dran, G., Blake, P., & Pipithsuksunt, V. (2000, August 10-13). A Comparison of the Most Important Website Features in Different Domains: An Empirical Study of User Perceptions. *Proceedings of Americas Conference on Information Systems (AMCIS'2000)*, Long Beach, CA (pp. 1367-1372).

APPENDIX

Please answer the following questions. They will help us understand your background and experience

Table 3. Pre–Test Questionnaire

Section One: Background and Experience Personal Information							
1	**Age**		9	Have you browsed the following websites before			
		18-29		www.flipkart.com	Yes	No	
		30-39		www.snapdeal.com	Yes	No	
		40-49		www.quikr.com	Yes	No	
		Over 50	10	Do you use the internet for purchasing products			
2	**Gender**			Yes			
		Male		No			
		Female		If no go to question 36			
3	**Education**						
		Postgraduate Degree		Section Two: Online shopping Experience			
		Higher Diploma	11	How frequently do you use the Internet for purchasing products?			
		Bachelors Degree		Weekly			
		Diploma		Monthly			
		12th Class or lower		Yearly			
Computer Experience			12	When was the first time you brought a product from the internet?			
4	How long have you had using a personal computer?			Less than a year ago			
		Under 1 year		One or two years ago			
		1-3 years		Over two years ago			
		More than 3 years	13	What was your last purchase online?			
5	How often do you use a personal computer tasks related to your work in a day?						
		Less than 2 years					
		2-4 hours					
		Mora than 4 years					
Internet Experience							
6	Which browser do you use normally		14	Which site did you use to make this purchase?			
		Internet Explorer					
		Nets cafe Navigator					
		Other					
7	How long have you been using the Internet?						
		Less than 1 year					
		1-3 years	15	Which method of payment did you use to pay for it?			
		More than 3 years			Credit Card		

continued on following page

Table 3. Continued

8	How often do you use the internet each week?			Cash on Delivery	
	Less than 2 hours			Cheque by Post	
	2-4 hours			Bank Transfer	
	More than 4 years			Other	

Table 4. A Matrix of user's profile

	Gender	**Female**			**Male**	
	Company 1	50%			50%	
	Company 2	50%			50%	
	Company 3	50%			50%	
	Average	50%			50%	
	Approximate number of users	10			10	
	Company 1	All levels, From house wife to Post Graduate				
	Company 2	All levels, From house wife to Post Graduate				
	Company 3	All levels, From house wife to Post Graduate				
	Education Level	**High School**	**Diploma**	**Bachelors Degree**	**Higher Diploma**	**Postgraduate Degree**
	Company 1	20%	20%	20%	20%	20%
	Company 2	20%	20%	20%	20%	20%
	Company 3	20%	20%	20%	20%	20%
	Average	20%	20%	20%	20%	20%
	Approximate number of users	3	4	5	4	4
Age	Company 1	20-45				
	Company 2	16-60				
	Company 3	25-60				
	Age	**18-29**	**30-39**	**40-49**	**Over 50**	
	Company 1	40%	40%	20%	0%	
	Company 2	25%	25%	25%	25%	
	Company 3	13%	29%	29%	29%	
	Average	27%	34%	26%	13%	
	Approximate number of users	5	7	5	3	
Experience using Computer	Company 1	More than one year				
	Company 2	97% more than one year				
	Company 3	More than three year				

continued on following page

Table 4. Continued

	Computer Experience	Under 1 year	1-3 years	More than 3 years
	Company 1	0%	50%	50%
	Company 2	10%	45%	45%
	Company 3	0%	0%	100%
	Average	3%	24%	73%
	Approximate number of users	0	6	14
Experience using internet	Company 1	More than one year		
	Company 2	97% more than one year		
	Company 3	More than three year		
	Internet Experience	Under 1 year	1-3 years	More than 3 years
	Company 1	0%	50%	50%
	Company 2	10%	45%	45%
	Company 3	0%	50%	50%
	Average	3%	49%	48%
	Approximate number of users	0	10	10

Table 5. User's characteristics and the frequency distribution

No	Characteristic	Range	Frequency Distribution	
			Novice Group	Expert Group
Personal Information				
1	Age	18-29	60%	70%
		30-39	30%	30%
		40-49	10%	0%
		Over 50	0%	0%
2	Gender	Male	50%	50%
		Female	50%	50%
3	Education	Postgraduate Degree	10%	20%
		Higher Diploma	0%	0%
		Bachelors Degree	40%	60%
		Diploma	40%	20%
		High School	10%	0%
Computer Experience				
4	Experience using Computer	Under 1 year	0%	0%
		1-3 years	30%	0%
		More than 3 years	70%	100%

continued on following page

Table 5. Continued

No	Characteristic	Range		Frequency Distribution	
				Novice Group	**Expert Group**
5	Daily use Computer	Less than 2 years		20%	0%
		2-4 hours		10%	30%
		More than 4 hours		80%	90%
		Internet experience			
6	Browser	Internet Explorer		90%	90%
		Nets cape Navigator		10%	10%
		Other		0%	0%
7	Experience using Internet	Less than 1 year		10%	0%
		1-3 years		90%	0%
		More than 3 years		0%	100%
8	Weekly use of internet	Less than 2 hours		0%	0%
		2-4 hours		20%	10%
		More than 4 hours		80%	90%
9	Have you browsed the following websites before?	Website 1	Yes	100%	100%
			No	0%	0%
		Website 2	Yes	100%	100%
			No	0%	0%
		Website 3	Yes	100%	100%
			No	0%	0%
10	Did the user used the internet for Purchasing	Yes		100%	100%
		No		0%	0%

Table 6. Likert scores of the pre-test questionnaire for novice and expert users and the result of Mann-Whitney test

No	Question	Likert Score		Mann-Whitney Test
		Novice Group	**Expert Group**	
Q 36	The cost of using the internet is generally reasonable	3.40	3.80	No (U=33.500, N1=10, N2=10, p=.218, two tailed)
Q 37	I am not interested in information about companies that is presented on their websites	3.60	5.80	No (U=17.000, N1=10, N2=10, p=.011, two tailed)
Q 38	I like websites to be easy to navigate	6.10	7.00	No (U=25.000, N1=10, N2=10, p=.063, two tailed)
Q 39	I am interested in well organized websites	7.00	7.00	No (U=50.000, N1=10, N2=10, p=1.000, two tailed)

continued on following page

Table 6. Continued

No	Question	Likert Score		Mann-Whitney Test
		Novice Group	Expert Group	
Q 40	Compulsory registration when shopping online is frustrating	5.60	5.40	No (U=28.000, N1=10, N2=10, p=.105, two tailed)
Q 41	I am worried about the security of my financial information while shopping online	7.00	7.00	No (U=50.000, N1=10, N2=10, p=1.000, two tailed)
Q 42	I would worried about the privacy of personal information when shopping online	7.00	7.00	No (U=50.000, N1=10, N2=10, p=1.000, two tailed)
Q 43	I am worried about the absence of legal regulations that govern online transaction	7.00	6.56	No (U=25.000, N1=10, N2=10, p=.063, two tailed)

Table 7. Experience of online shopping of expert users

No	Question	Range	Frequency Distribution
11	Frequently use of the internet for purchasing products	Weekly	0%
		Monthly	25%
		Yearly	75%
12	The first time a user purchased from the internet	Less than a year ago	50%
		One or two years ago	50%
		Over two years ago	0%
15	Method of payment a user used	Credit card	75%
		Cash on delivery	25%
		Cheque by post	0%
		Bank transfer	0%
		Other	0%
No.	Question	Answer	
13	What was your last purchase online?	Mobile Phone Digital Camera Books Dresses	
14	Which site did you use to make this purchase?	www.ebay.com www.flipkart.com www.snapdeal.com www.quikr.com	

Table 8. Likert scores for online shopping experience of expert users

No	Question	Likert Score Expert Group
Q 16	I shop online because it saves time	7.0
Q 17	I prefer to shop online from well known websites with a good reputation	6.8
Q 18	I do not find the website's search function useful when shopping online	6.5
Q 19	Generally I find it cheaper to shop online than to go to shops	5.8
Q 20	In general a detailed description of the product is not important to me	5.5
Q 21	I shop online because I can buy products at lower prices	4.3
Q 22	I prefer to research products in detail before purchasing	6.8
Q 23	I shop online because I can buy products at any time of day	7.0
Q 24	I shop online because I can buy products from anywhere	6.8
Q 25	I find it difficult to remember my password when shopping online	4.3
Q 26	In general products are received within the time period specified by the company	6.0
Q 27	In general I am satisfied with what I receive from Internet shopping and that products are accurately represented by websites	6.5
Q 28	Delivery costs are unreasonable	6.5
Q 29	In general I get good customer service from online companies	5.5
Q 30	Prices online are generally lower than elsewhere	4.8
Q 31	I find it encouraging to shop online from sites which have a clear return & refund policy	5.5
Q 32	It is important for me if a shopping site has the ability to deliver the order to an address other than my own	3.8
Q 33	It makes me feel more confident when the site keeps me informed about my order status	7.0
Q 34	I prefer to shop online from sites that provide alternative methods of ordering/payment/delivery	6.5
Q 35	I find it frustrating that some sites have limited delivery areas	5.8

Table 9. Mean time (in seconds) for each task across the three sites for novice and expert users

Task	Expert and Novice Groups	Site 1		Site 2		Site 3	
		Mean	Std. Deviation	Mean	Std. Deviation	Mean	Std. Deviation
Task 1	Novice Group	81.0000	36.72117	107.5000	42.28803	117.6000	58.10948
	Expert Group	53.4000	18.79835	83.0000	37.44032	99.0000	55.07409
	Total	**67.2000**	31.72679	**95.2500**	40.85388	**108.5000**	55.88758
Task 2	Novice Group	296.1000	79.11799	406.5000	28.76437	243.7000	111.85511
	Expert Group	247.3000	76.24529	326.9000	68.20793	169.3000	33.47653
	Total	**271.7000**	79.65855	**366.7000**	65.29214	**206.5000**	88.96096
Task 3	Novice Group	116.1000	46.29963	154.5000	44.28004	131.2000	42.12627
	Expert Group	71.3000	24.95796	97.8000	37.15373	72.8000	21.97878
	Total	**93.7000**	42.87939	**126.1500**	49.28144	**102.0000**	44.35028

continued on following page

Table 9. Continued

Task	Expert and Novice Groups	Site 1		Site 2		Site 3	
		Mean	Std. Deviation	Mean	Std. Deviation	Mean	Std. Deviation
Task 4	Novice Group	140.3000	32.23887	128.8000	50.74074	170.1000	15.37278
	Expert Group	123.4000	40.74092	127.1000	28.14822	168.3000	12.51710
	Total	**131.8500**	36.79284	**127.9500**	39.94532	**169.2000**	13.67518
Task 5	Novice Group	86.5000	39.39614	105.7000	14.56060	76.5000	35.31839
	Expert Group	80.7000	29.65749	73.5000	32.04944	82.1000	36.25052
	Total	**83.6000**	34.06866	**89.6000**	29.32288	**79.3000**	34.95124
Task 6	Novice Group	155.6000	43.06636	109.8000	54.05923	164.4000	21.59321
	Expert Group	112.8000	49.73664	80.5000	31.86865	159.4000	27.71762
	Total	**134.2000**	50.32275	**95.1500**	45.73065	**161.9000**	24.31785
Task 7	Novice Group	33.2000	21.82659	27.9000	29.08016	20.0000	11.84155
	Expert Group	31.2000	20.82093	17.6000	11.12754	17.2000	12.06280
	Total	**32.2000**	20.78613	**22.7500**	22.07136	**18.6000**	11.72222
Task 8	Novice Group	72.1000	45.01469	97.7000	33.25675	67.0000	45.69464
	Expert Group	62.2000	38.48752	68.8000	41.67013	50.2000	40.07992
	Total	**67.1500**	41.07666	**83.2500**	39.57521	**58.6000**	42.71127
Task 9	Novice Group	63.8000	40.26247	57.4000	23.33429	116.8000	8.50882
	Expert Group	33.2000	21.92310	35.9000	18.50195	99.9000	31.30655
	Total	**48.5000**	35.24127	**46.6500**	23.27473	**108.3500**	23.95231
Task 10	Novice Group	111.7000	70.16021	50.0000	62.85256	43.9000	36.80112
	Expert Group	74.6000	57.64296	34.1000	42.44591	18.0000	12.24745
	Total	**93.1500**	65.32854	**42.0500**	52.83188	**30.9500**	29.81782

Table 10. Tasks accuracy

Task	Expert and Novice Groups	Site 1	Site 2	Site 3
		Accuracy Score		
Task 1	Novice Group	100%	100%	60%
	Expert Group	100%	100%	80%
Task 2	Novice Group	100%	30%	80%
	Expert Group	100%	90%	100%
Task 3	Novice Group	70%	40%	70%
	Expert Group	90%	100%	100%
Task 4	Novice Group	100%	100%	50%
	Expert Group	100%	100%	80%
Task 5	Novice Group	70%	60%	80%
	Expert Group	90%	100%	80%

continued on following page

Table 10. Continued

Task	Expert and Novice Groups	Site 1	Site 2	Site 3
		Accuracy Score		
Task 6	Novice Group	10%	30%	0%
	Expert Group	60%	70%	0%
Task 7	Novice Group	100%	100%	100%
	Expert Group	100%	100%	100%
Task 8	Novice Group	50%	40%	60%
	Expert Group	70%	60%	80%
Task 9	Novice Group	100%	100%	20%
	Expert Group	100%	100%	40%
Task 10	Novice Group	60%	100%	80%
	Expert Group	80%	100%	90%

Table 11. Usability problem themes and sub-themes identified by performance data and observation and their locations per task

Problem Theme	Problem Sub-Theme	Site 1		Site 2		Site 3	
		Tasks Identified the Problem	Location	Tasks Identified the Problem	Location	Tasks Identified the Problem	Location
Navigation	**Misleading Links**	Task 2	Any product's page('Check out' link)	Task 2	Shipping page('go' link)	Task 10	Home page of the site('Our services' link)
		Task 2	Add to Cart End page('buy now' link)				
		Task 5	Entire site – Top Menu('sign in' and 'register' links)	Task 5	My account page('address book' link)		Home page of the Mall('Our Services' link)
		Task 10					
		Task 10	Entire site('advanced search' link)				
	Link are not obvious	Task 3	Entire site('Shopping cart' link)	Task 3	Entire site('Shopping cart' link)	Task 2	Any product's page('complete product' and 'shopping basket' links)
				Task 4	Order preview page('home page' link)	Task 3	Entire site('Shopping basket' link)
						Task 6	Home page of the Mall('online catalog' link)
	Weak Navigation Support	Task 3	Order preview page(did not have navigational menus or links to the home page or to other pages)	Not Exist	Not Exist	Task 3	Order page(did not have navigational menus or links to the home page or to other pages)
		Task 4				Task 2	Shopping cart page(did not have navigational menus or links to the home page or to other pages)
		Task 5				Task 3	
		Task 6					
Content	**Irrelevant Content**	Task 2	Shipping information page(confusing error message was displayed all the time)	Not Exist	Not Exist	Task 1	Online catalog sub section (displayed products which were not ready to selling)
		Task 4				Task 4	
						Task 6	
						Task 1	Search Mal Page(under construction page)
						Task 4	
						Task 9	

continued on following page

Table 11. Continued

Problem Theme	Problem Sub-Theme	Site 1		Site 2		Site 3	
		Tasks Identified the Problem	Location	Tasks Identified the Problem	Location	Tasks Identified the Problem	Location
Design	**Misleading Images**	Task 3	Order preview page(site's logo)	Not Exist	Not Exist	Task 3	Entire site(site's logo)
	Inappropriate page design	Not Exist	Not Exist	Task 1, Task 2, Task 4	Any product's page(inappropriate presentation of product's description)	Not Exist	Not Exist
				Task 2	Login page('new and current customer fields)		
					Address page('shipping and billing' fields)		
Architecture	**Poor Structure**	Not Exist	Not Exist	Not Exist	Not Exist	Task 1, Task 4, Task 9	Entire Site
Internal search	**Inaccurate results**	Task 6	Entire Site(product search)	Task 6	Entire Site(product search)	Not Exist	Not Exist
Purchasing Process	**Difficulty in knowing What was Required for some Fields**	Task 2	Free shipping coupon page('free shipping coupon' field)	Task 2	Shipping page('gift certificate code' field)	Not Exist	Not Exist
	Difficulty in Distinguishing between Required and Non-Required Fields	Not Exist	Not exist	Task 2	Login page('password' fiels)	Task 2	Personal information page (some field required)
					Address page(some required field)	Task 3	
						Task5	

continued on following page

Table 11. Continued

Problem Theme	Problem Sub-Theme	Site 1		Site 2		Site 3	
		Tasks Identified the Problem	Location	Tasks Identified the Problem	Location	Tasks Identified the Problem	Location
	Difficulty in Knowing what links were required to be clicked	Task 3	Shopping cart page('update order' link)	Not Exist	Not Exist	Task 3	Shopping cart page('ok' link)
	Session problem	Not Exist	Not Exist	Not Exist	Not Exist	Task 4 Task 9	Personal Information page(did not keep the users information)
	Required fields were not logical	Task 2	Registration page('state/province' field)	Task 2	Address page('state/region' field)	Not Exist	Not Exist
	Expected Information was not displayed after adding products to cart	Task 2 Task 4	Add to cart end page	Not Exist	Not Exist	Task 2	Product page
Accessibility and customer service	Not easy to find help/ customer support information	Task 8	Entire site	Task 8	Entire site	Task 8	Entire site
	Inappropriate information provide within a help section /customer service	Not Exist	Not Exist	Not Exist	Not Exist	Task 8	FAQ page

Table 12. Result of one-way within-subjects anova test for each task among the three sites

Task	ANOVA Test (One-Way within- Subjects)
	Was there a statistically significant difference among site 1, site 2 and Site 3
Task 1	**Yes** $F(2,38) = 6.021$, $p=.005$
Task 2	**Yes** $F(2,38) = 33.183$, $p=.000$
Task 3	**Yes** $F(2,38) = 4.471$, $p=.018$
Task 4	**Yes** $F(2,38) = 10.873$, $p=.000$
Task 5	**No** $F(2,38) = .502$, $p=.609$
Task 6	**Yes** $F(2,38) = 16.517$, $p=.000$
Task 7	**Yes** $F(2,38) = 4.369$, $p=.020$
Task 8	**No** $F(2,38) = 2.364$, $p=.108$
Task 9	**Yes** $F(2,38) = 40.407$, $p=.000$
Task10	**Yes** $F(2,38) = 8.814$, $p=.001$

Table 13. Usability problem themes and sub-themes identified by the post test questionnaire

Problem theme	Problem, Sub Theme	Statement Number in the Post Test questionnaire	Likert Score		
			Site 1	Site 2	Site 3
Navigation	Weak Navigation Support	9			2.55
		10			3.70
	Broken Links	24			3.85
Content	Irrelevant Content	14			3.50
		27			3.25
Design	Unaesthetic Design	20			3.80
	Inappropriate Page Design	25			2.95
Architecture	Poor Structure	1			2.95
		2			2.60
		8			2.70
Purchasing Process	Compulsory Registration	15	3.25	2.75	
		16			2.25

Table 14. Likert scores of the post-test questionnaire for the three sites for novice and expert users and the result of mann-whitney test

No	Site 1 Likert Score Novice Group	Site 1 Likert Score Expert Group	Site 1 Mann-Whitney test — Was there statistically a significant difference between Novice and Expert Groups	Site 2 Likert Score Novice Group	Site 2 Likert Score Expert Group	Site 2 Mann-Whitney test — Was there statistically a significant difference between Novice and Expert Groups	Site 3 Likert Score Novice Group	Site 3 Likert Score Expert Group	Site 3 Mann-Whitney test — Was there statistically a significant difference between Novice and Expert Groups
Q1	5.1	6.6	Yes (U=18.500,N1=10,N2=10, p=.015,two tailed)	4.5	5.8	Yes (U=22.500,N1=10,N2=10, p=.035,two tailed)	3.1	2.8	No (U=48.500,N1=10,N2=10, p=.912,two tailed)
Q2	5.6	6.6	No (U=24.000,N1=10,N2=10, p=.052,two tailed)	5.7	6.3	No (U=34.500,N1=10,N2=10, p=.247,two tailed)	2.6	2.6	No (U=44.500,N1=10,N2=10, p=.684,two tailed)
Q3	5.7	6.5	No (U=27.000,N1=10,N2=10, p=.089,two tailed)	5.0	6.2	No (U=26.500,N1=10,N2=10, p=.075,two tailed)	NA	NA	NA
Q4	5.2	6.5	Yes (U=20.500,N1=10,N2=10, p=.023,two tailed)	4.9	6.1	No (U=28.500,N1=10,N2=10, p=.105,two tailed)	3.7	2.0	No (U=27.500,N1=10,N2=10, p=.089,two tailed)
Q5	5.9	6.1	No (U=45.000,N1=10,N2=10, p=.739,two tailed)	5.4	5.8	No (U=43.500,N1=10,N2=10, p=.631,two tailed)	4.4	3.9	No (U=41.000,N1=10,N2=10, p=.529,two tailed)
Q6	4.9	5.7	No (U=39.000,N1=10,N2=10, p=.436,two tailed)	4.6	5.8	No (U=33.500,N1=10,N2=10, p=.218,two tailed)	3.8	2.9	No (U=37.500,N1=10,N2=10, p=.353,two tailed)
Q7	4.3	5.6	No (U=28.000,N1=10,N2=10, p=.105,two tailed)	4.4	5.5	No (U=29.500,N1=10,N2=10, p=.123,two tailed)	4.2	3.4	No (U=39.500,N1=10,N2=10, p=.436,two tailed)
Q8	5.5	6.6	Yes (U=22.000,N1=10,N2=10, p=.035,two tailed)	5.1	5.9	No (U=32.500,N1=10,N2=10, p=.190,two tailed)	3.4	2.0	No (U=25.500,N1=10,N2=10, p=.063,two tailed)
Q9	5.9	5.4	No (U=49.000,N1=10,N2=10, p=.971,two tailed)	3.5	4.8	No (U=31.500,N1=10,N2=10, p=.165,two tailed)	2.7	2.4	No (U=40.500,N1=10,N2=10, p=.481,two tailed)
Q10	4.9	6.3	Yes (U=23.000,N1=10,N2=10, p=.043,two tailed)	5.1	6.3	No (U=29.000,N1=10,N2=10, p=.123,two tailed)	4.1	3.3	No (U=39.500,N1=10,N2=10, p=.436,two tailed)

continued on following page

Table 14. Continued

No	Site 1			Site 2			Site 3		
	Likert Score		Mann-Whitney test	Likert Score		Mann-Whitney test	Likert Score		Mann-Whitney test
	Novice Group	Expert Group	Was there statistically a significant difference between Novice and Expert Groups	Novice Group	Expert Group	Was there statistically a significant difference between Novice and Expert Groups	Novice Group	Expert Group	Was there statistically a significant difference between Novice and Expert Groups
Q11	5.3	6.3	No (U=27.000,N1=10,N2=10, p=.089,two tailed)	5.4	6.1	No (U=35.500,N1=10,N2=10, p=.280,two tailed)	NA	NA	NA
Q12	5.6	6.5	No (U=22.000,N1=10,N2=10, p=.035,two tailed)	5.4	6.1	No (U=37.500,N1=10,N2=10, p=.353,two tailed)	NA	NA	NA
Q13	5.4	5.9	No (U=35.500,N1=10,N2=10, p=.280,two tailed)	5.8	5.6	No (U=50.000,N1=10,N2=10, p=1.000,two tailed)	NA	NA	NA
Q14	4.5	5.8	No (U=25.000,N1=10,N2=10, p=.063,two tailed)	4.5	5.6	No (U=32.000,N1=10,N2=10, p=.190,two tailed)	3.9	3.1	No (U=37.500,N1=10,N2=10, p=.353,two tailed)
Q15	3.4	3.1	No (U=46.500,N1=10,N2=10, p=.796,two tailed)	2.0	3.5	No (U=26.500,N1=10,N2=10, p=.075,two tailed)			
Q16							2.0	2.5	No (U=40.500,N1=10,N2=10, p=.481,two tailed)
Q17	4.7	6.2	No (U=26.500,N1=10,N2=10, p=.075,two tailed)	3.9	4.8	No (U=35.500,N1=10,N2=10, p=.280,two tailed)	2.5	2.0	No (U=40.500,N1=10,N2=10, p=.481,two tailed)
Q19	5.8	6.0	No (U=49.500,N1=10,N2=10, p=.971,two tailed)	5.6	5.2	No (U=35.500,N1=10,N2=10, p=.280,two tailed)	4.1	4.1	No (U=49.500,N1=10,N2=10, p=.971,two tailed)
Q20	5.9	6.0	No (U=44.500,N1=10,N2=10, p=.684,two tailed)	5.8	5.2	No (U=36.000,N1=10,N2=10, p=.315,two tailed)	4.1	3.5	No (U=40.500,N1=10,N2=10, p=.481,two tailed)
Q21	4.4	4.1	No (U=47.500,N1=10,N2=10, p=.853,two tailed)	5.7	4.8	No (U=41.000,N1=10,N2=10, p=.529,two tailed)	4.6	4.1	No (U=46.000,N1=10,N2=10, p=.796,two tailed)

continued on following page

Table 14. Continued

No	Site 1			Site 2			Site 3		
	Likert Score		Mann-Whitney test	Likert Score		Mann-Whitney test	Likert Score		Mann-Whitney test
	Novice Group	Expert Group	Was there statistically a significant difference between Novice and Expert Groups	Novice Group	Expert Group	Was there statistically a significant difference between Novice and Expert Groups	Novice Group	Expert Group	Was there statistically a significant difference between Novice and Expert Groups
Q22	5.5	6.1	No (U=47.000,N1=10,N2=10, p=.089,two tailed)	4.4	5.6	Yes (U=27.000,N1=10,N2=10, p=.089,two tailed)	4.8	4.7	No (U=43.500,N1=10,N2=10, p=.631,two tailed)
Q23	5.8	5.0	No (U=40.000,N1=10,N2=10, p=.481,two tailed)	4.7	5.5	No (U=33.000,N1=10,N2=10, p=.218,two tailed)	4.7	4.5	No (U=49.500,N1=10,N2=10, p=.971,two tailed)
Q24	5.5	4.7	No (U=45.500,N1=10,N2=10, p=.739,two tailed)	4.5	4.6	No (U=47.500,N1=10,N2=10, p=.853,two tailed)	4.8	2.9	No (U=25.500,N1=10,N2=10, p=.063,two tailed)
Q25	5.1	5.8	No (U=34.500,N1=10,N2=10, p=.247,two tailed)	4.0	4.7	No (U=36.500,N1=10,N2=10, p=.325,two tailed)	3.2	2.7	No (U=41.500,N1=10,N2=10, p=.529,two tailed)
Q26	4.3	6.2	Yes (U=18.000,N1=10,N2=10, p=.015,two tailed)	4.3	5.2	Yes (U=36.500,N1=10,N2=10, p=.315,two tailed)	2.6	2.5	No (U=50.000,N1=10,N2=10, p=1.000,two tailed)
Q27	5.2	5.3	No (U=47.500,N1=10,N2=10, p=.853,two tailed)	4.4	5.5	Yes (U=36.500,N1=10,N2=10, p=.315,two tailed)	3.1	3.4	No (U=46.500,N1=10,N2=10, p=.796,two tailed)
Q28	4.5	5.6	Yes (U=30.500,N1=10,N2=10, p=.143,two tailed)	4.8	4.9	No (U=49.500,N1=10,N2=10, p=.971,two tailed)	3.5	2.0	No (U=26.500,N1=10,N2=10, p=.075,two tailed)
Q29	5.7	5.9	No (U=46.000,N1=10,N2=10, p=.796,two tailed)	5.7	5.3	Yes (U=43.500,N1=10,N2=10, p=.631,two tailed)	5.2	5.0	No (U=48.500,N1=10,N2=10, p=.912,two tailed)
Q30	5.5	4.9	No (U=42.500,N1=10,N2=10, p=.579,two tailed)	5.0	5.2	No (U=47.500,N1=10,N2=10, p=.853,two tailed)	5.0	3.7	No (U=34.000,N1=10,N2=10, p=.247,two tailed)
Q31	5.5	5.3	No (U=47.000,N1=10,N2=10, p=.853,two tailed)	5.3	5.1	No (U=45.500,N1=10,N2=10, p=.739,two tailed)	4.6	3.4	No (U=32.000,N1=10,N2=10, p=.190,two tailed)

Table 15. Likert scores of the post-test questionnaire and the result of friedman test

No	Question	Likert Score			Friedman Test
		Site 1	Site 2	Site 3	Was there a statistically significant difference among site 1,site 2 and site 3
Architecture and Navigation					
Q 1	Finding the information related to the tasks(was very easy)	5.85	5.15	2.95	**Yes** X^2 (2, *N*=20)= 30.714, *p*=.000
Q 2	Finding the products(was very easy)	6.10	6.00	2.60	**Yes** X^2 (2, *N*=20)= 34.125, *p*=.000
Q 3	Using the internal search facility(was very easy)	6.10	5.60	NA	NA
Q 8	The organization of information of the website was clear	6.05	5.50	2.70	**Yes** X^2 (2, *N*=20)= 35.273, *p*=.000
Q 9	Moving around the website without getting lost was difficult	5.65	4.15	2.55	**Yes** X^2 (2, *N*=20)= 25.016, *p*=.000
Q 10	The table of contents was helpful	5.60	5.70	3.70	**Yes** X^2 (2, *N*=20)= 31.356, *p*=.000
Q 11	The site's search function was quick enough	5.80	5.75	**NA**	**NA**
Q 12	Accuracy of internal search result was good	6.05	5.75	**NA**	**NA**
Q 13	Results if internal search were poor	5.65	5.70	**NA**	**NA**
Q 21	It was difficult to go to the home page from any sub page of the sites	4.25	5.25	4.35	**Yes** X^2 (2, *N*=20)= 17.644, *p*=.000
Q 24	There were few broken/not working links	5.10	4.55	3.85	**Yes** X^2 (2, *N*=20)= 15.796, *p*=.000
Content					
Q 14	The information of the website was effective in helping me complete the purchasing tasks	5.15	5.05	3.50	**Yes** X^2 (2, *N*=20)= 22.172, *p*=.000
Q 27	The terminology/terms use throughout these website were clear	5.25	5.05	3.25	**Yes** X^2 (2, *N*=20)= 22.116, *p*=.000
Design					
Q 19	I liked the interface of this website	5.90	5.40	4.10	**Yes** X^2 (2, *N*=20)= 31.115, *p*=.000
Q 20	The interface of this website was pleasant/attractive	5.95	5.50	3.80	**Yes** X^2 (2, *N*=20)= 33.323, *p*=.000
Q 22	The choice of colors was appropriate	5.80	5.00	4.75	**Yes** X^2 (2, *N*=20)= 18.473, *p*=.000

continued on following page

Table 15. Continued

No	Question	Likert Score			Friedman Test
		Site 1	Site 2	Site 3	Was there a statistically significant difference among site 1,site 2 and site 3
Q 23	The size of the text made the site easy to read	5.40	5.10	4.60	Yes X^2 (2, N=20)= 12.792, p=.000
Q 25	It was clear to know the position of any page of the site	5.45	5.25	2.95	Yes X^2 (2, N=20)= 29.284, p=.000
Purchasing Process					
Q 4	Registering on the site(was very easy)	5.85	5.50	NA	NA
Q 5	Purchasing a product (was very easy)	6.00	5.60	4.15	Yes X^2 (2, N=20)= 30.632, p=.000
Q 6	Changing customer information (was very easy)	4.95	4.95	3.35	Yes X^2 (2, N=20)= 9.033, p=.011
Q 7	Changing the control of shopping cart (was very easy)	5.30	5.20	3.80	Yes X^2 (2, N=20)= 24.824, p=.000
Q 15	Compulsory registration in order to purchase products was convenient	3.25	2.75	NA	NA
Q 16	I prefer to register before purchasing products	NA	NA	2.25	NA
Q 29	I trust that the company will not misuse my personal information	5.80	5.50	5.10	Yes X^2 (2, N=20)= 14.176, p=.001
Q 30	I feel that the security of my financial information is protected while purchasing from this website	5.20	5.10	4.35	Yes X^2 (2, N=20)= 14.245, p=.001
Q 31	I have confidence in purchasing from this website	5.40	5.20	4.00	Yes X^2 (2, N=20)= 26.655, p=.000
The Overall Evaluation of the Sites					
Q 17	This website had all the functions and capabilities that I expected it to have	5.45	4.35	2.25	Yes X^2 (2, N=20)= 37.014, p=.000
Q 26	I felt comfortable using this website	5.25	4.75	2.55	Yes X^2 (2, N=20)= 25.400, p=.000
Q 28	I would recommend this site to a friend	5.05	4.85	2.75	Yes X^2 (2, N=20)= 28.212, p=.000

Table 16. Usability problem themes and sub-themes identified by the qualitative data of the post test questionnaire

Problem Theme	Problem Sub-Theme	Site 1 Location	Site 2 Location	Site 3 Location
Navigation	**Misleading Links**	Entire site – Top Menu('sign in' and 'register' links)	Shipping page('go' link)	Home page of the site('Our services' link)
	Link are not obvious	Not Exist	Not Exist	Not Exist
			Login page(Home page link)	
			Address page (Home page link)	
			Shipping and Payment Page(home page link)	
			Shipping cart problem (home page link)	
			Order preview page('home page' link)	
	Weak Navigation Support	Order preview page(did not have navigational menus or links to the home page or to other pages)	Not Exist	Not Exist
				Home page
				Online Catalog Subsection-search results page
	Broken links	Not Exist	Not Exist	Online Catalog subsection Banner
				Related Links pages
	Orphan pages	Not Exist	Not Exist	Product's Image page(Larger view)for any product's page
Content	**Irrelevant Content**	Not Exist	Not Exist	Entire site(most pages had repetitive/not concise content)
	Inaccurate Information	Any product's page(displayed out of stock products)	Any product's page(displayed out of stock products)	Not Exist
	Missing Information about the Products	Any product's page (availability)	Any product's page (availability)	Any product's page (availability)

continued on following page

Table 16. Continued

Problem Theme	Problem Sub-Theme	Site 1 Location	Site 2 Location	Site 3 Location
Design	Inappropriate page design	All product category pages(long pages with large number of images); Best/Most seller page (products are displayed at the bottom)	Any product's page(inappropriate presentation of product's description)	Not Exist
	Inappropriate choice of Fonts and colors	Not Exist	Entire site(small font size for menus and text, combination of background and link colors)	Not Exist
Architecture	Poor Structure	Not Exist	Not Exist	Entire Site
Internal search	Inaccurate results	Entire Site(product search)	Entire Site(product search)	Not Exist
	Limited option	Entire site(product and advanced search)	Entire site(product and advanced search)	Not Exist
Purchasing (Check out)Process	Difficulty in Distinguishing between Required and Non-Required Fields	Not exist	Login page('password' fields); Address page(some required field)	Personal information page (some field required)
	Long Ordering Process	Add to Cart End page; Checkout Page	Not Exist	Not Exist
	Session problem	Not Exist	Not Exist	Personal information page (did not keep the users information)
Accessibility and customer service	Not supporting the more than one language	Entire site	Entire site	Not Exist
Inconsistency	Inconsistent Design/Layout/ content	Not Exist	Not Exist	Not Exist
Missing Capabilities	Missing Information/Functions	Not Exist	Not Exist	Not Exist

Chapter 5
Quality Measures for Semantic Web Application

Adiraju Prasanth Rao
Anurag Group of Institution, India

ABSTRACT

The Semantic Web is a standard of Common Data Formats on WWW with aim to convert the current web data of unstructured and semi-structured documents into a common framework that allows data to be shared and reused across applications, enterprises. The main purpose of the Semantic Web is driving the evolution of the current Web by enabling users to find, share, and combine information more easily. Humans are capable of using the Web to carry out tasks such as searching for the lowest price for a LAPTOP. However, machines cannot accomplish all of these tasks without human direction, because web pages are designed to be read by people, not machines. The semantic web is a vision of information that can be readily interpreted by machines, so machines can perform more of the tedious work involved in finding, combining, and acting upon information on the web. The chapter presents the architecture of semantic web, its challenging issues and also data quality principles. These principles provide a better decision making within organization and will maximize long term data integration and interoperability.

INTRODUCTION

This is the age of information which can be gathered from different sources. Information-oriented communication networks, services and applications in various domains have recently undergone rapid changes due to sudden increases in number of network enabled devices and sensors deployed in physical environments. Within the next ten years, it is expected that billions of devices will generate large volumes of real world data for many applications and services in various domains such as smart phones, health care, transport environmental monitoring system, mobile applications etc. Data generated by these devices is expected to be mostly multimodal in nature (like temperature, light, sound and video) and manifold in character. This implies that the quality of data can change with devices, location and time.

DOI: 10.4018/978-1-4666-9764-5.ch005

The amount of data available on the world-wide-web is already huge and is increasing at a rapid pace. About 2.5 billion bytes of data is generated each day, which includes sensory data and data from various other sources. The generated data from different sources can be analyzed to extract actionable information which enables better understanding about the physical world and value added products and services provided by the manufacturers.

Currently, every business transaction or decision is data based. Data has also become more and more important for social activities. Large amount of business related data is published on the web with the development of internet from "Web of Documents" to "Web of Data". Today's web consists of large libraries of web documents and interconnected documents that are transmitted by systems and are available to the public. Applications let people view, search and combine data like calendars, address books, playlist and spreadsheet. This technology has been developed from hypertext systems to which anyone can contribute. They also reveal that the quality of information or the consistency of documents cannot be constantly assured. The present web or traditional web can be categorized into the 2nd generation. The traditional web was an association among internet users, content providers and enterprises. Originally, data was posted on web sites and users simply read or downloaded the content. This has led to the concept of the internet as a huge distributed database with users performing three major operations - search, integration and web data mining. These operations are expanded in the following paragraphs.

- **Search:** The main goal of search is to identify and access the information or resources on the web.
- **Integration:** Integration is the process of combining and aggregating different resources to accomplish a specialized task. For example, searching for Indian food in the United States of America requires two resources - a restaurant and Indian food items. By integrating these two resources, we can look forward to a nice dinner.
- **Web Data Mining:** Web data mining is the nontrivial extraction of useful information from large data sets or databases. The author's D. Artz & Y. Gil. (2007 [5]) discussed Special data mining techniques are used to automatically discover and extract information dynamically from web documents and services. This involves three main tasks viz. resource finding which retrieves the intended web documents, information selection and preprocessing which automatically selects and preprocesses specific information retrieved from web resources and lastly a generalization which dynamically discovers the patterns in individual web sites as well as across multiple sites.

For all three categories of internet users, the internet is entirely meant for reading and is purely display oriented and is therefore based on keyword matching only. The main reason for this is that the current internet contains mostly unstructured data. The current web involves too much manual work and needs to involve more automation. In its current version, the web data mining search mechanism could be very expensive because applications are highly specialized and application oriented.

We thus identify three major problems faced by all three internet user categories and would look for solutions to make these activities more efficient. The expected web has following features:

1. The output data from search results should be relevant
2. More automation is needed in the case of integration searching
3. Web data mining needs to be less expensive.

We thus conclude that the internet is constructed in such way that its documents only contain enough information for computers but there is not much comprehension of all available data. The main objective of this chapter is to improve the data quality of the current web and make it more machines understandable. The next section presents Overview of Semantic Web

OVERVIEW OF SEMANTIC WEB

Now a days, most of the web documents are written in Hypertext Markup Language (HTML).There is no correspondence between documents as requested by the user but it also displays many other unrelated documents (search engines will never deliver satisfactory performance).The degree dissimilarity and incompleteness of knowledge for a searching an item or documents leads to user dissatisfaction. The current web can be characterized as 2nd generation which generates active web pages for direct human processing (reading, browsing, form filling).Therefore machines have no idea about the meaning of the documents that are presented, no way to understand the documents and cannot make any intelligent decisions about these documents.

What Will Happen if Web Page Interprets the Meaning of the Data?

For example, we choose a scenario where on 20-03-2015, Johnson decides to undertake a business travel, visiting London, Sydney, Mumbai, Johannesburg and Paris. He needs to fix his air tickets, cabs, hotels and the appointments with his customers. He has planned to leave for London on Monday, March 23, 2015 at 8.20 am by Lufthansa Airlines. Johnson has booked Orange cabs both at his source and London and his stay at Hotel Marriott. He has two days work at London which might get extended by a day. Similarly Johnson plans a day's visit to Sydney but it can get extended by a day or two based on the progress of his business. Same is the case with his visits to Mumbai and Johannesburg. So, he needs to fix all his plans for air tickets, cabs, hotels and appointments dynamically. So Johnson needs to search for next available flights & tickets in his category, book cabs and check for availability at his preferred hotels. More importantly, he needs to check and fix appointments with his customers in all cities at frequently changing dates and times. This is possible using a Semantic Web, where in an agent takes up the job of checking the Web and fixing his travel itinerary. The agent carries out all these tasks on behalf of Johnson and this can be possible only with the semantic web.

Johnson could use his agents to carry out all these tasks thanks not to World Wide Web of today but rather the semantic web that will evolve into tomorrow. Most of the today web's content is designed for humans to read, not for computer programs to manipulate meaningfully.

What Is Semantic Web?

The current web data of unstructured and semi-structured documents is intended to transform into a common framework that aims for semantic web. The semantics will bring structure to meaningful content of web pages creating an environment where software agents roaming from one page to another page can readily carry out sophisticated tasks for users. The agent interprets the pages which it traverses and returns newly created tasks without changing its interpretation. The semantic web is not a separate web instance but an extension of the current web in which information is given a well defined meaning thus enabling computers and humans to work in cooperation. This leads to advancement in the current web and its enhancement leads to the semantic web. The Berners-Lee et(May 2001) were presented the definition of semantic web.

His vision of the Semantic Web as follows:

I have a dream for the web in which computers become capable of analyzing all the data on the web i.e. the content, links, and transactions between people and computers. A "semantic web", which makes this possible, has yet to emerge, but when it does, the day-to-day mechanisms of trade, bureaucracy and our daily lives will be handled by machines talking to machines. The "Intelligent Agent's people have publicized for ages will finally materialize the Berners-Lee et (May 2001[1]).

The block structure of the semantic web presented in next section.

BLOCK STRUCTURE OF THE SEMANTIC WEB

The semantic web is structure of few language specifications which represent a common framework on which an application can be built. Figure 1 illustrates the semantic web architectural components were discussed by authors D. Artz & Y. Gil. (2007).

The detailed mechanism of Figure1 is explained below:

Step 1 – Identification of Resource: The internet resources are identified with uniform resource identifier URI and internationalized resource identifier (IRI) harmonizes to URI. The IRI allows for use of characters from large range of writing systems in identifier.

Step2 – Data Interchange: Next step is to identify languages for the exchange of data among the resources. The Extensible Markup Language (XML) enables the preparation of both structured documents representing the information to be exchanged and metadata encapsulating its mean-

Figure 1. Semantic web Architectural Components

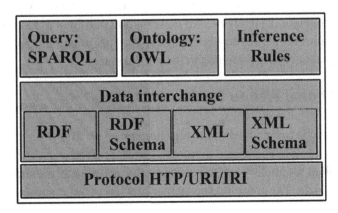

ing. So XML provides extensible, hierarchical, formatted information, and its required encoded metadata. The main goal of Resource Description Framework (RDF) is easy integration of data from multiple sources, automation of agents and automated services by supplying a rudimentary semantic capability. A graph-structured data format RDF was developed by the W3C standards for encoding such data.XML provides interoperability with in one application using given schema but RDF provides interoperability across multiple applications. Also RDF Schema (RDFS) used to express the class and its domain range of properties, hierarchies. This means that consistency check is required since data generates from different sources are heterogeneous in nature.

Step 3 – Mechanism Querying: The declarative query language allows for specifying queries against an integrated data in RDF by means of SPARQL (a recursive acronym for SPARQL and RDF query language) which similar to SQL. The SPARQL designed for querying against RDF data sets and handle complex structure queries, data stored in RDF repositories. The encoded data covers only part of meaning but adding inference rules to this data gives the better interpretation by the machine. The web ontology language (OWL) allows for automated inference rules by drawing conclusions based on existing facts.

The collection of semantic web technologies such as RDF, RDF Schema, SKOS, and SPARQL... etc. creates an environment where an application can query the data, apply inference rules on it using the controlled vocabulary.

There are many query languages such as OWL-QL, SWRL (Semantic Web Rule Language), RuleML (Rule Markup Language ORL (OWL Rules Language), OWL is based on Description Logic (DL) and RuleML is based on logic programs (LP).

Web Ontology Language (OWL) Query Language (QL)

The feature of OWL-QL:

1. Formal Language and protocol querying agents
2. Query answering dialogue using knowledge representation in the OWL
3. Use automated reasoning methods to derive answer to queries.
4. Use multiple Knowledge bases on the semantic web

The ontology for web defines the set inference rules to deduce new knowledge from previously established knowledge. The major design issues for constructing ontology to identify the key concepts in the domain and its structure, Properties and associated relationships among the concepts. The ontology spectrum for banking system can be presented in the next chapter.

How to Move Traditional Web to the Semantic Web?

The semantic web data needs to be added to the traditional web by following.

1. Construct a controlled vocabulary set that contains all important terms and synonyms for concepts within the given domain. The controlled vocabulary set has to be constructed using structured data.

2. Link the concepts or classes in a controlled vocabulary in a logical order or sort them into categories and establish relationship among those concepts or classes.
3. An Ontology spectrum should be constructed.

Following the above steps, we can link web pages to a structured data set that indicates the semantics of the linked page. A smart agent that is able to understand this structured data set will then be able to conduct intelligent actions and make intelligent decisions on a global state.

Different degrees of semantics can be achieved by adding approaches, models or methods to existing level of semantics. The levels of the semantics are as shown in Figure 2. Each of the levels is described in the paragraphs below.

Controlled vocabulary or Controlled lexicon

The list of terms or items that have been enumerated explicitly is known to be controlled lexicon or controlled vocabulary. The general terms that form a part of the vocabulary or lexicons for banking applications is given below.

Cheque facility, anywhere banking facility, trade, services, mobile banking, internet banking, credit card, debit/ATM card, real time gross settlement (RTGS), leverage financing, doorstep banking facilities, wealth management, equity trading, gold loan, home loan, personal loan, agriculture loan etc.

Figure 2. Semantic level of the web

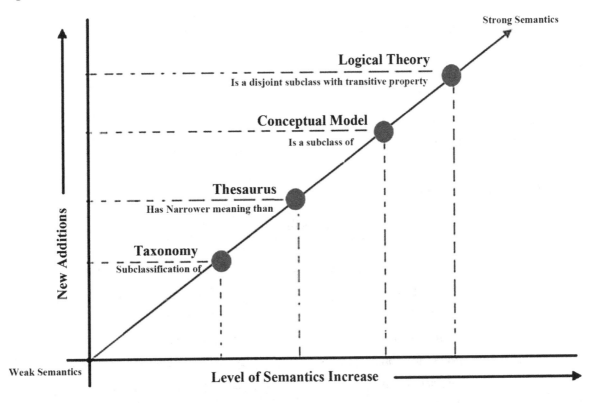

These vocabularies are used in markup language and these languages build the web. There are different markup languages such as HTML, XML, and XML Schema.

Taxonomy

After identifying the terms, we further categorize the terms into a tree like hierarchical structure. This means that a new structure and relationship is established among the terms, for example an inheritance relationship. The above banking terms can classified into two groups as shown in Figure 3

Thesaurus

The main objective of a thesaurus is to list words grouped together according to relationships between their meanings (synonyms / antonyms). A thesaurus can be implemented using SKOS (Simple Knowledge Organization System) which is a W3C recommendation. The thesaurus is a form of controlled vocabulary that seeks to dictate semantic manifestation of metadata in the indexing of controlled objects and classification schemes. SKOS is a part of a semantic family of standards built upon RDF and RDFS. This means that the thesaurus is a subject heading system or is another type of structured controlled vocabulary.

Based on the relation between the words or terms we can divide the words into different categories. Some examples are:

1. The words which have nearly the same meaning:
   Statement is a synonym for announcement or bill
2. Spelled the same way as a term but which has a different meaning
   Point: The pencil has a sharp point. It is not polite to point at people.
3. Terms which have a broader meaning
   A Bank has a broader meaning than financial organization
4. Terms which have narrower meaning
   Financial organization has a narrower meaning than bank
5. Terms that have some unspecified relationship between them
   Sunlight is associated with water

Figure 3. Classification of banking terms

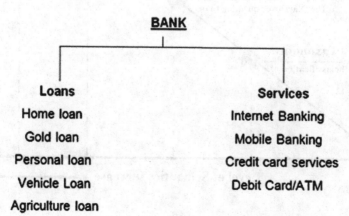

Ontology Spectrum

Ontology represents much richer semantic relationships among terms and attributes as well as inference rules to produce knowledge for the system. Ontology provides shared knowledge across many applications.

This is illustrated using the E-R model of a banking system as shown in Figure 4

The Figure 4 shows the ontology spectrum which is E-R Schema and also taxonomy with relationships. This defines class and properties of the classes. The many instances of classes and each instance carry the data. This possibly web may generate large amount of date.

WHAT ARE DATA QUALITY PROBLEMS AND ITS BASIC PRINCIPLES?

Data Quality refers to the state of completeness, validity, consistency, timeliness, and accuracy which represents the real world construct. Poor data quality may lead to errors which significantly affect business success. So, data quality problems can be summarized to identify proper solutions to resolve these problems. Based on these

Problems, we derived five basic principles for data quality in the semantic web. These principles are:

A. **Heterogeneity:** Heterogeneity generally occurs when data is generated from multiple sources & scenarios. Heterogeneity can be broken down into structural heterogeneity and semantic heterogeneity. Database schema or data sets generated from the same domain but resulting in differences in meaning and interpretation of data values are known to possess semantic heterogeneity. Structural

Figure 4. Ontology Spectrum

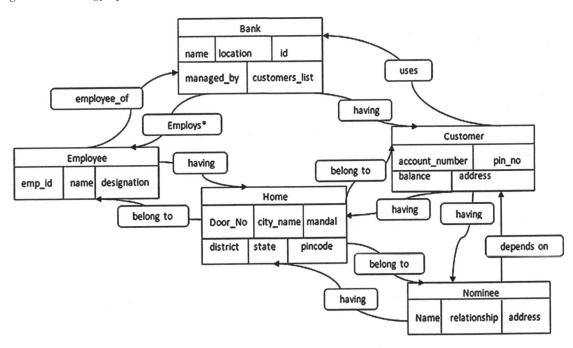

heterogeneity occurs when a different choice of modeling construct or integrity constraints is adopted. This occurs because two different schema elements are used to represent the same real world domain problem.

B. **Redundancy:** Redundancy occurs when more than one E-R diagram is used to represent the same real world domain. As a result and information for such systems is expressed more than once creating a redundancy problem. In the different representations, a few attributes of the redundant tuples will differ in meaning.

C. **Functional Dependency:** Functional dependencies can be defined as dependencies between the values of two or more different properties of controlled vocabulary. For example, we can express a functional dependency between the literal x for data type property A and the dependent literal y for the data type property B as shown below

$$A(x) \rightarrow B(y)$$
$$FD: \{y \mid y \in V_c \}$$

A functional dependency (FD) occurs when the dependent literal y obtains a value set and V_c consist of exactly one correct value or a set of correct values. The correct values of y are not available in the set V_c and there is violation in dependency known as functional dependency.

D. **Quality of semantic conversion:** Using controlled vocabulary the transformation of raw data into rich data.

E. **Comprehensibility:** Comprehensibility is a condition of data that can be correctly interpreted by other applications or users. Comprehensibility can be further divided into two types - one is ambiguity and the other, vacuity. The schema element or attribute can represent two or more meanings that are treated differently by a consumer of the data. The schema element or instances that have no meaning at all in the present context are known as vacuous.

How to Resolve Those Issues?

This is impossible to manage the huge web data even though there are many conventional tools available. There is need to invent new tools and technologies which are used to protect data and information from unauthorized access as well as malicious corruption. To provide data protection the web is characterized by interoperability as well as to ensure machine understandable web pages. This type web known to be a semantic web. The scientists accurately share data for given domain through structural relationship. The structure that defines contextual relationships on semantic web can achieved through ontology. The ontology is a hierarchical organization of knowledge domain that contains E-R schema.

Future Research Developments

1. The key properties of Internet of things are unstructured data generated from different sources, speed and streaming nature of data, fuzziness of data, and dynamic and heterogeneous in nature. These issues need to be controlled and interprets data, so an application needs to be developed using semantic technologies.

2. Meaningful combine Data Base management systems and semantic web query languages need be addressed. Need to identify real world problem where there real benefit having more expressive than SQL, SPARQL close to data.

CONCLUSION

This chapter introduces problems in the current web with three issues such as searching, integration and webmining. The mechanism to resolve these problems which results introduction of the semantic web. The semantic web features and its requirements elaborated with example. The basic components in order to develop semantic web application and principle quality of data were presented.

REFERENCES

DARPA Agent Markup Language (DAML) home page. (n. d.). Retrieved from www.daml.org/

Alesso, H.P., & Smith, C.F. (2009). Thinking on the Web: Berners-Lee, Godel and Turing. UK: John Wiley & Sons.

An introduction to ontologies. (n. d.). Semantic Web.org. Retrieved from www.SemanticWeb.org/knowmarkup.html

Artz, D., & Gil, Y. (2007). A Survey of Trust in Computer Science and the Semantic Web. *Journal of Web Semantics: Science, Services and Agents on the World Wide Web.*

Berners-Lee, T., Hendler, J., & Lassila, O. (2001, May). The Semantic Web, Scientific American. Retrieved from http://www.sciam.com

Fikes, R., P. Hayes, & I. Horrocks, (n. d.). OWL-QL - A Language for Deductive Query Answering on the Semantic Web. Stanford University, TR KS-03-14.

Fürber, C., & Hepp, M. (2005). The sociotechnical nature of mobile computing work: Evidence from a study of policing in the United States. *International Journal of Technology and Human Interaction, 1*(3), 1–14. doi:10.4018/jthi.2005070101

Hayes, P. (2004, February 10). RDF Semantics. W3C. Retrieved from http://www.w3.org/TR/rdf-mt/

Horrocks, I. (2004, April 30). SWRL: A Semantic Web Rule Language Combining OWL and Rule ML Version 0.6. Retrieved from http://www.daml.org/2004/04/swrl/rules-all.html

Yu, L. (2007). *Semantic Web and Semantic Web Services. Location/City, State*. Chapman & Hall/CRC.

Mika, P. (2007). *Social Networks and the Semantic Web*. Barcelona, Spain: Springer International.

Simple HTML Ontology Extensions Frequently Asked Questions (SHOE FAQ). (n. d.). Retrieved from www.cs.umd.edu/projects/plus/SHOE/faq.html

W3C Semantic Web Activity. (n. d.). Retrieved from www.w3.org/2001/sw/

World Wide Web Consortium (W3C). (n. d.). Retrieved from www.w3.org/

Section 2
Design Solutions for Web Usability

Chapter 6

Identification of Optimal Web Page Set based on Web Usage using Biclustering Optimization Techniques

R. Rathipriya
Periyar University, India

ABSTRACT

The primary objective of this chapter is to propose Biclustering Optimization Techniques (BOT) to identify the optimal web pages from web usage data. Bio-inspired optimization techniques like Firefly algorithm and its variant are used as optimization tool to generate optimal usage profile from the given web usage dataset. Finally, empirical study is conducted on the benchmark clickstream datasets like MSNBC, MSWEB and CTI and their results are analyzed to know the performance of the proposed biclustering optimization techniques with respect to optimization techniques available in the literature.

INTRODUCTION

The characterization of web users and their usage behaviors are the important issues in the design and maintenance of any web based recommendation systems and for targeted advertisement in the web pages. Understanding the interests and behaviors of web users serves as the base for many web usage data mining applications such as personalized search, recommendation, personalization, business decision, advertisement, targeting marketing, electronic commerce (E-commerce) and customer relationship management.

For past one decade, a lot of research is being done in the area of web usage mining based on the goals of the analyst and applications, various algorithms can be applied for cluster analysis. Very frequently, the clustering methods are used for grouping related web users of a web site, it typically partitions users according to their similar browsing behavior under all pages of a website. On the other hand, related web users do not necessarily express similar interest to every page in the website, or in other words, there are users who can be similar only for a subset of pages. On the contrary, it is also possible to discriminate

DOI: 10.4018/978-1-4666-9764-5.ch006

groups of pages by using different groups of users. From this point of view, clustering cannot only be addressed horizontally (users) or vertically (pages), but also in the two dimensions simultaneously. This approach is called biclustering, which is the one of the most popular data mining techniques that extracts browsing or usage patterns from a flood of web data by simultaneously clustering of rows(users) and columns (pages) of a web usage data. Owing to its computational complexity, it is constantly a matter of interest for machine learning researchers.

In this chapter, Biclustering Optimization Techniques(BOT) based biclustering approach is used to identify the optimal web page set of a web site from highly correlated user group over a subset of web pages (called bicluster).

RELATED WORK

More sophisticated systems and techniques for discovery and analysis of user browsing patterns are available in the literature.

All these works were concentrated in application of clustering and its variants for web usage mining in different perspective to identify the usage based clusters. These clusters may be user clusters or page clusters.

The major limitations of listed clustering above are:

1. The clustering algorithms described above are mainly manipulated on one dimension (i.e. either users or pages) of the web usage data only, rather than taking into account the correlation between web users and pages. Moreover, it is based on the assumption that all related users behave similarly across all set of pages of a website and vice versa. However, in most cases, the web clusters do often exist in the form of co-occurrence of pages and users, i.e. users from the same group are particularly interested in one subset of web pages.
2. The characteristic of the web usage data is that it is not necessary to include all the users or pages in the clusters. In fact, it may be more useful to identify a subset of pages where a subset of the users acts in a coherent manner.

The application of traditional clustering techniques for pattern (i.e. browsing pattern or usage pattern) discovery and data analysis poses significant problems. Consider a case of hundreds of web pages being viewed by the users. Typically, the pages browsed by one set of users will have a high level of mutual exclusivity when compared to pages browsed by other set of users. Discovering such similar local grouping of attributes (or pages) may be the key to uncover many interesting and useful browsing patterns that are not otherwise apparent. In-order to identify such browsing or usage patterns in terms of usage profile is possible by using biclustering of web usage data.

In Symeonidis. P et al. (2006), use biclustering approach to provide recommendation to the users based on the user and item similarity of neighborhood biclusters. Most of our pervious works were focused on the application of biclustering techniques for web usage data.

R. Rathipriya et al. (2011) introduced Binary Particle Swarm Optimization based biclustering to identify the global optimal web usage profile from the given web usage data. Similarly,

Table 1.

Author	Contribution
Cooley et al. (1997)	Introduced WEBMINER and proposed a general architecture for web usage mining (Cooley et al.1997). It's pioneer work in the web personalization.
Mobasher (1999)	The system architecture called WebPersonalizer is introduced. It has separated the offline tasks of data preparation and Web usage mining, and the online recommendation engine. Effective aggregate usage profiles are extracted from clustering of user transactions. This technique is used in this chapter.(Mobasher 1999)
Mobasheret al. (2001)	Technique for capturing common visitor profiles using association rule discovery and usage-based clustering of URLs were proposed. (Mobasheret al. (2001)
Joshi et al. (2000)	Shows how clustering can be done in case of discrepancy regarding two web sessions. A fuzzy clustering algorithm was developed in this paper that lead to the extraction of interesting user profiles. (Joshi et al. 2000)
Dai et al. (2002)	An efficient framework for Web personalization based on sequential and non-sequential pattern discovery from usage data. (Dai et al. 2002)
Mobasheret al. (2002)	Here, two techniques were evaluated experimentally, based on clustering of user transactions and clustering of page views, in order to discover overlapping aggregate profiles that can be effectively used by recommender systems for real-time Web personalization.(Mobasheret al. 2002)
Abraham (2003)	Proposed a novel approach called "intelligent-miner" that could optimize the concurrent architecture of a fuzzy clustering algorithm to discover web data clusters and a fuzzy inference system to analyze the web site visitor's trends.(Abraham 2003)
D Pierrakos et al. (2003)	Author has surveyed the work in web usage mining and focused on its application to web personalization. The survey is aimed to serve as a source of ideas for people working on the personalization of information systems, particularly those systems that are accessible over the Web.(D Pierrakos et al. 2003)
Ivancsy and Vajk (2005 a) Ivancsy and Vajk (2005 b).	An overview of using frequent pattern mining techniques for discovering different types of patterns in a web log database was presented by Ivancsy and Vajk (2005 a). The three patterns searched were: Frequent item sets, Sequences and Tree patterns, which was extended in Ivancsy and Vajk (2005 b).
Lee et al. (2008)	Author put forth a web usage mining technique based on clustering of browsing characteristics for an E-commerce application using hierarchical agglomerative clustering to cluster users' navigation patterns (Lee et al. 2008)
Zhang et al. (2009)	A web usage mining technique based on fuzzy clustering is presented in order to identify Target Group that share similar interests and behaviors by examining the data gathered in Web servers (Zhang et al. 2009).
G. Castellano et al. (2008)	Proposed a new work which has been focused on the application of major Computational Intelligent (CI) approaches to the context of web personalization. This paper emphasized the suitability of hybrid schemes deriving from the profitable combination of different CI methodologies for the development of effective Web personalization systems(G. Castellano et al. 2008).
Al Murtadha Y.M., et al. (2010)	A model has been developed using K-Means clustering approach for deriving usage profiles which followed by recommender systems to predict the next navigations profile (AlMurtadhaY.M., et al. 2010).
Tricia Rambharose et al. (2010)	The main computational intelligence methods (CI) (such as Fuzzy Systems, Genetic Algorithms, Neural Networks, Artificial Immune Systems and Swarm Intelligence which includes Particle Swarm Optimization, Ant Colony Optimization, Bee Colony Optimization and Wasp Colony Optimization) for personalization of web-based systems have been identified and reviewed critically by Authors' taxonomy for personalization of web systems based on CI methods is also proposed in this paper. It identifies two main approaches to personalize web-based systems as profile generation and profile exploitation which are further classified as either personalized navigation or personalized content. Future directions for application of CI modeling for personalization are discussed (Tricia Rambharose et al. 2010).
C.P. Sumathi et al. (2010)	Introduced a novel approach for recommendations of unvisited pages. In this work, an offline data preprocessing and clustering approach is used to determine groups of users with similar browsing patterns (C.P. Sumathi et al. 2010).
G. *Castellano et al. (2011)*	Usage-based web recommendation system is presented that exploits the potential of neuro-fuzzy computational intelligence techniques to dynamically suggest interesting pages to users according to their preferences(G. Castellano et al. 2011).
AlMurtadha et al.(2011)	Introduced a new method called iPACT, an improved recommendation system using Profile Aggregation based on Clustering of Transactions (PACT) which has better recommendation predictions accuracy than the PACT (AlMurtadha et al. 2011).
R Thiyagarajan et al. (2014)	This work focused on PSO-clustering method to extract the usage profiles from the web usage dataset. Based on these profile web page recommendations are done using hamming similarity measure(R Thiyagarajan et al. 2014).

R. Rathipriya et al. (2012) framed a new biclustering algorithm using Discrete Artificial Bees Colony algorithm to extract the optimal aggregated web usage profile from the global optimal bicluster. In the above two works, Average Correlation Value(ACV) based fitness function has been used to identify the potential bicluster.

K. Thangavel et al. (2014) presented a research work to mine correlated bicluster from the web usage dataset using Discrete Firefly Algorithm. The core part of these biclustering techniques is optimization of biclusterusing bio-inspired optimization techniques like Genetic Algorithm, Binary Particle Swarm Optimization and Discrete Artificial Bees Colony Optimization. The primary goal of these Biclustering Optimization Techniques (BOT) is to extract the optimal bicluster.

METHODOLOGY

The proposed methodology consists of following steps:

1. Preprocessing of Web log data or Generation of User Access Matrix.
2. Application of Biclustering Optimization Technique.
3. Generation of Usage Profile from the extracted biclusters.

This study used the biclusters produced by the biclustering step to build the usage profile with one profile for each bicluster. The usage profile is known as navigational profile or aggregated web usage profile. This navigation profile contains set of web pages and weights values. To summarize, construct a navigation profile as a set of web page-weight pairs:

profile = { p, weight(p) | p $\in$ P, weight(p) $\geq$ min_weight }.

where P ={p_1, p_2, . . ., p_n}, a set of n web page appearing in the log file with each web page uniquely represented by its associated URL and the weight(p) is the (mean) value of the attribute's value in the bicluster. This navigation profile consists of set of web pages based on their weights.

The primary objective of this chapter is to propose Biclustering Optimization Techniques (BOT) to identify the optimal web pages from web usage data. Bio-inspired optimization technique like Firefly algorithm and its variant are used as optimization tool to generate optimal usage profile from the given dataset. Finally, empirical study is planned to conduct on the benchmark clickstream data and the results is analyzed to know the performance of the proposed biclustering optimization techniques with respect to techniques available in the literature.

Brief Description of Firefly Optimization Algorithm

Firefly algorithm, developed by Xin-She Yang, is inspired by the light attenuation over the distance and fireflies' mutual attraction, rather than by the phenomenon of the fireflies' light flashing. Algorithm considers what each firefly observes at the point of its position, when trying to move to a greater light-source, than his own. The firefly meta-heuristic relies on a set of artificial fireflies which communicate with each other to solve optimization problems. The behavior of artificial fireflies is modeled according to the behavior of fireflies in nature, which searches for a mating partner by emitting a flashing light.

Firefly Optimization Algorithm

The Firefly Optimization algorithm is based on idealized behavior of the flashing characteristics of fireflies. For simplicity, summarize these flashing characteristics as the following three rules:

1. All fireflies are unisex, so that one firefly is attracted to other fireflies regardless of their sex.
2. Attractiveness is proportional to their brightness, thus for any two flashing fireflies, the less bright one will move towards the brighter one. The attractiveness is proportional to the brightness and they both decrease as their distance increases. If no one is brighter than a particular firefly, it moves randomly.
3. The brightness of a firefly is affected or determined by the landscape of the objective function to be optimized. For a maximization problem, the brightness can simply be proportional to the value of the objective function.

Based on these three rules, the basic steps of the firefly algorithm (FA) can be summarized as the pseudo code shown in algorithm 1. In this chapter, the behavior of fireflies is used to formulate the Biclustering Optimization algorithm for the identification of optimal web page set from the web log file.

Discrete Firefly Optimization Based Biclustering (DFOB) Algorithm

This section presents mapping the concepts of the firefly meta-heuristic to the problem of biclustering. Just as the real fireflies search for a mating partner by means of flashing lights, have a number of artificial fireflies which search for the optimal bicluster solution. Thus, map the attraction behavior of fireflies to the problem of selecting the optimal bicluster as follows:

1. a firefly becomes an artificial firefly
2. the position of a firefly becomes a bicluster solution
3. the brightness of a firefly becomes the quality of a bicluster solution evaluated with a fitness function
4. the attractiveness between two fireflies becomes the hamming distance between two biclusters
5. the movement of a firefly is mapped to a modification of the firefly's current position (i.e. bicluster)

Initial Population

Each bicluster is encoded as a binary string as shown in Figure 1. The length of the string is the number of users plus the number of pages of the user access matrix A (U, P). A bit is set to one when the corresponding user or page is included in the bicluster. These binary encoded biclusters are used as initial population for Firefly algorithm.

Figure 1. A Binary Encoded Bicluster

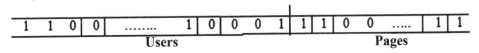

1	1	0	0	....	1	0	0	0	1	1	1	0	0	.....	1	1
			Users										**Pages**			

Directed Movement

In standard Firefly Optimization algorithm, firefly movement is based on light intensity and comparing it between each two fireflies. Thus for any two fireflies, the less bright one will move towards the brighter one. In Discrete Firefly algorithm, the movement is caused by the use of genetic crossover operator, and that is given as follows.

r = Hamming similarity (x_i, x_j)

x_i = crossover(x_i, x_j, r)

where function Hamming similarity(.) gives similarity between two fireflies x_i, x_j and r is used as crossover probability rate. But firefly x_{inew} position causes better cost, it will move to that new position. New firefly algorithm can be summarized as the pseudocode is shown in algorithm 1. This strategy makes a social behavior for all fireflies and they move towards global best.

Crossover Operator

The basic operator for producing new solutions in the GA is that of crossover. Like its counterpart in nature, crossover produces new individuals that have some parts of both parent's genetic material. In this study, Multi-point Crossover operator is used to move firefly towards brighter fly.

For multi-point crossover, mp crossover positions mp = $\{l_1, l_2, ..., l_{mp}\}$ are selected randomly and l is the length of the binary string. The bits between successive crossover points are exchanged between the two strings to produce two new offspring.

The idea behind multi-point, and indeed many of the variations on the crossover operator, is that the parts of the binary string representation that contribute to the most to the performance of a particular

Table 2.

Algorithm 1: Discrete Firefly Optimization based Biclustering algorithm
Input: N, number of fireflies,
Output: optimal bicluster
Step 3 Initialize the binary encoded biclusters as initial fireflies
X= {x₁, x₂, ..., xₙ).
Step 4 Do
for i = 1: N
for j =1: i
if fitness (xᵢ) < fitness (xⱼ) then
r= Compute_Distance(xᵢ, xⱼ)
xprob= r / number of bits in xᵢ
xᵢ= Crossover(xᵢ, xⱼ, xprob)
end if
end for
end for
until (Stopping_Condition())
Step 3 Return optimal bicluster

individual may not necessarily be contained in adjacent substrings. Further, the disruptive nature of multi-point crossover appears to encourage the exploration of the search space, rather than favoring the convergence to highly fit individuals (biclusters) early in the search, thus making the search more robust.

Description of Proposed DFOB Model

In the first step of the proposed algorithm, each firefly is associated with a generated bicluster solution. These initial solutions are further improved in an iterative process which stops when the best solution has been the same over the last iterations (Stopping Condition).

In each iteration, if the fitness of the solution associated to a firefly is better than the fitness of the solution associated to another firefly it means that the latter firefly will be attracted towards the first one and thus it will have its solution improved.

Hybrid Firefly Algorithm

Though Firefly algorithm is efficient, its parameters do not change during iterations, which result in stagnation of fireflies. To avoid this limitation, a hybrid model (algorithm 2) is proposed to improve the FA algorithm by combining Simulated Annealing algorithm (SA) to enlarge the search space and generate new solutions. It extracts the global optimal bicluster from web usage dataset at faster rate of convergence without sticking at local optima.

The detailed description of Simulated Annealing is given inK Bryan et al. 2005. SA has better scope of escaping local optima and reaches a global optimum in the search space. Thus introduction of SA into Firefly algorithm maintains a good balance between exploration and exploitation thus eliminating the problem of local optimum stagnation.

EXPERIMENTAL ANALYSIS

The performance of the proposed Firefly Optimization based Biclustering model and its hybrid model is tested on web usage datasets namely CTI, MSNBC and MSWEB.

CTI Dataset Description

The CTI dataset is taken from a University website log and was made available by the authors Mobasher2002, and Zhang et al..2009. The data is based on a random collection of users visiting university site for a 2-week period during the month of April 2002. After data preprocessing, the filtered data consist of 13745 sessions and 683 pages. Further preprocessed CTIdataset where the root pages are considered in the pageview of a session. This preprocessing step resulted in total of 16 categories namely, search, programs, news, admissions, advising, courses, people, research, resources, authenticate, cti, pdf, calendar, shared, forums, and hyperlink. These page views were given numeric labels as 1 for search, 2 for programs and so on. Each row of CTI web navigation data describes the hits of a single user. The session length in the dataset ranges from 2 to 68. Since comparing very long sessions with small sessions would not be meaningful, sessions of length between 3 and 7 only considered for this study. Finally, 5915 user sessions are taken for the experimentation.

Table 3.

Algorithm 2: Hybrid Discrete Firefly Optimization based Biclustering algorithm

Inputs: A, web access matrix, N, number of fireflies, T, T_{min}, α
Output: Optimal bicluster
  Step 4 Initialize the binary encoded biclusters as initial fireflies
    $X= \{x_1, x_2, ..., x_n\}$.
  Step 5 Do
    for i = 1: N
    for j =1: i
    if fitness (x_i) < fitness (x_j) then
                d. r= Compute_Distance(x_i, x_j)
                e. xprob = r /number of bits in x_i
                f. x_i= Crossover$(x_i, x_j, xprob)$
  end if
  end for
  end for
  current solution = X // SA Process
  current cost = fitness(X)
  while (T >T_{min}) do
  Neighbour = Generate_Random Vector (X) //Pick some neighbour
  Neighbour cost= Fitness (Neighbour)
  if Accept(current cost, Neighbour cost, T) then
                c. current solution = Neighbour
                d. current cost = Neighbour cost
  end
 	
  $T = \dfrac{T}{1+\alpha}$ // Reduce Temperature
  End (while)
  until (Stopping_Condition())
    Step 6 Return optimal bicluster

MSWEB Dataset Description

The *MSWEB* dataset is taken from the UCI KDD archive and records the logs within Microsoft website that users visited in one-week time frame during February 1998. Two separate data sets are provided, a training set and a test set. After data preprocessing, the filtered data consist of 32711 sessions and 285 pages. Further preprocessed MSWEB dataset where the root pages were considered in the pageview of a session. This preprocessing step resulted in total of 20 categories namely "library", "developer", "home", "finance", "repository", "gallery", "catalog", "mail", "ads", "education", "magazine", "support", "ms", "technology", "search", "country", "business", "entertainment", "news", "feedback".

MSNBC Dataset Description

The MSNBC data set from the UCI dataset repository that consists of Internet Information Server (IIS) logs for msnbc.com and news- related portions of msn.com for the entire day of September 28, 1999 (Pacific Standard Time).

Each sequence in the dataset corresponds to page views of a user during that twenty-four hour period. Each event in the sequence corresponds to a user's request for a page. Requests are not recorded at the finest level of detail but they are recorded at the level of page categories as determined by the site admin-

Figure 2. Flowchart for Hybrid Firefly Optimization based Biclustering Model

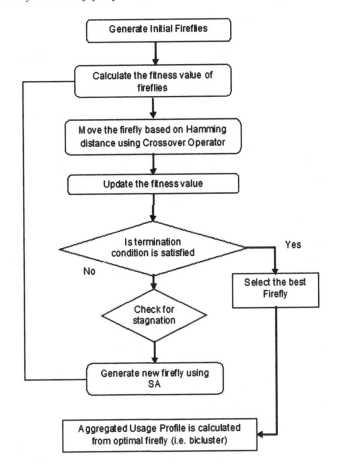

istrator. It consists of 17 pageview categories, namely, "front page", " news", "tech", "local", "opinion", "on-air", "misc", "weather", "health", "living", "business", "sports", "summary", "bbs" (bulletin board service), "travel", "msn-news", and "msnsports."

Each page category is represented by integer label. For example, "frontpage" is coded as 1, "news" as 2, "tech" as 3, etc. Each row describes the hits of a single user. For example, the fourth user hits "frontpage" twice, and the second user hits "news" once and so on. In the total dataset, the length of user sessions ranges from 1 to 500 and the average length of session is 5.7.

Result Discussion

The main characteristic feature of the firefly algorithm is the fact that it simulates a parallel independent run strategy, wherein every iteration, a swarm of n fireflies is generated from n solutions. Each firefly works almost independently, and as a result the algorithm, will converge very quickly with the fireflies aggregating closely to the optimal solution. Table 4 tabulates the characteristic of the optimal bicluster extracted from three datasets using Discrete Firefly Optimization Biclustering model. In which, Two-Way K-Means Clustering is used to generate the initial population.

Table 4. Performance of DFOB with Two-Way K-Means Clustering

	CTI	MSWEB	MSNBC
Volume	1926	1778	1840
ACV	0.9528	0.9521	0.9413
No. of Users	642	254	184
No. of Pages	3	7	10

The Performance of DFOB with Greedy Biclustering model is tabulated in the Table 5. It is evident from the values of ACV of the optimal bicluster in the second row that DFOB with Greedy Biclustering model extracts the larger volume bicluster with high correlation degree.

Though DFOB is efficient, its parameters do not change during iterations, which is also true for particle swarm optimization.Therefore, a hybrid DFOB model is proposed to improve the FA algorithm by introducing Simulated Annealing to adjust firefly behavior, and to enhance global search and generate new solutions. The performances of Hybrid Discrete Firefly Optimization Biclustering model with the initial populations using Two-Way K-Means clustering and Greedy Biclustering are tabulated in Tables 6 and 7 respectively.

In hybrid biclustering model, stagnated fireflies are enhanced using SA which results in high volume biclustering with high ACV than standard DFOB model. In Figures 3, 4, 5, 6 and 7, X-axis represents the pageview categories in the optimal bicluster extracted from each dataset viz., CTI, MSWEB and MSNBC. Y-axis represents the hit count value of each pageview category in the bicluster.

Figures 3 and 4 show the optimal usage pattern of the global optimal bicluster extracted from the CTI dataset using Discrete Firefly Optimization and Hybrid Discrete Firefly Optimization based biclustering models. It has been observed that, these two usage patterns are entirely different but their ACV values are high. In Figure 3, pageview categories such as Programs, News and Miscellaneous are visited fre-

Table 5. Performance of DFOB with Greedy Biclustering

	CTI	MSWEB	MSNBC
Volume	2576	8272	7065
ACV	0.9828	0.9892	0.9852
No. of Users	544	752	785
No. of Pages	4	11	9

Table 6. Performance of Hybrid DFOB with Two-Way K-Means Clustering

	CTI	MSWEB	MSNBC
Volume	1923	3296	3840
ACV	0.9529	0.9473	0.9535
No. of Users	641	412	884
No. of Pages	3	8	10

Table 7. Performance of Hybrid DFOB and Greedy Biclustering

	CTI	MSWEB	MSNBC
Volume	3606	11680	9540
ACV	0.9872	0.9903	0.9901
No. of Users	601	1168	954
No. of Pages	6	10	10

Figure 3. Usage Pattern of Optimal Bicluster for CTI Dataset using DFOB

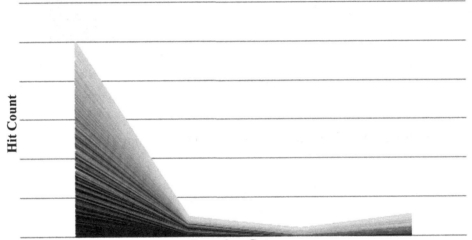

quently by the users in the optimal bicluster. Pageview categories such as Programs, News, Course and Miscellaneous are liked by the most of the users in the bicluster extracted using Hybrid DFOB and it constitutes the browsing pattern as shown in Figure 4.

Figures 5 and 6 show the usage pattern of the optimal bicluster extracted from the MSWEB dataset using DFOB and Hybrid DFOB models. It is evident from the figures 5 and 6 that, Hybrid DFOB extracts the high volume and High ACV optimal bicluster without trapping at local optimal.

The usage patterns of the optimal bicluster extracted from the MSNBC dataset using DFOB and Hybrid DFOB models are shown in Figures 7 and 8 respectively. From the figure 6, it is known that users are tightly correlated and their hit count value fluctuated highly. It has been seen that, hybrid DFOB extracts the optimal bicluster with high degree of correlation among the users and number of the users in it also high.

The performance of the Discrete Firefly Optimization based biclustering model is compared with other meta-heuristic approaches such as BPSO and DABC based biclustering models.ACV and Volume of the optimal biclusters are extracted by the biclustering models using standard meta-heuristic techniques such as BPSO(R. Rathipriya et al. 2011), DABC(R. Rathipriya et al. 2012) and DFOB (K. Thangavel et al. 2014)). Their performances are compared and represented graphically in Figures 9 and 10 respec-

Figure 4. Usage Pattern of Optimal Bicluster for CTI Dataset using Hybrid DFOB

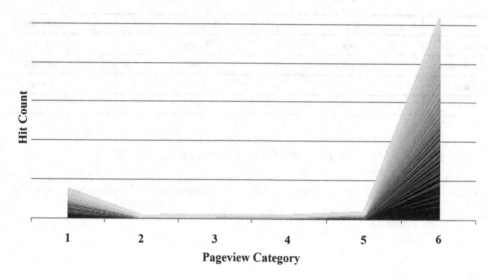

Figure 5. Usage Pattern of Optimal Bicluster for MSWEB Dataset using DFOB

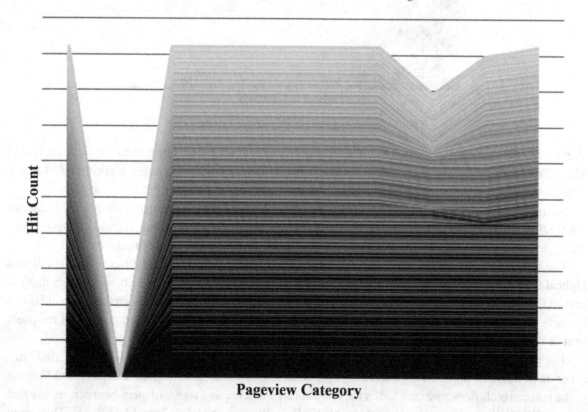

Figure 6. Usage Pattern of Optimal Bicluster for MSWEB Dataset using Hybrid DFOB

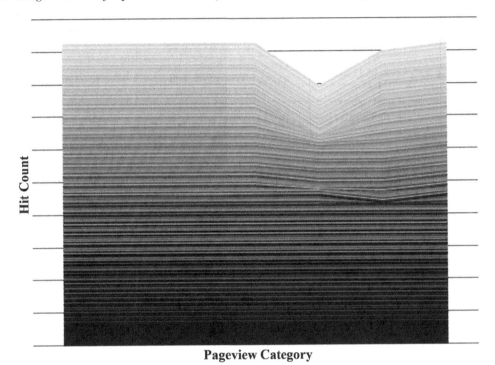

Figure 7. Usage Pattern of Optimal Bicluster for MSNBC Dataset using DFOB

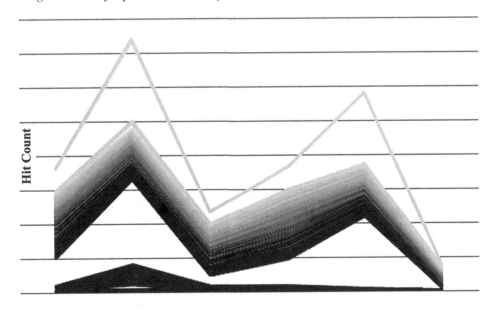

Table 8. List of Aggregated Usage Profile using DFOB Model

	Pageview Index	Weights	Aggregated Usage Profile
CTI	2, 3, 4, 10	0.9969, 0.7282, 0.827, 0.446	2, 3, 4
MSWEB	1, 2, 3, 5, 7, 10, 11, 12, 13, 14, 15	1.0000, 0.0196, 0.9022, 1.0000, 0.1397, 1.0000, 0.1098, 1.0000, 1.0000, 1.0000, 1.0000	1, 3, 5, 10, 12, 13, 14, 15
MSNBC	2, 3, 5, 6, 10, 11, 12, 14, 17	0.9560, 0.7240, 0.5400, 0.7880, 0.7440, 0.7880, 0.7920, 0.6200 0.3120	2, 3, 5, 6, 10, 11, 12, 14

Figure 8. Usage Pattern of Optimal Bicluster for MSNBC Dataset using Hybrid DFOB

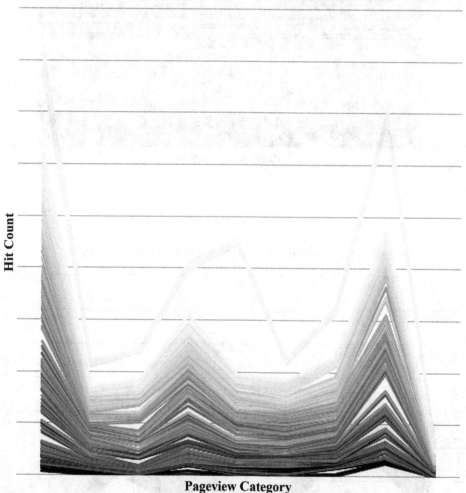

tively. It is observed that from Figure 9, Discrete Firefly Optimization based biclustering model extracts the bicluster with high correlation degree for the datasets CTI and MSWEB. BPSO based biclustering model extracts highly correlated bicluster in the MSNBC dataset. But, high volume bicluster is extracted by DABC based biclustering model for the datasets MSWEB and MSNBC and BPOS for CTI dataset.

Table 9. List of Aggregated Usage Profile using Hybrid DFOB Model

	Pageview Index	Weights	Aggregated Usage Profile
CTI	3, 5, 6, 7, 8, 9	0.9969, 0.8282, 0.427, 0.6446, 0.1322, 1.0000	3, 5, 7, 9
MSWEB	1, 2, 3, 5, 6, 10, 12, 13, 14, 15	1.0000, 0.514, 0.4003, 1.0000, 0.5325, 0.6201, 1.0000, 0.9990, 0.9927, 1.000	1, 2, 5, 6, 10, 12, 13, 14, 15
MSNBC	2, 3, 5, 6, 10, 11, 12, 14, 16, 17	0.9094, 0.7106, 0.5709, 0.8031, 0.6772, 0.7461, 0.7283, 0.6388, 0.2934, 0.5921	2, 3, 5, 6, 10, 11, 12, 14, 17

Figure 9. ACV based Comparison of Standard Meta-Heuristic techniques

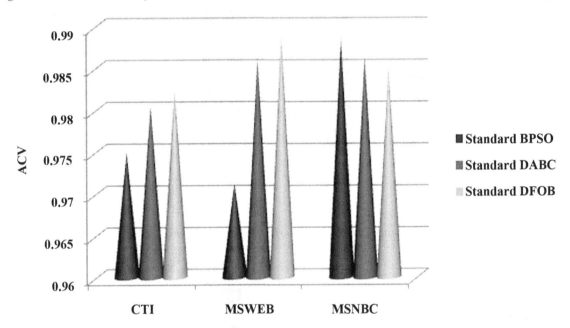

ACV and Volume of the optimal biclusters are extracted by the biclustering models using hybrid meta-heuristic techniques such as hybrid BPSO, hybrid DABC and hybrid DFOB are compared and represented graphically in Figures 10 and 11 respectively. From these figures, it is observed that Hybrid BPSO based biclustering model extracts the highly correlated bicluster with high volume. Hybrid DABC extracts high volume biclusters for MSNBC and MSWEB datasets and hybrid BPSO for CTI dataset. But, hybrid Discrete Firefly Optimization based biclustering does not show compete performance.

The average number of iterations required for convergence of optimal bicluster for each dataset is shown graphically in Figures 12 and 13. It shows that the performance of the presented discrete firefly is suitable and can reach to good-quality solutions within a less (reasonable) computational time than the other two meta-heuristic based biclustering model. Fast convergence of the optimal bicluster is achieved in Discrete Firefly optimization based biclustering model.

Figure 10. Volume based Comparison of Standard Meta-Heuristic techniques

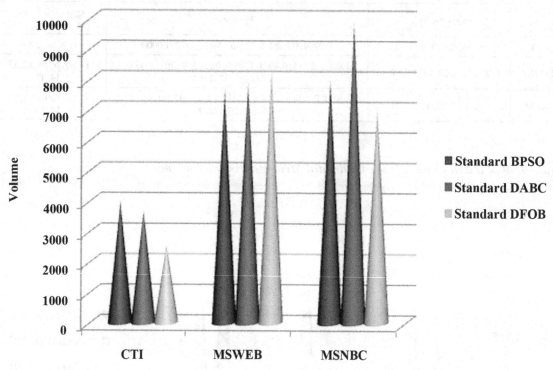

Figure 11. ACV based Comparison of Hybrid Meta-Heuristic techniques

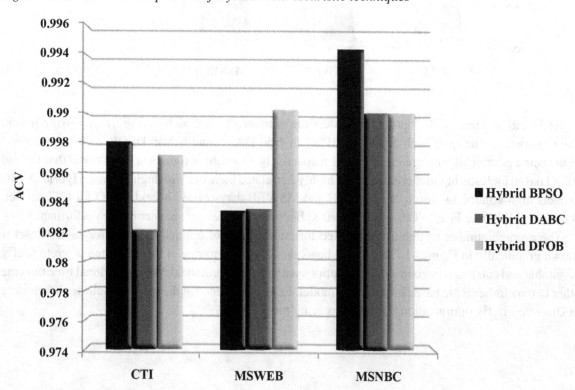

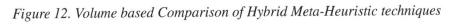

Figure 12. Volume based Comparison of Hybrid Meta-Heuristic techniques

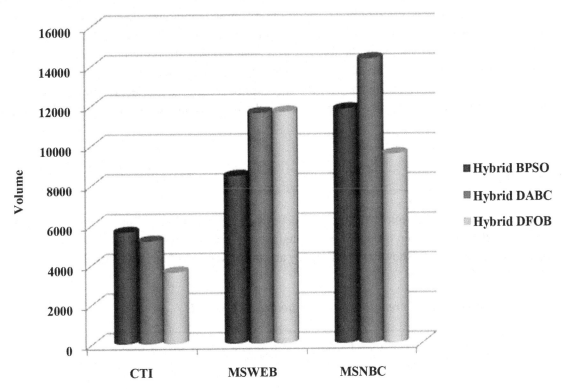

Figure 13. Convergence rate of Standard Meta-Heuristic Techniques

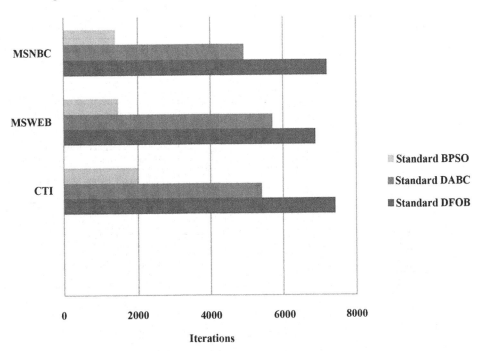

Table 10 summarizes the ACV, volume and optimal web page set for the optimal bicluster extracted from the three dataset using different bio-inspired optimization techniques. The Pageview Categories (i.e. web page) in the Optimal Browsing Patternfor the different datasets are tabulated. Optimal Browsing Pattern is collection of web pages (in the form of web page set) that are visited frequently by the huge set ofweb users of that web site. The main objective of optimization is to achieve larger size user group that shows correlated browsing behavior over the subset of pageview categories. Hence, it is concluded that in most case HDABC performs well in extracting the large volume (size) bicluster with high correlation degree.

SUMMARY

In this chapter, a new application of the recently developed Discrete Firefly Optimization algorithm to the web usage dataset has been proposed, presented, and tested. The results of the implementation of this proposed models clearly showed the efficiency and effectiveness of the DFOB model for extracting

Table 10. Performance of Different Bio-inspired Biclustering Models

Dataset	Optimization Algorithm	ACV of Optimal Bicluster	Volume of Optimal Bicluster	Pageview Categories in the Optimal Browsing Pattern
CTI	GA	0.981	2074	Search, Programs, People, Miscellaneous
	HBPSO	0.9881	5640	News, Advising, Courses, People, Authenticate, CTI
	HDABC	0.9882	6096	Programs, Admissions, People, Miscellaneous
	HDFOB	0.9872	3606	News, Advising, People, CTI
MSWEB	GA	0.9924	5154	Developer, finance, gallery, mail, ads, support, ms, technology, Country, Business
	HBPSO	0.9834	8452	Developer, gallery, ads, support, ms, technology, Search, Country, Business
	HDABC	0.9835	11619	Developer, Home, Respository, Mail, Support, ms, Technology, Business
	HDFOB	0.9903	11680	Developer, Home, Respository, Gallery, Mail, Support, Technology, Search, Country, Business
MSNBC	GA	0.9709	11715	Tech, on-air, living, business, sports, BBS, msn-sports
	HBPSO	0.9944	11818	News, Tech, Opinion, on-air, Living, Business, sports, BBS, Msnsports
	HDABC	0.9901	14336	News, Tech, Living, Business, sports, BBS
	HDFOB	0.991	9540	News, Tech, Opinion, on-air, Living, Business, sports, BBS

Figure 14. Convergence rate of Hybrid Meta-Heuristic Techniques

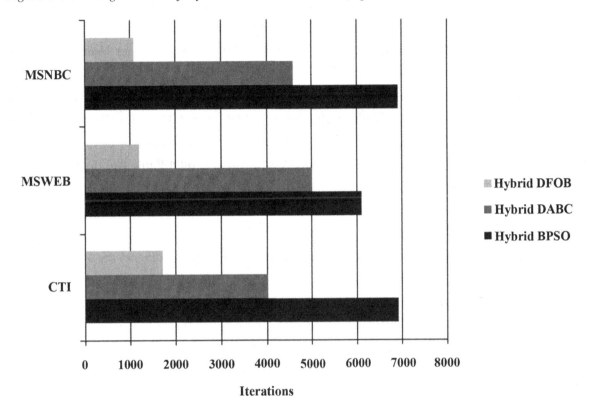

the larger volume bicluster with high correlation degree. Discrete Firefly algorithm is powerful in local search but sometimes it may trap into several local optimums as result it cannot search globally well. To overcome this problem, hybrid Discrete Firefly Optimization algorithm is used to extract the global optimal bicluster. Navigation profile orAggregated usage profile is calculated from the optimal bicluster. This identified usage profile is the optimal web page set for the web site.

REFERENCES

Abraham, A. (2003). Business Intelligence from Web Usage Mining. *Journal of Information & Knowledge Management, 2*(4), 375–390. doi:10.1142/S0219649203000565

Al Murtadha, Y. M., Sulaiman, M. N. B., Mustapha, N., & Udzir, N. I. (2010). Mining Web Navigation Profiles for Recommendation System. *Information Technology Journal, 9*, 790–796.

AlMurtadha, Y., Sulaiman, M. N. B., Mustapha, N., & Udzir, N. I. (2011). Ipact: Improved Web Page Recommendation System using Profile Aggregation Based on Clustering of Transactions. *American Journal of Applied Sciences*, 277–283.

Castellano, G., Fanelli, A. M., & Torsello, M. A. (2008). Computational Intelligence techniques for Web personalization. *Web Intelligent and Agent Systems, 6*(3), 253–272.

Castellano, G., Fanelli, A. M., & Torsello, M. A. (2011). NEWER: A system for Neuro-fuzzy Web Recommendation. *Applied Soft Computing, 11*(1), 793–806.

Cooley, R., Mobasher. B., & Srivatsava, J. (1997). Web Mining: Information and Pattern Discovery on the World Wide Web. *Proceedings of the 9th IEEE International Conference on Tools with Artificial Intelligence*, Newport Beach, CA, (pp. 558-567).

Iváncsy, R., & Vajk, I. (2005). Efficient Sequential Pattern Mining Algorithms. *WSEAS Transactions on Computers, 4*(2), 96–101.

Iváncsy, R., & Vajk, I. (2005). PD-Tree: A New Approach to Subtree Discovery. *WSEAS Transactions on Information Science and Applications, 2*(11), 1772–1779.

Joshi, A., & Krishnapuram, R. (2000). On Mining Web Access Logs. *Proceedings of the ACM SIGMOD* (pp. 63-69).

Lee, H. C., & Fu, H. Y. (2008). Web Usage Mining Based on Clustering of Browsing Features. *Proceedings of Eighth International Conference on Intelligent Systems Design and Applications* (Vol. 1, pp. 281-286). doi:10.1109/ISDA.2008.185

Mobasher, B., Cooley, R., & Srivastava, J. (1999). Creating Adaptive Web Sites Through Usage Based Clustering of URLs. *KDEX, 99*, 32–37.

Mobasher, B., Dai, H., Luo,T. and Nakagawa, M. (2001). Elective Personalization Based on Association Rule Discovery from Web Usage Data. *Proceedings of WIDM01*, Atlanta, (pp. 9-15).

Mobasher, B., Dai, H., Luo, T., & Nakagawa, M. (2002). Discovery and Evaluation of Aggregate Usage Profiles for Web Personalization. *Data Mining and Knowledge Discovery, 6*(1), 61–82. doi:10.1023/A:1013232803866

Pierrakos, D., Paliouras, G., Papatheodorou, C., & Spyropoulos, C. D. (2003). Web Usage Mining as a Tool for Personalization: A Survey. *User Modeling and User-Adapted Interaction, 13*(4), 311–372. doi:10.1023/A:1026238916441

Rambharose, T., & Nikov, A. (2010). Computational Intelligence-Based Personalization of Interactive Web Systems. *WSEAS Transactions on Information Science and Applications, 7*, 484–497.

Rathipriya, R., Thangavel, K., & Bagyamani, J. (2011). Binary Particle Swarm Optimization based Biclustering of Web usage Data. *International Journal of Computers and Applications, 25*(2).

Sumathi, C. P., Padmaja Valli, R., & Santhanam, T. (2010). Automatic Recommendation of Web Pages in Web Usage Mining. *International Journal on Computer Science and Engineering, 2*(9), 3046–3052.

Symeonidis, P., Nanopoulos, A., Papadopoulos, A. N., & Manolopoulos, Y. (2008). Nearest-Biclusters Collaborative Filtering Based on Constant and Coherent Values. [Kluwer Academic Publishers.]. *Information Retrieval*, 51–75.

Thangavel, K., & Rathipriya, R. (2012). A Discrete Artificial Bees Colony Inspired Biclustering Algorithm. *International Journal of Swarm Intelligence Research*, *3*(1), 30–42.

Thangavel, K., & Rathipriya, R. (2014). Mining Correlated Bicluster from Web Usage Data Using Discrete Firefly Algorithm Based Biclustering Approach. *International Journal of Mathematical, Computational, Natural and Physical Engineering, World Academy of Science. Engineering and Technology*, *8*(4), 705–709.

Thiyagarajan, R., Thangavel, K., & Rathipriya, R. (2014). Web Page Recommendation of Usage Profile Using Particle Swarm Optimization based Clustering. *International Journal of Applied Engineering Research*, *9*(23), 22641–22654.

Zhang, J., Zhao, P., Shang, L., & Wang, L. (2009). Web Usage Mining Based On Fuzzy Clustering in Identifying Target Group. *Proceedings of the International Colloquium on Computing, Communication, Control, and Management*, *4*, 209–212.

KEY TERMS AND DEFINITIONS

Biclustering: It is defined as the simultaneous clustering of rows and columns of the two- dimensional dataset.

Bio-Inspired Optimization Techniques: Optimization Techniques are designed based on inspiration from the biological systems or nature.

Clickstream Data: Clickstream data is a natural byproduct of a user accessing web pages, and refers to the sequence of pages visited and the time these pages were viewed.

Web Usage Dataset: A collection of web usage details in the form web log is called Web Usage Dataset.

Web Usage Profile: Web user profile or web usage model is the generalization of the collected data about the user behavior from web usage data.

Chapter 7
An Empirical study of Usability Metric for Websites

Sukhpuneet Kaur
Punjab Technical University, India

Hardeep Singh
Guru Nanak Dev University, India

Kulwant Kaur
Punjab Technical University, India

Parminder Kaur
Guru Nanak Dev University, India

ABSTRACT

A Concern is any important property or area of interest of a system that can treat in a modular way. One of the most important Concerns is Usability which is considered one of the key principles in Software Engineering. The importance of Usability Evaluation has dramatically increased due to extremely fast growth in Internet technology. The website design is directly related to the purpose of the website. Website with poor usability can easily destroy the purpose of website. So, the authors have chosen one of the concern "usability" which is the core component of web applications. The purpose of this chapter is to analysis and proposes an appropriate web usability metric for evaluation of universities website. The proposed method will be based partly on a literature study and partly on the survey analysis response by visitors.

1. INTRODUCTION

The term *separation of concerns* was probably coined by Edsger W. Dijkstra in 1982. Separation of Concerns (SoC) refers to the ability to identify, encapsulate and manipulate the software parts relevant to a particular concern. It has emerged as one of the important principles in Software Engineering. Separation of Concerns (SoC) is the principle for better control of software complexity, during development, maintenance and reuse. The main goal of SoC is the ability to deal with a concern (aspect) separately, during maintenance. A good SoC policy is useful to increase software quality and decrease the effort to test, maintain, understand, reuse and document software. For example, in object-oriented paradigm the separated concerns are modeled as objects and classes and in structural paradigm, concerns are represented as procedures(ISO 9241,1998). One of the most important concerns used in web applications is Usability.

DOI: 10.4018/978-1-4666-9764-5.ch007

1.1 Usability

1.1.1 Definitions

Usability is a quantitative and qualitative measurement of the design of a user interface, grouped into five key factors: learnability, efficiency, memorability, errors, and satisfaction. Usability measures of effectiveness, efficiency and satisfaction can be specified for overall goals. Basically Usability is a quality attribute of software that evaluates how easy user interfaces are to use. Usability also refers to the ease of use for a particular software application. Means how easily users can use the software to carry out their required task. The various definitions of Usability are as follows: ——

- "The capability of the software product to be understood learned, used and attractive to the user, when used under specified conditions." (ISO/IEC 9126-1, 2000) (Marchetto, 2005).
- "The extent to which a product can be used by specified users to achieve specified goals with effectiveness, efficiency and satisfaction in a specified context of use." (ISO9241-11, 1998) (ISO 9241, 1998).
- "The ease with which a user can learn to operate, prepares inputs for, and interprets outputs of a system or component." (IEEE Std.610.12-1990) (IEEE std. 1061, 1998).

Usability consists of five kinds of attributes (Nielsen J. & V.Philips,1993):

- **Learnability:** User should be able to start the work in first go which means that the software should be easily learnable.
- **Efficiency:** The software should be efficient to use, the user should be able to understand the software fully and thereafter the yield will be high.
- **Memorability:** Software should be easy to remember so that the user should be able to use the software even after some period of time.
- **Errors:** The software should have low error rate due to which the users will not be able to make errors while using the software.
- **Satisfaction:** The software should be easy and pleasant to use.

Examples of appropriate measures are given below in Table 1:

Web usability is a core component of web quality. Without good usability features the web quality will always be a question mark.

Likewise, McLaughin and Skinner break usability down into six related but distinct components (McLaughin, J., & Skinner, D., 2000):

Table 1.

Usability Objective	Effectiveness Measures	Efficiency Measures	Satisfaction Measures
Overall usability	Percentage of goals achieved; Percentage of users successfully completing task; Average accuracy of completed tasks	Time to complete a task Tasks completed per unit time	Rating scale for satisfaction Frequency of complaints

- **Checkability:** The system has or allows checks that ensure the correct information is going in and going out of it.
- **Confidence:** Users have confidence both in their capability to use the system and in the system itself.
- **Control:** Users have control over the operation of the system, particularly of the information fed into and out of the system.
- **Ease of Use:** The system is easy to use.
- **Speed:** The system can be used quickly.
- **Understanding:** The system and its outputs are understandable.

In general then, usability is potentially complex and wide ranging, but clearly "user-centered." In evaluating usability, it may be possible to measure each of these components separately or in combination using some form of metric or measure.

1.1.2 Importance of Usability

As Nielsen states, "Usability rules the Web. Simply stated, if the customer can't find a product, then he or she will not buy it" (Nielsen, J., 2000). In this sense, usability is an extremely important aspect of individual Web page and overall Web site design, particularly for the business-oriented Web site. In discussing e-commerce Web sites, Shacklett asserts that, "Twenty-eight percent of Web site transactions result in consumer failure and frustration. Six percent of users who leave a Web site in frustration say they won't return to the site or patronize the company" (Shackel, 2009). If usability is left unconsidered, then a business is likely to lose customers and miss out on profit opportunities-negatively impacting the cornerstones of any successful business. Similar in case with academic websites in which students seek information regarding admission process in various courses. The university websites also aims to facilitate their prospective students and scholars by providing the proper guidelines on the website to help them accordingly. A university website should serve the non-commercial information that is need of its current students and faculty. Information like the complexities of curriculum choices and the information about the daily events and procedures that happens within a University. Therefore, *usability*, is considered the key credentials of effective website design.

So from user's perspective, usability is important because it can make the difference between performing a task accurately and completely or not, and enjoying the process or being frustrated. From the developer's perspective, usability is important because it can mean the difference between the success or failure of a system. From a management point of view, software with poor usability can reduce the productivity of the workforce to a level of performance worse than without the system. In all cases, lack of usability can cost time and effort and can greatly determine the success or failure of a system.

1.1.3 User-Centered Design

User-centered design process (UCD) is also called Human-Centered Design process. User-Centered Design (UCD) is the process of designing a tool, such as a website's or application's user interface, from the perspective of how it will be understood and used by human user. In UCD, all "development proceeds with the user as the center of focus". Human centered design processes for interactive systems, ISO 13407 (1999), states: "Human-centered design is an approach to interactive system development that focuses specifically on making system usable. It is multi-disciplinary activity". Usability is one of the focuses of the field of Human-Computer Interaction. As the name suggests, usability has to do with bridging the gap between people and machines (Preece, 2007).

The Principles of UCD are as follows:

1. Early focus on users and tasks
   a. Structured and systematic information gathering (consistent across the board)
   b. Designers trained by experts before conducting data collection sessions
2. Empirical measurement and testing of product usage
   a. Focus on ease of learning and ease of use
   b. Testing of prototypes with actual users
3. Iterative Design
   a. Product designed, modified and tested repeatedly.
   b. Allow for the complete overhaul and rethinking of design by early testing of conceptual models and design ideas.

1.2 Dimensions of Usability

Usability of a product is normally demonstrated through interfaces. To ensure software products could meet this quality, a number of usability guidelines and standards have been introduced. These are the generic rules to guide the design and implementation for web applications. The various dimensions of usability (Nielsen J. & V. Philips.,1993) are:

- Ease Of Use
- User Friendly
- Efficiency
- Effective Satisfying
- Memorable Pleasure
- Accessible
- Learnability
- Findability
- Quality
- Usefulness
- Error rate
- Adaptability
- Acceptability
- Consistency
- Flexibility

1.2.1 The 5Es: Dimensions of Usability

a. Effective
b. Efficient
c. Engaging

d. Error tolerant
e. Easy to learn
    a. **Effective:** The completeness and accuracy with which users achieve their goals.
    Questions: Is the task completed successfully?
    Is the work completed correctly?
    Design considerations: Assistance in the UI for doing the job - checklists, scripts
    Language that creates clear choices
    Navigation that reduces backtracking and rework
    b. **Efficient:** The speed (with accuracy) in which users complete their tasks.
    Questions: How long does it take to complete a task?
    Can users work with minimal interaction?
    Does the interface feel efficient?
    Design considerations: Navigation shortcuts
    Visible menus or breadcrumbs
    Keyboard shortcuts
    Placement of controls
    c. **Engaging**: How pleasant or satisfying the interface is to use.
    Questions: What kind of work (or play) does the product support?
    What are the expectations for style and tone?
    What is the context of use?
    Design considerations: Frequent v. casual use
    Long sessions v. short interactions
    Physical environment - readability, visibility, accessibility
    Competitive environment
    d. **Error Tolerant:** The ability of the interface to prevent errors or help users recover from those that occur.
    Questions: Does the design help prevent errors?
    When an error occurs, is the interface helpful?
    Design considerations: Clarity of language in error messages
    Whether corrective actions are available when a problem occurs
    Providing duplicate or alternative paths to meet different needs
    e. **Easy-to-learn:** The website should be easy to learn.

1.3 Website Usability Guidelines

Several researchers have made an attempt at identifying which elements contribute towards good website design and usability. This led to the emergence of quite a few usability guidelines, or heuristics, that have been formulated both for generic user interfaces and for webpage design. Examples include those developed by Smith and Mosier (Smith, 1986), (Norman, 1988), (Nielsen, 1992) (Nielsen, 1999), (Nielsen, 1992), Comber (Comber, 1995), Sano (Sano, 1996), Borges *et al.* (Borges, 1996), Spool *et al.* (Spool, 1998), Fleming (Fleming, 1998), Rosenfeld and Morville (Rosenfeld, 1998), Shneiderman (Shneiderman, 1998), Dix *et al.* (Dix, 2004) and Loranger and Nielsen (Nielsen, 2006)

Despite the numerous website usability guidelines that have been developed throughout the years, there is currently no guideline set that has been established as a standard guiding framework. As a means of addressing this problem, Mifsud (Mifsud J., 2011) proposed a set of 242 research-based website usability guidelines compiled on the basis of the results from other usability studies carried out by researchers and experts in the fields.

1.4 Usability Framework and ISO Standards

Usability Framework is shown in the Figure 1. This framework considers usability as a Quality attribute, then various usability attributes are given, usability metrics, usability evaluation method and usability testing tools which are necessary for usability of web engineering research. The two major ISO standards (Abran, 2003) related to usability are:

- ISO 9126 -1
- ISO 9241-11

Figure 1. Usability Framework

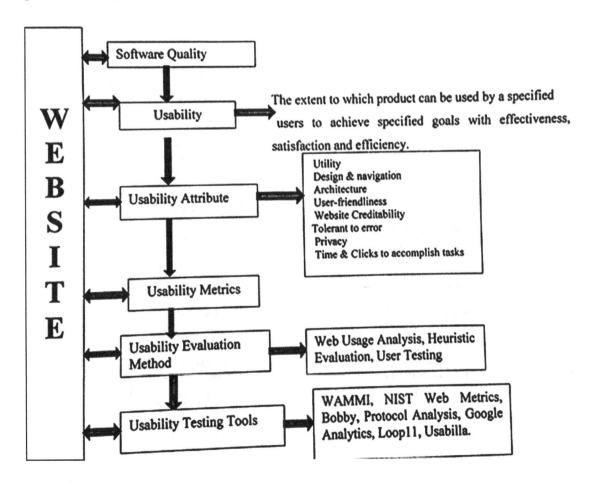

- **ISO 9126-1 Quality Model**

ISO 9126-1 defines a quality model that describes six categories of software quality which are relevant during product development (Abran, 2003). They are functionality, reliability, usability, efficiency, maintainability and portability (Figure 2).

- **ISO 9241-11 Guidance of Usability**

ISO 9241-11 explains the benefits of measuring usability in terms of user performance and satisfaction[6,2]. It emphasizes that visual display terminal usability is dependent on the context of use and that the level of usability achieved will depend on the specific circumstances in which a product is used. The context of use consist of the users, tasks and equipment.

- Effectiveness
- Efficiency
- Satisfaction

Figure 2. Software quality characteristics according to ISO 9126-1 (Abran, 2003).

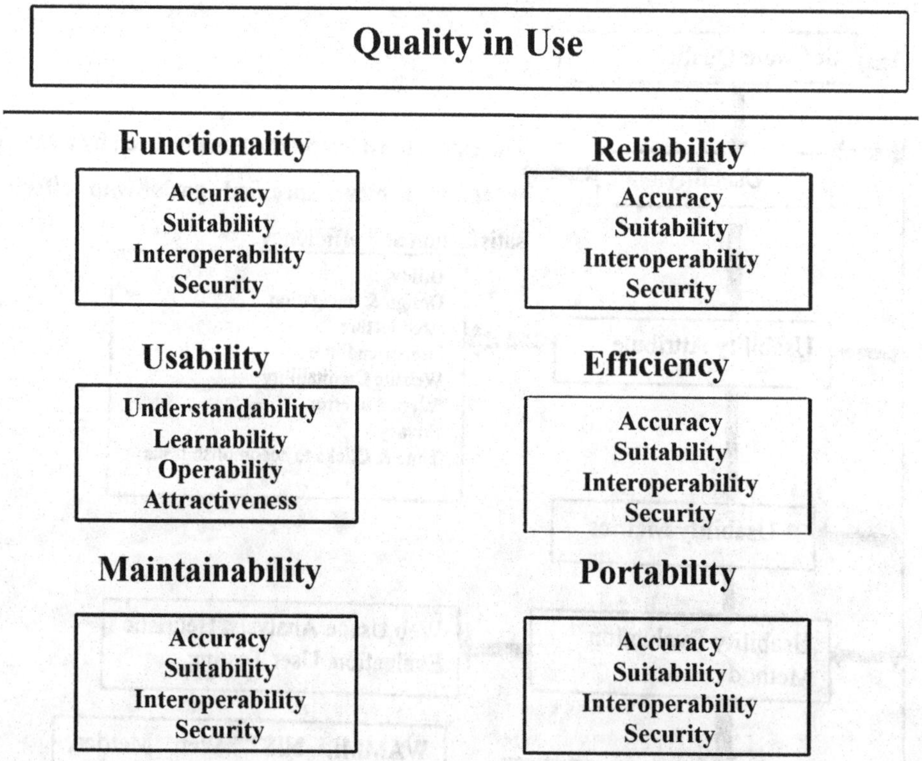

Quality in Use

Functionality
> Accuracy
> Suitability
> Interoperability
> Security

Reliability
> Accuracy
> Suitability
> Interoperability
> Security

Usability
> Understandability
> Learnability
> Operability
> Attractiveness

Efficiency
> Accuracy
> Suitability
> Interoperability
> Security

Maintainability
> Accuracy
> Suitability
> Interoperability
> Security

Portability
> Accuracy
> Suitability
> Interoperability
> Security

Figure 3. Usability Sub-Characteristics According to ISO 9241-11[2,6]

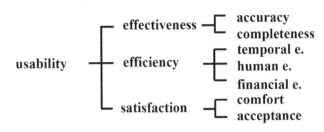

2. BACKGROUND

Usability of the system can be evaluated throughout the software's development life cycle. Shackel suggested that usability is the measure of how much the software is easy to use, effective, flexible and subjectively pleasing. Later on, Shackel's criteria(Shackel, 2009) was modified making usefulness, effectiveness, learnability and likeability of the software as the criteria's for the assessment of usability as flexibility of a software was difficult to measure and specify. Usability of software can be easily attributed to the combination of Learnability, Efficiency, Memorability, Errors and Satisfaction. The idea of Nielsen mainly focused on the attributes that constituted the usability. A new idea came into picture where usability aimed to give long term user satisfaction. Nielsen divided usability as the combination of learnability, retainability and the usage of advance feature. Another usability definition defined it as the combination of learnability, memorability, efficiency, flexibility, satisfaction, first impression, advance feature usage and evolvability (Wixon, 1997). The system should be relevant to user's needs, efficiency, user's subjective feelings, learnability and system's safety feature, such as grating user the right to undo actions that may lead to errors (Lecerof, 1998).

In an evaluation of Utrecht University, website carried out by Lautenbach *et al.* (1999), researchers proposed that 'surveyability' and 'findability' are reliable and effective measures of usability of web pages. Surveyability criteria are the users' satisfaction with the legibility and comprehensibility of the pages and findability is the users' ability to find information on the pages. A study was conducted during which the subjects were observed while they performed one of the four different set of search tasks for information on the university website. Each of these set of search tasks contained three sub-tasks. After completion of each search, subjects answered a questionnaire to measure the user's ability to survey the pages and find the information. A final score for usability of the web pages was calculated by taking the average of overall score for surveyability and findability.

Ahmed *et al.* (2001) have examined current approaches to usability metrics and proposed a new approach for quantifying software quality in use, based on modelling the dynamic relationships of the attributes that affect software usability. The Quality in Use Integrated Map (QUIM) is proposed for specifying and identifying quality in use components, which brings together different factors, criteria, metrics and data defined in different human computer interface and software engineering models (Ahmed, 2001).

According to Rashid Ahmad (2006), research is based on the empirical analysis of an experimental data obtained from the prospective students who were invited to interact with the websites of few world class educational institutions from four different countries. The data allows us to determine that despite active research in the area of usability engineering, the users still experience heavy 'navigational burden' while performing same task using similar systems (Rashid Ahmad, 2006).

Chaparro (2007) has discussed the university portal website at Wichita State was evaluated. Three groups of users – faculties, staff and students participated in the study. Tasks were identified which were representative of common activities conducted by each user group. These included searches for both general and specific information within the portal. The participants were asked to complete a series of tasks, one at a time. Post each task completion; participants rated its ease/difficulty on a 5-point scale. Performance data – success, task completion time and subjective data-perceived task difficulty, satisfaction were gathered for each participant. Post completion of all tasks, participants completed a satisfaction survey and was interviewed for overall comments (Chaparro Barbara S.,2008).

Mustafa and Al-Zoua'bi (2008) has focused on evaluating nine different Jordanian universities. The evaluation was performed using questionnaires and online automated tools. After a study of related literature, they came up with a list of 23 website usability criteria. The questionnaire was developed and designed based on identified usability criteria, which were divided into five categories - Content organization and readability, Navigation and links, User Interface design, Performance and effectiveness and Educational Information. Each of these categories deals with one usability aspect. Usability index for each category and the overall usability is computed and the usability levels are determined. Automated tools - HTML Toolbox and Webpage Analyzer were used to measure the websites internal attributes-load time, html check errors and browser compatibility issues of the websites, which cannot be perceived by users (Mustafa, 2008)

Lian Feldman *et al.* (2009) have conducted a total effort approach using usability study. The Authors interacts with three interfaces, the time and effort measures of time-on-task, total keystrokes, correctional keystrokes and gaze-path traversal were recorded and analysed. The finding of the study demonstrate a correlation between the intrinsic effort of an interface and its usability as predicted by extant interface layout guidelines (Feldman, 2009).

Tripathi *et al.* (2010) have presents a brief account of the development in the field usability of Web-applications. Usability has been considered most important factor amongst the other factors. Since Web based software are diverse and build by integrating numerous components it is not proper to have common quality model for all Web-applications. In this paper the researchers have proposed usability metrics of Web-applications for academic domain (Tripathi, 2010).

Chiang *et al.* (2010) have examined how different web metrics are related to each other and to the amount of Web 2.0 features used on the sites under evaluation. The results of the study indicate that the increasing number of visitors will result in even more new and return visits. When a website becomes more popular, a single visitor is more likely to visit the site more frequently. The total number of visits was positively associated with the average number of page views: the more visits, the more page views by a single user. The average number of page views was in turn negatively related to the average time on page: the more page views, the shorter the time spent on pages (Chiang, 2010).

Yogesh Singh *et al.* (2011) have used a set of fifteen web metrics to analyze a university website over a period of five months. The study focused on how to utilize web metrics to acquire as many visitors to the site as possible. Metrics like the number of page views, the number of files accessed, and number of entry pages were examined. The study identified the periods with the least amount of traffic and pointed out the need to find ways to acquire more visitors during the slow periods. The study also examined what are the most common exit pages (the page last visited by a visitor before leaving the site). It was proposed that these pages are driving away the visitors and efforts to improve the pages are needed (Singh, 2011).

Hasan *et al.* (2014) have investigated the evaluation of the usability of educational websites from the viewpoint of students. The author then evaluated the usability of nine educational websites based on student's preferences. The result showed that content and navigation were the first and second preferred design categories to be considered while the organization/architecture was the least important category (Hasan, 2012).

3. WEB METRICS

Quality is always an issue on which most of the researchers are working on, while developing the software. With the increase in the software market, customers are expecting software's of higher quality and they are even willing to pay higher prices for the software. With this increase in expectations and hike in the software market, companies and countries are continuing to invest great deal of money, time, and effort in improving the software quality (Marchetto, 2005). Software quality cannot be improved without knowledge of development process. The number of bugs and the errors occurred during the software development process have to be found in the early stages of development for better quality. If the errors are found late, then the corrective action will be very expensive . Software organizations will be greatly benefited if there is process to plan and predict the software development. The process of measuring the software is known as software metrics. Software metrics is defined as, "an objective, mathematical measure of software that is sensitive to differences in software characteristics. It provides a quantitative measure of an attribute which the body of Software exhibits". Its aim is to development process of software by controlling the different aspects. So it can be said that metrics are used to improve the ability to identify, control and measure the essential parameter during its development or it can also be said that measurement of software product and the process by which it is being developed.

Software metrics are studied as a way to access the quality of large system (Booth, P., 1989) (Wixon, 1997) and have been applied to object oriented systems. IEEE has published a standard for the software quality metrics methodology (Marinescu, 2001), which led to the development in this field. Its aim was to provide a systematic approach for the establishment of software quality metrics by identifying, implementing, analyzing and validating the software quality metrics of a system.

Metrics are very useful to analyze software applications or models, to study structural software quality, and to define prediction about software effort, such as for design effort, testing effort, and so on. However there is no consensus within the community on which metrics are to use or how to calculate metrics. In particular there are many empirically validated metrics suite and metrics. There are many papers describing different types of metrics involved in the different measurements, metrics definition, and analysis process. Several metrics-papers goal is to define and validate a set of high-level design metrics to evaluate the quality of the application design of a software system (Chidamber and Kemerer (C&K) OO metrics suite (Chidamber, 1994), and (Rosenberg, 1998)). Other papers Briand, L., Wust, J., Daly, J. and Porter, D. (Briand, 2000) focus on empirical validation of the relationships between design measurement in OO systems (coupling, cohesion, and inheritance) and the quality of the software (the probability of faults detection in system classes during testing). Fenton, N. and Neil, M (Fenton, N. & Neil, M., 2000) defines a software metrics roadmap for OO systems. Herder, E (Herder, E., 2002) studies Web metrics definition and analysis, while Dhyani, Keong and Bhowmick (Dhyani, 2002) proposes a Web metrics roadmap. Some papers study metrics for specific software quality aspect. Marinescu (Marinescu, 2001) defines a metrics-based approach for detecting design problems (well-known design flaws). Rosenberg, Hammer and Shaw (Rosenberg L., Hammer, T., and Shaw, J., 1998) defines metrics to promote and assess software reliability.

In the last few years a set of website metrics were defined and specified based on the data collection point of view. Among hundred and fifty automated web metrics catalogued up to now, metrics for Link and Page Faults, metrics for Navigation, metrics for Information, metrics for Media, metrics for Size and Performance and metrics for Accessibility are important categories for evaluation of quality of website.

4. EXPERIMENTAL DESIGN AND RESULTS

Based on the literature study, the evaluation method was determined, i.e. a Web-based usability evaluation questionnaire that allows the users to rate the usability of evaluated websites. A comprehensive literature study carried out by gathering material related to software usability in general and usability evaluation methods in particular. Questionnaire method are used in email survey for data collection. The Authors conducted a questionnaire survey in order to investigate usability analysis of three websites i.e., Guru Nanak Dev University Amritsar, Panjab University Chandigarh, Punjabi University Patiala. Questionnaires and interviews are two primary ways of conducting a survey. Questionnaire has been used in this research for data collection.

4.1 Questionnaire Design

The design of questionnaire consists of twenty three questions questionnaire in Microsoft word document (Appendix 1). The questionnaire was structured in such a way that it provided all possible answers to the rating scale. This was done in order to get quantitative data which is not possible to obtain if questions are asked without possible answer parameters. The evaluators just had to highlight the appropriate answers. The design of questionnaire was made simple because it is said that the quality of giving answers deteriorates with the passage of certain time (Dillman, 1993), (Dillman, 1998).

4.2 Usability Measurements

Usability measurements of GNDU Amritsar, Panjab University Chandigarh, Punjabi University Patiala Websites are given below. The following graphs shows the results of questionnaire, composed of 23 questions, evaluated by 30 participants. The participants were ask to navigate around the websites and answered a 23 questions questionnaire based on their experience during they navigate the website. The usability level of these websites are determined by using 1-5 Rating Scale.

On the basis of five attributes of usability i.e., Learnability, Efficiency, Error Rate, Memorability, and Satisfaction, the survey analysis of three websites are evaluated on these five attributes.

a. **Learnability**: The following graph (figure 4) shows the learnability measurement of three universities, which was evaluated by 30 participants in survey questionnaire.

Figure 4. Survey analysis graph for learnability of a website

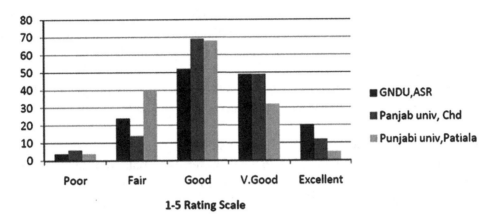

The above results in Table 2 show that Learnability of Guru Nanak Dev University, Amritsar is higher than Panjab University, Chandigarh and Punjabi University, Patiala. Learnability of Punjabi University, Patiala has to be improved. Maximum amount of poor ratio occurs in Panjab University, Chandigarh.

b.   **Efficiency:** The following graph (Figure 5) shows the efficiency measurement of three universities, which was evaluated by 30 participants in survey questionnaires.

Table 2. Survey analysis table for Learnability of a website

Univ.	Poor	Fair	Good	V.Good	Excellent
GNDU, ASR	2.67%	16%	34.67%	32.67%	13.33%
Panjab Univ, CHD	4%	9.33%	46%	32.67%	8%
Punjabi Univ, Patiala	2.67%	26.67%	45.33%	21.33%	3.33%

Figure 5. Survey analysis graph for efficiency of a website

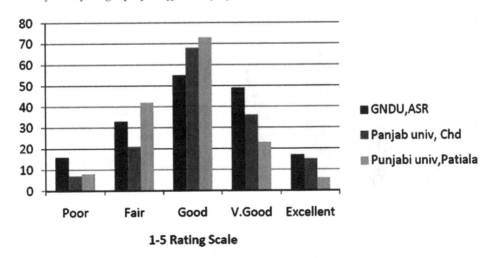

The above graph (figure 5) shows that the Guru Nanak Dev University, Amritsar is having higher efficiency but GNDU website has maximum amount of poor ratio also. Panjab University, Chandigarh also gives good results for efficiency than Punjabi University, Patiala. Overall percentage results conclude that efficiency of Punjabi University, Patiala has to be improved. Fast speedup, higher the efficiency (Table 3).

c.   **Error Rate:** The following graph (figure 6) shows the error prone measurement of three universities, which was evaluated by 30 participants in survey questionnaires.

The above graph (figure 6) shows that Panjab University, Chandigarh has minimum amount of error rate as compared to other two universities. But Punjabi University, Patiala website has to be improved. Guru Nanak Dev University, website also has to be improved in case of error proficiency. But it is better error prone than in Punjabi University, Patiala (Table 4).

d.   **Memorability:** The following graph (figure 7) shows the memorability measurement of three universities, which was evaluated by 30 participants in survey questionnaires.

The above graph (figure 7) shows that the memorability measurement is higher in Guru Nanak Dev University, Amritsar website as compared to other two universities. Punjabi University, Patiala websites shows poor results, so it needs to be improved. When visitor comes to access the website after long gap

Table 3. Survey analysis table for efficiency of a website

Univ.	Poor	Fair	Good	V. Good	Excellent
GNDU, ASR	8.89%	18.33%	30.55%	27.22%	9.44%
Panjab Univ, CHD	4%	11.67%	37.78%	20%	8.33%
Punjabi Univ, Patiala	4.44%	23.33%	40.55%	12.78%	3.33%

Figure 6. Survey analysis graph for error rate of a website

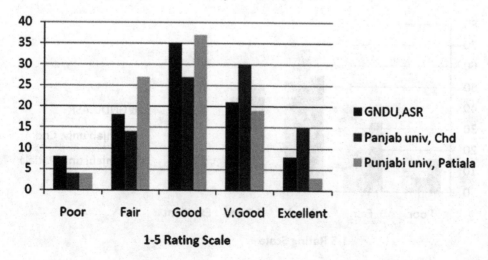

Table 4. Survey analysis table for error rate of a website

Univ.	Poor	Fair	Good	V. Good	Excellent
GNDU, ASR	8.89%	20%	38.89%	23.33%	8.89%
Panjab Univ, CHD	4%	15.55%	30%	33.33%	16.67%
Punjabi Univ, Patiala	4.44%	30%	41.11%	21.11%	3.33%

Figure 7. Survey analysis graph for memorability of a website

then they have to start from the initial step, they didn't remember the way from where they earlier do the work. So links and navigation has to be pointed cleared in Punjabi University, Patiala website. Panjab University, Chandigarh gives average results for this measurement (Table 5).

e.   **User Satisfaction:** The following graph (figure 8) shows the satisfaction measurement of three universities, which was evaluated by 30 participants in survey questionnaire.

The above graph (figure 8) shows that the maximum amount of satisfaction percentage is in Panjab University, Chandigarh. Guru Nanak Dev University, Amritsar has good user satisfaction percentage but it has higher poor percentage. Many of the visitors are not satisfied with Punjabi University, Patiala. This satisfaction measurement scale has to be improved in Punjabi University, Patiala (Table 6).

Table 7 concludes the usability measurement criteria of survey questionnaire result.

Table 5. Survey analysis table for memorability of a website

Univ.	Poor	Fair	Good	V. Good	Excellent
GNDU, ASR	6.67%	23.33%	37.78%	18.89%	13.33%
Panjab Univ, CHD	3.33%	25.55%	32.22%	15.55%	7.78%
Punjabi Univ, Patiala	13.33%	32.22%	27.77%	8.89%	2.22%

Figure 8. Survey analysis graph for user satisfaction of a website

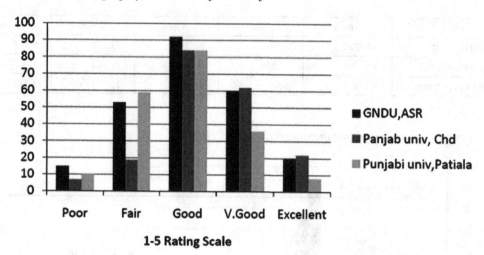

Table 6. Survey analysis table for user satisfaction of a website.

Univ.	Poor	Fair	Good	V.Good	Excellent
GNDU, ASR	6.25%	22.08%	38.33%	25%	8.33%
Panjab Univ, CHD	3%	8%	35%	26%	9.16%
Punjabi Univ, Patiala	4.16%	24.58%	35%	15%	3.33%

4.3 Proposed Metric for Usability Measurement

The proposed metric for usability measurement is given as:

Usability measure = w1*learnability+w2*efficiency+w3*errorrate+w4*memorability+ w5*satisfaction

where w1, w2, w3, w4, and w5 are assumed weights and based on the priority of the five attributes. Applying this newly proposed metric on survey usability analysis of three websites based on five usability attributes (Table 8).

Table 7. Usability Evaluation Measurement Criteria

Usability Criteria	GNDU, ASR	Panjab Univ. Chandigarh	Punjabi Univ. Patiala
Learnability	Excellent	V. Good	Good
Efficiency	V. Good	Excellent	Good
Error rate	Excellent	V. Good	Good
Memorability	V. Good	Excellent	Good
User Satisfaction	V. Good	Excellent	Good

Table 8. Proposed metric for Usability Measurement

Usability Attributes	Computed Value (cvi) where i=1 to 5	Assumed Weights (wi)	w=wi*cvi where i=1 to 5
Learnability	13.33	1.0	13.33
Efficiency	9.44	0.5	4.72
Error rate	16.67	0.2	3.334
Memorability	13.33	0.4	5.332
Satisfaction	9.16	1.0	9.16

These are arbitrary weights assigned to various Usability Attributes, in order to drive out a quantitative measure for Usability. However, in practice, depending upon the situation and the type of websites and users involved, these weights can be adjusted accordingly for driving the corresponding Usability measure.

From the above Table 7, the final weight calculated through wi*cvi of five Usability attributes is shown in Figure 9:

Usability measure:

$$= 13.33+4.72+3.334+5.332+9.16$$

$$= 35.876$$

Usability measure calculated as 35.876. This value gives average usability measure of these websites. In survey questionnaire of usability analysis of three websites, first 23 graphs are drawn as per questions in the questionnaire then evaluation is based on five usability attributes so these 23 graphs are reduced to five graphs. From the proposed metric of usability measurement, five graphs are reduced to single graph, having sum of products of weights and usability attributes.

Figure 9. Proposed Usability Measurement

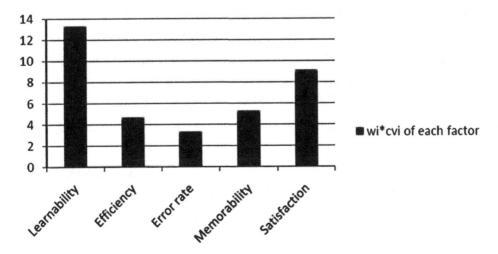

5. CONCLUSION

This chapter has proposed an appropriate usability evaluation metric for websites. It summarises website usability concepts as well as guidelines. The guidelines can be used to evaluate usability of websites as well as help Web designers and developers to build more usable websites. This chapter uses 1-5 Rating scale to measure Usability. Based on the responses provided by the students and visitors, webmasters will know the good and bad usability aspects of their websites. The more efficient a site is, the better the design is.Since it will take up less of the users' time and less things to remember, making it easier for them to reestablish proficiency even after a long period of not having visited the website.

This study is restricted to students and performing five tasks on the website, which were chosen based on a pilot study conducted early during this research. Some under-graduate and post graduate students were involved to identify the tasks that users normally perform while interacting with the academic websites. The results and analysis of the collected data indicates that the website of Panjab University, Chandigarh was seen to be exhibiting highest level of usability, followed by Guru Nanak Dev University, Amritsar website and Punjabi University, Patiala website. As per the results generated, Punjabi University, Patiala website was found to be relatively less usable among the three websites.

6. FUTURE RESEARCH DIRECTIONS

The future work consists of:

- **Finding Relative Accuracy:** During the survey of usability measurement of three websites, the accurate results can be find out through Usability Tools rather than Questionnaire method.
- **Development of Standard Framework Usability Evaluation Method (UEMs) Selection:** There is no standard framework for UEM selection in developing good usable software.

REFERENCES

Abran, A., Khelifi, A., Suryn, W., & Seffah, A. (2003). Consolidating the ISO Usability Models. *Proceedings of 11th International Software Quality Management Conference*. pp 1-17.

Ahmad, R., Zhang, Li, & Azam, F. (2006). Towards Generic User Interface for Web Based Systems Serving Similar Functions. *Proceedings of the IEEE Fourth International Conference on Software Engineering Research, Management and Applications* (pp. 297-306).

Booth, P. (1989). *An Introduction to Human-Computer Interaction*. Hillsdale, USA: Lawrence Erlbaum Associates Publishers.

Borges, J. A., Morales, I., & Rodriguez, N. J. (1996). Guidelines for designing usable World Wide Web pages. *Proceedings of the 1996 Conference on Human Factors in Computing Systems: Common Ground (CHI '96)*, Vancouver, Canada (pp. 277–278). doi:10.1145/257089.257320

Briand, L., Wüst, J., Daly, J., & Porter, D. (2000). Exploring the Relationships between Design Measures and Software Quality in Object-Oriented Systems. *Journal of Systems and Software, 51*(3), 245–273. doi:10.1016/S0164-1212(99)00102-8

Chaparro Barbara, S. (2008). Usability Evaluation of a University Portal Website. Usability News, 10(2), pp 1-7.

Chiang, I.-P., Huang, C.-Y., & Huang, C.-W. (2010). Traffic metrics and Web 2.0-ness In. *Online Information Review, 34*(1), 115–126. doi:10.1108/14684521011024155

Chidamber, S., & Kemerer, C. (1994). A Metrics Suite for Object Oriented Design. *IEEE Transactions on Software Engineering, 20*(6), 476–493. doi:10.1109/32.295895

Comber, T. (1995). Building Usable Web Pages: An HCI Perspective. *Proceedings of the Australian Conference on the Web (AusWeb '95)*, Ballina, Australia.

Dhyani, J., Keong, W., & Bhowmick, S. (2002). A Survey of Web Metrics. *Journal of ACM Computing Surveys, 34*(4), 469–503. doi:10.1145/592642.592645

Dillman, D., Sinclair, M., & Clark, J. (1993). Effects of Questionnaire Length, Respondent-friendly Design and a Difficult Question on Response Rates for Occupant-Addressed Census Mail Surveys. *Journal of Public Opinion Quarterly, 57*(3), 289–305. doi:10.1086/269376

Dillman, D., Tortora, R., & Bowker, D. (1998). *Principles for Constructing Web Surveys*. Joint Meetings of the American Statistical Association.

Dix, A., Finlay, J., Abowd, G. D., & Beale, R. (2004). *Human-Computer Interaction* (3rd ed.). Essex, UK: Pearson Education.

Feldman, L., Mueller, C. J., Tamir, D., & Komogortsev, O. V. (2009). An Economical Approach to Usability Testing. *Proceedings of the 2009 33rd Annual IEEE International Computer Software and Applications Conference* (Vol. 01, pp. 124-129).

Fenton, N., & Neil, M. (2000). Software Metrics: Roadmap. *Proceedings of the Conference on Software Engineering (ICSE 2000)*, Limerick, Ireland (pp 357-370).

Fleming, J. (1998). *Web Navigation: Designing the User Experience*. Sebastopol, Calif, USA: O'Reilly & Associates.

Hasan, L., Morris, A., & Probets, S. (2012). Morris A., Probets S. (2012). A Comparison of Usability Evaluation Methods for Evaluating e-commerce Websites. *Behaviour & Information Technology, 31*(7), 707–737. doi:10.1080/0144929X.2011.596996

Herder, E. (2002). Metrics for the Adaptation of Site Structure. *Proceeding of German Workshop on Adaptivity and User Modeling in Interactive Systems (ABIS02)*.

International Organisation for Standardisation. (1998). *ISO9241 Ergonomic, Part 11: Guidance on Usability* (1st ed.). Geneva, Switzerland. Retrieved from https://www.iso.org/obp/ui/#iso:std:iso:9241:-11:ed-1:v1:en

Krug, S. (2006). *Don't Make Me Think: A Common Sense Approach to Web Usability* (2nd ed.). Berkeley, Calif, USA: New Riders Press.

Lautenbach, M. A. E., Schegget, I. S., Schoute, A. M., & Witteman, C. L. M. (1999). *Evaluating the Usability of Web Pages: a Case Study* (pp. 1–13).

Leavitt, M., & Shneiderman, B. (2006). *The Research-Based Web Design & Usability Guidelines*. Washington, DC, USA: U.S. Government Printing Office.

Lecerof, A., & Paterno, F. (1998). Automatic Support for Usability Evaluation. *IEEE Transactions on Software Engineering, 24*(10), 863–888. doi:10.1109/32.729686

Loranger, H., & Nielsen, J. (2006). *Prioritizing Web Usability*. Berkeley, Calif, USA: New Riders Press.

Marchetto, A. (2005). *A Concerns-based Metrics Suite for Web Applications*. Retrieved from http://citeseerx.ist.psu.edu/viewdoc/summary?doi=10.1.1.59.9742

Marinescu, R. (2001). Detecting Design Flaws via Metrics in Object-Oriented Systems. Proceedings of the 39th Technology of Object-Oriented Languages and Systems (TOOLS USA 2001), Santa Barbara, CA, USA.

McLaughlin, J., & Skinner, D. (2000). Developing Usability and Utility: A Comparative Study of the User of New IT. *Technology Analysis and Strategic Management, 12*(3), 413–423. doi:10.1080/09537320050130633

Mifsud, J. (2011). *USEful: A Framework to Mainstream Web site Usability through Automated Evaluation* [B.Sc. thesis]. University of London, United Kingdom.

Mustafa, S. H., & Al-Zoua'bi, L. F. (2008). Usability of the academic websites of Jordan's Universities: An Evaluation Study. *Proceedings of the International Arab conference on information technology*, Tunisia (pp. 1–9).

Nielsen, J. (1992). The Usability Engineering Life Cycle. *Computer, 25*(3), 12–22.

Nielsen, J. (1999). User Interface Directions for the Web. *Communications of the ACM, 42*(1), 65–72. doi:10.1145/291469.291470

Nielsen, J. (2000). *Designing Web Usability: The Practice of Simplicity*. Indianapolis, IN: New Riders Publishing.

Nielsen, J., & Pernice, K. (2010). *Eyetracking Web Usability*. Berkeley, Calif, USA: New Riders Press.

Nielsen, J., & Philips, V. (1993). Estimating the relative usability of two interfaces: Heuristic, formal, and empirical methods compared. *Proceedings of ACM /IFIP Human Factors Computing Systems (INTERCHI)*, Amsterdam, The Netherlands (pp. 214-221).

Nielsen, J., & Tahir, M. (2002). *Homepage Usability: 50 Websites Deconstructed*. Berkeley, Calif, USA: New Riders Press.

Norman, D. (1988). *The Design of Everyday Things*. Broadway, NY, USA: Doubleday.

Preece, J., Rogers, Y., & Sharp, H. (2007). *Interaction Design Beyond Human-Computer Interaction* (pp. 224–301). Publishing House of Electronics Industry.

Rosenberg, L. (1998). Applying and Interpreting Object Oriented Metrics. *Proceedings of the Software Technology Conference '98*, Salt Lake City, UT. Retrieved from http://www.literateprogramming.com/ooapply.pdf

Rosenberg, L., Hammer, T., & Shaw, J. (1998). Software Metrics and Reliability. *Proceedings of the 9th International Symposium on Software Reliability Engineering*, Germany.

Rosenfeld, L., & Morville, P. (1998). *Information Architecture for the World Wide Web*. Sebastopol, Calif, USA: O'Reilly & Associates.

Sano, D. (1996). *Designing Large-Scale Websites: A visual Design Methodology*. New York, NY, USA: Wiley Computer Publishing, John Wiley & Sons.

Santos, L. (1999). Web-site Quality Evaluation Method: a Case Study on Museums. *Proceedings of the 2nd Workshop on Software Engineering over the Internet ICSE 99*.

Seffah, A., Gulliksen, J., & Desmarais, M. C. (2001). Human-Centered Software Engineering: Integrating Usability. *In Seffah, A., Fulliksen, J., & Desmarais, M.C. (Eds.), Human-Computer Interaction Series, 08*. Springer.

Shackel, B. (2009). Usability - context, framework, design and evaluation. *Journal Interacting with Computers, 21*(5-6), 339–346. doi:10.1016/j.intcom.2009.04.007

Shneiderman, B. (1998). *Designing the User Interface: Strategies for Effective Human-Computer Interaction*. Reading, Mass, USA: Addison-Wesley.

Singh, Y., Malhotra, R., & Gupta, P. (2011). Empirical Validation of Web Metrics for Improving the Quality of Web Page. *International Journal of Advanced Computer Science and Applications, 2*(5), 22–28. doi:10.5120/2414-3226

Smith, S., & Mosier, J. (1986). *Guidelines for Designing User Interface Software*. MITRE Corporation.

Spool, J., Scanlon, T., Snyder, C., & DeAngelo, T. (1998). *Website Usability: A Designer's Guide*. San Francisco, Calif, USA: Morgan Kaufmann Publishers.

IEEE Std. (1998). *IEEE Standard for a Software Quality Metrics Methodology*, New York, IEEE Computer Society Press. Retrieved from http://ieeexplore.ieee.org/xpl/articleDetails.jsp?arnumber=749159

Tripathi, P., Pandey, M., & Bharti, D. (2010). Towards the Identification of Usability Metrics for Academic Websites. *Proceedings of the 2nd International IEEE Conference on Computer and Automation Engineering (ICCAE),* Singapore (pp. 393-397).

Wixon, D., & Wilson, C. (1997). The Usability Engineering Framework for Product Design and Evaluation. In M. Helander (Ed.), *Handbook of Human-Computer Interaction* (2nd ed.). North Holland. doi:10.1016/B978-044481862-1.50093-5

KEY TERMS AND DEFINITIONS

Attribute: Attribute is a property, or a conclusion of a characteristic of an entity or any object.

Accessibility: Accessibility focuses on how a disabled person accesses or benefits from a site, system or application.

Concern: Area of interest or a matter of interest.

Efficiency: Once users have learned the design, how quickly can they perform tasks?

Error Rate: The Frequency in which errors occur in a given time period.

Guideline: A guideline is a statement by which to determine a course of action.

ISO Standard: The international standard, ISO 9241-11, provides guidance on usability and defines it as the extent to which a product can be used by specified users to achieve specified goals with effectiveness, efficiency and satisfaction in a specified context of use.

Learnability: How easy is it for users to accomplish basic tasks the first time they encounter the design?

Memorability: When users return to the design after a period of not using it, how easily can they reestablish proficiency?

Metrics: Metric is a quantitative measure of a degree to which a software system or process possesses some property.

Navigation: How to scroll items on websites or search systems for websites.

Quality Assurance: Quality assurance is any systematic process of checking to see whether a product or service being developed is meeting specified requirements.

Usability: Usability is a quality attribute that assesses how easy user interfaces are to use.

Usability Testing: Usability testing is a technique used in user-centered interaction design to evaluate a product by testing it on users.

Usability Tool: Usability Tools helps optimize websites for better user experience and higher conversion.

Website: A website is a related collection of World Wide Web (WWW) files or a set of related web pages typically served from a single domain.

APPENDIX

Questionnaire

Q1: The overall organization of the website is easy to understand.
- 0. Poor
- 1. Fair
- 2. Good
- 3. V.Good
- 4. Excellent

Q2: You can easily find what you want on this website.
- 0. Poor
- 1. Fair
- 2. Good
- 3. V.Good
- 4. Excellent

Q3: The language of the website is simple and understandable.
- 0. Poor
- 1. Fair
- 2. Good
- 3. V.Good
- 4. Excellent

Q4: Reading content at this website is easy.
- 0. Poor
- 1. Fair
- 2. Good
- 3. V.Good
- 4. Excellent

Q5: The design of the website makes sense and it is easy to learn how to use it.
- 0. Poor
- 1. Fair
- 2. Good
- 3. V.Good
- 4. Excellent

Q6: The website has all the functions and features you expect it to have.
- 0. Poor
- 1. Fair
- 2. Good
- 3. V.Good
- 4. Excellent

Q7: The content on the website is reliable and up-to-date.
- 0. Poor
- 1. Fair

   2.   Good

   3.   V.Good

   4.   Excellent

Q8: The links at this website are well maintained and updated.

   0.   Poor

   1.   Fair

   2.   Good

   3.   V.Good

   4.   Excellent

Q9: You like to scroll left and right when reading this website.

   0.   Poor

   1.   Fair

   2.   Good

   3.   V.Good

   4.   Excellent

Q10: This website provides useful links to get the desired information.

   0.   Poor

   1.   Fair

   2.   Good

   3.   V.Good

   4.   Excellent

Q11: You are comfortable with the colors used at this website.

   0.   Poor

   1.   Fair

   2.   Good

   3.   V.Good

   4.   Excellent

Q12: This website contains no features that irritates you such as scrolling or blinking text and looping animations.

   0.   Poor

   1.   Fair

   2.   Good

   3.   V.Good

   4.   Excellent

Q13: It is easy to move around at this website by using the links or back button of the browser.

   0.   Poor

   1.   Fair

   2.   Good

   3.   V.Good

   4.   Excellent

Q14: You can easily download syllabi, forms, prospectus, datesheet, gazattes and results.

   0.   Poor

   1.   Fair

.

    2.   Good

    3.   V.Good

    4.   Excellent

Q15: The interface of this website is pleasing. (Interface generally includes how the site can be navigated, menus available, search options etc)

    0.   Poor

    1.   Fair

    2.   Good

    3.   V.Good

    4.   Excellent

Q16: The search engines on the website provides useful results.

    0.   Poor

    1.   Fair

    2.   Good

    3.   V.Good

    4.   Excellent

Q17: The website responds to your actions as expected.

    0.   Poor

    1.   Fair

    2.   Good

    3.   V.Good

    4.   Excellent

Q18: You find the content useful.

    0.   Poor

    1.   Fair

    2.   Good

    3.   V.Good

    4.   Excellent

Q19: The website is free from technical problems (hyperlinks errors, programming errors etc).

    0.   Poor

    1.   Fair

    2.   Good

    3.   V.Good

    4.   Excellent

Q20: It is efficient to use this website.

    0.   Poor

    1.   Fair

    2.   Good

    3.   V.Good

    4.   Excellent

Q21: The website is easy to use.

    0.   Poor

    1.   Fair

2.   Good
3.   V.Good
4.   Excellent

Q22: Overall, you satisfied with the website.

0.   Poor
1.   Fair
2.   Good
3.   V.Good
4.   Excellent

Q23: How often you access this website?

Daily

More than once per day

Weekly

Monthly

Yearly

Q24: What else would you like to see available on the websites of Gndu, Amritsar, Panjab University, Chandigarh and Punjabi University, Patiala

Comment:

Chapter 8
Web Content Management in Institutions of Higher Learning in Emerging Economies

Gregory Wabuke Wanyembi
Mount Kenya University, Kenya

ABSTRACT

This chapter aims at examining the concept of content management (CM) and the need to identify it as a global best practice in light of its emergence in modern organizations, and specifically so in the context of institutions of higher learning in developing economies. The chapter also examines a number of models and approaches used in the adaptation of web content management systems (CMS), which provide a guide to the separation of digital content that is relevant to an institution of higher learning and also point out relevant management issues. The merits and demerits of these approaches are discussed. The stages in Content Life Cycle (CLC), information architecture and infostructure, quality of good online content, types of content suitable for a website, and are discussed. Content management tools and system have also been covered in some detail, which offers an institution part of the solution that they require to effectively manage and maintain their content. The chapter concludes with a set of recommendations and points at possible areas for further research.

INTRODUCTION

The emerging economies in Africa, Kenya included, are still at their infant stage insofar as technological development in general and content management systems in particular are concerned. However, these economies have become leaders in innovation of some of the modern information systems (IS). As Watson (2013) has noted, *Ushahidi.com*, a frugal IS for gathering information during a crisis situation, and which was developed in Kenya in 2007, has evolved into an "open source software for information collection, visualization, and interactive mapping" (Ushahidi.com, 2011). This information system has since been used in South Africa (to combat violence), the Democratic Republic of Congo (violence), Haiti (earthquake), New Zealand (earthquake), and Japan (earthquake). Further, according to the *Econo-*

DOI: 10.4018/978-1-4666-9764-5.ch008

mist, Kenya leads the world in mobile banking (The Economist, 2013) through its now world famous M-PESA (Ngugi, Pelowski, & Ogembo, 2010), which is an exemplar of frugal IS thinking. M-pesa is a mobile money transfer service with a cover of about 18 million customers in Kenya. These two examples point to Africa as a continent that is ready to play its leading role in technological advancement and innovation and, given the opportunity, could make more significant contributions that could benefit mankind as a whole

According to Kashorda and Waema (2007), the use of ICTs in higher education institutions has the potential of enhancing the quality of teaching and learning, the research productivity of the faculty and students, and the management and effectiveness of the institutions in general. In Kenya, ICT policies have already been put in place, which articulate the significance of ICT in education. ICT on its part is an enabler for content management as it facilitates the creation, manipulation, publishing, and the use of content in multiple forms, for example text and multimedia. Several initiatives are being made to implement content management systems in institutions of higher learning in these economies, as examples in Kenya and South Africa have shown. However, the main challenge is that web content management technology has had little impact on many institutions of higher learning due to inadequate ICT infrastructure, limited funding and lack trained manpower in the new technology.

Whereas there are a few enthusiastic advocates who are willing to champion the concept of content management in African countries, the reality is that most African educators generally have as yet had little knowledge about, or interest in, its implementation and usage. There remains very considerable infrastructural constraints to be overcome before the technology can be widely adopted for use in institutions of higher learning across the continent, and there is still a lot of reluctance in many institutions to develop systems that can enable information and storage resources to be made available. This does not mean that the potential of high quality digital content management systems should be ignored in Africa, but rather that much more sustained work needs to be done in human capacity development and infrastructural provision if African learners are truly to benefit from the interactive experiences that such systems as content management systems can deliver. This chapter examines various aspects of web content management in institutions of higher learning in emerging economies in Africa, and the role they play in enabling institutions of higher learning to effectively improve their web content and market themselves globally.

CONTENT IN WEB DEVELOPMENT

The term content in the context of web development is generally used to refer to electronic content (e-content) such as graphics, videos, images, sound, electronic journals, and so on that appear on web sites. In this chapter, content refers to pieces of information in the context of an institution of higher learning that appears in the form of documents such as reports, theses, dissertations, research papers and articles. Content is continuously generated internally by the institution and externally from outside the institution of higher learning. The generation of content may be categorized as either short term or long-term depending on how long it takes to generate it. The challenge that faces many institutions is how such huge amounts of content can be effectively and efficiently managed for them to receive returns on their investment. According to Mutula and Wamukoya (2007) define content management as a set of processes and technologies that support the generation, dissemination and use of content. Thus, content, in their view is any type of digital information. Cox (2002), on the other hand defines content management as benefits that organizations seek from it, which permits anyone without any technical knowledge to contribute to a website and yet allows for control to be maintained. Further, according to Cox (2002), content management is concerned with text, and especially with the management of websites, but a requirement exists equally to manage other types of content, e.g links, learning materials, and digital images.

TYPES OF CONTENT

Organizations can create and/or acquire different types of content in their efforts to share and make information accessible to its users. These types of content include websites, blogs and wikis, intranets and portals, and institutional repositories. These types are briefly describes in the following subsections.

Websites

Answers.com (2009) defines a website as a set of interconnected web pages, usually incorporating the home page generally located at the server, and prepared and maintained as a collection of information by a person, group of organization. Muske, Stanforth and Woods (n.d.) note that with the web so visible to us in writing, advertisements and casual conversations, many business owners believe that a web site is crucial to business growth. However, they advise that those thinking about setting up organizational web sites need to answer the following questions: Are it necessary? Will they help? How can it be done? They, however, note that the web market available to businesses considering online presence is potentially huge and a web site allows the business owner to reach this market using only limited resources. The authors further note that the number of users transacting business on the web is bound to grow as more and more people come online.

The authors also discuss the advantages and disadvantages of marketing on the web sites. The advantages according to them include:

1. Meeting a growing audience
2. Having a world-wide presence and access to buyers
3. Possible low cost marketing

while the disadvantages of web sites include:

1. Tremendous competition since competitors can also be found anywhere in the world
2. Attracting all sorts of people to one's site
3. Perpetual need to refresh and update one's site
4. Changing business operations to pay attention to the web site.
5. Security threats including viruses and cyber terrorism(Author's view)

Key issues to consider when building a web site, which include:

1. The need to understand the market
2. Understanding the purpose of your web site before you build it

3. Considering web site elements that will help users navigate the web site with relative ease to find relevant information
4. Site production issues such as expertise to man and maintain the web site and the resources needed for the initial set-up.

Blogs and Wikis

This type of content now forms part of the digital landscape known as Web 2.0. The term Web 2.0, according to Sharma (2008), is associated with the applications for the Internet and the web that enable information sharing, interoperability, user-centred design, dynamic content, collaboration, and generally offer users a richer online experience. A Web 2.0 site gives its users the free choice to interact or collaborate with each other in a social media dialogue as creators of user-generated content in a virtual community in sharp contrast to web sites where users are limited to the passive viewing of content that was initially created for them. Web 2.0 examples include social networks, wikis, video-sharing sites, hosted services, and web applications. It may help to note that the introduction of blogs and wikis (user-edited collaborative web sites) has brought about some of the earliest hopes for the Internet, i.e. an accessible, democratic community of users responsible for its own content, supported and aided by an open model of knowledge creation and communication. Also by assisting users who wish to shape and share their content while at the same allowing other users to access tools and other means of modifying the initial content, blogs and wikis continue to grow in utility and play a significant role on the Internet. Their ease of set-up and use daily contribute thousands of new pages of information, comments, and observations to the world wide web (WWW) and the Internet. The development of open source software (OSS), where users are allowed to contribute to and edit content created by others and new authoritative and comprehensive information results from the efforts of many rather than would not have been realized were it not for the growth and expansion of blogs and wikis.

Portals and Intranets

Businessdictionary.com (2010) defines a portal as a web site that serves as a gateway or a main entry point (cyber door) on the Internet to a specific field of interest or an industry. A portal provides at least four essential services:

1. Search engines(s)
2. E-mail
3. Links to other related sites, and
4. Personalized content.

It also provides facilities such as chat, members lists, and free downloads. Examples of common portals include AOL, MSN, Netcenter, and Yahoo, which earn their revenues from membership fees and/or by selling advertising space/rights on their web pages.

O'Brian (2002) defines an intranet as an Internet-like network within an organization. The author adds that in an intranet, web browser software provides easy access to internal web sites established by the organization's units, teams, and individuals, and other network resources and applications. The intranet as an internal or private network, is based on the Internet technology such as hypertext and TCP/IP protocols and accessed over the Internet. Further, the intranet is meant for the exclusive use of the organization and its associates, including employees, members, customers, suppliers, and partners), and is protected from unauthorized access with security systems that include the firewall. The services that intranets provide range from e-mail, data storage, search and retrieval functions, and, are, therefore, useful in disseminating information including policy manuals, and such other services as internal directories, price and product information for customers, and requirements and specifications for suppliers. Some intranets are confined into a room while in some other organizations, may span continents.

Institutional Repositories

The concept of Institutional Repository (IR) in the context of higher education may mean anything from 'irrelevant curiosity' to 'innovative solution' depending on whom one meets and asks. To professionals in the library, archivists, faculty, programmers, and systems analysts, who are publishing articles in journals and building information systems, an IE is, at the very least, a more convenient and reliable place to hold/store the output from scholarly communication. (Smith, in Conway, 2008). Davis and Connolly, in (Conway, 2008) made an observation that critics of the IR movement have their own arguments, including that the technologies and associated policy frameworks are too limited, too narrowly construed, too political or unconvincing.

However, Crow, in Hockx-Yu (2006), defines institutional repositories as digital collections that capture and preserve the intellectual output of a single or multi-university community. The author adds that while some repositories focus on particular subject domains, an institutional repository stores and makes accessible the educational, research and related assets of an institution. Despite the fact that most of the currently established repositories are e-print repositories offering open access to research outputs of an educational institution or research institute, the content may not need to be limited to e-prints but could include research data, learning materials, image collections, and many other different types of content. (Hockx-Yu, 2006).

Content Ownership

On the question of ownership of content, Chin (2003), observes that the technology behind an intranet lies within the domain and responsibility of the IT departments. However, the author adds that the content of an intranet needs to have an owner as well, someone who will be responsible for ensuring that information is accurate and up-to-date. In the author's opinion and as matter of rule, the owner should be someone within the department where the information originates. The author further explains that this will ensure that those best suited to represent their discipline are the ones responsible for managing their content and cautions against dumping this duty onto a third party, which is not only a wrong idea but a dangerous one as well. The reason for this is that third parties have no vested interests in seeing that such an important organization's asset is relevant and up-to-date. As a result, orphaned content may grow stale, users will lose confidence in the system, and the intranet will eventually lose its relevance. Chin further emphasizes the importance of ensuring that all content management facilities, in the form of in-house written applications or commercial off-the-shelf (COTS) software tools, are in place for content owners to update and modify the information.

CONTENT MANAGEMENT SYSTEMS AND TOOLS

Contenmanager.eu.com (2000) state that many organizations are now turning to content management because of three main reasons, namely, internal pressure to create and manage content in a more efficient manner, an awareness that solutions are available at affordable cost, and as a response to governments that are demanding that organizations comply to legislative requirements on issues of accessibility to information. The authors add that CMS solutions have evolved to the point where they are now genuinely easy to use and deploy, stable products, less costly and are strategically significant to an organization's operations. The authors further observe that with information being viewed as an asset, the only realistic method of storing and retrieving information is in electronic format, which in turn creates the need for a solution, or a combination of solutions, to manage the process and the content held, also known as Content Management Systems (CMS). Thus, those organizations that choose not to adopt CMS technology may suffer the same fate as those that thought they could carry on using the typing pool instead of implementing word processing systems. Hence, the ability of the organization to function at the same rate as its competitors and its ability to comply with legislation will require more resources and be less productive than if they had invested in a CMS.

Contentmanager.eu.com (2000) defines a CMS tool as a facility that enables a variety of centralized technical and de-centralised non-technical staff to create, edit, manage and publish in a number of formats a range of content, including text, graphics, video, documents and so on, whilst being constrained by a centralized set of rules, processes and workflows that ensure coherent, validated electronic content. With CMS tools, one is able to control what, when and how content is published and as business grows, more editors, writers and content creators will have access to the CMS.

Examples of such tools include Weblog Software, e.g. Blogger from Google and Bloglines from Ask Jeeves; Web Content Management Software (WCMS) which manages content in various formats that include text, graphics, links, etc. for ease of distribution to the web server. WCMS typically enforces a structure on the pages that are created, referred to often as templates. The structure is concealed from the editor or author so that the only task they have to complete is the insertion of content into a blank structure web page. The authors further state that a WCMS enables online information to be refreshed, consistent, and of a high quality, enables decentralized content creation thereby avoiding the IT bottlenecks that would otherwise delay the publishing of web content anf facilitates the re-use of content.

Mutula and Wamukoya (2007) describe the Document Sharing and Management Software which performs the functions of scanning, storage, management and retrieval of electronic records. The authors explain that this software is critical to enterprises or organizations that rely on fast access to their records. Another type of CMS is the Enterprise Content Management System, which supports both the web and content publication lifestyle. The software focuses on managing the capture, storage, security, revision control, distribution, preservation, and eventual destruction of documents and content. Finally, The Digital Asset Management software is also available, which manages digital media, e.g. graphics, photographs, video, and multimedia presentations. This software employs browsers and cataloguing software.

To be able to manage content effectively in an institution requires development or availability of content management system (CMS), which Byrne, in Souer et al (2007) defines as a system that supports the creation, collection, management/administration, publication and distribution of information. Thus, CMS can be considered to be a collection of business rules and editorial processes applied to content by individuals and institutions to align efforts of online publication with their goals. In general CMS may take different forms including web content management systems which manage websites, document management systems, workflow for management of journal publications, or single source content management system where content is stored in chunks within a relational database. As an enabler of content management, information and communication technology (ICT) can facilitate the creation, manipulation, dissemination, and use of content in a multiplicity of form, including text and multimedia. Several institutions of higher learning in emerging economies are making initiatives to incorporate ICTs in teaching, learning, research, communication, and administrative activities among others. An example is the VLIR-IUC-Moi University project in Kenya that seeks to improve ICT infrastructure, facilities and curriculum development at the university. Other projects include Kenya Education Network (KENET) that aims at creating awareness of various ICT issues and importance of their implementation in institutions of higher learning in Kenya. A number of institutions have also introduced open and distance learning initiatives which require sound ICT infrastructure.

ICTs have also created opportunities and platforms for scholars to engage in collaborative work over the Internet (Mutula 2008), and increasingly now universities that are rated highly are judged on the basis of the quality and utilization of their digital technologies, web content output and their web presence. According to Cybermetrics Lab (2009), which performs global ranking of universities, web presence measures the activities and visibility of the institutions and it is considered to be a good indicator of their impact and prestige. Ranking summaries the global performance of the university and provides information for students and faculty as to their global standing and reflects their commitment to the dissemination of knowledge. Cybermetrics Lab (2009) advises that if the web performance of a university is below an expected position in the ranking according to their academic excellence, the university authorities should reconsider their web policy and promote substantial increases of the volume and quality of their content, including electronic publications.

FACTORS TO CONSIDER WHEN ACQUIRING A CMS

Currently the trend is to acquire Content Management Software based on the following reasons:

- Extensive pre-built-in features
- Software upgrade availability, that is, you are notified when upgrades to the software occur, and that you have easy access to those upgrades
- Scalability of the software, that is, the need for additional content, functionality and the desire to branch off with niche sites
- Increased functionality
- Enhanced security
- Fewer software problems or issues
- Improved usability
- CMS is a mature product
- External support
- Availability of integration expertise
- Availability of resources to modify and/or develop additional functionality
- Lower total cost of ownership (TCO)
- Availability of user training
- Availability of user and technical documentation

- The software includes problem knowledge base
- Not reliant on employees with an organization
- The software supports modularity
- Clear product roadmap
- Availability of Application Program Interface (API)
- The software is compliant with standards such as W3C
- Availability of application help

The Pros and Cons of CMS

According to Iris Web Designs (http://www.iriswebdesigns.com/articles/pros-and-cons-of-content-management-systems-21/), there are advantages and disadvantage of CMSs, both for the client and for website designer or web developer, which are outlined below:

ADVANTAGES OF CONTENT MANAGEMENT SYSTEMS

- Larger firms may have several contributors and may monitor their contributions using a content management system. It streamlines the process.
- Content management systems can be used by almost anyone to create new pages. Many clients who engage a website designer are experts in their own fields but may be unfamiliar with how to create content pages on the internet. Most content management systems include a simple interface called a WSIWYG (what you see is what you get) editor that will allow the client or one of their staff members to create pages without knowing how to code. This is a distinct advantage to the expense of having to use the services of a web administrator.
- Web maintenance costs can be cut drastically by creating new content in the office as opposed to paying an administrator or developer to update the site.

Developer Advantages to Content Management Systems

- Many content management systems will have pre-made appliances, widgets and plugins available that will streamline the process of development.
- Developers can design a site and often turn it over to the site owner with no further involvement.
- A site may be faster to develop using a content management system as they often have solutions to common problems coded into them.

Disadvantages of Content Management Systems

- Content management systems do require training and can be broken if used incorrectly. A site that has been carefully designed and created can actually be broken by improper use of a CMS.
- Content management systems require time to update. If your organization does not contain persons with extra time to devote to updating the site then a content management system may go unused and be unnecessary.

- If you do not already have a web perceptive, computer oriented person on your team then extra training will be required to enable an employee to update it.
- Using the content management system like WordPress, Joomla! may hinder your ranking at search engines. Just think about it, why would a search engine reward your website if your code is same as million other websites?
- Popular content management systems like WordPress and Joomla! are often targeted by spammers and hackers. Since just about anyone can download the code and look for loopholes, security issues are inevitable. Not to mention that popularity of these systems give hackers an excellent incentive. Hackers know that many popular sites will be using these platforms. Thus, open one door and others will open by themselves.

Disadvantages in Using a Content Management System for the Developer

- A content management system will use more server resources as opposed to a static page and this should be balanced.
- Cost inflation due to training expenses are not preferred by clients or by developers but training may be necessary in order to teach the client to use the system effectively.
- Poor text design is possible using a content management system. Designers work hard on fonts, and text to give a website certain feel and flow and business owners pay for that polished professional look. CMS editors can permit poor text design and ruin the design the business owner paid for.

MODELS FOR WEB CONTENT MANAGEMENT

A number of models and approaches are used in the adaptation of web content management systems. The major models considered in this chapter include the Online Computer Library Centre (OCLC) Collection Materials Grid, the Stanford Model of Digital Collections and Services, Conway Content Landscape Model, and the General Knowledge Model. The models provide a guide to the separation of digital content that is relevant to an institution of higher learning. This chapter looks at these models and approaches and also point out relevant management issues related to them. Further, each model and approach has its merits and demerits.

The Online Computer Library Centre Collection Materials Grid (OCLC)

The Collections Grid model – developed by Lorcan Dempsey and Eric Childress of OCLC Research is a simple way of representing a complex universe (OCLC, 2003). The grid, shown in Figure 1, divides collection materials into 4 general areas, namely institutional content, open web content, published content, and special collections.

The vertical axis of the grid represents the degree of *uniqueness* of the content while the horizontal grid represents the *stewardship* that the resources need.

Figure 1. The OCLC Collection Grid
Source: OCLC (2003)

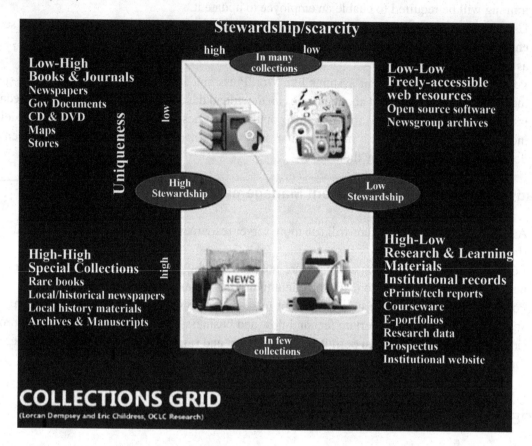

Description of the OCLC Grid

Dempsey and Eric Childress describe the quadrants according to the different types of content that is to be found in a given context such as a collection in a library. These quadrants include the 'published', 'open web content', 'special collections', and 'institutional content'.

Published content: The upper left quadrant depicts "published" content. Published content includes books, newspapers and magazines, journals, CDs, DVDs, video, maps, government records and similar documents. These materials may be in print form, electronic form or both. The authors argue that libraries have traditionally focused on acquiring, managing, and presenting these published materials, irrespective of whether they are purchased, licensed or linked to on the web site. Well-established practices have been used to manage these non-unique, published materials. Well-developed and mature standards and procedures have substantially reduced the libraries' burden of the creation of metadata.

Dempsey, Lorcan, Constance Malpas, and Brian Lavoie (2014) have pointed out that it is useful to think of three audience scales:

- Local or institution-scale, group-scale (where the intended audience is a consortium),
- Country, or "club" of some sort, and

- Webscale (where the intention is to reach the entire web population).

It is also useful to think of three sourcing approaches:

- Local or institutional (where an institution builds or provides a service itself),
- Group (where the approach is collaboratively sourced), and
- Third party (where an external provider is used).

Further, the authors argue that for any institution, it is possible to build a matrix of how they are building out services. In this context, they state that there is a general trend towards group as libraries try to build scale, and also a growing interest in leveraging webscale providers. The audience scales and sourcing approaches are depicted in Figure 2.

Open web content: Open web content quadrant includes freely accessible web sites, open-source software, images, newsgroup and archives. Although these materials are not unique, they are not published in the ordinary sense and are likely to be unmanaged or unmanageable. The libraries role in collecting, managing and presenting this type of content is yet to be clear. Emerging standards aimed at effectively managing this content are yet to mature and there are no published practices for managing their collection.

Figure 2. A partially built-out matrix for published materials
Source: Dempsey et al for OCLC Research (2014)

WebScale			Google Scholar; Google Books; WorldCat; Amazon
Group		WEST; OCUL; Orbis Cascade Alliance; HathiTrust	
Local	Course reserves		Locally available purchased and licensed materials
Audience Source	Institutional	Group	(Global) Third party

Special Collections: Special Collections quadrant represents content that is often found in the special collections of libraries, museums, and historical societies. The content may include rare books, local and historical newspapers, local history materials, manuscripts, theses and dissertations, photographs, and so on. They are usually described as high maintenance materials that require controlled physical environments, access and preservation. authors caution that using immature standards imply a high burden of metadata creation for libraries and archives. They further observe that institutional focus shifts from acquiring, managing and distributing published materials to acting as publisher and curator.

Institutional content: Institutional content quadrant for academic libraries includes where learning and research materials are to be found. Hence, learning objects, courseware, e-portfolios, e-prints, research data, and technical reports are included. Most institutional content is unique to the institutions. Lack of standards or poor standards, means that there is a huge burden of data/metadata creation. Much of institutional content is usually not published.

Merits and Demerits of the OCLC Collections Grid Model

The OCLC Collections Grid model, according to Conway (2008) gives priority value to those special collections materials with high stewardship and uniqueness values which confer upon research institutions their distinctive identities. However, Hazen, Horrell and Merrill-Oldham in Conway (2008), note that on the surface, the OCLC Collections Grid model's embedded value system contains the traditional view of preservation which emphasizes long-term preservation needs over short-term user needs. They further state that although the grids appears to be an accurate reflection of the collection behaviours of research libraries that are increasingly focusing their collection efforts and their institutions' collection revenue on digital resources, the grid may be less useful for engaging the broad array of academic stakeholders who do not value library-oriented stewardship that is unrelated to immediate scholarly requirements.

The OCLC Collections Grid model is, however, relevant to researchers and practitioners as it adequately describes categories of content normally found in institutions of higher learning. The usefulness of the model may not necessarily extend beyond this as contemporary scholars are rapidly moving away from traditional ways of seeking information in the library and prefer the ubiquitous nature of the Internet and digital libraries which permit them access to the global information regardless of their geographical locations.

The Stanford Model of Digital Collections and Services

Conway (2008) states that the Stanford Model of Digital Collections and Services shares with the OCLC Collections Grid awareness of stewardship responsibilities, which range from short-term need to long-term preservation. However, the Stanford model plots the second dimensions in terms of the 'compass direction' or the evolving orientation of digital services from individual to institutional requirements. Its main strength is the way it maps emerging academically oriented digital content on a suite of library digital repository and preservation services. The model explicitly presumes the library's role as a repository but does not address the management of digital assets that fall outside the library's scope.

Conway's Content Landscape Model (CLM)

Conway's Content Landscape Model (CLM) was first developed at Duke University as an alternative content landscape model to support campus conversations on the scope of digital library activities, Conway(2008). The model proposes 4 variables which together describe the core asset management challenges that universities contend with digital content, which are property rights, source, structure, and possession.

The Conway Content Landscape Model is intended to be a multi-dimensional framework that addresses three key issues with digital asset management in institutions of higher learning. First, the model acknowledges the broader academic mission within which digital content is created, acquired through purchase or license, managed and preserved, and distributed and utilized. Second, the model provides for selection processes and priority setting exercises through the dual perspectives of content creator/stakeholders and content user/stakeholders. Third, the model identifies four digital content property scales which provide an analytical foundation for assigning management properties to specific classes of digital content. More specifically, the model articulates four interacting variables which together describe the core asset management challenges that institutions of higher learning contend with which are *property rights, structure, source,* and *possession*. These are shown in Figure 3 below.

Conway (2008) observes that the first area, *property rights,* distinguishes campus digital assets based on the chances that the institution can retain the rights to capture, store, preserve, and make available digital content to its faculty and students. It must be observed that the rights of a university vis-a vis its digital content do not contradict one another, but rather depend on a number of factors that limit the options for access and preservation.

The *structure* variable recognizes that digital objects range from tightly structured, highly relational database elements to loosely coupled elements assembled for a variety of reasons. Conway (2008) argues that tight structure improves the chances that valuable asset can be identified and managed actively while loosely affiliated objects increase complexity.

Figure 3. The variable world of digital content
Adapted from Conway (2008)

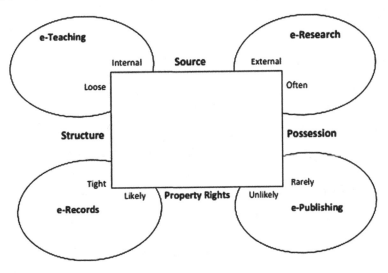

The third variable, *source of digital assets*, plays a significant role in content management priorities. Digital content that originates from a university campus (internal) may be simpler to identify and more technically capable of effective management than that originates from external sources. Furthermore, digital content that is generated locally has the value of being 'unique', which adds distinctive characteristic to a university in a similar fashion as special collections of a library have in the past.

The fourth variable, *possession*, points to the diversity of access models. It can be observed that despite the fact that some digital content often of critical value to faculty and students may be secured on campus-managed servers, the universities rarely have in their possession some of the most critical digital resources in which they have a continuing stake, specifically, licensed electronic journals and books. Hence, access to these resources is mostly through links to external databases with limited or no commitment to preserve them. These include e-journals and e-books over which the institution may have little or no control. Possession, it is to be noted, is quite often unassociated with property rights.

Conway (2008) explains that at its most abstract level, the model recognizes the information environment in which institutions of higher learning may carry out their mission to foster research, teaching, publication, and preservation (Waters, in Conway (2008). He further points out that this wider environment of e-research, e-teaching, e-publishing, and e-preservation is structurally similar to the digital framework which motivates research and development.

General Knowledge Model

Newman and Conrad (1999) defined knowledge management as a new discipline that seeks to improve the performance of individuals and organizations by maintaining and leveraging the present and future value of knowledge assets. Thus, knowledge managers need to understand and address the needs and interests of various stakeholders and the analysis of intertwined knowledge flows that link them. According to the authors, knowledge flows consist of a set of processes, events, and activities through which data, information, knowledge, and meta-data are transformed from one state to another. In simple terms, the General Knowledge Model organizes knowledge into 4 areas of activity as shown in Figure 4. These areas include:

- *Knowledge Creation,* which consists of activities associated with the entry of new knowledge into the system. This includes knowledge development, discovery, and capture;

Figure 4. The General Knowledge Model
Adapted from Newman and Conrad (1999)

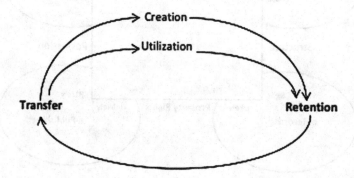

- *Knowledge Retention,* which comprises all activities that preserve knowledge and also permit it to remain in the system once captured. It also includes those activities that maintain the relevance and viability of knowledge in the system.
- *Knowledge Transfer* refers to those activities that are associated with the flow of knowledge from party to another and includes communication, translation, conversion, filtering, and rendering over a network.
- *Knowledge Utilization* includes those activities and events that are related to the application of knowledge to business processes.

The model is significant because it relates the individual and highly dynamic behaviors and processes to general activity areas and to each other by association. Furthermore, authors affirm that the model allows analysts to trace and follow individual knowledge flows by assisting them to assess and understand how knowledge enables certain actions and decisions to be made. Within each activity phase exists other smaller knowledge flows and cycles, resulting in layers that span a wide range of macro- and micro-behaviours, ranging from broad organizational and multi-organizational processes to discrete actions and decisions. These include all the varying intervening layers that comprise activities, tasks, workflows, systems, interfaces, and transformations.

In particular, the model relates closely to content management in that knowledge can be captured, stored, processed, and transmitted digitally in a system. In the process, knowledge bases can be created, which then directly draw upon content management strategies, processes and techniques to ensure that the knowledge becomes accessible to those who require it as and when the need arises.

A Comparison of Models

The overlapping characteristics and functions of digital content in academic environments and the unique requirements for management are well captured by the models. However, the OCLC and the Stanford Model tend to be limited for formal digital collections and the services such as the libraries and digital repositories. In addition to the formal setting, the modern environment for content management has to consider such aspects as user generated content and other decentralized information sources that include the Internet and other global sources. The Conway model opens up the content landscape to encompass more items but it does not incorporate emerging technologies such as the Web 2.0 and Web 3.0 that have given ordinary users the ability to create, access, and share information and content in the modern digital environment.

CONTENT LIFE CYCLE

Stuhler (2009) states that as IT becomes ever more prevalent in all aspects of our lives, the amounts of data generated and stored will continue to grow. Quoting IBM, the author added that worldwide data volumes were currently doubling every two years and observes that a major trend over the last few years has seen many organizations implementing enterprise resource planning and management and customer management solutions. This has in turn resulted in a dramatic increase in the amounts of data stored in organizations on customers, partners, suppliers, and prospects. Thus the ability to base business decisions on solid, reliable and timely management information has become a key determinant. In this scenario, organizations are faced with not only managing all of their own in-house generated data, both historic and current, but also an influx of additional data from external sources.

Stuhler (2009) also notes that technical trends and emerging technologies such as new capabilities within the databases used to store corporate data and information are yet another major driver of data growth. For example, DB2 now supports XML (eXtensible Markup Language) and LOBs ('Large Objects') such as graphics, images, audio, video, and so on. The ability to store this kind of data alongside the more traditional structured information can be useful but can also have a huge implication on the overall size of the database. The author adds that the technical trends that are contributing to database growth include storage of data in Unicode format, which can expand the overall database size by between 10 percent and 50 percent depending on the data, and the duplication of databases due to replication requirements associated with backup strategies.

Challenges of Expansion of Databases

The unprecedented growth in data volumes poses significant challenges to organizations, the most visible challenge being the operational costs. According to Stuhler (2009), this relates to more staff time required for routine maintenance and data-related exception handling such as out-of-space conditions and repartitioning. The author adds that as databases increase in size, so, too, does the central processing unit cost of running batch operations and routine housekeeping. Further, the ongoing running costs also increase due to the additional disk space requirements, as storage and processing capacity upgrades may be required.

As a solution to these data explosion problems, the author proposes data archiving. According to the Gartner report that the author quotes, database archiving significantly lowers storage costs for primary storage by moving older data to less costly storage. Archiving also reduces the size of primary storage, resulting in improved application performance and lower storage requirements for copies of the databases for testing, backup, and other purposes. In conclusion, implementing a thorough archiving policy and an intelligent archiving system, data, and thus content, can be managed throughout its life cycle.

CMC Review (2009) states that to better understand an otherwise complex business of content management, one needs to break it down into seven major stages involved in managing the content life cycle. These stages, shown in Figure 5, include:

1. **Organization:** Information is structured using tools such as XML (eXtensible Markup Language) or RDF (Resource Description Framework) both of which allow arbitrary metadata to be added to all elements of information. This further allows the information to be retrieved in a number of ways and reused in many more ways. In this stage, categories are created, vocabularies are controlled, taxonomic hierarchies are designed, and classification schemes developed. Without using such structuring, information will be collected in haphazard manner and stored in wrong places possibly never to be found by those who need it, which may then be required to be created afresh at great expense.

2. **Workflow:** For successful creation and use of content, there must be carefully designed albeit flexible rules that keep the content moving consistently with the organization's business requirements and rules, governing policies and procedures.

Figure 5. Stages in managing CLC
Source: CMC Review (2009)

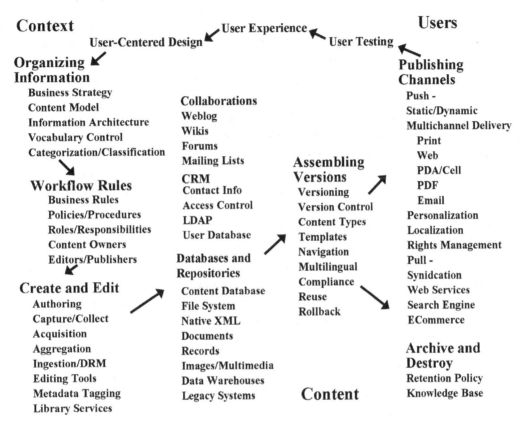

3. **Creation:** In this stage, all content is classified into the architectural categories initially designed in stage (a). This is irrespective of the methods and techniques used to capture the information into the system.

4. **Repositories:** In this stage, decisions are made on how the content will be stored, whether in a relational database structures, as file system objects, as unstructured text and binary graphic images, or as XML elements appropriately tagged with the metadata from stage (a).

5. **Versioning:** Since changes to content and presentation of the content are inevitable, versioning needs to be managed to allow authorized users to make changes to the content so that conflicts can be resolved and critical content is rolled back when errors creep into the system.

6. **Publishing:** The final content is delivered to users in many different ways both pull and push. Some will be through the traditional print formats, others over mobile devices such as PDAs and cell phones or via the web (Internet). All the delivery methods and techniques must be tested to insure the quality of user experience that stage (a) prepared.

7. **Archives:** Finally, the author concedes that in spite of publishing content as a major objective of the system, some of the content may not be short-lived and, therefore, may need to be protected as part of 'institutional memory'. This captures the organization's business knowledge and can be shared with future generations of users as a permanent base.

Information Architecture and Infostructure

The Institute of Information Architecture (2007) defines information architecture (IA) as the art and science of organizing and labeling websites, intranets, online communities and the software needed to support usability. The institute emphasizes that a good IA lays the necessary foundation for an information system that makes sense to users. To achieve this goal, best practices in information architecture support the development of interfaces that facilitate the flow of relevant and useful information to users. The institute further notes that IA is still an emerging community of practice at its infancy focused on bringing principles of design and architecture to the digital map.

Batley (2007) emphasizes that no matter how well designed and aesthetically pleasant the IA, it is only going to be of use only if it includes all the documentation and information its users will need, and that if those information and documentation can be easily retrieved. Thus, architecture is not only about creating robust physical structures, it is also about functionality.

Maurer (2004), on the other hand, points out that information architecture primarily relates to the design of information spaces such as sites (intranets, extranets, and search systems), and interactive spaces (business applications and browser-based transactional systems) in such a manner as to enable users to navigate the system and locate the information they need with ease. Towards this end, information can be arranged in ways such as by alphabetical order, by date, by geographical location, by topic, by hierarchy, by facet, organically and in a combination of other ways to permit multiple access methods. In this regard, the designer should arrange information in accordance with the needs of users so that the most appropriate content organization scheme is chosen, for instance, geographical location as an organizing scheme would be more appropriate where the content relates to spatiality and used with travel maps. In this chapter, infostructure is defined as the layout of information so that it can be navigated with ease. It is the result of organizing information in a useful manner and includes tables of content, bibliography or index (Tilton, 1994). The author explains that the important feature in an infostructure is to present a clear ordering of information by subject, creating a document that is as long as it needs to be and no more, ensure a document is richly cross-referenced, and provide a clear and consistent navigation structure.

The chapter will also examine Quality of good online content, and types of content suitable for a website. Further, advantages and disadvantages of marketing via websites as well as factors to consider when constructing a website and the need to understand the market will be considered. These will include organization, workflow, creation, repositories, versioning, publishing, and archives.

Qualities and Characteristics of Good Content

Gupta (1996), notes that information has several characteristics that make it very different from other commodities. These characteristics include the fact that information is reproducible and that its theft does not deprive its original owner its ownership. The cost of production of information is also low compared to the cost of production and transportation of other commodities. In terms of life time, information does not last long, and may be as short as when it is useful. Mohammadi and Moghaddam (2008) explored the qualities or features of information, which include immortality whereby information is permanent and can be increasingly produced over time; it can also be used simultaneously by several people including competitors at the same time especially in the electronic age; it creates value addition in products and services; it can be used and re-used repeatedly without losing its original value or qualities; it can be shared several times over thus optimizing its use greatly facilitated by advancement in computer technology and networks.

According to Muigai (2008), good content has the ability to engage, is timely, accurate, and useful. It should be detailed and focused, and that it should be search engine friendly, that is, it can be found and ranked. Further, the author points out that good content creates confidence, enriches user experience, and encourages repeat visits. However, for good content to be created and maintained, sound editorial guidelines are necessary. Oppenheim, Stenson, and Wilson (2001) observed that information is an asset which adds value to organizations that possess it. The authors note that information assets have various attributes that impact on the effectiveness of organizations, and these include attributes relating to economy, quality, and value. Additional attributes include accuracy, comprehensives, currency, and verifiability. Further, the authors note that while information can be, on one hand, dynamic, on the other hand it requires constant upkeep, maintenance and checks to ensure that quality is maintained. Often information acts as a catalyst; it has the ability to enhance productivity and reduce risk in innovation and so increases the value of traditional organizational resources.

Implementation of Content Management Systems in Universities in Kenya and South Africa

The implementation of content management systems in universities in emerging economies is growing despite the fact that it has had limited success. In her study (unpublished thesis 2012), Moseti carried out a study at Moi University, Kenya, which has implemented a content management system. The author noted that content management posed challenges to institutions of higher learning, and added that although the university has implemented several information systems, they were not effectively managed. This was attributed to the lack of formal and coherent strategies and frameworks to identify the digital content generated from its various administrative and academic units. The study also revealed that inadequate infrastructure had compromised effective creation and management of digital content, and the lack of a strategy and the absence of a content organizational approach had had a negative impact on accessibility and use of content in the university. Thus, despite the presence of extensive digital content in the university, users continue to experience problems in accessing digital content.

In another study conducted at the Stellenbosch University, South Africa, Steel (2012) conducted a needs-analysis study of how the University could effectively address the website and portal information needs of its users through the implementation of a content management system. The study further sought to understand the current perspectives and information needs of users of the university's corporate website, as well as the staff and student portals, and to propose ways in which the University could manage its content assets to address these needs. The results indicated a lack of modernization in the design of the portals and the importance of good information architecture to ensure an effective and user-centric content management solution. In addition the study found that portals were cluttered, difficult to navigate and the search features were ineffective.

Trends in Enterprise Content Management (ECM)

AIIM (2010) defines ECM as constituting *"strategies, methods and tools used to capture, manage, store, preserve and deliver content and documents related to organizational processes."* ECM applications and strategies allow the organization to manage its information more effectively (AIIM 2010). As Katuu (2014) observes, when these strategies, methods and tools are targeted at organizational processes, they manifest themselves in several modules. Ten (10) modules that may be considered fundamental for this purpose include:

- Document Management (DM),
- Records Management (RM),
- Workflow or Business Process Management (BPM),
- Collaboration,
- Imaging,
- Portal,
- Knowledge Management (KM),
- Digital Asset Management (DAM),
- Digital Rights Management (DRM), and
- Web Content Management (CMS Watch 2010, 21-86; Kampffmeyer 2004, 2006).

These modules are illustrated in Figure 6.

In a survey of ten (10) South African institutions that were considered to have successfully implemented ECM system, 5 considered themselves as having implemented ECM applications, nine of the institutions had both records and document management modules (Katuu 2012b). Katuu further observes that if these were the only modules implemented, then it would mean DRM applications were in place. However, most of these institutions had more than just DM and RM modules in place which demonstrated that institutions tend to go beyond just two ECM modules (Katuu 2012b, 50). These realities were important

Figure 6. Modules of a typical ECM application
Source: AIIM (2010)

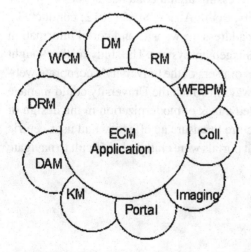

Key:

DM - Document Management
RM - Records Management
WFBPM - Work Flow Business Process Management
Coll. - Collaboration
KM - Knowledge Management
Dam - Digital Asset Management
DRM - Digital Rights Management
WCM - Web Content Management

to bear in mind when considering the preservation of digital content in the long-term and that this was because the more modules an ECM application has the more complex the transfer process tends to be.

A Model for Improving Enterprise Content Management

A concept that could be used to establish activities and routines at various levels of maturity and improve on rigor and details of rules for both ECM and DC applications is the capability maturity model (CMM). According to Katuu (2014), a maturity model is a management tool designed to help organizations implement effective processes in a given management discipline. It is a "structured collection of elements that describe characteristics of effective processes." It provides a place to start, the benefit of prior experience, a common language, a framework for prioritizing actions and a way to define improvement" (Murray and Ward 2007, 5).It provides a road map with which an organization can assess its maturity and the types of activities required to improve from one level of maturity to another.

Even though the concept has existed for more than three decades (Cameron 2011, 21), very little has been published in connection with ECM and DC applications. The most prominent early application of maturity models is in computer software engineering in the 1980s and 1990s (Liu 2002) which later spread to other disciplines including, financial management (McRoberts and Sloan 1998), human resources management (Curtis, Hefley, and Miller 1995), the health sector (Gillies 2000), project management (Kerzner 2001), and improving ICT management (Wanyembi 2009).

As Katuu (2014) observes, regardless of their disciplinary application, maturity models are developed on the basis that organizations do not move from zero capability to optimum capability in an instant, but rather progress along a journey of maturity (Murray and Ward 2007, 5). This journey of maturity is documented in a number of levels of maturity. The number of levels may vary from three to six but five and six are the most common levels. Sections 3.1 and 3.2 below will outline a number of maturity models that have been proposed for ECM and DC applications respectively.

There are at least three maturity models that have been developed for ECM to date. One was developed by an institution in South Africa (Katuu 2012a) while another was developed in the UK (Cameron 2011). Neither of these models have received much global attention. The third model, known as the ECM Maturity Model (ECM3), is probably the best well known and was developed in the US by four consulting firms as an open standard under creative commons license (MIKE2.0 2010). This section will highlight aspects of ECM3.

The first edition of ECM3 was published in March 2009 and a second edition in March 2010 (Pelz-Sharpe et al. 2010). ECM3 provides a structured framework from which to organize efforts by organizations to achieve business benefits from ECM, as well as to hold the attention of program stakeholders (Pelz-Sharpe et al. 2010, 7). It will be able to do this because it can be applied to audit, assess, and explain the current state within an organization, as well as form a roadmap for maturing organization capabilities (MIKE2.0 2010). The framework has 13 dimensions of maturity across three categories: human, information, and systems (Pelz-Sharpe et al. 2010, 8). The dimensions within the "Human" category relate to individual expertise in both business processes and information technology. Katuu (2014) argues that they relate to the extent of strategic alignment between business drivers and the ECM application to ensure institutional success. The dimensions within the "Information" category relate to attributes affecting the digital content itself, while those within the "Systems" category relate to attributes of the ECM applications technical features. Figure 7 provides a graphical representation of the maturity dimensions across three categories (MIKE2.0 2010).

The three categories and 13 dimensions are assessed in the five levels of maturity below:

Level 1: Unmanaged
Level 2: Incipient
Level 3: Formative
Level 4: Operational
Level 5: Pro-Active (Pelz-Sharpe et al. 2010, 6).

Katuu concludes that even though the ECM Maturity Model is reportedly used by a large number of institutions (ECM Maturity Model 2012) there has been little published about the experiences within these institutions (Katuu 2012a).

Maturity Model for Digital Preservation and Digital Repositories

Katuu (2014) notes that there are at least three maturity models that relate to either digital preservation or digital repositories. These are:

- *Digital Preservation Capability Maturity Model (DPCMM)* (Dollar and Ashley 2012),
- *Shaman/Scape Capability Model (Becker et al. 2011)* and the
- *Trusted Digital Repository Maturity Model (TDRMM)* (Cho 2012).

Figure 7. Maturity dimensions in the ECM maturity model
Source: MIKE2.0 2010).

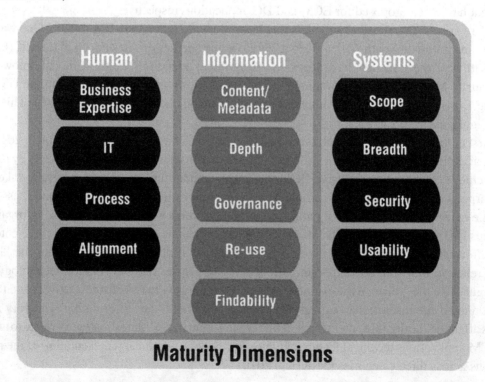

The author further notes that all the three models are at different stages of development and have different areas of emphasis due to their different perspectives. This is a reflection of how new the concept still is in content management discipline. The first has been developed to the point of being used in institutions while the second and third are still being developed. This chapter only highlights the first model.

According to Dollar and Ashley (2011, 8) in Katuu (2014), the objective of DPCMM is to "provide a process and performance framework…against best practice standards and foundational principles of records management, information governance, and archival science". DPCMM draws from the functional specifications and preservation services identified in ISO 1472, as well as checklist criteria found in TRAC guidelines (Trustworthy Repositories Audit and Certification: Criteria and Checklist). It is centered a trusted digital repository which is the results of digital preservation infrastructure as well digital preservation processes (Dollar & Ashley 2012). Figure 8 is a graphical representation of the model (Dollar & Ashley 2012).

The model has 15 process elements that are assessed using five maturity levels. According to Dollar and Ashley (2012), amongst the strengths of DPCMM is that it shows clearly defined components, which then enables priority setting based on risk, requirements, and resources for digital preservation processes.

Tips for Improving a Web Site

Gube (2011) suggests that there are seven (7) best practices that are available to a web designer for improving a website's usability. The author asserts that usable and readable web content is a marriage of efforts between web designers and web content writers. These practices include:

Figure 8. Digital preservation capability maturity model
Source: Dollar and Ashley (2012)

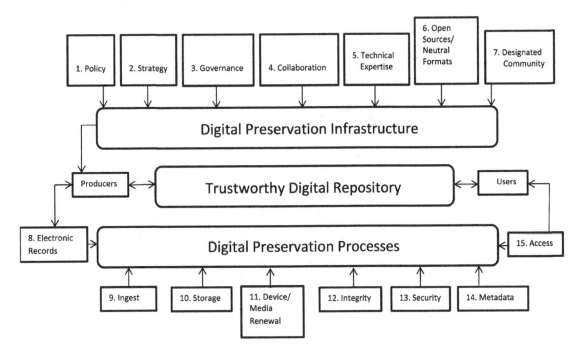

1. Keeping content as concise as possible. Users tend to skim webpages to find the information they want.
2. Use Headings to Break Up Long Articles. Gube (2011) observed that Internet readers inspect webpages in blocks and sections, or what is known as "block reading", in *F-shaped pattern as shown in Figure 9.*
3. Help Readers Scan Webpages Quickly. According to Gube (2011), there is evidence that web users tend to skim content, hence designing and structuring webpages with skimming in mind can improve usability.

To achieve this, Gube advises web content designers to:

*   Make the *first two words count*, because users tend to read the first few words of headings, titles and links when they're scanning a webpage.
*   Front-load keywords in webpage titles, headings and links by using the passive voice as an effective writing device.
*   *Use the inverted pyramid*, shown in Figure 10, writing style to place important information at the top of articles. `

4. Use Bulleted Lists and Text Formatting.

Gube (2011) further shows that users fixate longer on bulleted lists and text formatting (such as **bolding,** underlining, and *italics*).

Figure 9. F-Shaped pattern
Source: Gube (2011).

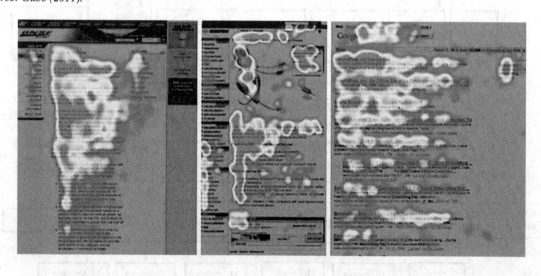

Figure 10. The inverted pyramid writing style
Source: Gube (2011).

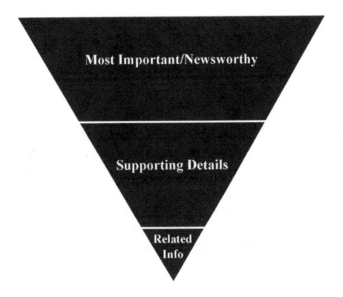

5. *Give Text Blocks Sufficient Spacing.*

Gube (2011) emphasizes that the spacing between characters, words, lines and paragraphs is important. How type is set on webpages can drastically affect the legibility (and thus, reading speeds) of readers.

6. Make Hyperlinked Text User-Friendly.

Nielsen (1997) observes that one big advantage of web-based content is our ability to use hyperlinks. The proper use of hyperlinks can aid readability. Web designers are thus urged to:

- Indicate which links have already been visited by the user by styling the: visited CSS selector differently from normal links, so that readers quickly learn which links they've already tried.
- Use the title attribute to give hyperlinks additional context and let users know what to expect once they click the link.

7. Use Visuals Strategically.

Photos, charts and graphs are worth a thousand words. Using visuals effectively can enhance readability when they replace or reinforce long blocks of textual content.

In an *eye-tracking study* conducted by Nielsen (1997) suggests that users pay "close attention to photos and other images that contain relevant information."

Further, in a study by *Meyer* (2015) on characteristics of minimalism in web design, an analysis of 112 minimalist websites revealed the defining features of minimalism as being flat design, limited color schemes, few UI elements, use of negative space, and dramatic typography, thus lending more to the concept of "less is more".

The Future of ECM Systems

According to an article posted by Rossi (2015), four major trends are likely to force a reshape of the entire enterprise Content Management (ECM) field and mandate a new approach to managing content. These trends are:

1. New Ways of Working

Rossi (2015) observes that allowing employees to work anywhere, anytime and on any device puts a lot of pressure on IT teams to support a new breed of networked employees, whose expectations for ease of use have already been shaped by consumer web services. Information and knowledge workers want to find documents as easily as they can browse for books and journals online. Over the next five years, organisations will increasingly need a solution that will support this increasingly dynamic working style whose share is projected to make up 75% of the global workforce by 2020. Currently most legacy ECM systems, which are already in failure mode due to poor user adoption, can't keep up and lack support for inter-organizational sharing and remote access.

2. Emergence of the extended Enterprise

According to Rossi (2015), organizations are extending their value chains and engaging more deeply with external companies, such as suppliers and distributors. It's becoming increasingly common to see product design, marketing, sales and service performed by remote contract workers and vendors that function as if they were part of the client firm.

However, this type of collaboration only works if there is controlled, two-way information flow across organizational boundaries. Legacy ECM, historically delimited by the firewall, does not serve modern enterprises that are not bound by the limits of IT infrastructure. This approach limits productivity and growth as mobile workers struggle with virtual private network (VPN) issues and external partners lack the access they need to collaborate effectively. The extended enterprise requires a new approach to ECM that supports easy, controlled sharing of content and process inside and outside the organization.

3. Massive Explosion in Digital Content

Rossi (2015) further observes that we live in a data-centric world, where the sheer volume of information and content flooding IT systems is leaving many organizations battling to manage it. This tidal wave of content being created isn't going to disappear anytime soon with some organizations projecting a 50-times growth in digital content from 2010 to 2020, with 90% of it in unstructured information such as emails, documents and video. It's, therefore, crucial that the new generation of ECM must put content in context so that people and processes work more efficiently and effectively.

4. New IT Infrastructure

The fourth trend, according to Rossi (2015) is the need for new IT infrastructure. He observes that sometimes trying to change enterprise IT is like changing direction of a supertanker: it changes slowly, but it is definitely on the move. The IT in today's businesses, especially in emerging economies, is being transformed by the adoption of public and private cloud, along with hybrid cloud deployments of core business systems. In tandem, the IT department has to manage support across a variety of new mobile platforms to meet growing demand from workers. The problem for old ECM systems is that they are trapped in software architectures from an earlier, more homogenous era. Their platforms are generally not built for cloud scale and offer only limited mobile support. By contrast, a modern ECM system needs to support the full range of deployment options and device types.

The Web

The development of the Web can be traced back to the PC era as illustrated in Figure 11.

This period was followed by Web 1.0, Web 2.0 and Web 3.0. It is envisaged that later generations of the Web, e.g. Web 4.0 and 5.0 will follow in a few years to come. Web 1.0, Web 2.0 and Web 3.0 are briefly described below.

Web 1.0

The first generation of the Web was Web 1.0. The focus of this phase was primarily on building the Web, making it accessible, and, for the first time, commercializing it. Important areas of interest were centered on protocols such as HTTP, open standard markup languages such as HTML and XML, In-

Figure 11. Growth of the Web
Source: Spivack (2015)

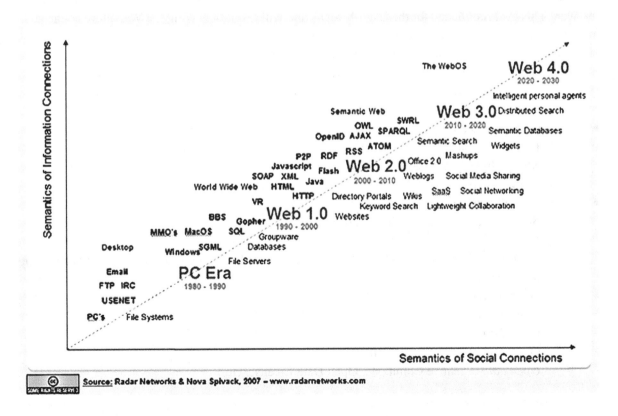

ternet access through ISPs, the first Web browsers, Web development platforms and tools, Web-centric software languages such as Java and Javascript, the creation of Web sites, the commercialization of the Web and Web business models, and the growth of key portals on the Web.

Web 2.0

The second phase of the development of the Web was Web 2.0, according to the Wikipedia. " a phrase coined by in 2004, refers to a supposed second generation of Internet-based services — such as, wikis, communication tools, and folksonomies — that emphasize online collaboration and sharing among users."

Web 3.0

According to Spivack (2015) the Web, as we know it, is entering a new phase of evolution. The world is witnessing the convergence of several growing technology trends that are outside the scope of what Web 2.0 has come to mean. The term *Web 3.0* was coined by Markoff of New York Times in keeping with the naming convention established by labeling the second generation of the Web as Web 2.0.

Following the same pattern as the above Wikipedia definition, Web 3.0 refers to a supposed third generation of Internet-based services that collectively comprise what might be called '*the Intelligent Web*' — such as those using semantic web, microformats, natural language search, data-mining, machine learning, recommendation agents, and artificial intelligence technologies — which emphasize machine-facilitated understanding of information in order to provide more productive and intuitive user experience."

The threshold to the third-generation Web was crossed in 2007. At this juncture the focus of innovation started to shift back from front-end improvements towards back-end infrastructure level upgrades to the Web. This cycle continued for the last 5-8 years, and will result in making the Web more connected, more open, and more intelligent. It will also transform the Web from a network of separately *siloed* applications and content repositories to a seamless and interoperable system.

Web 3.0 might further be defined as a third-generation of the Web enabled by the convergence of several key emerging technology trends including:

- Ubiquitous Connectivity
  - Broadband adoption
  - Mobile Internet access
  - Mobile devices
- Network Computing
  - Software-as-a-service business models
  - Web services interoperability
  - Distributed computing (P2P, grid computing, hosted "cloud computing" server farms such as Amazon S3)
- Open Technologies
  - Open APIs and protocols
  - Open data formats
  - Open-source software platforms
  - *Open data* (Creative Commons, Open Data License, etc.)

- Open Identity
    - ◦ Open identity (OpenID)
    - ◦ Open reputation
    - ◦ Portable identity and personal data (for example, the ability to port your user account and search history from one service to another)
      The Intelligent Web
- Semantic Web technologies (e.g. *RDF, OWL, SWRL, SPARQL*, Semantic application platforms, and statement-based datastores such as triplestores, tuplestores and associative databases)
- Distributed databases — e.g. "The World Wide Database - WWD" (wide-area distributed database interoperability enabled by Semantic Web technologies)
- Intelligent applications (including natural language processing, machine learning, machine reasoning, autonomous agents)

According to teachbytes.com, Web 3.0 will truly put the technology in the hands of the students, and will focus on using technology to help learners make their education their own. As illustrated in Figure 12, it will no longer be about producing new employees, but about encouraging students to be lifelong learners and engaging parents, teachers and students into a larger learning community.

Thus, universities in emerging economies especially in sub-Saharan Africa stand to benefit from the new features of the emerging and advanced technologies that will come with Web 3.0.

SOLUTIONS AND RECOMMENDATIONS

Content management in the context of emerging economies, especially in Sub-Saharan Africa, has began to attract a lot of attention due partly to the fact that these countries have widely adopted new technologies and are, therefore, keen stakeholders in the subject. Many institutions of higher learning are seeking ways of harnessing the new technologies as a part of the solution to surmount the problems associated with the huge digital assets that they generate internally, and receive from external sources. These institutions have started setting up digital repositories in varying degrees of success. Combined with integrated policies and balanced approaches, these solutions promise to help these institutions develop strong content management solutions which will see them compete favorably with the best institutions in the developed world. Towards this end, the following recommendations are made, that:

1. The development of ICT infrastructure geared towards strengthening institutions of higher learning be given top priority by the emerging economies through increased budgetary allocations to about 2%.
2. According to Lippert (2012), Collection Principle 4 states that good digital collections are *"broadly available and avoid unnecessary impediments to use"* and that *"Collections should be accessible to persons with disabilities,*
3. *and usable effectively in conjunction with adaptive technologies"*. It is, therefore, contingent upon institutions of higher learning in emerging economies to set up digital collections based on standards and best practices that maximize their availability, usefulness and accessibility by all including the disabled. Most institutions do not base the development of their digital collections on established standards and best practices, which often lead to problems of access to and use of content.

Figure 12. Evolution of the Web in education
Source: teachbytes.com (2015)

	Web 1.0	Web 2.0	Web 3.0
Meaning is...	Dictated	Socially constructed	Socially constructed & contextually reinvented
Technology is...	Confiscated at the classroom door (digital refugees)	Cautiously adopted (digital immigrants)	Everywhere (digital universe)
Teaching is done...	Teacher to student	Teacher to student & student to student	Teacher to student, student to student, & student to teacher
Schools are located...	In a building	In a building or online	Everywhere & thoroughly infused into society
Parents view schools as...	Daycare	Daycare	A place for them to learn, too
Teachers are...	Licensed professionals	Licensed professionals	Everybody, everywhere
Hardware & software in schools...	Are purchased at great cost and ignored	Are open source and available at lower cost	Are available at low cost and are used purposively
Industry views graduates as...	Assembly line workers	As ill-prepared assembly line workers in a knowledge economy	As co-workers or entrepreneurs

4. The institutions of higher learning develop and implement sound policies on education and training to ensure that their technical and management personnel are not left behind in the fast paced world of content management and maintenance technologies. Many institutions of higher learning in developing economies are not adequately funded to enable them keep abreast of these developments.

5. The widespread use and application of Web 2.0 and the emerging Web 3.0 tools in institutions of higher learning by both staff and faculty be encouraged and ways be found to acquire them where there are none through budgetary allocations and training.

6. A key benefit deriving from a repository of information is the ability to leverage an organization's capabilities through continuous learning and continuous improvement (Mnkandla, 2014). Use of models such as Capability Maturity Model applied to the improvement of web development and content management should be encouraged to market these institutions of higher learning and prepare them to compete effectively with their counterparts from the developed world, including global rankings. Currently this is left to a few individuals to determine the content, much of which is left unchanged for long periods on end on web sites and loses its relevance. Common practice in many universities does not include use of such models.

FUTURE RESEARCH DIRECTIONS

For future research and development, there is need to:

- Conduct surveys to assess the level of readiness in institutions of higher learning in Africa with the view to creating increased awareness of the importance of content management systems.
- An assessment of and training in the use of Web 2.0 and emerging Web 3.0 tools be conducted in institutions of higher learning in Africa.
- Studies in the development and implementation of models geared towards improving web content management be mounted to enable the institutions become more competitive.

CONCLUSION

The need for collaboration among a multitude of stakeholders in an organization coupled with the need for industry compliance with regulations as well as the need for consolidation of organizational data and the need to survive and secure a competitive advantage in a dynamic environment, are now increasingly considered to be the main drivers behind the emergence of web content management in organizations worldwide. Content is a key resource in any information economy and once created, it should to be documented, organized, managed, maintained, and conveyed to the right audience in affordable manner using appropriate technologies. Hence new models and approaches need to be adopted, developed and implemented to meet this increasing demand.

REFERENCES

AIIM. (2010). *What is Enterprise Content Management*. Retrieved from http://www.aiim.org/What-is-ECM-Enterprise-Content-Management.aspx

Answers.com/website. (2015, August 3). Retrieved from http://www.answers.com/topic/website

Batley, S. (2007). The I in information architecture: The challenge of content management. *Aslib Proceedings, 59*(2), 139–151. Retrieved from doi:10.1108/00012530710736654

Becker, C., Antunes, G., Barateiro, J., & Vieira, R. (2011). *A Capability Model for Digital Preservation: Analyzing Concerns, Drivers, Constraints, Capabilities and Maturities*. National Library Board Singapore and Nanyang Technological University. Retrieved from http://www.ifs.tuwien.ac.at/~becker/pubs/becker_ipres2011.pdf

Bellinger, G. (2004). *Knowledge Management – Emerging Perspectives*. Retrieved from http://www.systems-thinking.org/kmgmt/kmgmt.htm

Bitpipe Research Guide. (2000). *Content and Knowledge Management Overview*. Retrieved from http://www.bitpipe.com/data/web/bpmd/contmgmt/content-management.jsp

Businessdictionary.com. (2015). *Define Intranet*. Retrieved from http://www.businessdictionary.com/definition/intranet.html

Cameron, S. A. (2011). *Enterprise content management - a business and technical guide*. Swindon, UK: The Chartered Institute for IT.

Chin, P. (2003). *Intranet Content: Long Live the King*. Retrieved from http://www.intranetjournal.com/articles/.../pij_06_20_03a.html

Cho, N. (2012). *Trusted Digital Repositories Maturity Model (TDR-MM)* Retrieved from http://aeri2012.wordpress.com/conference-schedule/paper-presentations/trusteddigital-archives/

Contentmanager.eu.com. (2015). *What is Content Management?* Retrieved from http://www.content-manager.eu.com/

Conway, P. (2008). *Modeling the Digital Content Landscape in Universities*. Retrieved from http://www.emeraldinsight.com_Insight_ViewContentServiet_contentType=Article&Filename=_published_emeraldfulltextarticle_pdf_230260302

Dempsey, L., Malpas, C., & Lavoie, B. (2014). Collection Directions: The Evolution of Library Collections and Collecting. *Portal: Libraries and the Academy*, July, 393-423.

Dollar, C., & Ashley, L. (2011). *Digital Preservation Capability Maturity Model. A digital preservation maturity model in action*. Retrieved from http://lib.stanford.edu/files/pasigjan2012/12F2%20Digital%20Preservation%20Capability%20Maturity%20Model%20in%20Action.pdf

Gube, J. (2011). *7 Best Practices for Improving Your Website's Usability*. Retrieved from http://mashable.com/2011/09/12/website-usability-tips/

Gupta, G. (1996). *Characteristics of Information*. Retrieved from: http://www.cs.jcu.edu.au/subjects/cp2030/1997/Lecture_Notes/information/characteristics.html

Hockx-Yu, H. (2006). *Digital preservation in the context of institutional repositories*. Emerald Group Publishing Limited. Retrieved from http://www.emeraldinsight.com/Insight/ViewContentServiet>contentType=Article&Filename=_published/Emeraldfulltextarticle/Articles/2800400304.html

Institute of Information Architecture. (2007). *What is Information Architecture?* Retrieved 15 October 2009 from: http://www.iainstitute.org/en/learn/resources/what_is_ia.php

Kampffmeyer, U. (2004, September 28). *Trends in Record, Document and Enterprise Content Management*. Project Consult. Retrieved from http://www.projectconsult.net/Files/ECM_Handout_english_SER.pdf

Kashorda, M., & Waema, T. (2007). *ICT Strategy Brief Based on Findings of e-Readuiness Survey of Higher Education Institutions in Kenya*. Retrieved from www.kenet.or.ke/E-Readinesssurveyof_Kenya_highereducation_institutions2007.pdf0

Katuu, S. (2012a). Enterprise *Content Management– using maturity models to improve the quality of implementation*.

Katuu, S. (2012b). Enterprise Content Management (ECM) implementation in South Africa. *Records Management Journal*, 22(1), 37–56. doi:10.1108/09565691211222081

Katuu, S. (2014). *Enterprise Content Management and Digital Curation Applications*. Maturity Model Connections.

Lippert, R. (2012). *9 Guiding Principles - A Framework of Guidance for Building Good Digital Collections*. Retrieved from https://ezphotoscan.com/blog/9-guiding-principles-framework-guidance-building-good-digital-collections

Liu, R.Y.L. (2002). *Capability maturity model integration: origins and applications* [Masters dissertation]. California State University, Long Beach.

Maurer, D. (2004). *Information Architecture.* Retrieved from http://www.institute.org/tools/download/Maurer-IAItro.ppt

McGovern, G. (2001). *Re-establishing the Value of Content.* Retrieved from http://www.acm.org/ubiquity/views/g_mcgovern_1.html

McRoberts, H. A., & Sloan, B. C. (1998). "Financial management capability model." International. *Journal on Government Auditing, 25*(3), 8–11.

Meyer, K. (2015). *The Characteristics of Minimalism in Web Design.* Retrieved from http://www.nngroup.com/topic/web-usability/

MIKE2. 0. (2010). *ECM Maturity Model (ecm3)* Retrieved from http://mike2.openmethodology.org/wiki/ECM_Maturity_Model_%28ecm3%29

Mnkandla, E. (2014). A review of Communication Tools and Techniques for Successful ICT Projects. *The African Journal of Information Systems, 6*(1).

Mohammadi, M., & Moghadam, A. (2008). Some Issues on Impacts and Characteristics of Information as Wealth in the New Economy. *International Journal of Information science and Technology, 6*(2). Retrieved from http://www.srlst.com/ijist/ijism-Vol6No2/ijism62-37-47.pdf

Moseti, I. M. (2012). Digital Content Management and Use at Moi University [Unpublished MPhil Thesis]. Moi University, Kenya.

Mungai, A. (2008, November). *Local Content – an e-Tourism Perspective.* Paper presented at Tandaa 2008: The Kenya Content Conference held at Kenyatta International Convention Centre, Nairobi, Kenya.

Murray, A., & Ward, M. (2007). *Improving project performance using the PRINCE2 maturity model (P2MM).* Norwich: The Stationary Office.

Muske, G., Stanforth, N., & Woods, M. (n. d.). *The Internet as a Marketing Tool.* Retrieved from http://pods.dasnr.okstate.edu/docushare/dsweb/Get/Document-2491/AGEC-566web.pdf

Mutula, S., & Wamukoya, J. (2007). *Web Information Management: A Cross-disciplinary textbook.* Great Britain: Chandos Publishing. doi:10.1533/9781780631899

Newman, B., & Conrad, K. (1999). *A Framework for Characterizing Knowledge Management Methods, Practices, and Technologies* Retrieved from http://www.km-forum.org/KM-Characterization-Framework.pdf

Ngugi, B., Pelowski, M., & Ogembo, J. G. (2010). M-PESA: A Case Study of the Critical Early Adopters' Role in the Rapid Adoption of Mobile Money Banking in Kenya. *The Electronic Journal of Information Systems in Developing Countries*, 43.

O'Brien, J. (2002). *Management Information Systems: Managing Information Technology in the E-Business Enterprise* (5th ed.). India: Tata McGraw-Hill.

OCLC. (2003) Collections Grid. Retrieved from http://www.oclc.org/reports/escan/appendices/collectiongrid.html

Oppenheim, C., Stenson, J., & Wilson, R. M. S. (2001). *The Attributes of Information as an Asset*. Retrieved from http://www.emeraldinsight.com/journals.html?articleid=860097&show=html

Pelz-Sharpe, A., Durga, A., Smigiel, D., Hartman, E., Byrne, T., & Gingras, J. 2010. *ECM 3 - ECM maturity model* (2nd), June. Retrieved from http://ecmmaturity.files.wordpress.com/2009/02/ecm3-v2_0.pdf

Rao, Aditi. (2013). What Does Web 3.0 Look Like in Education? Retrieved from http://teachbytes.com/2013/03/24/what-does-web-3-0-look-like-in-education/

Review, C. M. S. (2015). *Seven Stages of the Content Lifecycle*. Retrieved from http://www.cmsreview.com/Stages/

Rossi, Ben. (2015). Retrieved from http://www.information-age.com/technology/information-management/123459381/4-trends-reshaping-traditional-content-management

Sharma, P. (2008). Core Characteristics of Web 2.0 services. Retrieved from http://www.techpluto.com/web-20-services/

Spivack, N. (2015). *The Third Generation Web is Coming*. Retrieved from http://lifeboat.com/ex/web.3.0

Steel, D. (2012). *Implementation of a content management system at the Stellenbosch University: an exploratory investigation* [Unpublished MPhil Thesis]. University of Cape Town.

Stuhler, J. (2009). *Managing the Data Explosion: The Causes, Effects and Solutions*. Retrieved from http://www.informationmanagement.com/infodirect/2009_129/data_management_archiving_storage_disaster_recovery-10015658-1.html

Tilton, J. (1994). *What is an infostructure?* Retrieved from http://www.library.creatifica.com/information-architecture-coining-the-term.pdf

VandenBos, G., Knapp, S., & Doe, J. (2001). *Role of reference elements in the selection of resources by psychology undergraduates*. Retrieved from http://jbr.org/articles.html

Wanyembi, G. (2009). *Improving ICT Management in Public Universities in Kenya, Answers to the problems arising from the rapid introduction and use of the new technology*. Germany: VDM Verlag.

Watson, R. T. (2013). Africa's Contributions to Information Systems. *The Africa Journal of Information Systems*, 5(4).

KEY TERMS AND DEFINITIONS

Content: The substance or what is contained therein and may be in any format such as animation, document, e-mail, image, e-journal, news, record, sound, text, video.

Content Management: A set of processes and technologies that are designed to support the generation, use, and dissemination of content.

Content Management System: A system that is designed to support the collection, creation, administration, publication and dissemination/distribution of content.

Extranet: A network similar in design and functions as the *intranet* only that it lies outside the intranet. It is to enable communication between an organization and its customers, partners, suppliers, often by providing limited access to its intranet.

Information Spaces: Sites such intranets, extranets, and search systems.

Infostructure: A layout of information so that it can be navigated with ease. It is the result of organizing information in a useful manner and includes tables of content, bibliography or index.

Interactive Spaces: Business applications and browser-based transactional systems that act in such a manner as to enable users to navigate the system and locate the information they need with ease.

Internet: A network of networks that spans the entire globe. It facilitates the development of applications on the world wide web (WWW). It is not owned by anyone.

Intranet: A private computer network that can be accessed only by authorized users, especially members or employees of the organization that owns it.

Website: A set of interconnected web pages, usually incorporating the home page generally located at the server, and prepared and maintained as a collection of information by a person, or group or organization.

World Wide Web (WWW): A maze of links that connect documents and through which one is able to navigate on the Internet.

Chapter 9
Website link Structure Optimization

Harpreet Singh
DAV University, India

Parminder Kaur
Guru Nanak Dev University, India

ABSTRACT

The structure of a website can be represented in the form of a graph where nodes represent pages and edges represent hyperlinks among those pages. The behaviour of website users changes continuously and hence the link structure of a website should be modified frequently. The problem of optimally rearranging the link structure of a website is known as Website Structure Optimization problem. It falls in the category of combinatorial optimization problems. Many methods have been proposed and developed by the researchers to optimize the web graph structure of a website. In this chapter taxonomy of the website link structure optimization models is presented. The formulation and explanation of the working of the models have also been provided so that the readers could easily understand the methodology used by the models.

INTRODUCTION

The size of the websites is growing with time and many firms are providing services through e-commerce applications. The burgeoning e-commerce market in the world has attracted the attention of researchers all over the world towards making the experience of a website user hassle free. Visitors visit a website at different times with different goals. The information needs of web users changes with time. Hence, there is need to frequently change the website structures according to changing needs of the users. Efficiently browsing a website means getting to the required webpage quickly. These days users tend to leave a website if it takes too long to get to the needed information. Increasing the efficiency refers to facilitating the browsing of a website for the users. The websites are classified mainly into two categories (Singh & Kaur, 2014c): Static websites and Dynamic websites. Static websites refer to the websites with textual material remaining unchanged for a long period of time. Websites of hotels, universities and

DOI: 10.4018/978-1-4666-9764-5.ch009

hospitals are examples of these kinds of websites. Dynamic websites refer to the websites with regularly changing content. E-commerce websites are examples of these kinds of websites where information about new products and schemes is added and information about old products is removed regularly. The link structure of a website can be considered as a directed graph where webpages are represented by nodes and edges represent the hyperlinks between webpages. Figure 1 represents such a structure. This structure is also known as a webgraph (Dhyani, Ng, & Bhowmick, 2002).

The algorithmic models to solve the Website Structure Optimization (WSO) problem are categorized into following classes:

Mathematical Programming Techniques- In these approaches, the problem is formed as 0-1 programming problem with some constraints to be satisfied. These methods use linear programming tools to solve the models.

Heuristic Methods- These methods are based on heuristics such as combining two nodes, removal or addition of links etc. Heuristic models do not guarantee to produce optimal or near optimal solutions. These methods also include the identification of frequently travelled path so that important links in a structure can be identified. These methods are very fast but are not successful in providing good results consistently.

Meta-Heuristic Techniques- Mostly, metaheuristics are derived from some natural process such as food foraging process of ants. These approaches use predefined strategy to find the near optimal solutions. In these techniques, the problem is transformed according to the natural process so that the technique could be easily applied to find the solutions. The problems that are not easily solved by heuristic methods or mathematical models have been found to be easily solvable by metaheuristic methods (Yin & Guo, 2013).

Every link structure optimization model follows certain constraints (Yin & Guo, 2013). Some of the constraints are:

Connectivity constraint- This constraint defines that every other webpage should be reachable from the home page. This constraint should be satisfied by every model.

Depth constraint- There should be a limit on maximum number of edges to be travelled to reach a particular page from home page. This constraint ensures that the user stays on the website for a long period of time.

Outdegree limit- There should be a limit on the number of hyperlinks out of a webpage. This is necessary because more hyperlinks on webpage can confuse a user about which link to follow.

Figure 1. Website graph structure example

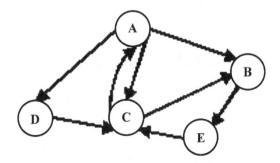

Link constraint- There are some links which should not be removed and there are also some links that should not be included in the link structure to maintain the service logics specified by website design.

Security constraint- Some webpages hold critical information for managerial personnel hence can be navigated through particular pages.

The websites that are restructured regularly according to changing browsing trends are known as adaptive websites (Perkowitz & Etzioni, 1997). The restructuring of the web graph can be performed in two ways (Perkowitz & Etzioni, 2000): Personalization and Transformation. In Personalization, additional web pages are generated which include links to another pages according to behaviour of a particular user. Transformation approaches include altering the link structure of a website to improve the browsing efficiency for all the users. Both these approaches mine web log data (Srivastava et al., 2002) at the web servers to get the browsing behaviour of users. Here, browsing behaviour of users refers to the webpage navigation patterns of web users. Web log data stores every click made by every web users. Web mining can be defined as the application of data mining techniques to find useful patterns from web content and user browsing behaviours. Web mining (Liu B., 2007) can be mainly categorized as: Web content mining, Web structure mining and Web usage mining. Web content mining refers to extraction of useful information from webpage contents. For example, customer reviews and product descriptions can be mined using web content mining. Web structure mining extracts useful information from link structure of a website. For example, web site link structure can be used to find important pages in a website. Web structure mining can also be used to find the user communities that share common interests. Web usage mining refers to the extraction of webpage access patterns from web log data stored at web servers. For example, web usage mining is used to find the sequence of webpages accessed in an E-commerce website to know the most traversed paths by the users.

Web usage mining mainly involves three tasks: preprocessing, discovery of patterns and analysis of patterns. In preprocessing, the sessionization of web access data is performed by using a time out technique (Cooley, Mobasher, & Srivastava, 1999). Here the browsing data is converted into sessions containing a sequence of webpages accessed by a user in specified time. Pattern discovery involves the use of algorithms from the fields of clustering, statistics, association rule mining to find the interesting patterns. Patterns analysis filters out useless patterns and presents important results to the user.

A basic web graph structure improvement model is shown in figure 2. The model is provided with two inputs: the browsing patterns of users and the current web graph structure. The algorithm generates the improved website graph structure as output. Only transformation based models will be discussed in this chapter. In the proposed chapter, four mathematical programming models have been presented. In the category of heuristic models, one model has been discussed. In the category of metaheuristic techniques, five models based on Ant Colony method and tabu search are described.

MATHEMATICAL PROGRAMMING TECHNIQUES

0-1 Programming Model Based on out Degree Constraint

Lin (2006) is the first researcher to introduce the use of 0-1 programming models for the solution of link structure optimization problem. The model is developed to tackle the problem of information overload. Information overload occurs when a user has too many options to choose from and he gets confused. For example, if a user finds too many hyperlinks on a webpage, he may find it difficult to choose the

Figure 2. Website graph structure improvement model

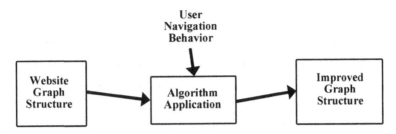

hyperlink that will lead to the goal webpage. This model uses the concept of access frequency of every edge to optimize the link structure of the website. The access frequency of a link refers to the number of users passing through that link to reach their target pages. The access frequency signifies the cohesion between webpages and it is obtained by applying web usage mining on webpage navigation patterns stored in web logs. Hence access frequency defines the importance of the link. This model states that the more important links should be kept in the structure and links with less importance should be eliminated. The goal of the model is to maximize the frequency summation of all the existing links along with the confirmation to some predefined constraints. In this model, an outdegree constraint is applied on every page so that the number of outward hyperlinks does not exceed a particular threshold. The outdegree constraint is applied to tackle the problem of information overload. The access frequency of a link from node i to node j is represented by symbol f_{ij}. The web graph is a directed graph, hence, f_{ij} is not same as f_{ji}. The model is described below.

$$Max \sum_{(i,j)\in E} f_{ij}x_{ij} \tag{1}$$

$$\text{Subject to } \sum_{v_j \in A(v_i)} x_{ij} \le d_i, i = 1,....n \tag{2}$$

$$\sum_{v_j \in A(v_1)} y_{ij} = n-1 \tag{3}$$

$$\sum_{v_i \in B(v_j)} y_{ij} - \sum_{v_k \in B(v_j)} y_{jk} = 1, j = 2,....,n, \tag{4}$$

$$y_{ij} \le (n-1)x_{ij} \forall (i,j) \in E, \tag{5}$$

$x_{ij} = 0,1; y_{ij} \geq 0,$

The parameter x_{ij} denotes the presence of link (i, j). If $x_{ij} = 1$, it means that a hyperlink exists from page i to j. If $x_{ij} = 0$ then page j cannot be accessed directly from i. The term d_i represents the maximal acceptable outward degree for v_i. Here, $A(v_i)$ stand for the set of the succeeding nodes of v_i. A transportation problem (Lin, 2006) is incorporated in the model to prevent the structure from generating inaccessible subgraphs. Node v_1 is the home page, and it is assumed that n -1 unit of pseudo-goods are to be transported from v_1 to the other nodes, with each node receiving just one unit. The parameter y_{ij} denote the units of the pseudo- goods flowing from v_i to v_j. Constraint (3) indicates that the total outflow from v_1 is n- 1. Constraint (4) specifies that the net flow received by each node should be exactly one unit, where $B(v_i)$ representing the set of the preceding nodes of v_i. Constraint (5) requires that the flow can only be transported on an available link. Hence at least one path must exist from the home page to every other webpage. The co-occurrence frequencies of all the edges are added to get the overall frequency sum and then the co-occurrence frequency of every edge is divided with frequency sum to obtain the access frequency value of every link. The value of the objective function lies between 0 and 1.

This model has been developed by using LINGO tool. Through this model, author gave encouragement to the future researchers about the use of techniques such as transportation problem to achieve the objectives of the link structure optimization problem. Lin (2006) performed the experiments on randomly generated web graph structures. These structures were modified to make sure that the constraints are satisfied. The method takes less computation time with graphs of less than hundred nodes. The computation time increases with increasing number of nodes in the link structure.

0-1 Programming Model Based on Shortest Path

Lin (2006) developed another 0-1 programming model for the solution of link structure problem that specifies that the length of the shortest path from home page to any other page should not be more than a specified length. The main goal of the shortest path constraint is to reduce the average number of links traversed by the user to reach a particular page from home page. This model is based on the generation of a spanning tree with the requisite level. The spanning tree is generated to satisfy the depth constraint. The proposed model reduces the information overload and distance of the webpages from the home page.

$$Max \sum_{(i,j)\in E} f_{ij} x_{ij} \tag{1}$$

$$Subject\ to\ \sum_{v_j \in A(v_i)} x_{ij} \leq d_i, i = 1,....,n, \tag{2}$$

$$z_{ij} \leq x_{ij} \forall (i,j) \in E, \tag{3}$$

$$\sum_{v_i \in B(v_j)} z_{ij} = 1, j = 2, ..., n, \tag{4}$$

$$\lambda_j + m(1 - z_{ij}) \ge \lambda_j + 1 \forall (i, j) \in E, \tag{5}$$

$$\lambda_i \le l \forall v_i \in V \tag{6}$$

$$x_{ij}, z_{ij} = 0, 1; \lambda_i \ge 0,$$

This model uses two 0–1 variables: one is z_{ij} and the other is x_{ij}. The parameter z_{ij} represents the participation of each link in the spanning tree. If $z_{ij} = 1$, then the link (i, j) is present as an edge in the spanning tree, otherwise, it is not. The parameter x_{ij} denotes the presence of link (i, j) as in the previous model. The parameter λ_i represents the level of a node i in the graph. The level of a node is defined as the length of shortest path from home page node to that node. Constraint (3) defines that a link can be selected as an edge in the spanning tree only if the link is present in the original webgraph structure. Constraint (4) maintains the connectivity and needs every node to participate in the expanding tree. Constraint (5) specifies that the level of node j should be greater than the level of node i, if an edge from v_i to v_j exists, where m is a sufficiently large positive number. Constraint (6) requires that the level of every node should be smaller than a specified depth *l*.

The model is successful in generating the improved webgraph link structure with specified outdegree and depth. This model is also implemented by using LINGO 8.0 tool. Lin (2006) observed that this model takes much more time than the previously explained model. It was observed that the reason for more computation time is the use of two 0-1 variables. The results obtained by Lin (2006) suggest that finding a spanning tree in a web link graph that satisfies the outdegree constraint is time consuming. It was also observed that the model generates solution within reasonable time for graphs of less than hundred nodes.

Two Phase 0-1 Programming Model

The model based on shortest path takes a lot of execution time due to the use of two 0-1 variables. Hence, to reduce the computation time, Lin (2006) developed a two stage model in which the spanning tree is generated first and then the outdegree constraint is satisfied in the second stage. Every phase uses only one 0-1 variable. The model is described below.

Phase 1

$$Max \sum_{(i,j) \in E} f_{ij} z_{ij} \tag{1}$$

Subject to $\sum\limits_{v_j \in A(v_i)} z_{ij} \leq d_i, i = 1, ..., n,$ (2)

$\sum\limits_{v_i \in B(v_j)} z_{ij} = 1, j = 2, ..., n,$ (3)

$\lambda_j + m(1 - z_{ij}) \geq \lambda_j + 1 \forall (i, j) \in E,$ (4)

$\lambda_i \leq l \forall v_i \in V$ (5)

$z_{ij} = 0, 1; \lambda_i \geq 0,$

Phase 2

$Max \sum\limits_{(i,j) \in E} f_{ij} x_{ij}$ (1)

Subject to $\sum\limits_{v_j \in A(v_i)} x_{ij} \leq d_{ij}, i = 1, ..., n,$ (2)

$z_{ij} \leq x_{ij} \forall (i, j) \in E,$ (3)

$x_{ij} = 0, 1; \lambda_i \geq 0,$

The parameter Z_{ij} represents the presence of edge (i, j) in the spanning tree. The parameter x_{ij} represents the presence of edge (i, j) in the obtained webgraph. The symbols used in the model represent the same parameters as in the previous two models and the description of constraints is also same as used in the previous models. A spanning tree satisfying degree and depth constraint is generated in the first phase. The spanning tree not only satisfies the outdegree constraint but also ensures that the link structure remains connected. In the second phase, the remaining links are selected to maximize the objective function. This model is also implemented by using LINGO 8.0 tool. The experiments performed with this model confirmed that it consumes less computation time than the model based on shortest path. Lin (2006) also observed that the solution quality is not better than the shortest path based model but in some cases this model produced high quality near optimal solutions. More experiments are needed further to analyze the solution quality. This model provides a good way of breaking the bigger problem into subproblems and obtaining the solutions in stages. A major limitation of this model is that like the above two models developed by Lin (2006), this model also cannot produce satisfactory results with webgraphs of more than hundred nodes.

Penalty Based Mathematical Model

A penalty based model has been developed recently by Chen and Ryu (2013) that tries to improve the structure rather than rearrange it. Chen and Ryu (2013) also stated that the website should be structured in a way such that the difference between its structure and user's expectations is minimized. This model relinks the webpages to make the navigability better for website users. A complete reorganization of a website could change the place of familiar items and could create navigation difficulty for users. This model tries to make minimum alterations to the original structure of the website by using user navigation data while improving the structure. In this model, the outdegree constraint is considered a soft constraint and the nodes are allowed to contain more than specified outward links if the cost of adding those links can be justified by the increased browsing convenience. If a node contains more than specified outward links then those extra links are penalized. In this model, more links are added in the structure if the addition of those links seems profitable. The discrepancy between the user's expectations and the link structure of a website is measured by the number of times a user attempted before getting to the target webpage (Chen & Ryu, 2013). A user visiting a website has to make a decision about which hyperlink to follow at every point. The user tries to follow the link that will most probably lead him to the target page. While navigating through a website if the user cannot locate the webpage he wants, he would backtrack to the already visited page to traverse a new path. This concept forms the basis of this model.

Analysis of the web server log data becomes the basis of the model. The log files are broken up into user sessions. A session can be defined as a group of actions performed by a user during his visit to a website. The evaluation metric used in this model is the number of paths traversed to find one target webpage. A session can have more than one target page. A path can be defined as the number of pages visited by a user without backtracking. Each node where the users backtrack becomes the end of the path. The more paths traversed by the users to get to the target pages, the more discrepancy is there between the link structure and the user's expectations. A group of pages visited by a user for only one target webpage is termed as a mini session. Hence, a session can contain one or more mini sessions, each of which comprises a set of paths traversed to reach the target webpage.

Suppose a user is browsing a website with ten webpages as shown in figure 3 where user starts from B, browses H and C, and then go back to B, from where he visits B, H, E, D and backtracks to E. Then, this user goes from E to J and then to F which is the target page. The mini session is denoted as S = {B, H, C}, {B, H, E, D}, {E, J, F}, where an element in S represents a path traversed by the user. In this example, mini session S has three paths as the user backtracks at C and D before reaching the target F.

The ease of navigation is assumed by the number of paths traversed by a user to get to the target page. If a user traverses less number of paths before getting to the target page, it means he may have faced less difficulty in navigation. More number of paths traversed by the user refers to difficulty faced by the user. The maximum number of paths allowed to reach the target page in a mini session is specified by

Figure 3. A website with 10 pages (Singh & Kaur, 2014b)

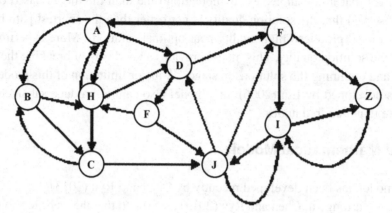

the user. This is termed as the path threshold. Therefore, to achieve the user navigation goal, the website structure is altered in a way such that the number of paths needed to locate the targets in the improved structure is not larger than the path threshold.

Web logs files are used to find the interaction between the user and website. Sessions are extracted from web log files by using timeout method discussed in previous sections. Mini sessions are demarcated by using the page stay time. It is assumed that a user spends more time on a page that is of interest to him. Hence, a page is considered as a target page if the time spent on that page is more than a specified threshold.

In the example, mini session S described above, the user has traversed three paths before reaching target webpage. When the model is applied on the website with path threshold of two paths then one of the solutions is to add link from page B to F. In this way the model tries to improve the user navigation. Let N be the set of all webpages and λ_{ij}, where $i, j \in N$, denote page connectivity in the current structure, with $\lambda_{ij} = 1$ indicating page i has a link to page j, and $\lambda_{ij} = 0$ otherwise. The set T of all mini sessions can be retrieved from log files. For a mini session $S \in T$, tgt(S) represents the target page of S. $L_m(S)$ denotes the length of S, i.e., the number of paths in S, and $L_p(k, S)$, for $1 \leq k \leq Lm(S)$, denotes the length of the kth path in S, i.e., the number of pages in the kth path of S. The model further defines parameter docno(r; k; S), for $1 \leq k \leq L_m(S)$ and $1 \leq r \leq L_p(k, S)$, as the rth page visited in the kth path in S. The symbol E represents the set of candidate links that can be chosen to improve the link structure to help users reach their targets faster. The problem is to decide whether to add a link from i to j for $(i, j) \in E$. Let $x_{ij} \in \{0, 1\}$ denote the decision variable such that $x_{ij} = 1$ indicates establishing the link. The parameter a^S_{ijkr} is defined to be 1 if docno(r, k, S) = i and tgt(S) = j, and 0 otherwise. It means $a^S_{ijkr} = 1$ if and only if page i is the rth visited page in the kth path in S and page j is the target of S. Further, the variable c^S_{kr} will be set to one if the solution specifies adding a link from the rth page in the kth path in S to the target page of S, i.e., tgt(S), and 0 otherwise. The model penalizes a webpage if its out-degree is larger than the specified threshold. Different weights of penalties can be imposed on pages with out-degree exceeding the threshold. The model is described below.

$$Minimize \sum_{(i,j) \in E} x_{ij} [1 - \lambda_{ij}(1 - \varepsilon)] + m \sum_{i \in N_g} p_i$$

Subject to

$$c_{kr}^{s} = \sum_{(i,j) \in E} a_{ijkr}^{s} x_{ij}; r = 1, 2, \ldots L_{p}$$

$$k = 1, 2, \ldots L_{m}(S), \forall S \in T^{R} \tag{1}$$

$$\sum_{k=1}^{b_{j}} \sum_{r=1}^{L_{p}(k,S)} c_{kr}^{s} \geq 1; \forall S \in T^{R}, j = tgt(S) \tag{2}$$

$$\sum_{(i,j) \in E} x_{ij} (1 - \lambda_{ij}) + W_{i} - p_{i} \leq C_{i}; \forall i \in N_{E} \tag{3}$$

$$x_{ij} \in \{0, 1\}, p_{i} \in \{0\} \cup Z^{+}, \forall (i,j) \in E, i \in N_{E} \tag{4}$$

The objective is to improve the website hyperlink structure by minimizing the cost. The cost consists of two parts: First part defines the number of new links to be added. Second part defines the penalties on pages containing more links than the out-degree threshold (C_i), in the improved structure (the second summation). Here m is the penalty imposed on the pages and p_i is the number of links exceeding the out-degree threshold C_i in page i.

Here ε is a very small number which is used to select the existing links. It is to be noted that if (1-ε) is not present, then there is no cost in choosing an existing link, and this could lead to a number of optima.

Constraint (1) defines variable c_{kr}^{S}, which is set to 1 if $a_{ijkr}^{s} = 1$ and $x_{ij} = 1$, for some $(i, j) \in E$, and 0 otherwise. The model uses parameter a_{ijkr}^{s} to make connections between variables x_{ij} and c_{kr}^{S}, because goal function is defined by variable x_{ij} that uses global indices (i and j) to label webpages, while the constraint (2) is defined by variable c_{kr}^{S} which uses local indices (S, k, and r) to identify position of the webpage in a mini session. Constraint (2) necessitates that the objective for user navigation be achieved for all relevant mini sessions, where the goal is defined as path threshold (b_j). Constraint (3) finds the number of links exceeding the outdegree threshold for a page. The parameter W_i denotes the current out degree of the page i. Constraint (4) defines that the decision variables are binary and p_i are nonnegative integers.

Website managers decide a navigation goal that should be met by the improved structure. The goal is the maximize number of paths allowed to get to the target page in a mini session. Take example of mini session S defined above. It is observed that B, H and C are visited in the first path. If the path threshold is set to one then the possible solution is to link either one of B, H or C to F. The link which would give the minimum cost will be added to the structure. If the path threshold is set to two then the candidate links would be the links from elements of second path to F. To improve the structure, first of all relevant mini sessions are identified. A mini session would be relevant if the total number of paths in that session is more than the path threshold. A set of candidate links is obtained from the database of sessions. Candidate links are the links that can be used to improve the structure. Every link in the candidate set cannot be used to improve the link structure. Hence a set of relevant candidate links out of candidate links is extracted. These are the links with target pages as the ending nodes. This model is concerned with relevant candidate links only, hence, the solution space is greatly reduced. Therefore the computation time is reduced.

Increasing the path threshold creates a large number of relevant links and thus increasing the solution space. The model has been tested on real dataset. The real dataset is divided into training and testing sets. The training dataset is used to generate the improved link structure and testing dataset is used to evaluate that structure. It is observed by the developers of this method that this model not only improves the navigation but also brings few changes to the original link structure. It has also been observed that the model improves the structure by adding few additional links. The change in the link structure after improvement is measured by the number of new links added to the structure. The biggest advantage of this model is that it is applicable on very large sized website containing more than one thousand webpages. The time taken to generate the solution is also remarkably low i.e. solutions are generated within seconds in most of the cases. The method needs to read the web log files which are in text form to get the mini sessions in the preprocessing phase that can be time consuming. Chen and Ryu (2013) have also stated that this model is appropriate for static websites with stable contents. The website managers need to maintain a balance between the extent of improvement and the number of new edges required to accomplish the task. Future works include the application of this model on dynamic websites and analyzing the results. More constraints can be tested with the model to analyze the behavior of the model.

HEURISTIC TECHNIQUES

Link Structure Improvement Based on User Access Patterns

Fu et al. (2002) presented a model that used splitting and merging of webpages as the basis of link structure improvement. This model contains three stages: preprocessing, page classification, reorganization. In the preprocessing stage, the log files are analyzed to identify the user sessions. In the page classification phase, the webpages are divided into two categories: index pages and content pages. The model uses a metric named frequency of a page that is defined as the number of sessions (Cooley et al.,1999) in which it occurs divided by the total number of sessions. A webpage is said to be frequent page if the frequency of a page is greater than minimum frequency; otherwise, it is called an infrequent page. An index page can be defined as a page containing hyperlinks to other webpages. The webpage that contains information for the web users is known as a content page.

A website user starts from the home page of a website and browses through index pages to get to the webpage that contains information that is of interest to the user. The objective of this model is to cut down on the number of intermediary index pages that has to be traversed by the user to get to the target webpage. This method uses the heuristic concept of merging and splitting the webpages to reduce the number index pages in the link structure. To achieve this goal, frequently accessed pages are positioned higher up in the link structure, i.e. nearer to the home page and pages that are not accessed frequently are placed lower in the website link structure.

The webpages are scanned sequentially starting from the home page. For every page, the predecessor and successor nodes are considered, where a predecessor is any page that has a link to it and successor nodes are pages that are pointed by the current page. There are different cases depending on the number of predecessor and successor nodes and for each case, different actions may be taken according to the frequency and category of the pages involved.

Example case: Consider the figure 4 (a). Here page B is an index page. Page B can be eliminated whenever possible. The easiest scenario is shown in Figure 4 (b) where two direct links from page A to page C1 and page C2 are added. However, since two links will be added in page. If page A does not have a free link, pages C1 and C2 are merged. Two or more pages can be merged if at most one of them is a content page and their total frequency does not exceed the minimum frequency.

Algorithm for site reorganization uses a queue as data structure and is described below:

1. Initialize all the nodes to the wait state
2. Add the nodes pointed to by home page node in the QUEUE
3. Repeat steps 4 to 7 until QUEUE is empty
4. P= Pop (QUEUE), Remove the front node of QUEUE
5. Adjustments are made in the structure according to various cases
6. Change the state of p to processed state
7. Add the nodes pointed to by p to the rear of queue

This heuristic method reduces the number of intermediary pages that are to be traversed to get desired information. The negative side of this method is that the authors of this method do not use any logical approach and the authors have also not discussed the effects of this approach on large sized websites. This method does not seem promising as there are many issues related to the content of the pages that may arise during the splitting or merging of pages.

METAHEURISTIC TECHNIQUES

Strategic Oscillation Based Model for E- Supermarket Websites

Wang et al. (2006) developed an efficient model for E-supermarket websites. E- supermarket websites fall in the category of dynamic websites. There are mainly two types of webpages in an E- supermarket

Figure 4. (a) Before processing (b) After processing (Singh & kaur, 2014b)

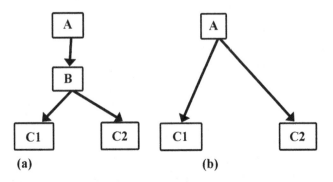

website: category pages and product pages. Product pages contain information about various products and category pages act as index pages that are essential to reach product pages. Hyperlinks are also divided into two categories: basic links and add on links. A link is a basic link if it has some category page as a source node and some other category page as destination node. A link may be a basic link if the source node is a category page and destination node is product page. A link would be an add-on if source and destination nodes are product pages. A link may be an add-on if source and destination nodes are category pages or the source node is a category page and destination node is a product page. A customer wants to get to the webpage containing information about the product of interest as quickly as possible, whereas the managers want the customers to browse the webpages that contain information about those products that generate bigger profits. The interests of both parties is reflected by the product of $c_{i,j}$ and p_j. For edge from node i to node j, the term $c_{i,j}$ represents the correlation coefficient which defines the interests of customers in products at node i and j. The term p_j represents the profit generated from product at node j. Association rule mining (Wang, Wang, & Ip, 2006) is used to find the correlation among different products. In the presented model, one product is represented by one webpage. A transaction is defined as a set of items bought by a customer. A transactional database is available that contains all the transactions. An association rule can be represented as $A \rightarrow B$. The support of rule $A \rightarrow B$ is defined as the number of transactions containing both A and B divided by the total number of transactions. The confidence of rule $A \rightarrow B$ is defined as the number of transactions containing both A and B divided by the total number of transactions containing item A. Correlation between products A and B is generated using following formula.

$$Correlation(A, B) = Support(A \rightarrow B) \times Confidence(A \rightarrow B)$$

Consider that the website contains n webpages. New links can be included in the graph structure. The objective function tries to minimize the overall weighted distance between nodes in the link structure of the webgraph. The model for E-supermarket contains more constraints than other models. A link cannot be inserted between webpages that are not correlated. A basic link matrix is defined where every element $b_{i,j} \in \{0,1\}$. Basic links cannot be removed from the link structure. The links that are added or deleted are add on links. There are also some links that are forbidden. It means forbidden links cannot be added in the graph. The formulation of the optimization model is described below:

$$Min\left(X\right) = \sum_{i \in V}\sum_{j \in V} c_{ij} p_j d_{ij}(X).(1 - \theta_{ij}(X)) + [\sum_{i \in V}\sum_{j \in V} \theta_{ij}(X)]^2 + \omega_1[\sum_{i \in V}\sum_{j \in V}(x_{ij} - e_{ij})]^+ - \omega_2[\sum_{i \in V}\sum_{j \in V}(e_{ij} - x_{ij})]^+ \quad (1)$$

$$st. \ x_{ij} - b_{ij} \geq 0, i, j \in V \quad (2)$$

$$u_{ij} - x_{ij} \geq 0, i, j \in V \quad (3)$$

$$\sum_{j \in V} \left| x_{ij} - e_{ij} \right| \le O_i, i \in V \tag{4}$$

$$\sum_{i \in V} \left| x_{ij} - e_{ij} \right| \le I_j, j \in V \tag{5}$$

$$\sum_{i \in V} \sum_{j \in V} \left| x_{ij} - e_{ij} \right| \le M \tag{6}$$

$$\theta_{ij}(X) = \begin{Bmatrix} 1, d_{ij}(X) = \infty \\ 0, otherwise \end{Bmatrix}$$

If link from node i to node j exist in the optimized structure then the variable $x_{i,j}$ is set to 1; otherwise $x_{i,j} = 0$. The element in the ith row and the jth column of adjacency matrix (Wang, Wang, & Ip, 2006) E of original structure is denoted by $e_{i,j}$. The link exist between node i and j if $e_{i,j} = 1$, otherwise not. Parameter b_{ij} represents a basic link, $b_{ij}=1$ means the basic link (i, j) exists; otherwise not. The profit factor for product j is represented by b_j. The terms c_{ij} and d_{ij} denote the correlation coefficient and distance between node i and j respectively. The objective is to minimize the overall weighted distance between the pages. The equation (1) represents the objective function. The first term in the objective function denotes that pages with larger correlation × product value should have less distance between them. The second term denotes the punishment for infinite-distance. The third term in the objective function denotes the penalty for adding an edge. The last term represents the inducement of removing an edge. Parameters ω_1 and ω_2 represent penalty and inducement factors, respectively. Constraint (2) prevents removal of basic links. Constraint (3) restricts the addition of add-on links that joins the web-pages without any relationship. The parameter u_{ij} take binary values. If $u_{ij}=1$, it means ith product or category is related with jth product or category; otherwise not. Constraints (4) and (5) correspond to the out-degree and in-degree variance respectively. The total-link-number variance is represented by constraint (6).

Tabu search (Glover, 1989) has been a very successful technique in finding solutions of combinatorial optimization problems. Tabu search works by exploring the neighboring solutions of current solution and moving towards the best solution out of those neighbors (Misevicius, 2005). Tabu search needs an initial solution to start with.

In the model, the initial structure is to be used as the initial solution. The methodology uses two types of moves to create the neighbor solution. One is add link operation and other is remove link operation. The add link operation consists of including the link that is not currently present in the solution. The removing link operation consists of removing an existing link. If there are N nodes in the graph then the neighborhood consists of $N^2 - N$ solutions. Very large neighborhood decreases the efficiency of the algorithm. To improve the efficiency of the algorithm, aspiration plus strategy is used. An aspiration threshold value is set, if the objective value becomes less than this value then that iteration is terminated. The neighbor search is terminated after certain iterations when the move evaluation exceeds the aspiration threshold. An upper bound is used on the number of overall moves.

The concept of critical events is also used in this model. A critical event is said to have occurred if a move generates an inferior solution that the previous one. The inferior solutions are generated until a maximum number is reached i.e. if the number successive critical events become more than a certain number, the current iteration is terminated.

The browsing information saved in the web logs is analyzed to identify the user browsing patterns. As explained earlier, data mining methods are used to establish a correlation between the product/category pages. The new links are added between only those pages that are correlated. A profit factor is associated with every product. This profit factor is decided by analyzing the profit generated by that particular product in the past sales.

A decision has to made at every move to about which link to be added out of many candidate links. This decision is taken by looking at the probability that is calculated by using the product of correlation and profit factor. The formula for adding a link is described below:

$$pro(i, j)^+ = \frac{c_{i,j} p_j}{\sum_{(i,j) \in H} c_{i,j} p_j}$$

The formula for removing a link is described below:

$$pro(i, j)^- = \frac{(cp_{max} - c_{i,j} p_j)}{\sum_{(i,j) \in H} (cp_{max} - c_{i,j} p_j)}$$

Here H denotes a set of candidate links that can be added or removed. C_{ij} denotes the correlation between webpage/product i and j. P_j denotes the profit factor related to product j. The links with more CP value has more probability of getting added and links with low CP value has more probability of getting deleted.

The developers of this model have performed all the experiments with artificially generated E-supermarket link structures. The profit factors of the products are generated between 1 and 7 using the random number generator function. To generate the correlation between nodes, a dummy transactional database is generated. Every transaction contains a set of products that are randomly generated. The parameters values used are fine tuned by performing experiments. To evaluate the performance of the algorithm, numbers of page pairs with different distances before and after the application of the algorithm are compared. It was observed that the number of page pairs with shorter distances increased. Hence, it is claimed that the customer convenience got increased after the application of the model (Wang, Wang & Ip, 2006).

Tabu search technique has been found to be a very fast method for optimizing the E-supermarket link structure. This method uses shortest paths to calculate the objective function value. With every move a new link is added or removed, hence the shortest paths between every pair of edges are needed to be calculated again and again. Therefore a lot of time is consumed by this step. Two new modules for the calculation of shortest paths are used by this model to reduce the time complexity. This model also uses two types of stopping criteria. One way is to terminate after a fixed number of iterations and other way is to stop when no better solutions are found for large number of iterations. This model is very promising for E- supermarket webgraph structures. Future works include the implementation of this model with ant colony, genetic algorithms or using some other metaheuristic technique. The application of this model on some real world E- supermarket website is still pending. Tabu search method should also be tested with larger and more complex artificially generated E- supermarket webgraph structures to find more issues related to tabu search. The problem with tabu search is that it does not always guarantee to provide the global optimal value. One solution to tackle this problem is to obtain the initial feasible solution with some other method and then the tabu search should be applied to enhance the quality of the solution.

Ant Colony System based Method for Web Graph Structure Improvement

Ant colony system (Colorni, Dorigo, & Maniezzo, 1992) has been found to be very successful for solving the combinatorial optimization problems. The metaheuristics such as ant colony system can be useful when finding a good solution quickly is more important than finding the optimal solution (Lin & Tseng, 2010). Website link structure rearrangement is also considered as a combinatorial optimization problem (Lin & Tseng, 2010). Many advanced versions of the ant colony system have been developed by various researchers. Lin & Tseng (2010) developed a model based on ant colony system that uses the food foraging behavior of ants to build the solution.

The method is divided into two stages. In the first stage, the Ant Colony based method is applied to generate a spanning tree and in the second stage, a simple method is used to form the optimal website link structure.

Ant colony method works like ants. When looking for food source, ants deposit pheromone on the path that they travel. The pheromone level released on a particular path rises with the number of ants passing through that path. Ants use pheromones to communicate with each another to identify shorter paths to the food source. In this way ants can find the shortest path from their home to the food source and vice versa. This shortest path is found with the help of the pheromone level that increases when more and more ants move through that path. The model presented in this section is based on ant colony system that is used to solve the travelling salesman problem. While finding solutions for travelling salesman problem, an ant standing at a node choose the next node according to some criteria.

In this approach, Ant colony algorithm chooses edges instead of nodes in the construction of the spanning tree. The ant repetitively selects a single edge to develop the spanning tree. A set of candidate edges is maintained, from which the ants select edges. A candidate edge is an edge having source node belonging to the tree being constructed and an end node that does not belong to the constructing tree. This model also follows two constraints. One is outdegree constraint which restricts the number of hyperlinks out of webpages. As explained earlier, outdegree constraint reduces the information overload. Second constraint is level constraint that limits the length of the shortest path from home webpage to every other page. This constraint is applied to minimize the number of clicks needed to get to the target page. Reorganizing the link structure of the website (Lin & Tseng, 2010) refers to finding a subgraph containing all nodes and maximizing the sum of edge access frequencies under the depth and outdegree constraints. Co-occurrence frequencies between webpages are obtained from web logs through web usage mining. Co-occurrence frequency corresponds to the number of visitors moving from page i to page j. The normalized access frequency f_{ij} values of the edges are obtained by dividing the co- occurrence frequency value of every edge with sum of co- occurrence frequency values of all the edges.

Suppose T be the tree being constructed. The set of candidate edges is defined by C = {(i, j) | $v_i \in$ T, $v_j \notin$ T}. The home page node is represented by v_1 and is added to the empty tree T in the beginning. Initially, the edges adjacent to v_1 are added to C. The ant picks an edge from C according to the following transition rule. If a random number $q \le q_0$, where q_0 is a predefined parameter between [0, 1] then the ant selects edge (x, y) according to the following rule.

$$f_{xy} = \max_{(i,j) \in C}\{f_{ij}\}, \text{ here } f_{ij} \text{ is the weight or access frequency of edge from node i to j}$$

If $q > q_0$, then an edge is randomly selected from C based on the probability distribution given by following equation.

$$P_{xy} = \begin{cases} \dfrac{\tau(x, y)}{\displaystyle\sum_{(i,j) \in C} \tau(i, j)}, if(x, y) \in C \\ 0, otherwise \end{cases}$$

The value of the parameter f_{ij} specifies the weight of the edge from node i to node j. All edges that leave v_y are added to C after edge (x, y) and node v_y are added to constructing tree T. The degree of V_x and the level of V_y are then checked. If the degree of V_x equals the prespecified limit then all edges that leave V_x are removed from C. Similarly, if the level of V_y equals the prespecified limit then all edges that leave V_y are ruled out. These actions help the tree to meet the degree and level constraints. Edges in C that result in loops in the tree are also removed. The tree construction stops when the set of candidate nodes becomes empty again.

When a spanning tree is generated by an ant then the second stage is started. A candidate edge set is also maintained in this stage containing the edges that are not present in the spanning tree but are present in the original structure. It is to be kept in mind that this model does not allow the addition of new edges. The edge with the largest frequency is taken out from remaining candidate edges one after another to add to the tree to form a subgraph that confirms to the degree and level constraints. The pheromones on the edges of the obtained subgraph are updated by the following local updating rule.

$$\tau_{ij} \leftarrow (1 - \rho)\tau_{ij} + \rho\Delta\tau$$

Here τ_{ij} denotes the pheromone (Dorigo & Blum, 2005) level on edge (i, j); $0 < \rho < 1$ is a parameter representing the local pheromone evaporation rate, and $\Delta\tau$ represents the variation in pheromone, which is set to be the initial pheromone level τ_0.

The global updating rule (2) is applied to update the pheromones on the edges of the globally best subgraph once the m ants have obtained their respective subgraphs.

$$\tau_{ij} \leftarrow (1-\alpha)\tau_{ij} + \alpha\Delta\tau$$

where $0 < \alpha < 1$ denotes the global pheromone evaporation rate, and

$$\tau_{gb} = \begin{cases} L_{gb}, if(i,j) \in global\ best\ solution \\ \tau_{ij}, otherwise \end{cases}$$

Here L_{gb} represents the objective function value of globally best solution.

Lin and Tseng (2010) performed most of the experiments on artificially generated web graph structures. First, complete graphs of N nodes were generated. Then, all the edges of the graph are assigned values between 0 and 1 using random number generator functions. The links of the largest K frequencies are selected and remaining links are deleted to form the subgraph containing N nodes and K edges. The graph structure is modified so that the link structure should remain connected i.e every node should have one incoming link. Then the frequencies of the links are normalized by dividing the frequency of the individual links with frequency sum of all the edges. The values of the parameters such as ρ, α, q_0 are decided after performing experiments on some instance of the problem as explained earlier. The experiments are performed to find the optimal values of these parameters. The model is implemented with LINGO 8.0. The ant colony system outperforms the 0–1 programming approaches by providing very good solutions in a short computation time. The ant colony system exhibits low time complexity, and can therefore be applied to reorganize large websites.

The major advantage of this model is: it takes very short computation time, it has less time complexity and is applicable on large sized webgraphs with more than 200 nodes and more than 3000 links. This method is also successful in reducing search depth and information overload for users browsing the website. Lin and Tseng (2010) conducted several experiments on a real world website and found that ant colony based model can generate near optimal solutions successfully. It is found that after application of this method, the average weighted shortest distance (Lin & Tseng, 2010) got reduced. More experiments with larger and complex link structures should be performed to discover issues not observed by the developers of this algorithm. Future work also includes the use of other metaheuristics to solve the above mentioned model. Lin & Tseng (2010) observed that as the values of the depth and oudegree constraints are increased, the computation time reduces and the low values of outdegree and depth prolongs the computation time. The quality of the solution decreases as the number of nodes and edges increases. Future work includes the implementation of this model with other metaheuristics. Ant Colony method presented in this section can also be merged with other local search methods to improve the quality of the solution.

Link Structure Improvement based on Quadratic Assignment Problem Approach

Saremi et al. (2008) proposed a model in which website link structure improvement approach is mapped as Quadratic Assignment Problem (QAP) and the ant colony method developed for QAP is used to solve the WSO problem. The method uses the web log data to identify the co occurrence between webpages. Mapping the WSO into QAP type of problem provides opportunity to the researchers to apply methods developed for QAP to solve the complex problem of WSO.

QAP Problem

The QAP is considered as facility location problem (Francis & White, 1976). The facilities location problem (Loiola, Abreu, Boaventura-Netto, Hahn, & Querido, 2007) is about placing the facilities at best locations if the distances between locations and the demand flows among the facilities are given. It can also be defined as the problem of allocation of facilities to locations at the minimum cost. Figure 5(a) shows three locations and distances between them and figure 5(b) shows three facilities which are to be assigned to these locations.

The QAP problem can be formulated as:

- Given N facilities $f_1, f_2,..., f_N$ and N locations $l_1, l_2,..., l_N$
- Let $A^{N \times N} = (a_{i,j})$ be a positive real matrix where $a_{i,j}$ is the flow between facilities f_i and f_j
- Let $B^{N \times N} = (b_{i,j})$ be a positive real matrix where $b_{i,j}$ is the distance between locations l_i and l_j
- Let p: $\{1,2,...,N\} \rightarrow \{1,2,...,N\}$ be an assignment of the N facilities to the N locations

The objective function (Singh & Kaur, 2014b) of QAP is formulated as,

$$Min(C(p)) = \sum_{i=1}^{N} \sum_{j=1}^{N} a_{i,j} b_{p(i),p(j)}$$

Here C(p) represents the cost function.

The above figure 6 shows one of the assignment situations in which the cost comes out to be: Cost = 10×10+ 30×5 + 40×1 = 290. The goal is to find the assignment with the lowest cost. The average connectivity metric (Zhou et al. 2001) is used to evaluate the link structure of the website. The user sessions are analyzed to count the number of sessions in which web pages are accessed.

Figure 5. (a) Location and distances (b) Facilities and flows (Singh & Kaur, 2014b)

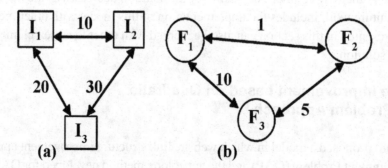

Figure 6. One of the solutions of problem in figure 5 (Singh & Kaur, 2014b)

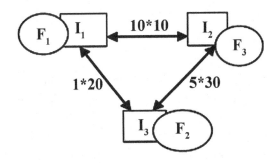

WSO as QAP Problem

The web pages represent facilities and the flow between the facilities is the connectivity between pages. The distance between locations is the shortest distance between two pages. The problem is to place the web pages at the possible locations in a website based on the connectivity and distance between web pages. The product of distance and connectivity represent the cost of two web pages. The structure with least possible overall cost would be the most efficient structure. The goal function of WSO problem modeled as QAP is defined as follows

$$Min\left(TC(a) = \sum_{1 \leq i < j \leq n} \left[C_{ij} \times d(a_i, aj)\right]\right)$$

here n denotes for the number of facilities, $d(a_i, a_j)$ shows the distance between two web pages, C_{ij} stands for the connectivity between web pages i and j and finally TC(a) represents the total cost of the website structure The less the total cost, the better the website structure.

The Ant Colony meta-heuristic technique is used to solve the QAP-modeled problem. In the employed Ant colony algorithm, the population of m artificial ants is dispersed in the original web link structure. In a single iteration, each ant goes through a sequence of nodes by traversing the edges to generate a candidate solution. Before the next iteration, the quantity of pheromone on each edge is updated by the pheromone updating rule as given below:

$$\tau_{ij}(t+1) = (1-\rho)\tau_{ij}(t) + \sum_{k \in colony\ that\ used\ edge(i,j)} \frac{Q}{L_k}$$

where $\tau_{ij}(t)$ is the primary amount of pheromone on edge (i, j). $\tau_{ij}(t+1)$ is the secondary amount of pheromone on the edge (i, j). Here parameter ρ is the evaporation rate of pheromone; Q is the overall amount of pheromone in the Ant System; L_k represents the objective function obtained by the kth ant. An ant chooses to go from current node to next node according to following criteria:

$$p_{ij}(t) = \frac{\tau_{ij}(t)^{\alpha}}{\displaystyle\sum_{j \in allowed\ nodes} \tau_{ij}(t)^{\alpha}}$$

here P_{ij} (t) is the probability of placing the ith facility at the jth location in the next step; $\tau_{ij}(t)$ is the current amount of pheromone on the edge (i,j) ; α is the weight of pheromone in probability computation.

Solution is generated in this way in every iteration. The objective value of the solution obtained in the current iteration is compared with the value of the global best solution. If the objective function value of the current solution is less than that of global best then the current solution becomes the global best. The method can be terminated by using some stopping criteria such as the running of maximum number of iterations. The method can also be terminated if a stagnation point is reached and the objective value does not change for last certain number of iterations.

The connectivity between webpages is calculated by analyzing the weblogs that contain the information about the webpages visited by various users. First, the users sessions are extracted from weblogs and then the user visiting session matrix is generated. The user visiting session matrix is shown in table 1.

User visiting session matrix is a binary matrix where columns represent the webpages and rows represent the user sessions. In the cells of matrix, the value of 1 represents that a particular session contains a particular page and 0 signifies that the page was not visited in that session. For example, in table 1, third session is represented as S3 and value of 1under columns of pages 1, 2, 4 and 8 signifies that these pages are visited in session 3. Then the associate degree between nodes is calculated. The associate degree represents the probability of visiting node j if the user have already visited node i. It is represented by the following formula:

$$R_{ij} = \frac{\left| P_{(i,j)} \right|}{\left| P_i \right|}$$

Here the term $\left| P_{(i,j)} \right|$ describes the number of sessions in which webpage i and j occurred together and $\left| P_i \right|$ represents the number of sessions in which page i occurred. Then the connectivity is obtained by using the following formulae:

Table 1. User Visiting Session matrix

	Page 1	Page 2	Page 3	Page 4	Page 5	Page 6	Page 7	Page 8
S1	1	0	0	1	1	0	1	1
S2	1	1	0	0	0	1	1	0
S3	1	1	0	1	0	0	0	1
S4	1	0	0	0	0	1	1	1
S5	1	1	1	1	0	0	0	1

$$C_{ij} = w_1 + w_2 + \ldots\ldots + w_m$$

Here m defines the number of possible routes from node i to node j. Here w_m represents the weights of mth route. The connectivity defines the amount of interaction between two webpages.

It is found that the QAP and ant colony technique is very efficient in solving website structure improvement problem. A lot of literature and research work about the ant colony technique and QAP is available that can provide assistance in the further improvements of the ant colony method for WSO.

This algorithm can optimize the website structures having too many web pages in less time. The developers of this method have claimed that it significantly reduces the navigation time for a user i.e. the time taken to get to the required webpage after entering the homepage of a website. The solution quality decreases as the number of hyperlinks in a link structure increases. A major problem in adopting this technique is that it cannot satisfy strict constraints and the number of links in the website structure cannot be increased or decreased. The ant colony can be merged with other methods such as tabu search to further improve the solution quality. Metrics should be developed that can evaluate the type of improvement made by the solution.

Link Structure Improvement based on Enhanced Tabu Search

It has been observed that the most successful hybrid methods use tabu search as a subroutine (James, Rego, & Glover, 2009). The authors also introduced several advanced intensification and diversification strategies (James, Rego, & Glover, 2009). Another tabu search based method has recently been developed by Yin & Guo (2013) in which the website structure optimization problem is modeled as quadratic assignment problem type problem. Tabu search technique has been employed to find the optimized structure.

Extraction of User Sessions

The method to extract the user sessions from the server log files is proposed by Cooley et al. (1999). The server files are extracted and scanned. Then the irrelevant information is removed. The time window technique is used to separate the different user sessions. If a user browses different pages in a specified time window of t minutes then all those pages are included in the session for that particular user. After the extraction of user sessions from web log, the paths visited by every user are extracted. The path consists of the sequential traversal of hyperlinks by a user.

Model Formulation

A website structure is represented by a directed graph, G = (P, L), where P = $\{p_i \mid i \in [1, N]\}$ is the set of webpages and L = $\{l_{ij} \mid i \neq j; i, j \in [1, N]\}$ is the set of hyperlinks.

The parameter τ_{ij} represents the total number of users going from webpage i to webpage j. The direct transition probability δ_{ij} on link l_{ij} is defined as follows.

$$\delta_{ij} = \frac{\tau_{ij}}{\sum_{\forall k} \tau_{ik}} \tag{1}$$

The parameter δ_{ij} is the conditional probability that the user would move to page p_j if he is currently at p_i.

The method uses a parameter named association degree R_{ij} which defines the associations from webpages p_i to p_j. Web server logs are used to extract the click through patterns (Yin & Guo, 2013). Click through patterns are used to generate the paths traversed by users. The main objective of the model is to make the frequently visited paths shorter. The symbol R_{ij} represents the association degree where p_i is the starting page and p_j serves as the end page. Let us assume there are m possible paths from p_i to p_j, denoted by $\{Path_1, Path_2, \ldots, Path_m\}$. Also let $|Path_u|$ represents the number of links contained in $Path_u$ and the permutation function $\pi_u(v)$ denotes the index of the v-th page in $Path_u$. The association degree R_{ij} is calculated by adding the multiplication product of the direct transition probability for each link along all feasible paths.

$$R_{ij} = \sum_{u=1}^{m} \prod_{v=1}^{|Path_u|} \delta_{\Pi_u(v)\Pi_u(v+1)} \tag{2}$$

The weighting sum of the webpage associations R_{ij} defines the usage estimation function where weight w_{ij} is the average length of all the simple paths from p_i to p_j in the improved link structure. The usage estimation function is defined as $\sum_{i \neq j} w_{ij} R_{ij}$. The problem is formulated as below:

Minimize $\sum_{i \neq j} w_{ij} R_{ij}$ \hfill (3)

Subject to $\sum_{\forall j} x_{ij} \leq k, \forall i \in O$ \hfill (4)

$d_{1j} \leq H, j > 1$ \hfill (5)

$x_{ij} = 1, \forall j \in U_i$ \hfill (6)

$\sum_{\forall j} x_{ij} \leq b_1, \forall i \in l$ \hfill (7)

$$\sum_{\forall j} x_{ij} \leq b_2, \forall i \in C \tag{8}$$

$$x_{rj} = 1, x_{kj} = 0, r \in R, j \in S, k \neq r \tag{9}$$

$$x_{ji} = 0, \forall j \notin F_i \tag{10}$$

$$x_{ij} \in \{0,1\}$$

The decision variable x_{ij} takes binary values where $x_{ij} = 1$ indicates that a hyperlink from page p_i to page p_j is present in the obtained website structure, and $x_{ij} = 0$ otherwise. Equation (4) defines that the number of outward hyperlinks from a webpage should not be greater than k. Equation (5) defines the connectivity and the website depth constraint. Here d_{ij} denotes the length of the shortest path from p_i to p_j. Equation (6) defines a basic links constraint that is used to maintain the service logics (Yin & Guo, 2013). Here U_i specifies the pages that must linked from p_i. Constraints (7) and (8) defines various out-degree upper limits b1 and b2 for index pages (p_i, $i \in I$) and content pages (p_i, $i \in C$), respectively. Equation (9) defines the security constraint where the secured pages (p_j, $j \in S$) should only be accessed immediately through the registration pages (p_r, $r \in R$). Constraint (10) is compatible link constraint that prevents some links between certain pages because of incompatibility with the service logics. There is a compatible page set F_i for every page p_i and p_i is not allowed to contain a hyperlink pointing to any page not belonging to set F_i.

Extended Tabu Search for WSO

Candidate solutions are represented by a binary matrix that contains binary values (0-1). In the extended tabu search method, the original structure is used as the initial solution. The structure is altered by two operations of link insertion and deletion. The authors have introduced the strategy to handle the constraints that defines the handling the infeasible solutions that are produced during the solution construction. During the link insertion or deletion operations, the constraints can get violated. Outward degree constraint can be violated by link insertion operations and the link deletion operation can defy connectivity constraint. If an edge insertion operation causes outward degree violation then a repairing link deletion operation is automatically triggered. And if some link deletion operation violates the connectivity constraint then some necessary links are added back to the web graph. These repairing operations help to generate high quality solutions. The simplified extended Tabu search algorithm (Yin & Guo, 2013) is given below.

Begin
Initialization of memory structures
Original website link structure is taken as initial solution

Repeat
Generate neighbors by link deletion and link insertion operations
Evaluate the neighborhood solutions
Select the best admissible solution among the neighborhood
Update tabu list
until stopping criteria is satisfied
end
Output the overall best solution

The algorithm is easy to implement and it can obtain a better value of web usage estimation than heuristic methods. The method maintains two tabu lists: delete tabu list and insert tabu list. Delete tabu list contains a list of links that should not be deleted from the link structure with in next u steps. Insert tabu list contains those links that should not be inserted in the structure with in next v steps. If a link is deleted from the structure then that link is inserted in the insert tabu list so that it is not inserted in next v steps. If a link is inserted in the structure then that link is inserted in the delete tabu list so that it is not deleted in next u steps. Enhanced tabu search also uses aspiration criteria to handle exceptional conditions. In the aspiration criteria, the tabu status can be changed if the addition or deletion of a link produces a solution having better objective value than the best solution obtained so far and also possesses the desired constraints. The tabu status of whole list can be changed if every link operation improves the solution. The stopping criteria are the execution of maximum number of iterations. The maximum number of iterations and the values of the other parameters are decided based on the experiments. These experiments are performed on some problem instance of a particular category so that the optimum values for every variable are decided to get the best performance from the algorithm. The developers of the method have used 1000 iterations as the stopping criteria.

It is also observed that the size of the problem instance directly affects the value of the objective function and number of constraints does not significantly affects the objective function value. The complexity of the problem depends upon the size of the problem and constraints applied. The authors have compared this approach with Genetic algorithms and observed that enhanced tabu search performs better than genetic algorithms in terms of consumed CPU time, average objective function value, standard deviation, minimum objective function value and maximum objective function value. Enhanced Tabu Search is found to produce lower objective function values and robust against the different problem instances in comparison to genetic algorithms. The method does not produce good quality solutions when structure is large and complex. The experiments are needed to be performed with artificially generated very large sized web graphs to evaluate the method under different conditions to find more performance related issues with this method. The developers of this method has used basic version of genetic algorithm for comparison whereas many improvements of the genetic algorithms have been proposed by many researchers. Hence comparisons should be done with improved versions of genetic algorithms to identify whether this method performs better than ETS.

Ant Colony System and Local Search based Hybrid Method for WSO

Singh & Kaur (2014a) have recently proposed a hybrid metaheuristic method which is an extension of ant colony based method (Lin & Tseng, 2010). It has been observed that this hybrid approach performs better than ant colony based approach. The objective of this model is same as that of ant colony based approach that is to maximize the frequency summation of all the links with certain constraints. Every edge has a weight f_{ij} that specifies the access frequency of webpage i to webpage j. Access frequency corresponds to the number of visitors moving from page i to page j. The proposed methodology works in two stages. First, initial improved website link structure is generated by applying the ant colony based method and then the resultant website structure is used as initial solution for the local search (Glover, 1989) algorithm to further improve the solution.

The local search is applied on the structure repeatedly to find if the objective value can be improved. The solution formation of the local search employs different neighborhood than ACS which increases the probability of getting an improved website structure. In website structure improvement problem, the decision variables have value of either 0 or 1 and candidate solutions are represented by a matrix having 0 or 1 as elements.

Link deletion and link insertion operations are used to generate the neighbourhood structures to analyze if some structure improves the objective function. First a candidate edge list is generated having only edges which exist in the original link structure but are excluded from the initial structure generated by the ant colony system. Every link in the candidate list has the source and destination nodes in the constructing tree. An edge from the candidate list is taken and inserted in the website structure. This insertion is also accompanied by an edge deletion operation so that the outward degree constraint is not violated. The edge to be deleted should be the edge of the lowest weight originating from a source webpage. Suppose a link with source node a and destination node b is picked from the candidate list for insertion, then out of all the outgoing edges from node a, the edge with the lowest weight should be removed to maintain the specified outdegree. In this approach, a link insertion move should be made only if the weight of the edge to be inserted is greater than the edge to be removed. In the link deletion and insertion operations, the connectedness of the structure should remain intact. The level constraint of the nodes should also be maintained during the neighbourhood generation. Suppose the deletion of link from x to z makes the level of node z more than the maximum allowed level then this deletion operation should be cancelled.

Procedure Local_search
Begin
Initialization of memory structures
Structure generate by ACS is taken as initial solution
Repeat
Generate neighbors by link deletion and link insertion operations
Evaluate the neighborhood link structures
Select the best admissible solution among the neighborhood
Update tabu list
if the best- found solution is better than the current structure then the current solution is replaced by the
   best found structure until stopping criteria is satisfied
end

This model produces better solutions than ant colony based approach because of an added local search module, but it uses more time that ACS. Future work includes the use of other metaheuristics to solve this problem. Future work also includes testing of this method on web graphs of upto 1000 nodes to find more problem related issues.

SUMMARY AND COMPARISON OF MODELS

Large sized E- supermarket based problem has been solved using Tabu Search based method which seems a promising approach. The 0-1 programming models developed by Lin (2006) are useful for websites containing less than100 nodes. The Ant Colony System based model developed by Lin (2010) is a promising model for websites of size greater than 200 nodes. The models based on QAP problem give the opportunity to apply rich literature related to QAP to solve WSO problem. Penalty based model is a promising model that does not introduce alterations to the structure beyond a certain point. The biggest advantage of penalty based model is that it works directly on sessions; hence, it is applicable on very large sized webgraphs. Hybrid approach based on Ant Colony and local search gives on improvement over ACS based method. Table 2 gives the main points of comparison between all the discussed models.

CONCLUSION

Website structure optimization problem is of combinatorial nature. The type of optimization method that is to be used depends on the nature of the website. Models based on metaheuristic seem the best methods for link structure improvement because a lot of literature is available about these techniques. A

Table 2. Comparison of models

Method	Constraints			Size of webgraph on which applicable	Approach used
	Connectivity constraint	Depth constraint	Outdegree constraint		
Model based on user access pattern (Fu et al., 2002)	Yes	No	Yes	Not specified	Heuristic
0-1 programming model based on out degree constraint by Lin (2006)	Yes	No	Yes	Less than 100 nodes	0-1 mathematical model
0-1 programming model based on shortest path (Lin, 2006)	Yes	Yes	Yes	Less than 100 nodes	0-1 mathematical model
Two Stage Mathematical programming model (Lin, 2006)	Yes	Yes	Yes	Less than 100 nodes	0-1 mathematical model
Penalty based mathematical model (Chen and Ryu, 2013)	Yes	No	Yes	Very large sized graph, greater than 1000 nodes	Mathematical model
ACS based method (Lin and Tseng, 2010)	Yes	Yes	Yes	Greater than 200 nodes	Ant colony technique
QAP based approach (Saremi et al., 2008)	Yes	No	Yes	Greater than 100 nodes	Ant colony technique
Tabu search based approach (Yin and Guo, 2013)	Yes	Yes	Yes	Greater than 100 nodes	Tabu search technique
Strategic oscillation based model for E- supermarket websites (Wang et al., 2006)	Yes	No	Yes	More than 350 nodes	Tabu search
ACS and Local Search based hybrid method for WSO (Singh & Kaur, 2014a)	Yes	Yes	Yes	More than 200 nodes	Ant Colony System

heuristic method that uses web log files and user paths is also very promising method that works with web graphs of very big sizes. Ant colony based techniques are also very successful in solving combinatorial optimization problems hence it is also a very promising approach for WSO. Hybrid methods that use combination of more than one metaheuristic have also been proved to be efficient methods for WSO. There is a need to develop models that can handle more constraints. Developments of metrics for the evaluation of these algorithms are also a research area. Other metaheuristics can also be used to solve the WSO problem.

REFERENCES

Chen, M., & Ryu, Y. U. (2013). Facilitating effective user navigation through web site structure improvement. *IEEE Transactions on Knowledge and Data Engineering*, *99*, 1–18.

Colorni, A., Dorigo, M., & Maniezzo, V. (1992). Distributed optimization by ant colonies. *Toward a practice of autonomous systems: Proceedings of the first European conference on artificial life* (pp. 134–142), Cambridge. MA: MIT Press.

Cooley, R., Mobasher, B., & Srivastava, J. (1999). Data Preparation for Mining World Wide Web Browsing Patterns. *Knowledge and Information Systems*, *1*(1), 1–27. doi:10.1007/BF03325089

Dhyani, D., Ng, W. K., & Bhowmick, S. S. (2002). A Survey of Web Metrics. *ACM Computing Surveys*, *34*(4), 469–503. doi:10.1145/592642.592645

Dorigo, M., & Blum, C. (2005). Ant colony optimization theory: A survey. *Theoretical Computer Science*, *344*(2-3), 243–278. doi:10.1016/j.tcs.2005.05.020

Francis, R. L., & White, J. A. (1976). *Facility Layout and Location: An Analytical Approach*. Prentice-Hall International Series.

Fu, Y., Shih, M. Y., Creado, M., & Ju, C. (2002). Reorganizing web sites based on user access patterns. *International Journal of Intelligent Systems in Accounting Finance & Management*, *11*(1), 39–53. doi:10.1002/isaf.209

Glover, F. (1989). Tabu search – Part I. *ORSA Journal on Computing*, 1, 190–206.

James, T., Rego, C., & Glover, F. (2009). Multistart tabu search and diversification strategies for the quadratic assignment problem. *IEEE Transactions on Systems, Man, and Cybernetics. Part A, Systems and Humans*, *39*(3), 579–596. doi:10.1109/TSMCA.2009.2014556

Lin, C. C. (2006). Optimal web site reorganization considering information overload and search depth. *European Journal of Operational Research*, *173*(3), 839–848. doi:10.1016/j.ejor.2005.05.029

Lin, C. C., & Tseng, L. C. (2010). Website reorganization using an ant colony system. *Expert Systems with Applications*, *37*(12), 7598–7605. doi:10.1016/j.eswa.2010.04.083

Liu, B. (2007). *Web Data Mining: Exploring Hyperlinks, Contents, and Usage Data. Springer-Verlag*. Berlin, Heidelberg: Springer-Verlag.

Loiola, E. M., deAbreu, N. M., Boaventura-Netto, P. O., Hahn, P., & Querido, T. (2007). A survey for the quadratic assignment problem. *European Journal of Operational Research, 176*(2), 657–690. doi:10.1016/j.ejor.2005.09.032

Misevicius, A. (2005). A tabu search Algorithm for the Quadratic assignment Problem. *Journal of Computational Optimization and Applications, 30*(1), 95–111. doi:10.1007/s10589-005-4562-x

Perkowitz, M., & Etzioni, O. (1997). Adaptive Web sites: An AI challenge. *Proceedings of International Joint Conference on Artificial Intelligence IJCAI-97*, Nagoya, Japan (pp. 16–21). Morgan Kaufmann.

Perkowitz, M., & Etzioni, O. (2000). Toward adaptive Web sites: Conceptual framework and case study. *Artificial Intelligence, 118*(1-2), 245–275. doi:10.1016/S0004-3702(99)00098-3

Saremi, H. Q., Abedin, B., & Kermani, A. M. (2008). Website structure improvement: Quadratic assignment problem approach and ant colony meta-heuristic technique. *Applied Mathematics and Computation, 195*(1), 285–298. doi:10.1016/j.amc.2007.04.095

Singh, H., & Kaur, P. (2014a). Website Structure Optimization Model Based on Ant Colony System and Local Search. *International Journal Information Technology and Computer Science, 6*(11), 48–53. doi:10.5815/ijitcs.2014.11.07

Singh, H., & Kaur, P. (2014b). A survey of transformation based Website Structure Optimization models. *Journal of Information and Optimization Sciences, 35*(5-6), 529–560. doi:10.1080/02522667.2014.961802

Singh, H., & Kaur, P. (2014c). Algorithms to Restructure the Websites for Efficient Browsing. *CSI Communications, 38*(9), 12–14.

Srivastava, J., Cooley, R., Deshpande, M., & Tan, P.-N. (2000). Web usage mining: Discovery and applications of usage patterns from Web data. *ACM SIGKDD Explorations Newsletter, 1*(2), 12–23. doi:10.1145/846183.846188

Wang, Y., Wang, D., & Ip, W. (2006). Optimal design of link structure for e-supermarket website, IEEE Transactions: Systems. *Man and Cybernetics – Part A, 36*(2), 338–355. doi:10.1109/TSMCA.2005.851336

Yin, P., & Guo, Y. (2013). Optimization of multi-criteria website structure based on enhanced tabu search and web usage mining. *Journal of Applied Mathematics and Computation, 219*(24), 11082–11095. doi:10.1016/j.amc.2013.05.033

Zhou, B., Jinlin, C., Jin, S., Hongjiang, Z., & Qiufeng, W. (2001). Website link structure evaluation and improvement based on user visiting patterns, The 12th ACM Conference on Hypertext and Hypermedia, pp. 241-242.

KEY TERMS AND DEFINITIONS

E- Supermarket: It is a website with a collection of webpages containing information about the various products to be sold.

Information Overload: It is a condition in which a user has many options to choose from and he gets confused.

Local Search: It is a method for solving hard optimization problems. It includes searching of neighboring solutions near current solution and going from one solution to another by applying some local changes.

Metaheuristic: These are approximate methods that explore the search space to find the near optimal solutions. These include mechanisms that search over a large set of feasible solutions.

Spanning Tree: A connected component in a graph that includes all the nodes and is a tree. If there are N nodes then the number of edges in spanning tree are N.

Web Graph: It is a directed graph in which nodes represent the webpages and edges represent the hyperlinks between the webpages.

Website Structure Optimization: The problem of rearranging or reorganizing the link structure of a website so that some objective function value is minimized or maximized.

Section 3
Design Solutions using Web Analytics

Chapter 10

Web Analytics:
Assessing the Quality of Websites Using Web Analytics Metrics

Balamurugan Balusamy
VIT University, India

Venkata Krishna P
VIT University, India

Jayashree Sridhar
VIT University, India

ABSTRACT

Over the decades, people are using internet for interconnecting distances across the universe which acts as an information hub. Internet changed the face of business, communication, etc. Consumers are overloaded with the abundance of websites and information offered. This creates a need to foster the quality of websites. Nowadays website designing trends has been evolved with numerous characteristics. This involves design simplicity, performance, improved bandwidth rate, content is designed first and device agnostic where interoperability and portability comes into action. Web analytics is a measure that can be utilized to optimize web usage and to improve the quality of websites. It is used to improve the effectiveness of the website and for optimizing web usage to an extent. This chapter deals with how website quality can be improved using web analytics. The quality of website is evaluated using web analytics with respect to the website metrics that matters.

INTRODUCTION

Web analytics is an art of improving websites which requires a deep level of creativity, balancing user-centric design, promotions, content, images and more. It helps to understand the site and to improve the site with continuous process. Web analytics supports webpage and site re-design, monitors information that the visitors expect, identifies how to improve access to environment information. Typically web metrics involves page tagging, visitors, top requests to pages, click streams, content improvement and

DOI: 10.4018/978-1-4666-9764-5.ch010

data values obtained from logs. The main aim of web analytics is to assist developers in improving the quality of websites. The quality of site depends on the performance and usability of sites. Increased quality reflects the effectiveness of the firm. The Web Analytics Association (WAA) defines web analytics as the practice of measuring, collecting, analyzing and reporting on internet data to understand how a site is used and how to optimize its usage. The goals of web analytics encompasses of better understanding of visitors, web design decisions relies on data, to improve website and to improve conversions and sales. It deals with large volume of data, understands the increased complexity of data and not time consuming which improves visitors or customer's satisfaction. Web analytics is purely based on behaviour of visitors. The logs are used to record the behaviour of visitors and client environment. Conversion is term that refers to how a visitor is transformed as customer of the particular site. This act of converting rate includes availability, improved layout, bandwidth which enforce the loading time of a site. A user once visits a website or webpage and later on by its content and look & feel, secure gateway paves a path to conversion rate, i.e. visitor to customer which reflects the quality of a website. Data collection for web analytics can be acquired via various sources of data. This involves server logs, JavaScript tagging, web beacons and packet sniffing (Waisberg et al., 2009). These data can be analyzed with the help of traffic sources. The traffic source involves various factors influencing the insights of the visitors and their actions. The quality and effectiveness of website can be improved by the web analytics process. The outcome of the process shows the factors of a website that need to be optimized to attain increased quality.

The website development should be goal-driven and user-centric, where the users are the parameter measured for the success of the site. The objectives of website leads to the metrics identified to increase the site performance. The website should be developed in such a way that it addresses the metrics associated with its quality, performance, availability and lifespan. Lifespan of a site refers to the time period of site existence. The existence of a site relies on number of users/visitors it holds. The other such site that fails to hold on the user needs vanishes without proper quality, maintenance and revenue. The business goals of the websites are the objective to the company which can be achieved by their customers. Content management is a key factor to an effective website development. The web metrics helps to improve the quality of web sites. The quality of any particular site can be illustrated into design metrics, user interface metrics, performance and content evaluation metrics. The eight common metrics for website analysis includes visitor type, visitor length, system statistics, visitor path, keyword search, top pages, referral logs and error logs (Booth, D., & Jansen, B. J, 2009). Website changes are based on environment or content change and customer changing needs. Therefore web analytics deals with collecting, analyzing and interpreting the web metrics. Web site quality is concerned from customer's or visitor's perspectives. The web quality characteristic includes efficiency, functionality, usability, availability, reliability and portability (Rio, et al., 2010).

Web analytics is a study of visitor, navigation and traffic patterns to evaluate the success of the website. There exists a plenty of web analytics tools available for developers to evaluate the website quality and effectiveness. Based on the evaluated metrics, steps are assigned to re-design or to optimize the site. The web metrics are categorized among the different type of websites. The main objective of this chapter is to elaborate how web analytics helps to the betterment of website quality. The chapter mainly focuses on the web analytics process, various data sources, the challenges of web analytics process, web analytics metrics involved in improving the quality of websites and a comparative analysis of web analytics metrics and website quality. It also defines the web analytic tools available in the market and the right choice on tools. The thresholds on the metrics identified helps to improve the quality of the evaluated website. This reflects ways to increase performance of a site. The developer gains knowledge on how to re-design the site in an effective way. Hence, web analytics provides insights of visitors and the changing environment to deploy enhanced and useful websites that addresses the web metrics to its estimated values or baselines. This results with defined baselines for web analytics metrics to attain quality websites. The challenges in web analytics process are actionable metric usage, to identify valid metrics, to make proper configuration, money, bounce rate, reporting and to find the right tool.

BACKGROUND

The literature review includes works on web design improvement, website quality improvement, navigability, content analysis and web analytics metrics for website improvement. Many research on web analytics implementation for effective web development is presented over the decades. Website designing is the important factor that ensures the key success factors. Gerry McGovern established ten rules for writing the web. These rules are concerned with how website content should be to gain better visitors in numbers. The rules are know your reader, valid content, keep content short and simple, metadata, keep on change the content, search efficiency, content in context, great summaries and great headings. Evaluate the quality of websites with effective designs. Yen B et al (2005) proposed a framework for website design evaluation and enhancement. The framework addresses the design objectives and constraints that are essential to enhance quality of the websites. The framework proposed is more applicable for content management while designing a website.

Quality attributes for websites are availability, performance, usability, reliability and maintainability. An artifact pattern matching framework is established to analyze the changing behaviour for service oriented architecture (Zhang et al, 2009). The pattern analyzed invokes best practices that can be utilized for designing with quality analytics. The multi-tier layers of websites are optimized to yield improved website quality that meets the visitor's requirements (Zhu M et al, 2009). Ying F et al (2010) proposed a balance scorecard based quality evaluation model for websites. Balance scorecard is a standard used for quality evaluation in corporate to manage performance. The quality factors are weighted using analytic hierarchy process and information theory. The model is illustrated with the glimpse of e-commerce websites. The quality metrics for websites defined by Mittal et al (2012) are load time, response time, mark-up validation, broken link, accessibility error, size, page rank, frequency of update, traffic and design optimization. The metrics identified are evaluated with the help of fuzzy logic. Fuzzy logic has the capability of handling inconsistent, incomplete, uncertain values. The metrics assessment is carried out with fuzzy membership functions. The proposed fuzzy model involves rule evaluation and regular fuzzification and defuzzification process. The proposed model is restricted to limited quality metrics. On evaluating those metrics will not be sufficient to yield enhanced quality of websites. Certain metrics that influences the quality of websites are suggested to be evaluated along with the existing quality metrics for better results. Wibowo S and Grandhi S (2014) have come up with performance based evaluation for websites which directs quality websites. The proposed performance based model is used to assess the quality of websites by using fuzzy technique and it is efficient for business websites. Information quality factors are defined for websites to ensure content analysis (Bahry S et al, 2014). Quality analytics based method to assess quality factors for dynamic websites. The quality components of learning environment are quality to be delivered, environment, memory constraints and technical aspects (Chhabra I, 2014). This involves the analytics process of the analytics tool which comprises of predicting, analyzing, monitoring and reporting. This method ensures quality assessment and optimized websites. Kopcso (2001) defined factors affecting the assessment of website quality. It involves the specific quality dimensions from user's perspectives. It uses quality model named WebQual for assessing the quality dimensions established. Eppler M and M P proposed a methodology for measuring information quality (2002). The problems associated with information quality are explored in web context. The hardware monitoring and software testing tools are used to evaluate the information quality of websites. The categories of tools for information quality measurement are performance monitoring, traffic analyzer, site analyzer and web mining (Eppler M and MP, 2002). Kohli et al (2012) presented a keyword similarity measure tool for content analysis based on keyword search approach. Involves Perl scripting language to implement the keyword similarity search algorithm for effective content analysis for websites. The keywords are evaluated with obtained visits and bounce rates to analyze the content improvement for websites. It enables how the tool can be utilized to increase the traffic rate and content optimization improves customer engagement. Content denotes the information quality that represents website goals to be attained and increase in conversion rates. A case study based approach to test the information quality of websites (Shpak, oleksandr et al, 2014).

Navigability of websites should be simple and the navigability metrics can be obtained from the referrer logs. The visitor's understandability and retention influences the navigation factor of the website. Navigation of website defines the structural complexity of websites. The navigation metrics and properties are addressed by Zhang et al (2004). The metrics calculated are limited in number and hence the website structure is designed in such a way that it addresses the metrics. The complexity of design is calculated to assess the navigation through the websites. The effectiveness of websites can be improved by measuring navigation metrics. Navigation patterns are introduced to improve the website quality (Verma et al, 2010). The web server log produces data for measuring process. The data obtained should be cleaned, processed and interpreted to gain knowledge sources for further decision making process in order to implement changes. Data mining algorithms are used for pattern mining and it shows that the algorithm used provides increased webpage analysis. The pattern obtained is used for designing solutions for navigability problems of dynamic websites.

The web metrics are collected together to employ web analytics process. Web analytics is a process of data collection, measuring visitor's insights and optimize the web usage. The data collection methods used in web analytics involves packet sniffing, page tagging, and java script tagging and web logs (Booth et al, 2009). The proposed work addresses how web metrics are used for website evaluation to improve the quality and customer engagement. A framework for web analytics is proposed by de Oliveira et al which diffuses the website metrics and ways to measure web performance. Web analytics is intended to achieve the business goal of the websites. Web analytics for security relevant information discovery is proposed by Glass K et al (2011). It addresses the web based security issues and resolves using predictive analytics. The security informatics involves cyber security, protocol validation and network attacks. Duncan seth (2010) establishes how web analytics can be utilized with public relations campaigns. Encompasses different methodologies to measure web analytics metrics concerned with public relations. The public relations involve the need of metrics to be post implemented for a website with four essential attribute ranks. The attributes defined drives visitor engagement. The work also addresses the technical limitations of web analytics. Weischedel et al (2006) introduced the web metrics for website optimization. The goal of web analytics is to assist companies in improving the quality of their websites. Quality of website can be defined as performance and usability. The data collected for analysis includes click stream data that helps for increasing the effectiveness of website. The work aims at improving manager's understandability and learning of various web metrics based on both click stream and customer interviews to improve the quality of websites. A case study is addressed to define the web metrics identification and those identified metrics are evaluated to optimize the website usage. The different challenges of web analytics are discussed in the next section.

CHALLENGES

The large amount of data that has traversed the internet since its creation leads to the information growth (in Exabyte). The terabytes of data paved to petabytes and that resulted with Exabyte of data, which developed in huge as zettabyte and yottabyte. Earlier times followed traditional metrics to analyze the internet data. Later, due to the abundance of data, web analytics came into existence in order to analyze unlimited data sources. This helps in better understanding of the visitors and steps to optimize the website standard. Dealing with web analytics is not easy unless the challenges are addressed.

Identify the Metrics that Matter

Trace the data that need to be analyzed, measured and optimized. Data when added meaning gives valid information. The information forms the metrics which are collected to analyze with respect to the improvement stated for a website. The data can be obtained from logs, tagging, customer interviews, traffic analysis, cookies and client side data collection. The assessment of qualitative and quantitative data values paves a path for the betterment of web development. In general web analytics metrics are counts, ratio and key performance indicator. Count is the basic unit of measurement, ratio is count divided by count and KPI refers to count or ratio which differs from site to site accordingly. Effective web analytics is to analyze web traffic data and to focus on the need for producing approximate results that determines the website quality and usefulness.

Actionable Metric Usage

Use metrics that are actionable, where actionable metrics are those which may lead to making a change for beneficial perspective. The metrics measured that leads to changes are actionable metrics. The changes made should be appropriate. Data analysis includes all kinds of available data sources. Pick data in particular for addressing the change mentioned. Measure the metrics that can be utilized for implementing changes that reflects quality websites.

Proper Configuration

The data acquired should be accurate on numbers, i.e. the data values accounted in form of counts or ratio should hold proper values. The web analytics employs various methods to acquire data and those data should be interpreted properly. The measurement process should be valid and the values reflect positivity. The web analytic tool used can also result with invalid or wrong inputs. The configuration of tool used is in need of validation. The changes need to be implemented in order to gain accurate data that matters.

Money

Making money through web analytics is related to the business strategy of a site. The return on investment should be increased against sales. The ratio of quality and sales is twice the other. The quality websites returns better revenues. The decision making relies on measured data which reflects on the money value on the website and business goals attained.

Understanding the Bounce Rate

Bounce rate is confused between exit rates. Bounce rate is single-page sessions (i.e. sessions in which the person left your site from the entrance page without interacting with the page). There are a number of factors that contribute to a high bounce rate. For example, users might leave your site from the entrance page if there are site design or usability issues. Alternatively, users might also leave the site after viewing a single page if they've found the information they need on that one page, and had no need or interest in going to other pages. To improve content, redesigning the entrance (or landing) pages, optimizing those pages so they correlate better with the search terms that bring users to your site, changing keywords to reflect better page content. The measure of bounces should be valid, accounts only single page sessions not last sessions which reflects exit rate.

Reporting

Web analytics is not only concerned with reporting on internet data, it is used for optimization of websites. Reporting intervals for conversion funnels, once defined, will most likely need to be decided based on the content being analyzed, taking into consideration the natural business cycles represented in that funnel. Reporting Methods addresses how would the marketing committee like to receive reports – in an emailed report, or a password protected web page, etc.

Finding the Right Tool

Once the company decides what it wants out of the Web analysis, it is time to find the right tool. Choosing right tool gives right measures for optimizing the website to its requirement. Selecting a tool is a difficult task to map the appropriate usage. This involves features available, version of tool, cost associated, time period of usage, open source tools available and methods to capture data.

Quality of Website

A good website should be easier to navigate through and understandable by the visitors. Each webpage should have a link to its homepage, colour and contrast of your websites, employ appropriate information needed and check whether the goal of the site is easily accomplished. Avoid using larger ratio of images, which may lead to confusion among the consumers. Increased traffic rate represents the visitor's count for a particular website. The quality of website can be categorized as user interface quality, information quality, design quality and performance quality (Table 1). The user interface quality includes time to learn (TL), retention over time (R), Subjective satisfaction (S) and rate of error (Er). TL must be less which intakes the understanding ability of the visitors, retention denotes the remembrance level,

Table 1. Quality attributes of websites

Website Quality	Attributes
User Interface Quality	TL, time to learn (TL $\propto$ 1/R)
	R, retention over time
	S, subjective satisfaction
	Er, error rate
Information Quality	Accurate
	Reliable
	Complete
	Timely
Design Quality	Navigability
	Look & Feel
	Contrast
Performance Quality	Loading time
	Response time
	Speed

subjective satisfaction is the need of different visitors attained or not, error involves broken links, page not found, etc. Information quality is content oriented which should be accurate, reliable, complete and timely (upgraded content). Design quality attributes are ease of navigation, look & feel, contrast and Key Performance Indicator (KPI's). Performance attribute is the bandwidth report that involves loading time, response time of the website.

Web pages are inter-linked to form a website which paves the path to navigation for the visitors to perceive information. This paper proposed the navigability metrics for complex structures by evaluating the path of incoming and outgoing links (Shpak, Oleksandr, et al., 2014).

C is the website complexity, e represents the number of links, where n and d is the nodes starting and ending.

C=e-n + d

C1=c / n ....from (Shpak, Oleksandr, et al., 2014)

Hu and Yuh Jong (2014) proposed a design paradigm to information flow and security services which can be applied for content management system. Website quality is domain dependent (Aivalis, et al., 2014). Websites can be classified into E-Commerce sites, healthcare sites, content oriented information sites, educational sites, business sites. In case of healthcare websites information clarity and security are the major consumer perspectives where Look & Feel (colour attributes) are not taken into account. Site repudiation and confidence level should be maintained (Tao, Donghua, et al., 2012). Log file data analysis method is used in business websites to track the visitors count and performance where visitor's behaviour is acquired via page tagging. Split testing is also done to increase the site performance that focuses on changes need to be performed to attain improved website. Website quality metrics forms broken links, number of links implemented, responsive and non-responsive pages, timed out operations, loading time of pages. Well structured websites provides effective user navigability. A model to improve navigability with minimal changes for effective website structuring is proposed (Chen, et al., 2013). The metrics involved are traversed path, links and backtracks. Backtracks are defined as number of revisits for a particular site. The navigability enforces the understandability of links, avoiding more links in single page. From (Chen, et al., 2013), the objective function minimizes the cost needed to improve the website structure, where the cost consists of two components: the number of new links to be established (the first summation), and the penalties on pages containing excessive links, i.e., more links than the out-degree threshold in the improved structure. Quality websites comprises of performance and usage of the data sources obtained by measuring the web metrics. The quality of business websites depends on the success of search engine optimization. Hence, a high quality website should provide relevant, useful, valid content and user satisfaction. Many individual factors are required to be considered to optimize the websites.

WEB ANALYTICS FOR WEBSITE QUALITY

Web analytics is utilized for improving website with increased revenue, marketing strategies, satisfy people and site performance (Figure 1). The revenue of a site indicates the return on investment, more money gained, marketing strategies can be achieved by optimizing resources, satisfy visitor needs and improve content and navigability. As per web analytics definition, collection involves accumulating data

Figure 1. Web Analytics Objectives

over a period of time, internet data is collected together for analysis, measuring the data collected and interpret, optimizing knowledge mined, understanding insights and reporting the analytics results. These are the basic steps in web analytics.

Web analytics determines the objectives of the websites to be achieved and formulates the online strategy on business goals. This results with improved efficiency and revenue sales. The web analytics process is depicted in figure2. It comprises of defining goals, data collection, building KPI's, analyzing data and implement changes until it achieves the metrics baselines.

Defining Goals

Define the business goals and certain required baselines to improve the website. Each website has its unique objectives to address the purpose of the site with user satisfaction. These objectives are inputs to establish the metrics that helps to measure the quality of websites. This is the startup for the web analytics process, followed by defining goals, build the key performance indicators. Continuous process improvement involves redefining goals constantly to optimize websites.

Build KPI

Key Performance Indicators (KPI) can be count or ratio, mostly ratio measure with associated business strategy. KPI will vary from different site and process types. Choosing KPI should be efficient to get the appropriate outcomes of web analytics. Choosing the most beneficial KPIs using this method is achieved by following "The Four M's of Operational Management" as outlined by Becher (2005) which facilitate effective selection of KPIs:

- **Motivate:** Ensure that goals are relevant to everyone involved.
- **Manage:** Encourage collaboration and involvement for achieving these goals.
- **Monitor:** Once selected, track the KPIs and quickly deal with any problems that may arise.
- **Measure:** Identify the root causes of problems and test any assumptions associated with the strategy.

Figure 2. Web Analytics Process

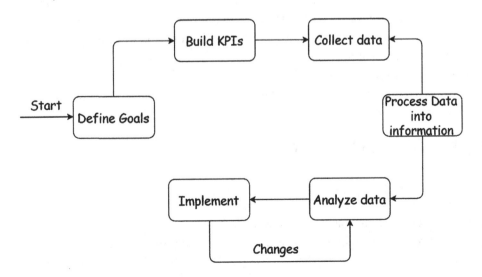

By carefully choosing a few, quality KPIs to monitor and making sure everyone is involved with the strategy, it becomes easier to align the goals of websites and addressing the actionable data. Good KPI's should maintain four attributes namely uncomplex, relevant, timely and instantly used.

Data Collection

Early web analytics data collection methods are traffic data which reflects web performance measurement, click through rate, page tags, etc. Nowadays, the most of the data sources are from server logs and other logs are referral logs, error logs and agent logs. Other than server side logging, there exists page tagging, image, cookies, flash cookies, etc. Web server delivers pages to the computer that requests information. The interaction between servers, site and visitor gets data to be stored in server log. Agent log holds the information of client side environment which includes browser, browser version and operating system. The referrer log points pages that link to documents on the server. The logs all together can be framed as web logs. The next method of collecting data is JavaScript tagging, a JavaScript is enabled in a website to cache the visitor's behavior when the visitor's access the site. Web beacons, also one of the data collection methods that includes links or banners that navigates through different websites. This in turn provides visitor's insights across different websites and third party servers. Packet sniffing contains data stored on packet that is sent to client side and it also appends JavaScript.

Analysis of data is a state where the data collected is processed into meaningful information that becomes the metrics. It defines a lot of metrics that can be measured and evaluated to optimize the websites. Analyze the data in such a way that it focus on outcomes, understands traffic sources and act on the data. Implement the actionable data, changes required for optimized outcomes and repeat analysis and implementation recursively until the optimized website is assured.

Web Analytics Metrics for Assessing the Quality of Websites

Different web analytics metrics for assessing the quality of websites are illustrated. Three types of web analytics metrics implementation envelopes count, ratio and KPI. Count is the basic unit of measure that reflects a single numerical value. Ratio denotes count divided by count. KPIs can be either a count or a ratio, frequently ratio. Dimensions can be represented as a visitor type or site dynamics. These web analytics metrics can be applied to three levels of granularity such as aggregate, segmented, individual. Aggregate defines total site traffic for a defined period of time, typically used for market comparisons. Segmented provokes greater insights through only a defined period of time, counts on traffic rate. Individual refers to unique visitors, activity of a single web visitor for a specific period of time. Figure 3 depicts the metrics analysis process.

The classification of metrics by web analytics association is depicted in figure 4. The metrics under each classified field is elaborated.

Building Blocks: Foundational Metrics

- Page: A page is an analyst definable unit of content
- Page Views: The number of times a page was viewed
- Visits/Sessions: A visitor interacts to a website
- Unique visitors: Single visitor to a site within a particular timeframe

Figure 3. Analytics metrics lifecycle process

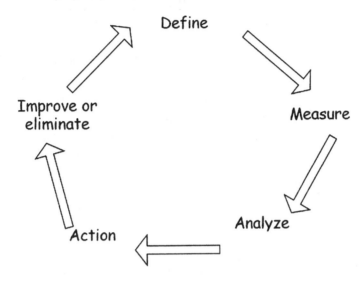

Figure 4. Metrics Classification

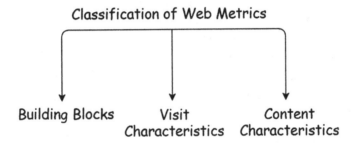

- New visitor: Number of unique visitors, first visit to a site
- Repeat visitor: Two or more visits to a particular website
- Return visitor: Visits during reporting time and also visited prior

Visit Characterization: Metrics Aimed at Understanding Visits, Either Single or Aggregate

- Entry Page: The first page of a visit
- Landing Page: A Page intended to identify the beginning of the user experience
- Exit Page: The end of a visit or session
- Visit duration: Time Period of session
- Referrer: Page URL that originally generated the request for the page view or object
- Click through: number of times a link was clicked by a visitor
- Click through rate: $\dfrac{number.of.clickthrough\_for\_a\_specific\_link}{number.of.times\_the\_link\_viewed}$

- Page views per visit: $\dfrac{number.of\_pageviews\_in\_reporting\_period}{number.of\_visits\_in\_reporting\_period}$

Content Characterization: Metrics Aimed at Understanding Content or its Use

- Page exit ratio: $\dfrac{number.of\_exits\_from\_a\_page}{total.number.of\_pageviews}$
- Single Page visits: Visits that consists of one page regardless of the page views
- Single page view visits (Bounces): Visits that consists of one page view
- Bounce rate: $\dfrac{single\_pageview\_visits}{entry\_pages}$

Conversion

Metrics aimed at linking visits and content. The completion of order represents the conversion. The number of visitors and the number of customers denotes the conversion rate of any website.

Translating these metrics into meaningful and accurate knowledge is a complex process. To improve the content of a site, the page views and agent log data sources are sufficient. More traffic rate in geographic reach explores optimization of web usage in particular area. Set up goals to improve the site effectiveness, increased page views results quality websites. The web analytics metrics for optimizing web usage and quality is depicted in Table 2.

The metrics measured can be a direct measure or metric, calculated metric, derived metric and indices. Measures are direct measure of an activity; examples are page views and visitors (unique count). Calculated metrics are obtained by dividing one measure by another measure; example: sessions (page views/user). Derived metrics are created by taking a metric and dimension (time). Indices are formed by normalizing a group of metric observed over a period of time; examples are top pages, customer engagement and click rates. Threshold values for metrics obtained should focus to business goals, which can have major impact on growth. Understand the metric usage, and average (mean, median, or mode) is the best way to present the metric. Where possible, break a metric out into different entity, based on frequency of observations noted. Map those changes to create a customized version of the "80/20" rule for that metric. Compare the annual observations recorded to attain threshold metrics specifications for

Table 2. Web analytics Metrics

Optimize Web Usage	Referrers	Content Analysis	Quality Metrics
• Numbers of visitors and sessions • Repeat visitors • Geographic information • Search Engine Activity	• Which websites are sending visitors to your site • The search terms people used to find your site • How many people place bookmarks to the site	• Top entry pages • Most popular pages • Top pages for single page view sessions • Top exit pages • Top paths through the site • Content Effectiveness	• Broken pages or server errors •Error log

performance improvements.

Type of Websites

Websites can be categorized into educational, business oriented, informative and service oriented. Some of their existences are in the form of e-commerce sites, blogs, RSS feeds, sharing sites, informative sites and gaming sites. The type of websites and its corresponding KPIs are illustrated in table 3.

E-commerce websites is business oriented where products are available for purchases. The visitor can view the products; buy them by placing an order. The completion of order triggers the conversion rate. The visitors became the customers of that site which involves average visit value and average order value. Increased bounce rate results with poor content. The content of these types of sites are expected to be valid. Hence bounce rate should be in minimal, so that it ensures increased visitor rate with valid content. Blogs are typical question and answers or information related content availability firms. Since content is the major component, bounce rate is concerned and new visitors, conversion rates are monitored to optimize its usage. RSS feeds displays headlines, links and reference to particular context. The referrer log is considered due to the usage of links in pages that points to another pages or site. Information site is similar to blogs. Gaming site are developed to attract more visitors, high conversion rates and repeat visitors. The KPIs mentioned are needed to be improved for the categorized websites.

Table 3. Type of websites and corresponding KPIs

Type of Websites	Key Performance Indicators
E-Commerce	Average visit value
	Average order value
	Bounce rate
	Conversion rates
Blogs	Conversion rates
	Page views per visit
	Bounce rate
	New visitor ratio
RSS feeds	Bounce Rate
	Referrer
	Top Pages
Content/Media	Returning visitors ratio
	Page depth
	Visit depth
	New visitors ratio
Information Site	Bounce Rate
	Visit depth
Gaming Site	Conversion rates
	New visitors ratio
	Top pages
	Repeat visitors rate

Evaluating Websites Using Web Analytics

Evaluating websites defines the success factors associated. These success factors denotes return on investment, profitability, effectiveness, reliability, utility, or competitive advantage (A. Phippen et al., 2004). The success of website varies in context to the goals of that particular site. Hence success factor differs from site to site. The success of a website can be measured with page views, visitor rate, sessions, etc. The web metrics are measured to assess the success of the site. Web analytics metrics discussed above are the useful parameters to measure and evaluate the site. Advanced web analytics aims to measure and understand the relationship between the customer and the Website (A. Phippen et al., 2004). The basic metrics for measuring web lead to web analytics. Web metrics are ambiguous by nature which may lead to improper conclusions while evaluating. Basic metrics are inadequate for evaluation and hence web analytics came into existence. The quality of websites can be improved by measuring the visitor actions and corresponding metrics. This makes web measurement as an essential feature of assessing the websites with unambiguous metrics and its associated values. These metrics and web analytics was establish to measure and evaluate the relationship and interaction between websites and its visitors. This involves the evaluation of customers or visitors' insights, i.e. customer behaviour analysis that monitors the actions of the customers during the session or visit to a site. The factors resulted on behavioural analysis are content validation, effective design and performance of the website. For example, content validation can be measured as content appropriateness C, which can be defined as,

$$C = \frac{number.of\_valid\_content\_consumed\_by\_visitors}{(Expected\_content)*(unique\_visitors)}$$

Web analytics is used for choosing the right metric to assess the website and to investigate on the factors influencing performance. The organization or the owner of the site can implement the web analytics to ensure site performance and to implement changes required for improving the quality constraints that are yet to be attained. The metrics need to be implemented for redesigning a website or to improve quality involves:

- Page views of the Web pages to be evaluated
- Page views of the that particular site in comparison to the page views of other Websites which of the same category of evaluating website
- Click stream analysis
- Conversion rates will help to map between the expected and actual return on investment with bookings made on the site
- "look to book ratio" – a metric designed to measure the ratio of number of page views to the number of bookings made as a result of a campaign (this metric was created by the company to perform a specific task, as they could not find an existing metric to suit their requirements) (A. Phippen et al., 2004).

Identify the goals of the website to be evaluated, get traffic sources measure. Web analytics utilizes web measurement to evaluate the different types of websites. The web measures considered are bounce rate, referrers, clicks shows how the visitors understand the site which reflects the design properties and conversion rates that shows visitor attention and profit of the website. Prioritize these metrics by means of ranks that provides the importance of each metric to be evolved. Conduct surveys on customer perspectives and develop prototype for customer understanding and check for the acceptance rate. Use alpha or beta testing to evaluate the website in terms interface quality that provides user-friendliness, retention, design pallets and navigability.

A sample website evaluation is done with a well known web analytics tool, Google analytics. The metrics calculated illustrates the page views, visitor rate, bounce rate and conversion rate with respect to time period of evaluation.

The metrics evaluated are of direct measure, calculated metric, derived metric and indices such as consumer engagement. This involves the total no. of unique visitors, page views, and average time, sessions and conversion rates. The evaluation of the metrics observed estimates the traffic of the site examined. By comparing the results with previous results can be utilized for website optimization or re-designing if required which reflects an increase in the popularity of the site and sales.

The key performance indicators are implemented for choosing the right metric that need to be evaluated. This can be defined with the three layers of testing (Kaushik A, 2007).

Key Performance Indicator: Percent of Repeat Visitors

Report and monitor the trend of repeat visitors for website. The repeat visitors rate should analyzed on monthly basis to identify the ups in repeat visitors. This defines the design efficiency of a website involving customer engagement.

Figure 5. Report generated for tested website

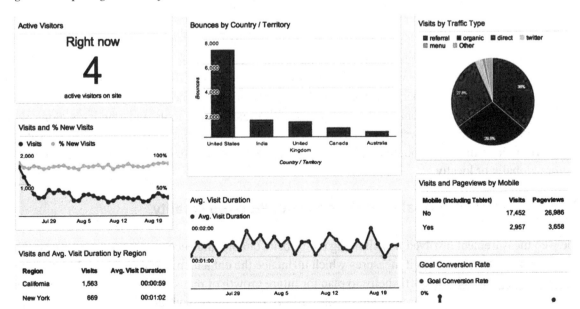

Table 4. Metrics Evaluation

Dimension	Metrics					
Consumer engagement (activity)	Total no. of unique visitors	Page views	Average time on page	Bounces	Bounce rate %	Exit %
avinash + kaushik	212	225	00:00:44	156	40.84	79.56
working + at + google	76	92	00:01:24	203	80.56	58.70
avinash	62	68	00:00:56	116	46.22	58.82
occam%27s + razor	27	32	00:00:18	196	60.73	75.00
survey + questions	15	155	00:02:36	133	92.45	52.63
customer + survey + questions	225	429	00:01:01	68	86.08	11.89
web + analytics + tools	338	16	00:00:17	35	49.3	37.50

Key Performance Indicator: Top Exit Pages on the Website

Report the top exit page ratio that involves the insight of the visitor on monthly basis. The web pages with leakage points are mapped to stop visitors from leaving the site. These actionable metrics are taken in to account for evaluating content patterns that are changing over time.

Key Performance Indicator: Conversion Rate for Top Search Keywords

Reports are in form of spreadsheet that consists of conversion rate of the website that are measured and evaluated. This is based on top keyword searches. This KPI is used for tracking the pay per clicks which denotes the positive outcome of the website.

The qualitative and quantitative data of web measurement is evaluated to drive the quality of established websites in order to gain customer insights and retention. This involves time committed for a particular site by a customer or visitor, cost per click, conversion rate, customer response, insight depth and testing strategies for comparing categories of sites or within the same category of sites. The metrics for evaluating site improvement can be compared with organization goals and standards along with emphasized customers. Any web analytics metric accounted for evaluation is subjected to measuring the return on investment and popularity. The popularity denotes the site consumed by large number of visitors globally or locally.

Comparison of Web Analytics Metrics with Website Quality

The web measurement involved in evaluating the website quality and success are discussed above. This can be elaborated by the ways it measures which influence the enhancement of websites. Measurement and monitoring of Web site traffic helps to plan for future growth of that site and customer expectations. Segmentation shows the differentiation of site visitors based on behaviour on the site and improves targeting, which enables the site to reach right customers with right message. Assessment of online initiatives (e.g. Web site redesign) and improvement to processes (e.g. online shopping processes) helps to assess, improve and plan future online strategy. Measuring revenue and popularity of online campaign improve promotions. Monitoring of external referrers identifies which search engines and affiliate partners produce the most profitable customers. Monitoring of click streams and paths Identifies unvisited or poorly performing sections of a Web site which helps with maintaining an efficient site. The metrics can be measured with respect to the case study illustrated. Case study referred from Rooms to go by Google analytics, 2014.

Case Study

Rooms To Go offers the nation's largest furniture marketing through nearly 150 retail showrooms as well as online. Products are sold as complete room packages—an approach that makes for a great shopping experience. Rooms To Go acts as a home furnishing retailer to satisfy the consumer shopping experience by offering completely designed room packages. To optimize their website, they planned to understand the insights of the users. In order to achieve this goal, they integrated Google Analytics Premium with BigQuery, Rooms To Go was able to identify the products that are often purchased together. With the insights obtained the page is customized with new features which are much simpler for consumers to experience better shopping and increased the revenue of sales. Extracted raw, visitor-level data about items purchased online. Performed statistical data mining to find products often purchased together. Expanded features of the site to increase the visitor rates and revenue increased parallel. A new view of the data is designed to help customers in querying massive datasets by enabling super-fast, SQL-like queries—all while using the processing power of Google's infrastructure. For Rooms To Go, this strategy enabled the extraction of data about items purchased in the site for analyzing which products were often bought together. "BigQuery allowed us to extract and organize large quantities of raw, visitor-level data from Google Analytics to use in this analysis," says Jonathan Weber, data evangelist at LunaMetrics. For example, the strategy has allowed Rooms To Go to find common purchase patterns among products. These insights have helped the company offer expanded functionality for customers to add accessory products (such as a nonslip rug pad with a rug) or coordinating pieces (such as extra dining chairs in a dining room) easily. By making customization smarter and easier, the company expects both increased sales and products and a better overall user experience.. The insights were quickly available and actionable. "Moving forward, the company is confident these data-driven options will continue to work in concert with the Rooms To Go tradition of giving online customers an easy, convenient way to decorate the rooms. In terms of ROI, Brown shared, "We had initially calculated ROI at 14 months. We have now seen additional benefits that would amount to a much quicker ROI of less than 12 months per store, and approximately 250% ROI over five years. "

Web Analytics Tools

The web analytics tools are provided by many companies for website evaluation; this includes free and paid web analytics tools. The open source tool for web analytics – Google Analytics; Google analytics is free web analytic software that uses page tagging to acquire the visitors behaviour. The KPIs of Google analytics includes visit depth, returning visitors, page depth. The top four players in web analytics are Coremetrics, Web trends, Omniture and Web side story HBX. The paid web analytics distributes cost on the use of tool such as administrative cost, data consumed rate, time of use, etc. To determine valid web metrics using web analytics tool relies on the right tool chosen. Choosing the right tool at a right time depends on ways to choose the optimal tool. Tools chosen can be free or paid tool, versions of tools are concerned to address the changing environment. Choose a tool that has its featured versions available in the market. Methods used by the tool to capture data such as log files and page tagging. Tools selected should involve creative solutions. Calculate the total cost of the tool opted. Cost of web analytics tools depends on the organization that provides. Cost can be calculated as cost per page view, incremental cost, annual cost (for a year subscription), support and maintenance cost, cost for troubleshooting and additional costs. Tools are expensive as it includes export cost for data exporting, segmenting data, integrating data and the tool selected should adapt to changes. Based on the changing needs, versioning of tools should be released for effective analytics.

There are different web analytics tools available according to the needs and improvements required for producing an efficient website. This can be classified into conversion tools that are all about how the customers are transformed into buyers, stat trackers that keeps track on visitors for a site, visitor's behavior tools and blog development or redesigning tools.

Right choice of tool for website optimization is essential. For the growing information, web analytics is increasingly essential to attain the business strategy of websites. The main objective for any web analytics tool is to perform its functionality on the acquired data to get valuable information that can be later used for decision making purposes. Tools are required to be design to meet the requirement of complex data or information abundance. The costs of web analytics tools are comparatively high when compared to traditional tools and concepts of web measurement. Optimize the cost associated with the tools with its pertained operations. The choice of right tool helps for the betterment of website quality is essential in order to get accurate qualitative and quantitative data.

Table 5. Classified Web analytics tools

Web Analytics Terminologies	Tools
Conversion tools	Web Trends http://www.webtrends.com/
	Hitslink http://www.hitslink.com/
	UserVue
	Clickfox http://www.clickfox.com/
Stat Trackers	Piwik http://piwik.org/
	Google Analytics
	Stat Counter http://statcounter.com/
	Visitor Vile http://www.visitorville.com/
Visitor behaviour tools	Coremetrics http://www-01.ibm.com/software/info/coremetrics-software/
	Deep log analyzer http://www.deep-software.com/
	Webstat http://www.webstat.com/
Blog tools	Google feed burner
	Conversation tracker
	Snoop
	Firestats

Figure 6. Sample Google analytics interface for website analysis

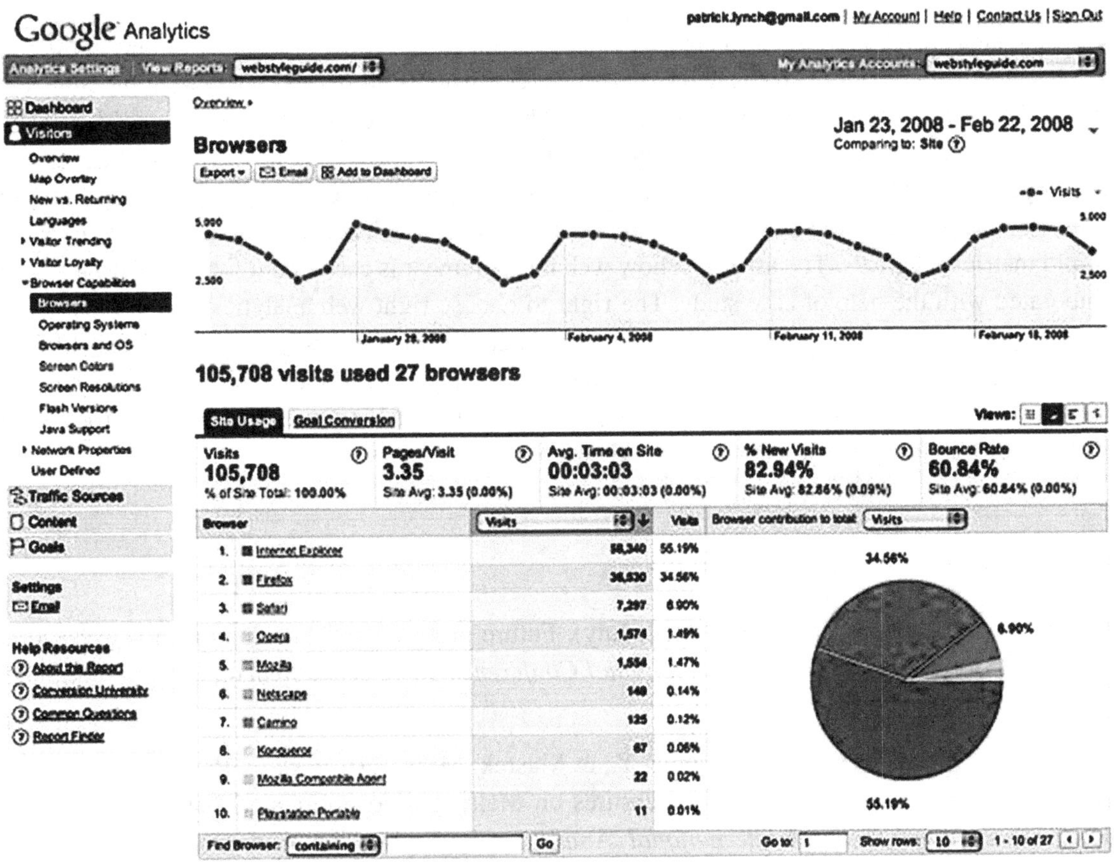

FUTURE RESEARCH DIRECTIONS

Future directions are concerned with focusing on the limitations of web analytics. The complex nature of growing information is not addressed by the existing web analytics methods. Web performance measures are predictive in nature such that it lacks in terms of security. The web analytics performed should not intrude the customers' identity. Since web analytics spies on customer behaviour towards websites, the customers' information can also be acquired that is possible due to the flaws in internet protocol standards. Most of the web analytics tools are provided by third party organization. There are no restrictions on access to visitor's details. In future, the methods involved to protect the privacy preserving attributes of the users can be focused. The ways in which organizations are benefited by using web analytics can be explored. Considering the future work, various cloud computing access control approaches that can be implemented in developing websites to avoid phishing and other side channel attacks, also methods for evaluating accuracy of measures obtained using web analytics tools can be elaborated.

CONCLUSION

Thus, the chapter explored how web analytics can be utilized for evaluating websites and to optimize the web usage. By integrating Web analytics with the company, a proper working environment and responsive developmental aspects for the Websites will be fostered. Web analytics transformed basic web metrics into performance measure of the websites. This chapter deals with how web analytics metrics are used for assessing the quality of websites. This also covers different categories of websites. The chapter also involves the web analytics process, associated data collection methods and how to choose the valid metrics for KPI's. The aspect on how web measurement is carried out for a particular website is elaborated with the help of case study. The right to choose right web analytics tool is the essential part for a successful web measurement. The interaction gap between users and a site is the root for creating interactive websites. An efficient web analytics should be able to make right decisions based on the outcomes of metrics for website redesigning or employing continuous improvement process. The limitations of web analytics process can be addressed in the future work.

REFERENCES

Aivalis, C. J., & Boucouvalas, A. C. (2014, July). Future proof analytics techniques for web 2.0 applications. *Proceedings of the 2014 International Conference on Telecommunications and Multimedia TEMU* (pp. 214-219). IEEE.

Bahry, S., Diana, F., Shahibi, M. S., Kamis, Y., & Masrek, M. N. (2014, May). Preferred information quality factors as a web content quality measures on Malaysian government websites: A conceptual paper. *Proceedings of the 2014 International Symposium on Technology Management and Emerging Technologies ISTMET* (pp. 400-405). IEEE.

Booth, D., & Jansen, B. J. (2009). A review of methodologies for analyzing websites. *Web Technologies: Concepts, Methodologies, Tools, and Applications: Concepts, Methodologies, Tools, and Applications*, 145.

Chen, M., & Ryu, Y. U. (2013). Facilitating Effective User Navigation through Website Structure Improvement. *IEEE Transactions on* Knowledge and Data Engineering, *25*(3), 571–588.

Chhabra, I. (2014, December). Quality analytics for evaluation of dynamic web based learning environment. *Proceedings of the 2014 IEEE International Conference on MOOC, Innovation and Technology in Education MITE* (pp. 138-141). IEEE.

de Oliveira, C. L. C., & Laurindo, F. J. B. (2011). A Framework of Web Analytics: Deploying the emergent knowledge of customers to leverage competitive advantage. *Proceedings of the 2011 International Conference on e-Business*, Seville, Spain (pp.1-6). IEEE.

Duncan, S. (2010). Using web analytics to measure the impact of earned online media on business outcomes: A methodological approach. *Context Analytics and Text100*.

Eppler, M. J., & Muenzenmayer, P. (2002). Measuring Information Quality in the Web Context: A Survey of State-of-the-Art Instruments and an Application Methodology. In IQ (pp. 187-196).

Mcgovern, G. (2001). *Writing for the web,* Retrieved from http://www.gerrymcgovern.com/new-thinking/writing-killer-web-headings-and-links

Glass, K., & Colbaugh, R. (2011, September). Web analytics for security informatics. *Proceedings of the 2011 European Intelligence and Security Informatics Conference EISIC* (pp. 214-219). IEEE. doi:10.1109/EISIC.2011.66

Hu, Y. J. (2014, August). Privacy-Preserving WebID Analytics on the Decentralized Policy-Aware Social Web. *Proceedings of the 2014 IEEE/WIC/ACM International Joint Conferences on Web Intelligence (WI) and Intelligent Agent Technologies IAT* (Vol. 2, pp. 503-510). IEEE Computer Society. doi:10.1109/WI-IAT.2014.140

Kaushik, A. (2007). Web Analytics: An Hour A Day (W/Cd). John Wiley & Sons.

Kent, M. L., Carr, B. J., Husted, R. A., & Pop, R. A. (2011). Learning web analytics: A tool for strategic communication. *Public Relations Review, 37*(5), 536–543. doi:10.1016/j.pubrev.2011.09.011

Kohli, S., Kaur, S., & Singh, G. (2012, December). A Website Content Analysis Approach Based on Keyword Similarity Analysis. *Proceedings of the 2012 IEEE/WIC/ACM International Joint Conferences on Web Intelligence and Intelligent Agent Technology* (Vol. 1, pp. 254-257). IEEE Computer Society. doi:10.1109/WI-IAT.2012.212

Kopcso, D., Pipino, L., & Rybolt, W. (2001). Factors affecting the assessment of web site quality. *Proceedings of ECIS 2001* (p. 65).

Mittal, H., Sharma, M., & Mittal, J. P. (2012, January). Analysis and modelling of websites quality using fuzzy technique. *Proceedings of the Second International Conference on Advanced Computing & Communication Technologies* (pp. 7-8). doi:10.1109/ACCT.2012.25

Phippen, A., Sheppard, L., & Furnell, S. (2004). A practical evaluation of Web analytics. *Internet Research, 14*(4), 284–293. doi:10.1108/10662240410555306

Rio, A., & e Abreu, F. B. (2010). Websites Quality.

Shpak, O., Lowe, W., Wingkvist, A., & Ericsson, M. (2014, October). A Method to Test the Information Quality of Technical Documentation on Websites. In *Quality Software (QSIC), 2014 14th International Conference on* (pp. 296-304). IEEE. doi:10.1109/QSIC.2014.48

Tao, D., LeRouge, C. M., Deckard, G., & De Leo, G. (2012, January). Consumer Perspectives on Quality Attributes in Evaluating Health Websites. In *System Science (HICSS), 2012 45th Hawaii International Conference on* (pp. 2675-2684). IEEE. doi:10.1109/HICSS.2012.180

Verma, B., Gupta, K., Panchal, S., & Nigam, R. (2010, September). Single level algorithm: An improved approach for extracting user navigational patterns to improve website effectiveness. In *Computer and Communication Technology (ICCCT), 2010 International Conference on* (pp. 436-441). IEEE.

Waisberg, D., & Kaushik, A. (2009). Web Analytics 2.0: empowering customer centricity. *The original Search Engine Marketing Journal, 2*(1), 5-11.

Weischedel, B., & Huizingh, E. K. (2006, August). Website optimization with web metrics: a case study. *Proceedings of the 8th international conference on Electronic commerce: The new e-commerce: innovations for conquering current barriers, obstacles and limitations to conducting successful business on the internet* (pp. 463-470). ACM. doi:10.1145/1151454.1151525

Wibowo, S., & Grandhi, S. (2014, April). A performance-based approach for assessing the quality of group buying websites. *Proceedings of the 2014 4th IEEE International Conference on Information Science and Technology ICIST* (pp. 71-74). IEEE. doi:10.1109/ICIST.2014.6920334

Yen, B., Hu, P., & Wang, M. (2005, March). Towards effective web site designs: A framework for modeling, design evaluation and enhancement. *Proceedings of the 2005 IEEE International Conference on e-Technology, e-Commerce and e-Service EEE '05* (pp. 716-721). IEEE. doi:10.1109/EEE.2005.137

Ying, F., & Chun, Q. R. (2010). Research on BSC-Based Quality Evaluation of Enterprise Business Websites. *Proceedings of the 2010 International Conference on Management and Service Science* (pp. 1-4). doi:10.1109/ICMSS.2010.5576863

Zhang, L. J., Mao, Z. H., & Zhou, N. (2009, July). Design Quality Analytics of Traceability Enablement in Service-Oriented Solution Design Environment. *Proceedings of the IEEE International Conference on Web Services ICWS '09* (pp. 944-951). IEEE. doi:10.1109/ICWS.2009.145

Zhang, Y., Zhu, H., & Greenwood, S. (2004, September). Web site complexity metrics for measuring navigability. *Proceedings of the Fourth International Conference on Quality Software QSIC '04* (pp. 172-179). IEEE.

Zhu, M., Liu, W., Hu, W., & Fang, Z. (2009, November). Application to improve the websites quality. *Proceedings of the Third International Symposium on Intelligent Information Technology Application9 IITA '09* (Vol. 3, pp. 535-537). IEEE. doi:10.1109/IITA.2009.330

KEY TERMS AND DEFINITIONS

Bounce Rate: Bounce rate is a web metric that measures the number of visits to a single page regardless of the page views. The rate of bounces denotes number of single page visits, i.e. visitors who visit a single page on a site and leaves the site due to lack of valid content.

Conversion Rates: The act of transforming visitors into customers is the conversion rate of a site that results in better return on investment.

Key Performance Indicator: Key performance Indicator forms the metrics identified to attain the business strategy.

Optimization: Continuous process improvement or activity performed repeatedly is known as optimization.

Quality Websites: Quality websites are sites that have reliable performance and usefulness.

Web Analytics: Web analytics is a process of measuring web metrics to report the visitors' behaviour toward the website.

Web Metrics: Web metrics are unit of web measurement that generally forms the countable characteristics of web pages.

Websites: Websites are a collection web page that addresses the user's needs and are user friendly.

Chapter 11
Web Analytics for Web Site Quality Improvement

Ambati Venkata Krishna Prasad
K.L. University, India

Varaprasad Rao M
Anurag Group of Institutions, India

ABSTRACT

Web plays an important role in running business organizations, governments, societies, education sector, scientific organizations, social networks etc. As soon as web application has been deployed into the production environment, some or all of its features are available to the users. Web analytics is used to understand the usage pattern and its behaviour of users. The Web analytics is a procedure of measuring, collecting, analyzing and reporting of Internet data to optimize the business processes and maximize their revenue. Web Analytics is processes of inspecting, analyzing, tracking, measuring and reporting of web data for the purpose of discovering useful information, understanding web site quality, assess and improve the effectiveness of a website.

INTRODUCTION

Web analytics is the measurement, collection, analysis and reporting of web data for purposes of understanding and optimizing web usage. Web Analytics is the science and the art of improving websites to increase their profitability and usability by improving the customer's website experience. It is a science because it uses statistics, data mining techniques, and a methodical process. It is an art because, like a brilliant painter, the analyst or marketer has to draw from a diverse pallet of colors (data sources) to find the perfect mix that will yield actionable insights. It is also an art because improving websites requires a deep level of creativity, balancing user-centric design, promotions, content, images, and more. Besides, the analyst is always walking the fine line among website designers, IT personnel, marketers, senior management and customers.

As soon as a Web application has been deployed into the production environment, typically by the end of its development, some or all of its features are available to the users. By observing and analyzing

DOI: 10.4018/978-1-4666-9764-5.ch011

the application usage over a certain period of time, it is possible to extract users' behavior patterns. Using these patterns to modify the application increases the chances to best meet users' expectations and thus improve their satisfaction. (Michael Beasley; Ypsilanti 2013)

BACKGROUND

History

Web analytics started about 10 years ago with the emergence of the Internet, when its audience started to grow significantly and other media were showing increasing interest and concern for the World Wide Web. Web analytics tools have been designed to gather and parse Web servers log files, compute metrics from the extracted data, and generate text reports. With technologies' evolutions, new data-gathering methods have been developed and reports have been enhanced with tables and graphics. It focuses on in-depth comparison of available visitor data, referral data and site navigation pattern. The diagram below (Figure-1) gives a visual look of how web analytics has advanced with time (Web Analytics & usability Blog).

Evolution of Web

Web is the largest transformable-information construct that its idea was introduced by Tim Burners-Lee in 1989. Much progress has been made about the web and related technologies in the past two decades. Web 1.0 as a web of cognition, web 2.0 as a web of communication, web 3.0 as a web of co-operation and web 4.0 as a web of integration are introduced such as four generation of the web since the advent of the web. Overall Evolution of the World Wide Web during its existence can be categorized into three phases (FIGURE 2).

Figure 1. Transformation of web with time

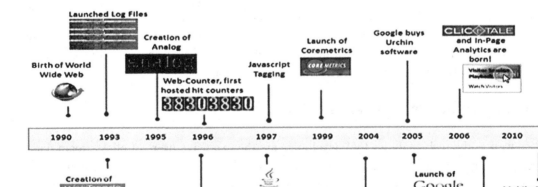

Figure 2. Evolution of Web

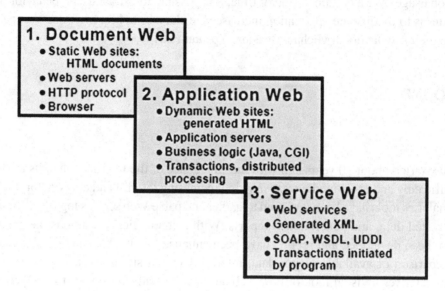

Web analytics can generate results for any kind of Web site:

Static Web sites: Web analytics tools have been designed from the ground-up to analyze the consultation of static Web sites. Web analytics tools are traditionally used for such Web sites, and literature abounds in explaining how to interpret the reports in this context.

Dynamic Web sites: Web analytics tools are used less for dynamic Web sites because in this case most of the reports are useless, incomplete, or must be interpreted differently.

Web services: Web analytics tools can bring into this context is a question that remains to be answered.

Why and When to Use Web Analytics

As web plays a remarkable role from the e-business perspective, the world of web is becoming exceedingly competitive and that calls for an urgency of constant monitoring of the web usage data and draw fruitful insight for the business. Simultaneously, when everybody around the world has access to the same tool and same infrastructures at a relatively low cost, the fight are always on to make e-business more efficient and attract more and more customers. The solution to all such concerns is well addressed by a collection of well-defined and well-structured click stream data.

By Whom and Where Web Analytics Is Used

Marketers as well as the web analytics tool developers are the extensive users of click stream data. A survey reveals that three-quarter of the marketers use website data. Web data are primarily used in the field of CRM, to develop marketing and advertising strategies, to optimize the website and to maximizing the investment they do in their website.

What It Does

Any sphere of business has variety of questions to be resolved. A proper analytical approach provides an appropriate answer to those concerns. Let us see the major questions in the world of e-business which are well answered by web analytics:

- Who are the visitors and how frequently they visit?
- What do they do they do and is there any pattern in their visit?
- Are the visitors satisfied with the site? What more they expect and what is not attracting them?
- Finally, how can more and more visitors be attracted?

MAIN FOCUS OF THE CHAPTER

Relevancy of Web Analytics

The 'how' can be seen from two different aspects viz; 'how it is measured' and 'how it is useful'. Let's start with the first part with a visual diagram (Figure -3) showing a typical flow of how such data is captured.

Step 1: The user requests for a browsing page.
Step 2: The request, in form of an HTML page, is sent to the host server.
Step 3 & 4: The server sends back the requested file to the web page & it is displayed.
Step 5: Simultaneously a JavaScript, which is embedded in the page, also get executed.
Step 6: The tracking system, on receiving the script, sends back a pixel tag to the page.
Step 7: The page in turn sends the page view details to the tracking server.
Step 8 & 9: In the meantime, a cookie is sent to the user through which his information is collected.
Step 10: Finally, based on the data collected, the in-built tool generates the report.

A web analytics data is captured in either of the following categories:

- **Web Logs:** The data here is captured in the form of a log file which gets created when a visitor request for a web page. When we type the URL in the browser, the server provides us that page and simultaneously creates a log of it.

Figure 3. Flow of Data capturing from web page

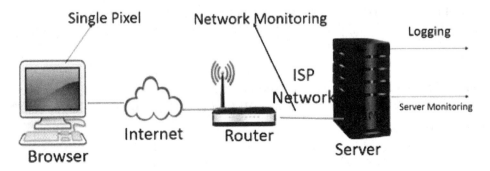

- **Web Beacon:** This measures the hit by a user on an add, banner or any graphics that pops up while opening a web page. The usual form of such data is the image on which the click is made.
- **Java Script Tags:** This is the most popular way of capturing the web data. When an URL is requested, the server furnishes the information along with a separate java script code embedded in it. The moment the page loads, the script gets executed and automatically sends the visitors information to a third party host server.

Now, proceeding with the second part of 'how', the most invaluable reason of data collection is decision support. [Phippen A., Sheppad L., Furnell S. (2004)] A proper and informatics data support the ability to make a right business decision. Click stream data serves the very same purpose in the field of web analytics. The most useful application of web analytics is in marketing and advertising where customer targeting is important. Constant and innovative efforts are made to attract new visitors through a fascinating and well-structured website design and relevant analysis is done on this data. Click stream data also serves the purpose of software testing, market research and analysing employee productivity. In Web server logging, data is logged by the Web server to files in one or more file formats. As Web server software has evolved, so has the variety of logging options and logging implementations. Some of the most widely spread log file formats are:

- NCSA Combined log format
- NCSA Separate log format (3-log format)
- NCSA Common log format (access log)
- Example 1 Combined log format log line
- 62.201.74.134 - - [29/Aug/2003:22:37:54 +0200] "GET /DisplayAccounts.do
- HTTP/1.1" 200 2972 "http://www.piggybank.com/MainMenu.do" "Mozilla/4.0 (compatible; MSIE 5.01; Windows NT)"

Separate log format combines all the Web usage data but splits the data into three log files in the following formats:

- Agent log format—agent data (Example 2)
- Referrer log format—referrer data (Example 3)
- Access log format (common log format)—the rest of the data (Example 4)
- Example 2 Agent log format
- Mozilla/4.0 (compatible; MSIE 5.01; Windows NT)
- Example 3 Referrer log format
- http://www.piggybank.com/MainMenu.do->/DisplayAccounts.do
- Example 4 Common log format (access log format)
- 62.201.74.134 - - [29/Aug/2003:22:37:54 +0200] "GET /DisplayAccounts.do HTTP/1.1" 200 2972

To produce all the reports, a complete log format such as the combined log format is needed in the Web server logging configuration. In Apache and IBM HTTP Server, this is done in the conf/httpd.conf configuration file (Example 5).

- Example 5 Combined log format configuration
- LogFormat "%h %l %u %t \"%r\" %>s %b \"%{Referer}i\"
- \"%{User-Agent}i\"" combined
- For e.g. an enterprise track the visitors' usage of their website along with a response study conducted for four months using click stream data. [L.Mich, M. Franch., L.Gaio (2003)] Following are the certain insights that were drawn from it:
  ○ A log transformation of the data would yield a better comparative study.
  ○ The historical data for an individual were not available.
  ○ One such user visited only once in the last 4 months.
  ○ 37% of users' visitor varies from one to four times.
  ○ 30% of visitor is more than 12 months old.
  ○ Lack of historical data & high variability in the data was an obstruction in finding a trend in the data.
  ○ Even 40% of the visitors didn't visit the site for at least 1 month. 16% of heavy user (3.2 hours of usage) was censored to zero (no visit in a month).
  ○ 14% of data points were missing.

Major Players and Their Feature

The web analytics tools can be broadly classified in two parts based on the features i.e. Conversion and Usability are explained below.

- **Conversion:** It measures the ratio of visitors who convert casual content views or website visits into desired actions based on subtle or direct requests from marketers, advertisers and content creators. Some eminent players helping in assessing the conversion rate are as follows:
  A. **Google Analytics:** Provides market based analysis with an excellent graphical representation. Gives a live view of what visitors are searching for and allow filtering click count from any specific domain. It is flexible in choosing the parameters and generates customized reports.
  B. **Web Trends:** It uses navigating behavior between pages to generate report. It helps to generate a comparative study between new and repeat visitors and generates reports based on demographic traits.
  C. **Compete:** Its utility is mainly based on competitor's analysis by comparing one site's usability to other. It can generate report for maximum of 5 website competitors and rank them based on the KPI's. It also generates alerts based on malicious website, site's popularity and discount offered in the site.
  D. **Stat Counter:** It offers charts and graphs for a better visualization of the statistics. Provides drill down analysis and its magnifying tool helps in zooming into individual visitors. It helps to set up multiple projects at a time.
  E. **Quantcast:** It accurately measures the visitors' information and helps in attracting advertisers. Generates graph for demographic variables. It also offers a free service that measures the usage of video, widgets and games. Finally it has the ability to generate one sentence summary.
- **Usability:** Certain web site tools focus on calculating the usability of the site. There are two main tools that do such a job.

A. **ClickTale:** It gives the analyzer to watch movie of user's individual browsing session it records every movement of the mouse, click and keystroke are tracked for better viewing. With such a tool the webmaster can improve usability and effectiveness of the site.

B. **Crazyegg:** It mainly focuses on capturing the page visited and its frequency along with volume of the click. The in-built feature 'overlay' count the number of click on every link or URL that is visited. Another feature 'Heatmap' compares the intensity of site visited by giving different color coding to them based on the volume.

Apart from the one mentioned above, there also more tools in the market which are free and have an excellent application to gather and analyze web data. Piwik, Firestats, Snoop, Yahoo Web Analytics, BBClone, Woopra, 4Q and Grape Web Statistics to name a few. [McFadden, C. (2005)].

The Web Analytics Process

Web Analytics is not a technology to produce reports; it is a process that proposes a virtuous cycle for website optimization. This section describes the Web analytics process applied to Web applications. As illustrated in Figure 4, the Web analytics process is composed of three phases:

1. Application users use the Web application; information about this usage is gathered
2. Web usage data is analyzed by the Web analytics tool to produce reports; the tool is configured and administered by the Web analytics tool administrator.

Figure 4. Web analytics Process Cycle

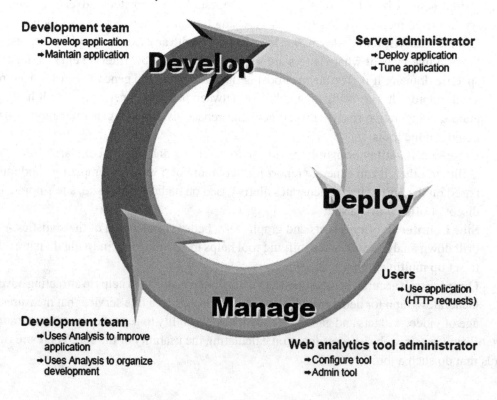

3. Developers analyze these reports to define Web application updates. Updated Web application is tested and deployed.

    Then the process cycles to phase 1.
    Roles:

-   Server administrator
-   Application user
-   Web analytics tool administrator
-   Developer

    Activities:

-   Deploy site
-   Configure and administrate Web analytics tool
-   View Web analytics reports
-   Define Web application updates
-   Update Web application

    Artifacts/Deliverables:

-   Reports
-   Web site

    Products/Tools:

-   Web content management tool
-   Web analytics tool
-   Web server/application server

Analysis Process

Inside the tool, the analysis and report generation process has four steps:

1. Gather Web usage data.
2. Parse data, and eventually store the data to a database and retrieve previously parsed data from the database.
3. Analyze data, and eventually store the results.
4. Generate and distribute the reports.

Figure 5. Analysis Process

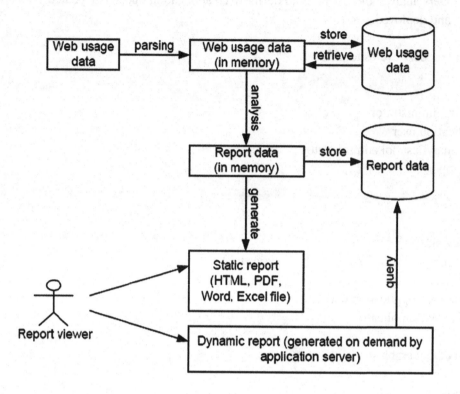

Distributing the Reports

Typically, the Web analytics tool provides a Web interface with a list of available reports, along with a calendar to select the time frame.

Reports usually contain a graphic, a table of numbers, and text explaining the meaning of these.

To distribute the reports to the report viewers, several methods can be used

- Print reports on paper and give them to the appropriate persons.
- Generate the reports as PDF, Word, or Excel documents and send them as e-mail attachments.

Figure 6. Distributing Reports

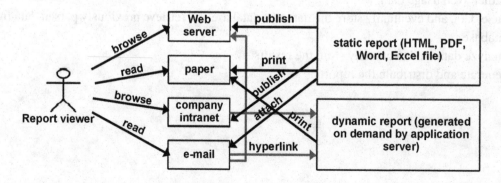

- Send an e-mail with a hyperlink to or the URL of the report-viewing interface.
- Insert a hyperlink to the report-viewing interface on the company intranet.

Troubleshooting

Every report is generated for a given time frame. If no report is available for a certain time frame, possible reasons are:

- The report generation for the corresponding time frame type (daily, weekly, monthly, quarterly, yearly) is not enabled in the configuration. Enable it and restart the analysis process.
- The analysis process is ongoing and the data for the time frame has not been analyzed yet. The solution is to wait for analysis process to be completed. Check the analysis progress status.
- The log files that have been analyzed contain no data for the time range. If this sounds wrong, check the log files content:
    - If no log line is present for the time frame, check the Web server logging configuration
    - If log lines are present for the time frame, check the tool configuration. Also look for an error in the result status of the analysis process.

Examining the Reports

The next sections show a number of interesting reports and explain how to analyze and exploit them to improve various aspects of a Web application, namely client compatibility, user navigation, robustness, bandwidth sizing, development, load-test plans, maintenance, and fat-client extensions. When activities of the Web application development process can benefit from feedback and how to apply the feedback will be explained in detail later.

Reports hereby presented have been generated from computer-generated log files, designed to be realistic and illustrative.

METRICS AND DIMENSIONS

Metrics and dimensions are key concepts in web analytics. Metrics are numeric measurements of various aspects of users' behaviour, like how long they spend viewing a page or how many times users viewed a page. Dimensions are the categories that user data may be grouped into, such as what browser they used or what keyword they searched for. Dimensions describe different attributes of users, their computers, how they enter in to this website, or even parts of the website that user's visit, how the users divided

Figure 7. Feedback from Webanalytics to development activity

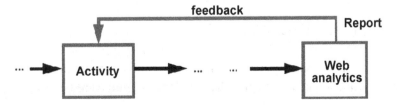

into segments. When dimensions are paired with metrics, we can learn things like how many users use each kind of browser, how many views each page receives, and how many visits came from specific location in specific day.

A metric can apply to three different universes:

- Aggregate — Total site traffic for a defined period of time.
- Segmented — A subset of the site traffic for a defined period of time, filtered in some way to gain greater analytical insight: e.g., by campaign (e-mail, banner, PPC, affiliate), by visitor type (new vs. returning, repeat buyers, high value), by referrer.
- Individual — Activity of a single Web visitor for a defined period of time.

Advantages and Disadvantages

The following are the benefits of click stream data from web analytics tool.

- Helps to track the flow of the website usage.
- Gives a sense of visitor's behavioural pattern. Helps to understand the need of the visitors.
- It also gives an indication of the most and the least viewed part of the website based on which actions can be taken.
- Based on such data, CRM can be easily implemented to optimize the site.
- Finally, it helps to keep the site updated with the competitive market. Though click stream data has been a revolution in the world of web analytics, its use has still been relatively low. Some of its drawbacks are listed below:
- It fails to capture user's activities on other websites.
- Sometimes it lacks in defining the user-specific information such as demographic profiles.
- Often the multiple file formats of click stream data becomes an issue of handling for integration.
- Also it is said that click stream data does not capture sub URL information which is one of its demerit.

The Need

Web analytics also serves to be exciting for the analyst to dig into. From such prospective, following are the broader area where analysis plays an important role: Measuring and maximizing ROI: Identifies which referral source generates more revenue and sales orders for the web business.

Customer targeting: Defines the visitors' group which has a possibility to get converted into a subscribed member.

Optimizing conversions: Study and maximize the rate of visitors' conversion to a subscription.

Saving on customer support: Reduce the offline cost by improving the online support.

SOLUTIONS AND RECOMMENDATIONS:

A website's success, all the same, relies on a company's ability to make the right choices. What new features and functionalities should be added to the site? What should be removed? What should be kept?

These are very difficult decisions, but web analytics can provide precious help in making the right ones. Below is a list of some problems and its possible solutions which should be considered as part of a site give a face-lift.

What Needs to be Corrected?

The website has an overall goal, for example to generate sales, registrations, requests for contact, bookings, and the list goes on. Each website must ensure that this main goal is accomplished by its visitors. The aim of a site revamp is to correct anything and everything that prevents the customers or prospects from doing what we would like the customers to do on the site.

The Conversion Funnel Analysis

Analysing conversion funnels reveals areas where prospects leave the site and also shows which pages they visit after they leave the funnel just a few steps before conversion. The pages from which Internet users leave the funnel can provide information on the funnel's potential problems.

The Internal Search Engine Analysis

The Internal search engine analyses show the search engine's ability to find and return searched content, and also shows the site's ability to efficiently direct visitors, without them needing to use the internal search engine. For example, we can see the pages on which users had the most difficulty finding what they were looking for by examining the page view analysis along with the internal search engine results analysis.

Which Content or Features Should be Removed?

Another aim of a site revamp is to get rid of part of the site in order to better meet your target audience's expectations. One of the pitfalls of many sites is that they try to please everyone and provide content to all audience types, at the risk of offering a poor user experience to the true target audience.

Analysing Traffic Volume of Different Site Sections

This analysis evaluates how often different sections of the site are used. Some site sections will not have a lot of traffic, meaning that these sections can be removed from the site.

Page Click Analyses

The Clickstream analyses counts the number of clicks made on the different links and zones that make up a page. We can verify which links are the most clicked and the most likely to direct users to targeted content. This analysis is most important on the home page, as the most difficult choices to make are those associated with the home page. Once again, one of the pitfalls of many websites is to suggest links to all different types of content available on the site. This analysis will help to make a firm decision, reduce the number of possibilities from the home page, and increase the chances of a click.

Page Scroll Analyses

The HeatScale analysis provides an image of what Internet users have viewed on a page by studying the vertical page scroll. In cumulative mode, we can obtain information on the percentage and number of visits having displayed each horizontal zone of the page.

Internal Hits

After the Web application is deployed, some requests are sent to the Web server by the internal development team (especially the testers). These hits should not be considered in data analysis. Some Web analytics offer the feature to exclude groups of client machines from data analysis. In WebTrends Log Analyzer, this feature is called *Intranet Domains*.

Data Volume

Large log files cause several problems:

- Writing logs into a big log file slows down the Web server performance. A solution is to rotate the log file periodically, usually daily. To avoid repeated administration overhead, the rotating task can be included in the server operating system task scheduler.
- Disk storage can become insufficient. Compress the log files. The compression ratio for log files is 95% to 98%. The commonly used compression algorithm is GZIP, which is supported by most platforms (including Windows and UNIX) and most tools, and is more free of rights than the ZIP algorithm.
- The duration of data analysis is an exponential function of the number of log lines. Use analysis time frames as short as possible.

Example: If the Web server is configured with the NCSA combined log file format, every request to a file makes the log file grow by about 200 bytes. If the Web server receives 2,000,000 hits a day, logging requires 400 MB disk storage a day, or 120 GB a year. Compression brings this number down to a reasonable size: about 4 GB a year. This takes days to be analyzed by a Web analytics tool. It is possible to reduce the log file size by deleting the log lines for images and CSS (Cascading Style Sheets). This can reduce the data volume by an order of magnitude depending on the number of images in the screens. A drawback is that some reports are not correct any more; for example, all hits must be analyzed to produce the report.

IP Multiplexing

In some organizations, browsers do not connect directly to Web sites, but pass on the requests to a proxycache

When a Web server receives a request from a proxy cache, it knows only the IP address of the proxy cache. The IP address of the requesting machine is hidden from the Web server. Therefore, all the browsers using the same proxy cache are seen by the Web servers as a single machine. This blurs the reports that exploit the IP addresses.

Figure 8. Proxycache

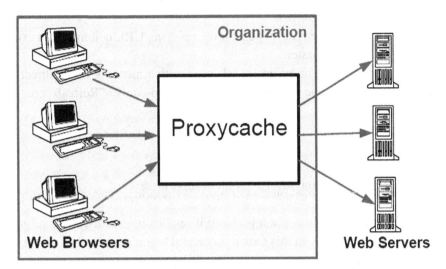

A solution to resolve IP multiplexing is to track client machines with an identifying cookie. This solution is implemented in the single-pixel data-gathering method.

HTTP Parameters

In standard Web analytics tools, HTTP parameters are not considered. A few specific tools on the market try to exploit information in HTTP parameters but fail to deliver a generic solution. For needs that are not covered by basic Web analytics software features, the best solution remains code instrumentation. Code instrumentation consists of developing custom logging inside the Web application. An interesting IBM framework for code instrumentation is ALS (Analytic Logging Service).

User Privacy

User privacy is a sensitive topic. Users are usually willing to share information for better service. However, users also typically prefer that they be asked for their permission to send them marketing e-mail or to share their contact information with partner companies. If a site provides a privacy statement documenting the intended uses, and gives users an e-mail address for comments, users can determine whether the policy is acceptable. To start, decide how to use the information that is recorded about the users. Then write privacy statement based on the users' point of view, and make that statement available on the Web site. A World Wide Web Consortium (W3C) project called *Platform for Privacy Protection* is helping to define and standardize the policies for data collection and the legitimate uses of this data.

Broken Links

Users may send requests to URIs that are not recognized by the application. In this case, the server returns a *HTTP 404 error*. When a user receives such an error page, he may be discouraged and stop using the application, especially in his first request.

These 404-type errors can be monitored with a Web analytics report (Figure 9).

Some possible solutions are as follows:

Fix the broken link or links in the referral page; if the referring URL belongs to an external Web site, contact the external Web site webmaster.

At a popular unrecognized URI insert an HTML page with a meta tag that redirects to a more appropriate resource, for example to the welcome page: <meta http-equiv="Refresh" content="0;URL=/index.html">

Entry Points

When a user enters a Web application, several problems may arise:

- The user is not logged in. This is not a problem if application security is configured to redirect unlogged users to a login page. In this case a successful logon seamlessly redirects the user to the expected response page.
- The user enters the application in the middle of a use case with wrong HTTP parameters. This leads to an error page, which is not a convenient way to welcome a user. Modify the controller component code to check the referrer and display a more appropriate page.
- The entry point does not exist anymore in the Web site; this case boils down to "Broken links"
- The list of entry points into the Web application can be found in a report as shown in Figure 10.

In Figure 10 we can see no entry in the middle of a use case, which is good. We can also see that about a third of the entries are not the welcome page, which is fine because unlogged users are redirected to the login page.

Figure 9. Unrecognized URIs

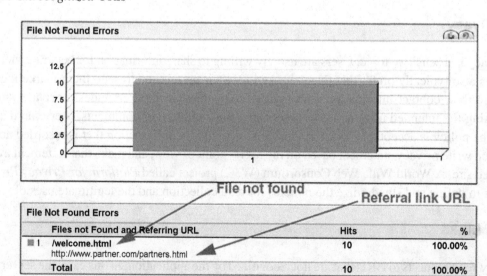

Figure 10. Top entry pages

Top Entry Pages

	Pages	Visits	%
1.	http://www.piggybank.com/index.jsp	542	67.50%
2.	http://www.piggybank.com/TransferAccounts.do	179	22.29%
3.	http://www.piggybank.com/DisplayAccounts.do	82	10.21%
	Total	803	100.00%

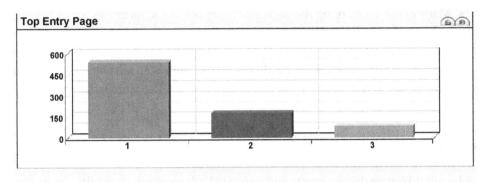

User Navigation Analysis

The report in Figure 11 shows what paths are followed by the visitors through the application.

This report presents a click-by-click view of user behaviour. Guidelines to modify the Web application are with the same objective of improving the users' experience. Top navigation paths can also be used to build realistic performance- and load-test plans.

FUTURE RESEARCH DIRECTIONS

In academia, current web analytics related research encompasses social search and mining, reputation systems, social media analytics, and web visualization. In addition, web based auctions, Internet monetiza-

Figure 11. Top paths through application

Top Paths Through Site

Starting Page	Paths from Start	Visits	%
All entry Pages	1. http://www.piggybank.com/index.jsp 2. http://www.piggybank.com/MainMenu.do 3. http://www.piggybank.com/DisplayAccounts.do 4. http://www.piggybank.com/TransferAccounts.do 5. http://www.piggybank.com/TransferForm.do	533	67.73%
	1. http://www.piggybank.com/TransferAccounts.do 2. http://www.piggybank.com/TransferForm.do 3. http://www.piggybank.com/Transfer.do	114	14.49%
	1. http://www.piggybank.com/DisplayAccounts.do	80	10.17%
	1. http://www.piggybank.com/TransferAccounts.do 2. http://www.piggybank.com/TransferForm.do	60	7.62%

tion, social marketing, and web privacy/security are some of the promising research directions related to web analytics. Many of these emerging research areas may rely on advances in social network analysis, text analytics, and even economics modelling research. Future work includes refining this model for a larger scale analysis to Web site design, product placement optimization, customer transaction analysis, and product recommendations can be easily accomplished through Web analytics. Finally Web analytics can be helpful from descriptive analysis to prescribe analysis i.e. (Recommendation systems).

CONCLUSION

We examined several Web analytics reports and presented a framework to modify the production environment, extract users' average behavior and anticipate future evolution of a Web application. We have found that the various data sources fulfil different purposes: clickstream data enable managers to answer 'when' and 'what' questions, customer surveys 'why' and 'how' questions, and external data to make competitor comparisons. Web metrics are the measures that reflect how customers are using a website. Companies use these metrics for further improvement of their website.

REFERENCES

Arikan, A. (2008). *Multichannel Marketing: Metrics and Methods for On and Offline Success*. Indiana: Wiley Publishing.

Beasley, M. (2013). *Practical Web Analytics for User Experience*. Ypsilanti: Morgan Kaufmann, Elsevier publications.

Cutler, M., & Sterne, J. (2000). *E-Metrics: Business Metrics for the New Economy*. Chicago, IL: NetGenesis. doi:10.1145/347090.347096

Dhyani, D., Ng, W.K. & Bhowmick, S.S. (2002). A survey of Web metrics. *ACM Computing Surveys*, 34(4), 469-503.

DuBois, L. (n. d.). 11 Best Web Analytics Tools. *Inc Magazine*. Retrieved from http://www.inc.com/guides/12/2010/11-best-web-analytics-tools.html

Hackman, J. R., & Woolley, A. W. (In press). Creating and leading analytic teams. In R. L. Rees & J. W. Harris (Eds.), *A handbook of the psychology of intelligence analysis: The human factor*. Burlington, MA: CENTRA Technology.

Kaushik, A. (2007). *Web Analytics: An Hour a Day*. Indiana: Wiley Publishing.

Kleinberg, J. M., Kumar, R., Raghavan, P., Rajagopalan, S., & Tomkins, A. (1999). The Web as a graph: Measurements, models, and methods. In T. Asano, H. Imai, D.T. Lee, S.-i. Nakano, & T. Tokuyama (Eds.), *Computing and Combinatorics*, LNCS (Vol. 1627, 1–17). Retrieved from www.webanalyticsassociation.org/aboutus/

Mavromoustakos, S., & Andreou, A. S. (2007, November). WAQE: A Web Application Quality Evaluation model. *International Journal of Web Engineering and Technology*, *3*(1), 96–120. doi:10.1504/IJWET.2007.011529

McFadden, C. (2005). Optimizing the Online Business Channel with Web Analytics.

Mendes, E. M., Mosley, N., & Counsell, S. (2001). Web Metrics -Estimating Design and Authoring Effort. *IEEE MultiMedia*, *8*(1), 50–57. doi:10.1109/93.923953

Mich, L., Franch, M., & Gaio, L. (2003, January-March). Evaluating and Designing the Quality of Web Sites. *IEEE MultiMedia*, *10*(1), 34–43. doi:10.1109/MMUL.2003.1167920

Phippen, A., Sheppad, L., & Furnell, S. (2004). A practical evaluation of web analytics. *Internet Research*, *14*(4), 284–293. doi:10.1108/10662240410555306

Phippen, A., Sheppad, L., & Furnell, S. (2004). A practical evaluation of web analytics. *Internet Research*, *14*(4), 284–293. doi:10.1108/10662240410555306

Sterne, J. (2002). *Web Metrics: Proven Methods for Measuring Web Site Success*. New York: John Wiley & Sons.

Sterne, J. (2002). *Web Metrics: Proven Methods for Measuring Web Site Success*. New York: John Wiley & Sons.

Verisign. (n. d.). Retrieved from http://www.verisign.com/static/040655.pdf

Web analytics Association. (n. d.). Retrieved from www.webanalyticsassociation.org

Weischedel, B., & Kelowna, Eelko K. R. E. (2006). Website optimization with web metrics: a case study. *Proceedings of the 8th international conference on Electronic commerce: The new e-commerce ICEC '06* (pp. 463-470).

KEY TERMS AND DEFINITIONS

Analytics: The science of logical analysis. Analytics often involves studying past historical data to research potential trends, to analyze the effects of certain decisions or events, or to evaluate the performance of a given tool or scenario. The goal of analytics is to improve the business by gaining knowledge which can be used to make improvements or changes.

Bounce Rate: Single page view visits divided by entry pages.

Click-through: Number of times a link was clicked by a visitor.

Click-through Rate/Ratio: The number of click-throughs for a specific link divided by the number of times that link was viewed.

Conversion: A visitor completing a target action.

Entry Page: The first page of a visit.

Event: Any logged or recorded action that has a specific date and time assigned to it by either the browser or server.

Exit Page: The last page on a site accessed during a visit, signifying the end of a visit/session.

External Referrer: The external referrer is a page URL where the traffic is external or outside of the website or a web-property defined by the user.

Hit: A 'hit' or a 'click' requests a page from the server. More the hits, more is the popularity of the website. Sometimes a viewer visits a page but navigate quickly because of not getting the proper information he is looking for. In such scenario hits can be misleading and over estimates the popularity.

Internal Referrer: The internal referrer is a page URL that is internal to the website or a web-property within the website as defined by the user.

Landing Page: A page intended to identify the beginning of the user experience resulting from a defined marketing effort.

New Visitor: The number of Unique Visitors with activity including a first-ever Visit to a site during a reporting period.

Original Referrer: The original referrer is the first referrer in a visitor's first session, whether internal, external or null.

Page: A page is an analyst definable unit of content.

Page Views: The number of times a page (an analyst-definable unit of content) was viewed.

Page Views per Visit: The number of page views in a reporting period divided by number of visits in the same reporting period.

Page Exit Ratio: Number of exits from a page divided by total number of page views of that page.

Repeat Visitor: The number of Unique Visitors with activity consisting of two or more Visits to a site during a reporting period.

Return Visitor: The number of Unique Visitors with activity consisting of a Visit to a site during a reporting period and where the Unique Visitor also Visited the site prior to the reporting period.

Referrer: The referrer is the page URL that originally generated the request for the current page view or object.

Single-Page Visits: Visits that consist of one page regardless of the number of times the page was viewed.

Search Referrer: The search referrer is an internal or external referrer for which the URL has been generated by a search function.

Single Page View Visits (Bounces): Visits that consist of one page-view.

Unique Visitors: The number of inferred individual people (filtered for spiders and robots), within a designated reporting timeframe, with activity consisting of one or more visits to a site. Each individual is counted only once in the unique visitor measure for the reporting period.

Visit Duration: The length of time in a session. Calculation is typically the timestamp of the last activity in the session minus the timestamp of the first activity of the session.

Visit Referrer: The visit referrer is the first referrer in a session, whether internal, external or null.

Visits/Sessions: A visit is an interaction, by an individual, with a website consisting of one or more requests for an analyst-definable unit of content (i.e. "page view"). If an individual has not taken another action (typically additional page views) on the site within a specified time period, the visit session will terminate.

Chapter 12
Web Analytics:
Boon for New Age Entrepreneurship

Himani Singal
Birla Institute of Technology, India

Shruti Kohli
Birla Institute of Technology, India

ABSTRACT

There is a remarkable association between an organization's analytics intricacy and its competitive enactment. The biggest problem to adopting analytics is the lack of knowledge of using it to improve business performance. A website is believed and considered as 'face' of the company. In present era, there are more than 200 million people who buy goods online across the globe. Business Analytics helps companies to find the most profitable customer and allows them to justify their marketing effort, especially when the competition is very high. Predictive analytics helps organizations to predict churn, default in loan payment, brand switch, insurance loss and even the outcome in a football match. There is ample evidence from the corporate world that the ability to make better decisions (by management executives) improves with analytical skills. This chapter will provide an in-depth knowledge of business analytic techniques and their applications in improving business processes and decision-making.

INTRODUCTION

Analytics is the application of computer expertise, domain knowledge and statistics to solve problems in business and industry; to aid efficient and effective decision-making. It is simply a scientific process of converting raw data into knowledge to support decision making by finding patterns in data. The goal of Analytics is to improve business, society or personal performance by gaining knowledge from data. It encourages well informed decision-making driven by data rather using gut-feeling or guessing estimates. It is reported that data is growing at 40% compound annual rate which will reach to 45 ZB (Zeta Bytes) by 2020. About 2.5 Quintillion bytes of data is created each year, out of which 90% data was created in last 2 years itself. With such huge amount of data, decisions of any kind cannot be taken randomly.

DOI: 10.4018/978-1-4666-9764-5.ch012

Proper analysis is required to undermine any pinning information which can increase customer base or revenues; to which insightful analytics is the solution. Analytics can be classified broadly along four dimensions as depicted in Figure 1.

Each of these dimensions of Analytics gives answer or insightful measures to a specific type of problem. These problems can be best described in the form of questions as follows:

1. Descriptive Analytics – What happened or happening in the business?
2. Inquisitive Analytics – Why did it happen?
3. Predictive Analytics – What is likely to happen based on historical information?
4. Prescriptive Analytics – What action should be taken?

Web analytics (WA) is the measurement, collection, analysis and reporting of internet data for purpose of understanding and optimizing web usage. It is a tool for measuring web traffic, business and market research by assessing and improving the effectiveness of a website. For instance, it helps to measure change of traffic to a website after the launch of a new advertising campaign, number of visitors on the website and number of pages viewed by the visitors. WA helps in measuring both on-site and off-site data (read site as website). Here, on-site data refers to the website data or direct data which is collected by tracking the visitors' behavior directly, whereas off-site data refers to the indirect data which cannot be determined online directly. The kind of data which Web Analytics helps to measure both on-site and off-site is depicted in Figure 2.

Figure 1. Dimensions of Analytics

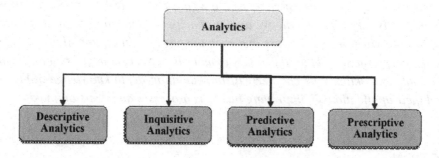

Figure 2. Web Analytics measures

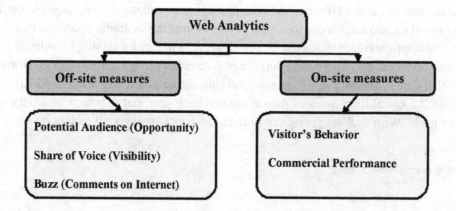

To sum up in simple words, 'systematic evaluation based on correct and precise data is known as analysis or analytics and if data is related to Internet (particularly websites), it is known as Web Analytics'. At conceptual level, Web Analytics is composed of different kinds of analysis activities, according to which it is categorized as depicted in Figure 3.

1. Statistical Analysis – Why is this happening?
2. Forecasting – What if these trends continues?
3. Predictive Modeling – What will happen next?
4. Optimization – What's the best that can happen?

These four components collectively help to measure five *Ws* and one *H*; which is fundamental for existence of any website.

Who: Identify people/customers/audience who interacts with the website.
Where: Identify the sources from where this traffic arrived on the website.
What: Identify the products/services/webpages the audience is looking for?
When: Identify the time of day/week/month/year when traffic is more.
Why: Identify the reason for which the website is being used.
How: Identify the pattern of usage of the website.

Thus, it can be summarized that 'Web Analytics is a procedure referred to gathering, measurement and exploration of user activity on a website to understand and help achieve the intended objective of the website. It is essential to use Web Analytics if the performance of the website is to be monitored, especially in terms of traffic sources, site behavior and online marketing'.

WEB ANALYTICS CONCEPTS

To track online activities from visitors in the best possible manner, WA works best when it undergoes the systematic approach as depicted in Figure 4. *(Kaushik, 2007)*

Figure 3. Composition of Web Analytics

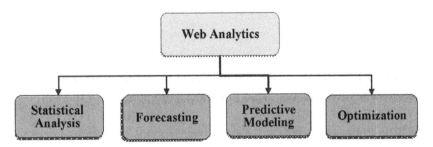

Figure 4. Steps of Web Analytics

Step 1: Define

To measure the success of a website, its goals should be predefined. Goals of a website may depend upon the kind or objective of a website for which analysis needs to be done. Generally, there are some common objectives for which a website is launched.

1. E-commerce websites – Their evident objective or goal is to sell their merchandises and amenities to make as much profit as they can.
2. Lead generation websites – These websites are hosted to gather information about the users for aiding people from sales to connect and target with potential leads.
3. Content websites - Their goal is to keep their visitors engaged by providing fresh and relevant content.
4. Support Websites – These websites aim to provide right and relevant information at right time to their users. They are also referred to as online information sites.

Apart from these, branding, driving awareness, engagement and loyalty are some objectives which are behind the hosting of almost every website.

Step 2: Measure

Once the goals are defined, they need to be measured to measure the overall performance of the website. By using any analytics tool, two types of data can be captured for this purpose:

1. Dimensions- It describes characteristics of users, their sessions and actions. For example, geographic location, traffic source, page views, etc.

2. Metrics- It is the quantitative measurements of users. For example, the total number of users on a website or app, averages like the average number of pages users sees or average time a user spends on a website*(Patton, 2002)*.

It is to be determined as to which of the metrics are best suitable for measuring the objectives defined in Step 1. These identified metrics are designated as Key Performance Indicators or KPIs. Identification of these key performance indicators and their effective tracking is the most basic and critical task as the further analysis depends on it.

Step 3: Analyze

After measuring the website, it may be noticed that some content or marketing activities are underperforming. If that happens, the data should be analyzed and the results should be explained in detail and accordingly action should be taken. It is basically an act of drilling down the metrics to the lowest level and pull out the core insights from it *(Alexander, Tate, 1999)*.

Step 4: Optimize

After being able to identify and explain why a particular area is underperforming, one should immediately think about ways to improve it. The solutions should be implemented in a planned manner and all the changes should be documented. By comparing these changes with the previous versions, optimized solution can be achieved.

KEY METRICS

As discussed in previous section, metrics is critical or central to analysis carried through any Web Analytics program. Ananalytics report consists of dimensions and metrics. The common dimensions available are: Geographic location of users (User Dimension), Traffic Source (Session Dimension), Name of Webpage (User Action Dimension). Similarly, the most common metrics available are: *(Booth, & Jansen, 2009)*

Visitors (Users)

It measures the "number of unique users that visit your site during a certain time period" *(Google Analytics Academy)*. This gives the overall size of the audience. This metric can be segmented to track "new users" and "returning users" for the website or for mobile app.

Visits (Sessions)

It is defined as "a period of consecutive activity by the same user" *(Google Analytics Academy)*. By default, a session persists if a user is inactive for 30 minutes or more. It is termed as "session timeout length". This can also be predefined in configuration settings if it is to be customized. For instance, in case of a website dealing with video streaming, it is apt to increase session timeout length to a little more than the size of longest video on the website.

Pageviews and Events

"The pageview metric literally counts every time a page is viewed on your site"*(Google Analytics Academy)*. Other activities or interactions can also be tracked using Web Analytics tools. These activities may involve video watching too.

Time-Based Metrics

All the time-based metrics rely on the stream or hits of user activity. It maintains history of all the interactions to calculate time metrics. For example, "to calculate the metric visit duration Google Analytics subtracts the time of the user's first interaction on your site from the time of the last interaction. To calculate the metric time on page Google Analytics takes the time that a user landed on a particular page, and subtracts that from the time of the next pageview"*(Google Analytics Academy)*.

Bounce Rate

Bounce rate is the percentage of sessions with only one user interaction. Traditionally, in web analytics, bounces are counted for users who land on a page of your site and leave immediately. It does not matter how much time they spend on the page. If they land on a page, and leave immediately from that page without viewing any other content, it counts as a bounce. Since bounced visits only consist of one interaction, Web Analytics tools does not have a second interaction to use for the calculation of visit duration or time on page. These visits, and the one pageview included in the visit, are assigned a visit duration and time on page of zero.

Why one might encounter with a high bounce rate value? First, it can be an indication that the right expectations have not been set for the users entering the site. Secondly, it could be an indication that they are not being provided with a good enough experience once they arrive. Alternatively, if it is expected by a user to view only one page, like on a blog, a high bounce rate is perfectly fine. This metric is especially useful when we are trying to measure our landing page effectiveness for marketing campaigns. Time metrics and bounce rate depend on keeping track of a user's activity throughout a session. This can actually be difficult for sites that don't load new pages frequently*(Google Analytics Academy)*.

Web Analytics tools can also be configured to track conversion metrics such as number of signs ups for a newsletter or purchases.

A common rule of thumb to identify key metrics is to associate them with the kind of website being analyzed. Some commonly used key metrics under this observation are Views, Visits, Bounce Rate, Conversion Rate, Time on Site, New vs. Returning Visitors and Depth of Visit for commercial websites, whereas Loyalty, Content Consumption Rate and Engagement of Web Applications for non-commercial

Figure 5. Components of Google Analytics

websites. Bounced visitors, time on last page and averages of any metrics are generally considered as potential pitfalls during analysis as they are prone to inaccurate calculations because of some hidden behavior of visitors *(Hong, 2007).*

Interaction with Google Analytics

Google Analytics is a freeware Web Analytics tool provided by Google with powerful analytical capabilities. In order to properly understand the data with the help of Google Analytics, it's important to know the basics of the data collection and the way it is managed prior to the generation of reports. There are four components in the Google Analytics system as depicted in Figure 5:*(Google Analytics Academy)*

We will review each of these components detailing the process of their working to generate the data required for acquiring the insights *(Hasan, Morris, Probets, 2009; Clifton, 2008; Google Analytics Academy).*

Collection

Google Analytics is a powerful tool to track user interaction data from websites, mobile apps and any digital environment that is connected and needs to be traced such as a kiosk. For data collection, it uses a small piece of JavaScript code, which needs to be placed or embed on each webpage of the website. Once a user lands on homepage or any other page of the website, this JavaScript code starts tracking information about users' engagement and their whereabouts with the website, such as URL of the visited pages, browser name and language used for browsing, device and its operating system, referring source, etc. All of this information is sent for processing to servers owned and hosted by Google. Every time a user clicks on any webpage or part of webpage, it is stated as a "hit" or an "interaction." The moment a user visits a new page, the JavaScript code gathers all the new or updated information and send it to the servers. This procedure alone helps to collect an unbelievable amount of data using Google Analytics. Google Analytics also provide many possible customizations to collect superfluous data required as per defined goals.

For example, if some airline company runs a loyalty program for their customers, it might want Google Analytics to keep track of all its customers' frequent flier status by collecting this information when a user logs onto its site. It is possible, using additional JavaScript code, to collect this data and send it back to Google Analytics' servers with the rest of its user interaction data.

Abstractly, data can be collected from mobile applications using similar lines through Google Analytics. But one should know some basic differences of mobile app tracking from website tracking. Similar JavaScript code cannot be used to track all mobile apps. Instead methods are used to do so which are customized according to the operating system, the device uses, on which the mobile app has been hosted or is used. Instead of data capturing on each hit on page, the data is collected after every "activity" on the mobile app. So, as JavaScript code should be added on each webpage of the website, similarly, while tracking mobile app, extra code should be added on each activity which one wants to track. It is always to be keep in mind that mobile devices are not continuously linked with the internet, so data cannot be sent to servers in real time. To overcome this problem, Google Analytics store the "hits" and dispatch them whenever the device is next connected with the internet.

Collecting data from digital environments besides websites and mobile applications requires assistance of a knowledgeable developer. Conceptually the collection process isn't much different from the data collection process from websites. To implement Google Analytics in any digital environment one has to simply define and choose what type of user interaction is to be considered as a "hit" for that specific environment and embed an extra code for it.

Processing

Regardless of the procedure and environment used for data ("hits") collection, it needs to be processed on the servers. Processing of data refers to transforming raw data into a usable form. For instance, data can be categorized according to the users' devices as mobile or non-mobile, their operating system, etc.

Configuration

Google Analytics can be customized using its configuration settings. These configuration settings are applied to the data. For instance, some data can be added or dropped using filters. After processing of data, the specified configurations are applied on it before storing it in a database. Once the data has been processed and changed according to the configurations, it cannot be further altered.

Reporting

Google analytics provide a web interface (www.google.com/analytics) to access the processed data stored in database according to the configurations. It can also be done through Google Analytics account using one's own application code and the Core Reporting API. This API is capable of building highly customizable reports.

Web Analytics Tools

There are numerous Web Analytics tools available in the market, both free and paid, which can help in analyzing the data to bits. Though Google Analytics is a freeware and is widely used WA tool; choice of tool solely depends on the factors and extent of data which one needs to analyze. Table 1 gives a comparative analysis between the vendors of different paid web analytics tools.

These vendors claim to solve various issues for their clients. Some of their interesting case studies are: *(Nabler, Marketelligent, Fractal, iCreate, Mu Sigma, Manthan)*

1. How to Identify Hot Leads?

    Need:

    To put in place a ranking system so as to classify each incoming lead into hot, warm or cold and convert hot leads into Customers.

    Challenges:

- Develop a predictive model that will tag each incoming lead as hot; warm or cold.
- Implement the predictive model in a real-time system so that hot leads get automatically routed to the appropriate dealer depending on the location of the lead and the dealer.

Table 1. Comparative Analysis of Different Web Analytics Vendors (Source: Nabler, Marketelligent, Fractal, iCreate, Mu Sigma, Manthan)

Vendor	Business Area Specialization	Services Offered	Prominent Clients	Tools
Nabler	- Marketing organizations - Digital agencies	- Site Analytics & Reporting - Testing and Optimization - Implementation Support - Campaign Analytics & Reporting - Social Media Analytics - Custom Analytics Software Development - Tool Specific Services	- Lenovo - Infosys - Dolby - StudioOne Networks - Triad Retail Media	- MapMyLead - NT WebStudio - DeepFish
Marketelligent	- Retail Banking & Consumer Finance - Consumer Packaged Goods (CPG) & Retail - Customer Relationship Management (CRM) - Media - Energy and Utility	- Strategic MIS Segmentation - Forecasting - Predictive Modeling - Customer Lifetime Value Optimization - Reporting and Desktop Solutions	- TimesOfMoney - Burgan Bank - Citigroup - Nestle - American Express - Pricewaterhouse Coopers - ICICI Bank	- Accurate Forecasting - ModelScape
Mu-Sigma	- Banking, Financial Services and Insurance - CPG and Retail - Pharmaceuticals - Healthcare - Technology, Media & Telecom	- Marketing - Supply chain - Risk Mitigation	Microsoft & Leading pharmaceutical, banking, retail, insurance companies (names undisclosed)	- muESP™ - muBuzz™ - muFlow™ - muMix™ - muPDNA™ - muRx™ - muXo™ - muHPC™ - muText™
Fractal Analytics	- Finance - CPG (Consumer Packed Goods) - Retail - Insurance	- Data & Trends - Predictive Analytics & Models - Solving Problem Optimization - Operational Analytics - Institutionalizing Analytics	Leading companies in almost all areas (names undisclosed)	- Customer Genomics - Concordia - Pincer
Manthan Systems	- e-Commerce - Finance - Human Resources - Store Operations - Fashion Retailers	- Manthan's 3rd i – Next Gen BI - Advanced Analytics - Performance Management - Role Based Analytics - Guided Analytics - Actionable Dashboards - ARC Demand Signal Repository - ARC eCommerce Analytics - ARC Store Operations	- Prada - ReadyPac - ecco - Woolworth - Vanity - PeavyMart	- ARC Merchandise Analytics - ARC Customer Analytics - ARC TargetOne - ARC Vendor Insights - ARC Vendor Link
i-Create	Banking	- DW / BI Services - Analytics Services - Core Banking Services	- Redhat - Informatica - Actian Corporation	- Biz$tart - Biz$core - BizManage - BizFactory - DRisk

Plan of Action:

- Analyze lead information along with purchase status over the past 2 years.
- Transform lead information variables like name, address, email, time frame of purchase etc. into derived variables.
- Build a predictive model to classify each lead into hot, warm or cold.
- Validate the model and implement as a SQL Stored Procedure to enable real-time delivery of hot leads to the right dealer.

2. How to Reduce Category Page Exit Rate?

Need:
To bring the high exit rate number of prominent page down and improve the overall revenue and margins.

Challenges:

- To identify the causes of high exit rate.
- To enlist the challenges to curb or lower down the problem areas.

Plan of Action:

- Evaluate the layout and the individual elements of the page on the basis of the following key factors:
  - Clarity
  - Value Proposition
  - Relevancy
  - Urgency
  - Positioning and messaging around CTA (Add to Cart)
- Create a few hypothesis based on which control and experiments needs to be defined.
- Perform quantitative data analysis using the Google Analytics solution and identify the sample test audience for the upcoming tests.
- Define the control and alternative content variations and conduct multiple A/B Tests and Multivariate Tests to determine the winning page layout.

3. How to unravel Purchase Behavior for Better Conversion?

Need:
To identify the most popular items and visitor behavior for tracking the conversion path of the products and to segment the most popular products on an e-commerce website.

Challenges:

- Various drop off points between the process of signing up and purchasing the product.
- The sign up form was asking the users to fill up too much of information and as a result bounce rate for the 'Sign Up' page was high.

Plan of Action:

- Define and create the funnel for the checkout process. (The funnel depicted engagement on the site, starting from the time a user enters a site until the end of the purchase process.)
- The 'Sign Up' process be made simpler.
- Cluster segmentation of purchase behavior of the users to identify which products and categories generated the highest revenue.

4. How to Measure the Impact of Social Media Programs?

Need:
To gather and analyze Consumer generated media (CGM) data to uncover consumers' perceptions of their brand and determine what actions may be necessary to bolster their brand.
Challenges:

- Rapid increase of social media proportionate CGM data.
- Lack of tools to extract relevant insights from high amount of unstructured data.

Plan of Action:

- Identify key competitors and relevant social media sites.
- Record the regular chatter between consumers on social media sites and categorize the CGM data.
- Classify the data as positive or negative themes and compare to competitors both pre- and post-recall.

5. How to Improve the Quality and Integrity of Web Analytics Data?

Need:
To get ROI (Return on Investment) or Actionable Business Insights after spending a significant percentage of online budget on Web Analytics Implementation and Upgrades.
Challenges:
Major challenges at Client end which compromises the data quality and integrity are:

- Lack of Governance around Content Updates
- Communication Gap between Business & IT
- Frequent Architectural changes by SEO Team
- Untagged Content Updates
- No Version Controlling of Analytics Code
- Lack of Weekly Data Audits
- Improper Web Analytics Tool Configuration
- Limited Web Analytics Product Knowledge

Plan of Action:

- Capitalize on what is available
  - ◦ Conduct weekly training programs
  - ◦ Validate tag integrity and simulate key conversion flows
  - ◦ Tool Configuration
  - ◦ Version Controlling
- Process Improvements and Audit Checkpoints
  - ◦ Updated Documentation
  - ◦ Active involvement of Analytics Team
- Formation of Centralized Web Analytics Team

WEB ANALYTICS IMPLEMENTATION GUIDE

Web Analytics Association, now renamed as Digital Analytics Association has laid down nine best key practices to form the blueprint for its analytics by any business. These key best practices can be best described with the help of Web Analytics process guide depicted in Figure 6.

Step 1: Identify Key Stake Holders

All the persons who have concern or interest with the website directly or indirectly should be identified as the part of very initial step of implementation of any Web Analytics program. They can be the special section of targeted customers (students for a University, females for lingerie shopping and women with 40+ age for anti-ageing products, etc.), persons involved in making or designing of website, management people, top executives or people who will directly get affected by the business for which the website is being analyzed.

Step 2: Define Primary Goals

The primary goals of stakeholders are directly linked with primary goals of the website as the existence of the website and the stakeholders' respective interests are related *(Booth, D., & Jansen, B. J. 2009)*. The goals could vary between increasing loyalty of customers, expanding business and increasing revenue or cutting expenses *(McFadden, 2005)*. The goals identified should be prioritized and further implementation of Web Analytics program should be made accordingly, giving preference to the highly prioritized goals first followed by low priority goals.

Step 3: Identify the Most Important Site Visitors

Customers are categorized into three types: "(1) customers a company wants to keep who have a high current value and high future potential, (2) customers a company wants to grow who can either have a high current value and low future potential or low current value and high future potential, and (3) cus-

Figure 6. Web Analytics Implementation Guide (Source: Booth, & Jansen, 2009; Digital Analytics Association, 2015)

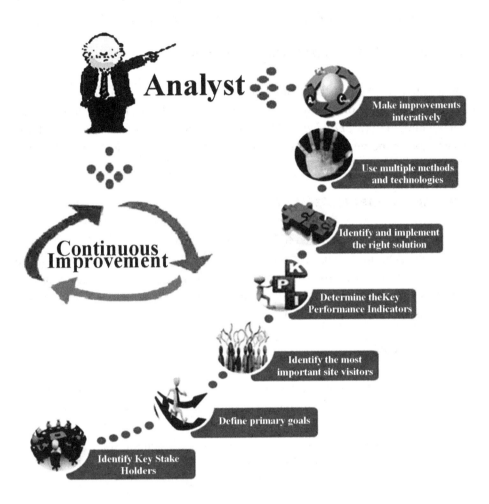

tomers a company wants to eliminate who have a low current value and low future potential"*(Booth, & Jansen, 2009).*The goals of all these kinds of customers should be kept in mind, both to prioritize them and to cater to their needs *(Peterson, 2004).*

Step 4: Determine the Key Performance Indicators

As already discussed in previous sections, identification of Key Performance Indicators is a precarious task and is critical for evaluation of performance of the website against its motive. They should be chosen wisely with utmost care according to the prioritized goals.

Step 5: Identify and Implement the Right Solution

Choose appropriate Web Analytics technology considering the website type and primary goals defined. One should also need to determine whether to use free tools or go for assistance packed paid tools. In the latter case, both budget constraint and technology used needs to be generously considered while former misses the professional or detailed guidance (in most cases). Thus, a trade-off needs to be set between the technology and constraints to fulfill all the requirements in the best possible manner.

Step 6: Use Multiple Methods and Technologies

It is advisable to use more than one method and more than one technology for Web Analysis, as variance in results (if any) can be get hold off before any disaster happens. At least two technologies and methods should be applied without fail *(McFadden, 2005)*. While technologies refers to different tools, methods refers to "focus groups, online surveys, usability studies, and customer services contact analysis" *(Booth & Jansen, 2009)*.

Step 7: Make Improvements Iteratively

Iterative improvements are always believed to be a better solution than applying all the changes at one go. Danielle Booth and Bernard J. Jansen from Pennsylvania State University, USA states that "When analyzing a Website's data, it is helpful to add gradual improvements to the Website instead of updating too many facets of the Website at once. By doing this one can monitor if a singular change is an improvement or if it is actually hurting the site" *(Booth, & Jansen, 2009)*.

Step 8: Employ an Analyst

"Web analyst works with web development programmers closely. The web developer and web analyst exchange ideas regarding structure, design, deployment of websites and software tools. A web analyst is also responsible for statistics and data collection for a website which range from website visits to performance of web server. He/she also reviews the system reports which are software generated and also analyzing and measuring keyword density, link management and search engine optimization statistics. They also provide reports on senior management efficiency so that strategic decisions can be made which concerns internet technology" *(Web Analytics, 2015)*.

Step 9: Establish a Process of Continuous Improvement

Continuous evaluation or continuous improvement is essential for the effective implementation of any Web Analytics program. It requires evaluation of any new goals, related or new metrics and key performance indicators according to any new changes incorporated. After each evaluation, it should be strictly cross checked that all the changes being made are effecting the website or business in a positive manner and bringing the stake holders nearer to their goals.

THE BIG PICTURE

As discussed, metrics is the fundamental unit of any Web analytics program, as it provides the basic information about the customer experience with the website. Different metrics when collected and collated helps to analyze web traffic and improve a website to better meet and serve its traffic. Thus, it is the center stage for any analysis of data. Keeping this in mind, authors have proposed a model, Evolutionary PRM model (*Singal & Kohli, 2013*), which helps to unearth the hidden insights and patterns from data very effectively. Web Analytics is a complex process that takes inputs, processes them and deliver outputs; so to overcome its challenges, the need of an hour is to introduce a unified, systematic and strategic approach which identifies what happens in each step of web merchandizing and who is responsible for that step. Evolutionary PRM Model will satiate this need as it is very simple, yet powerful in providing the solid understanding of what happens by measuring and optimizing its unique success metrics at each step.The model is discussed in detail here followed by a case study which shows the effectiveness of this model.

Evolutionary PRM model consists of three components as depicted in Figure 7:

1. Performance Breakdown (**PB**)
2. Resultant Breakdown (**RB**)
3. Maturity Breakdown (**MB**)

Performance Breakdown

It is the first component of Evolutionary PRM Model. The goal of PB is to study the motivation or intention behind the customers visiting the website under scrutiny. This is done with the help of data collected from basic metrics achievable generally through JavaScript Tags and site overlay reports. Their path analysis and search analysis reveals a lot amount of information which can further be segmented over identified KPIs (Key Performance Indicators) to procure valuable actionable insights.

Figure 7. Evolutionary PRM model

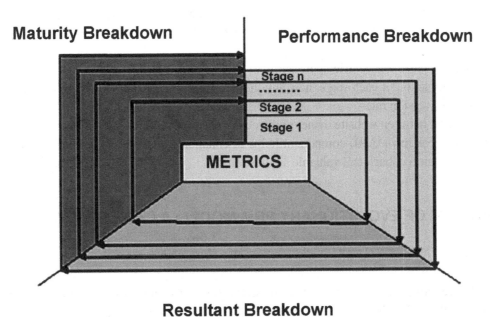

Resultant Breakdown

It is the second component of Evolutionary PRM Model. The goal of RB is to measure the aftermath of PB. In other words, this analytical breakdown is performed to analyze whether the purpose of existence of the website under scrutiny/optimization in the world of web is fulfilled or not, as every website has some purpose to exist. For e.g., e-commerce sites are for revenue generation, support sites are for timely problem resolution, non-profit sites are for generating leads and so on. In this phase, not only quantitative data is measured but also the qualitative data is analyzed and checked for its improvement over time.

Maturity Breakdown

This is the third and most critical component of Evolutionary PRM Model as it helps in driving CDI (Customer Driven Innovation) approach. This breakdown gives stress on analyzing competence of the website. It aims to identify how the customer's needs are being satiating with the help of surveys, market research and testing. It gives the customer's viewpoint about the presence of the website in the web-world thus making the approach fully customer-centric.

These three components of Evolutionary PRM model are spun across number of stages (n), where (n) is driven by the thirst and ability to find the valuable insights by the analysts and stakeholders of the web business being considered.

It is an ongoing process which gradually keeps on refining itself until and unless required/desired actionable insights are achieved from the metrics defining KPIs for the type of website under consideration. It is an iterative engineering paradigm where data from metrics is analyzed at all the three component levels to obtain the 'core insights' at stage 1, and iterating this process at higher and higher stages helps in refining these core insights to an ultimate level where ROI (Return on Investment) and conversion rates keeps on improving thus giving justice to enormous amount of efforts, time and money rinsed in carrying out the Web Analytics program by any organization.

The beauty of the proposed Evolutionary PRM model is:

1. It focuses on customer-centric approach.
2. On the completion of each stage, new actionable insights are achieved which helps in enhancing ROI and conversion rates.
3. Line of sight between website owner and website customer is reduced.
4. Maturity Breakdown (MB) component helps in enhancing customer experience at each stage by obtaining their feedback and valuable suggestions.

APPLICATION OF EVOLUTIONARY PRM MODEL: A CASE STUDY

Challenge

There is a University which understands the importance of hosting a website and possesses one of their own on World Wide Web for grabbing students' and parents' attention so that more number of enrollments could be targeted. The urgent need is to reform or restructure this website with an objective of easier navigation, succinct content and lead generation.

Solution

A minimum two stage plan is suggested based on Evolutionary PRM Model to combat the challenges faced by existing website in lead generation and their subsequent conversion. The two stages suggested corresponds to the stages depicted in the model and can be increased further to strengthen the quality and results of the solution.

Stage 1

First of all, before redesigning or restructuring of the website, behavior of current visitors needs to be checked and current inclinations in the concerned industry needs to be analyzed thoroughly. For this, the three components are divided as follows:

Performance Breakdown

Detailed analysis of all the concerned web metrics and the behavior of visitors needs to be done. Correspondingly, a sneak peak is to be made as to how other organizations or universities of similar kind host their websites and interact with their audience. This is necessary to unearth how strategies adopted by the company (here, University) are reflected by the web metrics.

Resultant Breakdown

Identified Web metrics of previous phase can be monitored using the existing account of Web Analytics tool being implemented by the University. This will lead to measure know-how of all the visitors visiting the existing website using the click-through reports for path analysis. For the current University scenario, it was found that generally visitors are inclined to fetch information about the course or program, fees, course description, duration and other related information before filling the enrollment form; which is the direct measure of generated leads.

Maturity Breakdown

As mentioned earlier, this is the most important phase. In stage 1, this phase aims at identifying the keywords which visitors/users use to land on the website. Those keywords are filtered which yield low bounce rates so that it could be determined that how the website is performing with respect to navigation and content consumption. This will set the platform for Stage 2. Research also needs to be done on how visitors, especially youth (prospective students) interacts with the current and other related similar websites to fix the design for a new website. It was found that the website content should bear clear and concise information about 'Life in University' and 'Careers' after the completion of course or tenure in the University.

Stage 2:

After a clear understanding of the present website, facts can be analyzed and recommendations for the new website can be laid down. This will yield the actual implementation of insights gathered from Stage 1.

Performance Breakdown

Analysis of Stage 1 should be reviewed by the senior analysts in consultation with some authorized and responsible persons from University. After this brainstorming, both present and new web metrics (if identified) should be designated as KPIs (Key Performance Indicators). Outline of the new website should be decided based on the findings. Goals and objectives should be clear and accordingly suggestions should be carried out to restructure the University's website.

Resultant Breakdown

Goals reiteration, identified audience and high level site navigation should be monitored and analyzed against the expectations of University stake holders. Keywords identified and filtered should again be analyzed for any unusual performance and the website should be restructured accordingly.

Maturity Breakdown

Further use cases should be identified for improvement. Assurance should be made by testing the new website for succinct content, easy navigation and lead conversions.

These two steps in accordance of Evolutionary PRM Model will form an integral part for the website design and any future incorporations can be made by expanding or spinning the model further along the stages, with each stage comprising of three phases: Performance Breakdown Phase, Resultant Breakdown Phase and Maturity Breakdown Phase. Further spinning will lead to more robust solution.

NEW AGE ANALYTICS AND FUTURE RESEARCH DIRECTIONS

In the current scenario, there is an ample dependability on the web channels for commercialization of products, due to which Business syndicates and enterprises in the web world spend billions of bucks on web analytics for tremendous online revenue. Yet the challenge of making optimal decisions for that invested money persists. Till recently, companies spent money on their websites just to maintain their brand value or rather because their competitors were doing so; but now the use of web analytics and web mining is maturing as this area has become the leading revenue fetchers of the nonhuman sales drive. Thus, an accurate estimate of success matrix is one of the most fundamental requirements for web investors and researchers planning for web analytics to attain the ultimate goal of earning revenue and satiating this need of business industry respectively. Analytics have moved on from Web Analytics (data about websites) to all other digital media and hence been renamed accordingly. For example, Mobile Analytics for mobile applications, Multi-Channel Analytics for collecting analytical data across heterogeneous platforms, Social Media Analytics for banking on Facebook Insights, Twitter Analytics and YouTube Analytics. Analytics has been made possible for almost all the digital environments. It is believed in Analytics market that 'You think of something and analytics companies will make it possible'.

To maintain a long term sustainable relationship with the customers rather than being content with short-term boost in the conversion rate by giving priority to customer over an expert's or analyst's view helps in decreasing the bounce rate and optimize global maxima rather than local maxima for every search, by focusing on key performance parameters (KPI's) for success and failure. To fulfill or achieve this it is advised to use analytics as a process, incorporating both traditional web analytics and new age analytics viz. Mobile Analytics, Multichannel Analytics, Social media Analytics etc.

This new age analytics which aim data from every possible medium including social media is helping business syndicates to access even the most personal information about their customers and future research aims in controlling of revelation of personal information and providing only those details which could increase their customer base. Appending semantic and sentiment analysis using various taxonomies and ontologies with itself, web analytics (rather digital analytics, as analytics can now be performed across all the digital media) is set to knock unreached heights and unravel new horizons.

CONCLUSION

Web Analytics has been aptly defined by Web Analytics Association (now renamed as Digital Analytics Association) as "objective tracking, collection, measurement, reporting and analysis of quantitative Internet data to optimize websites and web marketing initiatives." A report generated by Nasscom claims that Analytics outsourcing will grow from US$ 42bn to US$ 71bn in 2016. Data collection and its processing according to the configuration settings and reporting in user-friendly manner forms the basis for selection of any Web Analytics tool which in turn helps to improve the business by fortifying principles of Web Analytics implementation guide. Evolutionary PRM model proposed by the authors encourages customer-centric approach to gain actionable insights from the data lying underneath. Various Analytics tools have also been compared in detail sighting some important and interesting case studies solved in real-time.

REFERENCES

Alexander, J. E., & Tate, P. (1999). Web Wisdom: How to evaluate and create information quality on the web. *Paper presented at Mahwah*, Lawrence Erlbaum, NJ.

Booth, D., & Jansen, B. J. (2009). *A Review of Methodologies for Analyzing Websites*. IGI Global. doi:10.4018/978-1-59904-974-8.ch008

Clifton, B. (2008). *Advanced web metrics with Google Analytics*. Indianapolis, Indiana: Wiley Publishing Inc.

Digital Analytics Association. (2015). *What is Digital Analytics?* Retrieved from http://www.digitalanalyticsassociation.org/

Fractal Analytics. (2015). *Insight, Impact, Innovation*. Retrieved from http://www.fractalanalytics.com/

Google Analytics Academy. (2015). *Digital Analytics Fundamentals*. Retrieved from https://analyticsacademy.withgoogle.com/

Hasan, L., Morris, A., Probets, S. (2009). Using Google Analytics to Evaluate the Usability of E-Commerce Sites. *Human Centered Design* (pp. 697-706).

Hong, I. (2007). A survey of web site success metrics used by Internet-dependent organizations in Korea. *Internet Research*, *17*(3), 272–290. doi:10.1108/10662240710758920

iCreate. (2015). Banking Intellisense. Retrieved from http://www.icreate.in/

Kaushik, A. (2007). *Web Analytics: An hour a day*. Indianapolis, Indiana: Wiley Publishing Inc.

Manthan. (2015). *Analyze, Decide, Do*. Retrieved from https://www.manthan.com/

Marketelligent. (2015). *Analytics in action*. Retrieved from http://www.marketelligent.com/

McFadden, C. (2005). *Optimizing the Online Business Channel with Web Analytics*. Retrieved from http://www.Webanalyticsassociation.org/en/art/?9

Mu Sigma. (2015). *Do the Math*. Retrieved from http://www.mu-sigma.com/

Nabler. (2015). *Custom Digital Analytics software Solutions*. Retrieved from http://www.nabler.com/

Patton, S. (2002). *E-Commerce Tools: Web Metrics That Matter*. Retrieved from www.cio.com/article/31511/E_Commerce_Tools_Web_Metrics_That_Matter?page=2&taxonomyId=3181

Peterson, E. (2004). *Web analytics demystified: A marketer's guide to understanding how your web site affects your business*. Celilo Group Media and CafePress.

Singal, H., & Kohli, S. (2013). Evolutionary PRM Model: A Unified Strategic Approach to combat challenges of Web Analytics. *Paper presented at the meeting of International Workshop on Machine Learning and Text Analytics*, South Asian University, New Delhi, India.

Web Analytics. (2015). *Web Analytics*. Retrieved from http://www.webanalytics.in/?p=26

Section 4
Design Solutions for Website Effectiveness

Chapter 13
Architecture for Improving Security in Web Environment

Varaprasad Rao M
Anurag Group of Institutions, India

Ambati Venkata Krishna Prasad
K.L. University, India

ABSTRACT

Web security threats have undergone much sophistication compared to their initial introduction and they are becoming more & more evolved every day. The evolution might be in terms of new ways of attack or bringing in resistance to using simulated OS or VM environments. Web service architecture is a set of standard protocols to communicate secure web services. Which include policy, security, trust, secure conversation, reliable messaging and automatic transactions. Security is one of the major issues which reduces the growth of computing and complications with data privacy and data protection continue to plague the market. A new model targeting at improving features of an existing model must not risk or threaten other important features of the current model. The architecture of web poses such a threat to the security of the existing technologies when deployed in a web-based environment. In this chapter, the different security risks presented and specific to the different security issues that has emanated due to the nature of the service delivery models.

INTRODUCTION

Security is one of the major issues which reduces the growth of computing and complications with data privacy and data protection continue to plague the market. This chapter begins with a service and extends services to any application in Web environment. Now a days, every application is running on Web or Mobile is based on only service oriented. A comparative study on object orientation and service orientation is presented. Further, a new model targeting at improving features of an existing model must not risk or threaten other important features of the current model. The architecture of web poses such a threat to the security of the existing technologies when deployed in a web-based environment. This chapter organized the concepts of the key security requirements; the difference between threats, attacks,

DOI: 10.4018/978-1-4666-9764-5.ch013

vulnerabilities, and countermeasures; the key distinctions for web service architectures; the WSS Framework; the key principles and patterns for building secure services; the deployment of a new model and comparison with existing model.

BACKGROUND

Service

Patterns & Practices from Microsoft mentioned that a service is a public interface that provides access to a unit of functionality. Services literally provide some programmatic 'service' to the caller who consumes them. Services are loosely coupled and can be combined from within a client or from within other services to provide more complex functionality. Services are distributable and can be accessed from a remote machine as well as from the local machine on which they are running.

R. Chinnici, M. Gudgin, J-J. Moreau, J. Schlimmer, S. Weerawarana, (2003) and J. Cowan, R. Tobin, (2001) mentioned that services are message-oriented, meaning that service interfaces are defined by a Web Services Description Language (WSDL) file and operations are called using XML-based message schemas that are passed over a transport. Services support a heterogeneous environment by focusing interoperability at the message/interface definition. If components can understand the message and interface definition, they can use the service regardless of their base technology.

Common Services Scenarios

In MSDN; the services are flexible by nature and can be used in a wide variety of scenarios and combinations. The following are key scenarios that we will return to many times over the course of this guide:

- **Service Exposed Over the Internet:** This scenario describes a service that is consumed by Web applications or smart client applications over the Internet. Authentication and authorization decisions have to be made based upon Internet trust boundaries and credentials options. For example, username authentication is more likely in the Internet scenario than the intranet scenario. This scenario includes business-to-business as well as consumer-focused services. For example, a Web site that allows scheduling of your family's doctor visits could be included in this scenario.
- **Service Exposed Over an Intranet:** This scenario describes a service that is consumed by Web applications or smart client applications over an intranet. Authentication and authorization decisions have to be made based upon intranet trust boundaries and credentials options. For example, an Active Directory user store is more likely in the intranet scenario than in the Internet scenario. An enterprise Web-mail application could be included in this scenario.

M. Gudgin, M. Hadlcy, N. Mendelsohn, J-J. Moreau, H. Nielsen (2003) stated that now a days, every application is running on Web or Mobile is based on only service oriented. A comparative study on object orientation and service orientation is presented as follows.

Object Orientation vs. Service Orientation

Differences between object and service orientation are shown in Table 1.

The Key Security Requirements

H. Haas, A. Brown, (2004) mentioned any Service-Oriented Architecture (SOA) needs to support security features that provide auditing, authentication, authorization, confidentiality, and integrity for the messages exchanged between the client and the service.

As per Microsoft Patterns and Practices; Key security features include:

- **Auditing:** Effective auditing and logging is the key to non-repudiation. Non-repudiation guarantees that a user cannot deny performing an operation or initiating a transaction.
- **Authentication:** Authentication allows you to confidently identify the clients of your service. These might be end users, other services, processes, or computers. For example: Microsoft Windows supports mutual authentication, in preventing man-in-the-middle attacks.
- **Authorization:** Authorization determines what system resources and operations can be accessed by the authenticated user. This allows you to grant specific application and resource permissions for authenticated users.
- **Confidentiality:** Confidentiality is the process of making sure that data remains private and confidential, and that it cannot be viewed by unauthorized users. Encryption is frequently used to enforce confidentiality. Privacy is a key concern, particularly for data/messages passed across networks.
- **Integrity:** Integrity is the guarantee that data is protected from accidental or deliberate modification. Like privacy, integrity is a key concern, particularly for data/messages passed across networks. Integrity for data in transit is typically provided by using hashing techniques and message authentication codes.

Table 1. Differences between object and service orientation

Object Orientation	Service Orientation
Assumes a homogeneous platform and execution environment.	Assumes a heterogeneous platform and execution environment
Shares types, not schemas.	Shares schemas, not types
Assumes cheap, transparent communication.	Assumes variable cost, explicit communication.
Objects are linked: object identity and lifetime are maintained by the infrastructure.	Services are autonomous: security and failure isolation are a necessity.
Typically requires synchronized deployment of both client and server.	Allows continuous, separate deployment of client and server.
Is easy to conceptualize and thus provides a natural model to follow.	Builds on ideas from component software and distributed objects. Dominant theme is to manage/reduce sharing between services.
Provides no explicit guidelines for state management and ownership.	Owns and maintains state or uses the reference state.
Assumes a predictable sequence, timeframe, and outcome of invocations.	Assumes message-oriented, potentially asynchronous, and long-running communications.
Goal is to transparently use functions and types remotely.	Goal is to provide inter-service isolation and wire interoperability based on standards.

Difference between Threats, Attacks, Vulnerabilities, and Countermeasures

- **Asset:** A resource of value such as the data in a database, data on the file system, or a system resource.
- **Threat:** A potential occurrence — malicious or otherwise — that can harm an asset.
- **Vulnerability:** A weakness that makes a threat possible.
- **Attack:** An action taken to exploit vulnerability and realize a threat.
- **Countermeasure:** A safeguard that addresses a threat and mitigates risk.

The following explanations briefly describe some of the threats and attacks mentioned above:

- **Brute Force Attacks:** Attacks that use the raw computer processing power to try different permutations of any variable that could expose a security hole. For example, if an attacker knew that access required an 8-character username and a 10-character password, the attacker could iterate through every possible combination (256 multiplied by itself 18 times) in order to attempt to gain access to a system. No intelligence is used to shape or filter likely combinations.
- **Canonicalization Attacks:** There are multiple ways to access the same object and an attacker uses a method to bypass any security measures instituted on the primary intended methods of access. Often, the unintended methods of access can be less secure deprecated methods.
- **Cookie Manipulation:** Through various methods, an attacker will alter the cookies stored in the browser. Attackers will then use the cookie to fraudulently authenticate themselves to a service or Web site.
- **Cookie Replay Attacks:** Reusing a previously valid cookie to deceive the server into believing that a previously authenticated session is still in progress and valid.
- **Credential Theft:** Stealing the verification part of an authentication pair (identity + credentials = authentication). Passwords are a common credential.
- **Cross-Site Scripting:** An attacker is able to inject executable code (script) into a stream of data that will be rendered in a browser. The code will be executed in the context of the user's current session and will gain privileges to the site and information that it would not otherwise have.
- **Data Tampering:** An attacker violates the integrity of data by modifying it in local memory, in a data-store, or on the network. Modification of this data could provide the attacker with access to a service through a number of the different methods listed in this document.
- **Denial of Service:** Denial of service (DoS) is the process of making a system or application unavailable. For example, a DoS attack might be accomplished by bombarding a server with requests to consume all available system resources, or by passing the server malformed input data that can crash an application process.
- **Dictionary Attack:** Use of a list of likely access methods (usernames, passwords, coding methods) to try and gain access to a system. This approach is more focused and intelligent than the "brute force" attack method, so as to increase the likelihood of success in a shorter amount of time.
- **Disclosure of Sensitive/Confidential Data:** Sensitive data is exposed in some unintended way to users who do not have the proper privileges to see it. This can often be done through param-

eterized error messages, where an attacker will force an error and the program will pass sensitive information up through the layers of the program without filtering it. This can be personally identifiable information (PII) or system data.

- **Encryption:** The process of taking sensitive data and changing it in such a way that it is unrecognizable to anyone but those who know how to decode it. Different encryption methods have different strengths based on how easy it is for an attacker to obtain the original information through whatever methods are available.

- **Information Disclosure:** Unwanted exposure of private data. For example, a user views the contents of a table or file that he or she is not authorized to open, or monitors data passed in plaintext over a network. Some examples of information disclosure vulnerabilities include the use of hidden form fields, comments embedded in Web pages that contain database connection strings and connection details, and weak exception handling that can lead to internal system-level details being revealed to the client. Any of this information can be very useful to the attacker.

- **Man-in-the-Middle Attacks:** A person intercepts both the client and server communications and then acts as an intermediary between the two without each ever knowing. This gives the "middle man" the ability to read and potentially modify messages from either party in order to implement another type of attack listed here.

- **Network Eavesdropping:** Listening to network packets and reassembling the messages being sent back and forth between one or more parties on the network. While not an attack itself, network eavesdropping can easily intercept information for use in specific attacks listed in this document.

- **Password Cracking:** If the attacker cannot establish an anonymous connection with the server, he or she will try to establish an authenticated connection. For this, the attacker must know a valid username and password combination. If you use default account names, you are giving the attacker a head start. Then the attacker only has to crack the account's password. The use of blank or weak passwords makes the attacker's job even easier.

- **Repudiation:** The ability of users (legitimate or otherwise) to deny that they performed specific actions or transactions. Without adequate auditing, repudiation attacks are difficult to prove.

- **Session Hijacking:** Also known as man-in-the-middle attacks, session hijacking deceives a server or a client into accepting the upstream host as the actual legitimate host. Instead, the upstream host is an attacker's host that is manipulating the network so the attacker's host appears to be the desired destination.

- **Session Replay:** An attacker steals messages off of the network and replays them in order to steal a user's session.

- **Session Fixation:** An attacker sets (fixates) another person's session identifier artificially. The attacker must know that a particular Web service accepts any session ID that is set externally; for example, the attacker sets up a URL such as http://unsecurewebservice.com/?sessionID=1234567. The attacker then sends this URL to a valid user, who clicks on it. At this point, a valid session with the ID 1234567 is created on the server. Because the attacker determines this ID, he or she can now hijack the session, which has been authenticated using the valid user's credentials.

- **Spoofing:** An attempt to gain access to a system by using a false identity. This can be accomplished by using stolen user credentials or a false IP address. After the attacker successfully gains access as a legitimate user or host, elevation of privileges or abuse using authorization can begin.

MAIN FOCUS OF THE CHAPTER

Build Secure Services

MSDN and website-guardian.com gives the keys to building secure services include; Security requirements, threats, principles and deployment model.

- **Security Objectives / Requirements:** This includes identifying your security requirements.
- **Known Threats:** Know which threats are relevant for your particular scenarios and context. Threat modeling is an effective technique for helping you identify relevant threats and vulnerabilities. The objectives will help us to categorize threats and vulnerabilities. Using the threat model, developers address vulnerabilities, and testers verify that the developers closed the issues.
- **Apply Proven Principles, Patterns, and Practices:** Principles, patterns, and practices are a good starting point for building secure services. By using proven principles, patterns, and practices, you can eliminate classes of security problems. You can also leverage lessons learned. Patterns are effectively reusable solutions and typically encapsulate underlying principles. While principles, patterns, and practices are a good starting point, you should never blindly adopt them — you need to evaluate whether they make sense for your scenario.
- **Apply Effective Security Engineering throughout the Application Life Cycle:** You should consider security throughout your application life cycle. You should start with security objectives. Threat modeling will help you shape your design and make key trade-offs. Security design, code, and deployment inspections, along with testing, will improve your overall security posture.

Web Oriented Architecture

Definitions

1. Alex Newth stated that; "WOA is an architectural sub-style of service-oriented architecture that integrates systems and users via a web of globally linked hypermedia based on the architecture of the Web". This architecture emphasizes generality of interfaces (User interfaces and APIs) to achieve global network effects through five fundamental generic interface constraints:
   - Identification of resources
   - Manipulation of resources through representations (Web resource)
   - Self-descriptive messages
   - Hypermedia as the engine of application state
   - Application neutrality
2. Nick Gall also gives a mathematical formula for defining "WOA=SOA+WWW+REST".
3. Dion Hinchcliffe claims WOA to be:

"A core set of Web protocols like HTTP and plan XML, the only real difference between traditional SOA and the concept of WOA is that WOA advocates Representational state transfer (REST), an increasingly popular, powerful, and simple method of leveraging Hypertext Transfer Protocol (HTTP) as a Web service in its own right".

WOA vs. SOA

The main difference between SOA and WOA is that WOA supports REST whereas SOA uses SOAP. SOAP uses XML, a messaging format, which includes all headings and security information, and transfers information in a particular structure, but using REST eliminates the problem as it transfers information in URI form. SOA uses WS-Security, whilst WOA uses HTTP Secure (HTTPS), OAuth and Hash-based message authentication code (HMAC-SHA-1). REST allows for two systems to operate and function together efficiently using URIs.

OAuth is one of the highest security measures on the internet today, used by large websites, such as Twitter. Identity issues can be an issue for WOA applications. WOA style is used in many cloud based applications. Most WOA designs have included a federated login, which make it easier to confirm the identity of the user and easier for the user to move between programs.

WSS Framework

Security fundamentals for Web Sevices Security: Patterns & Practices from Microsoft and Anna Agnew (2011) stated that Web Services Security (WS-Security, WSS) is an extension to SOAP to apply security to Web services. It is a member of the Web service specifications and was published by OASIS. The Organization for the Advancement of Structured Information Standards (OASIS) is a global consortium that works on the development, convergence, and adoption of e-business and web service standards. With its headquarters in the United States, a trade association of SGML tool vendors to cooperatively promote the adoption of SGML through mainly educational activities, though some amount of technical activity was also pursued including an update of the CALS Table Model specification and specifications for fragment interchange and entity management.

The protocol specifies how integrity and confidentiality can be enforced on messages and allows the communication of various security token formats, such as Security Assertion Markup Language (SAML), Kerberos, and X.509. Its main focus is the use of XML Signature and XML Encryption to provide end-to-end security.

WS-Security describes *three* main mechanisms:

1. How to sign SOAP messages to assure integrity. Signed messages also provide non-repudiation.
2. How to encrypt SOAP messages to assure confidentiality.
3. How to attach security tokens to ascertain the sender's identity.

Table 2. WOA stack

Distribution (HTTP feeds)
Composition (Hypermedia Mashups)
Security (OpenID SSL)
Data Portability (XML RDF)
Data Representation (ATOM JSON)
Transfer Methods (REST, HTTP, BitTorrent)

Table 3. WS-Security stack

Identification **Authentication** **Authorization**	WS-Security Framework Extensible Access Control Markup Language (XACML) Extensible Rights Markup Language (XrML) XML Key Management (XKMS) Security Assertion Markup Language (SAML) .NET Passport
Confidentiality	WS-Security Framework XML-Encryption Secure Sockets Layer (SSL)
Integrity	WS-Security Framework XML-Digital Signatures

The specification allows a variety of signature formats, encryption algorithms and multiple trust domains, and is open to various security token models, such as: X.509 certificates, Kerberos tickets, User ID/Password credentials, SAML Assertions, and custom-defined tokens. The token formats and semantics are defined in the associated profile documents.

WS-Security incorporates security features in the header of a SOAP message, working in the application layer. These mechanisms by themselves do not provide a complete security solution for Web services. Instead, this specification is a building block that can be used in conjunction with other Web service extensions and higher-level application-specific protocols to accommodate a wide variety of security models and security technologies. In general, WSS by itself does not provide any guarantee of security. When implementing and using the framework and syntax, it is up to the implementer to ensure that the result is not vulnerable. Key management, trust bootstrapping, federation and agreement on the technical details (ciphers, formats, and algorithms) is outside the scope of WS-Security.

Transport-Level Security

Secure Socket Layer (SSL), otherwise known as Transport Layer Security (TLS), the Internet Engineering Task Force (IETF) officially standardized version of SSL, is the most widely used transport-level data-communication protocol providing:

- Authentication (the communication is established between two trusted parties).
- Confidentiality (the data exchanged is encrypted).
- Message integrity (the data is checked for possible corruption).
- Secure key exchange between client and server.

SSL provides a secure communication channel, however, when the data is not "in transit," the data is not protected. This makes the environment vulnerable to attacks in multi-step transactions. (SSL provides point-to-point security, as opposed to end-to-end security.)

Application-Level Security

Application-level security complements transport-level security. Application-level security is based on XML frameworks defining confidentiality, integrity, authenticity; message structure; trust management and federation.

Data confidentiality is implemented by XML Encryption. XML Encryption defines how digital content is encrypted and decrypted, how the encryption key information is passed to a recipient, and how encrypted data is identified to facilitate decryption.

Data integrity and authenticity are implemented by XML Signature. XML Signature binds the sender's identity (or "signing entity") to an XML document. Signing and signature verification can be done using asymmetric or symmetric keys.

Signature ensures non-repudiation of the signing entity and proves that messages have not been altered since they were signed. Message structure and message security are implemented by SOAP and its security extension, WS-Security. WS-Security defines how to attach XML Signature and XML Encryption headers to SOAP messages. In addition, WS-Security provides profiles for 5 security tokens: Username (with password digest), X.509 certificate, Kerberos ticket, Security Assertion Markup Language (SAML) assertion, and REL (rights markup) document.

The SOAP envelope body includes the business payload, for example a purchase order, a financial document, or simply a call to another Web service. SAML is one of the most interesting security tokens because it supports both authentication and authorization. SAML is an open framework for sharing security information on the Internet through XML documents.

SAML includes 3 parts:

1. SAML Assertion—How you define authentication and authorization information.
2. SAML Protocol—How you ask (SAML Request) and get (SAML Response) the assertions you need.
3. SAML Bindings and Profiles—How SAML assertions ride "on" (Bindings) and "in" (Profiles) industry-standard transport and messaging frameworks.

The full SAML specification is used in browser-based federation cases. However, web services security systems such as Oracle WSM only use SAML assertions. The protocol and bindings are taken care of by WS-Security and the transport protocol, for example HTTP.

SAML assertions and references to assertion identifiers are contained in the WS-Security Header element, which in turn is included in the SOAP Envelope Header element (described in the WS-Security SAML Token Profile). The SAML security token is particularly relevant in situations where identity propagation is essential.

Web Services Security Patterns

According to MSDN library framework, Web services security patterns are helpful for addressing various security concerns, like authentication, authorization, etc.

The following are patterns used in one of the web-based applications:

- Brokered Authentication
- Brokered Authentication: Kerberos
- Brokered Authentication: X.509 PKI
- Brokered Authentication: STS
- Data Confidentiality
- Data Origin Authentication
- Direct Authentication
- Exception Shielding
- Message Replay Detection
- Message Validator
- Perimeter Service Router
- Protocol Transition with Constrained Delegation
- Trusted Subsystem

PROTECT WEBSITE FROM MALWARE AND VIRUS ATTACKS

As per Anna Agnew (2011); a computer either in a home or business, website security is a crucial feature to get in order to protect your data. Any computer is prone to being attacked by viruses, malware or hackers. Now websites are easy targets for hackers because most of the people use free or/and open source software. Unfortunately, the software also becomes very popular with the hackers who have access to the open source code. By the intellectual worth of the hacker, the hacker finds a way to hack into these software platforms. Once they find a weakness or vulnerability in the code, they can negatively affect thousands of websites. Examples of popular open source platforms that are a favourite with the hackers are WordPress, OScommerce, Joomla and Magento to name just a few.

The following are 6 main strategies to consider in providing optimal website protection

1. Make sure your hosting control panel, FTP and platform software administration area is secure. Be sure to create 10 digit random passwords mixed with capital & small case alphabet letters and numbers. Refrain from sharing your passwords with anyone.
2. Delete access for those who do not need to log into the website. For example, if you have a staff member with administrator entry to the computer and they are no longer with the company, it is advisable to get rid of the user instead of having them on file. The greater number of people that have usage of the secure and safe information, the greater probability of that information falling into the wrong hands.
3. Keep updated anti-virus software with latest security patches. Each time a virus protection reminder appears on your desktop, take a minute to make sure things are current and working well.
4. Consider purchasing a security monitoring program that will alert you to any suspicious hacker activity. Make sure that you select experienced web developer, which can present you with valid references and testimonials, to properly install this security software. They should first clean your web site of all current viruses and then install software. Be sure they can offer you some kind of guarantee that indicates they stand behind the security software they are installing on your website.

5.   Establish a relationship with an experienced Webmaster / web development company that will be on hand to immediately assist you should you get hacked. This becomes even more important if you are not a particularly computer savvy person. Because an experienced Webmaster/ web developer deals with these kinds of hacker issues every day, they will be able to quickly hone in on your problem and help you get your web business back online as soon as possible.

6.   Make sure host computer is using the latest or updated versions of php / mySQL / Apache and other website server software.

Check your website's traffic regularly to figure out when and where traffic is coming from. If it is common to only have a small number of hits to your website every day and then you experience a higher volume of traffic for no reason at all, it might signal that your website is being attacked by a hacker or has been infected with a virus. Back up the information you have frequently to a separate system. In that way, you're protected in the instance of a harmful virus or an attack.

Each and every day your internet site is vulnerable to attacks from malware and viruses, so it is essential to install the proper website protection to stop such attacks. While there are several programs one can use to protect your pc against malware, you must be certain they're up-to-date to offer your personal computer and files the best and most effective protection. Attacks on your business doesn't just affect you, but they affect all the customers visiting your web site.

One of the most effective ways to secure your site from malware attack is by being sure your firewall plus virus safeguards are updated. Be sure to install the security patches as they become available as this aids in keeping the safeguards up to date. Sign up to receive reminders once you buy these programs in order for you to be alerted when an update becomes available. Having a computer virus protection program is actually a must-have when you're thinking of boosting your website security. Take time to spend on the best virus safety program. There are several you could choose from to maintain your website safety.

Creating a good password will help aid greatly in protecting your files. Work with a variations of uppercase as well as lowercase letters, numbers and perhaps symbols to make a password which will be difficult for hackers to break. Hackers make use of a number of password decoding programs in order to break into a website, so the more unique you make the password, the more protected your site is.

Try to avoid opening attachments on your server if you don't recognize the sender, or the email is sent to "bulk" recipients. Attachments may have malware code which is designed to infiltrate your data files when you down load the attachment. Ensure your personal computer features a firewall that'll protect your files from worm and also virus attacks. A computer hardware firewall may be installed within the computers router, but it really needs to be activated for it to be effective. The second form of protection, an application firewall, is the one that you can install yourself to give additional protection. Combine the software and hardware firewall programs for effective protection and website security.

Set up an anti-spyware program on your hard drive to ensure that you catch any malevolent software or dangerous files which could sneak beyond the antivirus or firewall. An anti-spyware program will regularly comb through your website files for added peace of mind.

In order to protect web site against malware or viruses, it is very important to research the website protection software offered in order to determine what will be best and most effective for you. The more informed you are about programs which prevent malware, the greater off your online business will be. Ultimately, a website that is down as a result of a hack will be detrimental to your business and ultimately your sales and profits.

Figure 1. Existing Web security model

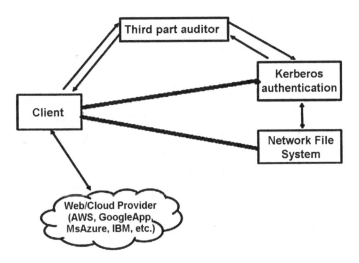

Existing Model

The existing model (figure 1) uses only authentication and authorization services to verify the client is correct or wrong executed by a third party after register with it. To maintain secrecy of the authenticated client there is no assurance service to check whether the key and sequence number is received properly by the client to access the required web or any service. Therefore to provide confidentiality service the authors are introduced an AES algorithm.

System Model

Representation network architecture for cloud data storage with effect of Kerberos authentication service is illustrated in Figure 2. This deals with six different network entities as Client, Third party, AES algorithm, Kerberos authentication procedure, Network file system and Web or Cloud provider.

The entity roles are as follows:

- **Client:** Any client, who should get registered in third party and obtain the password, session key.
- **Third party:** The third party defines who has the correctness, expertise, capabilities to access and utilize the service provider.
- **Advanced Encryption Standard:** AES is based on a design principle known as a substitution-permutation network, combination of both substitution and permutation, and is fast in both software and hardware. Unlike its predecessor DES, AES does not use a Feistel network. AES is a variant of Rijndael which has a fixed block size of 128 bits, and a key size of 128, 192, or 256 bits. By contrast, the Rijndael specification *per se* is specified with block and key sizes that may be any multiple of 32 bits, both with a minimum of 128 and a maximum of 256 bits. AES operates on a 4×4 column-major order matrix of bytes, termed the *state*, although some versions of Rijndael have a larger block size and have additional columns in the state. Most AES calculations are done

Figure 2. New Deployment model for improving Web Security

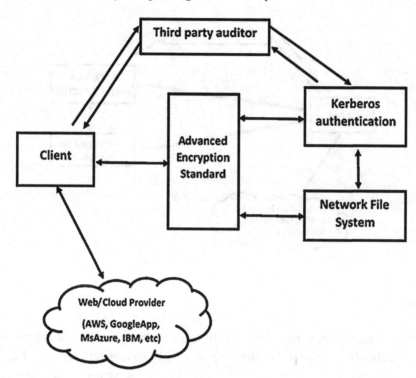

in a special finite field. The key size used for an AES cipher specifies the number of repetitions of transformation rounds that convert the input, called the plaintext, into the final output, called the cipher text. The number of cycles of repetition are as follows:

- ◦ 10 cycles of repetition for 128-bit keys.
- ◦ 12 cycles of repetition for 192-bit keys.
- ◦ 14 cycles of repetition for 256-bit keys.

Each round consists of several processing steps, each containing four similar but different stages, including one that depends on the encryption key itself. A set of reverse rounds are applied to transform cipher text back into the original plaintext using the same encryption key.

- • **Kerberos operation:** Kerberos is an authentication mechanism that provides a secure means of authentication for network users. It prevents transmission of clear text passwords over the network by encrypting authentication messages between clients and servers. In addition, Kerberos provides a system for authorization in the form of administering tokens, or credentials. Kerberos is an authentication protocol for trusted hosts on non-trusted networks. Kerberos provides two services as *Authentication Service (AS)*, Authentication Service that know the password of all user and stores these in a centralized database. In addition, the AS shares a unique secret key with each server. The second service is *Tickets Granting Service (TGS)*, TGS provide and issue tickets to user who have been authentication to AS. Once these two phases are completed then the service is granted from *Service Granting Token (SGT)* to user to access the required Web service.

- **Data Base:** The database is the container the entries information related with users and services. The data base is shared between third party and Kerberos. Each entry/principal contains the following information:
  - The principal to which the entry is associated.
  - The maximum validity duration for a ticket associated to the principal.
  - The encryption key.
  - The maximum time a ticket associated to the principal may be renewed.
  - The attributes or flags characterizing the behavior of the tickets.
  - The password expiration date.
  - The expiration date of the principal, after which no tickets will be issued.
- **Web/Cloud Service Provider:** Web Services are accessed by SOAP with XML parsing code. The Web oriented architecture offer service solutions; these may contains virus, threat or vulnerable. The services do install on local hardware to access for further services or applications in the form of cookies. These cookies are generated for every session. Cloud service providers offer cloud solutions, like Google Apps, Amazon Web Services that are delivered electronically over the internet. Unlike a managed service provider, cloud service providers do not sell or install hardware everything they offer is stored online and accessible securely from anywhere. There are many advantages with a cloud service provider like Cloud Sherpa, Cloud era when switching from your old email and collaboration software.
- **Network File System**: The users can directly access the Web Environment across all types of networks. A file system is a system which represents an addressability of the storage.

Design Goals

To ensure the security of storage the data in web server we design a mechanism with the following goals:

- Each user can perform storage and register in minimum time results easiness of work.
- To ensure the users that, the user's data is store in trusted manner and can execute their job in accurate type will results trustworthiness.

Implementation

In web, the users store their data in the web server and for accessing any data in the web they must refer to web service provider. Thus the correctness of the user is being referred to the distributed web server, because the data stored in the web server may be frequently updated with users, including the operations as insertion, deletion, modification, append, reorder, etc. To ensure this updating, correctness of user is important. In this part we have introduced a model based on Kerberos and AES algorithms.

In this model each user must be registered and get authenticated by the third party. Once a user authenticated then he should referred to the Kerberos Authentication Service for authentication and ticket granting services. The TGS will issue a token, is encrypted by AES algorithm. This token is submitted to service granting to obtain client required service.

The Service Granting Ticket/Token Algorithm is as follows:

Step 1: Get the UID and PWD from third party
Step 2: Get authorized from AS and obtain TGS-ID for accessing of a TGS service

Step 3: TGS will issue encrypted form of Token using AES

Step 4: Submit TGS-ID to TGS ticket

Step 5: Obtain Service Granting Ticket (SGT) in encrypted form using AES

Step 6: Then client will access requested service by decrypt using AES and access corresponding service through SGT

FUTURE DIRECTIONS

This model is very useful for Web environment for improving security in terms of authentication and confidentiality services. The proposed model can be implemented in easily in any programming languages like in Java, Python. The model is not focused on maintaining of database in which it can store sub keys and sequence numbers. Its size may be rapidly increased due to storage of huge number of user's data.

CONCLUSION

Computer security is becoming more important because the world is interconnected. The environment in which machines must survive has changed radically since the popularization of the Internet. Deciding to connect a local area network (LAN) to the Internet is a security-critical decision. The root of most security problems is software architecture. This chapter deals with both symmetric and asymmetric algorithms in cryptography and network security. The goal of this chapter is to familiarize you with the current best practices for keeping security flaws out of your software architecture. A model has designed with Kerberos and AES algorithms for providing secured data transmission over Web environment. Authentication and authorization are achieved through Kerberos algorithm and confidentiality is achieved through AES algorithm.

ACKNOWLEDGMENT

Words cannot express my gratitude to Editor Prof. G Sreedhar for his professional advice and assistance in polishing this manuscript. Thanks to all the technical reviewers who reviewed this chapter and made me in strengthen the chapter not only by catching mistakes but also by suggesting those additions. I place on record, my sense of gratitude to one and all, who directly or indirectly, have lent their hand in this venture. I would like to express my sincere gratitude to my advisor Prof. B Vishnu Vardhan for the continuous support to complete this chapter, for his patience, motivation, and immense knowledge. I take this opportunity to express gratitude to all of the Department faculty members, Principal, Director, and Management of Anurag Group of Institutions for their help and continuous support. I'd like to thank my parents for allowing me to follow my ambitions throughout my childhood. This chapter would not have been possible without the support, motivation and encouragement of my wife, Mrs. PV Prajwala. For understanding my long nights at the computer, I'd like to thank my children, Karthikeya and Harshith. Finally, my sincere thanks to IGI Publisher to publish the chapter/book.

REFERENCES

Agnew, A. (2011, December 2) How to Protect Your Website from Malware and Virus Attacks Retrieved from http://www.website-guardian.com/how-to-protect-your-website-from-malware-and-virus-attacks-va-4.html

Agnew, A. (2011, October 24). How to improve your website Security against dangers on the Web? Retrieved from http://www.website-guardian.com/how-to-improve-your-website-security-against-dangers-on-the-web-va-2.html

Chinnici, R., Gudgin, M., Moreau, J.-J., Schlimmer, J., & Weerawarana, S. (2003, November 10). *Web Services Description Language (WSDL) Version 2.0 Part 1: Core Language*. W3C Working Draft. Retrieved from http://www.w3.org/TR/2003/WD-wsdl20-20031110/

Cowan, J., & Tobin, R. (2001, October 24). *XML Information Set*, W3C Recommendation, Retrieved from http://www.w3.org/TR/2001/REC-xml-infoset-20011024/

Curphey, M., Scambray, J., & Olson, E. (2003). *Improving Web Application Security Threats and Countermeasures: Patterns & Practices*. Microsoft Corporation.

Gall, N. (2014, October 28). Web-oriented architecture and the rise of pragmatic SOA Retrieved from http://www.cnet.com/uk/news/web-oriented-architecture-and-the-rise-of-pragmatic-soa/

Gall, N. (2014, October 28). WOA: Putting the Web Back in Web Services Retrieved from http://blogs.gartner.com/nick_gall/2008/11/19/woa-putting-the-web-back-in-web-services/

Gudgin, M., Hadley, M., Mendelsohn, N., Moreau, J.-J., & Nielsen, H. (2003, June 24) *SOAP Version 1.2 Part 1: Messaging Framework*. W3C Recommendation. Retrieved from http://www.w3.org/TR/2003/REC-soap12-part1-20030624/

Haas, H., & Brown, A. (2004, February 11). *Web Services Glossary*, W3C Working Group Note. Retrieved from http://www.w3.org/TR/2004/NOTE-ws-gloss-20040211/

Hinchcliffe, D. (2009). Web-Oriented Architecture (Speech). London QCon. Retrieved from http://qconlondon.com/london-2009/qconlondon.com/dl/qcon-london-2009/slides/DionHinchcliffe_WebOrientedArchitectureWOA.pdf

Hinchcliffe, D. (2014, October 27). The SOA with reach: Web-Oriented Architecture Retrieved from http://qconlondon.com/london-2009/qconlondon.com/dl/qcon-london-2009/slides/DionHinchcliffe_WebOrientedArchitectureWOA.pdf

Newth, A. (n. d.). What Is Web Oriented Architecture? Retrieved from https://en.wikipedia.org/wiki/Web-oriented_architecture

Security fundamentals for Web Services Security: Patterns & Practices from MSDN library. (n. d.). Retrieved from https://msdn.microsoft.com/en-us/library/ff648318.aspx

Understanding Web Services Security Concepts. (n. d.). Oracle. Retrieved from http://docs.oracle.com/cd/E17904_01/web.1111/b32511/intro_security.htm#WSS

Website Guardian. (n. d.). Retrieved from http://www.website-guardian.com

Wikipedia. (n. d.). Retrieved from http://www.wikipedia.org

ADDITIONAL READING

Agnew, A. (2012, November 16) What are htaccess files? Retrieved from http://www.website-guardian.com/what-are-htaccess-files-va-12.html

Agnew, K. (2012, October 19). What is key difference between Hackers and Crackers?

Austin, D., Barbir, A., Ferris, C., & Garg, S. (2004, February 11). Web Services Architecture Requirements. *W3C Working Group Note*. Retrieved from http://www.w3.org/TR/2004/NOTE-wsa-reqs-20040211

Berners-Lee, T., Fielding, R., & Masinter, L. (1998, August). *Uniform Resource Identifiers (URI): Generic Syntax*, IETF RFC 2396. Retrieved from http://ietf.org/rfc/rfc2396.txt

Bray, T., Paoli, J., Sternberg-McQueen, C. M., & Maler, E. (2000, October 6). *Extensible Markup Language (XML) 1.0 (Second Edition)*, W3C Recommendation, Retrieved from http://www.w3.org/TR/2000/REC-xml-20001006

Cole, E. (2009). *Network Security Bible 2 edition*. New Delhi, India: Wiley.

Fielding, R. (2000). *Architectural Styles and the Design of Network-based Software Architectures* [Ph.D. Dissertation]. Retrieved from http://www.ics.uci.edu/~fielding/pubs/dissertation/top.htm

Forouzan, B. (2007). *Cryptography and Network Security, New Delhi, India*. Tata: McGraw-Hill.

Gudgin, M., Hadley, M., Mendelsohn, N., Moreau, J.-J., & Nielsen, H. (2003, June 24). SOAP Version 1.2 Part 1: Messaging Framework. *W3C Recommendation*. Retrieved from http://www.w3.org/TR/2003/REC-soap12-part1-20030624/

Gudgin, M., Hadley, M., Mendelsohn, N., Moreau, J.-J., & Nielsen, H. (2003, June 24). SOAP Version 1.2 Part 2: Adjuncts. *W3C Recommendation*. Retrieved from http://www.w3.org/TR/2003/REC-soap12-part2-20030624/

He, H., Haas, H., & Orchard, D. (2004, February 11). Web Services Architecture Usage Scenarios. *W3C Working Group Note*. Retrieved from http://www.w3.org/TR/2004/NOTE-ws-arch-scenarios-20040211/

Jacobs, I. (2003, December 9). Architecture of the World Wide Web, First Edition. *W3C Working Draft*. Retrieved from http://www.w3.org/TR/2003/WD-webarch-20031209/

Kahate, A. (2003). *Cryptography and Network Security, New Delhi, India*. Tata: McGraw-Hill.

Kendall, S. C., Waldo, J., Wollrath, A., & Wyant, G. (1994, November). *A Note on Distributed Computing*. Retrieved from http://research.sun.com/techrep/1994/abstract-29.html

Parnami, P., Ruchi, D., & Verma, A. (2013, February). WOA Based Implementation of SOA. Department of Computer Science and Engineering, Suresh Gyan Vihar University, Jaipur.

Stallings, W. (2005). *Cryptography and Network Security: Principles and Practice.* NY: Pearson.

Verma, A., Bhatnagar, V., & Jain, S. (2014, January). A Comparative Performance Analysis of WOA vs. SOA (Report).

KEY TERMS AND DEFINITIONS

Policy: A policy is a deliberate system of principles to guide decisions and achieve rational outcomes. A policy is a statement of intent, and is implemented as a procedure or protocol.

Reliable: A reliable service is one that notifies the user if delivery fails, while an "unreliable" one does not notify the user if delivery fails.

Security Risks: A security risk is any event that could result in the compromise of organizational assets i.e. the unauthorized use, loss, damage, disclosure.

Security: Security is the degree of resistance to, or protection from, harm. It applies to any vulnerable and valuable asset, such as a person, dwelling, community, nation, or organization.

SOA: A service-oriented architecture (SOA) is an architectural pattern in computer software design in which application components provide services to other components via a communications protocol, typically over a network. The principles of service-orientation are independent of any vendor, product or technology.

Threat: In computer security a threat is a possible danger that might exploit a vulnerability to breach security and thus cause possible harm. A threat can be either "intentional" (i.e., intelligent; e.g., an individual cracker or a criminal organization) or "accidental" (e.g., the possibility of a computer malfunctioning, or the possibility of a natural disaster such as an earthquake, a fire, or a tornado) or otherwise a circumstance, capability, action, or event.

Virtual Machine: In computing, a virtual machine (VM) is an emulation of a particular computer system. Virtual machines operate based on the computer architecture and functions of a real or hypothetical computer, and their implementations may involve specialized hardware, software, or a combination of both. A virtual machine (VM) is a software implementation of a machine (for example, a computer) that executes programs like a physical machine. Virtual machines are separated into two major classes, based on their use and degree of correspondence to any real machine.

Web Service: A Web service is a method of communication between two electronic devices over a network. It is a software function provided at a network address over the Web with the service always on as in the concept of utility computing.

WSDL: The Web Services Description Language (WSDL) is an XML-based interface definition language that is used for describing the functionality offered by a web service.

WSS: Web Services Security (WS-Security, WSS) is an extension to SOAP to apply security to Web services. It is a member of the Web service specifications and was published by OASIS.

Chapter 14
Web based Privacy Disclosure Threats and Control Techniques

Tithi Hunka
KIIT University, India

Sital Dash
KIIT University, India

Prasant Kumar Pattnaik
KIIT University, India

ABSTRACT

Due to advancement of internet technologies, web based applications are gaining popularity day by day. Many organizations maintain large volumes of web site based data about individuals that may carry information that cannot be revealed to the public or researchers. While web-based applications are becoming increasingly pervasive by nature, they also present new security and privacy challenges. However, privacy threats effects negatively on sensitive data and possibly leads to the leakage of confidential information. More ever, privacy preserving data mining techniques allow us to protect the sensitive data before it gets published to the public by changing the original micro-data format and contents. This chapter is intended to undertake an extensive study on some ramified disclosure threats to the privacy and PPDM (privacy preserving data mining) techniques as a unified solution to protect against threats.

INTRODUCTION

Many organizations say example: industries, hospitals, railways, banks, credit card companies, etc. maintains a huge web site related data (micro-data) about individuals and organizational statics. These data may contain sensitive information so releasing the data to the public and to the researchers for data mining purpose may be a great risk. Privacy preserving data mining techniques is seeking attention these days because of privacy issues on sensitive web site related data.

Any micro-data set contains mainly three common attributes, namely identifying attributes (that uniquely identify the individual), quasi-identifying attributes (the set of data values that is sufficient to

DOI: 10.4018/978-1-4666-9764-5.ch014

recognize a person on the database), and sensitive attribute (attribute containing secret data). Many of the individuals from the U.S. may be recognized by the quasi-identifying attributes (Sweeney, 2002, pp. 557-570).

Section 2 deals with the privacy and privacy threats, and a list of control techniques for threats; section 3 deals with a description of the privacy disclosure control techniques; lastly, section 4 include conclusion and future scope of the work.

PRIVACY[1]

The American Institute of Certified Public Accountants (AICPA) and Canadian Institute of Charted Accountants (CICA) define that, "Privacy is the right and the obligation of individuals and organizations with respect to the collection, use, retention, and disclosure of personal information" (Joseph, Daniel, & Vasanthi, 2013, p. 1). Privacy aims to less risk of disclosure of confidential value in a micro-data file, less information loss and high utility of micro-data for analysis purpose.

Privacy Disclosure Threats

There can be four types of privacy disclosure threats commonly identified while publishing the micro-data 1) Identity Disclosure 2) Membership Disclosure 3) Attribute Disclosure 4) Statistical Disclosure. A novel technique should protect against all the disclosure while maintaining the trade-off between data utility, information loss and risk of disclosure.

A.SOME OF THE PRIVACY CONTROL TECHNIQUES

Some of the privacy control techniques like k-anonymity, l-diversity, t-closeness, etc. are discussed below:

1. **k-anonymity:** k-anonymity is an anonymization approach of privacy preservation. The micro-data table is said to be k-anonymized if a particular record matches with the other k-1 records released in the same data set with respect to quasi-identifiers. Generalization and suppression technique is used for hiding the individual identity. k- Anonymity is simple and easy to understand and also for each record, there are k-1 matching records so it provides sufficient protection against linking attacks. It does not work well in case of high dimensional data and suffers from similarity and background knowledge attack (Sweeney, 2002a).This experiment has been performed on the toy set by using ARX TOOL version 2.3.0.

2. **l-diversity:** l-diversity is the improvement on k-anonymity. It gives protection against linking and similarity attack and focus on the diversity of the sensitive attributes within an equivalence class. A micro-data table is said to be l-diverse if for each equivalence class there should be l distinct values of sensitive data. Increasing value of l requires more knowledge of adversary to find out the sensitive attribute. There may be three types of l-diversity methods 1) Distinct l-diversity, 2) Entropy l-diversity, 3) Recursive (c, ℓ)-diversity (Machanavajjhala, Kifer, & Venkitasubramaniam, 2007).

Table 1. Control techniques for Privacy Disclosure threats

Serial No.	Privacy Disclosure Threat	Description	Privacy Disclosure Control Techniques
1	Identity Disclosure (Templ, Meindl, & Kowarik, 2013)	Identity disclosure occurs when adversaries are able to recognize a particular person in the released data set.	• k-anonymity • l-diversity • t-closeness with k-anonymity • slicing
2	Statistical Disclosure (Templ, Meindl, & Kowarik, 2013)	In this, if adversaries are able to estimate the confidential data from the released statics than it is said that statistical disclosure has been taking place. For disclosure control either data are modified (Perturbation of data) or reduced (broad banding of data) to an acceptable level. The method chosen depends upon the data to be released.	• Global Recoding • Local Suppression • Top/Bottom Coding • Adding Noise • Swapping • PRAM(Post Randomization method) • Micro aggregation • Resampling
3	Membership Disclosure (Templ, Meindl, & Kowarik, 2013)	In a specific database (such as dataset containing cancer patients) If someone is unable to decide whether the record of any individual is present in the dataset or not, then the dataset is free from membership disclosure. In some cases it is better to use the identity disclosure control technique when the adversary is unknown about the membership of individuals, and in cases when adversary knows the individual's record than membership disclosure control technique is not sufficient.	• Slicing
4	Attribute Disclosure (Templ, Meindl, & Kowarik, 2013)	Attribute Disclosure occurs, when any additional information about an individual is revealed from the released data set. Identity Disclosure leads to Attribute Disclosure .Attribute Disclosure can occur with or without identity disclosure (If someone knows the identity of a person in a dataset, he can easily find out the sensitive information or for all matching tuples there are the same sensitive attribute).	• Randomization • Bucketization • l-diversity • Slicing

Table 2. Original Patients Table

	Zip code	Sex	Disease
1.	47677	29	Heart Disease
2.	47602	22	Heart Disease
3.	47678	27	Heart Disease
4.	47905	43	Flu
5.	47909	49	Heart Disease
6.	47906	47	Cancer
7.	47605	30	Heart Disease
8.	47673	36	Cancer
9.	47607	32	Cancer

Table 3. 3-Anonymous Patients Table

	Zip code	Age	Disease
1.	476**	2*	Heart Disease
2.	476**	2*	Heart Disease
3.	476**	2*	Heart Disease
4.	4790*	4*	Flu
5.	4790*	4*	Heart Disease
6.	4790*	4*	Cancer
7.	476**	3*	Heart Disease
8.	476**	3*	Cancer
9.	476**	3*	Cancer

3.   **t-closeness:** t-closeness is improved technique of l-diversity. This method gives sufficient protection against similarity and background knowledge attack. A micro-data table is said to have t-closeness if the distribution of sensitive values in any equivalence class is close to the distribution of attribute in the overall table (not more than threshold t). For identity disclosure control it is suggested to use the t-closeness with k-anonymity. It can be said that t-closeness is the best if one is to release

Table 4. Original Patients Table

	Zip code	Age	Salary	Disease
1.	47677	29	3K	Gastric ulcer
2.	47602	22	4K	Gastric ulcer
3.	47678	27	5K	Stomach cancer
4.	47905	43	6K	Gastric
5.	47909	52	11K	Flu
6.	47906	47	8K	Bronchitis
7.	47605	30	7K	Bronchitis
8.	47673	36	9K	Pneumonia
9.	47607	32	10K	Stomach cancer

Table 5. 3-diverse Patients Table

	Zip code	Age	Salary	Disease
1.	476**	2*	3K	Gastric ulcer
2.	476**	2*	4K	Gastric ulcer
3	476**	2*	5K	Stomach cancer
4.	4790*	>=40	6K	Gastric
5.	4790*	>=40	11K	Flu
6.	4790*	>=40	8K	Bronchitis
7.	476**	3*	7K	Bronchitis
8.	476**	3*	9K	Pneumonia
9.	476**	3*	10K	Stomach cancer

the data. In (Li, Li, & Venkatasubramanian, 2007, pp. 106-115) author used EMD (Earth Movers Distance) to calculate the distance between categorical and numerical attribute values i,e between two distributions.

4. **Global Recoding:** Global Recoding technique use to mask micro-data while the information loss remains minimum. In this technique the detailed variables (identifying or non-identifying variables) can be globally recoded by disclosing only less detailed values .For instance, all cities of city/town variable can be re-coded by the associated province (Hundepool, & de Wolf, 2011).

5. **Local Suppression:** In some micro-data file set of variables (Identifying or Non-identifying) might present that combined are used to identify a particular respondent. These variables are generally set of categorical variables that can identify a rare or unique person. In this technique, at least one of the variables from a risky record is locally suppressed (By providing a score of "unknown"), so that the risky record is no longer being unique and identifying. For instance (Mayor, Ambsterdam, Male, High Qualification) the unique record can be locally suppressed to (Mayor, Unknown, Man, High Qualification).The record which is risky and going to be suppressed that is having a rare combination of scores on identifying variables. (Hundepool, & de Wolf, 2011)

6. **Top/Bottom Coding:** Top coding is one of the simple methods to protect the numerical variable of micro-data. In this the value above (Top coding) and below (Bottom coding) the predefined threshold is converted to a new value or mean of all the values above the threshold can be used as a new value. For instance, an age above 80 can be converted to 80+ (Hundepool, & de Wolf, 2011).

Table 6. Original Patients Table

	Zip code	Age	Salary	Disease
1.	47677	29	3K	Gastric ulcer
2.	47602	22	4K	Gastric ulcer
3.	47678	27	5K	Stomach cancer
4.	47905	43	6K	Gastric
5.	47909	52	11K	Flu
6.	47906	47	8K	Bronchitis
7.	47605	30	7K	Bronchitis
8.	47673	36	9K	Pneumonia
9.	47607	32	10K	Stomach cancer

Table 7. t-closeness Patients Table

	Zip code	Age	Salary	Disease
1.	4767*	<=40	3K	Gastric ulcer
3.	4767*	<=40	5K	Stomach cancer
8.	4767*	<=40	9K	Pneumonia
4.	4790*	<=40	6K	Gastric
5.	4790*	<=40	11K	Flu
6.	4790*	<=40	8K	Bronchitis
2.	4760*	<=40	4K	Gastric
7.	4760*	<=40	7K	Bronchitis
9.	4760*	<=40	10K	Stomach cancer

7. **Swapping:** Data swapping techniques first reference found in Delenius and reiss in 1978 in which the records of the sensitive variables are interchanged among individuals without changing the marginal frequency counts. This technique is used for masking categorical variables. Subsets of the records may be chosen if the records have greater risk than other records. This method is easy to implement and preserve confidentiality, but even at low swapping rates analytical properties may be destroyed (Fienberg, & McIntyre, January 2004, pp. 14-29).

In rank swapping, the particular variable is selected, sorted and swapped in k-percentage range and typically without replacement. If k will large then re identification will be small and at small k value distortion will be small.

NISS (National institute of statistical science) and US federal agencies made a web based tool for masking categorical variables. It takes swap variable and swap rate as user input. Records are randomly selected and swapped if it differs on at least one of the unswapped attributes and the loop continues until specified number of records gets swapped. Risk-Utility frontier is for calculating the maximum protection available for swap rate and swap variable combination. The software can be downloaded from www.niss.org (Sanil, Gomatam, Karr, & Liu, 2003).

8. **Slicing:** Slicing is the best anonymization technique and used as a technique for membership disclosure protection technique. Slicing technique goes through partitioning of attributes (column partitioning), partitioning of records (tuple partitioning) and after this each column is randomly permuted to break the linking between columns. Column generalization may be the addition step in slicing. Advantages of the slicing are that it can handle high dimensional data, it preserves the better data utility than generalization and also prevents attribute disclosure and also it is more efficient than bucketization in workloads involving the sensitive attributes (Neha v. Mogre, & Sulbha Patil, 2013, pp.103-108).

9. **Bucketization:** Bucketization is a special case of slicing. It is the technique, which does not apply to data that have a clear separation between quasi-identifying attributes and sensitive attributes. In the first step, the identifying attribute of the original data set is removed and then the tuples are distributed between buckets. In bucketization Sensitive attributes are separated from quasi identifiers and then randomly permuting the sensitive attribute values in the bucket so that the correlation between Sensitive Attribute's and Quasi Identifiers are preserved. This technique ignores the adversary's background knowledge so it is not an ideal technique. Bucketization does not work against membership disclosure. The main disadvantage of this technique their must a clearly defined

Table 8. Original Patients Table

Zip code	Age	Sex	Disease
47906	22	M	Dyspepsia
47906	22	F	Flu
47905	33	F	Flu
47905	52	F	Bronchitis
47302	54	M	Flu
47302	60	M	Dyspepsia
47304	60	M	Dyspepsia
47304	64	F	Gastric

Table 9. Sliced Table

(Age, Sex)	(Zip code, Disease)
(22,M)	(47905, Flu)
(22,F)	(47906, Dyspepsia)
(33,F)	(47905, Bronchitis)
(52,F)	(47906, Flu)
(54,M)	(47304, Gastric)
(60,M)	(47302, Flu)
(60,M)	(47304, Dyspepsia)
(64,F)	(47302, Dyspepsia)

Sensitive Attribute's and Quasi Identifying attributes which is tough to detect in some datasets (Mohiddin, & Kiran Kumar, 2013, pp. 387-391; Vijay R. Sonawane, & Kanchan S. Rahinj, 2013).

10. **PRAM:** PRAM stands for post randomization method. It is a perturbation technique used for statistical disclosure protection. It is an alternative technique of data swapping. In this technique the score of a particular attribute is changed according to some predefined probability mechanism (A Markov matrix). This technique works for securing categorical variables, but can be generalised for numerical variables as well (Hundepool, & de Wolf, 2011).

11. **Microaggregation**: Microaggregation is a perturbation approach originally defined for statistical disclosure control of continues data. If a micro data file contains a number of variables, then there are two types of microaggregation possible, they are univariate and multivariate microaggregation. In univariate micro aggregation, single variable get involved while in multivariate microaggregation multiple variables get involved, also satisfies k-anonymity for the dataset.

Microaggregation can be fixed sized or variable sized based on the number of records in a group. In fixed sized microaggregation the records get divided into groups of size k where one group may have greater than k records if number of records are not multiple of k and in variable sized microaggregation the group size varies from k to 2k-1.

In microaggregation, firstly the total no of records are grouped into a set of records of size k (User defined parameter) then original data values are replaced by the centroid of the corresponding cluster. The larger the value of k, the disclosure risk will be minimized and information loss will be high (Sweeney, 2002, pp. 557-570).

12. **Resampling:** Resampling is a perturbation approach originally defined for statistical disclosure control of numerical data. In this technique, Firstly if the data set contains n records, then take t samples with replacement (i,e values can be taken more than once). Secondly, each sample is sorted in increasing order. Then, For first value, the average of all first values from different samples are taken, for second value the average of all second values from different samples are taken, and so on. Author of (Templ, Meindl, & Kowarik, 2013) has modified the Resampling technique so that the data set can satisfy k-anonymity property.

Noise Addition: Noise addition is a perturbation technique used for the statistical disclosure control applicable in continuous data. For noise addition, the first process is the de-identification (By removing the attribute that can uniquely identify a person) and then second process is to find the confidential at-

Table 10. Original Patients Table

Zip code	Age	Sex	Disease
47906	22	M	Dyspepsia
47906	22	F	Flu
47905	33	F	Flu
47905	52	F	Bronchitis
47302	54	M	Flu
47302	60	M	Dyspepsia
47304	60	M	Dyspepsia
47304	64	F	Gastric

Table 11. Bucketized Table

Zip code	Age	Sex	Disease
47906	22	M	Flu
47906	22	F	Dyspepsia
47905	33	F	Bronchitis
47905	52	F	Flu
47302	54	M	Gastric
47302	60	M	Flu
47304	60	M	Dyspepsia
47304	64	F	Dyspepsia

Table 12. Some Statistical Disclosure Control techniques Vs their applicability on data

Method	Continuous Data	Categorical Data
Additive Noise	*	
Micro aggregation	*	(*)
Rank Swapping	*	
Resampling	*	
PRAM		*
Top/Bottom Coding	*	*
Global Recoding	*	*
Local Suppression		*

tribute for adding a random number ε with zero mean and predefined variance to protect its confidentiality. Various noise addition are possible i,e, additive noise, multiplicative noise, and logarithmic multiplicative noise (Mivule, 2013).

B: Some Statistical Disclosure Control Techniques vs. Their Applicability on Data

Statistical Disclosure control techniques differ according to the applicability for continuous or categorical variables. Continuous variable means the variable that is numeric, numerical and arithmetic operations can be performed with it. Continuous variable may not have an infinite range. For example, in case of Age; And Categorical variable take values in a finite range, standard arithmetic operations cannot be applied. For example Gender, Marital Status are the categorical variables. In the table given below, * denotes application and (*) denotes application with some adaptation.

CONCLUSION AND FUTURE SCOPE OF THE WORK

In this chapter, we carry out the survey of the different disclosure threats, and their control techniques available in privacy preserving data mining on web site based data for improving a website quality and effectiveness. This study of different techniques helps in developing a new system of privacy preservation that may combine two or more techniques to secure website based data against different threats. The method chosen to secure micro-data depends upon the data inside the micro-data, the disclosure risk one wants to preserve and the level of information loss and data utility can be compromised. In future we can add more detail about each technique and new techniques of privacy preservation can be added.

REFERENCES

Chettri, S. K., Paul, B., & Dutta, A. K. (2013). Statistical Disclosure Control for Data Privacy Preservation. *International Journal of Computers and Applications*, *80*(10), 38–43. doi:10.5120/13899-1880

Fienberg, S. E., & McIntyre, J. (2004, January). Data swapping: Variations on a theme by dalenius and reiss. In *Privacy in statistical databases* (pp. 14–29). Springer Berlin Heidelberg. doi:10.1007/978-3-540-25955-8_2

Hundepool, A., & de Wolf, P. P. (2011). Methods Series: Statistical disclosure control.

Joseph, N. M., Daniel, E., & Vasanthi, N. A. (2013). Survey on privacy-preserving methods for storage in cloud computing. *Proceedings on Amrita International Conference of Women in Computing IJCA '13* (pp. 1-4).

Li, N., Li, T., & Venkatasubramanian, S. (2007, April). t-closeness: Privacy beyond k-anonymity and l-diversity. *Proceedings of the IEEE 23rd International Conference on Data Engineering ICDE '07* (pp. 106-115). IEEE.

Machanavajjhala, A., Kifer, D., Gehrke, J., & Venkitasubramaniam, M. (2007). l-diversity: Privacy beyond k-anonymity. *ACM Transactions on Knowledge Discovery from Data*, *1*(1), 3. doi:10.1145/1217299.1217302

Martínez, S., Sánchez, D., & Valls, A. (2012). Towards k-anonymous non-numerical data via semantic resampling. In *Advances in Computational Intelligence* (pp. 519–528). Springer Berlin Heidelberg. doi:10.1007/978-3-642-31724-8_54

Mivule, K. (2013). Utilizing noise addition for data privacy, an overview. *arXiv preprint arXiv:1309.3958*.

Mohiddin, S. K., & Kiran Kumar, M. (2013). A Novel Approach for Data Publishing In Mining. *IJRCCT*, *2*(7), 387–391.

Neha v. M., & Sulbha, P. (2013). Slicing: An Approach For Privacy Preservation in High-Dimensional Data Using Anonymization Technique. *Proceedings of Fifth IRAJ International Conference*, Pune, India (pp.103-108).

Sanil, A. P., Gomatam, S., Karr, A. F., & Liu, C. (2003). NISSWebSwap: A Web Service for data swapping. *Journal of Statistical Software*, *8*(7). doi:10.18637/jss.v008.i07

Sonawane, V. R., & Rahinj, K. S. (2013). A New Data Anonymization Technique used For Membership Disclosure Protection. *International Journal of Innovative Research in Science Engineering and Technology*, *2*(4), 1230–1233.

Sweeney, L. (2002). Achieving k-anonymity privacy protection using generalization and suppression. *International Journal of Uncertainty, Fuzziness and Knowledge-based Systems*, *10*(05), 571–588. doi:10.1142/S021848850200165X

Sweeney, L. (2002). k-anonymity: A model for protecting privacy. *International Journal of Uncertainty, Fuzziness and Knowledge-based Systems*, *10*(05), 557–570. doi:10.1142/S0218488502001648

Templ, M., Meindl, B., & Kowarik, A. (2013). Introduction to statistical disclosure control (sdc). *Project: Relative to the testing of SDC algorithms and provision of practical SDC, data analysis OG.*

Chapter 15

Reliability and Scalability of Service Oriented Architecture in Web Services:
Signature Verification

Madana Kumar Reddy C
Annamacharya PG College of Computer Studies, India

ABSTRACT

The use of Information Technology through Web services has been a major technology trend in the IT industry. IT promoted as a means of reducing costs, increasing reuse, simplifying integration and creating more active infrastructures. Web services replace other methods and technologies used in design, development, deployment and integration, and management services. It also allows different applications to exchange data with one another. SOA separates functions into distinct units or services, thus users can combine and reuse them in the production of various applications via modularity of functions. Here we are taken Signature verification application for dealing all these activities like online verification, offline verification, pressure, thickness, strength, etc. Software is componentized and the components are distributed among the devices available in the distributed environment with respect to their computational strength.

LITERATURE REVIEW

Handwritten signature verification is the process of confirming the identity of a user based on the handwritten signature of the user as a form of behavioral biometrics. Automatic handwritten signature verification is not a new problem. Many early research attempts were reviewed in the survey papers. The primary advantage that signature verification has over other types of biometric technologies is that handwritten signature is already the most widely accepted biometric for identity verification in daily use. The long history of trust over signature verification means that people are very willing to accept a signature-based biometric authentication system. However, there has not been any major interna-

DOI: 10.4018/978-1-4666-9764-5.ch015

tional effort that aims at comparing different signature verification methods systematically. As common benchmark databases and benchmarking rules are often used by researchers in such areas as information retrieval and natural language processing, researchers in biometrics increasingly see the need for such benchmarks for comparative studies.

INTRODUCTION

Many applications in image science require similarity retrieval of an image from a large collection of images. This project deals with this issue in the context of a database of handwritten signature images and describes a system for similarity retrieval and identification of handwritten signature images. Similarity retrieval of images has two components.

1. What should be the measure of similarity?
2. How should similar images be identified?

Linked to both these components are the issues of image representation, Indexing and matching. So that images similar to the query image can be retrieved without excessively searching the database. The aim of this work is to address these issues in the context of a database of handwritten signature images to provide a solution to the problem of handwritten signature identification which refer to the process of identifying an individual on the basis of his or her signature. It is important problem in practical applications in banking, commerce and law. The advantage of these features is that they give the virtual model of the signature irrespective of the size and orientation.

The other advantage is that it is tolerant of missing features and allows even partial signatures. The proposed system can be further developed by adding few more features in future. The hand written signature has long held position of importance in society. It is a symbol of consent, authentication, responsibility and authorization. The prime incentive to duplicate a signature has remained constant: financial gain.

BACKGROUND

With the development of widely dispersed networks of computer terminals, automatic tellers and databanks, there has been a corresponding increase in computer crime and growing need to protect the sensitive information assets. An important aspect of this problem is personal identification, that is, the ability to ensure that only the authorized people get access to resources (Fox, 2004). A method of personal identification that cannot be lost, stolen or forgotten is required for control of computer access, building access or automated banking. Because the signature is the normal and customary way of identifying an individual, it has many natural advantages over other techniques such as fingerprints or voice recognition. How in the sense, suppose a person has cold then his voice would not be same as his original voice. Signatures are the most popular validation tools for documents or commercial transactions.

If computers can be made intelligent enough to understand human handwriting it will be possible to make man-computer interfaces more ergonomic and attractive. With this motivation considerable research efforts have been invested in the recognition of human handwriting include characters, numerals and signatures. Signatures are a special case of handwriting in which special characters and flourishes are available, and the ratio between middle zone width and the letter heights is sometimes abnormal.

In many cases a signature is not readable even by a human being. Therefore, it is necessary to deal with a signature as a complete image that has a typical distribution of pixels representing different writing styles and not as a collection of letters and words. Signature data can be utilized by a computer provided reliable techniques are available for solving signature recognition and verification problems. Signature verification problem is concerned with determining whether a particular signature truly belongs to a particular person. So that forgeries can be detected. In the signature recognition problem a signature database is searched to establish identity of a given signature. Techniques used for solving these problems can be grouped into two broad classes: Online using an electronic tablet. In this case dynamic information like speed of writing, pressure applied, number of strokes etc., are available.

In Offline technique, image of a signature written on a paper is obtained either through a camera or a scanner and obviously dynamic information is not available. Since the volume of information available is less, signature analysis using offline techniques is relatively more difficult. Offline signature verification and recognition techniques use global, statistical or geometric and topological features. Global features are extracted from the global aspect of the signature. These features include transforms, image gradients, polygonal descriptions, etc. Statistical features are derived from statistical distribution of pixels from the image. Features like pressure measurement's proportionalities between upper, middle, lower and initial signature zones belong to this category. Geometrical and topological features described local and structural properties of the signatures.

Classes of Signature Verification System

Signatures can be verified either on-line or off-line.

Online Verification

On-line methods of signature verification are those, which involve measurement of various signature dynamics such as pen position, velocity and tip pressure as a function of time. The most successful of the on-line approaches is that reported by Asto and Kogure in 1982(Asto & Kogure, 1982). Their system performs almost perfectly even when tested against forgeries. This and other on-line techniques have enjoyed considerable success. First, each requires substantial amount of data post processing to facilitate an accurate decision. Second each requires some type of special equipment (graphics tablet, accelometric pen) at the point of signature generation.

Offline Verification

On the other hand, Off-line verification determines the genuineness of the signature through examining the overall shapes of the signatures. Off-line techniques involve only a picture of the signature and do not suffer from various limitations like pressure, etc. They offer the potential of centralized verification, though at the cost of inferior performance with the restriction of dynamic measurement removed, the off-line method shows a greater variety of approaches (Frederick Hirsh, John Kemp & Jani Ilkka,

2006). For example, run length histograms, character height-to-width ratio and slant angle values have been used to perform the task with varying degrees of success. All works involving off-line methods are intended to catch the casual forgery, i.e., a signature that is not a concerted attempt to duplicate a target.

The justification is clear with only the image of the signature to observe, any two images that look sufficiently alike will be attributed to the same writer. It is the casual forgery; however that is a leading contributor to lost assets in the banking and credit world today. Since the human eye easily catches causal forgeries, an automated system that could reduce the volume of the signatures that require inspection would be beneficial. An improved off-line system designed to detect such forgeries would therefore be of benefit.

DESCRIPTION

The Ultimate aim of any Signature Verification System is to distinguish the genuine signature of a person to its forged counterpart. Like in any commercial bank, a customer is given an account number and his specimen signature is taken. Whenever any person comes to bank carrying a cheque signed by the account holder, the clerk there in the bank verifies on the cheque by comparing it with the specimen signature, which we have. We are interested in automating this process. Let us assume that in our automated system, at the time of creating an account we receive a couple of signatures from the account-holder and let us call them as training signatures. A computer would process these and the resulting features are stored in the database along with the original signatures for verifying any new signature. Feature of signature is a vector defining the characteristics of the signature.

It can be length and width of the signature along with vertical or horizontal projection or pressure factor or tilt or slant direction or ratio or coefficients of some other transaction etc. In on-line methods features such as the pressure factor velocity at a point or the dynamic slope are mainly used. It is the choice of feature that differentiates various implementations of the system. Whenever a test signature is entered into the system, the features of the test signature are derived using the same method as that used for training signatures. If the test feature is in the neighborhood of the trained features it is decided that the test signature is genuine. The total process of signature verification can be briefly described with the following illustration.

The total signature verification system appears as shown in the above figure. The "Data Acquisition" block includes procedures for extracting the raw signature information form the image file by following its file format. The "Preprocessing" block includes many image-processing algorithms as a signature is treated as a digital image in off-line verification. "Feature extraction" block derives the appropriate features of the test signature which are then compared with the trained features in the decision making

Figure 1. Process of Signature verification

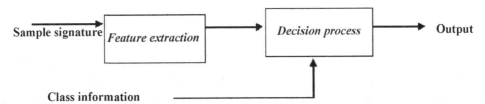

345

block. "Matching" includes the process in which the features of the test signature are compared with that of trained features which are accessed by the USER-ID (Jang, C.T.Sun & Mizutani,E, 2004). If the features are within the range of threshold then the output of the system is "Genuine" else it is "Forged".

PREPROCESSING

Preprocessing is required to eliminate noise, distortions etc. From the original image depending on the features needed in the next stage the processing algorithms perform more specific operations on the extracted image. Off-line signature verification is related to the validation and processing of specific paper forms. In this context one may have two problems: finding the signature on the cheque and separating signature from the background. In most of the practical cases specimens are noisy, so one may require noise elimination techniques to enhance the image quality.

In the earlier works considerable importance has not been given to the processing steps. With the help of window operator detection of the signature can be done, to separate signature form background thresholding is proposed and to process the thresholded image two more processing smoothing and thinning were proposed. So finally we have three processing steps. They are,

1. Thresholding
2. Smoothing
3. Thinning

Thresholding

Thresholding is a method to convert a gray-level image into binary image so, that object of interest are separated from background. For effective thresholding, it is necessary that the object and background have sufficient contrast. The intensity levels of pixels and intensity characteristics determine the value of threshold. The brightness of the each pixel is compared to a threshold value and the pixel is assigned to one of the two categories depending on whether the threshold is exceeded or not. Many thresholding algorithms have been proposed to select the value of threshold, but no single algorithm is proved best.

Smoothing

Smoothing operations are used primarily for diminishing spurious effects that may be present in a digital image as a result of poor sampling system or transmission channel. Smoothing can be done by comparing the sum of object pixels in 8 pixel neighborhood around each pixel in the image, when this sum is grater than threshold the pixel is made object pixel else it is background pixel. This operation is fills out the rough regions of the noisy image, while thresholding out smaller speckles of noise.

Thinning

An important approach to representing the structural shape of a plane region is to reduce it to a graph. This reduction may be accomplished by obtaining the skeleton of the region via a thinning (also called skeletonizing) algorithm. Thinning procedures play a main role in a broad range of problems in image processing, ranging from automated inspection of printed circuit boards to counting of asbestos fibers in air filters. The thinning algorithms that delete edge points of a region subject to the constraints that deletion of the following points:

1. Does not remove end points
2. Does not break connectedness, and
3. Does not cause excessive erosion of the region.

FEATURE EXTRACTION

In a signature verification system, Feature extraction phase is carried out in the enrollment process, to build up the reference database of the system, and at run time for verifying the authenticity of a given signature (Prasad Subodh, 2014). It provides the information about the signature in terms of features and their locations. Once the feature set is extracted from the signature, these features can represent the signature itself, which reduces the complexity in matching process. Almost all the dynamic information is lost in the Off-line techniques. By the use of gray scale image it is possible to extract some of the dynamic information. In the present work I used the gray scale images and I extracted one dynamic feature like High Pressure Regions. I also extracted some global features like Width to Height Ratio, Tilt and Slant. Width to Height Ratio accounts for variation in space viable for the individual to sign. Slant and Tilt are dependent on the penmanship and these are important characteristic features of individual.

Slant

Although slant angle represents a prominent, idiosyncratic feature of a signature it is mainly a psycho-physical concept. Ammar counted the number of pixels that were 'positively, negatively and vertically' connected to provide a more global estimation of the slant property. To estimate the slant of the signature the algorithm proposed by Ammar is used.

Width to Height Ratio

This feature is the external feature of the signature. Proportionally exists between Width and Height of the signature. Width and Height of the signature are measured in terms of number of pixels and the calculated the ratio.

Tilt

Slope of the baseline is considered as the tilt of the signature. Base is the median of the body of the Image.

MATCHING PROCESS

The matching process compares the test signature with the reference signature stored in the database and the given test signature may be accepted or rejected according to its similarities to the reference signature set.

1. Slant Direction.
2. Slant Number.
3. Tilt.
4. Width to Height Ratio.
5. Pressure Factor.

PROCESSING OF IMAGES

However, when the data consist of pictures or portions of visual images, there is a need to first measure various features of the images or of the objects contained in the images, before they can be classified. Before features are extracted from an image, it may be useful to preprocess the image to reduce irrelevant information or noise and to enhance the image properties that will make feature measurement easier or more reliable. Such an operation can be called an image-to image transformation because the original image is replaced by a new image. In the simplest situation, the image-to-image transformations will then be followed by image-to-feature transformations which extract small number of features from the image, and finally by a feature-to-decision transformation. This uses one or more features to classify the image or the objects in it.

In more complicated cases there will be several cycles of image processing, image analysis and decision making before the final results are scanned first to see if it contains any regions that might of interest. If so, these regions could be examined more closely, using different features, to see if they contain objects to be classified (Rajasekaran, S., & G.A.V. Pai, 2003). Next, additional image processing and feature measurement steps may require providing features for classifying the objects. We call a one dimensional array of data a sampled wave form, sampled waveforms can be obtained by measuring the values of a continuous wave form at a series of uniformly spaced points $x1, x2\ldots xn$ produce the sampled waveform $g(x)$, $X=x1,x2\ldots,xn$. Sampled waveforms could be obtained from sound waves, seismic disturbances, stock market levels, or temperature readings taken at a fixed location. The sampled brightness of a scene as a function of distance along a single scans line through the image is also a sampled waveform.

Three-dimensional arrays are called volume images and can be obtained from some medical imaging equipment, in which case the individual data points are called voxels ("volume elements").The brightness at each point in an ordinary flat-film x-ray indicates the degree to which the photons are absorbed along a line through the three-dimensional object being x-rayed. The x-rayed image can be thought of as a projection of 3D object onto a plane. A CAT (computerized axial topography) scan is volume image that shows the degree to which photons are absorbed by each small volume of the 3D object being x-rayed. Images are obtained from a video camera in which the light from a scene passes through a lens and onto a matrix of sensors. Each sensor records the average rate at which photons are striking it during the time that the image is being acquired, In other video cameras, an optical image formed in a vidicon tube is scanned by an electron beam, and its voltage is sampled by an analog-to-digital converter.

Photographs and other images may also be digitized by various types of scanners, In all these cases, a finite matrix of brightness value is produced. The brightness values are called gray levels and the points of the matrix are called pixels.

There are two common conventions in use for representing the position of a pixel in an image. Usually the ordinary Cartesian coordinate system is used. In this system, g(x,y) is the gray level the pixel(x,y) and the pixel(1,1) (some times(0,0)) is at the lower left corner of the image as x(horizontal component) increases(x,y) moves to the right, and a y(the vertical component) increases,(x,y) moves upward. Images can alternatively be thought of as ordinary matrices in which the gray level of a pixel represented as g(i,j).In this case, the pixel(i,j) moves downward as I(row index) increases, and (i,j) moves to the right as j(the column index) increases. Typical image sizes for low-cost commercial image processing systems range from 256 x 256 pixels to 512 x 512 pixels. Formats such as 640 X 480 Pixels are also used and are closer to the size and shape used for television images some systems with high geometric resolution must be distinguished from gray scale resolution, which refers to the number of different gray levels that can be represented at a given pixel in an image. Image acquisition and display devices always have limited gray level resolution.

When general-purpose computers are used to process images, the precision to which the gray levels can be represented internally is not normally a constraining factor, but fast special purpose commercial and military image processing hardware usually has more limited precision. Care must be taken to design algorithms that avoid overflow or underflow of the intermediate results when using this type of equipment. Care must be taken to ensure the proper orientation of the images and efficiency of the algorithms used when transferring data and algorithms from one system to another. For example, if the gray levels in an image have been stored as a series of horizontal stripes, it may not be efficient to access them as series of vertical stripes.

Gray levels are often represented by integers between 0 and k-1 inclusive, where the number of gray level k is often a power of 2. Usually, black is represented by the gray level 0 and white by gray level k-1. Often one byte (8 bits) of memory per pixel is used, which can encode 256 different gray levels. Human cannot distinguish between more gray levels than this on a monochrome (gray level) video display. Eight bits per color (red, green, and blue) are sufficient for color displays operations on images can yield non-integer gray levels. When using general-purpose computers these values need not be rounded except possibly for display or compact storage.

In a pseudo color image, the gray levels are replaced by colors. The color that corresponds to each gray level can be assigned arbitrarily one common scheme is to use the blue hues to represent the lowest gray levels, green the intermediate gray levels, and red the highest gray levels. Other hues are interpolated as in the visible light spectrum. For example, it in a certain type of medical image the normal liver varies only from blue to green, it is easy to recognize any yellow or orange areas as abnormalities. These regions would not be as noticeable in a gray-level image.

RECOGNITION

Recognition or more specifically pattern recognition is a typical characteristic of human beings and other living organisms. The term pattern means something that is setup as an ideal to be imitated. For example, in our childhood a shape 'A' is shown to us and we are asked to imitate that. So the shape is the ideal one. On the other hand, if what we produce or draw obeying that instruction is close to that shape, our teacher identifies that as 'A'. This identification step is called recognition and the shapes we draw (i.e., objects we made) may be termed as patterns. Thus, the pattern recognition means identification of the ideal object. Recognition should therefore be preceded by development of the concept of the ideal or model or prototype. This process is called learning. In most real-life problems no ideal example is available. In that case, the concept of ideal is abstracted from many near-perfect examples.

Under this notion learning is of two types:

1. Supervised learning
2. Unsupervised learning

Supervised Learning

If appropriate label is attached (by a teacher) to each of these examples, it is called as 'supervised learning'.

Unsupervised Learning

If no such labeling is available; it is called as 'unsupervised learning'. It is obvious that for recognizing an object we must receive (or sense) some information or features from that object. Based on these features we assign the object being considered to one of the possible classes each of which represents a pattern. Hence, classification is the actual task to be done and we call it recognition if the classes are labeled with particular patterns. Some times, learning and recognition work together; outcome of recognition process modifies knowledge about the pattern classes. Unsupervised methods usually fall in this category.

Usually recognition process deals with physical items. Thus it depends on features from the items. Such process is called sensory pattern recognition or visual pattern recognition. Since objects are assigned to the classes based on the invariant features associated with them, it is obvious that objects of the same class must possess similar features and those which belong to different classes possess different features. Therefore, the set of features that distinguishes objects of different classes and is common to objects of the same classes is the key for classification and recognition. Identifying such a minimal feature set is an important step in the process of recognition. The process is called feature selection.

Another major step is designing the decision process. The decision procedure should be optimum in a sense that the classification error must be minimum (Madana Kumar Reddy, C., 2009). This is developed usually through learning. That means given a set of training data, a set of decision rules is to be devised so that the training data are separated into the given set of classes in an optimum way. Note that each training data is a feature vector along with the class label, which the object actually belongs to. This is an example of supervised training.

IMPLEMENTATION DETAILS

For our work, signature images acquired using a hand-held scanner that provides binary images. Signature specimens written on a white sheet of paper using ordinary black ink were considered. It was found that the binary image obtained from the scanner was corrupted due to noise. There were isolated regions of white pixels causing intermediate discontinuities in the strokes firming the signature. These imperfections were due to non-uniform smoothness of the writing surface or paper and/or improper spread of the ink. So background subtraction and noise reduction are applied to get thin image. After getting the thin image, features are to be extracted. The features are two types.

1. Moment features
2. Envelope features

Moment Features

These are flatness of distribution, asymmetry of distribution and pixels intensity over a region. This remains unaltered irrespective of the size of the image.

Envelope Features

The envelope features are obtained about the principal axis of signature (above and below). The basic idea is that irrespective of the size (small or larger) and transformation, envelopes structure always locks similar.

METHODOLOGY

The signature image, which is basically a collection of points distributed over a well-related area, possesses distinct shape characteristics. Global features which can be capture nature of the distribution of these points in space are ideally suited for gross characterization of the signatures. These features, obviously, cannot capture the fine structural aspects of the signature images essential for detection of tracing forgeries or photocopies, but possesses sufficient discriminatory power to eliminate substitution errors. In addition, consideration of different types of global features can increase reliability of the identification decisions.

With the above motivation three types of features were selected for this purpose.

1. Horizontal and vertical projection moments
2. Upper envelope of signature component
3. Lower envelope of signature component

1. Projection Moments

A signature is characterized by writer specific horizontal and vertical flourishes at individual characters and/or typical curves or loops at end zones. Horizontal and vertical projection images of the signatures reflect the typical nature of this distribution of data points along x and y directions. Features like kurtosis (measure of flatness of distribution) and skewness (measure of asymmetry of distribution) provide appropriate numeric measures for the distribution characteristic of the points in the projection images. Also, relation between these measures for vertical and horizontal projection images indicates the nature of relative flourishes along these directions.

Projection images can be defined in the following way

Horizontal projection image
$X(i) = \Sigma j\ im(i,j)$
Vertical projection image
$Y(i) = \Sigma i\ im(i,j)$

Where $im(i,j)$ is either 1/0 and I is the row index and j refers to the column. An rth order moment measures μr for the projection image is defined as

$\mu r = \Sigma(xi-xc)r\ G(xi)$

Where x-centroid of corresponding projection image

$G()$ can be either $X()$ or $Y()$.

The following moment measures are also calculated (V indicates moments captured from vertical image, and H horizontal moment)

1. Kurtosis measures
    $K_V = \mu^V_4 / (\mu^V_2)^2$
    $K_H = \mu^H_4) / (\mu^H_2)^2$
2. Skewness measures:
    $S_V = \mu^V_3 / (\mu^V_2)^{1.5}$
    $S_H = \mu^H_3 / (\mu^H_2)^{1.5}$
3. Relative kurtosis and skewness measures
    $R_V = \mu^V_3 / (\mu^V_4)^{0.75}$
    $R_H = \mu^H_3 / (\mu^H_4)^{0.75}$
4. Relative vertical and horizontal projection measures
    $VH_1 = \mu^V_2 / (\mu^H_2)^{1.5}$
    $VH_2 = \mu^V_4 / (\mu^H_4)^{1.5}$

Thus from the definition of moment measures it is clear that if the signature is not properly aligns; erroneous measures will be obtained because projection images will be different.

2. Envelope Characteristics

External points of a signature image are positioned in a characteristic pattern on both sides of the principal axis of the signature pattern on both sides of the principal axis of the signature. Relative position of these external points represents the typical writing style of the individuals. It two curves are constructed by connecting these points, taking the points on one side of the axis a time, then the shape of the signature can be described in terms of these curves. Features extracted from these curves can capture both global and local shape properties of the signature. The curve constructed with points lying on the upper side of the principal axis is referred to as upper envelope and that on the lower is called lower envelope.

We constructed enveloped by sampling external points at regulate intervals. For smaller sampling intervals envelopes exhibit local variations of the signature pattern, some of these variations may be due to the noise. To reduce the effect of noise a sampling interval of two pixels was used. For extracting the shape information from these curves a m * n grid was formed with enveloped bounded. The grid boundaries were coincident with the bounding box of the signature. Depending on the nature of the envelope clipped within an element of the grid following numerical values assigned.

0: If envelope does not pass through the region
1: If envelope passes through the region, but no prominent peak/valley lies inside the region (or both prominent peak and valley lies in the region)
2: If a prominent peak (curvature maxima) lies inside the region.
3: If a prominent valley (curvature minima) lies inside the region.

Valleys and peaks were determined by considering the y-coordinates of the sampled points over a local neighborhood. Peaks or a valley having height or depth more than 25% of the height of the grid cell has been considered prominent. Largest peak or the deepest valley has been considered if multiple peaks or valleys occur in the neighborhood defined by the grid. These numerical values constitute a 12-dimensional future vector.

APPLICATIONS OF SIGNATURE VERIFICATION

Credit cards deal with very large amounts of funds each day. Perhaps as much as $5-$10 billon worth of purchases are charged to credit cards every day. It has been reported that credit card issuers lost $800 million in 1989, about $1 billion in 1990 and about $1.6 billion in 1991. Present credit card fraud in the United States alone has been reported to be well over $2 billion per year. Although these sums are substantial, they are quite small when expressed as percentage of the total credit card purchases, certainly well below 1% . Credit card issuers however get only a small commission of the purchase price and therefore the total losses due to credit card fraud are significant for the credit card issuers.

It has been reported that half of all credit card fraud involved lost or stolen cards while the rest involves counterfeit cards, the non-receipt of cards, or fraudulent credit card applications. A number of techniques have been used in an attempt to curb this fraud, some based on identifying sudden surges of spending, but it appears none of these have been particularly successful. Most banks therefore do little to control credit card fraud. A reliable HSV (High Security Verification) technique could have applications in reducing credit card fraud although there appears to be some hurdles that must be overcome if the technology is to be useful (Peng, Z.R. & M. Tsou, 2003). A stolen card has the owner's signature on the back and this makes it particularly easy to forge the signature given minimal checking of signatures at the place of purchase.

This problem of forging the signature does not even arise if a credit card has been intercepted in mail since any signature could be used and put on the back arise if a credit card has been intercepted in mail since any signature could be used and put on the back of the card. One possible approach to reducing credit card fraud would be to require the owner of a new credit card to visit the bank and supply sample signatures so that information from the signatures could be put electronically on the card making it unnecessary to have the owner's signature on the card at all, a signature that may be viewed and forged by a person who has stolen the card.

The above scheme of course has a problem. If one credit card issuer require that a person that is being issued a new card must go to the bank and produce identification and give sample signatures while other credit card issuers continue with the present procedure of requiring no such visit to the bank, the credit card issuer requiring signatures would not have many customers. The suggested approach is therefore not particularly convenient for the customer and is likely to be adopted in a very competitive market place where the customers are being bombarded with offers of new credit cards almost every day.

Another approach might be possible. When the owner of a new card makes the first purchase using the card, the check-out staff be asked (by the credit card terminal) to check the customers identification(e.g. drivers license) and provide the identification number, as is done when cashing a cheque. This scheme does have some merit in that it only creates a minor nuisance when the customer is asked the first time for an identification but using this approach the HSV technique may not work very well since the system has only one signature to base its reference signature on. Further signatures will of course become available as the customer makes more purchases but then it is possible that those signatures are those of the genuine customer and not a forger.

Yet another approach might be possible. In this approach, the customer uses the credit card as he or she would normally but his/her signatures are captured electronically and compared with a signature profile that has been built over the last few weeks or months. When the result of comparison shows a significant mismatch then a suitable action is taken which may include either rejecting the purchase being charged to the card or, preferably bringing the mismatch information to the attention of a human operator who can take appropriate action.

HSV might also have uses in computer authentication. If a HSV technique could be designed that provided a high level of security against intruders through a zero or near zero FAR (False Acceptance Ratio). It might be suitable for user authentication not only at log-in time but also for accessing sensitive applications e.g., sensitive databases or exclusive software. A typical dynamic HSV system will of course require that a signature input device like graphics tablet be connected to each workstation to capture signature details.

This technique has the potential to replace the password mechanisms for accessing computer system in some situations (R. Eberhart, P. Simpson & R. Dobbins, 1996). The major disadvantage of this approach of course is the requirement that a graphics tablet be attached to each workstation. Reliable HSV could well have other applications. For example, it might assist in reducing the forging of passports. An application form and signatures be certified in the presence of an authorized officer. It is thus not unreasonable that the office where a passport application is filed may require the applicant to provide a set of sample signatures which are captured electronically and used for building a referenced signature. That reference signature could then be placed on a magnetic strip on the passport, moreover passports in the future are likely to have magnetic strips for faster processing anyway.

At the port of entry, at the immigration counter, the person entering the country is then required to sign his or her name on the graphics tablet and the signature is compared with the reference signature on the passport strip. Forging of passports will then be almost impossible. A number of commercial products in HSV are already being advertised and some are listed here. The list is not comprehensive since growth in this field is quite fast and there is no simple mechanism to find a list of all products in the field. A product called PENOP is being marketed by Peripheral Vision of New York and it is claimed that the software may be used in configuring systems so that users must login using handwritten signatures. Another product called Sign-On it is claimed allows HSV to be built-in to a variety of widely used software enabling the system to use a handwritten signature instead of a password. It uses, besides the signature image, acceleration, stroke angles, start and stop pressures (if available) and other factors.

CONCLUSION

A new approach for verification and recognition of signatures is presented in this work by using Service Oriented Architecture in web services. Projection moments and envelope features have been used for characterizing the signatures. Combination of these features is used to enhance reliability of the conclusions. Consequently, in case of confusion in classification on the basis of one of feature set, other feature sets can help in a symbolic fashion. It was typically found that many signatures are composed of multiple components. Some of these components do not carry significant shape information. For example, a curved line drawn below the main body of the signature must be separated out because it does not convey significant information about the identity of the writer. SOA separates functions into distinct units or services, thus users can combine and reuse them in the production of various applications via modularity of functions. The SOA features used in the approach makes it more effective. This would also reduce computational overhead of the scheme.

REFERENCES

Adriaana, P., & Zantinge, D. (2002). *Data Mining*. Pearson Education Asia.

Bragg, R., Rhodes-ousley, M., & Strassberg, K. (2004). Network security. *TataMc-GrawHill*.

Eberhart, R., Simpson, P., & Dobbins, R. (1996). *Computational Intelligence- PC Tools*. Boston: AP Professional.

Feldman, A., Greenberg, A., Lund, C., Reingold, N., Rexford, J., & True, F. (2001). Deriving traffic demands for operational IP Networks: Methodology and Experience. *IEEE/ACM Transactions on Networking*, 9(3), 265–280.

Fox, G. (2004). Grids of Grids of Simple Services. *Computing in Science & Engineering*, 6(4), 84–87.

Han, J., Kamber, M., & Pei, J. (2011). *Data Mining: Concepts and Techniques* (pp. 192–203). New Delhi: Morgan Kaufmann.

Hashimi, S. (2004). *Service-Oriented Architecture Explained*. O'Reilly.

Hirsh, F., Kemp, J., & Ilkka, J. (2006). *Mobile Web Services - Architecture and Implementation*. John Wiley and Sons. doi:10.1002/9780470017982

Information technology - Vocabulary - Part 1: Fundamental terms. (2005). International Standards Organization (ISO).

ISO/IEC 2382-01 Information Technology - Open Distributed Processing - Use of UML for ODP system specifications. (2005). International Standards Organization (ISO), committee draft v02.00 edition.

Jang, J. S. R., Sun, C. T., & Mizutani, E. (2004). *Neuro-Fuzzy and soft computing. PHI*. Pearson Education.

Koenen, R.H., Lacy, J., Mackay, M., & Mitchell, S. (2006). The long march to interoperable digital rights management. *Proceedings of the IEEE*, 92(6), 883-897. Retrieved from http://ieeexplore.ieee.org/iel5/5/28864/01299164.pdf

Madana Kumar Reddy. C. (2009). Operating Systems Made easy (pp. 23-49). New Delhi: University Science Press.

Oriezy, P. et al.. (1999). An Architecture-Based Approach to Self-Adaptive Software. *IEEE Intelligent Systems*, 14(3).

Peng, Z.R., & Tsou, M. (2003). Internet GIS: Distributed Geographic Information Services for the Internet and Wireless Networks. Wiley.

Prasad, S. (2014). Signature Analysis and Trait Prediction. LAP Lambert Academic Publishing.

Pressman R., S., & Maxim, B. (2008). *Software Engineering: A Practitioner's Approach*. McGraw Hill.

Rajasekaran, S., & Pai, G. A. V. (2003). Neural Networks, Fuzzy Logic and Genetic Algorithms. PHI, Pearson Education.

Reference Model for Service Oriented Architecture. (2006). OASIS. Retrieved from http://www.oasis-open.org/committees/download.php/19679/soa-rm-cs.pdf

Yeung, D.-Y., *Chang, H., Xiong, Y., George, S., Kashi, R., Matsumoto, T., & Rigoll, G.* (2004). *SVC2004: First International Signature Verification Competition. In D. Zhang, A.K. Jain (Eds.), Biometric Authentication*, LNCS (Vol. 3072, pp. 16–22). .

Chapter 16
Quantitative Evaluation of Web2.0 Application

Jibitesh Mishra
College of Engineering and Technology, India

Kabita Rani Naik
College of Engineering and Technology, India

ABSTRACT

Web 2.0 is a new generation of web applications where the users are able to participate, collaborate and share the created artefacts. Web 2.0 is all about the collective intelligence. Web 2.0 applications are widely used for all the educational, professional, business and entertainment purposes. But a methodology for quantitative evaluation of web2.0 application quality is still not available. With the advancement of web technology various dimensions to evaluate web2.0 application quality is changing. So studies will be made to select a quality model that is required for web 2.0 application. Then the quantitative analysis will be done on the basis of questionnaire method and statistical formula. Quantitative analysis is necessary to know the weakness and strength of a website and then to improve the web quality. Quantitative evaluation can also be used for comparing two or more websites. In this study, quantitative analysis is done for each quality attribute of two social networking sites. Then the two sites are compared on the basis of the quantitative value of quality.

INTRODUCTION

Quality in all the fields like business, manufacturing and engineering has a pragmatic interpretation as the superiority of something. Quality is also defined as fitness for purpose. Quality is a perceptual, conditional, and subjective attribute and may be different for different people. Every user focuses on the quality and specification of a product or service. They compare the product or service with the competitors in the market. The producers might measure the conformance quality, or the degree to which the product or service was produced correctly. A quality product or service has the ability to attract users and perform satisfactorily in the market. So, the evaluation of quality is very much important. But there is not a consolidated methodology for the evaluation of website quality. Web-based applications are fast

DOI: 10.4018/978-1-4666-9764-5.ch016

becoming larger, more widespread, more interactive, and more essential. The most successful Web-based application companies are realizing that the critical factors for success or failure of any Website must be dependable on delivering a high-quality website. To achieve the desired quality of a Web-based application, it is necessary to suggest a model that organizes and enables the identification of Web-based application quality perspectives. The development and usage of Web applications in different platforms and devices are continuously increasing. Web 2.0 applications have become the most popular in mobile phones now a day.

Web 2.0 describes the website that uses technology beyond the static pages of earlier web1.0 websites. The term Web2.0 was coined by Darcy Dinucci and was popularized by Tim O'Reilly (O'Reilly, 2005) at the O'Reilly Media Web 2.0 conference in late 2004. Although Web 2.0 suggests a new version of the World Wide Web, but it does not refer to any upgrade of any technical specification. It refers to cumulative changes in the way web pages are made and used. A Web 2.0 application may allow the user to interact and collaborate with each other in a social media. Web2.0 allows the users to create their own content in a virtual community where as web1.0 is only limited to the passive viewing of content. In web1.0 there is a content provider who publishes something on the websites and the users read it or download it. So web1.0 is read only application which allow only download of content. But in web2.0 there is active participation of users. Web2.0 supports both upload and download. Web2.0 is about sharing information and knowledge. The content of web2.0 applications are highly dynamic and changes continuously with time. Examples of Web 2.0 include social networking sites, blogs, wikis, video sharing sites, hosted services, web applications, mashups etc.

According to Tim O'Reilly (O'Reilly,2005, O'Reilly,2006), the Web 2.0 is considered as a new version of the Web and it does no longer consider the user as a consumer of information, but rather as a producer who is a potential for the realization of the contents of the Web (Hussher,2006). The quantity of information is increasing significantly, which will offer the possibility of production, communication, sharing and dissemination of content by users. Thus, a collective intelligence on the network is necessary. According to Cavazza (Cavazza, 2005) "Web 2.0 is a marketing concept for some people, a vague term for others, Web 2.0 suffers from a lack of explanation of its impact."

The Web 2.0 is not a standard. But it is a series of principles for the use of existing technology. Web 2.0 allows users to modify and renew the contents making it an area of information storage, which is not only flexible but also in continuous movement. Taking into consideration that the amount of data has never been more important, the function of information dissemination is exploding with the advent of collaborative applications and platforms of wikis and blogs (Hussher, 2006).

Web 2.0 applications are generally a combination of one or more technologies such as AJAX (Asynchronous JavaScript and XML (Extended Mark-up Language)), Flux, Mash up etc. in website development. Web2.0 applications provide richer user experiences through robust functions and elegant user interfaces (O'Reilly, 2005, Ogawa, 2006). The aim of Web2.0 application development is the real-time communication between websites and the users or among various users and thereby enhancing the website quality and rich user experience. Web 2.0 environments are all about collective intelligence. Collective intelligence applications depend on understanding, managing, and responding to monolithic amounts of user-generated data in real-time. Thus, real-time data usage is the backbone of the next generation of web 2.0 applications (Saha, 2011).

According to Rajeev Saha and Sandeep Grover (Saha, 2011) the most significant characteristics of Web 2.0 service are the Web as Platform, User-centred Design, Rich User Experience, Crowd-sourcing and Collaboration.

1. **The Web as Platform:** Applications based on web 2.0 do not depend on the browser or operating system. It can be run in any operating system like Window and Mac. It can also be run in any web browser like Mozilla Firefox, Google chrome, Internet Explorer. Web 2.0 application runs in desktop, laptop as well as mobile phones. In Web 1.0 user had to download supportive programs onto the desktop for accessing various web applications, but Web 2.0 application doesn't require any auxiliary software to run a service. The web 2.0 applications are self-reliant with its own working environment acts as its platform. Using cloud computing technique, more and more web services are taking the route of SaaS (Software as a Service). The Software is available as a web service with no platform dependency at all.

2. **User-Centred Design:** The attraction of a web page depends upon the degree of user's capability to perform certain customizations within the design of the website. The appearance of the design may be modified according to a user's need and choice. User-centred designs are the main attraction of web2.0 application. One of the most appropriate examples of a User-cantered design is iGoogle, a customizable Google homepage.

3. **Rich User Experience:** A great user experience is a main reason for a user to come back again to the web service. Use of XHTML, Ajax, CSS 2.0, Mashups, flex, and other rich media producing technologies have helped to make web services faster, lighter, less cluttered and more appealing to the end user.

4. **Crowd-Sourcing:** Web 2.0 services are proactive and highly dynamic in nature due to user's contribution and active participation towards its contents. A large number of such contributions lead the website to the state of higher relevance. Blogs are producing relevant content frequently as millions of users are acting as a contributor, and it helps in building up a large resource within the much lesser span of time.

5. **Collaboration:** Collaboration is the process of extraction of useful content from the content provider website and displaying it on some another website. The content being regularly checked and updated by content providers or concerned users. The provided information is of good quality. One of the best examples of collaboration is Wikipedia.

The success of web 2.0 applications depends on their capability to attract more users and satisfy the user's needs. This has led to increase attention on quality models, processes and methods that facilitate understanding, evaluating the overall quality of products, service and processes. By quantifying the quality of websites one can compare it with other websites, competitor; one can know the strength and weakness of a website and use it according to his needs. The designers of a website can also know their strength and weakness and this encourage them to improve the website quality. So efforts are made in this chapter to use the quality model proposed by Tihomir Orehovacki, Andrina Granic, Dragutin Kermek in 2013 to quantify the quality.

BACKGROUND

A great amount of work is done in the area of Web 2.0 quality in the last decade. As the dependency on Web 2.0 increases, the need to assess the characteristics of Web 2.0 quality increases. Recently, research and studies are gathering on different models to evaluate the quality of Web2.0 application.

Since the 1970s, researchers and practitioners have been looking for ways to characterize software quality. They found that software artefact can be breakdown into constructs that can be assured and measured. This enables evaluation of quality through the evaluation of more detailed characteristics (ELdesouky, 2008). There are a significant number of quality models.

One of the first well-known quality models was James McCall's quality model (ELKorany, 2009). This quality model aimed towards the system developers and described the system development process. In this quality model, McCall tries to reduce the gap between developers and users. He has focused on a number of Software quality factors that reflect both the developers' priorities and the users' views. In McCall quality model, there are three major perspectives for identifying and defining the quality of software product. These are product revision, product transition and product operation. The model further explains detail about the three perspectives in a hierarchy of factors, criteria and metrics. The quality factors explain different types of system behavioural characteristics. The quality criterions are the attributes to one or more of the quality factors. The quality metric aims to capture some of the aspects of a quality criterion.

The ISO 9126 standard was first introduced in 1991. ISO/IEC 9126/2001 (ISO/IEC, 2003) standard defined software quality. Originally it was a thirteen page document. It elaborated the internal and external software qualities and their relation to software attributes. The software quality model defined in ISO 9126 follows the factor-criteria-metrics model proposed by McCall (Cavano, 1978). It identifies six major external quality factors, which are refined into criteria. These criteria are assessed by metrics measuring the design and the development process and the software itself. The ISO 9126 quality factors include functionality, reliability, usability, efficiency, maintainability and portability. These factors are further subdivided into sub-characteristics. For example, sub-characteristic of functionality are suitability, accuracy, security and interoperability. These sub-characteristics are comprehensive, that is, any component of software quality can be described in terms of some aspects of one or more of these six factors.

The ISO 9126 standard for software engineering product quality states that the main aim of software quality evaluation is to provide the quantitative reference for software products quality such as reliability, understandability and acceptability. The main weakness point here is the lack of a formal specification of key factors for the Web-based application quality. Traditional quality models are not suitable for Web-based applications because they do not address all the problems associated with the new features of Web-based applications. Therefore, ISO 9126 and different quality models of software were partially used as an initial step to identify a conceptual quality model for a Web-based application. Web 2.0 applications have some common characteristics with traditional software packages and other distinct characteristics that are particular to Web 2.0 application.

Web 2.0 applications are rapidly expanding into all sectors of our society and becoming a vitally necessary platform of any computer applications. Web 2.0 applications are ever-evolving, complex and rapidly updated software systems. Since 1994, many Web-based application quality models had appeared aiming to assess Web-based application quality characteristics.

Further many quality factors and attributes were studied to ensure having a comprehensive list of quality factors for web based application. Scalability and availability were added in quality models proposed for a web application. According to Pang (Pang, 2009), E-commerce websites are large and complex, but quality requirements demand the key performance of factors such as scalability, availability, performance, and security. This provides the biggest influence on the effective implementation of any Web 2.0 application.

In 2002, Albuquerque and Belchior (Albuquerque AB, Belchior AD, 2006) have identified a comprehensive set of software quality attributes and organised it into objectives where each objective is composed of a set of quality factors. Each quality factor is further divided into sub-factors.

During 2002, Eppler and Muenzenmayer (Beg, 2005, Burn,2005, Gabriel,2007, Cappiello,2009, Mich,2003) proposed Web 2.0 application content quality model. Content quality is a very important concern that must be taken into consideration when discussing the quality factors of Web 2.0 application. Content quality is commonly thought as a multi-dimensional concept with varying characteristics and attributes. Eppler's model divided quality of Web 2.0 application into two quality perspective: content quality and media quality. Content quality subdivided into two categories that are relevant information and sound information. Each category consists of dimensions. These mentioned content quality model framework varied in their approach and application. However, they share a number of same characteristics.

In 2000, Fitzpatrick presented Web-based application quality model considering five quality characteristics related to the World Wide Web domain, their sub-characteristics (sub-factors), and a checklist which can be used by all IS professionals as essential issues to be addressed when creating quality web applications. These characteristics are intelligibility, visibility, credibility, engaging the visitor and differentiation. Visibility refers to the degree to which a user can visit websites. Intelligibility refers to the ease with which a user can interpret and assimilate web content. Credibility refers to the level of user confidence with the content of the website. Engaging the visitor refers to the extent to which a user achieve a complete experience. And differentiation refers to the extent to which a website demonstrates corporate superiority.

Early in 2000, Luisa and Mariangela (Mich, 2003) proposed an original model for evaluating and designing the quality of the Web-based application. The model is named 2QCV3Q. It has been developed using classic rhetorical principles. It can be used for evaluation of the quality of the Web-based application and provide suggestions for improvements. Symmetrically, the model provides guidelines for the design of the Web-based application and allows identification and classification of the users' and owners' requirements.

Lu and Hong(Lu & Hong, 2005) introduced Interactivity quality model that is focused on the importance of interactivity factor in Web 2.0 application environment that can satisfy visitors. Interactivity features are extremely important to improve the communication quality, improve user satisfaction, engage users and hence make the application more usable and more acceptable. Ha and James' Interactivity model present five Web quality dimensions. These dimensions are connectedness, playfulness, choice, reciprocal communication and information collection. These dimensions require two-way communication.

There are a number of researches addressing the evaluation of usability, user experience, and quality in use of Web2.0 applications. Silva and Dix (Silva, 2007), Hart (Hart, 2008), Thompson and Kemp (Thompson, 2009) suggested that the reason for that might be the inappropriateness of current approaches for the evaluation of those applications. A research on usability assessment carried out by Hart (Hart, 2008) revealed that the popular social networking site Facebook complies with only two of ten heuristics originally proposed by Nielsen (Nielsen, 1995). They also described that the attributes such as usefulness, ease of use, and playfulness have a major impact on users' loyal behaviour. In conventional usability evaluation, YouTube scores badly, meeting only two of previously mentioned traditional heuristics (Silva, 2007). Thompson and Kemp (Thompson, 2009) reported that one of the main reasons for having a large number of active user in Web 2.0 applications such as Flicker, Wikipedia and YouTube is their focus on user experience. They modified and extended a set of Nielsen's traditional heuristics with an objective to evaluate the usability of Web 2.0 applications. However, the validity of the proposed set of heuristics has so far not been empirically confirmed. Based on twenty-eight studies related to the evaluation of websites, Pang (Pang, 2009) has proposed a model for evaluating the quality of Web 2.0 applications. This model consists of five first-order dimensions and twenty-five second-order dimensions. But till now, the authors have not provided any empirical evidence that their model is actually appropriate for evaluating the Web 2.0 applications. In 2011, Rajeev Saha and Sandeep Grover (Saha, 2011) proposed a quality model where web2.0 quality dimensions are classified into five major categories interface, performance, information, service, emotional and twenty-eight second-order dimensions. There are various researches mostly focused on the development of methods and models aimed for the evaluation of particular aspects of the quality in use for example accessibility (Brown, 2012) or information quality (Almeida, 2010) or types of Web 2.0 applications like mashups (Cappiello, 2009).

Several Web 2.0 application quality factors have recently been proposed. However, most of them are built upon the previously Web-based quality models and devoted for empirically validating. In 2013, the quality model proposed by Tihomir Orehovacki, Andrina Granic, Dragutin Kermek (Orehovački, 2013) was mainly used for Web 2.0 applications. The developed conceptual model classifies quality attributes into six basic categories: system quality, service quality, information quality, performance, effort and acceptability. The qualities are further divided into 33 sub-attributes. This quality model covers all most all the quality attribute of web2.0 application. So, in this study the quality model is followed for quality evaluation.

METHODOLOGY

To quantify the quality attribute, some step by step procedure is followed in this study. There are already large numbers of quality models present in literature. So, here main focus has been given to quantify the quality of web2.0 application. Before that, a suitable quality model is selected from previously proposed models. Here the researchers present a generalised methodology which can be used in all types of web 2.0 application. So questionnaire method is the best choice for this study.

Figure 1 represents the Block Diagram of methodology employed for quantification of web 2.0 application quality. This study aims to identify a quality model and to quantify various quality attribute by a numerical index. Then analysis and comparison of various quality factors of web 2.0 application are done.

The first step of this study is to identify a quality model for web 2.0 application. Here the quality model proposed by Tihomir Orehovacki, Andrina Granic, Dragutin Kermek is followed. As this study is based on a survey, the second step is to select the measuring scale and method. In previous studies, Quantification of web quality is done for a particular application. So to avoid this limitation in this study the questionnaires method and Likert scale is used. In the third step, various questionnaires are prepared. The questions are prepared in such a way that it can be used for any type of web 2.0 application. The fourth step is to select web 2.0 applications for the survey. In this study, the authors have selected the two popular social networking sites Facebook and Twitter. One major limitation of the previous study was the homogeneity of participants so in this study the fifth step is to select participant coming from the different background. Then the next steps are to conduct the survey and quantify the quality. In the survey, some questions are asked to participants. Five options are given for a question and participant has to select one option. The options are the parameter of Likert scale. Then quantification is done by finding the mean of the collected value.

Figure 1. Block Diagram of Methodology for Quantification of Web 2.0 application Quality

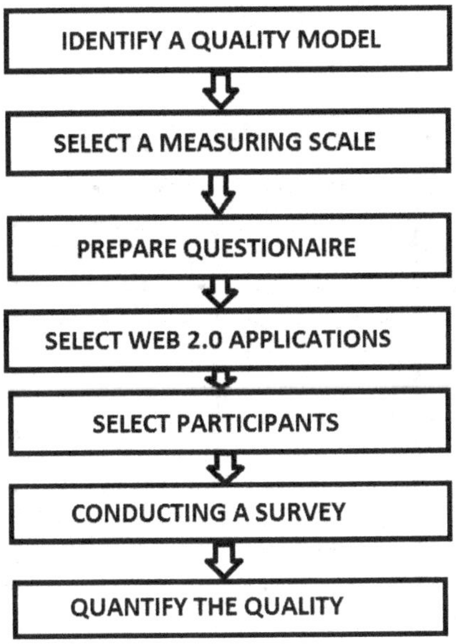

Identify a Quality Model

According to ISO/IEC 25000:2005, a quality model is a "defined set of characteristics, and relationships between them, which provides a framework for specifying quality requirements and evaluating quality." In this study, the quality model proposed by Tihomir Orehovaˇcki, Andrina Granic, Dragutin Kermek (Orehovaˇcki, 2013) was chosen as the reference point. They proposed a conceptual quality model which classifies quality attributes into six basic categories: system quality, service quality, content quality, performance, effort and acceptability. Figure 2 shows the quality model for evaluating the quality in use of web 2.0 applications proposed by Tihomir Orehovacki, Andrina Granic, Dragutin Kermek.

System Quality measures quality in use of Web 2.0 application at the level of its interface features. It is again subdivided into six attributes: navigability, consistency, aesthetic, familiarity, customizability, and security. Navigability is the degree to which interface elements are well organized and offers alternative navigation mechanisms. Consistency may be defined as the degree to which the same design, structure, terminology and components are used throughout of a Web 2.0 application. Aesthetic means visual attractiveness of web interface. Familiarity is the degree to which web interface is similar to previously used applications. Customizability refers to the degree to which interface elements can be adapted to the characteristics of the task or user. Security is the extent to which personal data and files are protected from unauthorized access.

Service quality is an extent of quality of interaction and communication between user and Web 2.0 application. This quality is further decomposed into eight sub-attributes: helpfulness, availability, interactivity, error prevention, reliability, recoverability, responsiveness, feedback. Helpfulness is the degree to which web application contains features for user's assistance and help. Availability is the extent to which interface elements are continuously accessed and websites are almost always available without a frequent period of unavailability. Interactivity feature means the degree to which Web 2.0 application creates a feeling for the use of the desktop application. Error prevention is the degree to which Web ap-

Figure 2. Quality Model for evaluating the quality in use of Web 2.0 applications proposed by Tihomir Orehovacki, Andrina Granic, Dragutin Kermek

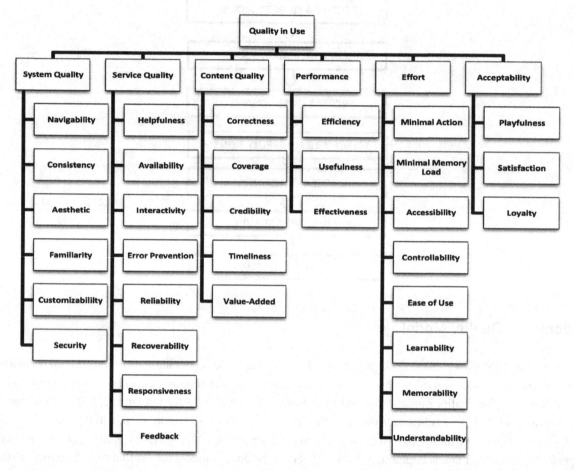

plication prevents the occurrences of errors. Reliability means the extent to which Web 2.0 application works without errors or interruptions. Recoverability is the degree to which Web 2.0 application can recover from errors and interruptions in its running. Responsiveness implies the extent of the speed of Web 2.0 application response to users' requests, query and actions. Feedback means the extent to which Web 2.0 application displays its status or progress at any time.

Content Quality refers to the quality of content which is the result of using a Web 2.0 application. This quality further decomposes into five sub-attributes: correctness, coverage, credibility, timeliness, value-added. Correctness corresponds to the degree to which information content is free of errors. Coverage means the extents to which information content is complete, appropriate, and compactly represented. Credibility means the degree to which information content is unbiased, trustworthy and verifiable. Timeliness attribute represents the degree to which information content is up to date. Value-added is the degree to which information content is advantageous and fresh.

The performance captures the quality of performing assignments by means of Web 2.0 application interface functionalities. This category contains three attributes: effectiveness, usefulness, efficiency. Effectiveness is the degree to which assignment can be achieved accurately and completely. Usefulness refers to the degree to which user perceives Web 2.0 application as the most appropriate solution for performing an assignment. Efficiency implies the degree to which goal can be achieved with the minimal consumption of resources.

Effort can be defined as an extent of perceived and estimated physical and mental energy when executing a task with Web 2.0 applications. This category is sub-classified into eight attributes: minimal action, minimal memory load, accessibility, and controllability, ease of use, learnability, memorability and understandability. Minimal action means the degree to which assignment solution can be achieved in a minimum number of steps. Minimal memory load means the amount of information the user needs to remember when carrying out a specific task in web2.0 application. Accessibility is the degree to which Web 2.0 application can be used by people with the widest range of disabilities. Controllability is the level of user's freedom while completing the task. As the name suggests ease of use means the degree to which Web 2.0 application can be used without help. Learnability measures how easily the user can learn to use Web 2.0 application functionalities. Memorability measures how easy it is to remember and memorize the steps to use the Web 2.0 application. Understandability refers to the extent to which interface elements are clear and unambiguous to the user.

Acceptability directly contributes to the success of a Web 2.0 application. Acceptability is the attribute which measures likeability and behavioural intentions related to the Web 2.0 application usage. It includes playfulness, satisfaction, and loyalty. Playfulness is the extent to which using a Web 2.0 application is fun and stimulating. Satisfaction is the degree to which Web 2.0 application can meet user's expectations. Loyalty means the users' intention to continue to use Web2.0 application or to recommend it to their colleagues.

In this study, this quality model is chosen because it covers almost all the web2.0 application quality.

Select a Measuring Scale

This study is based on a Survey and for this questionnaire method is followed. There are varieties of scale to measure user's response. At a first glance, all the different scales look similar and seem easily replaceable by each other. But after studying and analyzing them in depth, one can realize the diversity of their natures. They are different in their uses and findings. There are more than 20 different types of scales that are used by researchers in surveys.

There are a number of factors to be considered in choosing an appropriate scale. According to Ivana Taylor (Taylor, 2012) some of the factors are, the type of data that is required from the respondent such as ratio, interval, ordinal or nominal, number of divisions in the scale such as even or odd, how the information will be analyzed once it is acquired, type of statistical analysis methods and process to be used after data is collected, the physical form of the scale like vertical, linear, horizontal, whether response to a question is mandatory or not mandatory.

Taylar (Taylor, 2012) describes 4 types of scales for a survey. These scales are given below.

Graphic Rating Scale: A graphic rating scale is a scale where the two ends of the scale are sometimes labeled with opposite values. This scale is also known as a continuous rating scale. In this scale, the respondents have to mark at a point on the scale that they consider appropriate. Sometimes, there are also numbers or values along with the markings of the line. Sometimes, there are no markings at all on the line and only two values at both the end of the line. This scale is suitable for the online survey. For the offline survey, this scale is not appropriate. So in this study this scale is not used.

Semantic Differential Scale (Max Diff): Semantic Differential Scale is also known as Max Diff scale. A semantic scale is a combination of more than one continuum. It usually contains an odd number of radio buttons with labels at opposite ends. Semantic Differential Scales are often used in trade-off analysis such as conjoint. Max Diff analysis mainly used in new product features research or in market segmentation research. It is used to get accurate orderings of the most important product features. So the authors ruled out this scale for this survey.

Side-by-Side Matrix: Another type of scale used in research is a side-by-side matrix. This scale is very commonly used in questionnaires. The side-by-side matrix is used for the importance/satisfaction type of question. This type of scale is a combination of two type of matrix. The first matrix is about the importance and the second matrix is about satisfaction. First, questions are asked to the respondents about the importance of an attribute. Then the respondents have to answer how satisfied they are with the performance in that area. But this scale is also not fitted in this survey. Because here the authors need only one response for one question, not both importance/satisfaction responses.

Likert Scale: A Likert scale is a psychometric scale. It is commonly used in research that employs questionnaires. A Likert scale generally contains an odd number of options for a question, usually 5 to 7. Like the Graphic Rating Scale, here also the two ends of the scale are labeled with opposite values. One end is labelled as the most positive option while the other end is labelled as the most negative option and the middle of the scale is labelled as 'neutral'. The phrases like 'mostly negative', 'purely negative', 'extremely disagree' and 'slightly disagree' are used in this scale. Likert scale was invented by Rensis Likert and the scale was named after him. This scale is appropriate for this survey.

Likert Scale is the most widely used approach to scaling responses in survey research when questionnaires are used. In simple words, it is a type of rating scale. When responding to a Likert questionnaire item, the respondents stipulate their level of agreement or disagreement on a symmetric agrees disagrees scale for a series of questions or statements. Thus, the range captures the intensity of their feelings for a given item. A Likert item is simply a statement that the respondent is asked to evaluate by giving it a quantitative value on any kind of subjective or objective dimension, with level of agreement or disagreement being the dimension most commonly used. Well-designed Likert items exhibit symmetry and balance property. Symmetry means the scale contains equal numbers of positive and negative responses whose respective distances are bilaterally symmetric from the "neutral" or zero position. Balance means the distance between each candidate value is the same. This allows good quantitative comparisons such as averaging being valid across items containing more than two candidate values. Generally five ordered response levels are used most of the time. But many surveyors advise to use seven or nine ordered response levels. Likert scaling is a bipolar scaling method, measuring either positive or negative response to a statement. Sometimes an even point scale is used, where the middle option of "Neutral" is not available. A recent empirical study found that items with five or seven levels may produce slightly higher mean scores relative to the highest possible attainable score, compared to those produced from the use of 10 levels. This difference was statistically significant. When considering other data characteristics, there was a very small difference among the scale formats in terms of variation about the mean, skewness.

In this study five-level Likert scale is used. The Likert scale is very simple and easy to use. One can take any level of Likert scale according to their need. The surveyor can decide values of parameters independently. One can take any type of phrases in scale as desired. In this survey, four types of attributes are used in Likert scale. In one type 'strongly disagree', 'disagree', 'neither agree nor disagree', 'agree', 'strongly agree' phrases are used where value of 'strongly disagree' is 1, value of 'disagree' is 2, value of 'neither agree nor disagree' is 3, value of 'agree' is 4 and value of 'strongly agree' is 5. In another scale the options are 'Not Similar', 'Less Similar', 'Average', 'Similar', 'Very Similar' where 'Not Similar' choice means rating is 1, 'Less Similar 'choice means rating is 2, 'Average 'choice means rating is 3, 'Similar 'choice means rating is 4, 'Very Similar' choice means rating is 5. Similarly in the third type of Likert like scale the phrases include 'extremely satisfied', 'satisfied', 'average', 'dissatisfied', 'extremely dissatisfied' where 'extremely satisfied' means 5, 'satisfied' means 4, 'average' means 3, 'dissatisfied' means 2, 'extremely dissatisfied' means 1. In the fourth type of Likert-like scale the phrases include 'very good', 'good', 'average', 'bad', 'very bad' where 'very good' means 5, 'good' means 4, 'average' means 3, 'bad' means 2, 'very bad' means 1. After the questionnaire is completed, each item may be analyzed separately. In some cases, the item responses are summed to create a score for a group of items. Hence, Likert scales are otherwise called as summative scales.

Prepare Questionnaire

Generally, selecting a measuring scale and preparing questionnaire is a parallel process. The Questionnaire is prepared in such a way that it can be used for any type of web2.0 application. This Questionnaire can be asked for either social networking site or informative and educational web application or video sharing site. About 4 to 10 questions are asked to participants for each quality attribute. When large numbers of questions are asked in questionnaire method the participants may feel bored and the answers may be biased. So to avoid this problem the questions for different qualities are asked on different days.

The Prepared Questionnaire and respective Likert scale options for the survey are given below.

System Quality

- **Navigation:** (Question number 1 to 5 the options are 'extremely satisfied', 'satisfied', 'average', 'dissatisfied', 'extremely dissatisfied', Question number 6 to 7 the options are 'strongly disagree', 'disagree', 'neither agree nor disagree', 'agree', 'strongly agree')
    1. Ability to navigate within the website?
    2. Stylist indication of the clickable item?
    3. Readability? Consider type of face, font size, color contrast
    4. Availability of link to the opening page on each subsequent page or keyword-based search feature?
    5. The Layout of the site?
    6. It avoids opening of unnecessary new browser windows.
    7. The system track where the user was in the last session (and any progress made).
- **Consistency:** (Question number 1 to 5 the options are 'Not Similar', 'Less Similar', 'Average', 'Similar', 'Very Similar')
    1. How similar are the organization and layout of pages with the opening page? Stylist indication of the clickable item?
    2. IIow is the use of the same terminology throughout the application?
    3. How alike is the use of spacing, layers, tables, borders, dividers and backgrounds throughout the application?
    4. How similar is the use of colour and shapes in all pages of the website?
    5. How similar the fonts and letter size throughout the application?

- **Aesthetic:** (Question number 1 to 5 the options are 'very good', 'good', 'average', 'bad', 'very bad')
  1. How is the site's design? (Aesthetically appealing, pleasing)?
  2. How are the colours used in the website? (Harmonious and logically related)?
  3. How are the graphic and multimedia content of the website (likely to attract and appeal people or distract from the content)?
  4. How are the audio and video component's qualities?
  5. How is the graphics in the website? (Clear and easy to understand or access)?
- **Familiarity:** (Question number 1 to 4 the options are 'Not Similar', 'Less Similar', 'Average', 'Similar', 'Very Similar')
  1. How similar is the terminology with the previously used application?
  2. How similar is the structure or layout with the previous application?
  3. How similar is the execution of the task with the previous application?
  4. How similar is the icons and symbols with other application?
- **Customizability:** (Question number 1 to 5 the options are 'extremely satisfied', 'satisfied', 'average', 'dissatisfied', 'extremely dissatisfied')
  1. Support for choosing language
  2. Support for changing the background?
  3. Support for choosing layout?
  4. Support for changing colour?
  5. Support for marking, deleting, viewing by own choice?
- **Security:** (Question number 1 to 5 the options are 'extremely satisfied', 'satisfied', 'average', 'dissatisfied', 'extremely dissatisfied')
  1. The presence of the mechanism to avoid obvious security flaws?
  2. The resiliency of forms to special characters?
  3. Password protection of private files?
  4. Availability of setting to block access?
  5. Safeguarded of customer data appropriately against external access?

Service Quality

- **Helpfulness:** (Question number 1 to 5 the options are 'extremely satisfied', 'satisfied', 'average', 'dissatisfied', 'extremely dissatisfied')
  1. Availability of various types of help?
  2. The presence of FAQ?
  3. The presence of video tutorials?
  4. How clear and comprehensible are the instruction?
  5. The presence of large-print or audio options for the visually impaired?
- **Availability:** (Question number 1 to 5 the options are 'strongly disagree', 'disagree', 'neither agree nor disagree', 'agree', 'strongly agree')
  1. The site is almost always available (no frequent periods of unavailability)?
  2. Heavy traffic and/or limited connections do not affect site access?
  3. It notifies the user about the close of a site due to upgrade and maintenance?

4. The Site does not need any proprietary software, helper applications or plug-ins?

5. Downtime of the site is satisfactory?

- **Interactivity:** (Question number 1 to 5 the options are 'extremely satisfied', 'satisfied', 'average', 'dissatisfied', 'extremely dissatisfied')

  1. Facility of a text message?
  2. Availability of bulletin boards?
  3. Facility of video chat and audio chat?
  4. Facility of giving comments?
  5. Message sending technique?

- **Error Prevention:** (Question number 1 to 5 the options are 'strongly disagree', 'disagree', 'neither agree nor disagree', 'agree', 'strongly agree')

  1. It asks user approval for any action.
  2. It asks for confirmation message for action like the update, delete, upload.
  3. It shows the warning message.
  4. It verifies the content, check grammar and spelling before posting.
  5. Undo, the redo feature is available.

- **Reliability:** (Question number 1 to 5 the options are 'strongly disagree', 'disagree', 'neither agree nor disagree', 'agree', 'strongly agree')

  1. The website is free from server side errors.
  2. The scripts are free from errors.
  3. It avoids breakdown.
  4. It does not repeat the same error.
  5. The information has been reviewed by others to ensure accuracy.

- **Recoverability:** (Question number 1 to 2 the options are 'extremely satisfied', 'satisfied', 'average', 'dissatisfied', 'extremely dissatisfied', Question number 3 the options are 'strongly disagree', 'disagree', 'neither agree nor disagree', 'agree', 'strongly agree')

  1. How does it react to interrupt?
  2. How fast will it recover from error and interrupt?
  3. The Work was done before an interrupt is not lost.

- **Responsiveness:** (Question number 1 to 5 the options are 'extremely satisfied', 'satisfied', 'average', 'dissatisfied', 'extremely dissatisfied')

  1. How fast you get reply for your query?
  2. How quickly the pages are loaded?
  3. How fast upload is done?
  4. How fast download is done?
  5. How fast is the action like delete, update and post?

- **Feedback:** (Question number 1 to 5 the options are 'strongly disagree', 'disagree', 'neither agree nor disagree', 'agree', 'strongly agree')

  1. The website has a Contact Us page with real address, phone number.
  2. Contact form or email available, basically a clear and easy to use feedback/contact mechanism.
  3. It notifies user regularly about what is going on.
  4. For each activity done, the application displays an appropriate message.
  5. Show status of loading, uploading, downloading.

Content Quality

- **Correctness:** (Question number 1 to 6 the options are 'strongly disagree', 'disagree', 'neither agree nor disagree', 'agree', 'strongly agree')
    1. The material of this site is unique, useful, and accurate. It is not derivative, repetitious, or doubtful.
    2. The content of the page is well written, with no grammar, typographical error and no spelling mistakes.
    3. The website is free of errors and disproven theories.
    4. For primary source information, the research methods are adequately described and explained. And for secondary source information, the sources of information are given.
    5. It generally agrees with other sources for similar information.
    6. The information of the site is valid.
- **Coverage:** (Question number 1 to 6 the options are 'strongly disagree', 'disagree', 'neither agree nor disagree', 'agree', 'strongly agree')
    1. The purpose of the resource is clearly stated.
    2. The site contains original information, not simply links.
    3. The representation of information is in a well-defined order.
    4. The information is subjective, not objective.
    5. It is totally free and there is no fee to obtain the information.
    6. There is no under construction page.
- **Credibility:** (Question number 1 to 5 the options are 'strongly disagree', 'disagree', 'neither agree nor disagree', 'agree', 'strongly agree')
    1. The information is trustworthy.
    2. It is full of fact, not opinion.
    3. The experience and skills of the author are satisfactory.
    4. The source of information is given and verified.
    5. The author can be contacted anytime for clarification.
- **Timeliness:** (Question number 1 to 6 the options are 'strongly disagree', 'disagree', 'neither agree nor disagree', 'agree', 'strongly agree')
    1. The content of the page need not to be updated (It contains Historical Data).
    2. The content is produced recently.
    3. The resource is frequently updated.
    4. There are no dead links on the page.
    5. The information on the pages is not outdated.
    6. The links in the site are up-to-date.
- **Value-Added:** (Question number 1 to 5 the options are 'strongly disagree', 'disagree', 'neither agree nor disagree', 'agree', 'strongly agree')
    1. Using this Website helps me to get a better decision.
    2. The information is very much useful.
    3. The site offers things not found elsewhere.
    4. The website encourages ongoing learning and further investigation.
    5. The facts contribute something new or add value to your knowledge of the subject.

Performance

- **Efficiency:** (Question number 1 to 5 the options are 'strongly disagree', 'disagree', 'neither agree nor disagree', 'agree', 'strongly agree')
  1. All of the pages within the site load quickly.
  2. The graphic content does not load a long time after the textual content has loaded.
  3. The information is quick to access.
  4. Searching for information in this website is an efficient way to manage my time.
  5. The website processing is fast.
- **Usefulness:** (Question number 1 to 7 the options are 'strongly disagree', 'disagree', 'neither agree nor disagree', 'agree', 'strongly agree')
  1. Using this website makes my job easier.
  2. It enhances performance in executing a task.
  3. It improves my task quality.
  4. It increases my task productivity.
  5. Using World Wide Web enables me to access a lot of information.
  6. The site is technologically impressive.
  7. Using this website saves my money.
- **Effectiveness:** (Question number 1 to 3 the options are 'strongly disagree', 'disagree', 'neither agree nor disagree', 'agree', 'strongly agree')
  1. Using the website enables me to accomplish tasks more quickly and accurately?
  2. The website supports to execute the critical part of my Tasks accurately?
  3. This Site enables me to have more accurate Information?

Effort

- **Minimal Action:** (Question number 1 to 4 the options are 'strongly disagree', 'disagree', 'neither agree nor disagree', 'agree', 'strongly agree')
  1. The page is well designed and easy to navigate, without too much clicking.
  2. The individual pages are not so long that excessive scrolling is necessary.
  3. It takes less number of links to get to something useful.
  4. Information can be searched by minimal key typing.
- **Minimal Memory Load:** (Question number 1 to 4 the options are 'strongly disagree', 'disagree', 'neither agree nor disagree', 'agree', 'strongly agree')
  1. Using this Web requires less mental effort.
  2. To achieve a particular task, users should keep a minimal deal of information in mind.
  3. Minimal memorizing is required to use the website.
  4. Minimal thinking and decision making is needed to use the website.
- **Accessibility:** (Question number 1 to 6 the options are 'strongly disagree', 'disagree', 'neither agree nor disagree', 'agree', 'strongly agree')
  1. It is viewable in different browsers.
  2. It viewable in different operating systems.
  3. The page doesn't require special software to view the information. Less amount of information is missing without the software.

4. The user is not required to divulge personal information or to pay a usage fee.
5. The site is available for people with disabilities.
6. The site has a text-based alternative.

- **Controllability:** (Question number 1 to 5 the options are 'strongly disagree', 'disagree', 'neither agree nor disagree', 'agree', 'strongly agree')
  1. The user has full control on the site.
  2. The user has full freedom to the site.
  3. There are facilities provided to return to the top level at any stage (e.g. links back to the homepage).
  4. I find it easy to get this Web to do what I want it to do.
  5. I find this Website user-friendly.

- **Ease of Use:** (Question number 1 to 6 the options are 'strongly disagree', 'disagree', 'neither agree nor disagree', 'agree', 'strongly agree')
  1. Navigation within the website is fairly easy.
  2. The content is easy to read (both font style and size).
  3. It is easy to find information and services within the website.
  4. It is easy to search the website.
  5. The information is well-organized including a table of contents, index, menu, and other easy-to-follow tools for navigation.
  6. Background knowledge and experiences are not necessary to use the website.

- **Learnability:** (Question number 1 to 5 the options are 'strongly disagree', 'disagree', 'neither agree nor disagree', 'agree', 'strongly agree')
  1. Learning this Website is easy for me.
  2. It can be understood by people with various levels of education or/and from different cultural backgrounds.
  3. It is easy for me to become skilful by using this Website.
  4. The information of the site is clear and easy to understand.
  5. I can comprehend most components of a page within seconds.

- **Memorability:** (Question number 1 to 3 the options are 'strongly disagree', 'disagree', 'neither agree nor disagree', 'agree', 'strongly agree')
  1. I can easily remember how to reach the same page when I visit next time.
  2. As time passes, I am more accustomed to the website with less effort.
  3. I can easily remember the location of the particular feature even if the application is not used for a longer period of time.

- **Understandability:** (Question number 1 to 5 the options are 'strongly disagree', 'disagree', 'neither agree nor disagree', 'agree', 'strongly agree')
  1. How to use the website is clear and easy to understand.
  2. It is clearly stated why the page was written and for whom.
  3. The website does not have unnecessary components.
  4. There are not redundant components in the website.
  5. The website can be used without expert help.

Acceptability

- **Playfulness:** (Question number 1 to 12 the options are 'strongly disagree', 'disagree', 'neither agree nor disagree', 'agree', 'strongly agree')
    1. I find this portal overall an entertaining site.
    2. I browse the site for my pleasure.
    3. The index page attracts a visitor deeper into the site.
    4. The information is presented in an interesting manner, but not so creatively as to obscure its meaning.
    5. I find it enjoyable to use the site.
    6. When interacting with the website, my full attention is focused on the site.
    7. When interacting with the website, I do not realize the time elapsed and I forget the other work I must do.
    8. When interacting with the website, I am not aware of any noise.
    9. Using the site gives me enjoyment and fun for my task.
    10. Using the site keeps me happy for my task.
    11. Using the site stimulates my curiosity.
- **Satisfaction:** (Question number 1 to 5 the options are 'strongly disagree', 'disagree', 'neither agree nor disagree', 'agree', 'strongly agree', Question number 6 the options are 'excellent', 'good', 'similar', 'worse', 'worst')
    1. This site is appropriate for your needs. It fulfils its purpose.
    2. Using this site is a good and positive idea.
    3. Using this site is a wise idea.
    4. Using this site is a satisfactory idea.
    5. How does our website compare to similar websites you have visited?
- **Loyalty:** (Question number 1 to 6 the options are 'strongly disagree', 'disagree', 'neither agree nor disagree', 'agree', 'strongly agree')
    1. I recommend this website to friends or colleague in the future.
    2. The site is distinct and memorable.
    3. It encourages me to return to this site in the future.
    4. I feel that I have personal ties to the website.
    5. I feel as though I am emotionally connected to the website.
    6. I feel as though I am taking part with the website.

Select Web 2.0 Application

The prepared questionnaire can be asked for any web 2.0 application. But social networking sites are used for various purposes. Some users use it for communicating with friends in a virtual society. Some users use it for sharing information and some users use it for entertainment. Some users use it for finding some information like current news. For a comparative study of two similar web2.0 applications, Twitter and Facebook are selected. In this century, all are familiar with the two social networking sites. These names stir up feelings, opinions, and experiences in just about all of us. Some love Twitter or Facebook more than life itself while some others use it for time pass. Regardless of the level of involvement, there is no denying of the immense popularity of Facebook and Twitter. These two sites have a large number of users all over the world, and the users are from different educational and professional background. The two websites have almost all web 2.0 features. So in this study, these two popular social networking sites are chosen.

Twitter

Twitter is an online social networking site that enables users to send and read short 140-character messages called "tweets". Twitter was created in March 2006 by Jack Dorsey, Evan Williams, Biz Stone and Noah Glass. The website was launched in July 2006. The head office of Twitter is in San Francisco and over 35 offices around the world. Twitter is a free micro blogging website. In twitter, the registered users can read and post tweets, but unregistered users can also read them. But to post tweets users have to register in the website. The users can access Twitter through the website interface, SMS, or mobile device app. The service rapidly gained worldwide popularity, with more than 100 million users who in 2012 posted 340 million tweets per day. The service can also handle 1.6 billion search queries per day. In 2013, Twitter was one of the ten most-visited websites and has been described as "the SMS of the Internet." According to the data published in official twitter website as on June 30, 2015, Twitter has 316 million monthly active users, around 500 million tweets sent per day. There are 80% active users on mobile, 4100 employees around the world and 50% of the employees are the engineers. Over 35 languages are supported by twitter. Twitter has a search bar and a sidebar of "trending topics" the most common phrases appearing in messages. Biz Stone explains that all messages are instantly indexed and it reported "with this newly launched feature, Twitter has become something unexpectedly important – a discovery engine for finding out what is happening right now." Twitter experienced many security attacks, outages and error but it recovered from those and now it is a stable site with less downtime. The theme of twitter is "Discover what's happening in your world" and the mission of twitter is "To give everyone the power to create and share ideas and information instantly, without barriers".

Twitter messages are public, but users can also send private messages. Twitter collects personally identifiable information about its users and shares it with third parties. While Twitter displays no advertising, advertisers can target users based on their history of tweets and may quote tweets in ads directed specifically to the user. Twitter has also launched the beta version of their "Verified Accounts" service on June 11, 2009. It allows the famous or notable people to announce their Twitter account name. The home pages of these accounts display a badge indicating their status. Twitter has a "report abuse" button for all versions of the site. Twitter has also reporting and blocking policies. Twitter has its own integrated photo-sharing service that allows users to upload a photo and attach it to a tweet. Users can also add pictures to Twitter's search by adding hash tags to the tweet. These are some features of twitter. Besides these features twitter has many more features. So twitter is very popular now a day. People use Twitter to follow their favourite celebrities and know about them. People use twitter to know the current news as well as to share information. People can talk with each other in this virtual society.

Facebook

Facebook is also an online social networking service. The Headquarter of facebook is in Menlo Park, California. The website was launched on February 4, 2004, by Mark Zuckerberg with his college roommates and fellow Harvard University students Andrew McCollum, Eduardo Saverin, Chris Hughes and Dustin Moskovitz. Mark Zuckerberg is popularly known as the founder of Facebook. The mission of

Facebook is "to give people the power to share and make the world more open and connected". According to the official website of Facebook, "people use Facebook to stay connected with friends and family, to discover what's going on in the world, and to share and express what matters to them". Facebook allows anyone who claims to be at least 13 years old to become a registered user of the website. After registering to use the site, users can create their user profile, add other users as friends, following other users, post status updates and photos, exchange messages, share videos and receive notifications when others update their profiles. Facebook has its news Feed and Facebook Notes. Facebook provides messaging, voice calling, video calling, video viewing facility. The users can create various communities and join it. The users may also join common-interest user groups, organized by workplace, school or college, or other characteristics. The users can categorize their friends into different lists such as People from Work, family or Close Friends. There is facebook messenger which can be used for messaging, that is sending and receiving the text message, image, audio, and video. There is Facebook Lite for android. The user can play various games using facebook account. Facebook had over 1.3 billion active users as on June 2014. Due to the large volume of data collected about users, the service's privacy policies have faced scrutiny, among other criticisms. It also provides Tor hidden service for privacy purpose. There are many more features of facebook. Now a day facebook is very popular among user.

Participants

For this study, a survey is conducted and the participants in the survey are the users of Facebook and Twitter. According to Holzinger (Holzinger, 2005) thirty subjects are sufficient to reach 80% discovery rate when the questionnaire method is applied. A total of 50 participants aged 18 to 35 years, 23 (i.e. 46%) male and 27 (54%) female participated in the study. All of them are the users of both Facebook and Twitter. Figure 3 represents bar graph of age detail of the participants participated in the survey.

Figure 3. Bar graph of age detail of the participants

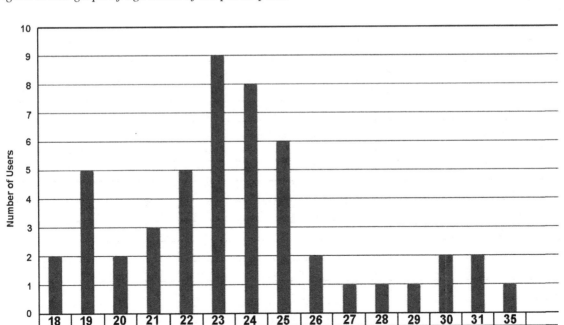

	18	19	20	21	22	23	24	25	26	27	28	29	30	31	35		
■Total	2	5	2	3	5	9	8	6	2	1	1	1	2	2	1		

Age

Table 1 shows the age and gender detail of the participants. Figure 4 shows corresponding bar graph of the age and gender detail of participants. Since one major limitation in the previous studies was the homogeneity of participants. When conducting a survey on participants of same the locality or the same age group, their thinking was also matched up to some extents. So for a bias-free survey in this study the survey in conducted on the user coming from the different background. Among the 50 participants 4 are faculty, 28 are M.Tech students, 12 are B.Tech students, 2 are B.Sc students, 1 is CS student, 1 is MCA student, 1 is MBA student, 1 is Marketing executive. Some of the M.Tech students have experience in software development and web development field. The detail about qualification and occupation of the participants is given in Table 2. Figure 5 shows the respective bar graph for qualification and occupation detail of participants.

Conducting a Survey

For this study, a survey is conducted. As already mentioned here the questionnaire method and Likert scale is used. So after preparing questionnaire the Likert scale is added for each question. Then the Questionnaire is printed in the paper and given to different participants. The questionnaire is given to 50 participants. They have to mark tick against their choice for each question. For bias free survey, the questionnaire for different quality is given to participants in different days. Sufficient time is given to the participant for thinking and marking correct response. The Surveyor explained detail about the survey and meaning of each and every question to the participants. After collecting all the responses, analysis of data is done.

Table 1. Gender and age detail of participant

Age	M(23)	F(27)
18	2	-
19	-	5
20	-	2
21	1	2
22	1	4
23	2	7
24	4	4
25	4	2
26	2	-
27	1	-
28	1	-
29	1	-
30	1	1
31	2	-
35	1	-

Figure 4. Bar graph of age and gender detail of the participants

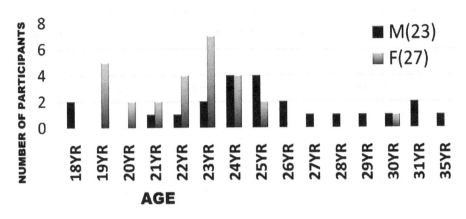

Table 2. Qualification and Occupation detail of participant

Qualification	Student	Faculty	Marketing Executive
PhD.(CONT)		3	
M.TECH		1	
M.TECH(Cont..)	28		
B.TECH(Cont..)	12		
B.SC(Cont..)	2		
C.S(Cont..)	1		
MCA(Cont..)	1		
MBA(Cont..)	1		
MIMC			1

Figure 5. Bar graph of qualification and occupation detail of the participants

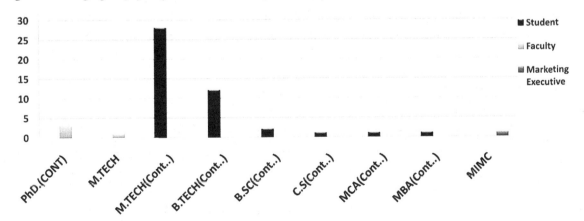

FINDINGS

After the questionnaire is completed, each question is analyzed separately. Responses of the questions are summed up to create a score. Then the average is calculated for each question.

Average of a question (score) = (Total sum of responses for the question) / (number of participants)

It is otherwise written as the formula (1) given below.

$$\text{Score for a question} = \frac{\left(\sum_{i=1}^{n} \text{response of the participant i for a question}\right)}{n} \tag{1}$$

Where n=number of participants

After finding the score for each question, the score of each quality attribute is calculated.

Score of a quality attribute = (Total sum of score for each question in a quality attribute) / (number of question for that quality attribute)

This can be otherwise written by the formula (2) given below.

$$\text{Score of a quality attribute} = \frac{\left(\sum_{i=1}^{m} \text{Score for question } i\right)}{m} \tag{2}$$

Where m is the number of question for a quality attribute.

After calculating these values, the finding for each quality attribute for Facebook and twitter is given in the table below. Table 3 shows the score of each quality attributes for System quality. Figure 6 represents respective bar graph for score of quality attributes of System quality. Table 4 shows the score of each quality attributes for Service quality. Figure 7 represents respective bar graph for score of quality attributes of Service quality. Table 5 shows the score of each quality attributes for Content quality. Figure 8 represents respective bar graph for score of quality attributes of Content quality. Table 6 shows the

Table 3. Detail Score of Quality attributes of System Quality

System quality	Facebook	Twitter
Navigation	4.077	3.868
Security	3.972	3.772
Aesthetic(Attractiveness)	4.164	4.004
Consistency	4.088	4.02
Customizability	3.46	3.348
Familiarity	3.48	3.275

Figure 6. Bar graph of Score of quality attributes of System Quality

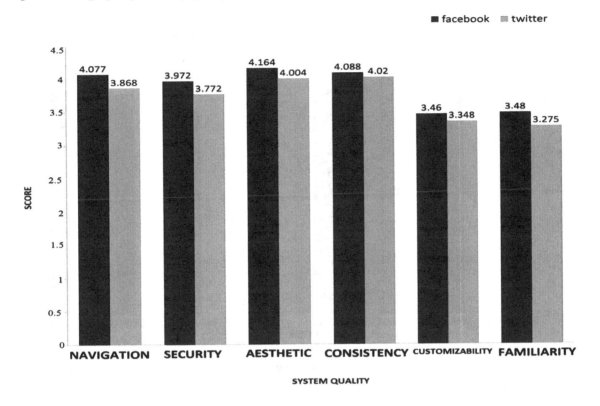

Table 4. Detail Score of Quality attributes of Service Quality

Service quality	Score of Facebook	Score of twitter
Helpfulness	3.488	3.372
Availability	3.74	3.644
Interactivity	4.2	3.92
Error Prevention	3.768	3.552
Reliability	3.348	3.24
Recoverability	3.326	3.233
Responsiveness	3.696	3.712
Feedback	3.78	3.644

Table 5. Detail Score of Quality attributes of Content Quality

Content quality	Score of Facebook	Score of Twitter
Correctness	3.41	3.3967
Coverage	3.928	3.812
Credibility	3.196	3.1
Timeliness	3.72	3.6933
Value-Added	3.408	3.448

Figure 7. Bar graph of Score of quality attributes of Service Quality

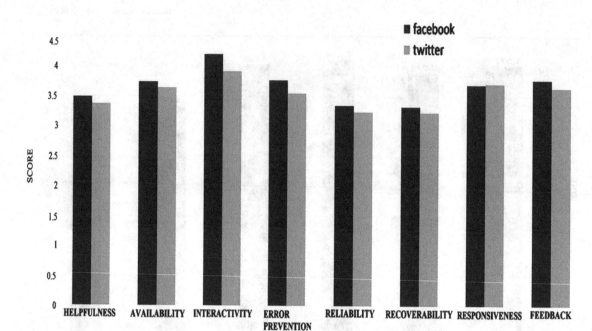

Figure 8. Bar graph of Score of quality attributes of Content Quality

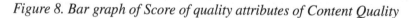
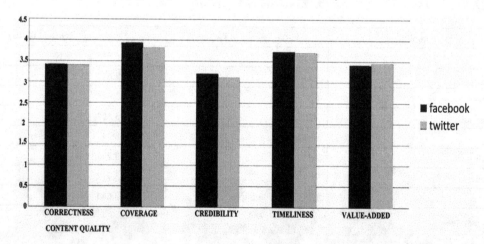

score of each quality attributes for Performance. Figure 9 represents respective bar graph for score of quality attributes of Performance. Table 7 shows the score of each quality attributes for Effort. Figure 10 represents respective bar graph for score of quality attributes of Effort. Table 8 shows the score of each quality attributes for Acceptability. Figure 11 represents respective bar graph for score of quality attributes of Acceptability.

Table 6. Detail Score of Quality attributes Performance

Performance	Score for Facebook	Score of Twitter
Efficiency	3.78	3.808
Effectiveness	3.28	3.2933
Usefulness	3.482	3.417

Figure 9. Bar graph of Score of quality attributes of Performance

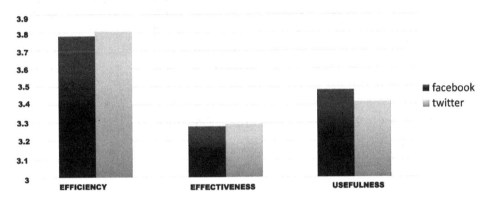

Table 7. Detail Score of Quality attributes of Effort

Effort	Score of Facebook	Score of twitter
Minimal Action	3.93	3.9
Minimal Memory Load	3.87	3.795
Accessibility	3.8	3.71667
Controllability	3.84	3.756
Understandability	3.916	3.804
Ease of Use	4.16	4.093
Learnability	4.028	3.736
Memorability	4.106666667	3.893

Table 8. Detail Score of Quality attributes of Acceptability

Acceptability	Score of Facebook	Score of Twitter
Satisfaction	4.008	3.616
Playfulness	3.912	3.574
Loyalty	3.82667	3.5333

Figure 10. Bar graph of Score of quality attributes of Effort

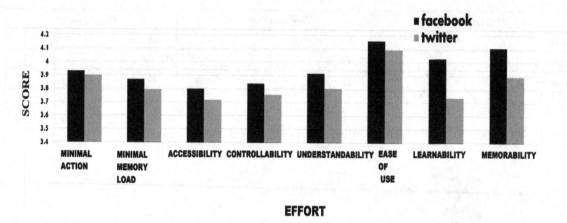

Figure 11. Bar graph of Score of quality attributes of Acceptability

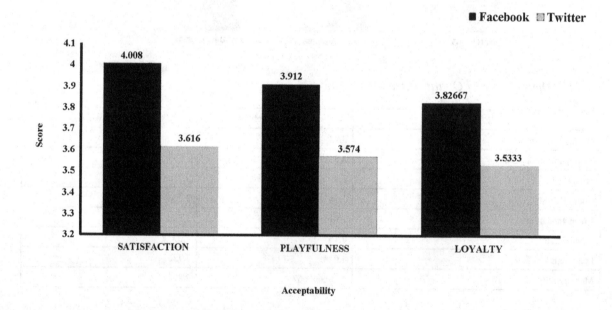

FUTURE RESEARCH DIRECTIONS

Considering these points of views this study presents the results of an on-going research, future work will be focused on, more analysis of collected data to improve website quality attribute which score badly in this quantitative evaluation. Representing the website quality with a single numerical index should be done in future researches. Another future work of this study will be focused on validating the method to what extends it produce good result.

Web 2.0 app is a social web application which deals with retrieval of information syntactically, but it does not provide meaningful information. This is because web 2.0 application is a syntactic web app.

But the desktop or computers and mobile apps can't process the data semantically as they are not human beings. Hence, there is a need to design the data in a consistent and semantic way to provide a better quality design. The semantic web app is built by using ontologies in the web. Ontologies specify meaning of annotations and also provide a vocabulary of terms. To build ontology in web app RDF, RDFS and OWL language are used to achieve the efficient quality design in mobile web system.

CONCLUSION

In this study, a quality model for web 2.0 application is identified. A survey is conducted on 50 Facebook and twitter users by using questionnaire method. In previous studies, one limitation was the homogeneity of participants. In this study, this limitation is avoided by conducting a survey on the different types of user coming from the different backgrounds. In previous study, quality evaluation is done for a particular web 2.0 application. To avoid this limitation, in this study, the survey is done by questionnaire method and the questions are prepared in such a way that, it can be used for any type of web 2.0 application. In this study, the survey is only done for the two popular social networking site Facebook and twitter.

From the findings and graph, it is found that Facebook scores more than twitter for every quality attribute except responsiveness, value added, effectiveness and efficiency. But the difference between the score of the two websites is very low but cannot be ignored. This may be one reason that Facebook has more users compared to twitter. While considering the quality attributes of individual websites, all the quality attributes of both the side score above average. But some quality attributes score poor and some score more. So the poor scoring quality can be improved by giving more focus on that area while designing and modifying the websites. Interactivity scores the highest and credibility scores the lowest for Facebook. Ease of use scores highest and credibility score lowest for twitter. So the focus should be given while designing and updating these websites to achieve more score in credibility.

REFERENCES

Albuquerque, A. B., & Belchior, A. D. (2002). E-commerce Website quality evaluation. *Proceedings of the 28th 2002 Euromicro Conference* (pp. 294-300). IEEE.

Almeida, J. M., Goncalves, M. A., Figueiredo, F., Pinto, H., & Belem, F. (2010). On the quality of information for web 2.0 services. *IEEE Internet Computing*, *14*(6), 47–55. doi:10.1109/MIC.2010.102

Beg, M. S. (2005). A subjective measure of web search quality. *Information Sciences*, *169*(3), 365–381. doi:10.1016/j.ins.2004.07.003

Brown, A., Jay, C., Chen, A. Q., & Harper, S. (2012). The uptake of Web 2.0 technologies, and its impact on visually disabled users. *Universal Access in the Information Society*, *11*(2), 185–199. doi:10.1007/s10209-011-0251-y

Burns, A.C., & Bush, R.F. (2008). Basic Marketing Research (2nd ed., p. 245). New Jersey: Pearson Education.

Cappiello, C., Daniel, F., & Matera, M. (2009). *A quality model for mashup components* (pp. 236–250). Springer Berlin Heidelberg.

Cavano, J. P., & McCall, J. A. (1978, January). A framework for the measurement of software quality. *Performance Evaluation Review, 7*(3-4), 133–139. doi:10.1145/1007775.811113

Cavazza, F. (2005). *Web 2.0: la révolution par les usages*. Journal du Net Solutions.

ELdesouky. A. I., Hesham, A., & Hazem, R. (2008). Toward complex academic websites quality evaluation method (QEM) framework: quality requirements phase definition and specification. Cairo, Egypt: Mansoura University, Faculty of Engineering. Computer and Systems Engineering Department.

ELKorany, A., Nabil, D., & ELDin, A. S. (2009). Quality measurement model for KADS domain knowledge. *J Softw Eng*, 1-14.

Gabriel, I. J. (2007, April). Usability metrics for measuring usability of business-to-consumer (b2c) e-commerce sites. *Proceedings of the 6th Annual ISOnEworld Conference* (pp. 74-1).

Guide to Software Product Quality Requirements and Evaluation (SQuaRE). (2010, December). ISO, Geneva.

Hart, J., Ridley, C., Taher, F., Sas, C., & Dix, A. (2008, October). Exploring the Facebook experience: a new approach to usability. *Proceedings of the 5th Nordic conference on Human-computer interaction: building bridges* (pp. 471-474). ACM. doi:10.1145/1463160.1463222

Holzinger, A. (2005). Usability engineering methods for software developers. *Communications of the ACM, 48*(1), 71–74. doi:10.1145/1039539.1039541

Hussher. (2006). *F. Le nouveau pouvoir des internautes* (Timée-Editions).

Lu, Y. H., Hong, Y., Varia, J., & Lee, D. (2005, March). Pollock: automatic generation of virtual web services from websites. *Proceedings of the 2005 ACM symposium on Applied computing* (pp. 1650-1655). ACM. doi:10.1145/1066677.1067052

Mich, L., Franch, M., & Gaio, L. (2003). Evaluating and designing website quality. *Multimedia, IEEE, 10*(1), 34–43. doi:10.1109/MMUL.2003.1167920

Nielsen, J. (1995, May). Usability inspection methods. *Conference companion on Human factors in computing systems* (pp. 377–378). ACM. doi:10.1145/223355.223730

O'Reilly, T. (2006). *Web 2.0 Principles and Best Practices*. O'Reilly Media.

O'Reilly, T. (2005). What is Web 2.0: Design Patterns and Business Models for the Next Generation of Software. *Proceedings of the Web 2.0 Conference.*

O'Reilly, T. (2006). *Seven principles of Web 2.0 make a lot more sense if you change the order*. Open Gardens.

Ogawa, H., & Goto, Y. (2006). *Web 2.0 book*. Tokyo, Japan: Impress Japan Corporation.

Orehovački, T., Granić, A., & Kermek, D. (2012). Exploring the quality in use of Web 2.0 applications: the case of mind mapping services. *Current Trends in Web Engineering* (pp. 266–277). Springer Berlin Heidelberg. doi:10.1007/978-3-642-27997-3_26

Orehovački, T., Granić, A., & Kermek, D. (2013). Evaluating the perceived and estimated quality in use of Web 2.0 applications. *Journal of Systems and Software, 86*(12), 3039–3059. doi:10.1016/j.jss.2013.05.071

Pang, M., Suh, W., Hong, J., Kim, J., & Lee, H. (2009). A new website quality assessment model for the Web 2.0 Era. Handbook of research on Web, 2(3.0), 387-410.

Pang, M. S., Suh, W., Kim, J., & Lee, H. (2009). A benchmarking-based requirement analysis methodology for improving websites. *International Journal of Electronic Commerce, 13*(3), 119–162. doi:10.2753/JEC1086-4415130305

Ricca, F., & Chao, L. (2009). Special section on web systems evolution. *International Journal of Software Tools and Technology Transfer, 11*(6), 419–425. doi:10.1007/s10009-009-0127-0

Saha, R., & Grover, S. (2011). Quantitative evaluation of website quality dimension for web2. 0 environment. *International Journal of u-and e-Service Science and Technology, 4*(4), 14–35.

Sbihi, B., El Jazouli, S., & El Kadiri, K. E. (2009). Web 2.1: Toward a large and qualitative participation on the Web. *Journal of Information and Organizational Sciences, 33*(1), 191–204.

Shirleen, K., & Burn, J. (2005). Developing a framework for assessing information quality on the World Wide Web. *Inform Sci J, 8*, 159–172.

Silva, P. A., & Dix, A. (2007, September). Usability: not as we know it! *Proceedings of the 21st British HCI Group Annual Conference on People and Computers: HCI... but not as we know it (Vol. 2*, pp. 103-106). British Computer Society.

Taylor, I. (2012, January). *4 Measurement Scales Every Researcher Should Remember*. Retrieved from http://blog.questionpro.com/2012/01/04/4-measurement-scales-every-researcher-should-remember/

Thompson, A. J., & Kemp, E. A. (2009, July). Web 2.0: extending the framework for heuristic evaluation. *Proceedings of the 10th International Conference NZ Chapter of the ACM's Special Interest Group on Human-Computer Interaction* (pp. 29-36). ACM. doi:10.1145/1577782.1577788

TR 9126-3 Software engineering product quality Part3: internal metrics. (2003). *International Organization for Standardization.*

KEY TERMS AND DEFINITIONS

Quality Attributes: Quality attributes are the overall factors that affect run-time behaviour, system design, and user experience. They represent areas of concern that have the potential for application wide impact across layers and tiers. In this study, web 2.0 applications have various qualities attribute that affect web 2.0 application.

Quality Model: Quality models are structured and well-defined classification and sub-classification of various quality and sub-quality. Web quality model classify various quality attribute affecting the website. There are a large number of quality models and standards. Generally web quality models are used for evaluating the quality of a website.

Quantitative Analysis: Quantitative analysis is a business or financial analysis technique that seeks to understand behavior by using complex mathematical and statistical modeling, measurement and research. By assigning a numerical value to variables, quantitative analysts try to replicate reality mathematically.

Questionnaire: Questionnaire is a research instrument consisting of a series of questions and other prompts for the purpose of gathering information from respondents. It is devised for the purpose of the survey or statistical study. It serves four basic purposes: to collect the appropriate data, make data comparable and amenable to analysis, minimize bias in formulating and asking the question, and to make questions engaging and varied.

Social Networking Sites: Social network sites are web-based services that allow individuals to create a public profile, create a list of users with whom to share connections, and view and cross the connections within the system. Social networking sites can be used to describe community-based Websites, online discussions forums, chartrooms and other social spaces online. Facebook, Twitter, Google+ and LinkedIn are the leading social sites.

Web 2.0: Web 2.0 describes World Wide Websites that emphasize user-generated content, usability and interoperability. Web 2.0 is the term given to describe a second generation of the World Wide Web that is focused on the ability for people to collaborate and share information online. Web 2.0 basically refers to the transition from static HTML Web pages to a more dynamic Web that is more organized and is based on serving Web applications to users.

Compilation of References

Artz, D., & Gil, Y. (2007). A Survey of Trust in Computer Science and the Semantic Web. *Journal of Web Semantics: Science, Services and Agents on the World Wide Web.*

Abraham, A. (2003). Business Intelligence from Web Usage Mining. *Journal of Information & Knowledge Management, 2*(4), 375–390. doi:10.1142/S0219649203000565

Abran, A., Khelifi, A., Suryn, W., & Seffah, A. (2003). Consolidating the ISO Usability Models. *Proceedings of 11ᵗʰ International Software Quality Management Conference.* pp 1-17.

Adriaana, P., & Zantinge, D. (2002). *Data Mining.* Pearson Education Asia.

Agarwal, R., & Venkatesh, V. (2002). Assessing a Firm's Web Presence: A Heuristic Evaluation Procedure for the Measurement of Usability. *Information Systems Research, 13*(2), 168–186. doi:10.1287/isre.13.2.168.84

Agnew, A. (2011, December 2) How to Protect Your Website from Malware and Virus Attacks Retrieved from http://www.website-guardian.com/how-to-protect-your-website-from-malware-and-virus-attacks-va-4.html

Agnew, A. (2011, October 24). How to improve your website Security against dangers on the Web? Retrieved from http://www.website-guardian.com/how-to-improve-your-website-security-against-dangers-on-the-web-va-2.html

Ahmad, R., Zhang, Li, & Azam, F. (2006). Towards Generic User Interface for Web Based Systems Serving Similar Functions. *Proceedings of the IEEE Fourth International Conference on Software Engineering Research, Management and Applications* (pp. 297-306).

AIIM. (2010). *What is Enterprise Content Management.* Retrieved from http://www.aiim.org/What-is-ECM-Enterprise-Content-Management.aspx

Aivalis, C. J., & Boucouvalas, A. C. (2014, July). Future proof analytics techniques for web 2.0 applications. *Proceedings of the 2014 International Conference on Telecommunications and Multimedia TEMU* (pp. 214-219). IEEE.

Akao, Y. (1990). *Quality Function Deployment.* Cambridge, MA: Productivity Press.

Al Murtadha, Y. M., Sulaiman, M. N. B., Mustapha, N., & Udzir, N. I. (2010). Mining Web Navigation Profiles for Recommendation System. *Information Technology Journal, 9,* 790–796.

Aladwani, A. M. (2003). Key Internet characteristics and e-commerce issues in Arab countries. *Information Technology & People, 16*(1), 9–20. doi:10.1108/09593840310462998

Aladwani, A. M., & Palvia, P. C. (2002). Developing and validating an instrument for measuring user-perceived web quality. *Information & Management, 39*(6), 467–476. doi:10.1016/S0378-7206(01)00113-6

Albuquerque, A. B., & Belchior, A. D. (2002). E-commerce Website quality evaluation.*Proceedings of the 28th2002 Euromicro Conference*(pp. 294-300). IEEE.

Aldridge, S., & Rowley, J. (1998). Measuring customer satisfaction in higher education. *Quality Assurance in Education, 6*(4), 197–204. doi:10.1108/09684889810242182

Alesso, H.P., & Smith, C.F. (2009). Thinking on the Web: Berners-Lee, Godel and Turing. UK: John Wiley & Sons.

Alexander, J. E., & Tate, P. (1999). Web Wisdom: How to evaluate and create information quality on the web. *Paper presented at Mahwah*, Lawrence Erlbaum, NJ.

Almeida, J. M., Goncalves, M. A., Figueiredo, F., Pinto, H., & Belem, F. (2010). On the quality of information for web 2.0 services. *IEEE Internet Computing, 14*(6), 47–55. doi:10.1109/MIC.2010.102

AlMurtadha, Y., Sulaiman, M. N. B., Mustapha, N., & Udzir, N. I. (2011). Ipact: Improved Web Page Recommendation System using Profile Aggregation Based on Clustering of Transactions. *American Journal of Applied Sciences*, 277–283.

Alsmadi, S. (2002) Consumer attitudes towards online shopping in Jordan: opportunities and challenges. *Proceedings of theMarketing Workshop*, UAE.

An introduction to ontologies. (n. d.). Semantic Web.org. Retrieved from www.SemanticWeb.org/knowmarkup.html

Answers.com/website . (2015, August 3). Retrieved from http://www.answers.com/topic/website

Arasli, H., Mehtap-Smadi, S., & Katircioglu, S. T. (2005). Customer Service Quality In The Greek Cypriot Banking Industry. *Managing Service Quality: An International Journal, 15*(1), 41–56. doi:10.1108/09604520510575254

Arikan, A. (2008). *Multichannel Marketing: Metrics and Methods for On and Offline Success*. Indiana: Wiley Publishing.

Athiyaman, A. (1997). Linking student satisfaction and service quality perceptions: The case of university education. *European Journal of Marketing, 31*(7), 528–540. doi:10.1108/03090569710176655

Bahry, S., Diana, F., Shahibi, M. S., Kamis, Y., & Masrek, M. N. (2014, May). Preferred information quality factors as a web content quality measures on Malaysian government websites: A conceptual paper. *Proceedings of the 2014 International Symposium on Technology Management and Emerging Technologies ISTMET* (pp. 400-405). IEEE.

Bailey, H. J., & Milheim, W. D. (1991). A comprehensive model for deigning interactive video based materials.*Proceeding for the Night Conference on Interactive Instruction Delivery at the 2991 Society for Applied Learning Technology Conference*. Orlando, FL.

Balakrishnan, V., Liew, T. K., & Pourgholaminejad, S. (2015). Fun learning with Edooware – A social media enabled tool. *Computers & Education, 80*(1), 39–47. doi:10.1016/j.compedu.2014.08.008

Barnard, L., & Wesson, J. (2003) Usability issues for e-commerce in South Africa: an empirical investigation. *Proceedings of SAICSIT 2003* (pp. 258-267).

Barnes, S., & Vidgen, R. (2002). An integrative approach to the assessment of ecommerce quality. *Journal of Electronic Commerce Research, 3*(3), 114–127.

Barutcu, S. (2006). Quality Function Deployment in Effective Website Design, An Application in E-Store Design. *İşletme Fakültesi Dergisi, 7*(1), 41-63.

Batley, S. (2007). The I in information architecture: The challenge of content management. *Aslib Proceedings, 59*(2), 139–151. Retrieved from doi:10.1108/00012530710736654

Beasley, M. (2013). *Practical Web Analytics for User Experience*. Ypsilanti: Morgan Kaufmann, Elsevier publications.

Becker, C., Antunes, G., Barateiro, J., & Vieira, R. (2011). *A Capability Model for Digital Preservation: Analyzing Concerns, Drivers, Constraints, Capabilities and Maturities*. National Library Board Singapore and Nanyang Technological University. Retrieved from http://www.ifs.tuwien.ac.at/~becker/pubs/becker_ipres2011.pdf

Beg, M. S. (2005). A subjective measure of web search quality. *Information Sciences, 169*(3), 365–381. doi:10.1016/j.ins.2004.07.003

Beirekdar, A., Vanderdonckt, J., & Noirhomme-Fraiture, M. (2002). Kwaresmi – Knowledge based Web Automated Evaluation with reconfigurable guidelines optimization. In P. Forbig, Q. Limbourg, B. Urban, & J. Vanderdonckt (Eds.), *DSV-IS 2002, LNCS, 2545* (pp. 362–376). Heidelberg: Springer.

Bellinger, G. (2004). *Knowledge Management – Emerging Perspectives*. Retrieved from http://www.systems-thinking.org/kmgmt/kmgmt.htm

Berger, C., Blauth, R., Boger, D., Bolster, C., Burchill, G., DuMouchel, W., & Walden, D. et al. (1993). Kano's Methods for Understanding Customer - defined Quality. *Center for Quality Management Journal, 2*(4), 3–36.

Berners-Lee, T., Hendler, J., & Lassila, O. (2001, May). The Semantic Web, Scientific American. Retrieved from http://www.sciam.com

Bevan, N., & Macleod, M. (1994) Usability measurement in context, Behaviour and Information Technology, Taylor & Francis Ltd. Basingstoke, UK, 1&2.

Bevan, N. (1998). Usability Issues in Website Design. *Proceedings of UPA'98, Washington DC*, USA.

Bharadwaj, S., & Menon, A. (1997). Discussion in applying the Kano methodology to meet customer requirements. *Quality Management Journal, 4*(3), 107–109.

Bitpipe Research Guide. (2000). *Content and Knowledge Management Overview*. Retrieved from http://www.bitpipe.com/data/web/bpmd/contmgmt/content-management.jsp

Black, P., & Wiliam, D. (1998). Assessment and classroom learning. *Assessment in Education: Principles, Policy & Practice, 5*(1), 7–74. doi:10.1080/0969595980050102

Bobby. (n. d.). Retrieved from http://webxact.watchfire.com/

Booth, D., & Jansen, B. J. (2009). A review of methodologies for analyzing websites. *Web Technologies: Concepts, Methodologies, Tools, and Applications: Concepts, Methodologies, Tools, and Applications*, 145.

Booth, D., & Jansen, B. J. (2009). *A Review of Methodologies for Analyzing Websites*. IGI Global. doi:10.4018/978-1-59904-974-8.ch008

Booth, P. (1989). *An Introduction to Human-Computer Interaction*. Hillsdale, USA: Lawrence Erlbaum Associates Publishers.

Borges, J. A., Morales, I., & Rodriguez, N. J. (1996). Guidelines for designing usable World Wide Web pages. *Proceedings of the 1996 Conference on Human Factors in Computing Systems: Common Ground (CHI '96)*, Vancouver, Canada (pp. 277–278). doi:10.1145/257089.257320

Boud, D., & Falchikov, N. (1989). Quantitative studies of self-assessment in higher education: A critical analysis of findings. *Higher Education, 18*(5), 529–549. doi:10.1007/BF00138746

Bragg, R., Rhodes-ousley, M., & Strassberg, K. (2004). Network security. *TataMc-GrawHill*.

Brajnik, G. (2001). Towards Valid Quality Models for Websites. *Proceedings of the7th Conference onHuman Factors and the Web*, Madison, Wisconsin.

Bramall, C., Schoefer, K., & McKechnie, S. (2004). The determinants and consequences of consumer trust in e-retailing: A conceptual framework. *Irish Marketing Review*, *17*(1/2), 13–22.

Bressolles, G., Durrieu, F., & Senecal, S. (2014). A consumer typology based on e-service quality and e-satisfaction. *Journal of Retailing and Consumer Services*, *21*(6), 889–896. doi:10.1016/j.jretconser.2014.07.004

Briand, L., Wüst, J., Daly, J., & Porter, D. (2000). Exploring the Relationships between Design Measures and Software Quality in Object-Oriented Systems. *Journal of Systems and Software*, *51*(3), 245–273. doi:10.1016/S0164-1212(99)00102-8

Brinck, T., Gergle, D., & Wood, S. D. (2001). *Usability for the web: designing websites that work*. Morgan Kaufmann Publishers.

Brown, A., Jay, C., Chen, A. Q., & Harper, S. (2012). The uptake of Web 2.0 technologies, and its impact on visually disabled users. *Universal Access in the Information Society*, *11*(2), 185–199. doi:10.1007/s10209-011-0251-y

Brysland, A., & Curry, A. (2001). Service Improvements in Public Services Using SERVQUAL. *Managing Service Quality: An International Journal*, *11*(6), 389–401. doi:10.1108/09604520110410601

Burch, R. O. (2001). Effective web design and core communication issues: The missing components in web-based distance education. *Journal of Educational Multimedia and Hypermedia*, *10*(4), 357–367.

Burns, A.C., & Bush, R.F. (2008). Basic Marketing Research (2nd ed., p. 245). New Jersey: Pearson Education.

Businessdictionary.com. (2015). *Define Intranet*. Retrieved from http://www.businessdictionary.com/definition/intranet.html

Büyüközkan, G., & Çifçi, G. (2012). A combined fuzzy AHP and fuzzy TOPSIS based strategic analysis of electronic service quality in healthcare industry. *Expert Systems with Applications*, *39*(3), 2341–2354. doi:10.1016/j.eswa.2011.08.061

Byun, H., Lee, B., & Rye, J. (2014). A Comparative Study on Evaluating the Service Quality Attributes based on Kano Model: A Case of Low-cost Carrier and Full-service Carrier. *SHS Web of Conferences 12*.

Calderhead, J. (1989). Reflective teaching and teacher education. *Teaching and Teacher Education*, *5*(1), 43–51. doi:10.1016/0742-051X(89)90018-8

Calero, C., Ruiz, J., & Piattini, M. (2005). Classifying Web Metrics Using the Web Quality Model. Online Information Review, 29(3), 227–248. doi:10.1108/14684520510607560

Cameron, S. A. (2011). *Enterprise content management - a business and technical guide*. Swindon, UK: The Chartered Institute for IT.

Cappiello, C., Daniel, F., & Matera, M. (2009). *A quality model for mashup components* (pp. 236–250). Springer Berlin Heidelberg.

Carlson, J., & O'Cass, A. (2011). Developing A Framework For Understanding E-Service Quality, Its Antecedents, Consequences, And Mediators. *Managing Service Quality: An International Journal*, *21*(3), 264–286. doi:10.1108/09604521111127965

Carrasco, R. A., Muñoz-Leiva, F., Sánchez-Fernández, J., & Liébana-Cabanillas, F. J. (2012). A model for the integration of e-financial services questionnaires with SERVQUAL scales under fuzzy linguistic modeling. *Expert Systems with Applications*, *39*(14), 11535–11547. doi:10.1016/j.eswa.2012.03.055

Castellano, G., Fanelli, A. M., & Torsello, M. A. (2008). Computational Intelligence techniques for Web personalization. *Web Intelligent and Agent Systems, 6*(3), 253–272.

Castellano, G., Fanelli, A. M., & Torsello, M. A. (2011). NEWER: A system for Neuro-fuzzy Web Recommendation. *Applied Soft Computing, 11*(1), 793–806.

Cavano, J. P., & McCall, J. A. (1978, January). A framework for the measurement of software quality. *Performance Evaluation Review, 7*(3-4), 133–139. doi:10.1145/1007775.811113

Cavazza, F. (2005). *Web 2.0: la révolution par les usages*. Journal du Net Solutions.

Chang, H., & Kim, D. (2010). A Quality Function Deployment Framework for the Service Quality of Health Information Website. *Healthcare Informatics Research, 16*(1), 6–14. doi:10.4258/hir.2010.16.1.6 PMID:21818418

Chaparro Barbara, S. (2008). Usability Evaluation of a University Portal Website. Usability News, 10(2), pp 1-7.

Chawda, B., Craft, B., Cairns, P., Ruger, S., & Heesch, D. (2005). Do "Attractive Things Work Better"? An Exploration of Search Tool Visualisations. *Proceedings of British HCI Group Annual Conference* Edinburgh, UK, (pp. 46-51). The Bigger Picture.

Cheng, B., Wang, M., Mørch, A. I., Chen, N.-S., Kinshuk, , & Spector, J. M. (2014). Research on e-learning in the workplace 2000–2012: A bibliometric analysis of the literature. *Educational Research Review, 11*(1), 56–72. doi:10.1016/j.edurev.2014.01.001

Chen, M., & Ryu, Y. U. (2013). Facilitating effective user navigation through web site structure improvement. *IEEE Transactions on Knowledge and Data Engineering, 99*, 1–18.

Chen, M., & Ryu, Y. U. (2013). Facilitating Effective User Navigation through Website Structure Improvement. *IEEE Transactions on* Knowledge and Data Engineering, 25(3), 571–588.

Chen, Z.-Y., Fan, Z.-P., & Sun, M. (2015). Behavior-aware user response modeling in social media: Learning from diverse heterogeneous data. *European Journal of Operational Research, 241*(2), 422–434. doi:10.1016/j.ejor.2014.09.008

Chettri, S. K., Paul, B., & Dutta, A. K. (2013). Statistical Disclosure Control for Data Privacy Preservation. *International Journal of Computers and Applications, 80*(10), 38–43. doi:10.5120/13899-1880

Chhabra, I. (2014, December). Quality analytics for evaluation of dynamic web based learning environment. *Proceedings of the 2014 IEEE International Conference on MOOC, Innovation and Technology in Education MITE* (pp. 138-141). IEEE.

Chiang, I.-P., Huang, C.-Y., & Huang, C.-W. (2010). Traffic metrics and Web 2.0-ness In. *Online Information Review, 34*(1), 115–126. doi:10.1108/14684521011024155

Chidamber, S., & Kemerer, C. (1994). A Metrics Suite for Object Oriented Design. *IEEE Transactions on Software Engineering, 20*(6), 476–493. doi:10.1109/32.295895

Chin, P. (2003). *Intranet Content: Long Live the King*. Retrieved from http://www.intranetjournal.com/articles/.../pij_06_20_03a.html

Chinnici, R., Gudgin, M., Moreau, J.-J., Schlimmer, J., & Weerawarana, S. (2003, November 10). *Web Services Description Language (WSDL) Version 2.0 Part 1: Core Language*. W3C Working Draft. Retrieved from http://www.w3.org/TR/2003/WD-wsdl20-20031110/

Cho, N. (2012). *Trusted Digital Repositories Maturity Model (TDR-MM)* Retrieved from http://aeri2012.wordpress.com/conference-schedule/paper-presentations/trusteddigital-archives/

Chu, C.-J., Wang, S.-L., & Lai, Y.-C. (2010). A Study of Web 2.0 Based Digital Archives System Using Kano Model. *Paper presented at the 2010 International meeting of the Computer Symposium*, Tainan.

Clifton, B. (2008). *Advanced web metrics with Google Analytics*. Indianapolis, Indiana: Wiley Publishing Inc.

Clutter Consortium. (2000). Poor Project Management – Problem of E-Projects. Cutter Consortium: The Cutter Edge.

Colorni, A., Dorigo, M., & Maniezzo, V. (1992). Distributed optimization by ant colonies. *Toward a practice of autonomous systems:Proceedings of the first European conference on artificial life* (pp. 134–142), Cambridge. MA: MIT Press.

Comber, T. (1995). Building Usable Web Pages: An HCI Perspective. *Proceedings of the Australian Conference on the Web (AusWeb '95)*, Ballina, Australia.

Conover, W. J. (1971). *Practical nonparametric statistics*. New York, Chichester: Wiley.

Contentmanager.eu.com. (2015). *What is Content Management?* Retrieved from http://www.contentmanager.eu.com/

Conway, P. (2008). *Modeling the Digital Content Landscape in Universities*. Retrieved from http://www.emeraldinsight.com_Insight_ViewContentServiet_contentType=Article&Filename=_published_emeraldfulltextarticle_pdf_230260302

Cooley, R., Mobasher. B., & Srivatsava, J. (1997). Web Mining: Information and Pattern Discovery on the World Wide Web. *Proceedings of the 9th IEEE International Conference on Tools with Artificial Intelligence*, Newport Beach, CA, (pp. 558-567).

Cooley, R., Mobasher, B., & Srivastava, J. (1999). Data Preparation for Mining World Wide Web Browsing Patterns. *Knowledge and Information Systems*, *1*(1), 1–27. doi:10.1007/BF03325089

Cowan, J., & Tobin, R. (2001, October 24). *XML Information Set*, W3C Recommendation, Retrieved from http://www.w3.org/TR/2001/REC-xml-infoset-20011024/

Cox, J., & Dale, B. G. (2001). Service Quality And Ecommerce: An Exploratory Analysis. *Managing Service Quality: An International Journal*, *11*(2), 121–131. doi:10.1108/09604520110387257

Curphey, M., Scambray, J., & Olson, E. (2003). *Improving Web Application Security Threats and Countermeasures: Patterns & Practices*. Microsoft Corporation.

Cutler, M., & Sterne, J. (2000). *E-Metrics: Business Metrics for the New Economy*. Chicago, IL: NetGenesis. doi:10.1145/347090.347096

DARPA Agent Markup Language (DAML) home page. (n. d.). Retrieved from www.daml.org/

de Jager, J., & Gbadamosi, G. (2013). Predicting students' satisfaction through service quality in higher education. *The International Journal of Management Education*, *11*(3), 107–118. doi:10.1016/j.ijme.2013.09.001

de Oliveira, C. L. C., & Laurindo, F. J. B. (2011). A Framework of Web Analytics: Deploying the emergent knowledge of customers to leverage competitive advantage.*Proceedings of the 2011 International Conference on e-Business*, Seville, Spain (pp.1-6). IEEE.

de Reuver, M., Nikou, S., & Bouwman, H. (2015). The interplay of costs, trust and loyalty in a service industry in transition: The moderating effect of smartphone adoption. *Telematics and Informatics*.

DeMarco, T. (1999). *Management Can Make Quality (Im) possible*. Boston: Cutter IT Summit.

Dempsey, L., Malpas, C., & Lavoie, B. (2014). Collection Directions: The Evolution of Library Collections and Collecting. *Portal: Libraries and the Academy*, July, 393-423.

Department of Health and Human Services. (2006). *Research-based web design & usability guidelines*. Washington: U.S. Government Printing Office.

Dhyani, D., Ng, W.K. & Bhowmick, S.S. (2002). A survey of Web metrics. *ACM Computing Surveys, 34*(4), 469-503.

Dhyani, J., Keong, W., & Bhowmick, S. (2002). A Survey of Web Metrics. *Journal of ACM Computing Surveys, 34*(4), 469–503. doi:10.1145/592642.592645

Digital Analytics Association. (2015). *What is Digital Analytics?* Retrieved from http://www.digitalanalyticsassociation.org/

Dillman, D., Sinclair, M., & Clark, J. (1993). Effects of Questionnaire Length, Respondent-friendly Design and a Difficult Question on Response Rates for Occupant-Addressed Census Mail Surveys. *Journal of Public Opinion Quarterly, 57*(3), 289–305. doi:10.1086/269376

Dillman, D., Tortora, R., & Bowker, D. (1998). *Principles for Constructing Web Surveys*. Joint Meetings of the American Statistical Association.

Dix, A., Finlay, J., Abowd, G. D., & Beale, R. (2004). *Human-Computer Interaction* (3rd ed.). Essex, UK: Pearson Education.

Djajadikerta, H., & Trireksani, T. (2006). Measuring University Web Site Quality: A Development of a User-Perceived Instrument and its Initial Implementation to Web sites of Accounting Departments in New Zealand's Universities. *School of Accounting, Finance and Economics & FIMARC Working Paper Series*, 1-23.

Dochy, F., Segers, M., & Sluijsmans, D. (1999). The use of self-, peer and co-assessment in higher education: A review. *Studies in Higher Education, 24*(3), 331–350. doi:10.1080/03075079912331379935

Dollar, C., & Ashley, L. (2011). *Digital Preservation Capability Maturity Model. A digital preservation maturity model in action*. Retrieved from http://lib.stanford.edu/files/pasigjan2012/12F2%20Digital%20Preservation%20Capability%20Maturity%20Model%20in%20Action.pdf

Dorigo, M., & Blum, C. (2005). Ant colony optimization theory: A survey. *Theoretical Computer Science, 344*(2-3), 243–278. doi:10.1016/j.tcs.2005.05.020

Dreyfus, P. (1998). Principles of usability. Retrieved from http://www.devedge.netscape.com/viewsource/arcive/editior98.3.23.htm

DuBois, L. (n. d.). 11 Best Web Analytics Tools. *Inc Magazine*. Retrieved from http://www.inc.com/guides/12/2010/11-best-web-analytics-tools.html

Duncan, S. (2010). Using web analytics to measure the impact of earned online media on business outcomes: A methodological approach. *Context Analytics and Text100*.

Eberhart, R., Simpson, P., & Dobbins, R. (1996). *Computational Intelligence- PC Tools*. Boston: AP Professional.

Edvardsson, B. (1997). Quality in new service development: Key concepts and a frame of reference. *International Journal of Production Economics, 52*(1-2), 31–46. doi:10.1016/S0925-5273(97)80765-7

ELdesouky. A. I., Hesham, A., & Hazem, R. (2008). Toward complex academic websites quality evaluation method (QEM) framework: quality requirements phase definition and specification. Cairo, Egypt: Mansoura University, Faculty of Engineering. Computer and Systems Engineering Department.

ELKorany, A., Nabil, D., & ELDin, A. S. (2009). Quality measurement model for KADS domain knowledge. *J Softw Eng*, 1-14.

Eppler, M. J., & Muenzenmayer, P. (2002). Measuring Information Quality in the Web Context: A Survey of State-of-the-Art Instruments and an Application Methodology. In IQ (pp. 187-196).

EvalIris. (n. d.). Retrieved from http://www.sc.ehu.es/acwbbpke/evaliris.html

Falchikov, N. (1986). Product comparisons and process benefits of collaborative peer group and self assessments. *Assessment & Evaluation in Higher Education*, *11*(2), 146–166. doi:10.1080/0260293860110206

Farkas, D. K., & Farkas, J. B. (2000). Guidelines for designing web navigation. *Technical Communication (Washington)*, *4*(3), 341–358.

Feldman, A., Greenberg, A., Lund, C., Reingold, N., Rexford, J., & True, F. (2001). Deriving traffic demands for operational IP Networks: Methodology and Experience. *IEEE/ACM Transactions on Networking*, *9*(3), 265–280.

Feldman, L., Mueller, C. J., Tamir, D., & Komogortsev, O. V. (2009). An Economical Approach to Usability Testing. *Proceedings of the 2009 33rd Annual IEEE International Computer Software and Applications Conference* (Vol. 01, pp. 124-129).

Fenton, N., & Neil, M. (2000). Software Metrics: Roadmap.*Proceedings of the Conference on Software Engineering (ICSE 2000)*, Limerick, Ireland (pp 357-370).

Field, A. (2009). *Discovering statistics using SPSS* (2nd ed.). London: Sage.

Fienberg, S. E., & McIntyre, J. (2004, January). Data swapping: Variations on a theme by dalenius and reiss. In *Privacy in statistical databases* (pp. 14–29). Springer Berlin Heidelberg. doi:10.1007/978-3-540-25955-8_2

Fikes, R., P. Hayes, & I. Horrocks, (n. d.). OWL-QL - A Language for Deductive Query Answering on the Semantic Web. Stanford University, TR KS-03-14.

Fitzpatrick, R., & Higgins, C. (1998). Usable software and its attributes: A synthesis of software quality, European Community law and human-computer interaction.*Proceedings of HCI'98 Conference*, Springer, London, UK. doi:10.1007/978-1-4471-3605-7_1

Fleming, J. (1998). *Web Navigation: Designing the User Experience*. Sebastopol, Calif, USA: O'Reilly & Associates.

Fogg, B. J., Soohoo, C., Danielson, D. R., Marable, L., Stanford, J., & Tauber, E. R. (2003). How do users evaluate the credibility of Web sites?: a study with over 2,500 participants.*Proceedings of the 2003 conference on Designing for user experiences* (pp. 1-15). doi:10.1145/997078.997097

Fox, G. (2004). Grids of Grids of Simple Services. *Computing in Science & Engineering*, *6*(4), 84–87.

Fractal Analytics. (2015). *Insight, Impact, Innovation*. Retrieved from http://www.fractalanalytics.com/

Francis, R. L., & White, J. A. (1976). *Facility Layout and Location: An Analytical Approach*. Prentice-Hall International Series.

Freeman, M. B., & Hyland, P. (2003). *Australian online supermarket usability (Technical report). Decision Systems Lab*, University of Wollongong.

Fürber, C., & Hepp, M. (2005). The sociotechnical nature of mobile computing work: Evidence from a study of policing in the United States. *International Journal of Technology and Human Interaction*, *1*(3), 1–14. doi:10.4018/jthi.2005070101

Fu, Y., Shih, M. Y., Creado, M., & Ju, C. (2002). Reorganizing web sites based on user access patterns. *International Journal of Intelligent Systems in Accounting Finance & Management*, *11*(1), 39–53. doi:10.1002/isaf.209

Gabriel, I. J. (2007, April). Usability metrics for measuring usability of business-to-consumer (b2c) e-commerce sites. *Proceedings of the 6th Annual ISOnEworld Conference* (pp. 74-1).

Gall, N. (2014, October 28). Web-oriented architecture and the rise of pragmatic SOA Retrieved from http://www.cnet.com/uk/news/web-oriented-architecture-and-the-rise-of-pragmatic-soa/

Gall, N. (2014, October 28). WOA: Putting the Web Back in Web Services Retrieved from http://blogs.gartner.com/nick_gall/2008/11/19/woa-putting-the-web-back-in-web-services/

Garner, K. H. (1990). 20 rules for arranging text on screen. *CBT Directions*, *3*(5), 13–17.

Gefen, D. (2002). Reflections on the dimensions of trust and trustworthiness among online consumers. *The Data Base for Advances in Information Systems*, *33*(3), 38–53. doi:10.1145/569905.569910

Geissler, G., Zinkhan, G., & Watson, R. T. (2001). Web home page complexity and communication effectiveness. *Journal of the Association for Information Systems*, *2*, 1–46.

Glass, K., & Colbaugh, R. (2011, September). Web analytics for security informatics. *Proceedings of the2011 EuropeanIntelligence and Security Informatics Conference EISIC* (pp. 214-219). IEEE. doi:10.1109/EISIC.2011.66

Gledec, G. (2005). Quality Model for the World Wide Web. *Proceedings of the8th International Conference on Telecommunications - ConTEL2005*, Zagreb, Croatia (pp 281-287). doi:10.1109/CONTEL.2005.185873

Glover, F. (1989). Tabu search – Part I. *ORSA Journal on Computing*, *1*, 190–206.

Goldstein, S. M., Johnston, R., Duffy, J., & Rao, J. (2002). The service concept: The missing link in service design research. *Journal of Operations Management*, *20*(2), 121–134. doi:10.1016/S0272-6963(01)00090-0

Google Analytics Academy. (2015). *Digital Analytics Fundamentals*. Retrieved from https://analyticsacademy.withgoogle.com/

Gray, W., & Salzman, C. (1998). Damaged merchandise? a review of experiments that compare usability evaluation methods. *Human-Computer Interaction*, *13*(3), 203–261. doi:10.1207/s15327051hci1303_2

Gronroos, C. (1984). A service quality model and its marketing implications. *European Journal of Marketing*, *18*(4), 36–44. doi:10.1108/EUM0000000004784

Gronroos, C. (1992). *Service Management and Marketing*. Massachusetts: P Lexington Books.

Gube, J. (2011). *7 Best Practices for Improving Your Website's Usability*. Retrieved from http://mashable.com/2011/09/12/website-usability-tips/

Gudgin, M., Hadley, M., Mendelsohn, N., Moreau, J.-J., & Nielsen, H. (2003, June 24) *SOAP Version 1.2 Part 1: Messaging Framework*. W3C Recommendation. Retrieved from http://www.w3.org/TR/2003/REC-soap12-part1-20030624/

Guide to Software Product Quality Requirements and Evaluation (SQuaRE). (2010, December). ISO, Geneva.

Gupta, G. (1996). *Characteristics of Information*. Retrieved from: http://www.cs.jcu.edu.au/subjects/cp2030/1997/Lecture_Notes/information/characteristics.html

Haas, H., & Brown, A. (2004, February 11). *Web Services Glossary*, W3C Working Group Note. Retrieved from http://www.w3.org/TR/2004/NOTE-ws-gloss-20040211/

Habermas, J. (1973). *Knowledge and Human Interests*. London: Heineman.

Hackman, J. R., & Woolley, A. W. (In press). Creating and leading analytic teams. In R. L. Rees & J. W. Harris (Eds.), *A handbook of the psychology of intelligence analysis: The human factor*. Burlington, MA: CENTRA Technology.

Han, J., Kamber, M., & Pei, J. (2011). *Data Mining: Concepts and Techniques* (pp. 192–203). New Delhi: Morgan Kaufmann.

Hannafin, M. J., & Hooper, S. (1989). An integrated framework for CBI screen design and layout. *Computers in Human Behavior*, *5*(3), 155–165. doi:10.1016/0747-5632(89)90009-5

Harper, S., & Yesilada, Y. (2008). Web accessibility and guidelines. In S. Harper & Y. Yesilada (Eds.), *Web Accessibility* (pp. 61–78). London: Springer-Verlag. doi:10.1007/978-1-84800-050-6_6

Hart, J., Ridley, C., Taher, F., Sas, C., & Dix, A. (2008, October). Exploring the Facebook experience: a new approach to usability.*Proceedings of the 5th Nordic conference on Human-computer interaction: building bridges* (pp. 471-474). ACM. doi:10.1145/1463160.1463222

Hartmann, J., Angeli, A. D., & Sutcliffe, A. (2008). Framing the User Experience: Information Biases on Website Quality Judgement. *Proceeding of the Twenty-sixth Annual SIGCHI Conference on Human Factors in Computing Systems*, Florence, Italy (pp 855-864). doi:10.1145/1357054.1357190

Hasan, L., Morris, A., Probets, S. (2009). Using Google Analytics to Evaluate the Usability of E-Commerce Sites. *Human Centered Design* (pp. 697-706).

Hasan, L., Morris, A., & Probets, S. (2012). Morris A., Probets S. (2012). A Comparison of Usability Evaluation Methods for Evaluating e-commerce Websites. *Behaviour & Information Technology*, *31*(7), 707–737. doi:10.1080/0144929X.2011.596996

Hashimi, S. (2004). *Service-Oriented Architecture Explained*. O'Reilly.

Hayes, P. (2004, February 10). RDF Semantics. W3C. Retrieved from http://www.w3.org/TR/rdf-mt/

Herder, E. (2002). Metrics for the Adaptation of Site Structure.*Proceeding of German Workshop on Adaptivity and User Modeling in Interactive Systems (ABIS02)*.

Herrera-Viedma, E., Lopez-Herrera, A. G., & Porcel, C. (2006). Evaluating the information quality of Web sites: A methodology based on fuzzy computing with words. *Journal of the American Society for Information Science and Technology*, *57*(4), 538–549. doi:10.1002/asi.20308

Herzwurm, G., Schockert, S., & Mellis, W. (1999). Higher Customer Satisfaction With Prioritizing And Focused Software Quality Function Deployment. *Proceedings of theSixth European Conference on Software Quality*, Vienna.

Hew, K. F., & Cheung, W. S. (2013). Use of Web 2.0 technologies in K-12 and higher education: The search for evidence-based practice. *Educational Research Review*, *9*(1), 47–64. doi:10.1016/j.edurev.2012.08.001

Hidayanto, A. N., Rofalina, F., & Handayani, P. W. (2015). Influence of Perceived Quality of Official University Websites to Perceived Quality of University Education and Enrollment Intention. In P. Isaias, P. Kommers, &T. Issa (Eds.), The Evolution of the Internet in the Business Sector: Web 1.0 to Web 3.0. Hershey, PA, USA: IGI Global Publishing. doi:10.4018/978-1-4666-7262-8.ch013

Hidayanto, A.N., Mukhodim, W.M., Kom, F.M., & Junus, K.M. (2013). Analysis of Service Quality and Important Features of Property Websites in Indonesia. *Pacific Asia Journal of AIS*, *5*(3).

Hinchcliffe, D. (2009). Web-Oriented Architecture (Speech). London QCon. Retrieved from http://qconlondon.com/london-2009/qconlondon.com/dl/qcon-london-2009/slides/DionHinchcliffe_WebOrientedArchitectureWOA.pdf

Hinchcliffe, D. (2014, October 27). The SOA with reach: Web-Oriented Architecture Retrieved from http://qconlondon.com/london-2009/qconlondon.com/dl/qcon-london-2009/slides/DionHinchcliffe_WebOrientedArchitectureWOA.pdf

Hirsh, F., Kemp, J., & Ilkka, J. (2006). *Mobile Web Services - Architecture and Implementation*. John Wiley and Sons. doi:10.1002/9780470017982

Hockx-Yu, H. (2006). *Digital preservation in the context of institutional repositories*. Emerald Group Publishing Limited. Retrieved from http://www.emeraldinsight.com/Insight/ViewContentServiet>contentType=Article&Filename=_published/Emeraldfulltextarticle/Articles/2800400304.html

Holsapple, C. W., & Wu, J. (2008). Building effective online game websites with knowledge-based trust. *Information Systems Frontiers*, *10*(1), 47–60. doi:10.1007/s10796-007-9060-5

Holzinger, A. (2005). Usability engineering methods for software developers. *Communications of the ACM*, *48*(1), 71–74. doi:10.1145/1039539.1039541

Hong, I. (2007). A survey of web site success metrics used by Internet-dependent organizations in Korea. *Internet Research*, *17*(3), 272–290. doi:10.1108/10662240710758920

Horrocks, I. (2004, April 30). SWRL: A Semantic Web Rule Language Combining OWL and Rule ML Version 0.6. Retrieved from http://www.daml.org/2004/04/swrl/rules-all.html

Hsu, C. M., Yeh, Y. C., & Yen, J. (2009). Development of design criteria and evaluation scale for web-based learning platforms. *International Journal of Industrial Ergonomics*, *39*(1), 90–95. doi:10.1016/j.ergon.2008.08.006

Hu, Y. J. (2014, August). Privacy-Preserving WebID Analytics on the Decentralized Policy-Aware Social Web. *Proceedings of the 2014 IEEE/WIC/ACM International Joint Conferences on Web Intelligence (WI) and Intelligent Agent Technologies IAT* (Vol. 2, pp. 503-510). IEEE Computer Society. doi:10.1109/WI-IAT.2014.140

Human, G., & Naudé, O. (2014). Heterogeneity in the quality–satisfaction–loyalty framework. *Industrial Marketing Management*, *43*(6), 920–928. doi:10.1016/j.indmarman.2014.05.006

Hundepool, A., & de Wolf, P. P. (2011). Methods Series: Statistical disclosure control.

Hussher. (2006). *F. Le nouveau pouvoir des internautes* (Timée-Editions).

iCreate. (2015). Banking Intellisense. Retrieved from http://www.icreate.in/

IEEE Std. (1998). *IEEE Standard for a Software Quality Metrics Methodology*, New York, IEEE Computer Society Press. Retrieved from http://ieeexplore.ieee.org/xpl/articleDetails.jsp?arnumber=749159

Information technology - Vocabulary - Part 1: Fundamental terms. (2005). International Standards Organization (ISO).

Institute of Information Architecture. (2007). *What is Information Architecture?* Retrieved 15 October 2009 from: http://www.iainstitute.org/en/learn/resources/what_is_ia.php

International Organisation for Standardisation. (1998). *ISO9241 Ergonomic, Part 11: Guidance on Usability* (1st ed.). Geneva, Switzerland. Retrieved from https://www.iso.org/obp/ui/#iso:std:iso:9241:-11:ed-1:v1:en

Ioannou, G., Pramataris, K. C., & Prastacos, G. (2004). Quality Function Deployment Approach to Web Site Development: Applications for Electronic Retailing. *Les Cahiers du Management Technologique*, *13*(3), 1–18.

Islam, R., Ahmed, M., & Alias, M. H. (2007). Application of Quality Function Deployment in redesigning website: A case study on TV3. *International Journal of Business Information Systems*, *2*(2), 195–216. doi:10.1504/IJBIS.2007.011619

ISO. (1997). *ISO 9241: Ergonomics Requirements for Office Work with Visual Display Terminal (VDT)* Parts 1–17.

ISO/IEC 2382-01 Information Technology - Open Distributed Processing - Use of UML for ODP system specifications. (2005). International Standards Organization (ISO), committee draft v02.00 edition.

Iváncsy, R., & Vajk, I. (2005). Efficient Sequential Pattern Mining Algorithms. *WSEAS Transactions on Computers*, *4*(2), 96–101.

Iváncsy, R., & Vajk, I. (2005). PD-Tree: A New Approach to Subtree Discovery. *WSEAS Transactions on Information Science and Applications*, *2*(11), 1772–1779.

Ivory, M. Y., & Hearst, M. A. (2002). Towards quality checkers for web site designs. *IEEE Internet Computing*, *6*(2).

James, T., Rego, C., & Glover, F. (2009). Multistart tabu search and diversification strategies for the quadratic assignment problem. *IEEE Transactions on Systems, Man, and Cybernetics. Part A, Systems and Humans*, *39*(3), 579–596. doi:10.1109/TSMCA.2009.2014556

Jang, J. S. R., Sun, C. T., & Mizutani, E. (2004). *Neuro-Fuzzy and soft computing. PHI*. Pearson Education.

Ji, P., Jin, J., Wang, T., & Chen, Y. (2014). Quantification and integration of Kano's model into QFD for optimising product design. *International Journal of Production Research*, *52*(21), 6335–6348. doi:10.1080/00207543.2014.939777

Jonassen, D. H., & Hannum, W. H. (1987). Research based principles for designing computer software. *Educational Technology*, *27*(11), 7–14.

Joseph, N. M., Daniel, E., & Vasanthi, N. A. (2013). Survey on privacy-preserving methods for storage in cloud computing. *Proceedings on Amrita International Conference of Women in Computing IJCA '13* (pp. 1-4).

Joshi, A., & Krishnapuram, R. (2000). On Mining Web Access Logs. *Proceedings of the ACM SIGMOD* (pp. 63-69).

Juran, J. M., & Godfrey, A. B. (1999). *Juran's Quality Handbook*. New York: McGraw-Hill Professional.

Kampffmeyer, U. (2004, September 28). *Trends in Record, Document and Enterprise Content Management*. Project Consult. Retrieved from http://www.projectconsult.net/Files/ECM_Handout_english_SER.pdf

Kano, N., Seraku, N., Takahashi, F., & Tsuji, S. (1984). Attractive quality and must-be quality. Hinshitsu. *The Journal of the Japanese Society for Quality Control*, *14*(2), 39–48.

Kantner, L., & Rosenbaum, S. (1997). Usability Studies of WWW sites: Heuristic Evaluation vs. Laboratory Testing. *Proceedings of ACM 15th International Conference on Systems Documentation*, Salt Lake City, UT, USA (pp. 153-160). doi:10.1145/263367.263388

Kashorda, M., & Waema, T. (2007). *ICT Strategy Brief Based on Findings of e-Readiness Survey of Higher Education Institutions in Kenya*. Retrieved from www.kenet.or.ke/E-Readinesssurveyof_Kenya_highereducation_institutions2007.pdf0

Katuu, S. (2012a). Enterprise *Content Management– using maturity models to improve the quality of implementation*.

Katuu, S. (2012b). Enterprise Content Management (ECM) implementation in South Africa. *Records Management Journal*, *22*(1), 37–56. doi:10.1108/09565691211222081

Katuu, S. (2014). *Enterprise Content Management and Digital Curation Applications*. Maturity Model Connections.

Kaushansky, K. (2012). *Designing With Audio: What Is Sound Good For?* Retrieved from http://www.smashingmagazine.com/2012/04/18/designing-with-audio-what-is-sound-good-for/

Kaushik, A. (2007). Web Analytics: An Hour A Day (W/Cd). John Wiley & Sons.

Kaushik, A. (2007). *Web Analytics: An Hour a Day*. Indiana: Wiley Publishing.

Kaushik, A. (2007). *Web Analytics: An hour a day*. Indianapolis, Indiana: Wiley Publishing Inc.

Keeker, K. (1998). Improving Website Usability and Appeal. *MSN Usability Research*. Retrieved from http://www.microsoft.com/workshop/management/planning/

Kent, M. L., Carr, B. J., Husted, R. A., & Pop, R. A. (2011). Learning web analytics: A tool for strategic communication. *Public Relations Review, 37*(5), 536–543. doi:10.1016/j.pubrev.2011.09.011

Khalid, M. S., Mustafa, A., & Haque, I. (2008). Application of Kano's Model for Evaluating Information Quality of University Websites.*Proceedings SWWS* (pp. 277-280).

Kleinberg, J. M., Kumar, R., Raghavan, P., Rajagopalan, S., & Tomkins, A. (1999). The Web as a graph: Measurements, models, and methods. In T. Asano, H. Imai, D.T. Lee, S.-i. Nakano, & T. Tokuyama (Eds.), *Computing and Combinatorics*, LNCS (Vol. 1627, 1–17). Retrieved from www.webanalyticsassociation.org/aboutus/

Koenen, R.H., Lacy, J., Mackay, M., & Mitchell, S. (2006). The long march to interoperable digital rights management. *Proceedings of the IEEE, 92*(6), 883-897. Retrieved from http://ieeexplore.ieee.org/iel5/5/28864/01299164.pdf

Kohli, S., Kaur, S., & Singh, G. (2012, December). A Website Content Analysis Approach Based on Keyword Similarity Analysis. *Proceedings of the 2012 IEEE/WIC/ACM International Joint Conferences on Web Intelligence and Intelligent Agent Technology* (Vol. 1, pp. 254-257). IEEE Computer Society. doi:10.1109/WI-IAT.2012.212

Kopcso, D., Pipino, L., & Rybolt, W. (2001). Factors affecting the assessment of web site quality. *Proceedings of ECIS 2001* (p. 65).

Krug, S. (2006). *Don't Make Me Think: A Common Sense Approach to Web Usability* (2nd ed.). Berkeley, Calif, USA: New Riders Press.

Kuniavsky, M. (2003). *Observing the user experience: a practitioner's guide to user research*. San Francisco, Calif; London: Morgan Kaufmann.

Kuo, H.-M. (2006). Discussion of the interfering factors for internet shopping.*Conference on Theories and Practices in International Business*, Chang Jung Christian University (p. 52).

Kuo, H.-M., & Chen, C.-W. (2011). Application of quality function deployment to improve the quality of Internet shopping website interface design. *International Journal of Innovative Computing, Information, & Control, 7*(1), 253–268.

Kuo, Y. F. (2003). A study on service quality of virtual community websites. *Total Quality Management & Business Excellence, 13*(4), 461–473. doi:10.1080/14783360320000047237a

Kuppelwieser, V. G., & Sarstedt, M. (2014). Exploring the influence of customers' time horizon perspectives on the satisfaction–loyalty link. *Journal of Business Research, 67*(12), 2620–2627. doi:10.1016/j.jbusres.2014.03.021

Kyrnin, J. (2015). *Pros and Cons of Adding Sound to Web Pages*. Retrieved from http://webdesign.about.com/od/sound/a/aa080607.htm

Lai, Y. C., & Ng, W. S. (2011). Nurturing information literacy of early childhood teachers through web-based collaborative learning activities. *Hong Kong Journal of Early Childhood, 10*(1), 77–83.

Lautenbach, M. A. E., Schegget, I. S., Schoute, A. M., & Witteman, C. L. M. (1999). *Evaluating the Usability of Web Pages: a Case Study* (pp. 1–13).

Lazar, J. (2006). *Web usability: a user-centered design approach. Pearson*. Addison: Wesley.

Leavitt, M.O., & Shneiderman, B. (n. d.). Research-Based Web Design & Usability Guidelines.

Leavitt, M., & Shneiderman, B. (2006). *The Research-Based Web Design & Usability Guidelines*. Washington, DC, USA: U.S. Government Printing Office.

Lecerof, A., & Paterno, F. (1998). Automatic Support for Usability Evaluation. *IEEE Transactions on Software Engineering*, *24*(10), 863–888. doi:10.1109/32.729686

Lee, W.-I., Shih, B.-Y., & Tu, L.-J. (2002). The Application of Kano's Model for Improving Web-based Learning Performance. *Paper presented at the meeting of the 32nd ASEE/IEEE Frontiers in Education Conference*, Boston. doi:10.1109/FIE.2002.1157975

Lee, D., Moon, J., Kim, Y. J., & Yi, M. Y. (2015). Antecedents and consequences of mobile phone usability: Linking simplicity and interactivity to satisfaction, trust, and brand loyalty. *Information & Management*, *52*(3), 295–304. doi:10.1016/j.im.2014.12.001

Lee, G.-G., & Lin, H.-F. (2005). Customer perceptions of e-service quality in online shopping. *International Journal of Retail & Distribution Management*, *33*(2), 161–176. doi:10.1108/09590550510581485

Lee, H. C., & Fu, H. Y. (2008). Web Usage Mining Based on Clustering of Browsing Features.*Proceedings of Eighth International Conference on Intelligent Systems Design and Applications* (Vol. 1, pp. 281-286). doi:10.1109/ISDA.2008.185

Lee, Y. C., & Chen, J. K. (2009). A new service development integrated model. *Service Industries Journal*, *29*(12), 1669–1686. doi:10.1080/02642060902793573

Lewis, J. R. (1995). IBM computer usability satisfaction questionnaires: Psychometric evaluation and instructions for use. *International Journal of Human-Computer Interaction*, *7*(1), 57–78. doi:10.1080/10447319509526110

Li, N., Li, T., & Venkatasubramanian, S. (2007, April). t-closeness: Privacy beyond k-anonymity and l-diversity. *Proceedings of the IEEE 23rd International Conference on Data Engineering ICDE '07* (pp. 106-115). IEEE.

Liburne, B., Devkota, P., & Khan, K. M. (2004). Measuring Quality Metrics for Web Applications. *Proceedings of the 2004 IRMA International Conference*, New Orleans, USA.

Lin, C. C. (2006). Optimal web site reorganization considering information overload and search depth. *European Journal of Operational Research*, *173*(3), 839–848. doi:10.1016/j.ejor.2005.05.029

Lin, C. C., & Tseng, L. C. (2010). Website reorganization using an ant colony system. *Expert Systems with Applications*, *37*(12), 7598–7605. doi:10.1016/j.eswa.2010.04.083

Lindgaard, G., Fernandes, G. J., Dudek, C., & Brownet, J. (2006). Attention web designers: You have 50 ms to make a good first impression! *Behaviour & Information Technology*, *25*(2), 115–126. doi:10.1080/01449290500330448

Lin, L.-Z., Yeh, H.-R., & Wang, M.-C. (2015, February). Integration of Kano's model into FQFD for Taiwanese Ban-Doh banquet culture. *Tourism Management*, *46*, 245–262. doi:10.1016/j.tourman.2014.05.007

Lippert, R. (2012). *9 Guiding Principles - A Framework of Guidance for Building Good Digital Collections*. Retrieved from https://ezphotoscan.com/blog/9-guiding-principles-framework-guidance-building-good-digital-collections

Liu, R.Y.L. (2002). *Capability maturity model integration: origins and applications* [Masters dissertation]. California State University, Long Beach.

Liu, B. (2007). *Web Data Mining: Exploring Hyperlinks, Contents, and Usage Data. Springer-Verlag*. Berlin, Heidelberg: Springer-Verlag.

Li, Y., Tan, K., & Xie, M. (2002). Measuring Web-based Service Quality. *Total Quality Management, 13*(5), 685–700. doi:10.1080/0954412022000002072

Loiola, E. M., deAbreu, N. M., Boaventura-Netto, P. O., Hahn, P., & Querido, T. (2007). A survey for the quadratic assignment problem. *European Journal of Operational Research, 176*(2), 657–690. doi:10.1016/j.ejor.2005.09.032

Loranger, H., & Nielsen, J. (2006). *Prioritizing Web Usability*. Berkeley, Calif, USA: New Riders Press.

Lu, Y. H., Hong, Y., Varia, J., & Lee, D. (2005, March). Pollock: automatic generation of virtual web services from websites. *Proceedings of the 2005 ACM symposium on Applied computing* (pp. 1650-1655). ACM. doi:10.1145/1066677.1067052

Machanavajjhala, A., Kifer, D., Gehrke, J., & Venkitasubramaniam, M. (2007). l-diversity: Privacy beyond k-anonymity. *ACM Transactions on Knowledge Discovery from Data, 1*(1), 3. doi:10.1145/1217299.1217302

Madana Kumar Reddy. C. (2009). Operating Systems Made easy (pp. 23-49). New Delhi: University Science Press.

Madu, C. N., & Madu, A. A. (2002). Dimensions of e-Quality. *International Journal of Quality & Reliability Management, 19*(3), 246–258. doi:10.1108/02656710210415668

Manthan. (2015). *Analyze, Decide, Do*. Retrieved from https://www.manthan.com/

Mao, J. (2014). Social media for learning: A mixed methods study on high school students' technology affordances and perspectives. *Computers in Human Behavior, 33*(1), 213–223. doi:10.1016/j.chb.2014.01.002

Marchetto, A. (2005). *A Concerns-based Metrics Suite for Web Applications*. Retrieved from http://citeseerx.ist.psu.edu/viewdoc/summary?doi=10.1.1.59.9742

Marentakis, C., & Emiris, D. (2010). Location aware auctions for tourism services. *Journal of Hospitality and Tourism Technology, 1*(2), 121–143. doi:10.1108/17579881011065038

Marinescu, R. (2001). Detecting Design Flaws via Metrics in Object-Oriented Systems. Proceedings of the 39th Technology of Object-Oriented Languages and Systems (TOOLS USA 2001), Santa Barbara, CA, USA.

Marketelligent. (2015). *Analytics in action*. Retrieved from http://www.marketelligent.com/

Martínez, S., Sánchez, D., & Valls, A. (2012). Towards k-anonymous non-numerical data via semantic resampling. In *Advances in Computational Intelligence* (pp. 519–528). Springer Berlin Heidelberg. doi:10.1007/978-3-642-31724-8_54

Marucci, L., & Patrno, F. (2000, March 27-31). Adaptive Interfaces for Web Museums Applications: the Virtual Marble Museum. Proceedings of EVA2000 – electronic Imaging & the Visual Arts, Conference, Training & Workshops, Firenze (pp. 151-155).

Mathwick, C., Wiertz, C., & de Ruyter, K. (2008). Social capital production in a virtual P3 community. *The Journal of Consumer Research, 34*(6), 832–849. doi:10.1086/523291

Maurer, D. (2004). *Information Architecture*. Retrieved from http://www.institute.org/tools/download/Maurer-IAItro.ppt

Mavromoustakos, S., & Andreou, A. S. (2007, November). WAQE: A Web Application Quality Evaluation model. *International Journal of Web Engineering and Technology, 3*(1), 96–120. doi:10.1504/IJWET.2007.011529

May So, W. C., Danny Wong, T. N., & Sculli, D. (2005). Factors affecting intentions to purchase via the Internet. *Industrial Management & Data Systems, 105*(9), 1225–1244. doi:10.1108/02635570510633275

Mayer, R. E. (2009). *Multimedia learning*. Cambridge: Cambridge University Press. doi:10.1017/CBO9780511811678

McFadden, C. (2005). Optimizing the Online Business Channel with Web Analytics.

McFadden, C. (2005). *Optimizing the Online Business Channel with Web Analytics.* Retrieved from http://www.Webanalyticsassociation.org/en/art/?9

McGovern, G. (2001). *Re-establishing the Value of Content.* Retrieved from http://www.acm.org/ubiquity/views/g_mcgovern_1.html

Mcgovern, G. (2001). *Writing for the web,* Retrieved from http://www.gerrymcgovern.com/new-thinking/writing-killer-web-headings-and-links

McLaughlin, J., & Skinner, D. (2000). Developing Usability and Utility: A Comparative Study of the User of New IT. *Technology Analysis and Strategic Management, 12*(3), 413–423. doi:10.1080/09537320050130633

McRoberts, H. A., & Sloan, B. C. (1998). "Financial management capability model." International. *Journal on Government Auditing, 25*(3), 8–11.

Mebrate, T. W. (2010). *A Framework for Evaluating Academic Website's Quality From Students' Perspective.* Netherlands: Delft University of Technology.

Mendes, E. M., Mosley, N., & Counsell, S. (2001). Web Metrics -Estimating Design and Authoring Effort. *IEEE MultiMedia, 8*(1), 50–57. doi:10.1109/93.923953

Merriam, S. (1998). *Qualitative research and case study applications in education.* Jossey-Bass Publishers.

Meyer, K. (2015). *The Characteristics of Minimalism in Web Design.* Retrieved from http://www.nngroup.com/topic/web-usability/

Mich, L., Franch, M., & Gaio, L. (2003, January-March). Evaluating and Designing the Quality of Web Sites. *IEEE MultiMedia, 10*(1), 34–43. doi:10.1109/MMUL.2003.1167920

Mifsud, J. (2011). *USEFul: A Framework to Mainstream Web site Usability through Automated Evaluation* [B.Sc. thesis]. University of London, United Kingdom.

Mika, P. (2007). *Social Networks and the Semantic Web.* Barcelona, Spain: Springer International.

MIKE2. 0. (2010). *ECM Maturity Model (ecm3)* Retrieved from http://mike2.openmethodology.org/wiki/ECM_Maturity_Model_%28ecm3%29

Misevicius, A. (2005). A tabu search Algorithm for the Quadratic assignment Problem. *Journal of Computational Optimization and Applications, 30*(1), 95–111. doi:10.1007/s10589-005-4562-x

Mittal, H., Sharma, M., & Mittal, J. P. (2012, January). Analysis and modelling of websites quality using fuzzy technique. *Proceedings of theSecond International Conference on Advanced Computing & Communication Technologies* (pp. 7-8). doi:10.1109/ACCT.2012.25

Mivule, K. (2013). Utilizing noise addition for data privacy, an overview. *arXiv preprint arXiv:1309.3958.*

Mnkandla, E. (2014). A review of Communication Tools and Techniques for Successful ICT Projects. *The African Journal of Information Systems, 6*(1).

Mobasher, B., Dai, H., Luo,T. and Nakagawa, M. (2001). Elective Personalization Based on Association Rule Discovery from Web Usage Data. *Proceedings of WIDM01,* Atlanta, (pp. 9-15).

Mobasher, B., Cooley, R., & Srivastava, J. (1999). Creating Adaptive Web Sites Through Usage Based Clustering of URLs. *KDEX, 99,* 32–37.

Mobasher, B., Dai, H., Luo, T., & Nakagawa, M. (2002). Discovery and Evaluation of Aggregate Usage Profiles for Web Personalization. *Data Mining and Knowledge Discovery*, *6*(1), 61–82. doi:10.1023/A:1013232803866

Mohammadi, M., & Moghadam, A. (2008). Some Issues on Impacts and Characteristics of Information as Wealth in the New Economy. *International Journal of Information science and Technology,* 6(2). Retrieved from http://www.srlst.com/ijist/ijism-Vol6No2/ijism62-37-47.pdf

Mohiddin, S. K., & Kiran Kumar, M. (2013). A Novel Approach for Data Publishing In Mining. *IJRCCT*, *2*(7), 387–391.

Moogan, Y. J., Baron, S., & Bainbridge, S. (2001). Timings and trade-offs in the marketing of higher education courses: A conjoint approach. *Marketing Intelligence & Planning*, *19*(3), 179–187. doi:10.1108/02634500110391726

Moseti, I. M. (2012). Digital Content Management and Use at Moi University [Unpublished MPhil Thesis]. Moi University, Kenya.

Mu Sigma. (2015). *Do the Math*. Retrieved from http://www.mu-sigma.com/

Mungai, A. (2008, November). *Local Content – an e-Tourism Perspective*. Paper presented at Tandaa 2008: The Kenya Content Conference held at Kenyatta International Convention Centre, Nairobi, Kenya.

Murray, A., & Ward, M. (2007). *Improving project performance using the PRINCE2 maturity model (P2MM)*. Norwich: The Stationary Office.

Muske, G., Stanforth, N., & Woods, M. (n. d.). *The Internet as a Marketing Tool*. Retrieved from http://pods.dasnr.okstate.edu/docushare/dsweb/Get/Document-2491/AGEC-566web.pdf

Mustafa, S. H., & Al-Zoua'bi, L. F. (2008). Usability of the academic websites of Jordan's Universities: An Evaluation Study. *Proceedings of theInternational Arab conference on information technology*, Tunisia (pp. 1–9).

Mustafa, S., & Al-Zoua'bi, L. (2008). Usability of the Academic Websites of Jordan's Universities. *Proceedings of the International Arab Conference on Information Technology*, Tunisia (pp. 2-9).

Mutula, S., & Wamukoya, J. (2007). *Web Information Management: A Cross-disciplinary textbook*. Great Britain: Chandos Publishing. doi:10.1533/9781780631899

Nabler. (2015). *Custom Digital Analytics software Solutions*. Retrieved from http://www.nabler.com/

Negash, S., Ryan, T., & Igbaria, M. (2003). Quality and effectiveness in web-based customer support systems. *Information & Management*, *40*(8), 757–768. doi:10.1016/S0378-7206(02)00101-5

Neha v. M., & Sulbha, P. (2013). Slicing: An Approach For Privacy Preservation in High-Dimensional Data Using Anonymization Technique. *Proceedings of Fifth IRAJ International Conference*, Pune, India (pp.103-108).

Newman, B., & Conrad, K. (1999). *A Framework for Characterizing Knowledge Management Methods, Practices, and Technologies* Retrieved from http://www.km-forum.org/KM-Characterization-Framework.pdf

Newth, A. (n. d.). What Is Web Oriented Architecture? Retrieved from https://en.wikipedia.org/wiki/Web-oriented_architecture

Ng, W. S. (2011). Innovative pedagogy for enhancing web-based collaborative learning in tertiary teacher education using wikis. *Proceedings of the Work-in-Progress Poster of the International Conference on Computers in Education: ICCE 2011*. Chiang Mai: National Electronics and Computer

Ngugi, B., Pelowski, M., & Ogembo, J. G. (2010). M-PESA: A Case Study of the Critical Early Adopters' Role in the Rapid Adoption of Mobile Money Banking in Kenya. *The Electronic Journal of Information Systems in Developing Countries*, 43.

Ng, W. S. (2014). Critical design factors of developing a high-quality educational website: Perspectives of preservice teachers. *Issues in Informing Science and Information Technology*, *11*, 101–113.

Nielsen, J. (1995). *10 Usability Heuristics for User Interface Design*. Retrieved from http://www.nngroup.com/articles/ten-usability-heuristics/

Nielsen, J. (2006). *Quantitative studies: how many users to test?*. Useit.com.

Nielsen, J., & Philips, V. (1993). Estimating the relative usability of two interfaces: Heuristic, formal, and empirical methods compared. *Proceedings of ACM /IFIP Human Factors Computing Systems (INTERCHI)*, Amsterdam, The Netherlands (pp. 214-221).

Nielsen. (1998). Using link titles to help users predict where they are going. Retrieved from www.useit.com/alertbox/990530.html

Nielsen, J. (1992). The Usability Engineering Life Cycle. *Computer*, *25*(3), 12–22.

Nielsen, J. (1993). *Usability engineering*. London: Aademic Press.

Nielsen, J. (1994). Heuristic Evaluation. In J. Nielsen & R. L. Mack (Eds.), *Usability Inspection Methods* (pp. 25–64). New York: John Wiley & Sons.

Nielsen, J. (1995, May). Usability inspection methods. *Conference companion on Human factors in computing systems* (pp. 377–378). ACM. doi:10.1145/223355.223730

Nielsen, J. (1998). *Content usability, NPL: Usability Forum-Making Webs Work (Tutorial)*. Middlesex, UK: NPL.

Nielsen, J. (1999). User Interface Directions for the Web. *Communications of the ACM*, *42*(1), 65–72. doi:10.1145/291469.291470

Nielsen, J. (2000). *Designing Web Usability: The Practice of Simplicity*. New Riders Publishing.

Nielsen, J., & Pernice, K. (2010). *Eyetracking Web Usability*. Berkeley, Calif, USA: New Riders Press.

Nielsen, J., & Tahir, M. (2002). *Homepage Usability: 50 Websites Deconstructed*. Berkeley, Calif, USA: New Riders Press.

Norman, D. A. (2002). Emotion and design: attractive things work better. *Interactions Magazine*, 36-42.

Norman, D. (1988). *The Design of Everyday Things*. Broadway, NY, USA: Doubleday.

O'Brien, J. (2002). *Management Information Systems: Managing Information Technology in the E-Business Enterprise* (5th ed.). India: Tata McGraw-Hill.

O'Reilly, T. (2005). What is Web 2.0: Design Patterns and Business Models for the Next Generation of Software. *Proceedings of the Web 2.0 Conference*.

O'Reilly, T. (2006). *Web 2.0 Principles and Best Practices*. O'Reilly Media.

O'Reilly, T. (2006). *Seven principles of Web 2.0 make a lot more sense if you change the order*. Open Gardens.

Obeidat, M. (2001). Consumer protection and electronic commerce in Jordan (an exploratory study). *Proceedings of the Public Voice in Emerging Market Economies Conference*, Dubai, UAE.

OCLC. (2003) Collections Grid. Retrieved from http://www.oclc.org/reports/escan/appendices/collectiongrid.html

Offutt, J. (2002). Quality Attributes of Web Software Applications. *Software, IEEE, 19*(2), 25–32. doi:10.1109/52.991329

Ogawa, H., & Goto, Y. (2006). *Web 2.0 book*. Tokyo, Japan: Impress Japan Corporation.

Oh, J.-C., Yoon, S.-J., & Park, B.-I. (2012). A structural approach to examine the quality attributes of e-shopping malls using the Kano model. *Asia Pacific Journal of Marketing and Logistics, 24*(2), 305–327. doi:10.1108/13555851211218075

Oldfield, B. M., & Baron, S. (2000). Student perceptions of service quality in a UK university business and management faculty. *Quality Assurance in Education, 8*(2), 85–95. doi:10.1108/09684880010325600

O'Leary, D. E. (2008). Wikis: From each according to his knowledge. *IEEE Computer, 41*(2), 34–41. doi:10.1109/MC.2008.68

Oppenheim, C., Stenson, J., & Wilson, R. M. S. (2001). *The Attributes of Information as an Asset*. Retrieved from http://www.emeraldinsight.com/journals.html?articleid=860097&show=html

Orehovački, T., Granić, A., & Kermek, D. (2012). Exploring the quality in use of Web 2.0 applications: the case of mind mapping services. *Current Trends in Web Engineering* (pp. 266–277). Springer Berlin Heidelberg. doi:10.1007/978-3-642-27997-3_26

Orehovački, T., Granić, A., & Kermek, D. (2013). Evaluating the perceived and estimated quality in use of Web 2.0 applications. *Journal of Systems and Software, 86*(12), 3039–3059. doi:10.1016/j.jss.2013.05.071

Orel, F. D., & Kara, A. (2014). Supermarket self-checkout service quality, customer satisfaction, and loyalty: Empirical evidence from an emerging market. *Journal of Retailing and Consumer Services, 21*(2), 118–129. doi:10.1016/j.jretconser.2013.07.002

Oriezy, P. et al.. (1999). An Architecture-Based Approach to Self-Adaptive Software. *IEEE Intelligent Systems, 14*(3).

Oztekin, A., Nikov, A., & Zaim, S. (2009). UWIS: An assessment methodology for usability of web-based information systems. *Journal of Systems and Software, 82*(12), 2038–2050. doi:10.1016/j.jss.2009.06.047

Panda, S. K., Swain, S. K. Mall, R. (2015). An Investigation into Usability Aspects of E-Commerce Websites Using Users' Preferences. Advances in Computer Science: an International Journal, 4(13), 65-73.

Panda, S. K. (2014). A Usability Evaluation Framework for B2C E-Commerce Websites. *Journal of Computer Engineering and Intelligent System, 5*(3), 66–85.

Pang, M., Suh, W., Hong, J., Kim, J., & Lee, H. (2009). A new website quality assessment model for the Web 2.0 Era. Handbook of research on Web, 2(3.0), 387-410.

Pang, M. S., Suh, W., Kim, J., & Lee, H. (2009). A benchmarking-based requirement analysis methodology for improving websites. *International Journal of Electronic Commerce, 13*(3), 119–162. doi:10.2753/JEC1086-4415130305

Parasuraman, A., Zeithaml, V. A., & Berry, L. L. (1985). A Conceptual Model of Service Quality and It's Implication for Future Research. *Journal of Marketing, 49*(4), 41–50. doi:10.2307/1251430

Parasuraman, A., Zeithaml, V. A., & Berry, L. L. (1988). SERVQUAL: A Multiple-item Scale for Measuring Consumer Perception of Service Quality. *Journal of Retailing, 64*(1), 12–40.

Parasuraman, A., Zeithaml, V. A., & Malhotra, A. (2005). E-S-QUAL: A Multiple-Item Scale for Assessing Electronic Service Quality. *Journal of Service Research, 7*(3), 213–233. doi:10.1177/1094670504271156

Patton, S. (2002). *E-Commerce Tools: Web Metrics That Matter*. Retrieved from www.cio.com/article/31511/E_Commerce_Tools_Web_Metrics_That_Matter?page=2&taxonomyId=3181

Pearrow, M. (2000). *Website usability handbook*. Charles River Media.

Pearson, J., Pearson, A., & Green, D. (2007). Determining the Importance of Key Criteria in Web Usability. *Management Research News*, *30*(11), 816–828. doi:10.1108/01409170710832250

Pelz-Sharpe, A., Durga, A., Smigiel, D., Hartman, E., Byrne, T., & Gingras, J. 2010. *ECM 3 - ECM maturity model* (2nd), June. Retrieved from http://ecmmaturity.files.wordpress.com/2009/02/ecm3-v2_0.pdf

Peng, Z.R., & Tsou, M. (2003). Internet GIS: Distributed Geographic Information Services for the Internet and Wireless Networks. Wiley.

Perkowitz, M., & Etzioni, O. (1997). Adaptive Web sites: An AI challenge.*Proceedings of International Joint Conference on Artificial IntelligenceIJCAI-97*, Nagoya, Japan (pp. 16–21). Morgan Kaufmann.

Perkowitz, M., & Etzioni, O. (2000). Toward adaptive Web sites: Conceptual framework and case study. *Artificial Intelligence*, *118*(1-2), 245–275. doi:10.1016/S0004-3702(99)00098-3

Peterson, E. (2004). *Web analytics demystified: A marketer's guide to understanding how your web site affects your business*. Celilo Group Media and CafePress.

Phippen, A., Sheppard, L., & Furnell, S. (2004). A practical evaluation of Web analytics. *Internet Research*, *14*(4), 284–293. doi:10.1108/10662240410555306

Pierrakos, D., Paliouras, G., Papatheodorou, C., & Spyropoulos, C. D. (2003). Web Usage Mining as a Tool for Personalization: A Survey. *User Modeling and User-Adapted Interaction*, *13*(4), 311–372. doi:10.1023/A:1026238916441

Poncelet, G. M., & Proctor, L. F. (1993). Design and development factors in the production of hypermedia based courseware. *Canadian Journal of Educational Communication*, *22*(2), 91–111.

Prasad , S. (2014). Signature Analysis and Trait Prediction. LAP Lambert Academic Publishing.

Preece, J., Rogers, Y., & Sharp, H. (2007). *Interaction Design Beyond Human-Computer Interaction* (pp. 224–301). Publishing House of Electronics Industry.

Preece, J., Sharp, H., & Rogers, Y. (2002). *Interaction design: beyond human computer interaction*. John Wiley & Sons, Inc.

Pressman R., S., & Maxim, B. (2008). *Software Engineering: A Practitioner's Approach*. McGraw Hill.

Rajasekaran, S., & Pai, G. A. V. (2003). Neural Networks, Fuzzy Logic and Genetic Algorithms. PHI, Pearson Education.

Rambharose, T., & Nikov, A. (2010). Computational Intelligence-Based Personalization of Interactive Web Systems. *WSEAS Transactions on Information Science and Applications*, *7*, 484–497.

Ranganathan, C., & Ganapathy, S. (2002). Key dimensions of business-to-consumer web sites. *Information & Management*, *39*(6), 457–465. doi:10.1016/S0378-7206(01)00112-4

Rao, Aditi. (2013). What Does Web 3.0 Look Like in Education? Retrieved from http://teachbytes.com/2013/03/24/what-does-web-3-0-look-like-in-education/

Rashid, M. M., Tamaki, J., Ullah, A. M. M. S., & Kubo, A. (2011). A Kano Model Based Linguistic Application for Customer Needs Analysis. *International Journal of Engineering Business Management*, *3*(2), 29–36.

Ratanasawadwat, N. (2015). E-Service Attribute Analysis: An Application of Kano's Model. *Journal of Economics. Business and Management, 3*(11), 1076–1079.

Rathipriya, R., Thangavel, K., & Bagyamani, J. (2011). Binary Particle Swarm Optimization based Biclustering of Web usage Data. *International Journal of Computers and Applications, 25*(2).

Reference Model for Service Oriented Architecture. (2006). OASIS. Retrieved from http://www.oasis-open.org/committees/download.php/19679/soa-rm-cs.pdf

Reichenstein, O. (2006). *Web design is 95% typography*. Retrieved from http://informationarchitects.net/blog/the-web-is-all-about-typography-period/

Reilly, N. B. (1999). *The Team Based Product Development Guidebook*. Milwaukee, Wisconsin: ASQ Quality Press.

Review, C. M. S. (2015). *Seven Stages of the Content Lifecycle*. Retrieved from http://www.cmsreview.com/Stages/

Ricca, F., & Chao, L. (2009). Special section on web systems evolution. *International Journal of Software Tools and Technology Transfer, 11*(6), 419–425. doi:10.1007/s10009-009-0127-0

Rio, A., & e Abreu, F. B. (2010). Websites Quality.

Rodger, K., Taplin, R. H., & Moore, S. A. (2015, October). Using a randomised experiment to test the causal effect of service quality on visitor satisfaction and loyalty in a remote national park. *Tourism Management, 50*, 172–183.

Rosenberg, L. (1998). Applying and Interpreting Object Oriented Metrics. *Proceedings of the Software Technology Conference '98*, Salt Lake City, UT. Retrieved from http://www.literateprogramming.com/ooapply.pdf

Rosenberg, L., Hammer, T., & Shaw, J. (1998). Software Metrics and Reliability. *Proceedings of the9th International Symposium on Software Reliability Engineering*, Germany.

Rosenfeld, L., & Morville, P. (1998). *Information Architecture for the World Wide Web*. Sebastopol, Calif, USA: O'Reilly & Associates.

Rossi, Ben. (2015). Retrieved from http://www.information-age.com/technology/information-management/123459381/4-trends-reshaping-traditional-content-management

Rubin, J. (1994). *Handbook of usability testing:how to plan, design, and conduct effective tests*. Wiley.

Saha, R., & Grover, S. (2011). Quantitative evaluation of website quality dimension for web2. 0 environment. *International Journal of u-and e-Service Science and Technology, 4*(4), 14–35.

Sanil, A. P., Gomatam, S., Karr, A. F., & Liu, C. (2003). NISSWebSwap: A Web Service for data swapping. *Journal of Statistical Software, 8*(7). doi:10.18637/jss.v008.i07

Sano, D. (1996). *Designing Large-Scale Websites: A visual Design Methodology*. New York, NY, USA: Wiley Computer Publishing, John Wiley & Sons.

Santos, L. (1999). Web-site Quality Evaluation Method: a Case Study on Museums. *Proceedings of the2nd Workshop on Software Engineering over the Internet ICSE 99*.

Saremi, H. Q., Abedin, B., & Kermani, A. M. (2008). Website structure improvement: Quadratic assignment problem approach and ant colony meta-heuristic technique. *Applied Mathematics and Computation, 195*(1), 285–298. doi:10.1016/j.amc.2007.04.095

Sauerwein, E., Bailom, F., Matzler, K., & Hinterhuber, H. H. (1996). The Kano Model: How to delight your customers. *Proceedings of the International Working Seminar on Production Economics*, Innsbruck, Austria (pp. 313-327).

Sbihi, B., El Jazouli, S., & El Kadiri, K. E. (2009). Web 2.1: Toward a large and qualitative participation on the Web. *Journal of Information and Organizational Sciences, 33*(1), 191–204.

Scharl, A. (2000). *Evolutionary Web Development (Applied Computing)*. Springer.

Schenkman, B. N., & Jonsson, F. U. (2000). Aesthetics and preferences of web pages. *Behaviour & Information Technology, 19*(5), 367–377. doi:10.1080/014492900750000063

Schon, D. A. (1991). *The reflective practitioner: how professionals think in action*. Aldershot, England: Ashgate.

Security fundamentals for Web Services Security: Patterns & Practices from MSDN library. (n. d.). Retrieved from https://msdn.microsoft.com/en-us/library/ff648318.aspx

Seffah, A., Gulliksen, J., & Desmarais, M. C. (2001). Human-Centered Software Engineering: Integrating Usability. *In Seffah, A., Fulliksen, J., & Desmarais, M.C. (Eds.), Human-Computer Interaction Series, 08*. Springer.

Shackel, B. (2009). Usability - context, framework, design and evaluation. *Journal Interacting with Computers, 21*(5-6), 339–346. doi:10.1016/j.intcom.2009.04.007

Sharma, P. (2008). Core Characteristics of Web 2.0 services. Retrieved from http://www.techpluto.com/web-20-services/

Shergill, G., & Chen, Z. (2005). Web-based shopping: Consumers' attitudes towards online shopping in New Zealand. *Journal of Electronic Commerce Research, 6*(2).

Shin, D-H. (2014). Effect of the customer experience on satisfaction with smartphones: Assessing smart satisfaction index with partial least squares. *Telecommunications Policy*.

Shirleen, K., & Burn, J. (2005). Developing a framework for assessing information quality on the World Wide Web. *Inform Sci J, 8*, 159–172.

Shi, Y., Prentice, C., & He, W. (2014, July). Linking service quality, customer satisfaction and loyalty in casinos, does membership matter? *International Journal of Hospitality Management, 40*, 81–91. doi:10.1016/j.ijhm.2014.03.013

Shneiderman, B. (1998). *Designing the user interface, strategies for effective human computer interaction* (3rd ed.). Addison Wesley.

Shneiderman, B. (1998). *Designing the User Interface: Strategies for Effective Human-Computer Interaction*. Reading, Mass, USA: Addison-Wesley.

Shostack, G. L. (1982). How to Design a Service. *European Journal of Marketing, 16*(1), 49–63. doi:10.1108/EUM0000000004799

Shostack, G. L. (1984). Designing services that deliver. *Harvard Business Review, 62*(1), 134–135.

Shpak, O., Lowe, W., Wingkvist, A., & Ericsson, M. (2014, October). A Method to Test the Information Quality of Technical Documentation on Websites. In*Quality Software (QSIC), 2014 14th International Conference on* (pp. 296-304). IEEE. doi:10.1109/QSIC.2014.48

Signore, O., & Bartoli, R. Fresta Ga, Loffredo M (1997, September 3-5). Implementing the Cognitive Layer of a Hypermedia – Museum Interactive Multimedia 1997: Cultural Heritage Systems Design and Interfaces. In D. Bearman and J. Trant (Ed.), *Selected papers from ICHIM 97 the Fourth International Conference on Hypermedia and InterActivity in Museums*, Paris, France (pp. 15-22).

Signore, O., Marucci, L., & Leporini, B. (2004). Web accessibility: principles, international context and Italian regulations. *Proceedings of Euro CMG 2004*, Vienna.

Silva, P. A., & Dix, A. (2007, September). Usability: not as we know it!*Proceedings of the 21st British HCI Group Annual Conference on People and Computers: HCI... but not as we know it (Vol. 2*, pp. 103-106). British Computer Society.

Simple HTML Ontology Extensions Frequently Asked Questions (SHOE FAQ). (n. d.). Retrieved from www.cs.umd. edu/projects/plus/SHOE/faq.html

Singal, H., & Kohli, S. (2013). Evolutionary PRM Model: A Unified Strategic Approach to combat challenges of Web Analytics. *Paper presented at themeeting of International Workshop on Machine Learning and Text Analytics*, South Asian University, New Delhi, India.

Singh, H., & Kaur, P. (2014a). Website Structure Optimization Model Based on Ant Colony System and Local Search. *International Journal Information Technology and Computer Science*, *6*(11), 48–53. doi:10.5815/ijitcs.2014.11.07

Singh, H., & Kaur, P. (2014b). A survey of transformation based Website Structure Optimization models. *Journal of Information and Optimization Sciences*, *35*(5-6), 529–560. doi:10.1080/02522667.2014.961802

Singh, H., & Kaur, P. (2014c). Algorithms to Restructure the Websites for Efficient Browsing. *CSI Communications*, *38*(9), 12–14.

Singh, Y., Malhotra, R., & Gupta, P. (2011). Empirical Validation of Web Metrics for Improving the Quality of Web Page. *International Journal of Advanced Computer Science and Applications*, *2*(5), 22–28. doi:10.5120/2414-3226

Skaalid, B. (1999). *Multimedia & Web Page Design Principles*. Retrieved from http://www.usask.ca/education/coursework/skaalid/page/design/webdsgn.htm

Smith, S., & Mosier, J. (1986). *Guidelines for Designing User Interface Software*. MITRE Corporation.

Sohn, S. Y., Park, H. Y., & Chang, S. I. (2009). Assessment of a Complementary Cyber Learning System to Offline Teaching. *Expert Systems with Applications*, *36*(3), 6485–6491. doi:10.1016/j.eswa.2008.07.075

Sonawane, V. R., & Rahinj, K. S. (2013). A New Data Anonymization Technique used For Membership Disclosure Protection. *International Journal of Innovative Research in Science Engineering and Technology*, *2*(4), 1230–1233.

Spivack, N. (2015). *The Third Generation Web is Coming*. Retrieved from http://lifeboat.com/ex/web.3.0

Spool, J., Scanlon, T., Snyder, C., & DeAngelo, T. (1998). *Website Usability: A Designer's Guide*. San Francisco, Calif, USA: Morgan Kaufmann Publishers.

Sqrum, H., Medaglia, R., & Normann Andersen, K. (2009). Assessment of Website Quality: Scandinavian Web Awards Right on Track? *Proceedings of the 8th International Conference on Electronic Government*, Linz, Austria (pp. 198 – 209). Springer-Verlag.

Srivastava, J., Cooley, R., Deshpande, M., & Tan, P.-N. (2000). Web usage mining: Discovery and applications of usage patterns from Web data. *ACM SIGKDD Explorations Newsletter*, *1*(2), 12–23. doi:10.1145/846183.846188

Steel, D. (2012). *Implementation of a content management system at the Stellenbosch University: an exploratory investigation* [Unpublished MPhil Thesis]. University of Cape Town.

Steeples, G. P. (1998). Creating shareable representations of practice. *Advance Learning Technology Journal*, *6*(3), 16–23.

Stemler, L. K. (1997). Educational characteristics of multimedia: A literature review. *Journal of Educational Multimedia and Hypermedia*, *6*(3/4), 339–359.

Sterne, J. (2002). *Web Metrics: Proven Methods for Measuring Web Site Success*. New York: John Wiley & Sons.

Stern, J. (1995). *World Wide Web marketing*. New York, USA: John Wiley & Sons Inc.

Stockdale, R., & Borovicka, M. (2006, Autumn). Ghost towns or vibrant villages? Constructing business-sponsored online communities. *International Journal of Communications Law & Policy, 11*, 1–22.

Stodberg, U. (2012). A research review of e-assessment. *Assessment & Evaluation in Higher Education, 37*(5), 591–604. doi:10.1080/02602938.2011.557496

Stone, D., Jarrett, C., Woodroffe, M., & Minocha, S. (2005). *User interface design and evaluation.* The Open University, Morgan Kaufmann.

Stuhler, J. (2009). *Managing the Data Explosion: The Causes, Effects and Solutions.* Retrieved from http://www.informationmanagement.com/infodirect/2009_129/data_management_archiving_storage_disaster_recovery-10015658-1.html

Sumathi, C. P., Padmaja Valli, R., & Santhanam, T. (2010). Automatic Recommendation of Web Pages in Web Usage Mining. *International Journal on Computer Science and Engineering, 2*(9), 3046–3052.

Swaid, S., & Wigand, R. T. (2009). Measuring the Quality Of E-Service: Scale Development and Initial Validation. *Journal of Electronic Commerce Research, 10*(1), 13–28.

Sweeney, L. (2002). Achieving k-anonymity privacy protection using generalization and suppression. *International Journal of Uncertainty, Fuzziness and Knowledge-based Systems, 10*(05), 571–588. doi:10.1142/S021848850200165X

Sweeney, L. (2002). k-anonymity: A model for protecting privacy. *International Journal of Uncertainty, Fuzziness and Knowledge-based Systems, 10*(05), 557–570. doi:10.1142/S0218488502001648

Symeonidis, P., Nanopoulos, A., Papadopoulos, A. N., & Manolopoulos, Y. (2008). Nearest-Biclusters Collaborative Filtering Based on Constant and Coherent Values.[Kluwer Academic Publishers.]. *Information Retrieval*, 51–75.

Tan, A. R., Matzen, D., McAloone, T. C., & Evans, S. (2010). Strategies for designing and developing services for manufacturing firms. *CIRP Journal of Manufacturing Science and Technology, 3*(2), 90–97. doi:10.1016/j.cirpj.2010.01.001

Tan, K. C., & Pawitra, T. A. (2001). Integrating SERVQUAL and Kano's model into QFD for service excellence development. *Managing Service Quality: An International Journal, 11*(6), 418–430. doi:10.1108/EUM0000000006520

Tao, D., LeRouge, C. M., Deckard, G., & De Leo, G. (2012, January). Consumer Perspectives on Quality Attributes in Evaluating Health Websites. In*System Science (HICSS), 2012 45th Hawaii International Conference on* (pp. 2675-2684). IEEE. doi:10.1109/HICSS.2012.180

Tarafdar, M., & Zhang, J. (2005). Analyzing the Influence of Website Design Parameters on Website Usability. *Information Resources Management Journal, 18*(4), 62–80. doi:10.4018/irmj.2005100104

Taylor, I. (2012, January). *4 Measurement Scales Every Researcher Should Remember.* Retrieved from http://blog.questionpro.com/2012/01/04/4-measurement-scales-every-researcher-should-remember/

Templ, M., Meindl, B., & Kowarik, A. (2013). Introduction to statistical disclosure control (sdc). *Project: Relative to the testing of SDC algorithms and provision of practical SDC, data analysis OG.*

Thangavel, K., & Rathipriya, R. (2012). A Discrete Artificial Bees Colony Inspired Biclustering Algorithm. *International Journal of Swarm Intelligence Research, 3*(1), 30–42.

Thangavel, K., & Rathipriya, R. (2014). Mining Correlated Bicluster from Web Usage Data Using Discrete Firefly Algorithm Based Biclustering Approach. *International Journal of Mathematical, Computational, Natural and Physical Engineering, World Academy of Science. Engineering and Technology, 8*(4), 705–709.

Thatcher, J. e. (2006). *Web Accessibility: Web Standards and Regulatory Compliance.* New York: Friends of ED.

Thiyagarajan, R., Thangavel, K., & Rathipriya, R. (2014). Web Page Recommendation of Usage Profile Using Particle Swarm Optimization based Clustering. *International Journal of Applied Engineering Research, 9*(23), 22641–22654.

Thompson, A. J., & Kemp, E. A. (2009, July). Web 2.0: extending the framework for heuristic evaluation.*Proceedings of the 10th International Conference NZ Chapter of the ACM's Special Interest Group on Human-Computer Interaction* (pp. 29-36). ACM. doi:10.1145/1577782.1577788

Tilson, R., Dong, J., Martin, S., & Kieke, E. (1998). Factors and principles affecting the usability of four e-commerce sites. *Proceedings of the 4th Conference on Human Factors and the Web (CHFW).* AT&TLabs, USA.

Tilton, J. (1994). *What is an infostructure?* Retrieved from http://www.library.creatifica.com/information-architecture-coining-the-term.pdf

Tjiptono, F. (2003). *Strategi Pemasaran, Edisi Kedua.* Yogyakarta: Penerbit Andi.

Toit, M., & Bothma, C. (2010). Evaluating the Usability of an Academic Marketing Department's Website from a Marketing Student's Perspective. *International Retail and Marketing Review, 5*(1), 15–24.

Topping, K. (1998). Peer assessment between students in colleges and universities. *Review of Educational Research, 68*(3), 249–276. doi:10.3102/00346543068003249

TR 9126-3 Software engineering product quality Part3: internal metrics. (2003). *International Organization for Standardization.*

Tractinsky, N., Cokhavi, A., & Kirschenbaum, M. (2004). Using Ratings and Response Latencies to Evaluate the Consistency of Immediate Aesthetic Perceptions of Web Pages. Workshop Program & ProceedingsAIS SIGHCI, Washington. *HCI Research in MIS, 04,* 40–44.

Tractinsky, N., Cokhavi, A., Kirschenbaum, M., & Sharfi, T. (2006). Evaluating the consistency of immediate aesthetic perceptions of web pages. *International Journal of Human-Computer Studies, 64*(11), 1071–1083. doi:10.1016/j.ijhcs.2006.06.009

Tripathi, P., Pandey, M., & Bharti, D. (2010). Towards the Identification of Usability Metrics for Academic Websites. *Proceedings of the 2nd International IEEE Conference on Computer and Automation Engineering (ICCAE),* Singapore (pp. 393-397).

Udo, G. J., Bagchi, K. K., & Kirs, P. J. (2011). Using SERVQUAL to assess the quality of e-learning experience. *Computers in Human Behavior, 27*(3), 1272–1283. doi:10.1016/j.chb.2011.01.009

Understanding Web Services Security Concepts. (n. d.). Oracle. Retrieved from http://docs.oracle.com/cd/E17904_01/web.1111/b32511/intro_security.htm#WSS

Valet. (n. d.). Retrieved from http://valet.webthing.com/access/url.html

Van Doorn, J., Lemon, K. E., Mittal, V., Naß, S., Pick, D., Pirner, P., & Verhoef, P. C. (2010). Customer Engagement Behavior: Theoretical Foundations and Research Directions. *Journal of Service Research, 13*(3), 253–266. doi:10.1177/1094670510375599

van Iwaarden, J., van der Wiele, T., Ball, L., & Millen, R. (2003). Applying SERVQUAL to Web sites: An exploratory study. *International Journal of Quality & Reliability Management, 20*(8), 919–935. doi:10.1108/02656710310493634

VandenBos, G., Knapp, S., & Doe, J. (2001). *Role of reference elements in the selection of resources by psychology undergraduates.* Retrieved from http://jbr.org/articles.html

Verhagen, T., Swen, E., Feldberg, F., & Merikivi, J. (2015, July). Benefitting from virtual customer environments: An empirical study of customer engagement. *Computers in Human Behavior, 48*, 340–357. doi:10.1016/j.chb.2015.01.061

Verisign. (n. d.). Retrieved from http://www.verisign.com/static/040655.pdf

Verma, B., Gupta, K., Panchal, S., & Nigam, R. (2010, September). Single level algorithm: An improved approach for extracting user navigational patterns to improve website effectiveness. In *Computer and Communication Technology (ICCCT), 2010 International Conference on* (pp. 436-441). IEEE.

VideoAktiv. (2006). *Handbook on Digital Video and Audio in Education*. UK: The VideoAktiv Project.

W3C Semantic Web Activity. (n. d.). Retrieved from www.w3.org/2001/sw/

W3C. (2008). *Web content accessibility guidelines (WCAG) 2.0*.

Wagner, C., & Majchrzak, A. (2007). Enabling Customer Centricity Using Wikis and the Wiki Way. *Journal of Management Information Systems, 23*(3), 17–43. doi:10.2753/MIS0742-1222230302

Waisberg, D., & Kaushik, A. (2009). Web Analytics 2.0: empowering customer centricity. *The original Search Engine Marketing Journal, 2*(1), 5-11.

Wan, A. H. (2000). Opportunities to enhance a commercial Website. *Information & Management, 38*(1), 15–21. doi:10.1016/S0378-7206(00)00048-3

Wang, Y., Wang, D., & Ip, W. (2006). Optimal design of link structure for e-supermarket website, IEEE Transactions: Systems. *Man and Cybernetics – Part A, 36*(2), 338–355. doi:10.1109/TSMCA.2005.851336

Wanyembi, G. (2009). *Improving ICT Management in Public Universities in Kenya, Answers to the problems arising from the rapid introduction and use of the new technology*. Germany: VDM Verlag.

Watson, R. T. (2013). Africa's Contributions to Information Systems. *The Africa Journal of Information Systems, 5*(4).

Web analytics Association. (n. d.). Retrieved from www.webanalyticsassociation.org

Web Analytics. (2015). *Web Analytics*. Retrieved from http://www.webanalytics.in/?p=26

Web Content Accessibility Guidelines. W3C Recommendation (2008). retrieved from http://www.w3.org/TR/WCAG20/

Website Guardian. (n. d.). Retrieved from http://www.website-guardian.com

Website Standards and Guidelines. (n. d.). Release 2012, version 6.0. Retrieved from http://www.state.nj.us/it/ps/web/index.html

Weinberg, G. M. (1997). *Quality Software Management: Anticipating Change*. USA: Dorset House Publishing Co Inc.

Weischedel, B., & Kelowna, Eelko K. R. E. (2006). Website optimization with web metrics: a case study. *Proceedings of the 8th international conference on Electronic commerce: The new e-commerce ICEC '06* (pp. 463-470).

Weischedel, B., & Huizingh, E. K. (2006, August). Website optimization with web metrics: a case study.*Proceedings of the 8th international conference on Electronic commerce: The new e-commerce: innovations for conquering current barriers, obstacles and limitations to conducting successful business on the internet* (pp. 463-470). ACM. doi:10.1145/1151454.1151525

Wibowo, S., & Grandhi, S. (2014, April). A performance-based approach for assessing the quality of group buying websites. *Proceedings of the 2014 4th IEEE International Conference on Information Science and Technology ICIST* (pp. 71-74). IEEE. doi:10.1109/ICIST.2014.6920334

Wikipedia. (n. d.). Retrieved from http://www.wikipedia.org

Wixon, D., & Wilson, C. (1997). The Usability Engineering Framework for Product Design and Evaluation. In M. Helander (Ed.), *Handbook of Human-Computer Interaction* (2nd ed.). North Holland. doi:10.1016/B978-044481862-1.50093-5

Won, S. G. L., Evans, M. A., Carey, C., & Schnittka, C. G. (2015). Youth appropriation of social media for collaborative and facilitated design-based learning. *Computers in Human Behavior*, *50*(1), 385–391. doi:10.1016/j.chb.2015.04.017

World Wide Web Consortium (W3C). (n. d.). Retrieved from www.w3.org/

Xiao, Y., & Lucking, R. (2008). The impact of two types of peer assessment on students' performance and satisfaction within a Wiki environment. *The Internet and Higher Education*, *11*(3-4), 186–193. doi:10.1016/j.iheduc.2008.06.005

Yang, B., & Lester, D. (2004). Attitudes toward buying online. *Cyberpsychology & Behavior*, *7*(1), 85–91. doi:10.1089/109493104322820156 PMID:15006173

Yen, B., Hu, P., & Wang, M. (2005, March). Towards effective web site designs: A framework for modeling, design evaluation and enhancement. *Proceedings of the 2005 IEEE International Conference on e-Technology, e-Commerce and e-Service EEE '05* (pp. 716-721). IEEE. doi:10.1109/EEE.2005.137

Yeung, D.-Y., *Chang, H., Xiong, Y., George, S., Kashi, R., Matsumoto, T., & Rigoll, G.(2004). SVC2004: First International Signature Verification Competition. In D. Zhang, A.K. Jain (Eds.), Biometric Authentication, LNCS (Vol. 3072, pp. 16–22). .*

Ying, F., & Chun, Q. R. (2010). Research on BSC-Based Quality Evaluation of Enterprise Business Websites. *Proceedings of the 2010 International Conference on Management and Service Science* (pp. 1-4). doi:10.1109/ICMSS.2010.5576863

Yin, P., & Guo, Y. (2013). Optimization of multi-criteria website structure based on enhanced tabu search and web usage mining. *Journal of Applied Mathematics and Computation*, *219*(24), 11082–11095. doi:10.1016/j.amc.2013.05.033

Yu, L. (2007). *Semantic Web and Semantic Web Services. Location/City, State.* Chapman & Hall/CRC.

Zakon, R.H. (2003). *Hobbes' Internet Timeline.* Retrieved from www.zakon.org/robert/internet/timeline/

Zaphiris, P., Ghiawadwala, M., & Mughal, S. (2005). Age-centered research-based web design guidelines. *Proceedings of the conference on Human Factors in Computing SystemsChi 2005: Technology, Safety, Community*, Portland, Oregon, USA (pp. 1897-1900).

Zeithaml, V. A., Parasuraman, A., & Berry, L. L. (1990). *Delivering Quality Service: Balancing Customer Perceptions and Expectations.* New York: The Free Press.

Zhang, L. J., Mao, Z. H., & Zhou, N. (2009, July). Design Quality Analytics of Traceability Enablement in Service-Oriented Solution Design Environment. *Proceedings of the IEEE International Conference on Web Services ICWS '09* (pp. 944-951). IEEE. doi:10.1109/ICWS.2009.145

Zhang, P., Von Dran, G., Blake, P., & Pipithsuksunt, V. (2000, August 10-13). A Comparison of the Most Important Website Features in Different Domains: An Empirical Study of User Perceptions. *Proceedings of Americas Conference on Information Systems (AMCIS'2000)*, Long Beach, CA (pp. 1367-1372).

Zhang, Y., Zhu, H., & Greenwood, S. (2004, September). Web site complexity metrics for measuring navigability. *Proceedings of the Fourth International Conference on Quality Software QSIC '04* (pp. 172-179). IEEE.

Zhang, J., Zhao, P., Shang, L., & Wang, L. (2009). Web Usage Mining Based On Fuzzy Clustering in Identifying Target Group. *Proceedings of the International Colloquium on Computing, Communication, Control, and Management*, *4*, 209–212.

Zhang, T. (2006). *A Study of Government e-Service Quality and Its Effect on Public Satisfaction*. China: Macau University of Science and Technology.

Zhao, M., & Dholakia, R. R. (2009). A multi-attribute model of web site interactivity and customer satisfaction: An application of the Kano model. *Managing Service Quality: An International Journal, 19*(3), 286–307. doi:10.1108/09604520910955311

Zhou, B., Jinlin, C., Jin, S., Hongjiang, Z., & Qiufeng, W. (2001). Website link structure evaluation and improvement based on user visiting patterns, The 12th ACM Conference on Hypertext and Hypermedia, pp. 241-242.

Zhu, M., Liu, W., Hu, W., & Fang, Z. (2009, November). Application to improve the websites quality. *Proceedings of the Third International Symposium on Intelligent Information Technology Application9 IITA '09* (Vol. 3, pp. 535-537). IEEE. doi:10.1109/IITA.2009.330

About the Contributors

G. Sreedhar is working as an Associate Professor in the Department of Computer Science, Rashtiya Sanskrit Vidyapeetha (Deemed University), Tirupati, India since 2001. G. Sreedhar received his Ph.D in Computer Science and Technology from Sri Krishnadevaraya University, Anantapur, India in the year 2011. He has over 15 years of Experience in Teaching and Research in the field of Computer Science. He has published more than 15 research papers related to web engineering in reputed international journals. He has published 4 books from reputed international publications and he has presented more than 15 research papers in various national and international conferences. He has handled research projects on computer science funded by the University Grants Commission, Government of India. He is a member of various professional bodies like the academic council, the board of studies and editorial board member in various international journals in the field of computer science, Information Technology and other related fields. He has proven knowledge in the fields of Computer Science and allied research areas.

***

Balamurugan Balusamy is working as Assistant Professor(SG) in the school of Information Technology and Engineering at VIT University, Vellore, India. He completed his B.E at Bharathidasan University and his M.E at Anna University. His research interests are Cloud computing, Cloud security and Web services.

Dina Chahyati obtained her master's degree in Computer Science from Universitas Indonesia. Currently, she is working as a lecturer in the Faculty of Computer Science, Universitas Indonesia. Her research interests are related to image processing and information systems.

Sital Dash has a M.Tech in Information Security and is working as an Assistant Professor, School Of Computer Engineering, KIIT University, India. Areas of interest include mobile computing and cloud computing.

Achmad Nizar Hidayanto is the Head of Information Systems/Information Technology Stream, Faculty of Computer Science, Universitas Indonesia. He received his PhD in Computer Science from Universitas Indonesia. His research interests are related to information systems/information technology, e-learning, information systems security, change management, technology adoption and information retrieval.

Tithi Hunka obtained her M.Tech degree in Computer Science from the KIIT University at Bhubaneshwar in 2015. She received her B.E degree in Information Technology from Chhattisgarh Swami Vivekanand Technical University at Bhilai in 2012.Her major research interests include privacy-preservation data mining and cloud computing.

Kulwant Kaur is Dean, School of Information Technology, Apeejay Institute of Management Technical Campus, Jalandhar. She received master's degree from M.B.M. Engineering College, Jai Narian Vyas University, Jodhpur. She received her Ph.D. (Computer Science and Engineering) from Guru Nanak Dev University, Amritsar, India. Her career spans about two decades of research guidance, and teaching Bachelor and Master level courses in the field of Computer Science/Applications. Her expertise areas include Artificial Intelligence and Software Engineering. As an ingenious researcher, she has presented several research papers in national conferences and seminars. She has also organised national conferences and seminars. She has edited three books and has contributed numerous papers to several journals and chapters to edited books. She is Life Member of Computer Society of India.

Parminder Kaur is working as an Assistant Professor, Department of Computer Science, Guru Nanak Dev University, Amritsar. She has completed her post graduation work in Mathematics as well as System Software and a Doctorate in the field of Component-Based Systems, a branch of Software Engineering. She has around 45 international/national publications related to component certification, component versioning, version-control tools, software architecture, and software security. She is an editorial review committee member for the International Arab Journal of Information Technology (IAJIT), Zarqa University, Jordan. She is a life member of the Punjab Science Congress and the Computer Society of India.

Sukhpuneet Kaur received her M.Tech. (Information Technology) from the Guru Nanak Dev University, Amritsar in 2009. Currently, working as an Assistant Professor in Department of Computer Science, Khalsa College, Amritsar. Also pursuing Ph.D in Computer Science Engineering from Punjab Technical University, Kapurthala. Her research areas are Usability, User-Centered Design, Software Engineering.

Dorie Pandora Kesuma obtained his bachelor's degree in System Information from STMIK MDP in 2008 and a master's degree in Information Technology from Universitas Indonesia in 2014. Currently he is working as a lecturer in STMIK GI MDP. His research interest are related to information systems, information technology, and IT service quality.

Shruti Kohli is an assistant professor at Birla Institute of Technology, India.

P. Venkata Krishna is a Professor at department of Computer Science and Engineering, Padmavathi University, Tirupati, India. He received his B. Tech in Electronics and Communication Engineering from Sri Venkateswara University, Tirupati, India, M. Tech in Computer Science & Engineering from REC, Calicut, India and he received his Ph.D. from VIT University, Vellore, India. Dr. Krishna has several years of experience working in the academia, research, teaching, consultancy, academic administration and project management roles. His current research interests include Mobile and wireless systems, cross layer wireless network design, QoS and Grid Computing.

Meyliana has been a faculty member of the School of Information Systems at Bina Nusantara University since 1997. Her research interests are business process management, enterprise systems, customer relationship management, e-business, knowledge management, and information system development. She graduated with a Master's degree in Management of Information Systems from Bina Nusantara University, and now, she is a PhD candidate in Computer Science at the University of Indonesia. Currently, she is the Deputy Vice Rector Operational of Alam Sutera Campus and Rector's Office Manager of Bina Nusantara University.

Jibitesh Mishra has more than 20 years of teaching and research experience. His research interests are fractal graphics and web engineering. He has written many books and published papers with reputed publishers.

Kabita Rani Naik is a Master's student in Information Technology. She is working in the area of evaluation of quality of web 2.0 websites.

Wing Shui Ng is a teaching fellow at The Hong Kong Institute of Education for training and assessing pre-service and in-service teachers as well as conducting educational research. He has the experience of being seconded to Technology Education Section of Curriculum Development Institute of Education Bureau to develop New Senior Secondary Information and Communication Technology Curriculum, participate in school-based curriculum development, organize teacher training programmes and was invited as a speaker in educational seminars. He also contributed his efforts to serve as a reviewer of Computer Education Textbook Review Panel and as a setter as well as marker of public examination papers for the Hong Kong Examinations and Assessment Authority. In addition, he was appointed as the School Development Officer in Education Bureau. He also taught computer subjects and served as the coordinator in secondary schools for many years. He was in charge of Information Technology in the Education Committee and a member of the School Administrative Council. His research areas include Information Technology in Education and Assessment for Learning.

Sandeep Kumar Panda is a Ph.D scholar in the School of Computer Engineering at KIIT University, Bhubaneswar, Odisha, India. He has presented lectures, and workshops on Software Engineering. His active research interests are in Software Engineering, Web Engineering, Web Sizing, Cost Estimation, and on Web Quality and Productivity Measurement.

Prasant Kumar Pattnaik, M.Tech, Ph.D in Computer Science, is a Senior Member of the IEEE(USA), Fellow of IETE (India), is working as a Professor, School Of Computer Engineering, KIIT University, India. He is area of interest includes mobile computing and cloud computing.

Kongkiti Phusavat is an Associate Professor of the Faculty of Engineering, Kasetsart University. He received his doctoral degree from Virginia Tech's Department of Industrial and Systems Engineering, USA. His research areas include productivity and quality management, and acquisition logistics.

Ambati Venkata Krishna Prasad is working as a Professor in Department of Computer Science and Engineering at KL University. He completed his Ph.D in Computer Science from Sri Venkateswara University, Tirupati in 2012. He is an Editorial Board Member and Reviewer for several International Journals. He published several papers in national and international journals. His Interested Research areas are Mining, Big Data and Analytics.

Adiraju Prashantha Rao has 9 years of experience in the industry and 10 years of teaching experience.

M. Varaprasad Rao is a Doctor in Computer Science & Engineering. He obtained a postgraduate degree in M.Sc Computer Science in 2000. After, an MTech in CSE in 2006. He previously worked with MIPGS for 7 years and the AVPG Centre with 7 years. His areas of research are Information Security, Data Mining, Algorithms, Cloud Computing and Big Data.

R. Rathipriya is an Assistant Professor, Department of Computer Science, Periyar University, India. Her research area is Web Mining. She is reviewer of reputed journals.

C. Madana Kumar Reddy has a M.C.A., a M.Phil. and is currently working as Associate Professor in the Department of Computer Applications in Annamacharya P.G. College of Computer Studies, Rajampet, Kadapa(Dt), Andhra Pradesh. He has 16 years' experience in teaching computer-related subjects to M.C.A., M.Tech. and B.Tech. students. His speeches related to Computer field and other educational areas are broadcast through All India Radio, Kurnool. He has also presented a number of papers at various national and international level conferences. Presently, he is pursuing his Doctoral research in Computer Science under the guidance of Dr. A. Rama Mohan Reddy, S. V. University, Tirupathi.

Himani Singal is ardently captivated by the world of big data, cloud computing and web analytics. She has a corporate experience of more than two years; thus having hands on experience of live projects. Due to zealous inclination towards academics, she then moved to pursue her doctorate from BIT, Mesra, India. She has many national and international publications in the area of cloud computing and web analytics. She has been a remote centre coordinator for various workshops conducted by IIT Bombay and has qualified UGC NET. She has augmented her academics by her research findings which have been accepted in various conferences of IEEE, ACM and International Workshop of Machine Learning and Text Analytics held in South Asian University, New Delhi.

Hardeep Singh is presently a Professor in the Department of Computer Science, Guru Nanak Dev University, Amritsar. Having throughout first class academic career, Dr Singh is an M.S. (Software Systems) from Birla Institute of Technology and Science (BITS), Pilani and has received his Ph. D from Guru Nanak Dev University, Amritsar, India. His career spans more than two decades' of research, research guidance at doctoral, M.Tech, MCA & B.Tech and university teaching in field of Computer Science. During his this professional career, he has also been visiting faculty to different universities, institutes and corporations, apart from associating as a member of UGC teams, AICTE panels, governing boards of various educational institutions and as a member of academic bodies like the Board of Studies, R.D.C.s and Academic Councils of different universities viz. H.P. University, Shimla; Kurukshetra University, Kurukshetra; Punjab Technical University, Jalandhar; HNB Gharwal University, Srinagar, Uttrakhand; Panjab University, Chandigarh; etc. An active researcher and a prolific writer, Dr. Singh has authored five books and has contributed around 100 papers to several journals. He is also an active member many of Professional Societies such as he is fellow of the British Computer Society (FBCS); member of the Association for Computing Machinery (ACM); member of the International Association of Engineers (IAENG); Global Member of the Internet Society; Life Member of the Punjab Science Congress and Computer Society of India, etc. He is a frequent reviewer, discussant, and session chair for seminars and conferences.

Jayashree Sridhar is pursuing a MS degree in Software Engineering at VIT University, Vellore. Her research interests are cloud computing, cloud security and web development.

Santosh Kumar Swain is an Associate Professor of School of Computer Engineering at the KIIT University, Bhubaneswar, Odisha, India. He has presented numerous lectures, conference presentations and workshops on Software Engineering, Object Oriented Analysis. His active research interests are in Software Engineering, Web Engineering, Web Sizing, Cost Estimation, and on Web Quality and Productivity. He has published 25 peer reviewed international journal papers and several conference papers.

Gregory W. Wanyembi is an associate professor of ICT management at Mount Kenya University. He obtained his B.Sc. at the University of Nairobi (1974), Kenya, Diploma in Computer Science at the University of Dundee (1989), Scotland, and a PhD in ICT management at Delft University of Technology (2002) in the Netherlands. He has taught and held positions as chairman of the department and director of ICT at Moi University, Kenya, Masinde Muliro University of Science and Technology, Kenya, University of Kabianga, Kenya, and Mount Kenya University, Kenya. He has published widely in refereed journals in the areas of ICT management and authored a book. He is currently a reviewer with the African Journal of Information Systems (AJIS). In 2013, he was won a Distinguished Scholar Award in ICT in Kenya. He has also successfully supervised several Master theses and four PhD theses. His research interests include strategic utilization of ICTs in emerging economies.

Index

Become an IRMA Member

Members of the **Information Resources Management Association (IRMA)** understand the importance of community within their field of study. The Information Resources Management Association is an ideal venue through which professionals, students, and academicians can convene and share the latest industry innovations and scholarly research that is changing the field of information science and technology. Become a member today and enjoy the benefits of membership as well as the opportunity to collaborate and network with fellow experts in the field.

IRMA Membership Benefits:

- **One FREE Journal Subscription**

- **30% Off Additional Journal Subscriptions**

- **20% Off Book Purchases**

- Updates on the latest events and research on Information Resources Management through the IRMA-L listserv.

- Updates on new open access and downloadable content added to Research IRM.

- A copy of the Information Technology Management Newsletter twice a year.

- A certificate of membership.

IRMA Membership $195

Scan code to visit irma-international.org and begin by selecting your free journal subscription.

Membership is good for one full year.

Printed in the United States
By Bookmasters